Quick Reference Directory

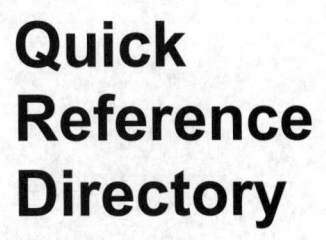

This directory should be used to quickly locate legislation in this volume.

To use the directory, place right thumb on the outer edge of this page against the required legislation. Then fold back the remaining pages to align the directory with the corresponding page tab.

For content not included in the directory, consult the full subject index.

IAA 1974 — Part II

IAA 1974 — Part III

IAA 1974 — Part IV

IAA 1974 — Part V

IAA 1974 — Sch 1 NY Convention

IAA 1974 — Sch 2 Model Law

IAA 1974 — Sch 3 ICSID Convention

To: HEW R. DUNDAS
From: MALCOLM HOLMES

LEXISNEXIS ANNOTATED ACTS

THE INTERNATIONAL ARBITRATION ACT 1974: A COMMENTARY

2011 EDITION

Dear Hew,

With many thanks for your friendship

Best wishes

Malcolm

LEXISNEXIS ANNOTATED ACTS

THE INTERNATIONAL ARBITRATION ACT 1974: A COMMENTARY

Malcolm Holmes

Chester Brown

LexisNexis Butterworths
Australia
2011

	LexisNexis
AUSTRALIA	LexisNexis Butterworths
	475–495 Victoria Avenue, Chatswood NSW 2067
	On the internet at: www.lexisnexis.com.au
ARGENTINA	LexisNexis, BUENOS AIRES
AUSTRIA	LexisNexis Verlag ARD Orac GmbH & Co KG, VIENNA
BRAZIL	LexisNexis Latin America, SAO PAULO
CANADA	LexisNexis Canada, Markham, ONTARIO
CHILE	LexisNexis Ltd, SANTIAGO
CHINA	LexisNexis China, BEIJING, SHANGHAI
CZECH REPUBLIC	Nakladatelství Orac sro, PRAGUE
FRANCE	LexisNexis SA, PARIS
GERMANY	LexisNexis Germany, FRANKFURT
HONG KONG	LexisNexis Hong Kong, HONG KONG
HUNGARY	HVG-Orac, BUDAPEST
INDIA	LexisNexis, NEW DELHI
ITALY	Dott AGiuffrè Editore SpA, MILAN
IRELAND	LexisNexis UK, DUBLIN
JAPAN	LexisNexis Japan KK, TOKYO
KOREA	LexisNexis, SEOUL
MALAYSIA	LexisNexis Malaysia Sdn Bhd, PETALING JAYA, SELANGOR
NEW ZEALAND	LexisNexis, WELLINGTON
POLAND	Wydawnictwo Prawnicze LexisNexis, WARSAW
SINGAPORE	LexisNexis, SINGAPORE
SOUTH AFRICA	LexisNexis Butterworths, DURBAN
SWITZERLAND	Staempfli Verlag AG, BERNE
TAIWAN	LexisNexis, TAIWAN
UNITED KINGDOM	LexisNexis UK, LONDON, EDINBURGH
USA	LexisNexis Group, New York, NEW YORK
	LexisNexis, Miamisburg, OHIO

National Library of Australia Cataloguing-in-Publication entry

Title: The International Arbitration Act 1974: A Commentary
Edition: 1st ed.
ISBN: 9780409327472 (pbk).

©2012 Reed International Books Australia Pty Limited trading as LexisNexis

This book is copyright. Except as permitted under the Copyright Act 1968 (Cth), no part of this publication may be reproduced by any process, electronic or otherwise, without the specific written permission of the copyright owner. Neither may information be stored electronically in any form whatsoever without such permission.

Inquiries should be addressed to the publishers.
Typeset in Palatino and Times New Roman.
Printed in Australia by Ligare Pty Ltd (NSW).

Visit LexisNexis Butterworths at www.lexisnexis.com.au

Contents

Foreword	vii
Preface	ix
Authors' Acknowledgments	x
Table of Cases	xi
Table of Statutes	xix

International Arbitration Act 1974

Legislative Background	3
Table of Provisions	9
Table of Amendments	13
Part I — Preliminary	15
Part II — Enforcement of Foreign Awards	27
Part III — International Commercial Arbitration	89
Part IV — Application of the Convention on the Settlement of Investment Disputes Between States and Nationals of Other States	125
Part V — General Matters	133
Schedule 1 — United Nations Conference on International Commercial Arbitration Convention on the Recognition and Enforcement of Foreign Arbitral Awards	135
Schedule 2 — UNCITRAL Model Law on International Commercial Arbitration (as Adopted by the United Nations Commission on International Trade Law on 21 June 1985, and as Amended by the United Nations Commission on International Trade Law on 7 July 2006)	139
Schedule 3 — Convention on the Settlement of Investment Disputes Between States and Nationals of Other States	241
Index	339

Foreword
Justice James Allsop[1]

I am honoured to have been asked to write a foreword for a publication that is both a timely and an important work of legal scholarship. It provides an up-to-date and comprehensive comparative analysis of one of Australia's most important pieces of legislation, the International Arbitration Act 1974 (Cth). Before saying something of the work, something should be said about the subject of the work. The International Arbitration Act is Australia's legislative response to the 1958 New York Convention on the recognition and enforcement of arbitral awards and the 1985 UNCITRAL Model Law on International Commercial Arbitration (revised in 2006). Put thus, the subject seems prosaic. It is not. The New York Convention is one of the most important conventions ever done. It makes enforceable a valid arbitral award in over 140 countries. It makes international arbitral dispute resolution work in a way national courts cannot. Arbitration, and not judicial hearing, provides a practical structure for the widespread enforceability of rights and duties in international commerce by peaceful, civilised means engaging the international rule of law.

Why is this important? Need we understand it? International commerce carried on in good faith according to acceptable legal rules is fundamental to a peaceful and prosperous world. High-flown rhetoric is dangerous, if it distracts from the truth. But think for one moment about how one can find a satisfactory way of creating a structure for dispute resolution acceptable to a majority of the vast number of participants in international commerce. What system of dispute resolution would merchants from different cultures and legal systems who are to enter a bargain but do not know each other, or, do know, but do not trust, each other, choose? Preferably not force, whether gunboat diplomacy or private force. The words of the resolution of the General Assembly of the United Nations on 11 December 1985 (40/72) requesting the Secretary-General to transmit the Model Law to States for their due consideration reflect, in restrained terms, the high international public policy involved:

> *Recognizing* the value of arbitration as a method of settling disputes arising in international commercial relations. *Convinced* that the establishment of a model law on arbitration that is acceptable to States with different legal, social and economic systems contributes to the development of harmonious international economic relations ... *Convinced* that the Model Law, together with the [New York Convention] significantly contributes to the establishment of a unified legal framework for the fair and efficient settlement of disputes arising in international commercial relations ...

The Australian Parliament recognised this as important national policy in 1974 and has done so ever since. The Commonwealth Parliament, after a review carried out by the Commonwealth Attorney-General, the Hon Robert McClelland, has recently brought the International Arbitration Act into line with the most recent international instruments found in the 2006 amendments to the Model Law.

It is vital that Australian businesspeople, lawyers and judges understand how international arbitration works. Australia is a great trading nation. An ordered, efficient dispute resolution mechanism leading to an enforceable award is an essential underpinning of commerce. Disputes are regrettable, but they are part of commerce. Their possibility and the cost of their resolution are factors affecting price and value.

---

1 President, New South Wales Court of Appeal.

That the vast majority of all international disputes go to arbitration and not national courts bespeaks the will of the commercial community to resolve disputes applying international standards. It should be respected by legal systems (mature and young alike), which should not encourage legal particularism or parochialism or exceptionalism.

The reasons for this approach need not detain us. They are obvious — trust and enforceability are keys to international dispute resolution. Commerce is ultimately based on trust; so is the strength of any legal system or structure of dispute resolution. The international commercial community has placed its trust in international arbitration. Australian lawyers who do not understand the need to be skilled in participation in that choice will be left to their own devices.

There should be no suspicion of a process whose underpinning function is the prompt, honest, efficient and fair resolution of disputes. The international arbitration conventions and Model Law have been enacted into national law for the purpose of fostering, assisting and supervising an international structure of dispute resolution that is vital to the rule of law in living contemporary international society and to Australia's vital national interests. This is not propaganda; it is recognised international public policy, translated into high national public policy.

This work is founded on the recognition of the importance of the subject. The approach of the authors is not provincial. The commentary draws its ideas from jurisdictions all around the world to give content to the provisions of the International Arbitration Act and the adopted conventions. Having said that, the authors have resisted the temptation to descend too far into the detail of the vast body of jurisprudence on the topic. Rather, what is provided is an overview of the key decisions (both Australian and foreign) and discussion of the issues likely to arise in international arbitrations, as they fall thematically under each of the sections or schedules of the Act. Unlike other erudite commentaries on the Model Law, such as Howard M Holtzmann and Joseph E Neuhaus, *A Guide to the UNCITRAL Model Law on International Commercial Arbitration* (Kluwer Law International, The Hague, 1989), this work is not limited to the *travaux préparatoires* of the UNCITRAL Working Group and drafting history of the instruments. That is not a criticism of Holtzmann, which was published before much of the body of international arbitral law on the Model Law had been decided. The benefit of a publication such as this one is that it incorporates the history of the provisions of the international instruments, the Australian explanatory material from the enactment and review of the International Arbitration Act and the global body of jurisprudence, as it has developed.

This is a work of legal scholarship of which the authors and publishers are to be proud. It is essential reading and an essential point of reference for any practitioner, Australian or international, in the understanding not only of the Australian legislation, but also of the international conventions underpinning international commercial arbitration.

Preface

As the title of this work may suggest, we have endeavoured to provide the reader with an informed and analytical commentary on each of the provisions of the International Arbitration Act 1974 (Cth) (the Act). The work commences with an outline of the context and background against which the Act was enacted and its major revisions were made, and the sources of the text found in the Act. The balance of the book essentially provides a provision-by-provision commentary to the Act and its Schedules. The exception is Schedule 1 of the Act, which contains the New York Convention. The book does not include a commentary to the New York Convention, as its provisions have been specifically implemented into Australian law by their individual restatement in the sections comprising Part II of the Act. Schedule 2 of the Act contains the UNCITRAL Model Law, and Schedule 3 of the Act contains the ICSID Convention, and the provisions of these international instruments are, like those of the Act, subjected to detailed analysis, and reference is made to the case law of Australian courts, other national courts, international arbitral tribunals and the writings of respected authors.

We have been conscious of the international origins and context of the text used in the Act and the need to give effect to the legislative directions found in the Act with respect to its interpretation. In this regard we have endeavoured to adopt a balanced approach in the work including all Australian case law on the provisions of the Act, and relevant recent case law from other jurisdictions which have enacted or implemented the same international legal instruments.

This book is the product of a fruitful collaboration between the authors. Although it is a co-authored work, Malcolm Holmes took responsibility for drafting the commentary to Parts I, II, III and V of the Act, and half of the provisions of the UNCITRAL Model Law. Chester Brown took on the task of drafting the commentary to Part IV of the Act, half of the provisions of the UNCITRAL Model Law, and the ICSID Convention. The authors are, of course, jointly responsible for the outcome.

The law as stated is correct as at the time of writing, although an effort has been made to include later material where possible. In this regard, reference has been made to an amendment to section 15AA of the Acts Interpretation Act 1901 (Cth), which received the Royal Assent on 27 June 2011, and is due to commence either on the date of proclamation or six months after Royal Assent was received (ie, 28 December 2011). We have also been able to include discussion of the Supreme Court of Victoria Court of Appeal's judgment in *IMC Aviation Solutions Pty Ltd v Altain Khuder LLC* [2011] VSCA 248; BC201106268, which was delivered on 22 August 2011, and the High Court of Australia's judgment in *Westport Insurance Corporation v Gordian Runoff Ltd* [2011] HCA 37, which was delivered on 5 October 2011.

MALCOLM HOLMES QC
CHESTER BROWN

22 August 2011

Authors' Acknowledgments

The authors have benefited from various forms of assistance in the preparation of the text, and we are pleased to record our thanks and appreciation. Malcolm Holmes would like to express his thanks to Peter McQueen, Michael Holmes and Greg Nell SC and to acknowledge the inspiration that he has drawn from the students of the Diploma of International Commercial Arbitration. Chester Brown is grateful to Sydney Law School, which granted him an Early Career Researcher Grant in 2010, thus enabling him to dedicate time to this project, and to Sydney Law School's Research Development Fund for financial assistance. Chester Brown also wishes to record his sincere thanks to Emanuel Blum for his dedicated and thorough research assistance throughout the duration of this project, as well as to a number of interns in the Sydney Centre for International Law — Steve Hind, Bryce Williams and Jason Wong — who assisted with various tasks in the final stages of the preparation of the text. Both authors are grateful to Associate Professor Luke Nottage of Sydney Law School, who subjected a draft of the manuscript to a thorough critique, and also to Linda Boer, Philippa Huxley, Desanka Vukelich, and the team at LexisNexis Australia, for having ensured the smooth publication of this volume. We are also particularly indebted to Justice James Allsop, President of the New South Wales Court of Appeal — and someone who has made an enormous contribution to the study and development of international arbitration in Australia — for having done us the honour of writing the Foreword to this book.

We would also like to acknowledge the intellectual debt that we owe to the writers of a number of other texts to which we have referred in researching and preparing various sections of this book. In this regard, it is appropriate to mention specifically Martin Davies and Anthony Dickey, *Shipping Law*, 3rd ed, Lawbook Company, Australia, 2004, which was especially useful in the preparation of the commentary to section 2C of the Act; Howard Holtzmann and Joseph Neuhaus, *A Guide to the UNCITRAL Model Law on International Commercial Arbitration*, Kluwer Law International, The Hague, 1989, a key text on the drafting of the UNCITRAL Model Law; and Christoph Schreuer, Loretta Malintoppi, August Reinisch and Anthony Sinclair, *The ICSID Convention: A Commentary*, 2nd ed, Cambridge University Press, Cambridge, 2009, on the ICSID Convention.

Last, but not least, we wish to express our sincere thanks to our families for their support and encouragement throughout the formulation, writing and publication of this book. Malcolm Holmes would like to thank Helen, Gavin and Kirsty, David and Leticia, and Holly and Mitch, and Chester Brown would like to thank his wife Catherine and daughter Caroline. It is to our families that this book is dedicated.

MALCOLM HOLMES QC
CHESTER BROWN

22 August 2011

Table of Cases

References are to paragraph numbers

114 Nepean Highway Pty Ltd v Abnote Australasia Pty Ltd [2009] VSCA 317 . . . .[s 28-5]
2 Roslyn Street Pty Ltd, In the Matter of; 2 Roslyn Street Pty Ltd v Leisure Inn Hospitality Management Pty Ltd [2011] NSWSC 512; BC201103981 . . . .[s 7-4]
429545 BC Ltd v Joseph B Herlihy (1998 unreported) . . . .[Sch 2 Art 8-6]
Abdroikov; R v [2008] 1 All ER 315; [2007] All ER (D) 226 (Oct); [2007] 1 WLR 2679 . . . .[s 18A-3]
Abigroup Contractors Pty Ltd v Transfield Pty Ltd (1998) 217 ALR 435 . . . .[s 7-13], [s 7-15]
ABB Service Pty Ltd v Pyrmont Light Rail Company Ltd (2010) 77 NSWLR 321; [2010] NSWSC 831; BC201005359 . . . . .[Sch 2 Art 32-1],
ABN Amro Bank v Krupp Mak Maschinenbau GmbH (1996) 135 DLR (4th) 130 . . . .[Sch 2 Art 8-4], [Sch 2 Art 8-6]
— v — (1995 unreported) . . . . .[Sch 2 Art 8-6]
ACD Tridon Inc v Tridon Australia Pty Ltd [2002] NSWSC 896; BC200206142 . . . . .[s 7-12], [s 7-21]
ACN 006 397 413 Pty Ltd v International Movie Group (Canada) Inc [1997] 2 VR 31 .[s 8-3], [s 8-18], [s 8-28]
ACN 103 753 484 Pty Ltd (in liq) formerly Blue Chip Development Corporation Pty Ltd, In the Matter of [2011] QSC 64; BC201108440 . . . .[s 7-17]
Administration of Norfolk Island v SMEC Australia Pty Ltd BC200404489 . . .[s 2A-3], [s 2B-3]
AED Oil Ltd v Puffin FPSO Ltd (2010) 27 VR 22; 265 ALR 415 . . .[s 7-12], [s 7-14], [s 7-21], [s 8-6], [s 8-21]
— v Puffin FPSO Ltd (No 2) [2009] VSC 534; BC200910755 . . .[s 7-12], [s 7-14], [s 7-21]
Aerospatiale Holdings Australia v Elspan International Ltd (1992) 28 NSWLR 321 . . . .[s 7-15]
AES Ust-Kamenogorsk Hydropower Plant LLP v Ust-Kamenogorsk Hydropower Plant JSC [2011] EWCACiv 647 . . . .[s 3-6]
Agromet v Maulden Engineering Ltd [1985] 1 WLR 762 . . . .[s 8-31]
Aguas del Tunari SA v Bolivia (2005 unreported) . . . .[Sch 3 Art 43-5]
AJU v AJT [2011] SGCA 41 . . . .[s 8-21]
Allergan Pharmaceuticals Inc v Bausch & Lomb Inc (1985) AIPC 90-262; (1985) ATPR 40-636; 3 BCL 61 . . . . . .[s 7-9], [s 7-12], [s 7-17]

Altain Khuder LLC v IMC Mining Inc (2011) 276 ALR 733; 246 FLR 47 . . . .[s 8-10]
Amaltal Corp Ltd v Maruha (NZ) Corp Ltd [2003] 2 NZLR 92 . . . .[s 8-21]
American Diagnostica Inc v Gradipore Ltd (1998) 44 NSWLR 312 . . . .[Sch 2 Art 20-8], [s 7-5], [s 21-3]
Ansett Australia Ltd v Malaysian Airline System Berhad (2008) 217 FLR 376 .[s 7-9], [s 7-11], [s 7-13], [s 7-15], [s 7-17]
Antclizo Shipping Corp v The Food Corp of India BC9806040 . . . .[s 8-31]
Arris Investments Pty Ltd v Fahd [2010] NSWSC 309; BC201002666 . . . .[s 7-4]
Associated Electric & Gas Insurance Services Ltd v European Reinsurance Co of Zurich [2003] All ER (D) 308 (Jan); [2003] 1 All ER (Comm) 253; [2003] 1 WLR 1041 . . . . . .[s 8-32]
Astel-Peiniger Joint Venture v Argos Engineering & Heavy Industries Co Ltd [1995] 1 HKLR 300 . . . .[Sch 2 Art 7-8]
ATA Construction, Industrial and Trading Co v Jordan (2011 unreported) . . . . . .[s 31-3]
Attorney-General v Feary [2007] NZHC 112 . . . .[Sch 2 Art 16-7]
Australia v France (Nuclear Test Cases) [1974] ICJ 253 . . . .[Sch 3 Art 25-5]
Australia Pacific Airports (Melbourne) Pty Ltd v Nuance Group (Australia) Pty Ltd [2005] VSCA 133; BC200503467 . .[Sch 2 Art 1-5]
Australian Granites Ltd v Eisenwerk Hensel Bayreuth Dipl-Ing Burkhardt GmbH [2001] 1 Qd R 461 . . . .[s 7-5], [s 21-3]
Autopista Concesionada de Venezuela, SA v Venezuela (2003 unreported) . . . .[Sch 3 Art 42-3]
Azurix Corp v Argentina (2009 unreported) . . . .[Sch 3 Art 52-3]
Bakri Navigation Co Ltd v Owners of Ship 'Golden Glory' Glorious Shipping SA (1991) 217 ALR 152 . . . . .[Sch 2 Art 8-4], [s 7-6], [s 7-19], [s 7-21], [s 7-22]
Bank Mellat v Helliniki Techniki SA [1984] QB 291; [1983] 3 All ER 428; (1983) 133 NLJ 597; [1983] 3 WLR 783 .[Sch 2 Art 20-2], [s 7-5]
Banro American Resources, Inc v Democratic Republic of the Congo (2000 unreported) . . . .[Sch 3 Art 27-2]
Barclays Bank PLC v Nylon Capital LLP [2011] EWCACiv 826 . . . .[s 7-11]
Best (A) Floor Sanding Pty Ltd v Skyer Australia Pty Ltd [1999] VSC 170; BC9903185 . .[s 7-12]

BHP Billiton Ltd v Oil Basins Ltd [2006] VSC 402; BC200608700 . . . .[Sch 2 Art 31-3]
BHP Trading Asia Ltd v Oceaname Shipping Ltd (1996) 67 FCR 211 . . . .[s 2C-4]
BHPB Freight Pty Ltd v Cosco Oceania Chartering Pty Ltd (2008) 168 FCR 169; 247 ALR 369 . . . .[s 7-14], [s 7-21]
Biloune and Marine Drive Complex Ltd v Ghana Investments Centre and the Government of Ghana 95 ILR 184 . . . . . .[Sch 3 Art 51-2]
Biwater Gauff (Tanzania) Ltd v Tanzania (2006 unreported) . . . .[Sch 3 Art 43-6]
— v — (2008 unreported) . . . .[Sch 3 Art 25-12]
Bloemen (F J) Pty Ltd v City of Gold Coast Council (1972) 26 LGRA 78; [1973] AC 115; (1972) 46 ALJR 366 . . . .[s 8-31]
Bradken Consolidated Ltd v Broken Hill Company Pty Co Ltd (1979) 145 CLR 107; 24 ALR 9; 53 ALJR 452 . . . .[s 2B-2]
Braes of Doune Wind Farm (Scotland) Ltd v Alfred McAlpine Business Services Ltd [2008] All ER (D) 222 (Mar); [2008] BLR 321; [2008] 1 Lloyd's Rep 608 . . . . . .[Sch 2 Art 20-3], [Sch 2 Art 20-5]
Brali v Hyundai Corp (1988) 15 NSWLR 734; 84 ALR 176 . . . .[s 8-3], [s 8-31]
Brandes Investment Partners, LP v Venezuela (2009 unreported) . . . .[Sch 3 Art 41-10]
Bremer Handelsgellschaft v Westzucker (No 2) [1981] 2 Lloyd's Rep 130 . . . . . .[Sch 2 Art 31-3]
Bremer Oeltransport GmbH v Drewry [1933] 1 KB 753 . . . .[s 8-31]
Briginshaw v Briginshaw (1938) 60 CLR 336; [1938] ALR 334; (1938) 12 ALJR 100 . . . .[s 8-10]
British American Tobacco Australia Services Ltd v Laurie (2011) 242 CLR 283; 273 ALR 429 . . . .[s 18A-2], [s 18A-3]
Brunswick Bowling & Billiards Corp v Shanghai Zhonglu Industrial Co Ltd [2009] HKCFI 94 . . .[s 3-5], [s 8-8], [s 8-14], [Sch 2 Art 19-2], [Sch 2 Art 34-6]
Bulk Chartering & Consultants Australia Pty Ltd v T & T Metal Trading Pty Ltd (1993) 31 NSWLR 18; 114 ALR 189 . . . . . .[s 2C-3], [s 2C-4], [s 2C-6], [s 2C-9], [s 2C-11]
C v D [2007] All ER (D) 365 (Jun); [2007] 2 All ER (Comm) 557 . . . .[Sch 2 Art 20-7]
— v — [2007] All ER (D) 61 (Dec); [2008] 1 All ER (Comm) 1001; [2008] 1 Lloyd's Rep 239 . . . .[Sch 2 Art 20-7]
— v — [2007] EWCAC 1282 . . . .[s 3-6], [Sch 2 Art 20-4]
Caratube International Oil Co LLP v Kazakhstan (2009 unreported) . . . . . .[Sch 3 Art 47-6]
Cardile v LED Builders Pty Ltd (1999) 198 CLR 380; 162 ALR 294 . . . .[s 8-33]

Cargill International SA v Peabody Australia Mining Ltd [2010] NSWSC 887; BC201005660 . . . .[s 7-5], [s 21-3]
Carter Holt Harvey Ltd v Genesis Power Ltd [2006] 3 NZLR 794 . .[Sch 2 Art 5-2], [Sch 2 Art 8-1]
Carus-Wilson and Greene, Re (1887) 18 QBD 7 . . . .[Sch 2 Art 1-5]
CEMEX Caracas Investments BV v Venezuela (2010 unreported) . . . .[Sch 3 Art 47-5]
Chalbury MccOuat International Ltd v PG Foils Ltd [2011] 1 All ER (Comm) 435; [2011] 1 Lloyd's Rep 23; [2010] BLR 593 . . .[Sch 2 Art 20-4]
Channel Tunnel Group Ltd v Balfour Beatty Construction Ltd [1993] AC 334; [1993] 1 All ER 664; [1993] 2 WLR 262; [1993] 1 Lloyd's Rep 291 . . . .[Sch 2 Art 28-2]
China Ocean Shipping Co v Mitrans Maritime Panama SA [1994] 2 HKC 614 . . . .[Sch 2 Art 11-14]
China Sichuan Changhong Electric Co Ltd v CTA International Pty Ltd [2009] FCA 397; BC200903081 . . . .[s 8-28]
Chloe Z Fishing Co Inc v Oydessey Re (London) Ltd (2000) 109 F Supp 2d 1236 . . . . . .[s 3-2]
Christian Mutual Life Insurance Co v ACE Bermuda Insurance Ltd [2002] Bda LR 1 . . . . .[Sch 2 Art 16-4], [Sch 2 Art 16-6], [Sch 2 Art 16-7]
Chu Kheng Lim v Minister for Immigration Local Government & Ethnic Affairs (1992) 176 CLR 1; 110 ALR 97; 67 ALJR 125 . . . .[s 31-10]
Chugg v Pacific Dunlop Ltd (1990) 170 CLR 249; 95 ALR 481; 64 ALJR 599 . . . .[s 2D-4]
CMS Gas Transmission Co v Argentina (2003 unreported) . . . .[Sch 3 Art 42-2]
Codelfa Construction Pty Ltd v State Rail Authority of NSW (1982) 149 CLR 337; 41 ALR 367; 56 ALJR 459; (1982) NSW ConvR 55-070 . . . .[s 7-21], [s 25-2]
Comandate Marine Corp v Pan Australia Shipping Pty Ltd (2006) 157 FCR 45; 238 ALR 457 . . . .[s 2C-1], [s 3-1], [s 3-2], [s 7-4], [s 7-9], [s 7-11], [s 7-12], [s 7-15], [s 7-17], [s 7-20], [s 7-21], [s 16-2], [s 17-2], [Sch 2 Art 7-1], [Sch 2 Art 8-3], [Sch 2 Art 9-4], [Sch 2 Art 16-2]
Commonwealth Development Corp v Montague [2000] QCA 252; BC200003514 . . . .[s 3-5]
Compagnia de Aguas del Aconquija SA and Vivendi Universal v Argentina (2002 unreported) . . . .[Sch 3 Art 52-8]
Compagnie des Messageries Maritimes v Wilson (1954) 94 CLR 577; [1954] ALR 1095; (1954) 28 ALJR 465 . . .[s 2C-2], [s 2C-3], [s 2C-9]
Compagnia de Aguas del Aconquija SA and Vivendi Universal v Argentina (2001 unreported) . . . .[Sch 3 Art 57-3]
Conagra International Fertiliser Co v Lief Investments Pty Ltd (1997) 141 FLR 124 . . . . . .[s 7-12]

TABLE OF CASES

Coppee Lavalin v Ken-Ren [1995] 1 AC 38; [1994] 2 All ER 449; [1994] 2 Lloyd's Rep 109; [1994] 2 WLR 631 . . . .[Sch 2 Art 5-4]
Corvetina Technology Ltd v Clough Engineering Ltd (2004) 183 FLR 317 . . . . .[s 2D-2], [s 8-21]
CRW Joint Operation v PT Perusahaan Gas Negara (Persero) TBK [2011] SGCA 33 . . . .[s 8-15]
Cypressvale Pty Ltd v Retail Shop Leases Tribunal [1996] 2 Qd R 462 . . . . . .[Sch 2 Art 31-3]
Dalimpex Ltd v Janicki (2003) 64 OR (3d) 737; 228 DLR (4th) 179; [2003] CanLII 34234 .[s 7-11], [s 8-24], [Sch 2 Art 8-4]
Dallah Real Estate and Tourism Holding Company [2011] UKSC 46 . . . . . .[Sch 2 Art 16-3]
Dallah Real Estate and Tourism Holding Company v Govt of Pakistan [2011] 1 AC 763; [2010] All ER (D) 36 (Nov); [2011] 1 All ER 485 . . . .[s 3-7], [s 8-2], [s 8-5], [s 8-8], [s 8-11], [s 8-13]
Dalmia v National Bank [1978] Lloyd's Rep 223 . . . .[s 3-5]
Dardana Ltd v Yukos Oil Co [2002] All ER (D) 126 (Apr); [2002] 1 All ER (Comm) 819; [2002] 2 Lloyd's Rep 326 . . .[s 8-2], [s 8-24], [s 8-25]
Desert Line v Yemen (2008 unreported) . . . .[Sch 3 Art 41-5]
Desputeaux v Editions Chouette (1987) Inc 2003 SCC 17 . . . .[s 7-12]
Discovery Beach Project Pty Ltd v Northbuild Construction Pty Ltd [2011] QSC 306; BC201108127
. . . . . .[s 8-15], [s 8-32], [Sch 2 Art 32-1]
Dobbs v National Bank of Australasia Ltd (1935) 53 CLR 643; [1935] ALR 360; (1935) 9 ALJR 112 . . . .[s 2C-3]
Dodwell & Co (Aust) Pty Ltd and Moss Security Ltd, Re (1990 unreported) . . . .[s 7-9]
Donald Fleming, Florence Fleming and Donna Moran v Space Homes Ltd [1985] CanLII 1458 . . . .[Sch 2 Art 11-4]
Doshion Ltd v Sembawang Engineers and Constructors Pte Ltd [2011] SGHC 46 . . . .[s 7-11], [Sch 2 Art 16-8]
Dowans Holding SA v Tanzania Electric Supply Co Ltd [2011] EWHC 1957 . . .[s 8-8], [s 8-17], [s 8-25]
Downer-Hill Joint Venture v Government of Fiji [2005] 1 NZLR 554 . . . . .[Sch 2 Art 34-5], [Sch 2 Art 34-7], [s 8-21]
Du Toit v Vale (1993) 9 WAR 138 . . . . .[s 28-4]
Dubai Islamic Bank PJSC v Paymentech Merchant Services Inc [2001] 1 Lloyd's Rep 65 .[s 7-5]
Effect of Awards of Compensation of the United Nations Administrative Tribunal [1954] ICJ Rep 47 . . . .[Sch 3 Art 51-2]
El Nasharty v J Sainsbury PLC [2007] EWHC 2618 . . . .[s 7-22]

Elders CED Ltd v Dravo Corp (1984) 59 ALR 206; 2 BCL 68 . . . .[s 7-8], [s 7-9], [s 7-17]
Electra Air Conditioning BV v Seeley International Pty Ltd ACN 054 687 035 [2008] FCAFC 169; BC200808797 . . . .[s 7-11]
Emmott v Michael Wilson & Partners Ltd [2008] 2 All ER (Comm) 193; [2008] All ER (D) 162 (Mar); [2008] 1 Lloyd's Rep 616 . .[s 23C-2]
Enron Corp and Ponderosa Assets LP v Argentina (2004 unreported) . . . . . .[Sch 3 Art 54-3]
Enron Creditors Recovery Corp v — (1989 unreported) . . . .[Sch 3 Art 52-4]
— v — (2010 unreported) . . . .[Sch 3 Art 52-4]
— v Argentine Republic (2008 unreported) . . . .[Sch 3 Art 52-13]
ESCO Corp v Bradken Resources Pty Ltd [2011] FCA 905; BC201105961 . . . . .[s 8-24], [s 8-26]
Esso Australia Resources Ltd v Plowman (1995) 183 CLR 10; 128 ALR 391; 69 ALJR 404 . . . .[s 23C-2], [s 23C-3]
Eton Properties Ltd [2011] HKCFA 31 . . .[s 8-31]
Excalibur Ventures LLC v Texas Keystone Inc [2011] EWHC 1624 . . . .[Sch 2 Art 16-10], [s 3-5], [s 8-11]
Fedax NV v Venezuela (1997 unreported) . . . . .[Sch 3 Art 25-8], [Sch 3 Art 25-12]
Ferris v Plaister (1994) 34 NSWLR 474; 11 BCL 417 . . . .[Sch 2 Art 16-2]
Fiona Trust & Holding Corp v Privalov [2007] 4 All ER 951; [2007] All ER (D) 233 (Oct); [2008] 1 Lloyd's Rep 254 .[s 7-11], [Sch 2 Art 16-2]
Fisheries Jurisdiction (Interim Protection) [1972] ICJ Rep 12 . . . .[Sch 3 Art 47-3]
Flakt Australia Ltd v Wilkins and Davies Construction Co Ltd [1979] 2 NSWLR 243; (1979) 25 ALR 605; 39 FLR 267 . . .[s 7-5], [s 7-9], [s 7-15], [s 7-17], [s 7-23]
Fox v Welfair Ltd [1981] 2 Lloyd's Rep 514 . . . .[s 8-14]
Francis Travel Marketing Pty Ltd v Virgin Atlantic Airways Ltd (1996) 39 NSWLR 160 .[s 7-11]
Fulham Football Club (1987) Ltd v Richards [2011] EWCACiv 855 . . . .[s 7-12], [s 7-21]
Fung Sang Trading Ltd v Kai Sun Sea Products and Food Co Ltd [1991] HKCFI 190 . . . . . .[Sch 2 Art 1-3], [Sch 2 Art 11-13], [Sch 2 Art 16-2]
Furness Withy (Aust) Pty Ltd v Metal Distributors (UK) Ltd ("The Amazonia") [1990] 1 Lloyd's Rep 236 . . . .[s 2C-4], [s 2C-7]
Galsworthy Ltd v Glory Wealth Shipping Pte Ltd [2011] 1 SLR 727 . . . .[s 8-11]
Gao Haiyan v Keeneye Holdings Ltd [2011] HKCFI 240 . . . .[Sch 2 Art 4-5], [s 8-22], [s 18A-4]
— v — [2011] HKCFI 767 . . . .[s 8-21]
Gascor v Ellicott [1996] VR 332 .[Sch 2 Art 12-4]

References are to paragraph numbers

Gater Assets Ltd v Nak Naftogaz Ukrainiy [2008] All ER (D) 232 (Oct); [2008] 1 All ER (Comm) 209; [2007] 2 Lloyd's Rep 558 . . . .[s 8-30]
Gay Constructions Pty Ltd v Caledonian Techmore (Building) Ltd [1995] 2 HKLR 35 . . . .[Sch 2 Art 7-6], [Sch 2 Art 7-7], [Sch 2 Art 7-8]
GE Transportation SpA v Republic Of Albania (2010) 693 F Supp 2d 132 . . . .[s 8-24]
Gordian Runoff Ltd v Westport Insurance Corp (2010) 267 ALR 74 . . . .[Sch 2 Art 31-3]
Gough; R v [1993] AC 646; [1993] 2 All ER 724; (1993) 97 Cr App Rep 188; [1993] 2 WLR 883 . . . . .[Sch 2 Art 12-7], [s 18A-1], [s 18A-3]
Government Insurance Office of New South Wales v Atkinson-Leighton Joint Venture (1981) 146 CLR 206; 55 ALJR 212; 1 ANZ Ins Cas 60-425 . . . .[s 25-2]
Grimaldi SpA v Sckihyo Lones Ltd [1990] 1 WLR 708 . . . .[s 7-22]
Gruslin v Malaysia (2000 unreported) . . . .[Sch 3 Art 25-15]
Gulf Canada Resources v Arochem International [1992] CanLII 4033 (BC CA); (1992) 43 CPR (3d) 390 . . . .[Sch 2 Art 8-4]
Habas Sinai VE Tibbi Gazlar Isthisal Endustri AS v Sometal SAL [2010] All ER (D) 99 (Jan); [2010] 1 All ER (Comm) 1143; [2010] 1 Lloyd's Rep 661 . . . .[Sch 2 Art 7-8]
Hallen v Angledal [1999] NSWSC 552; BC9903040 . . . .[s 8-24]
Harbour Assurance Co (UK) Ltd v Kansa General International Insurance Co Ltd [1993] QB 701; [1993] 3 All ER 897; [1993] 3 WLR 42; [1993] 1 Lloyd's Rep 455 . . . . . .[Sch 2 Art 16-2]
Hashwani v Jivraj [2011] All ER (D) 246 (Jul); [2011] 1 WLR 1872 . . . .[s 28-4], [Sch 2 Art 11-1]
Hebei Import & Export Corp v Polytek Engineering Co Ltd [1991] 1 HKLRD 665 (CFA) .[s 8-11], [s 8-22], [Sch 2 Art 4-5]
— v — [1996] 3 HKC 725 . . . . .[s 8-24], [s 8-25]
— v — [1999] 2 HKC 205 . . . .[s 8-21]
Heller Financial Services Ltd v Thiess Contractors Pty Ltd [2000] FCA 802; BC200003220 . .[s 7-14]
Hi-Fert Pty Ltd v Kiukiang Maritime Carriers Inc (1998) 155 ALR 94 . . . .[s 7-16]
— v Kiukiang Maritime Carriers Inc (No 5) (1998) 90 FCR 1; 159 ALR 142; [1999] 2 Lloyd's Rep 782 . . . .[s 2C-9], [s 7-3], [s 7-17], [s 7-21]
— v United Shipping Adriatic Inc (1998) 89 FCR 166; 165 ALR 265 . . . . .[s 2C-9], [s 2C-10]
HIH Casualty & General Insurance Ltd (in liq) v Wallace (2006) 68 NSWLR 603; 204 FLR 297 . . . .[s 7-21]
Hiscox v Outhwaite [1992] 1 AC 562; [1991] 3 All ER 124; [1991] 2 Lloyd's Rep 1; [1991] 2 WLR 1321 . . . .[Sch 2 Art 20-9]

— v — [1991] 3 All ER 641; [1991] 2 Lloyd's Rep 435; [1991] 3 WLR 297 . . .[Sch 2 Art 31-6]
Hrvatska Elektroprivreda v Slovenia (2008 unreported) . . . .[Sch 3 Art 44-2]
Hussmann (Europe) Ltd v Ahmed Pharaon [2003] All ER (D) 17 (Mar); [2003] 1 All ER (Comm) 879 . . . .[Sch 2 Art 34-9]
IBM Australia v National Distribution Services (1991) 22 NSWLR 466; 100 ALR 361; 20 IPR 95; ATPR 41-094 . . . .[Sch 2 Art 16-2]
IBM Word Trade Corp v Ecuador (2003 unreported) . . . .[Sch 3 Art 39-4]
ICT Pty Ltd v Sea Containers Ltd [2002] NSWSC 77; BC200200385 . . . .[s 18A-2]
IMC Aviation Solutions Pty Ltd v Altain Khuder LLC [2011] VSCA 248; BC201106268 . .[s 2D-2], [s 2D-4], [s 8-2], [s 8-7], [s 8-10], [s 8-11], [s 8-13], [s 8-14], [s 8-21], [s 8-23], [s 9-2]
Imperial Leatherware Co Pty Ltd v Macri & Marcellino Pty Ltd (1991) 22 NSWLR 653 . . . . . .[Sch 2 Art 5-4], [Sch 2 Art 31-3]
Inceysa Vallisoletana SL v El Salvador (2006 unreported) . . . .[Sch 3 Art 41-3]
Incitec Ltd v Alkimos Shipping Corp (2004) 138 FCR 496; 206 ALR 558 . . . . . .[s 7-11], [s 7-13]
Industries Ltd v Western Bulk Ltd [2011] EWHC 93 (Comm) . . . .[Sch 2 Art 29-2]
Insigma Technology Co Ltd v Alstom Technology Ltd [2008] SGHC 134 . . . . .[Sch 2 Art 16-9]
IPCO (Nigeria) Ltd v Nigeria National Petroleum Corp [2008] EWHC 797 . . . .[s 8-18]
— v Nigerian National Petroleum Corp [2005] EWHC 726 . . . .[s 8-24], [s 8-25]
Ispat Industries Ltd v Western Bulk Pte Ltd [2011] EWHC 93 .[Sch 2 Art 9-4], [Sch 2 Art 31-4]
IW v City of Perth (1997) 191 CLR 1; 94 LGERA 224; 146 ALR 696 . . . .[s 2D-3]
James Miller & Partners Ltd v Whitworth Street Estates (Manchester) Ltd [1970] AC 583; [1970] 1 All ER 796; [1970] 2 WLR 728; [1970] 1 Lloyd's Rep 269 . . . . . .[Sch 2 Art 20-1]
Jebsens International (Aust) Pty Ltd v Interfert Australia Ltd (2011 unreported) . . .[s 2C-10]
Kanoria v Guiness [2006] 2 All ER (Comm) 413; [2006] 1 Lloyd's Rep 701 . .[s 8-12], [s 8-14]
— v — (2005 unreported) . . . .[s 8-12]
Karaha Bodas Co, LLC v Perusahaan Pertambangan Minyak Dan Gas Bumi Negara (2004) 364 F 3d 274 . . . .[s 2D-2]
Kempinski Hotels SA v PT Prima International Development [2011] SGHC 171 . . . .[s 8-15], [Sch 2 Art 32-1], [Sch 2 Art 33-1], [Sch 2 Art 34-9]
Kim Meller Imports Pty Ltd v Eurolevent Spa (1986) 7 NSWLR 269; 87 FLR 247 . . . . .[s 2C-5]
Klöckner Industrie-Anlagen GmbH v Cameroon and Société Camerouaise des Engrais (1985 unreported) . . . .[Sch 3 Art 52-4]

References are to paragraph numbers

TABLE OF CASES

Klöckner Pentaplast GmbH & Co v Advance Technology (H.K.) Co Ltd [2011] HKCFI 48 ....[s 7-22]
La Donna Pty Ltd v Wolford AG (2005) 194 FLR 26 ....[s 7-21]
Lafarge Redland Aggregates Ltd v Shepherd Hill Civil Engineering Ltd [2001] 1 All ER 34; [2000] 1 WLR 1621 ....[s 24-3]
Larkden Pty Ltd v Lloyd Energy Systems Pty Ltd (2011) 279 ALR 772 .....[Sch 2 Art 16-8], [s 7-12]
Larsen Oil and Gas Pte Ltd v Petroprod Ltd [2011] SGCA 21 ....[s 7-11], [s 7-12]
Lehigh Valley Railroad Co v Board of Public Utility Commissioners (1928) 278 US 24 ....[Sch 3 Art 51-2]
Lesotho Highlands Development Authority v Impregilio SpA [2006] 1 AC 221; [2005] All ER (D) 363 (Jun); [2005] 3 All ER 789 .[s 3-5], [Sch 2 Art 34-5]
Leung v Minister for Immigration and Multicultural Affairs (1997) 74 FCR 430; 46 ALD 519; 25 AAR 113 ....[Sch 2 Art 32-1]
LG&E v Argentina (2006 unreported) ....[Sch 3 Art 42-6]
Liberian Eastern Timber Company (LETCO) v Liberia (1986 unreported) .[Sch 3 Art 42-5], [Sch 3 Art 45-2]
Liberty Re-insurance Canada v QBE Insurance and Re-insurance (Europe) Ltd (2002) 42 CCLI (3d) 249 ....[Sch 2 Art 28-4]
Lief Investments Pty Ltd v Conagra International Fertiliser Co [1998] NSWCA 481; BC9803166 ....[s 3-3], [s 7-12], [Sch 2 Art 7-8]
Lightsource Technologies Australia Pty Ltd v Pointsec Mobile Technologies AB (2011) 250 FLR 63 ....[s 7-5], [s 7-8], [s 7-22], [s 21-3]
Lindow v Barton McGill Marine Ltd (2002) 16 PRNZ 796 .....[Sch 2 Art 9-3], [Sch 2 Art 17-6]
Lipman Pty Ltd v Emergency Services Superannuation Board [2011] NSWCA 163; BC201104482 ....[s 7-11]
Lkt v Chun [2004] NSWSC 820; BC200406102 ....[s 8-3], [s 8-13], [s 8-14]
Louis Dreyfus Trading Ltd v Bonarich International (Group) Ltd [1997] HKCFI 312 ....[Sch 2 Art 8-6]
McConnell Dowell Constructors (Aust) Pty Ltd v Ship 'Asian Atlas' [2011] FCA 174; BC201100867 ....[s 7-6]
McHutchinson v Western Research and Development Ltd [2004] FCA 1234; BC200406153 .[s 7-14]
MCI Power Group LC and New Turbine, Inc v Ecuador (2009 unreported) .[Sch 3 Art 52-12]
Maffezini v Spain (1999 unreported) ....[Sch 3 Art 47-6]
Malaysian Historical Salvors Sdn Bhd v Malaysia (2007 unreported) .....[Sch 3 Art 25-11], [Sch 3 Art 25-12]

— v — (2009 unreported) ..[Sch 3 Preamble-1], [Sch 3 Art 25-12]
Mareva Companania Naviera SA v International Bulkcarriers SA [1975] 2 Lloyd's Rep 509 ....[s 8-33]
Margulead Ltd v Exide Technologies [2004] All ER (D) 94 (May); [2004] 2 All ER (Comm) 727 ....[s 8-14], [Sch 2 Art 33-2]
Margulies Brothers Ltd v Dafnis Thomaides & Co (UK) Ltd [1958] 1 Lloyd's Rep 205 .[s 8-6]
Maritime International Nominees Establishment v Guinea (1989 unreported) .[Sch 3 Art 52-4], [Sch 3 Art 52-7]
Marnell Corrao Associates Inc v Sensation Yachts Ltd (2000 unreported) ......[Sch 2 Art 8-5], [Sch 2 Art 9-3]
Maybury v Atlantic Union Oil Co Ltd (1953) 89 CLR 507; 28 ALJR 254 ....[s 3-3]
Menna v HD Building Pty Ltd (1986 unreported) ....[Sch 2 Art 31-3]
Meshlawn Pty Ltd v Qld [2010] QCA 181; BC201005136 ....[s 28-4]
Methanex Motunui Ltd v Spellman [2004] 1 NZLR 95 .....[Sch 2 Art 18-1], [Sch 2 Art 24-6], [Sch 2 Art 31-5], [Sch 2 Art 34-2], [Sch 2 Art 34-5], [s 8-14], [s 8-23]
Metrocall Inc v Electronic Tracking Systems Pty Ltd (2000) 52 NSWLR 1; 101 IR 66 ....[s 7-12]
Michael Wilson & Partners Ltd v Emmott [2008] EWHC 2684 ....[Sch 2 Art 16-7]
Michel Rhéaume v Société d'Investissements l'Excellence Inc 2010 QCCA 2269 ....[Sch 2 Art 36-4]
MINE Maritime International Nominees Establishment v Guinea (1989 unreported) ....[Sch 3 Art 52-8]
Minister for Immigration and Ethnic Affairs v Teoh (1995) 39 ALD 206; 183 CLR 273; 128 ALR 353 ....[s 31-10]
Minmetals Germany v Ferco Steel [1999] 1 All ER (Comm) 315 ....[s 8-14], [s 8-15], [s 8-25]
— v — [1999] 1 All ER 315 ....[s 8-24]
Mitsui Engineering and Shipbuilding Co Ltd v Easton Graham Rush (2004) SLR 14 .[Sch 2 Art 5-2]
ML Ubase Holdings Co Ltd v Trigem Computer Inc (2007) 69 NSWLR 577 ....[s 8-28]
— v — [2005] NSWSC 224; BC200501412 .[s 8-2], [s 9-2]
Momcilovic v R (2011) 280 ALR 221 ....[s 8-6]
Mond v Berger (2005) 21 BCL 125 .....[s 28-4], [s 28-5]
MTD Equity Sdn Bhd & MTD Chile SA v Chile (2007 unreported) .....[Sch 3 Art 52-5], [Sch 3 Art 52-8]
Murrumbidgee Irrigation Ltd v Goodwood Services Pty Ltd [2010] NSWSC 914; BC201006113 ....[s 7-17]

References are to paragraph numbers

Najjar v Haines (1991) 25 NSWLR 224; 10 BCL 272;
11 BCL 315 . . . .[s 28-4]
Nanjing Cereals, Oils and Foodstuffs Import & Export
Corp v Luckmate Commodities Trading Ltd
[1994] HKCFI 140 . . . . . .[Sch 2 Art 36-4]
Nanjing Tianshun Shipbuilding Co Ltd v Orchard
Tankers PTE Ltd [2011] EWHC 164 .[s 7-22]
Naviera Amazonica Peruana SA v Compania
International De Seguros Del Peru [1988] 2
Lloyd's Rep 116 . . . .[Sch 2 Art 20-1]
Nicola v Ideal Image Development Corp Inc (2009)
261 ALR 1 . . . .[s 7-11], [s 7-12]
Nigerian National Petroleum Corp v IPCO (Nigeria)
Ltd [2008] All ER (D) 197 (Oct); [2009] 1 All
ER (Comm) 611; [2009] 1 Lloyd's Rep 89
. . . .[s 8-18], [s 8-24]
Northbuild Construction Pty Ltd v Discovery Beach
Project Pty Ltd [2010] QSC 94; BC201002049
. . . .[Sch 2 Art 31-3]
Northern Cameroons (Cameroon v United Kingdom)
[1963] ICJ Rep 15 . . . . . .[Sch 3 Art 25-5]
O'Brien v Tanning Research Laboratories Inc (1988)
14 NSWLR 601; 84 ALR 221; (1989) 7 ACLC
182; (1988) 93 FLR 270 . . . .[s 7-17]
Occidental Petroleum Corp and Occidental
Exploration and Production Co v Ecuador (2007
unreported) . . . .[Sch 3 Art 47-5],
[Sch 3 Art 47-6]
Ocean Steamship Company v Queensland State
Wheat Board [1941] 1 KB 402 . . . .[s 2C-3]
Oil Basins Ltd v BHP Billiton Ltd (2007) 18 VR 346;
[2007] VSCA 255; BC200709808
. . . .[Sch 2 Art 31-3], [s 28-4]
ONGC Ltd v Saw Pipes Ltd (2003) 5 SCC 705
. . . .[Sch 2 Art 34-4]
Opotiki Packing v Opotiki Fruitgrowers [2003] 1
NZLR 205 . . . .[Sch 2 Art 32-1],
[Sch 2 Art 33-1], [Sch 2 Art 34-7]
Origin Energy Resources Ltd v Benaris International
NV [2002] TASSC 50; BC200204520 .[s 7-15]
Pacific China Holdings Ltd v Grand Pacific Holdings
Ltd [2011] HKCFI 424 . . . .[s 8-8], [s 8-14],
[s 18C-2], [Sch 2 Art 34-6]
Paczy v Haendler & Natermann GmbH [1981] 1
Lloyd's Rep 302 . . . .[s 7-22]
Paharpur Cooling Towers Ltd v Paramount (WA) Ltd
[2008] WASCA 110; BC200803347 . .[s 7-11],
[s 7-12]
Paklito Investment Ltd v Klockner East Asia Ltd
[1993] 2 HKLR 39 .[Sch 2 Art 34-6], [s 8-14]
Pamphilos, The [2002] 2 Lloyd's Rep 681 .[s 8-14]
Parsons & Whittemore Overseas Co Inc v Société
Générale De L'Industrie Du Papier (1974) 508 F
2d 969 . . . .[s 2D-2]
Pathak v Tourism Transport Ltd [2002] 3 NZLR 681
. . . .[Sch 2 Art 8-6]
Petersville Ltd v Peters (WA) Ltd (1997) ATPR
41-566 . . . .[s 7-12]

Phoenix Action v Czech Republic (2009 unreported)
. . . .[Sch 3 Art 25-12]
PMT Partners Pty Ltd (In Liq) v Australian National
Parks & Wildlife Service (1995) 184 CLR 301;
131 ALR 377; 69 ALJR 829 . . . . . .[s 3-3]
Porter v Magill [2002] 2 AC 357; [2002] 1 All ER
465; [2002] 2 WLR 37 . .[s 8-21], [s 18A-3],
[s 18A-4]
Powerex Corp v Alcan Inc [2004] BCCA 504
. . . .[s 8-24]
Private Company "Triple V" Inc v Star (Universal) Co
Ltd [1995] 3 HKC 129 . . .[Sch 2 Art 11-11]
Property People Ltd v Housing New Zealand Ltd
(1999) 14 PRNZ 66 . . . . . .[Sch 2 Art 8-6]
PSEG Global Inc v Turkey (2004 unreported)
. . . .[Sch 3 Art 25-19]
PT Asuransi Jasa Indonesia (Persero) v Dexia Bank
SA [2006] SGCA 41 . . . . .[s 8-14], [s 8-21],
[Sch 2 Art 16-7]
PT Garuda Indonesia v Birgen Air [2002] 1 SLR(R)
401 . . . .[Sch 2 Art 1-8], [Sch 2 Art 20-1],
[Sch 2 Art 20-2], [Sch 2 Art 34-2]
PT Thiess Contractors Indonesia v PT Kaltim Prima
Coal [2011] EWHC 1842 . . .[s 7-9], [s 7-11]
QH Tours Ltd v Ship Design & Management (Aust)
Pty Ltd (1991) 33 FCR 227; 105 ALR 371; 22
IPR 447 . [s 7-4], [s 8-24], [Sch 2 Art 16-2]
Queensland Power Trading Corp v Xstrata
Queensland Ltd [2005] QCA 477;
BC200510862 . . . .[Sch 2 Art 1-5]
R v Abdroikov [2008] 1 All ER 315; [2007] All ER
(D) 226 (Oct); [2007] 1 WLR 2679 .[s 18A-3]
— v Gough [1993] AC 646; [1993] 2 All ER 724;
(1993) 97 Cr App Rep 188; [1993] 2 WLR 883
. . . . .[Sch 2 Art 12-7], [s 18A-1], [s 18A-3]
Raguz v Sullivan (2000) 50 NSWLR 236
. .[Sch 2 Art 20-6], [Sch 2 Art 20-8], [s 3-5],
[s 7-5], [s 21-3]
Ram International Industries, Inc v Air Force of Iran
29 Ir-USCTR 383 . . . .[Sch 3 Art 51-2]
Ranko Group v Antarctic Maritime SA (1998
unreported) . . . .[Sch 2 Art 16-7]
Recyclers of Australia Pty Ltd v Hettinga Equipment
Inc (2000) 100 FCR 420; 175 ALR 725
. . . .[s 7-9], [s 7-13], [s 7-17]
Repsol YPF Ecuador SA v Empresa Estatal Petroleos
del Ecuador (2007 unreported)
. . . .[Sch 3 Art 52-5]
Resort Condominiums Inc v Bolwell [1995] 1 Qd R
406; (1993) 118 ALR 655 . .[s 3-7], [s 8-5],
[s 8-7], [s 8-21], [s 8-31], [Sch 2 Art 5-4]
Road Regenerating and Repair Services v Mitchell
Water Board BC9000777 . . . .[s 28-3]
Ron Fuchs v Georgia (2010 unreported) . .[s 31-4],
[Sch 3 Art 52-13]
Rosseel NV v Oriental Commercial & Shipping Co
(UK) Ltd [1991] 2 Lloyd's Rep 625 . .[s 8-2],
[s 8-10]

References are to paragraph numbers

TABLE OF CASES

— v Oriental Shipping Ltd [1990] 1 WLR 1386 ....[s 8-33]
RSM Production Corp v Grenada (2009 unreported) ....[Sch 3 Art 44-2]
— v — (2011 unreported) ....[Sch 3 Art 52-10]
Saba Fakes v Turkey (2010 unreported) ....[Sch 3 Art 25-12]
Safond Shipping Sdn Bhd v East Asia Sawmill Corp [1993] HKCFI 151 .....[Sch 2 Art 11-14]
Salini Costruttori SpA and Italstrade SpA v Morocco (2001 unreported) .....[Sch 3 Art 25-12]
Santos Ltd v Pipelines Authority of South Australia (1996) 66 SASR 38; BC9601565 ....[Sch 2 Art 1-5]
Seeley International Pty Ltd v Electra Air Conditioning BV (2008) 246 ALR 589 ....[s 7-11]
Seimens Ltd v Origin Energy Uranquinty Power Pty Ltd (2011) 279 ALR 759 ..[s 7-12], [s 7-21]
Sempra Energy International v Argentina (2007 unreported) ....[Sch 3 Art 42-7]
Shangdong Hongri Acron Chemical Joint Stock Co Ltd v Petrochina International (Hong Kong) Corp Ltd [2011] HKCA 124 ......[s 8-30]
Shanghai Foreign Trade Corporation v Sigma Metallurgical Co Pty Ltd (1996) 133 FLR 417 ....[s 7-21], [Sch 2 Art 8-4]
Shashoua v Sharma [2009] All ER (D) 64 (May); [2009] 2 All ER (Comm) 477; [2009] 2 Lloyd's Rep 376 ......[s 7-5], [Sch 2 Art 20-7]
Shoalhaven City Council v Firedam Civil Engineering Pty Ltd [2011] HCA 38; BC201107576 ....[Sch 2 Art 1-5]
Sinclair & Lindsay Sinclair Pty Ltd v Bayly & Earle (1994) 11 BCL 439 ....[s 28-4]
Skips Nordheim v Syrian Petroleum [1984] 1 QB 599 ....[Sch 2 Art 7-8]
Slaughter v American Arbitration Association (2011 unreported) ....[s 28-3]
Société Nationale d'Opérations Petrolières de la Cote d'Ivoire — Holding v Keen Lloyd Resources Ltd [2001] HKCFI 173 ....[s 8-17]
Soleh Boneh v Uganda Govt [1993] 2 Lloyd's Rep 208 ....[s 8-25]
Soleimany v Soleimany [1999] QB 785; [1999] 3 All ER 847; [1998] 3 WLR 811 .....[s 8-21]
Sonmez Denizcilik Ve Ticaret Anonim Sirketi v The Blooming Orchard (1990) 22 NSWLR 273 ....[s 2C-4]
SOS Corporación Alimentaria SA v Inerco Trade SA [2010] 2 Lloyd's Rep 345 ...[Sch 2 Art 4-6]
Soufraki v United Arab Emirates (2004 unreported) ....[Sch 3 Art 42-2]
South West Africa Cases [1962] ICJ 319 ....[Sch 3 Art 25-5]
Sovarex SA v Alvarez SA [2011] EWHC 1661 ....[Sch 2 Art 16-10], [s 8-11]

State Government Insurance Corporation v Government Insurance Office of NSW (1991) 28 FCR 511; 101 ALR 259; 21 IPR 65 ..[s 2B-2]
Stericorp Ltd v Stericycle Inc [2005] VSC 203; BC200504017 ....[s 7-13], [s 7-21]
Stern v National Australia Bank [1999] FCA 1421; BC9907269 ....[s 8-21]
Suez, Sociedad General de Aguas de Barcelona SA and InterAguas Servicios Integrales del Agua SA v The Argentine Republic (2007 unreported) ......[Sch 3 Art 14-2], [Sch 3 Art 57-3]
Swift-Fortune Ltd v Magnifica Marine SA [2006] SGCA 42 ....[Sch 2 Art 9-3]
Tan Boon Jek Jeffrey v Tan Poh Lang Stanley [2001] 3 SLR 237 ....[Sch 2 Art 32-1]
Tanning Research Laboratories Inc v O'Brien (1990) 169 CLR 332; 91 ALR 180; 64 ALJR 211 ..[s 7-9], [s 7-11], [s 7-12], [s 7-13], [s 7-14], [s 7-15], [s 7-17]
Television New Zealand Ltd v Langley Productions Ltd [2000] 2 NZLR 250 ......[s 23C-3]
The Bay Hotel and Resort Ltd v Cavalier Construction Co Ltd [2001] All ER (D) 229 (Jul); [2001] 5 LRC 376 ......[s 24-2], [Sch 2 Art 31-3], [Sch 2 Art 31-5]
Thoroughvision Pty Ltd v Sky Channel Pty Ltd [2010] VSC 139; BC201002353 ...[Sch 2 Art 31-3]
Tjong Very Sumito v Antig Investments [2009] 4 SLR (R) 732 ....[s 7-12]
Tokios Tokeles v Ukraine (2003 unreported) ....[Sch 3 Art 47-6]
Tommy CP Sze & Co v Li & Fung (Trading) Ltd [2002] HKCFI 682 ..[Sch 2 Art 8-4], [s 7-22]
Toyo Engineering Corp v John Holland Pty Ltd [2000] VSC 553; BC200007910 ....[s 8-24]
Trade Fortune Incorporated v Amalgamated Mill Supplies Ltd (1994) 89 BCLR (2d) 132; 113 DLR (4th) 116 ....[Sch 2 Art 17J-3]
Trail Smelter Case (1911 unreported) ......[Sch 2 Art 17-3], [Sch 3 Art 47-2]
Transfield Philippines Inc v Pacific Hydro Ltd [2006] VSC 175; BC200609991 ..[s 7-11], [s 7-15]
Transpac Capital Pte Ltd v Buntoro [2008] NSWSC 671; BC200805307 .....[s 8-28], [s 9-2]
Trave Schiffahrtsgesellschaft mbH & Co KG v Ninemia Maritime Corp [1986] QB 802; [1986] 2 All ER 244; [1986] 2 WLR 773; [1986] 1 Lloyd's Rep 393 ....[Sch 2 Art 31-3]
Tridon Australia Pty Ltd v ACD Tridon Inc (2004) 20 BCL 413 ....[s 8-3], [s 8-6]
Trustees of Rotoaira Forest Trust v Attorney-General [1999] 2 NZLR 452 .....[Sch 2 Art 18-4], [Sch 2 Art 18-5], [s 8-14]
Trygg Hansa Insurance Co Ltd v Equitas Ltd [1998] 2 Lloyd's Rep 439 ....[Sch 2 Art 7-8]
TW Thomas & Co v Portsea Steamship Co [1912] AC 1 ....[Sch 2 Art 7-8]

References are to paragraph numbers

Uganda Telecom Ltd v Hi-Tech Telecom Pty Ltd (2011) 277 ALR 415 . . . . .[s 2D-2], [s 8-8], [s 8-13], [s 8-14], [s 8-21], [s 8-28]
— v Hi-Tech Telecom Pty Ltd (No 2) (2011) 277 ALR 441 . . . .[s 8-4], [s 8-6], [s 8-27], [s 8-28]
Union of India v McDonnell Douglas Corp [1993] 2 Lloyd's Rep 48 . . . .[Sch 2 Art 20-1], [Sch 2 Art 20-5], [Sch 2 Art 20-8]
United Mexican States v Metalclad Corp (2001) BCSC 664 (CanLii); 14 BLR (3d) 285 . . . .[Sch 2 Art 1-4]
Vantage Holdings Pty Ltd v JHC Developments Group Pty Ltd [2011] QSC 155; BC201103834 . . . .[s 7-4]
Vee Networks Ltd v Econet Wireless International Ltd [2004] All ER (D) 209 (Dec); [2005] 1 All ER (Comm) 303; [2005] 1 Lloyd's Rep 192 . . . .[Sch 2 Art 16-2]
— v Econonet Wireless International Ltd [2004] EWHC 2909 . . . .[s 8-14]
Veerman v Germany 25 ILR 522 .[Sch 2 Art 17-3], [Sch 3 Art 47-2]
Velásquez Rodríguez (Merits) 95 ILR 259 . . . . . .[Sch 2 Art 17-3], [Sch 3 Art 47-2]
Vibroflotation AG v Express Builders Co Ltd (1994 unreported) . . . .[Sch 2 Art 27-3]
Victims Compensation Fund v Brown (2002) 54 NSWLR 668; 129 A Crim R 538 . . .[s 2D-3]
Victims Compensation Fund Corp v — (2003) 201 ALR 260; 77 ALJR 1797 . . . .[s 2D-3]
Victor Pey Casado and President Allende Foundation v Chile (2001 unreported) .[Sch 3 Art 47-6]
— v — (2009 unreported) . . . .[s 31-4]
Wagners Nouvelle Caledonie Sarl v Vale Inco Nouvelle Caledonie SAS [2010] QCA 219; BC201005964 . . . .[s 7-5], [s 21-3]

Walter Rau Neusser Oel und Fett v Cross Pacific Trading Ltd [2005] FCA 1102; BC200505922 . . . .[s 7-11], [s 7-17]
Wena Hotels v Egypt (2005 unreported) . . .[s 31-3]
— v Egypt (2002 unreported) . . .[Sch 3 Art 52-7]
— v — (2005 unreported) . . . . .[Sch 3 Art 50-3]
Wena Hotels Ltd v — (2002 unreported) . . . .[Sch 3 Art 42-6]
West Tankers Inc v Allianz SpA [2011] EWHC 829 . . . .[s 8-6]
Westacre Investments Inc v Jugoimport-SPDR Holding Co Ltd [2000] 1 QB 288; [1999] 3 All ER 864; [1999] 3 WLR 811 . . . . . .[s 8-21]
— v Jugoimport-SPDR Ltd [1999] QB 740; [1998] 4 All ER 570; [1998] 3 WLR 770; [1998] 2 Lloyd's Rep 111 . . . .[s 8-21]
Westport Insurance Corp v Gordian Runoff Ltd [2011] HCA 37; BC2011075079 . . .[Sch 2 Art 31-3]
WesTrac Pty Ltd v Eastcoast OTR Tyres Pty Ltd (2008) 219 FLR 461 . .[s 3-2], [s 7-8], [s 7-9], [s 7-11], [s 7-15], [s 7-17]
White Industries Ltd v Trammel (1983) 51 ALR 779; 76 FLR 48; (1983) ATPR 40-429 . . .[s 7-17]
Wires Jolley LLP v Wong [2010] BCSC 391 . . . .[s 8-24], [s 8-25]
Yang v S & L Consulting Pty Ltd [2009] NSWSC 223; BC200902011 . . . .[s 9-2]
Yugraneft Corp v Rexx Management Corp [2010] 1 SCR 649 . . . .[Sch 2 Art 5-5], [s 8-29]
Yukos Oil Co v Dardana Ltd [2001] EWCACiv 1007 . . . .[s 8-25]
Zermalt Holdings SA v Nu Life Upholstery Repairs Ltd [1985] 2 EGLR 14 . . . .[s 8-14]
Zhang v Shanghai Wool and Jute Textile Co Ltd (2006) 201 FLR 178 . . . . .[s 7-15], [s 7-21]

Table of Statutes

References are to paragraph numbers

COMMONWEALTH

Acts Interpretation Act 1901
s 15AA . . . .[s 2D-4]
s 15AB . . . .[s 17-4], [s 31-10]

Arbitration (Foreign Awards and Agreements) Act 1974 . . . .[s 3-1], [s 13-1]
s 14 . . . .[s 14-1]

Ashmore and Cartier Islands Acceptance Act 1933
. . . .[s 2A-2]

Australian Antarctic Territory Act 1954 . .[s 2A-2]

Carriage of Goods by Sea Act 1991 . . . .[s 2C-8], [s 7-21]
s 2 . . . .[s 2C-13]
s 6 . . . .[s 2C-13]
s 11 . . . .[s 2C-9], [s 2C-12]
s 11(1) . . . .[s 2C-9]
s 11(2) . . . .[s 2C-9], [s 2C-10]
s 16 . . . .[s 2C-13]
s 20 . . . .[s 2C-8]
s 20(2) . . . .[s 2C-1]

Competition and Consumer Act 2010
s 7(2) . . . .[s 7-11]
s 52 . . . .[s 7-11]
s 87 . . . .[s 7-11]

Consular Privileges and Immunities Act 1972
s 12 . . . .[s 36-3]

Coral Sea Islands Act 1969 . . . .[s 2A-2]

Corporations Act 2001
s 459G . . . .[s 7-4]

Diplomatic Privileges and Immunities Act 1967
. . . .[s 31-7]
s 7 . . . .[Sch 3 Art 20-1]
s 14 . . . .[s 36-3]

Federal Court of Australia Act 1976 . . . .[s 7-16]
s 8(7) . . . .[s 8-27]
s 52 . . . .[s 8-27]
s 52(1) . . . .[s 8-27]

Foreign States Immunities Act 1985
. . . .[Sch 3 Art 55-3]
s 31 . . . .[Sch 3 Art 55-3]

Heard Island and McDonald Islands Act 1953
. . . .[s 2A-2]

International Arbitration Act 1974
. . .[Sch 3 Art 69-1], [Sch 3 Art 70-1], [s 31-1]
Pt II . . . .[s 34-2]
Pt III . . . .[s 34-2]

Pt IV . . . .[s 31-1]
s 2A . . . .[s 2A-1]
s 2B . . . .[s 2B-2]
s 3(1) . . . .[s 2A-1]
s 4 . . . .[s 2A-1]
s 5 . . . .[s 2A-1]
s 7(2) . . . .[s 2A-3]

International Organisations (Privileges and Immunities) Act 1963 .[Sch 3 Art 19-2], [Sch 3 Art 20-3], [Sch 3 Art 21-6], [Sch 3 Art 23-2], [Sch 3 Art 24-3]
s 9A . . . .[Sch 3 Art 19-2]

Judiciary Act 1903
Pt II . . . .[s 13-2]
s 13 . . . .[s 13-2]
s 38 . . . .[s 13-2], [s 38-2], [s 38-3]

Norfolk Island Act 1979 . . . .[s 2A-2]

Sea-Carriage of Goods Act 1924 . . . . . .[s 2C-8]
s 2C . . . .[s 2C-1]
s 9 . . . .[s 2C-1], [s 2C-2], [s 2C-3], [s 2C-4], [s 2C-5], [s 2C-7], [s 2C-8], [s 2C-11]
s 9(1) . . . .[s 2C-2], [s 2C-6]
s 9(2) . . . .[s 2C-2], [s 2C-3], [s 2C-9]

Statute Law Revision Act 2011 . . . .[s 31-1]
s 10(1) . . . .[s 31-7]
s 10A(1) . . . .[s 31-7]
s 10A(5) . . . .[s 31-7]
s 77 . . . .[s 31-8]

ENGLAND, WALES AND NORTHERN IRELAND

Arbitration Act 1996 . . .[s 8-2], [s 8-12], [s 8-13], [s 8-18], [Sch 2 Art31-3]
s 7 . . . .[Sch 2 Art 16-2]
s 12 . . . .[Sch 2 Art 4-6]
s 29 . . . .[s 28-2]
s 29(1) . . . .[s 28-1]
s 33(1)(a) . . . .[s 18C-2]
s 30 . . . .[Sch 2 Art 16-3]
s 36 . . . .[s 37-2]
s 65 . . . .[s 27-3]
s 69 . . . .[Sch 2 Art 34-5]
s 101 . . . .[s 8-2]
s 103(2)(c) . . . .[s 8-14]

NEW SOUTH WALES

Arbitration (Foreign Awards and Agreements) Act 1973 . . . .[s 7-23]

Commercial Arbitration Act 1984
s 42 . . . .[s 21-3]

NEW SOUTH WALES —*continued*
Commercial Arbitration Act 1984 —*continued*
s 44 . . . .[s 21-3]
s 50 . . . .[s 28-1]
s 51 . . . .[s 28-5]

VICTORIA

Supreme Court Act 1986
s 27A . . . .[s 28-5]

CHRISTMAS & COCOS (KEELING) ISLANDS

Cocos (Keeling) Islands Act 1955 . . . . .[s 2A-2]

NEW ZEALAND

Arbitration Act 1996
s 14 . . . .[s 23C-3]

UNITED KINGDOM

Arbitration Act 1979
s 7 . . . .[Sch 2 Art 7-8]

References are to paragraph numbers

International Arbitration Act 1974

Legislative Background

The starting point when considering the proper construction of the provisions of the International Arbitration Act 1974 (Cth) (the Act) is to construe the language of the Act in its natural and ordinary meaning but the language used in the Act, and the Act itself, must be put in context. This necessarily involves explanation of how the Act has evolved and the various sources of the text found in the Act. The legal nature and status of the various instruments from which the text of the Act has been drawn also need to be considered as they engage a number of different principles of statutory construction. The legislative purpose of, and background to, the Act are also relevant considerations.

The provisions of the Act relating to international commercial arbitration are primarily based on two international legal instruments, each of a distinctly different legal character and status. Part IV of the Act deals with the subject of the settlement of investment disputes between States and nationals of other States, which for present purposes may be considered separately. The first international instrument on which the Act is based is the Convention on the Recognition and Enforcement of Foreign Arbitral Awards made in New York on 10 June 1958 — commonly referred to as the New York Convention. The second is the 1985 United Nations Commission on International Trade Law Model Law on International Commercial Arbitration — commonly referred to as the Model Law.

In broad terms, the New York Convention first addresses the entry into the arbitration process — the arbitration agreement — and second, the outcome of the arbitration process — the award. The entry is facilitated and enforced by the States parties to the New York Convention agreeing to recognise an arbitration agreement by requiring that a court of a State party, when seized of an action in a matter in respect of which the parties have made an arbitration agreement, will, at the request of one of the parties, refer the parties to arbitration, unless the court finds that their arbitration agreement is null and void, inoperative or incapable of being performed. The outcome of the process is affirmed and enhanced by the contracting States agreeing to recognise foreign arbitral awards as binding and to enforce such awards except in specified and limited circumstances.

Australia was present at the conference when the Convention was signed in New York in 1958, but it was not until 1974 when the Act, then titled the Arbitration (Foreign Awards and Agreements) Act 1974 (Cth) was passed that Australia acceded to the New York Convention. Section 7 of the Act sets out the circumstances in which a foreign arbitration agreement will be enforced in similar but not identical terms to the New York Convention. Section 8 sets out the circumstances in which a foreign arbitration award will be recognised and enforced, again in terms slightly different to those used in the New York Convention. The New York Convention itself was attached as Schedule 1 to the Act.

In 1966, the United Nations General Assembly created the United Nations Commission on International Trade Law (UNCITRAL), which is based in Vienna (GA Resolution 2205 (XXI) of 17 December 1966). The United Nations General Assembly gave UNCITRAL the task of harmonising and modernising the rules of international business and the reform of commercial law. In this context, an internationally uniform system of resolving disputes by impartial and independent arbitration was, and continues to be, seen as a way of facilitating international trade and commerce, thereby advancing the objectives of the United Nations.

At the time, the procedures of international arbitration were usually governed by ad hoc arbitration rules, or by the different procedural rules of the various international arbitration institutions. Part of UNCITRAL's early work was to prepare a set of arbitration rules based upon international best practice. UNCITRAL published its Arbitration Rules in 1976. These rules were concerned with the regulation of the process from the time of the notice of dispute up until the final award. Whilst the New York Convention had addressed the entry into, and the outcome of, the process, UNCITRAL used the text and principles of the Convention to draft a set of rules which would regulate the process in a manner consistent with the New York Convention. An example can be seen in Article V(1)(b) of the New York Convention, which recognises that an award may be refused enforcement if a party was not given proper notice of the appointment of the arbitrator or the proceedings, or was otherwise unable to present its case to the arbitral tribunal. The requirement of notice was adopted in the 1976 UNCITRAL Arbitration Rules in provisions requiring parties to be given proper notice of the appointment of the arbitrator and of the proceedings (see Articles 3 and 6). The requirement of an opportunity to present a case was adopted and enhanced in Article 15(1) which gave the arbitral tribunal the freedom to conduct the arbitration in such manner as it considered appropriate, provided the parties are treated with equality and that each party is given a full opportunity of presenting that party's case.

The UNCITRAL Arbitration Rules have no force of law and are not the product of, or in the form of, an international treaty. Nor are they are a recommended form of draft legislation. They are different in their nature and effect from, and do not perform the role of, a national law on arbitration. They are merely a comprehensive set of procedural rules which the parties may agree to incorporate into their arbitration agreement as contractual terms to regulate the conduct of the arbitration of any dispute which may exist, or may arise between the parties. The description "procedural" understates their significance in that once incorporated into the parties' agreement, the terms of these rules become a source of substantive contractual rights and obligations.

UNCITRAL subsequently considered the problems caused by the inadequacies and disparities which existed in and between the various national laws dealing with international commercial arbitration. These domestic laws varied in content and understandably reflected parochial national interests rather than perhaps a more altruistic objective of facilitating international trade and commerce without an emphasis on one particular legal system or a particular form of arbitration. The outcome of this work was the 1985 UNCITRAL Model Law on International Commercial Arbitration (the Model Law). The approach and text of the Model Law draws heavily on the New York Convention and on the 1976 UNCITRAL Arbitration Rules. To give but two examples, Article 18 of the Model Law states that the parties shall be treated with equality and each party shall be given a full opportunity of presenting its case which mirrors the text of Article 15 of the 1976 UNCITRAL Arbitration Rules. Further, the text of Article 34 of the Model Law which sets out the limited grounds upon which an award may be challenged mirrors the text of Article V of the New York Convention setting out the same limited grounds on which enforcement of an award may be refused by a court of a contracting State.

The Model Law was not an operative law in itself. It was not a convention or treaty or compact between contracting States. It was not a model for a contract to be incorporated into the parties' arbitration agreement. Rather, it was, as its name suggests, a template for legislation which dealt with the subject of international commercial arbitration. It did not purport to address every aspect or issue which might arise in the course of an international arbitration. It did not purport to be a comprehensive arbitration law. The Model Law was merely an international best practice template which sovereign States could use when drafting their own laws dealing with the subject of international commercial arbitration. It has since been used as a template for arbitration laws in a diverse range and an increasing number of countries. As at the time of writing, UNCITRAL reports that the Model Law has been adopted in 73 jurisdictions (UNCITRAL, "Status of Conventions and Model Laws", UN Doc No A/CN.9/723, 4 May 2011, p 18).

Australia's adoption of the Model Law in 1989 prompted a major revision of the Act which amounted to the first attempt to enact a national arbitration law in Australia. The existing provisions of the Act which had implemented the New York Convention became Parts I and II of the Act, and a new Part III was introduced to accommodate the Model Law. In contrast to the approach taken to implement the New York Convention, the legislature implemented the Model Law verbatim. The new Part III included section 16(1), which provided, "Subject to this Part, the Model Law has the force of law in Australia". As a result the literal terms of the Model Law became the terms of an Act of the Commonwealth Parliament. The Model Law was inserted as Schedule 2 to the Act.

Part III also introduced a number of other provisions which were supportive of international arbitration and designed to encourage international arbitration to take place in Australia. These included section 28, which sought to limit the liability of an arbitrator, and section 29, which sought to attract overseas arbitration practitioners and their arbitrations. Section 29 gave a party a right to be represented by any person of that party's choice regardless of whether or not that person was a duly qualified legal practitioner practicing in the state or territory where the arbitration was held.

Part III also contained a number of provisions which were described as optional in the sense that the parties could, either in their arbitration agreement or otherwise, agree that the provisions would apply to the arbitration (the opt-in provisions). This was an unusual approach for the legislature to adopt as some of these optional provisions related to procedural matters such as interest and costs which were, and are unsurprisingly, normally accepted as part and parcel of the powers given to an arbitrator under Australian common law. On the other hand, Part III included the contentious section 21, which provided that where the parties had agreed that their dispute was to be settled "otherwise than in accordance with the Model Law", then the Model Law did not apply in relation to the settlement of that dispute (an opt-out provision).

In 1996, UNCITRAL created another significant influence on the harmonisation of the processes of international arbitration with its publication of a guide to the conduct of an international arbitration for parties, their representatives and arbitrators entitled "Notes on Organising Arbitral Proceedings" ("Report of the United Nations Commission on International Trade Law on the Work of its Twenty-ninth Session", *Official Records of the General Assembly, Fifty-first Session, Supplement No 17* (UN Doc No A/51/17)). This publication, as its name suggests, comprehensively described in practical terms how the process might be conducted and has become a standard reference point for those involved in international arbitration. The process regulated by the UNCITRAL Arbitration Rules (1976) is reflected in this publication.

Other major harmonising factors in international commercial arbitration, which have influenced the work of UNCITRAL and the text of the Model Law, include the standard practice guidelines issued by representative bodies such as the International Bar Association. Examples of their output in the area are the IBA Rules on the Taking of Evidence in International Arbitration, which were first published in 1999, and the IBA Guidelines on Conflict of Interest in International Arbitration, which were first published in 2004.

UNCITRAL (and its Working Group established to consider international arbitration) continued to examine and review the terms of the 1985 Model Law. On 7 July 2006, UNCITRAL "amended" the 1985 Model Law. As the Model Law was a template for sovereign States to use, the "amendments" made in 2006 to the Model Law did not automatically become part of, or change, the law of Australia. The records of the work of UNCITRAL and its Working Group leading to the 2006 "amendments", and the 2006 "amendments", had no immediate effect, direct or indirect, on the Act or on the proper construction of its provisions. Any effect was dependent upon the use made of these documents and changes to the Model Law by the Commonwealth Parliament.

On 21 November 2008, the Commonwealth Attorney-General announced a review of the Act and released a discussion paper to stimulate debate about the future of the Act (the Review). The Review resulted in first, the Federal Justice System Amendment (Efficiency Measures) Act (No 1) 2009 (Cth), which conferred jurisdiction under the Act on the Federal Court of Australia concurrently with that of the Supreme Courts of the States and Territories, and second, the International Arbitration Amendment Act 2010 (Cth), which involved a major revision of the Act and the adoption of the 2006 amendments to the Model Law.

The International Arbitration Amendment Act 2010 (Cth) repealed the contentious opt-out provisions of section 21 and inserted a new section 21, which provides that if the Model Law applies to an arbitration, the law of a State or Territory relating to arbitration does not apply to the arbitration. Prior to the amendment, the view had been taken that the Act did not evince an intention to cover the field and nor did the Model Law. As noted above, the Model Law did not purport to be a comprehensive law on arbitration; the parties could opt-out of the Model Law, and the Act lacked certain provisions which were needed to support the process such as provisions to issue subpoenas to compel attendance and the production of documents.

The 2010 amendments introduced a raft of supplementary provisions which support an arbitration to which the Model Law applies, such as section 23: "Parties may obtain subpoenas"; section 23A: "Failure to assist arbitral tribunal"; section 23B: "Default by party to an arbitration agreement"; section 23J: "Evidence" (the arbitral tribunal can make an order allowing a party or expert to inspect, examine and take samples of evidence in another party's possession); and section 23K: "Security for costs". These provisions apply unless the parties agree that they shall not apply to the arbitration (ie, unless the parties choose to opt out of these provisions).

The provisions in the Act relating to the power of the arbitral tribunal to award interest up to the making of an award (section 25), to award interest on the debt under the award (section 26) and the power to award costs (section 27) which previously only applied where the parties had made a specific agreement that they would apply (ie, on an opt-in basis) were changed so as to apply unless the parties agreed they would not apply (ie, the parties choose to opt out of these provisions). The arbitral tribunal is also given the additional power under the new section 27(d) to limit the amount of costs that a party is to pay.

The amendments also seek to address the subject of confidentiality in the arbitration process. The High Court, in *Esso Australia Resources Ltd v Plowman (Minister for Energy & Minerals)* (1995) 183 CLR 10; 128 ALR 391; [1995] HCA 19; BC9506416, had determined that although arbitration was a private process, an arbitration agreement did not contain any implied term that it was a confidential process. By inserting a definition of "confidential information" in section 15(1) and inserting sections 23C, 23D, 23E, 23F and 23G into the Act, the legislature has sought to introduce a new regime of statutory confidentiality with which parties may cloak their arbitration. These provisions are not mandatory and only apply if the parties agree in writing that they will apply (ie, on an opt-in basis).

The amendments also introduced a statement of the objects of the Act in section 2D, which is complemented by section 39. Under section 39(2)(b), when exercising the powers under Parts II and III of the Act, courts "must" have regard to:

    (b) the fact that:
        (i) arbitration is an efficient, impartial, enforceable and timely method by which to resolve commercial disputes; and
        (ii) awards are intended to provide certainty and finality.

The potential effect of the statement of the objects of the Act has been further enhanced by the amendment made to section 15AA of the Acts Interpretation Act 1901 (Cth) by the Acts Interpretation Amendment Act 2011 (Cth). Section 15AA now provides that in interpreting a provision of an Act, the interpretation that would "best achieve" the purpose or object of the Act (whether or not that purpose is expressly stated in the Act) is to be preferred to each other interpretation.

The amendments added a regulation power in the new section 40. This power was added with the intention of prescribing the Australian Centre of International Commercial Arbitration (ACICA) under the new section 18(1) and (2), as a "competent authority" to appoint arbitrators and replacement arbitrators under Articles 11(3) and 14(3) of the Model Law. This intention was realised when the International Arbitration Regulations 2011 (Cth) prescribed ACICA as an appointing authority.

Part III of the Act was given an extended operation under section 30A. This new section sets out the various constitutional heads of power upon which Part III can draw if its operation were expressly confined to arbitrations involving:

    (a) places, persons, matters or things external to Australia; or
    (b) disputes arising in the course of trade or commerce with another country, or between the States; or
    (c) disputes between parties at least one of which is a corporation to which paragraph 51(xx) of the Constitution applies; or
    (d) disputes arising in the course of trade or commerce in a Territory.

Part IV of the Act is concerned with the related subject matter of the arbitration of investor-State disputes which may arise between foreign investors and the host States in which the investment is made. Concerns as to how these disputes could be resolved without recourse to the national courts of the investor or the host State led to an international convention which created the International Centre for Settlement of Investment Disputes (ICSID), made in Washington in 1965, also known as the ICSID Convention, or the Washington Convention. This convention, which was negotiated under the auspices of the World Bank (also known as the International Bank for Reconstruction and Development) provides a facility for the conciliation and arbitration of investment disputes between contracting States and nationals of other contracting States. In 1990, the Act was amended to insert a new Part IV, which gave effect to the ICSID Convention. Chapters II to VII of the ICSID Convention, which was inserted as Schedule 3, were given the force of law in Australia under section 32 of the Act.

It is against this legislative background, which now spans more than 50 years from the time of the making of the New York Convention, that each provision in the Act must now be considered.

International Arbitration Act 1974

TABLE OF PROVISIONS

Section — Title

PART I — PRELIMINARY

1	Short title of Principal Act	[s 1]
2	Commencement	[s 2]
2A	Territories	[s 2A]
2B	Crown to be bound	[s 2B]
2C	Carriage of goods by sea	[s 2C]
2D	Objects of this Act	[s 2D]

PART II — ENFORCEMENT OF FOREIGN AWARDS

3	Interpretation	[s 3]
7	Enforcement of foreign arbitration agreements	[s 7]
8	Recognition of foreign awards	[s 8]
9	Evidence of awards and arbitration agreements	[s 9]
10	Evidence relating to Convention	[s 10]
10A	Delegation by Secretary of the Foreign Affairs Department	[s 10A]
12	Effect of this Part on other laws	[s 12]
13	Judiciary Act	[s 13]
14	Application of Part	[s 14]

PART III — INTERNATIONAL COMMERCIAL ARBITRATION

DIVISION 1 — PRELIMINARY

15	Interpretation	[s 15]

DIVISION 2 — MODEL LAW

16	Model Law to have force of law	[s 16]
17	Interpretation of Model Law — use of extrinsic material	[s 17]
18	Court or authority taken to have been specified in Article 6 of the Model Law	[s 18]
18A	Article 12 — justifiable doubts as to the impartiality or independence of an arbitrator	[s 18A]
18B	Article 17B — preliminary orders	[s 18B]
18C	Article 18 — reasonable opportunity to present case	[s 18C]
19	Articles 17I, 34 and 36 of Model Law — public policy	[s 19]

Section	Title	
20	Chapter VIII of Model Law not to apply in certain cases	[s 20]
21	Model Law covers the field	[s 21]

DIVISION 3 — ADDITIONAL PROVISIONS

22	Application of additional provisions	[s 22]
22A	Interpretation	[s 22A]
23	Parties may obtain subpoenas	[s 23]
23A	Failure to assist arbitral tribunal	[s 23A]
23B	Default by party to an arbitration agreement	[s 23B]
23C	Disclosure of confidential information	[s 23C]
23D	Circumstances in which confidential information may be disclosed	[s 23D]
23E	Arbitral tribunal may allow disclosure in certain circumstances	[s 23E]
23F	Court may prohibit disclosure in certain circumstances	[s 23F]
23G	Court may allow disclosure in certain circumstances	[s 23G]
23H	Death of a party to an arbitration agreement	[s 23H]
23J	Evidence	[s 23J]
23K	Security for costs	[s 23K]
24	Consolidation of arbitral proceedings	[s 24]
25	Interest up to making of award	[s 25]
26	Interest on debt under award	[s 26]
27	Costs	[s 27]

DIVISION 4 — MISCELLANEOUS

28	Immunity	[s 28]
29	Representation in proceedings	[s 29]
30	Application of Part	[s 30]
30A	Severability	[s 30A]

PART IV — APPLICATION OF THE CONVENTION ON THE SETTLEMENT OF INVESTMENT DISPUTES BETWEEN STATES AND NATIONALS OF OTHER STATES

DIVISION 1 — PRELIMINARY

31	Interpretation	[s 31]

DIVISION 2 — INVESTMENT CONVENTION

32	Application of Investment Convention to Australia	[s 32]
33	Award is binding	[s 33]
34	Investment Convention awards to prevail over other laws	[s 34]
35	Recognition of awards	[s 35]

DIVISION 3 — MISCELLANEOUS

36	Evidence relating to Investment Convention	[s 36]

Section	Title	
37	Representation in proceedings	[s 37]
38	Judiciary Act	[s 38]

PART V — GENERAL MATTERS

39	Matters to which court must have regard	[s 39]
40	Regulations	[s 40]
	SCHEDULE 1 — UNITED NATIONS CONFERENCE ON INTERNATIONAL COMMERCIAL ARBITRATION CONVENTION ON THE RECOGNITION AND ENFORCEMENT OF FOREIGN ARBITRAL AWARDS	[Sch 1]
	SCHEDULE 2 — UNCITRAL MODEL LAW ON INTERNATIONAL COMMERCIAL ARBITRATION (AS ADOPTED BY THE UNITED NATIONS COMMISSION ON INTERNATIONAL TRADE LAW ON 21 JUNE 1985, AND AS AMENDED BY THE UNITED NATIONS COMMISSION ON INTERNATIONAL TRADE LAW ON 7 JULY 2006) .	[Sch 2]
	SCHEDULE 3 — CONVENTION ON THE SETTLEMENT OF INVESTMENT DISPUTES BETWEEN STATES AND NATIONALS OF OTHER STATES	[Sch 3]

International Arbitration Act 1974

TABLE OF AMENDMENTS

Arbitration (Foreign Awards and Agreements) Act No 136 of 1974, given Royal Assent on 9 December 1974 as amended by:

Amending Legislation	Date of Assent	Date of Commencement
Arbitration (Foreign Awards and Agreements) Act 1974 No 136	9 December 1974	ss 1–3: Royal Assent Remainder: 24 June 1975 (see Gazette 1975, No G24, p 2)
Jurisdiction of Courts (Miscellaneous Amendments) Act 1979 No 19	28 March 1979	Parts II–XVII (ss. 3–123): 15 May 1979 (see Gazette 1979, No S86) Remainder: Royal Assent
Statute Law (Miscellaneous Provisions) Act 1987 No 141	18 December 1987	s 3: Royal Assent (a)
International Arbitration Amendment Act 1989 No 25	15 May 1989	12 June 1989
ICSID Implementation Act 1990 No 107	18 December 1990	Parts 2 and 3 (ss 3–8): 1 June 1991 (see s 2(2) and Gazette 1991, No S98) Remainder: Royal Assent
Carriage of Goods by Sea Act 1991 No 160	31 October 1991	s 21: Royal Assent (b)
Law and Justice Legislation Amendment Act 2004 No 62		Schedule 1 (items 40–42): 27 May 2004
Statute Law Revision Act 2008 No 73		Schedule 4 (items 348–350): 4 July 2008
Federal Justice System Amendment (Efficiency Measures) Act (No 1) 2009 No 122	7 December 2009	Schedule 2: Royal Assent
International Arbitration Amendment Act 2010 No 97	6 July 2010	Schedule 1 (items 6, 25): (c) Schedule 1 (item 8): 7 Dec 2009 (see s 2(1)) Remainder: Royal Assent
Statute Law Revision Act 2011 No 5	22 March 2011	Schedule 6 (items 67, 68) and Schedule 7 (items 77–79): 19 Apr 2011

An Act relating to the recognition and enforcement of foreign arbitral awards, and the conduct of international commercial arbitrations, in Australia, and for related purposes

PART I — PRELIMINARY

[s 1] Short title of Principal Act

1 This Act may be cited as the International Arbitration Act 1974.

COMMENTARY ON SECTION 1
Title .... [s 1-1]

[s 1-1] Title The title of the Act when enacted in 1974 was the Arbitration (Foreign Awards and Agreements) Act 1974 (Cth). The Act was renamed the International Arbitration Act 1974 (Cth) when s 1 was amended by the International Arbitration Amendment Act 1989 (Cth).

[s 2] Commencement

2 (1) Sections 1, 2 and 3 shall come into operation on the day on which this Act receives the Royal Assent.

(2) The remaining provisions of this Act shall come into operation on a date to be fixed by Proclamation, being a date not earlier than the date on which the Convention enters into force for Australia.

COMMENTARY ON SECTION 2
Commencement .... [s 2-1]

[s 2-1] Commencement Sections 1, 2, 3 and 4 of the Act commenced on 9 December 1974, the date of assent. The reference to s 4 was removed from s 2 of the Act by the Law and Justice Legislation Amendment Act 2004 (Cth), when s 4 was repealed.

[s 2A] Territories

2A This Act extends to all external Territories.

COMMENTARY ON SECTION 2A
History of section .... [s 2A-1]
External Territories .... [s 2A-2]
Extended operation of Act .... [s 2A-3]

[s 2A-1] History of section When enacted in 1974, s 3(1) of the Act defined the use of the word "Australia" in the Act to include "the Territories other than Papua New Guinea." There was a similar exclusion in s 4 which contained a declaration (made under Article X of the New York Convention) that the

Convention extended to all the external Territories other than Papua New Guinea. Section 5 stated that the Act extended to all the external Territories other than Papua New Guinea.

Papua New Guinea ceased to be a territory of Australia on 16 September 1975 and became an independent sovereign State and was admitted to membership of the United Nations on 10 October 1975.

The International Arbitration Amendment Act 1989 (Cth) repealed ss 5 and 6 and introduced s 2A into the Act. The 1989 Act also deleted the phrase "other than Papua New Guinea" from the definition in s 3(1) and from s 12(1).

[s 2A-2] **External Territories** The "external Territories" of Australia are the Ashmore and Cartier Islands, the Australian Antarctic Territory, Christmas Island, the Cocos (Keeling) Islands, the Coral Sea Islands, Heard Island and McDonald Islands, and Norfolk Island. Each of the external Territories owes its status as an external Territory to an Act of the Commonwealth Parliament (see, respectively, the Ashmore and Cartier Islands Acceptance Act 1933 (Cth); the Australian Antarctic Territory Act 1954 (Cth); the Christmas Island Agreement Act 1958 (Cth); the Cocos (Keeling) Islands Act 1955 (Cth); the Coral Sea Islands Act 1969 (Cth); the Heard Island and McDonald Islands Act 1953 (Cth); and the Norfolk Island Act 1979 (Cth)).

[s 2A-3] **Extended operation of Act** An example of the extended application of the Act is seen in *Administration of Norfolk Island v SMEC Australia Pty Ltd* [2004] NFSC 1 (Supreme Court of Norfolk Island, 21 July 2004, BC200404489, unreported), where an application was brought under s 7(2) of the Act to stay proceedings commenced in the Court in Norfolk Island.

[s 2B] **Crown to be bound**

2B This Act binds the Crown in right of the Commonwealth, of each of the States, of the Northern Territory and of Norfolk Island.

COMMENTARY ON SECTION 2B

History of section .... [s 2B-1]
Presumption .... [s 2B-2]
Extended operation of Act .... [s 2B-3]

[s 2B-1] **History of section** Section 2B was introduced into the Act by the International Arbitration Amendment Act 1989 (Cth).

[s 2B-2] **Presumption** At the time the Act was enacted there was a general rule of the common law that "the Crown is only bound by statute where there exists express mention or necessary implication" (*Bradken Consolidated Ltd v Broken Hill Company Pty Co Ltd* (1979) 145 CLR 107 at 127; 24 ALR 9; 53 ALJR 452; BC7900047 (Stephen J)). As a result s 2B reverses the presumption. Although as French J later observed in *State Government Insurance Corp v Government Insurance Office of NSW* (1991) 28 FCR 511 at 557; 101 ALR 259; 21 IPR 65; BC9103102: "[t]he common law presumption that statutes are intended not to bind the Crown remains in force, but as a more flexible guide to construction which may be displaced without the stringent requirements that previously existed".

[s 2B-3] Extended operation of Act An example of the application of s 2B is seen in *Administration of Norfolk Island v SMEC Australia Pty Ltd* [2004] NFSC 1 (Supreme Court of Norfolk Island, 21 July 2004, BC200404489, unreported), where the court noted (at [3]) that by the operation of s 2B, the Act "binds the Crown in right of Norfolk Island."

[s 2C] Carriage of goods by sea

2C Nothing in this Act affects:
 (a) the continued operation of section 9 of the Sea-Carriage of Goods Act 1924 under subsection 20(2) of the Carriage of Goods by Sea Act 1991; or
 (b) the operation of section 11 or 16 of the Carriage of Goods by Sea Act 1991.

COMMENTARY ON SECTION 2C

History of section	[s 2C-1]
Sea-Carriage of Goods Act 1924 (Cth) s 9	[s 2C-2]
Effect of s 9 on arbitration agreement	[s 2C-3]
Application of s 9 to documents relating to carriage of goods by sea	[s 2C-4]
Operation of s 9 is confined to "parties" to bill of lading or document	[s 2C-5]
Section 9 does not apply to an award	[s 2C-6]
Party may be estopped from relying on s 9	[s 2C-7]
Limited continued operation of s 9 under 1991 Act	[s 2C-8]
Carriage of Goods by Sea Act 1991 (Cth) s 11	[s 2C-9]
Application of s 11(1) to charterparties and contracts of affreightment	[s 2C-10]
Introduction of s 11(3) in 1997	[s 2C-11]
Current terms of Carriage of Goods by Sea Act 1991 (Cth) s 11	[s 2C-12]
Continued reference to s 16 in s 2C of the Act is unnecessary as s 16 has been repealed	[s 2C-13]

[s 2C-1] History of section Section 2C was introduced into the Act by the International Arbitration Amendment Act 1989 (Cth) to allow for the continued operation of s 9 of the Sea-Carriage of Goods Act 1924 (Cth). When introduced in 1989, s 2C simply stated that "[n]othing in this Act affects the operation of section 9 of the Sea-Carriage of Goods Act 1924".

The Carriage of Goods by Sea Act 1991 (Cth) repealed s 2C. This Act also substituted the current wording of s 2C. The new wording introduced a reference to the continued, but limited, operation of s 9 of the Sea-Carriage of Goods Act 1924 (Cth) under s 20(2) of the Carriage of Goods by Sea Act 1991 (Cth) and a reference to ss 11 and 16 of the later Act.

As Allsop J noted in *Comandate Marine Corp v Pan Australia Shipping Pty Ltd* (2006) 157 FCR 45; 238 ALR 457; [2006] FCAFC 192; BC200610833 at [196]:

> This section [s 2C] preserves the primacy of the Australian national interest in ensuring the availability of Australian courts or Australian arbitral tribunals in the resolution of disputes arising from the carriage of goods by sea in the circumstances set out in the

provisions referred to in s 2C. These circumstances will often involve the vindication of rights under bills of lading or similar documents ... What is important for present purposes is to appreciate that Parliament has chosen one area to exclude from the operation of the *International Arbitration Act*.

[s 2C-2] Sea-Carriage of Goods Act 1924 (Cth) s 9 Section 9 of the Sea-Carriage of Goods Act 1924 (Cth) provided:

(1) All parties to any bill of lading or document relating to the carriage of goods from any place in Australia to any place outside Australia shall be deemed to have intended to contract according to the laws in force at the place of shipment, and any stipulation or agreement to the contrary, or purporting to oust or lessen the jurisdiction of the Courts of the Commonwealth or of a State in respect of the bill of lading or document, shall be illegal, null and void, and of no effect.

(2) Any stipulation or agreement, whether made in the Commonwealth or elsewhere, purporting to oust or lessen the jurisdiction of the Courts of the Commonwealth or of a State in respect of any bill of lading or document relating to the carriage of goods from any place outside Australia to any place in Australia shall be illegal, null and void, and of no effect.

Section 9 was aimed at clearing away any intended contractual impediments to the jurisdiction of Australian courts. Under s 9 any stipulation or agreement "purporting to oust or lessen the jurisdiction of" any Australian court in respect of any bill of lading or document relating to the carriage of goods was declared to "be illegal, null and void, and of no effect."

Subsection 9(1) of the Sea-Carriage of Goods Act 1924 (Cth) operated in relation to and in connection with the carriage of goods by sea from any port in Australia to any other port, whether in or outside Australia and to preserve the Australian courts' jurisdiction over such matters. The subsection had effect only in respect of outward bills of lading or similar documents of title.

Subsection 9(2) extended the legislative preservation of the jurisdiction of Commonwealth and State courts over to include inward carriage. In the case of s 9(2), "its object was to insure that Australian consignees of goods imported might enforce in Australian courts the contracts of sea-carriage evidenced by the bills of lading which they held" (*Compagnie des Messageries Maritimes v Wilson* (1954) 94 CLR 577 at 583; [1954] ALR 1095; (1954) 28 ALJR 465; BC5400110 (Dixon CJ)).

[s 2C-3] Effect of s 9 on arbitration agreement Although an arbitration agreement does not oust the jurisdiction of the courts (eg, *Dobbs v National Bank of Australasia Ltd* (1935) 53 CLR 643 at 652; [1935] ALR 360; (1935) 9 ALJR 112; BC3500024 (Rich, Dixon, Evatt and McTiernan JJ)), nonetheless the High Court in *Compagnie des Messageries Maritimes v Wilson* (1954) 94 CLR 577 at 592; [1954] ALR 1095; (1954) 28 ALJR 465; BC5400110 (Taylor J), held that the provisions of s 9(2) rendered an agreement for foreign arbitration in the bill of lading null and void because "the section applies to stipulations which *purport* to oust or lessen the jurisdiction and not only to stipulations which have that effect".

A reference by agreement of a dispute to a foreign court or foreign arbitration purports to oust or lessen the jurisdiction of Commonwealth and State courts and therefore is invalid under s 9 (*Bulk Chartering v T&T Metal Trading* ("*The Krasnogrosk*") (1993) 31 NSWLR 18 at 41.A; 114 ALR 189 (Sheller JA); *Ocean*

Steamship Company v Queensland State Wheat Board [1941] 1 KB 402). It was also suggested in *"The Krasnogrosk"* that an arbitration agreement made in Australia providing for arbitration in Australia might not be invalid under s 9. It was argued that in those circumstances, the parties have not, by their agreement, "purported to oust the jurisdiction". It was reasoned that it was the Australian arbitration statute, and not the parties, which controlled and lessened the jurisdiction of the courts (*"The Krasnogrosk"* at NSWLR 41.D (Sheller JA)).

[s 2C-4] Application of s 9 to documents relating to carriage of goods by sea Section 9 is not limited to bills of lading. The Supreme Court of NSW in *The "Blooming Orchard" [No 2]* (1990) 22 NSWLR 273 held that a voyage charterparty was also covered by s 9 as it was a "document relating to the carriage of goods". The decision to apply s 9 to a voyage charterparty was followed by the Federal Court in *BHP Trading Asia Ltd v Oceaname Shipping Ltd* (1996) 67 FCR 211 at 235; BC9601387, with the result that the requirement in the charterparty that the parties submit to arbitration was void (see also the discussion of the case in M Davies, "Fruits of the Blooming Orchard" [1991] *Australian Business Law Review* 217–32).

The Court of Appeal (England) in *Furness Withy (Australia) Pty Ltd v Metal Distributors (UK) Ltd ("The Amazonia")* [1990] 1 Lloyd's Rep 236 held that s 9 applied to a clause paramount in a charterparty and that s 9 rendered void the agreement for arbitration in London and the choice of English law as the governing law of the charterparty. In addition, the court found that the parties, by their conduct, had made a second agreement when jointly appointing a sole arbitrator to arbitrate the dispute. One line of reasoning was that under the first agreement in the charterparty, each party "makes an offer to agree to an individual reference [to arbitration] if, when and as often as the other party calls upon [that party] to do so" (*"The Amazonia"* at 244 (Staughton LJ) and at 248 (Dillon LJ)). The court indicated that had the second agreement to arbitrate the particular dispute been subject to Australian law it would also be void under s 9.

In *Bulk Chartering v T&T Metal Trading ("The Krasnogrosk")* (1993) 31 NSWLR 18; 114 ALR 189, one member of the NSW Court of Appeal expressed the view that, as a matter of construction, s 9 did not apply to such a fresh ad hoc submission agreement because the section "has no application to agreements to refer existing disputes" to arbitration (*"The Krasnogrosk"* at NSWLR 28–9 (Handley JA)). Such an agreement would not be one relating to a contract for carriage of goods. In these circumstances, Handley JA had (at NSWLR 29) "considerable reservations about the reasoning", but not the result in *"The Amazonia"*.

[s 2C-5] Operation of s 9 is confined to "parties" to bill of lading or document As a matter of the proper construction of s 9, the carve-out of the Act effected by s 9 is limited, in that it only applies to "[a]ll parties to any bill of lading or document relating to the carriage of goods". As a result, the section was held not to apply to a shipowner who was sued only as a bailee of goods which were the subject of a bill of lading. The shipowner was not a "party" to the bill of lading, but was a person under a clause in the bill of lading who received the benefit of the contract. Accordingly the shipowner was able to rely on the arbitration clause in the bill of lading and to insist on arbitration (*Kim Meller Imports Pty Ltd v Eurolevent Spa* (1986) 7 NSWLR 269 at 271–2; 87 FLR 247).

[s 2C-6] Section 9 does not apply to an award Problems may arise if the operation of the section is overlooked and not called in aid until after an award is made. In *Bulk Chartering v T&T Metal Trading ("The Krasnogrosk")* (1993) 31 NSWLR 18; 114 ALR 189 the parties were bound by a charterparty agreement which contained a clause requiring all disputes to be referred to arbitration in London. Subsection 9(1) applied to this agreement. When a dispute arose it was agreed that the dispute could be resolved, not pursuant to the arbitration clause, "but by an Australian arbitrator pursuant to a fresh ad hoc agreement". The arbitration was then held and an award made. The unsuccessful party commenced proceedings seeking a declaration that the ad hoc arbitration agreement and the award were void because of the operation of s 9(1). The claim failed. The court focused not on the arbitration agreement, but on the standing and effect of the award, which had been made. "The award should be regarded as being of the character of an accord and satisfaction by substituted agreement and imposing a new obligation on [the unsuccessful party] which sprang from the act of the arbitrator in making it" and not from the original charterparty ("*The Krasnogrosk*" at NSWLR 41 (Sheller JA)). The court held the award neither ousted, nor lessened, (nor purported to oust or lessen) the jurisdiction of the Australian court.

[s 2C-7] Party may be estopped from relying on s 9 If because of a mistaken belief, the parties have a common shared assumption that the arbitration agreement is valid and they have proceeded to arbitrate their dispute for some time, and at some cost, a party may be estopped from relying on s 9 to assert the invalidity of the agreement (*Furness Withy (Australia) Pty Ltd v Metal Distributors (UK) Ltd ("The Amazonia")* [1990] 1 Lloyd's Rep 236 at 246–7 (Staughton LJ) and at 251 (Dillon LJ)).

[s 2C-8] Limited continued operation of s 9 under 1991 Act The two-stage objective of the Carriage of Goods by Sea Act 1991 (Cth) was initially to adopt The Hague-Visby Rules and subsequently to consider the adoption of the Hamburg Rules. The history of The Hague-Visby and Hamburg Rules in Australia is beyond the scope of this work. For a detailed discussion, see M Davies and A Dickey, *Shipping Law*, 3rd ed, Lawbook Company, Australia, 2004, pp 171–9 and more generally, R Burnett and V Bath, *Law of International Business in Australasia*, The Federation Press, Sydney, 2009, pp 130–76.

Under the first stage, the Carriage of Goods by Sea Act 1991 (Cth) repealed the Sea-Carriage of Goods Act 1924 (Cth) but s 20 provided for a limited continued operation of s 9 of the 1924 Act.

Section 20 of the Carriage of Goods by Sea Act 1991 (Cth) provides:

    (1) The Sea-Carriage of Goods Act 1924 is repealed.
    (2) The Sea-Carriage of Goods Act 1924, as in force immediately before the commencement of this section, continues to apply to a contract of carriage of goods by sea after that commencement if:
        (a) the contract was made before that commencement; and
        (b) that Act would have applied but for the operation of subsection (1).

[s 2C-9] Carriage of Goods by Sea Act 1991 (Cth) s 11 Section 11, which is headed "Construction and jurisdiction" as originally enacted provided:

(1) All parties to:
  (a) a bill of lading, or similar document of title, relating to the carriage of goods from any place in Australia to any place outside Australia; or
  (b) a non-negotiable document of a kind mentioned in subparagraph 10(1)(b)(iii), relating to such a carriage of goods;
are taken to have intended to contract according to the laws in force at the place of shipment.

(2) An agreement (whether made in Australia or elsewhere) has no effect so far as it purports to:
  (a) preclude or limit the effect of subsection (1) in respect of a bill of lading or a document mentioned in that subsection; or
  (b) preclude or limit the jurisdiction of a court of the Commonwealth or of a State or Territory in respect of a bill of lading or a document mentioned in subsection (1); or
  (c) preclude or limit the jurisdiction of a court of the Commonwealth or of a State or Territory in respect of:
    (i) a bill of lading, or similar document of title, relating to the carriage of goods from any place outside Australia to any place in Australia; or
    (ii) a non-negotiable document of a kind mentioned in subparagraph 10(1)(b)(iii) relating to such a carriage of goods.

Significantly, s 11(1) is confined in its operation to be a mandatory choice of law clause. The parties are taken to have intended to contract according to the laws in force at the place of shipment in Australia (outbound shipments only). Section 11(2) continues the preservation of the jurisdiction of Australian courts (outbound and inbound shipments).

In *Bulk Chartering v T&T Metal Trading ("The Krasnogrosk")* (1993) 31 NSWLR 18 at 42–3; 114 ALR 189 (Sheller JA) there was a question of whether the 1991 legislation applied, as the events giving rise to the action occurred from 1989 to 1992. The court held that even if s 11(2) did apply, it did not operate to avoid or nullify the award for the same reasons set out above that s 9 did not apply. In terms of the 1991 legislation, the award neither precluded, nor limited (nor purported to preclude or limit) the jurisdiction of the Australian court within the meaning of s 11(2).

In *Hi-Fert Pty Ltd v Kiukiang Maritime Carriers Inc (No 5)* (1998) 90 FCR 1; 159 ALR 142; [1999] 2 Lloyd's Rep 782; BC9806222 the full court of the Federal Court considered the application of s 11(2) and applied the reasoning in *Compagnie des Messageries Maritimes v Wilson* (1954) 94 CLR 577; [1954] ALR 1095; (1954) 28 ALJR 465; BC5400110 notwithstanding the differences in the wording between s 9(2) of the 1924 Act and s 11(2) of the 1991 Act (see also *Hi-Fert Pty Ltd v United Shipping Adriatic Inc* (1998) 89 FCR 166 at 178.F; 165 ALR 265; BC9806853). The full court (Emmett J at 24–6 with whom Beaumont and Branson JJ agreed) held that as the relevant clause in the bills of lading provided that any dispute "shall" be settled in accordance with the Arbitration Act in London, the clause purported to "preclude or limit" the court's jurisdiction. An argument that s 11(2) only struck down the requirement to arbitrate in London and left the submission to a London arbitration intact, was rejected. The arbitration clause was therefore of no effect.

[s 2C-10] Application of s 11(1) to charterparties and contracts of affreightment When s 11(1) was introduced in 1991, its operation was confined to bills of lading and "a similar document of title". As such, the section did not apply to a charterparty or to a contract of affreightment, which is not a document of title.

Regulation 6 of the Carriage of Goods by Sea Regulations 1998 (Cth), which came into force on 1 July 1998, amended s 11(1)(a) and s 11(2)(c)(i) by omitting "a bill of lading or similar document of title" and substituting "a sea carriage document to which, or relating to a contract of carriage to which, the amended Hague Rules apply..." (see the discussion of the amendment in *Hi-Fert Pty Ltd v United Shipping Adriatic Inc* (1998) 89 FCR 166 at 178-83; 165 ALR 265; BC9806853). The phrase "sea carriage document" was not defined by the Act but the Regulations also introduced as Schedule IA, the "Amended Hague Rules," which, in Art I(1)(g) defined the words "sea carriage document" when used "in these Rules" but not in the Act, as follows:

> **'Sea carriage document'** means:
> (i) a bill of lading; or
> (ii) a negotiable document of title that is similar to a bill of lading and that contains or evidences a contract of carriage of goods by sea; or
> (iii) a bill of lading that, by law, is not negotiable; or
> (iv) a non-negotiable document (including a consignment note and a document of the kind known as a sea waybill or the kind known as a ship's delivery order) that either contains or evidences a contract of carriage of goods by sea.

Sections 11(1)(a) and 11(2)(c)(i) were further amended by the Carriage of Goods by Sea Regulations 1998 (No 2) (Cth). As a result of this further amendment, the operation of these two provisions now applies to "a sea carriage document relating to the carriage of goods from any place in Australia to any place outside Australia" and "a sea carriage document relating to any place outside Australia to any place in Australia" respectively. A voyage charter party and a contract of affreightment would be covered by the phrase "sea carriage document" in s 11 if the meaning given to the phrase by Sch 1A to the Act is used. On this construction, any provision in such a document which purported to compel a foreign arbitration would be null and void and of no effect (see generally the discussion in M Davies and A Dickey, *Shipping Law*, 3rd ed, Lawbook Company, Australia, 2004, pp 177–9).

A contrary view was expressed in a ruling made by the Supreme Court of South Australia in *Jebsens International (Australia) Pty Ltd v Interfert Australia Ltd* (Anderson J, 25 August 2011, unreported). The court reasoned (at p 2 of the typescript ruling) that the "COGSA in its current form deals with the rights of persons holding bills of lading or similar instruments. A charter party is a document of a different genus". The court concluded that the "voyage charter party" was not a "sea carriage document" within Art I(1)(g)(iv).

[s 2C-11] Introduction of s 11(3) in 1997 The Court of Appeal in *Bulk Chartering v T&T Metal Trading ("The Krasnogrosk")* (1993) 31 NSWLR 18 at 43; 114 ALR 189 (Sheller JA) also noted that there was a possible inconsistent operation between s 11(2) of the Carriage of Goods by Sea Act 1991 (Cth) and Art 22 of the Hamburg Rules if those rules were to be implemented.

The court noted that on the one hand, s 11(2), like its predecessor, s 9 of the Sea-Carriage of Goods Act 1924 (Cth), appeared to deny effect to a reference to an Australian arbitrator of a dispute under a bill of lading or document relating to the carriage of goods by sea, and yet on the other hand, Art 22 of the Hamburg Rules, if adopted by the legislature, would enable parties, subject to the provision of the article, to provide by agreement evidenced in writing, that any dispute that may arise relating to carriage of goods under the Hamburg Rules may be referred to arbitration. The court stated an intention to draw the legislature's attention to the potential conflict (at NSWLR 43.E).

Although subsequently no action was taken to implement or adopt the Hamburg Rules, including Art 22, the legislature responded to the decision in *"The Krasnogrosk"* (1993) 31 NSWLR 18; 114 ALR 189 and s 11(3) was inserted by the Carriage of Goods by Sea Amendment Act 1997 (Cth).

[s 2C-12] Current terms of Carriage of Goods by Sea Act 1991 (Cth)
s 11 As a result of the changes discussed above, s 11 currently provides:

(1) All parties to:
  (a) a sea carriage document relating to the carriage of goods from any place in Australia to any place outside Australia; or
  (b) a non negotiable document of a kind mentioned in subparagraph 10(1)(b)(iii), relating to such a carriage of goods;
are taken to have intended to contract according to the laws in force at the place of shipment.

(2) An agreement (whether made in Australia or elsewhere) has no effect so far as it purports to:
  (a) preclude or limit the effect of subsection (1) in respect of a bill of lading or a document mentioned in that subsection; or
  (b) preclude or limit the jurisdiction of a court of the Commonwealth or of a State or Territory in respect of a bill of lading or a document mentioned in subsection (1); or
  (c) preclude or limit the jurisdiction of a court of the Commonwealth or of a State or Territory in respect of:
    (i) a sea carriage document relating to the carriage of goods from any place outside Australia to any place in Australia; or
    (ii) a non negotiable document of a kind mentioned in subparagraph 10(1)(b)(iii) relating to such a carriage of goods.

(3) An agreement, or a provision of an agreement, that provides for the resolution of a dispute by arbitration is not made ineffective by subsection (2) (despite the fact that it may preclude or limit the jurisdiction of a court) if, under the agreement or provision, the arbitration must be conducted in Australia.

[s 2C-13] Continued reference to s 16 in s 2C of the Act is unnecessary as s 16 has been repealed Section 16 of the Carriage of Goods by Sea Act 1991 (Cth) headed "Construction", provided:

(1) All parties to a contract of carriage by sea relating to the carriage of goods from any place in Australia to any place outside Australia are taken to have intended to contract according to the provisions of this Act.

(2) An agreement (whether made in Australia or elsewhere) has no effect so far as it purports to preclude or limit the effect of subsection (1) in respect of such a contract.

As no decision has been taken to adopt the Hamburg Rules, s 16 was repealed on 31 October 2001 by the sunset operation of s 2 of the Carriage of Goods by

Sea Act 1991 (Cth). The Carriage of Goods by Sea Amendment Act 1997 (Cth) amended s 2. The amended s 2 provided that if, within 10 years of the commencement of the section (referring back to 31 October 1991), the Minister had not tabled a statement in accordance with s 2A(4) setting out a decision that The Hague-Visby Rules should be replaced by the Hamburg Rules, Pt 3 of the legislation (which contained ss 12–16), Sch 2 (ie, the Hamburg Rules), and s 2A, were to be repealed on the first day after the end of that 10-year period, which had commenced on 31 October 1991. No such statement was tabled and accordingly s 16 was repealed on 31 October 2001. Therefore the continued reference in s 2C of the Act to s 6 of the Carriage of Goods by Sea Act 1991 (Cth) appears to be in error.

[s 2D] Objects of this Act

2D The objects of this Act are:
  (a) to facilitate international trade and commerce by encouraging the use of arbitration as a method of resolving disputes; and
  (b) to facilitate the use of arbitration agreements made in relation to international trade and commerce; and
  (c) to facilitate the recognition and enforcement of arbitral awards made in relation to international trade and commerce; and
  (d) to give effect to Australia's obligations under the Convention on the Recognition and Enforcement of Foreign Arbitral Awards adopted in 1958 by the United Nations Conference on International Commercial Arbitration at its twenty-fourth meeting; and
  (e) to give effect to the UNCITRAL Model Law on International Commercial Arbitration adopted by the United Nations Commission on International Trade Law on 21 June 1985 and amended by the United Nations Commission on International Trade Law on 7 July 2006; and
  (f) to give effect to the Convention on the Settlement of Investment Disputes between States and Nationals of Other States signed by Australia on 24 March 1975.

COMMENTARY ON SECTION 2D

History of section .... [s 2D-1]
Effect of s 2D .... [s 2D-2]
Section 2D must be considered in context .... [s 2D-3]
Acts Interpretation Act 1901 (Cth) s 15AA .... [s 2D-4]
Other interpretation provisions .... [s 2D-5]

[s 2D-1] History of section Section 2D was introduced into the Act by the International Arbitration Amendment Act 2010 (Cth). The Revised Explanatory Memorandum to the International Arbitration Amendment Bill 2010 (Cth) (at [5]) stated that "the primary purpose of the Act is to facilitate international trade and commerce by encouraging the use of arbitration as a method of resolving disputes. The Act does this by facilitating the use of arbitration agreements to manage disputes — particularly by giving force to the Model Law — and by facilitating the enforcement and recognition of foreign arbitration agreements and awards by giving effect to the New York Convention".

[s 2D-2] Effect of s 2D This section must be considered in conjunction with s 39 of the Act, which states that a court must have regard to the objects of the Act when a court is considering exercising a power or performing a function as outlined in s 39(1). The objectives of the New York Convention are also a relevant consideration. The uniform construction of the New York Convention and the provisions of the Act "accords with the Act's stated purpose to facilitate the use of arbitration as an effective dispute resolution process" (*IMC Mining Solutions Pty Ltd v Altain Khuder LLC* [2011] VSCA 248; BC201106268 (*IMC Mining Solutions*) at [35] (Warren CJ)). Nonetheless, whilst international case law may be useful and instructive, it is the words used by the Parliament which must be construed in accordance with the applicable principles of statutory construction (see *IMC Mining Solutions* at [35] (Warren CJ) and at [127]–[133] (Hansen JA and Kyrou AJA)).

The influence of s 2D has been immediate and significant. The section was the basis for the Federal Court decision in *Uganda Telecom Ltd v Hi-Tech Telecom Pty Ltd* (2011) 277 ALR 415; [2011] FCA 131; BC201100586, not to follow the earlier decision of the Supreme Court of NSW in *Corvetina Technology Ltd v Clough Engineering Ltd* (2004) 183 FLR 317; [2004] NSWSC 700; BC200404900. The Federal Court held (at [132]) that s 8(7)(b) of the Act "should be narrowly interpreted consistently with the United States cases" of *Parsons & Whittemore Overseas Co Inc v Société Générale De L'Industrie Du Papier* (1974) 508 F 2d 969; [1974] USCA2 836 (2nd Circuit, 1974); and *Karaha Bodas Co, LLC v Perusahaan Pertambangan Minyak Dan Gas Bumi Negara* (2004) 364 F 3d 274; [2004] USCA5 66, 306 (5th Circuit, 2004). The reasoning of the Federal Court for following the narrower interpretation adopted in the United States decisions was that the "principles articulated in those cases sit more comfortably with the purposes of the [New York] Convention and the objects of the Act" (at [132]).

[s 2D-3] Section 2D must be considered in context "In other words, like any other provision in legislation, a purpose or objects clause must be interpreted in its context": DC Pearce and RS Geddes, *Statutory Interpretation in Australia*, LexisNexis, Sydney, 2011 at [2.11] and see also [4.49], although it should be noted that this work was written before the commencement of the Acts Interpretation Amendment Act 2011 (Cth) discussed below at [s 2D-4]. A similar view was expressed in *IW v City of Perth* (1997) 191 CLR 1 at 12; 94 LGERA 224; 146 ALR 696; BC9703257, where Brennan CJ and McHugh J said that an objects clause should be understood by reference to the other provisions contained in the legislation. The objects of a statute must not be pursued at all costs. (See the discussion by Spigelman CJ in *Victims Compensation Fund v Brown* (2002) 54 NSWLR 668 at 672; 129 A Crim R 538; [2002] NSWCA 155; BC200203034, which was endorsed on appeal by Heydon J in *Victims Compensation Fund Corp v Brown* (2003) 201 ALR 260; 77 ALJR 1797; [2003] HCA 54; BC200305654 at [12], with whom McHugh, Gummow, Kirby and Hayne JJ agreed.)

The context of the Act generally, in the sense of the "Legislative Background", is outlined above at p 3. The current Australian approach to statutory interpretation has been described in terms of "the attribution of meaning to the words of a statutory text in the totality of the 'context' in which the statutory text was enacted", subject to the recent view that the word "context" should be expanded to include the way the statutory text has been applied in the courts after the text is enacted (see "Common Law Statutes and Judicial Legislation: Statutory Interpretation as a Common Law Process" by SG Gageler SC, Fiat Justitia Lecture, Monash University Law School, 24 August 2011, p 2 of the typescript).

[s 2D-4] Acts Interpretation Act 1901 (Cth) s 15AA The relationship between s 2D of the Act and s 15AA of the Acts Interpretation Act 1901 (Cth) should also be considered, eg, *IMC Aviation Solutions Pty Ltd v Altain Khuder LLC* [2011] VSCA 248; BC201106268 at [174] (Hansen JA and Kyrou AJA). Section 15AA originally required that regard be had to the purpose and object of a statute in the following terms:

> (1) In the interpretation of a provision of an Act, a construction that would promote the purpose or object underlying the Act (whether that purpose or object is expressly stated in the Act or not) shall be preferred to a construction that would not promote that purpose or object.

Section 15AA was repealed by the Acts Interpretation Amendment Act 2011 (Cth), which received the Royal Assent on 27 June 2011 (due to commence on 28 December 2011), and the following wording substituted:

> (1) In interpreting a provision of an Act, the interpretation that would best achieve the purpose or object of the Act (whether or not that purpose or object is expressly stated in the Act) is to be preferred to each other interpretation.

The reason for the amendment was that the original wording of the section had been expressed in absolute terms, ie, a construction that would promote the purpose of an Act was to be preferred to one that would not. Section 15AA did not address the situation where there was a choice between two or more constructions that would promote Parliament's purpose. The limited nature of s 15AA had been noted in a case on the equivalent Victorian provision (*Chugg v Pacific Dunlop Ltd* (1990) 170 CLR 249 at 262; 95 ALR 481; 64 ALJR 599; BC9002934 at [20]–[23] (Dawson, Toohey and Gaudron JJ, with whom Brennan CJ and Deane J agreed)). As a result, the amendment was made to s 15AA to prefer the construction of an Act that would "best achieve" the purpose or object of the Act over each other interpretation: see Explanatory Memorandum to the Acts Interpretation Amendment Bill 2011 (Cth) at [99]–[101].

[s 2D-5] Other interpretation provisions The operation of s 17 of the Act and Art 2A of the Model Law are specifically directed to interpretation of the provisions of the Model Law. Section 17 directs attention to the documents of UNCITRAL and its working group used in the preparation of the Model Law. Article 2A requires regard to be had to its international origin and the need to promote uniformity in its application.

PART II — ENFORCEMENT OF FOREIGN AWARDS

[s 3] Interpretation

3 (1) In this Part, unless the contrary intention appears:

agreement in writing has the same meaning as in the Convention.

arbitral award has the same meaning as in the Convention.

arbitration agreement means an agreement in writing of the kind referred to in sub-article 1 of Article II of the Convention.

Australia includes the Territories.

Convention means the Convention on the Recognition and Enforcement of Foreign Arbitral Awards adopted in 1958 by the United Nations Conference on International Commercial Arbitration at its twenty-fourth meeting, a copy of the English text of which is set out in Schedule 1.

Convention country means a country (other than Australia) that is a Contracting State within the meaning of the Convention.

court means any court in Australia, including, but not limited to, the Federal Court of Australia and a court of a State or Territory.

data message means information generated, sent, received or stored by electronic, magnetic, optical or similar means, including, but not limited to, electronic data interchange (EDI), email, telegram, telex or telecopy.

electronic communication means any communication made by means of data messages.

Foreign Affairs Department means the Department administered by the Minister administering the Diplomatic Privileges and Immunities Act 1967.

foreign award means an arbitral award made, in pursuance of an arbitration agreement, in a country other than Australia, being an arbitral award in relation to which the Convention applies.

(2) In this Part, where the context so admits, *enforcement*, in relation to a foreign award, includes the recognition of the award as binding for any purpose, and *enforce* and *enforced* have corresponding meanings.

(3) For the purposes of this Part, a body corporate shall be taken to be ordinarily resident in a country if, and only if, it is incorporated or has its principal place of business in that country.

(4) For the avoidance of doubt and without limiting subsection (1), an agreement is in writing if:
  (a) its content is recorded in any form whether or not the agreement or the contract to which it relates has been concluded orally, by conduct, or by other means; or
  (b) it is contained in an electronic communication and the information in that communication is accessible so as to be usable for subsequent reference; or
  (c) it is contained in an exchange of statements of claim and defence in which the existence of an agreement is alleged by one party and not denied by the other.

(5) For the avoidance of doubt and without limiting subsection (1), a reference in a contract to any document containing an arbitration clause is an arbitration agreement, provided that the reference is such as to make the clause part of the contract.

COMMENTARY ON SECTION 3

Introduction to requirement for agreement in writing .	[s 3-1]
Meaning of "agreement in writing"	[s 3-2]
"arbitration agreement"	[s 3-3]
Incorporation by reference (s 3(5) of the Act; Art 7(6) of the Model Law)	[s 3-4]
Arbitration agreement may arise in course of arbitration .	[s 3-5]
Law governing the agreement to arbitrate	[s 3-6]
"arbitral award"	[s 3-7]
"Australia"	[s 3-8]
"court"	[s 3-9]
"electronic communication" and "data message"	[s 3-10]
"Foreign Affairs Department"	[s 3-11]
"ordinarily resident"	[s 3-12]

[s 3-1] Introduction to requirement for agreement in writing The definition for the phrase an "agreement in writing" was inserted into the Act in 1974 by the Arbitration (Foreign Awards and Agreements) Act 1974 (Cth). The phrase has "the same meaning as in the Convention". Article II.1 of the New York Convention requires recognition of an "agreement in writing" under which the parties undertake to submit to arbitration differences which have arisen or may arise between them. "The drafters of the Convention wished to exclude oral or tacit acceptance of the arbitration agreement thereby leaving its terms and the assent to it without written proof" (*Comandate Marine Corp v Pan Australia Shipping Pty Ltd* (2006) 157 FCR 45; 238 ALR 457; [2006] FCAFC 192; BC20061083 at [152] (Allsop J)). Article II.2 of the Convention uses an inclusive definition for an "agreement in writing" and is expressed in language reflective of the technology and means of communication used in 1958: "contained in an exchange of letters and telegrams".

An attempt to expand and modernise the definition was made in 1985 by UNCITRAL in Art 7 of the Model Law. Relevantly, the Model Law provided that an agreement was in writing if it was "in an exchange of letters, telex, telegrams or other means of telecommunication which provide a record of the agreement, or in an exchange of statements of claim and defence in which the existence of an agreement is alleged by one party and not denied by another . . .".

In 2006, the requirement for writing in the definition of an arbitration agreement in the Model Law was further liberalised by UNCITRAL. Article 7 of the Model Law was amended "to better conform to international contract practices" (Explanatory Note by UNCITRAL Secretariat on the 1985 Model Law on International Commercial Arbitration as amended in 2006, para 19) and two options were adopted in the revised Art 7. No preference was expressed by UNCITRAL in favour of Option I or II. Option I was adopted by Australia (see s 16(2) of the Act).

Option I follows the structure of the original 1985 text. Consistently with the New York Convention, it requires a written form of the arbitration agreement but recognises a record of the "contents" of the agreement "in any form" as equivalent to traditional "writing". The agreement to arbitrate may be entered into in any form (including orally) as long as the content of the agreement is recorded. It no longer requires signatures of the parties or an exchange of messages between the parties. It modernises the language by adopting wording from the 1996 UNCITRAL Model Law on Electronic Commerce and the 2005 United Nations Convention on the Use of Electronic Communications in International Contracts. It also covers the situation where there has been "an exchange of statements of claim and defence in which the existence of the agreement is alleged by one party and not denied by another". It also covers the situation where there is a reference in a contract to a document, such as general conditions, which contains an arbitration clause "provided that the reference is such as to make that clause part of the contract".

A further attempt to expand the definition as found in the New York Convention was made by UNCITRAL in its Report (A/61/17) of 14 July 2006. UNCITRAL adopted a recommendation "that article II, paragraph (2) of the Convention be applied recognising that the circumstances described therein are not exhaustive." This recommendation was adopted by the General Assembly of the United Nations, in its resolution 61/33 of 4 December 2006, which also noted that "in connection with the modernisation of articles of the Model Law, the promotion of a uniform interpretation and application of the [New York Convention] is particularly timely".

While the meaning of agreement in writing in the New York Convention is inclusive, it was said in 2010 when the amendments were made to the Act that there was a "growing concern amongst Contracting Parties to the Convention that Article II(2) is being construed too narrowly by legislators and domestic courts. This concern has arisen primarily in response to the growing reliance on electronic communications in international trade and commerce. Overly narrow interpretations of the writing requirement have the potential to undermine the ongoing effectiveness of the Convention" (Revised Explanatory Memorandum to the International Arbitration Amendment Bill 2010 (Cth) at [14]).

These circumstances led to the insertion of a new s 3(4) into the Act by the International Arbitration Amendment Act 2010 (Cth), which "clarifies that *agreement in writing* is to be given an expansive interpretation that takes into account modern means of communication . . . The new provision builds on the existing meaning of *agreement in writing* in the Convention and the Act by clarifying that an agreement will be in writing if 'its content is recorded in any form' regardless of whether the agreement or contract to which it related 'has been concluded orally, by conduct, or by other means' . . . Further, an agreement is in writing if 'it is contained in an electronic communication and the information in that communication is accessible so as to be usable for subsequent reference'" (Revised Explanatory Memorandum to the International Arbitration Amendment Bill 2010 (Cth) at [16]–[18]).

The changes to these definitions in the section, which were made in 2010 and the adoption of Option I of Art 7 of the 2006 Model Law, were to ensure "consistency between the application of the enforcement and recognition provisions in the New York Convention and those in the Model Law as given force under the Act" (Revised Explanatory Memorandum to the International Arbitration Amendment Bill 2010 (Cth) at [21]). As a result, it is necessary to bear in mind the changes to the Act made in 2010 when considering decisions before the amendments took effect on 6 July 2010.

[s 3-2] Meaning of "agreement in writing" The requirement that there be "an agreement in writing" was considered in *Comandate Marine Corp v Pan Australia Shipping Pty Ltd* (2006) 157 FCR 45; 238 ALR 457; [2006] FCAFC 192; BC20061083. Allsop J, with whom Finn and Finkelstein JJ agreed, held (at [148]) that the requirement was "clearly addressed to the agreement to arbitrate, not to the wider substantive legal relationship, which may or may not be contractual". Thus even though the ultimate "act of formation" of the substantive contract may have been by conduct, as the agreement to the arbitration clause was contained in an earlier exchange of letters and telegrams, the requirement in Article II was satisfied. "Where there is clear mutual documentary exchange as to the terms of, and assent to, the arbitration agreement the purpose of Article II is fulfilled. If the agreement so reached was conditional, in the sense of being operative only upon an event occurring, the arbitration agreement can, nonetheless, be said to be contained in the exchange of relevant documents" (at [152]).

The expression "letters or telegrams" should be taken to extend to all "forms of written communications regularly utilised to conduct commerce in the various signatory countries" to the New York Convention (*WesTrac Pty Ltd v Eastcoast OTR Tyres Pty Ltd* (2008) 219 FLR 461; [2008] NSWSC 894; BC200807689 at [16] referring to *Chloe Z Fishing Co Inc v Oydessey Re (London) Ltd* (2000) 109 F Supp 2d 1236 at 1250).

[s 3-3] "arbitration agreement" The agreement must contain an agreement to "arbitrate". In the case of *Lief Investments Pty Ltd v Conagra International Fertiliser Company* [1998] NSWCA 481; BC9803166, during the negotiations leading to the contract, a facsimile was sent which included a statement "other terms and conditions as per . . . standard contract". The standard contract contained an arbitration clause. Some days later the parties signed a contract in which "no mention was made of any" standard contract. When the court proceedings were commenced to recover damages for breach of the contract an application was made for a stay under s 7. The court applied the decision in *Maybury v Atlantic Union Oil Co Ltd* (1953) 89 CLR 507 at 517; (1954) 28 ALJR 254; BC5300750 (Dixon CJ, Fullagar and Taylor JJ) where it was said "once an agreement is made in writing it is treated, unless the parties are shown otherwise to intend, as the full expression of their obligations". The court held that the contractual document, which was executed by the parties, was executed with the objective intention of superseding entirely all prior negotiations in relation to the subject matter dealt with by the document. There was no continuing intention of the parties to include the standard terms in the formal executed contract. As there was a written agreement, which did not contain an arbitration clause, there was no arbitration agreement and no stay could be ordered under s 7.

An agreement may be an "arbitration" agreement even though only one party to the agreement has a right to compel arbitration. In *PMT Partners Pty Ltd (In Liq) v Australian National Parks & Wildlife Service* (1995) 184 CLR 301; 131 ALR 377; 69 ALJR 829 (*PMT Partners*), the High Court was considering the definition of arbitration agreement in the uniform commercial arbitration legislation. There it was defined as an "agreement to refer present or future disputes to arbitration".

The court found that the ordinary and natural meaning of these words are "wide enough to encompass agreements by which the parties are bound to have their dispute arbitrated if an election is made or some event occurs or some condition is satisfied, even if only one party has the right to elect or is in a position to control the event or satisfy the condition" (*PMT Partners* at 310 as per Brennan CJ and Gaudron and McHugh JJ). See also the debate whether the domain name dispute resolution process organised by WIPO, which may only be initiated by one party, is an arbitration or an administrative process, L Nottage, "Is (International) Commercial Arbitration ADR?", *The Arbitrator and Mediator*, Vol 20, 2002, pp 84–5.

[s 3-4] Incorporation by reference (s 3(5) of the Act; Art 7(6) of the Model Law) The 2010 amendments introduced s 3(5), which recognised that many arbitration agreements are contained in documents separate from the main agreement between the parties. The terms of s 3(5) are taken from the definition of "arbitration agreement" found in Art 7(6) of the Model Law, which was introduced as part of the 2006 revision of the Model Law. The Model Law in Art 2(e) also contains a similar provision relating to the incorporation by reference of the arbitration rules of an arbitration institution. For an analysis of incorporation by reference see the commentary to Art 7(6) of the Model Law below.

[s 3-5] Arbitration agreement may arise in course of arbitration An ad hoc arbitration agreement may arise in the course of an international arbitration. A third party may submit to the jurisdiction of the arbitral tribunal by actively taking on the role of a party to the arbitration. The question "of submission to the jurisdiction of the arbitrators depends on whether, on an objective analysis, the [third party] intended to take any part in" the arbitration process (*Excalibur Ventures LLC v Texas Keystone Inc* [2011] EWHC 1624 (Comm) at [61]). As was noted by the court in *Brunswick Bowling & Billiards Corp Ltd v Shanghai Zhonglu Industrial Co Ltd* [2009] HKCFI 94 at [107], "the parties had by conduct agreed to confer jurisdiction on the [Arbitral] Tribunal to deal with [the counterclaims]. Participation in arbitral proceedings without challenging the jurisdiction of the tribunal is a submission to arbitration".

Further, an arbitration agreement may arise when the parties come before the arbitral panel at an early stage of the arbitration and agree upon the future conduct of the arbitration. In an arbitration conducted under the International Chamber of Commerce (the ICC), a document known as the Terms of Reference is drawn up and signed by or on behalf of the parties at an early stage of the proceedings under Art 13 of the ICC Arbitration Rules. This document may also amount to an ad hoc arbitration agreement.

The Queensland Court of Appeal in *Commonwealth Development Corp v Montague* [2000] QCA 252; BC200003514 held that the Terms of Reference was an enforceable agreement. In that case, the defendant resisted an application to enforce a costs award by an arbitrator who had dismissed the claim after finding that there was no arbitration agreement between the parties. The court found that an agreement to arbitrate had been made during the course of the proceedings and enforced the award.

Fryberg J said:

> Article 13 of the rules of arbitration of the International Chamber of Commerce ... required the arbitrator to draw up terms of reference and required the arbitrator and the parties to sign the terms of reference. It contained no requirement that the terms of reference be formulated as an agreement between the parties. It is therefore possible to imagine a case where a party signs terms of reference not as indicating an agreement to anything, but simply in compliance with the rules and in furtherance of the arbitration. However that is not this case. Here, the terms of reference recorded, immediately above the signature of the appellant's solicitor, that they 'were agreed and signed in Auckland, New Zealand on the 13th day of September 1996.' ... For these reasons, the agreement made by the terms of reference was in my judgment one under which the parties undertook to submit a difference which might arise between them in respect of a defined legal relationship (namely, participants in an arbitration) to arbitration. It therefore fell within the definition of 'arbitration agreement' in the [International Arbitration] Act.

Lord Steyn expressed a similar view in *Lesotho Highlands Development Authority v Impregilo SpA* [2005] All ER (D) 363 (Jun); [2006] 1 AC 221; [2005] 3 All ER 789; [2005] UKHL 43 at [21]. Lord Steyn, referring to the same instrument under the ICC Arbitration Rules, said: "the terms of reference may ... amend or supplement the terms of the arbitration agreement. The terms of reference are a source of the powers of the arbitrators ...".

Kerr J made a contrasting finding in relation to the Terms of Reference in *Dalmia v National Bank* [1978] Lloyd's Rep 223 at 233, where, notwithstanding the fact that the Terms of Reference had been signed by the parties, it was held in the particular circumstances of that case not to amount to a separate ad hoc submission agreement to arbitrate. The Court of Appeal in *Raguz v Sullivan* (2000) 50 NSWLR 236 at 250; [2000] NSWCA 240; BC200005212, considered the status of an analogous instrument, which had been signed by the parties at a preliminary conference at an early stage of the arbitration. In the circumstances of that case, it was held not to be an arbitration agreement but merely "an agreed set of steps for the conduct of the arbitration".

[s 3-6] Law governing the agreement to arbitrate The law governing the main transaction may be different to the law governing the agreement to arbitrate; see, eg, *C v D* [2007] EWCA 1282, where the underlying contract was governed by New York law but the arbitration clause in the contract was governed by English law; and *AES Ust-Kamenogorsk Hydropower Plant LLP v Ust-Kamenogorsk Hydropower Plant JSC* [2011] EWCA Civ 647, where the underlying contract was governed by Kazakhstan law but the arbitration clause in the contract was governed by English law.

[s 3-7] "arbitral award" The definition of an "arbitral award" was enacted by the Arbitration (Foreign Awards and Agreements) Act 1974 (Cth). An award is defined as having the same meaning as in the New York Convention. Article I(1) states that the Convention "shall also apply" to arbitral awards not considered as domestic awards in the country in which enforcement is sought. Article I(2) states that the term "arbitral award" includes not only those awards made by arbitrators appointed for each case but also those made by permanent arbitral bodies to which the parties have submitted.

The term "award" would not usually include an order made by an arbitrator in the nature of procedural directions or a "decision on a procedural point" (*Resort Condominiums International Inc v Bolwell* [1995] 1 Qd R 406 at 420; (1993) 118

ALR 655; BC9303445). The New York Convention in Art V(1)(c) speaks of "differences" referred to arbitration and not to orders dealing with procedural matters. Lord Mance expressed a similar view in *Dallah Real Estate and Tourism Holding Company v Govt of Pakistan* [2010] All ER (D) 36 (Nov); [2011] 1 AC 763; [2011] 1 All ER 485; [2010] UKSC 46 at [22]: "I do not regard the New York Convention as concerned with preliminary awards on jurisdiction." Thus an award may be interim or final providing it determines finally at least some of the matters in dispute, which have been referred to the arbitrator for determination. See also the discussion of an award in s 8 below.

[s 3-8] **"Australia"** The definition of the word "Australia" was enacted by the Arbitration (Foreign Awards and Agreements) Act 1974 (Cth). The terms of the original definition were "includes the Territories other than Papua New Guinea". The words "other than Papua New Guinea" were deleted by the International Arbitration Amendment Act 1989 (Cth). That amending Act also introduced a new s 2A, which extended the operation of the Act to all external territories and a new s 2B, which provided that the Crown was bound by the Act in the right of the Commonwealth, of each of the States, of the Northern Territory and of Norfolk Island.

[s 3-9] **"court"** When the Arbitration (Foreign Awards and Agreements) Act 1974 (Cth) was enacted it defined the word "court" as meaning "any court in Australia including a court of a State or Territory". The definition was changed in 2009 by the Federal Justice System Amendment (Efficiency Measures) Act (No 1) 2009 (Cth), which deleted the words after the word "including" quoted above and substituted "but not limited to, the Federal Court of Australia and a court of a State or Territory". This definition was not changed in 2010 with the enactment of the International Arbitration Amendment Act 2010 (Cth).

[s 3-10] **"electronic communication" and "data message"** Definitions for "electronic communication" and "data message" were inserted into s 3(1) of the Act by the International Arbitration Amendment Act 2010 (Cth). The definition for data message includes a number of examples such as email but is not intended to be confined to the examples given; rather, it "should be interpreted to take account of new means of communication as they emerge". (Revised Explanatory Memorandum to the International Arbitration Amendment Bill 2010 (Cth) at [16]–[18]).

[s 3-11] **"Foreign Affairs Department"** The Statute Law Revision Act 2011 (Cth) inserted a definition for the "Foreign Affairs Department". This was brought about by the change in the reference to the "Department of Foreign Affairs" in ss 10(1), 10A(1) and 10A(5) to "Foreign Affairs Department".

[s 3-12] **"ordinarily resident"** The restricted meaning contained in s 3(3) for the phrase "ordinarily resident" in relation to a body corporate was enacted by the Arbitration (Foreign Awards and Agreements) Act 1974 (Cth).

NOTE: **Section 4** "Accession to Convention" was repealed by the Law and Justice Legislation Amendment Act 2004 (Cth) and has not been replaced. **Section 5** "Territories" and **section 6** "Crown to be bound" were repealed by the International Arbitration Amendment Act 1989 (Cth) and have not been replaced.

[s 7] Enforcement of foreign arbitration agreements

7 (1) Where:
  (a) the procedure in relation to arbitration under an arbitration agreement is governed, whether by virtue of the express terms of the agreement or otherwise, by the law of a Convention country;
  (b) the procedure in relation to arbitration under an arbitration agreement is governed, whether by virtue of the express terms of the agreement or otherwise, by the law of a country not being Australia or a Convention country, and a party to the agreement is Australia or a State or a person who was, at the time when the agreement was made, domiciled or ordinarily resident in Australia;
  (c) a party to an arbitration agreement is the Government of a Convention country or of part of a Convention country or the Government of a territory of a Convention country, being a territory to which the Convention extends; or
  (d) a party to an arbitration agreement is a person who was, at the time when the agreement was made, domiciled or ordinarily resident in a country that is a Convention country;

this section applies to the agreement.

(2) Subject to this Part, where:
  (a) proceedings instituted by a party to an arbitration agreement to which this section applies against another party to the agreement are pending in a court; and
  (b) the proceedings involve the determination of a matter that, in pursuance of the agreement, is capable of settlement by arbitration;

on the application of a party to the agreement, the court shall, by order, upon such conditions (if any) as it thinks fit, stay the proceedings or so much of the proceedings as involves the determination of that matter, as the case may be, and refer the parties to arbitration in respect of that matter.

(3) Where a court makes an order under subsection (2), it may, for the purpose of preserving the rights of the parties, make such interim or supplementary orders as it thinks fit in relation to any property that is the subject of the matter to which the first-mentioned order relates.

(4) For the purposes of subsections (2) and (3), a reference to a party includes a reference to a person claiming through or under a party.

(5) A court shall not make an order under subsection (2) if the court finds that the arbitration agreement is null and void, inoperative or incapable of being performed.

COMMENTARY ON SECTION 7

Introduction	[s 7-1]
Cautionary note	[s 7-2]
Constitutional validity	[s 7-3]
A stay under Art 8 of the Model Law or under inherent jurisdiction of a Supreme Court	[s 7-4]
"the procedure in relation to arbitration ... is governed ... by the law of" (s 7(1)(a) and (b))	[s 7-5]
"arbitration agreement" (s 7(1), (2) and (5))	[s 7-6]
"Convention country" (s 7(1))	[s 7-7]
"domiciled or ordinarily resident" (s 7(1))	[s 7-8]
"determination of a matter" (s 7(2))	[s 7-9]

"that, in pursuance of the agreement, is capable of
    settlement by arbitration" (s 7(2)(b)) .... [s 7-10]
Scope of arbitration agreement .... [s 7-11]
Arbitrability of matters in dispute .... [s 7-12]
"on the application of a party" (s 7(2)(b)) .... [s 7-13]
"a person claiming through or under a party" (s 7(4)) .. [s 7-14]
"the court shall" (s 7(2)) .... [s 7-15]
An order under s 7 is interlocutory .... [s 7-16]
"upon such conditions (if any) as it thinks fit" (s 7(2)) . [s 7-17]
"may, for the purpose of preserving the rights of the
    parties, make such interim or supplementary orders
    . . . in relation to any property that is the subject of the
    matter" (s 7(3)) .... [s 7-18]
"null and void, inoperative or incapable of being
    performed" (s 7(5)) .... [s 7-19]
"null and void" .... [s 7-20]
"inoperative" .... [s 7-21]
"incapable of being performed" .... [s 7-22]
Time for making application .... [s 7-23]
"the court" .... [s 7-24]

[s 7-1] **Introduction** The wording of s 7 has remained unaltered from the time of its enactment in 1974 to the time of writing, apart from the minor drafting amendment made by the International Arbitration Amendment Act 1989 (Cth), which introduced the Model Law into the Act, when the word "Act" in s 7 was replaced with the word "Part".

[s 7-2] **Cautionary note** When considering decisions which have considered this section of the Act and which were made prior to 6 July 2010, account needs to be taken of the amendments made elsewhere in the Act by the International Arbitration Amendment Act 2010 (Cth). These amendments relevantly include the statement of the objects of the Act inserted in s 2D, and the matters set out in s 39(2), which a court now must have regard to when exercising its powers under the Act (see s 39(1)(a)(vi), (1)(a)(vii) and (1)(c)).

[s 7-3] **Constitutional validity** The constitutional validity of the section was upheld by the Federal Court in *Hi-Fert Pty Ltd v Kiukiang Maritime Carriers Inc (No 5)* (1998) 90 FCR 1; 159 ALR 142; [1999] 2 Lloyd's Rep 782; BC9806222.

[s 7-4] **A stay under Art 8 of the Model Law or under inherent jurisdiction of a Supreme Court** Section 7 is not an exclusive code regulating applications for a stay of proceedings. An application for a stay of proceedings may also be brought under Art 8(1) of the Model Law. Section 7 and Art 8 are "independent operative provisions" (see s 16(1) of the Act and the discussion in *Comandate Marine Corp v Pan Australia Shipping Pty Ltd* (2006) 157 FCR 45; 238 ALR 457; [2006] FCAFC 192; BC200610833 at [50], [188] and [198]–[205] (Allsop J)).

In addition, a Supreme Court of a State or Territory "has the inherent power to stay proceedings pending the outcome of an arbitration . . . The inherent power is, however, rarely invoked because of the extensive statutory jurisdiction to stay which is available for domestic and international arbitrations" (*Vantage Holdings Pty Ltd v JHC Developments Group Pty Ltd* [2011] QSC 155; BC201103834 at [36]). A court may also be able to rely on a power to stay proceedings for an abuse of process and a general power to control its own proceedings (*QH Tours Ltd v Ship Design and Management (Aust) Pty Ltd* (1991) 33 FCR 227 at 231; 105 ALR 371; 22 IPR 447; BC9103569).

The power to stay proceedings may arise in the context of an application to proceed on a Statutory Demand for payment of a debt under s 459G of the Corporations Act 2001 (Cth). As was stated by Palmer J in *Arris Investments Pty Ltd v Fahd* [2010] NSWSC 309; BC201002666 at [19]–[20]:

> an express agreement that the parties' disputes must be determined by arbitration rather than by any other form of litigious proceeding should carry great discretionary weight in considering whether a Statutory Demand should be set aside under s 459J(l)(b). There are often good commercial reasons for parties to agree to air their disputes only in the privacy of an arbitration. There are considerations also of savings in time and legal expense in such proceeding. If the dispute is fairly and squarely within the purview of a compulsory arbitration clause, the Court should not lightly permit one party to ignore the clause and precipitate legal proceedings by the issue of a Statutory Demand. In short, the Court should not encourage parties to breach their contracts.

This approach was endorsed by Ward J in *In the Matter of 2 Roslyn Street Pty Ltd; 2 Roslyn Street Pty Ltd v Leisure Inn Hospitality Management Pty Ltd* [2011] NSWSC 512; BC201103981 at [107].

[s 7-5]   "the procedure in relation to arbitration ... is governed ... by the law of" (s 7(1)(a) and (b))   The procedural law, sometimes referred to as the *lex arbitri*, or curial law, is the law which governs the procedure in an arbitration. Under the "rules of private international law, in the absence of any contractual provision to the contrary, the procedural (or curial) law governing arbitrations is that of the forum of the arbitration, [whether it be a local or foreign law] ... since this is the system of law with which the agreement to arbitrate in the particular forum will have its closest connection" (*Bank Mellat v Helliniki Techniki SA* [1984] QB 291; [1983] 3 All ER 428; (1983) 133 NLJ 597; [1983] 3 WLR 783 (*Bank Mellat*) at QB 301 (Kerr LJ)). There must be an applicable arbitration law regulating the procedure of the arbitration. Common law jurisprudence "does not recognise the concept of arbitral procedures floating in the transnational firmament, unconnected to any municipal system of law": *Bank Mellat* at QB 301 applied in *American Diagnostica Inc v Gradipore Ltd* (1998) 44 NSWLR 312 at 324; BC9800877, and for a discussion about the concept of "delocalisation", see S Greenberg, C Kee and R Weeramantry, *International Commercial Arbitration: An Asia-Pacific Perspective*, Cambridge University Press, Melbourne, 2011, pp 66–80 and J Paulsson, "Delocalisation of International Commercial Arbitration: When and Why it Matters" (1983) 32 *International and Comparative Law Quarterly* 53–61.

The arbitration law and the arbitration forum may be an obvious choice if all matters, including procedural matters, occur in one jurisdiction. The difficulties which might otherwise arise where the procedure of an international arbitration takes place in several jurisdictions are minimised by the parties' choice, either express or implied, of a juridical home or seat for their arbitration. This is also referred to as "the place of the arbitration" under the Model Law (see the commentary on Art 20 of the Model Law below). Usually, the law of the seat of arbitration governs matters of procedure.

Procedural problems may only be minimised as the local laws of jurisdictions other than the seat may still apply, eg, *Raguz v Sullivan* (2000) 50 NSWLR 236 at 249; [2000] NSWCA 240; BC200005212 at [54], Spigelman CJ and Mason P, where it was said that the parties' agreement on Lausanne, Switzerland as the seat of the arbitration, "cannot oust the Court's jurisdiction to police arbitrators' misconduct" conferred by the provisions of the since repealed Commercial Arbitration Act 1984 (NSW).

Where the parties have failed expressly to choose the juridical home or law governing the conduct of the arbitration, this law will be the law of the country or jurisdiction presumed to have been selected by the parties to govern the arbitration, eg, *Dubai Islamic Bank PJSC v Paymentech Merchant Services Inc* [2001] 1 Lloyd's Rep 65. If the arbitration is held in one country, prima facie it will be the law of that country, eg, *Flakt Australia Ltd v Wilkins and Davies Construction Co Ltd* [1979] 2 NSWLR 243 at 246; (1979) 25 ALR 605; 39 FLR 267, where the application of s 7(1)(b) was common ground. The parties are presumed to have chosen the country most closely connected to the arbitration (*American Diagnostica Inc v Gradipore Ltd* (1998) 44 NSWLR 312 at 324; BC9800877).

An agreement as to the seat of arbitration brings in the law of that country as the curial law and is analogous to an exclusive jurisdiction clause. Not only is there agreement on the curial law of the seat, but also on the courts of the seat having supervisory jurisdiction over the arbitration. Thus by agreeing to the seat, the parties agree that any challenge to an interim or final award is to be made only in the courts of the place designated as the seat of the arbitration (*Shashoua v Sharma* [2009] 2 Lloyd's Rep 376; [2009] EWHC 957 (Comm) at [23]). Where proceedings are brought in another jurisdiction in breach of such agreement, an anti-suit injunction or a stay may be granted.

The parties may incorporate the procedural rules of an international or domestic arbitration institution but the mere choice of such contractual terms (absent any provision in the nature of a choice of seat contained in those rules) will not determine which "law" governs the procedure of the arbitration (*Wagners Nouvelle Caledonie Sarl v Vale Inco Nouvelle Caledonie SAS* [2010] QCA 219; BC201005964 (*Wagners*); *Cargill International SA v Peabody Australia Mining Ltd* [2010] NSWSC 887; BC201005660 (*Cargill*)). A contrary view was recently expressed by the ACT Supreme Court in *Lightsource Technologies Australia Pty Ltd v Pointsec Mobile Technologies AB* (2011) 250 FLR 63; [2011] ACTSC 59; BC201102227 at [108]–[112] which, it is submitted, was wrongly decided. The ACT Supreme Court followed without question the decision in *Australian Granites Ltd v Eisenwerk Hensel Bayreuth Dipl-Ing Burkhardt GmbH* [2001] 1 Qd R 461; BC9904474, notwithstanding that it had been noted by White JA in *Wagners* at [51] that Ward J in *Cargill* at [42]–[91] had "argued, persuasively, that *Eisenwerk's* reasoning was plainly wrong and should not be followed".

[s 7-6] "arbitration agreement" (s 7(1), (2) and (5)) See the discussion of the definition of "arbitration agreement" in s 3(1) above.

The question of whether there was in effect an arbitration agreement giving rise to a stay under s 7 is to be answered "by looking at the state of affairs as it exists when the application for a stay is made" (*Bakri Navigation Co Ltd v Owners of Ship*

'Golden Glory' Glorious Shipping SA (1991) 217 ALR 152 at 167; BC9103216, [46]). Absent an arbitration agreement in writing at that time between the parties, a stay is not available under s 7 or under Art 8(1) of the Model Law, eg, *McConnell Dowell Constructors (Aust) Pty Ltd v Ship 'Asian Atlas'* [2011] FCA 174; BC201100867 at [21].

[s 7-7] "Convention country" (s 7(1)) The phrase "Convention country" is defined in s 3(1) as a "Contracting State within the meaning of the [New York] Convention".

[s 7-8] "domiciled or ordinarily resident" (s 7(1)) The phrase "ordinarily resident" in relation to a body corporate has been given a limited meaning by s 3(3) of the Act. A body corporate is taken to be ordinarily resident in a country, if and only if, it is incorporated or has its principal place of business in that country, eg, *Elders CED Ltd v Dravo Corp* (1984) 59 ALR 206 at 207–8; 2 BCL 68; *Lightsource Technologies Australia Pty Ltd v Pointsec Mobile Technologies AB* (2011) 250 FLR 63; [2011] ACTSC 59; BC201102227 at [107]. If a foreign company incorporated in a Contracting State obtains a limited local presence through a local registration under the Business Names Act 1962 (NSW) or local registration as a foreign company, it does not cease to be ordinarily resident at its place of incorporation (*Elders CED Ltd v Dravo Corp* (1984) 59 ALR 206 at 207–8; 2 BCL 68).

The requirement of "domiciled" is satisfied if the domicile is the place of incorporation (*WesTrac Pty Ltd v Eastcoast OTR Tyres Pty Ltd* (2008) 219 FLR 461; [2008] NSWSC 894; BC200807689 at [11]). The circumstance of incorporation is alone sufficient to warrant a finding of domicile in the place of incorporation and that the company has no domicile anywhere else.

[s 7-9] "determination of a matter" (s 7(2)) The word "matter" is a word of wide import. The expression "matter . . . capable of settlement by arbitration . . . requires that there be some subject matter, some right or liability in controversy which, if not co-extensive with the subject of the controversy which falls for determination in those proceedings, is at least susceptible of settlement as a discrete controversy" (*Tanning Research Laboratories Inc v O'Brien* (1990) 169 CLR 332 at 351; 91 ALR 180; 64 ALJR 211; BC9002954 (Deane and Gaudron JJ)). The court must consider the substance of the controversy as it appears from the circumstances in evidence and not just the particular terms in which it has been formulated in the court process (*PT Thiess Contractors Indonesia v PT Kaltim Prima Coal* [2011] EWHC 1842 at [35], following *Tanning Research Laboratories Inc v O'Brien* (1990) 169 CLR 332 at 352–3; 91 ALR 180; 64 ALJR 211; BC9002954 (Deane and Gaudron JJ)).

The meaning of the word "matter" is derived from its use in Art II(3) of the New York Convention in the context of the agreement between the Contracting States in Art II(1) to recognise foreign arbitration agreements. The word "matter" in s 7(2)(b) is "a reference to the differences between the parties or the controversy that are or is covered by the terms of the arbitration agreement. That is, such part (or all) of the differences that fall within the scope of the arbitration agreement. It is that body of differences which is to be capable of settlement by arbitration"

(*Comandate Marine Corp v Pan Australia Shipping Pty Ltd* (2006) 157 FCR 45; 238 ALR 457; [2006] FCAFC 192; BC200610833 at [235] (Allsop J, with whom Finn and Finkelstein JJ agreed)).

An argument that the "matter" means the ultimate subject matter at issue in the proceedings, which can only be ascertained when the pleadings are closed, was rejected by the court in *Flakt Australia Ltd v Wilkins and Davies Construction Co Ltd* [1979] 2 NSWLR 243 at 250; (1979) 25 ALR 605; 39 FLR 267; and in *Recyclers of Australia Pty Ltd v Hettinga Equipment Inc* (2000) 100 FCR 420; 175 ALR 725; [2000] FCA 547; BC200002851 at [11]–[20].

When an application is made, it is necessary, first, to examine the nature and scope of the proceedings to identify each matter to be determined in the proceeding and, second, to construe the agreement so as to identify each matter that, in pursuance of it, is capable of settlement by arbitration. To the extent that there is correspondence between the results of the two enquiries, the matters concerned will be matters in respect of which the Act will require the proceedings to be stayed (*WesTrac Pty Ltd v Eastcoast OTR Tyres Pty Ltd* (2008) 219 FLR 461; [2008] NSWSC 894; BC200807689 at [18]).

In undertaking this process, the court is concerned to identify a matter which "denotes any claim for relief of a kind proper for determination in a court. It does not include every issue which would, or might, arise for decision in the course of the determination of such a claim" (*Flakt Australia Ltd v Wilkins and Davies Construction Co Ltd* [1979] 2 NSWLR 243 at 250; 25 ALR 605; 39 FLR 267; and see also *Elders CED Ltd v Dravo Corp* (1984) 59 ALR 206 at 210; 2 BCL 68; *Allergan Pharmaceuticals Inc v Bausch & Lomb Inc* (1985) AIPC 90-262; (1985) ATPR 40-636 at 47–173; 3 BCL 61; *Recyclers of Australia Pty Ltd v Hettinga Equipment Inc* (2000) 100 FCR 420; 175 ALR 725; [2000] FCA 547; BC200002851 at [11]–[12]; *Ansett Australia Ltd v Malaysian Airline System Berhad* (2008) 217 FLR 376; [2008] VSC 109; BC200802403 at [20]; and see also the discussion in *Re Dodwell & Co (Australia) Pty Ltd and Moss Security Ltd* (FCA No G649 of 1989, 11 April 1990, Wilcox J, unreported, at [5]–[8])).

[s 7-10] **"that, in pursuance of the agreement, is capable of settlement by arbitration" (s 7(2)(b))** Once the matter or matters have been identified it is necessary to consider whether the "matter" or "matters" as identified, are capable of settlement by arbitration under the terms of the arbitration agreement. The court cannot grant a stay unless it is satisfied that the proceedings involve the determination of a matter that is "capable of settlement by arbitration". The phrase where it appears in s 7(2)(b) conveys two distinct concepts, both of which must be established. First, there is the question of the "scope" of the arbitration clause, which must be considered, and the related question of whether the matter so identified falls within the scope of the clause, and second, there is a question of the "arbitrability" of the matters in dispute.

[s 7-11] **Scope of arbitration agreement** The first issue raised by the phrase "in pursuance of the agreement, is capable of settlement by arbitration" requires consideration of the "scope" of the arbitration clause. This issue also arises under Arts 34(2)(a)(iii) and 36(1)(iii) of the Model Law. The controversy "must be one falling within the scope of the arbitration agreement" (*Tanning Research*

Laboratories Inc v O'Brien (1990) 169 CLR 332 at 351; 91 ALR 180; 64 ALJR 211; BC9002954 (Deane and Gaudron JJ)).

The question of the scope of an arbitration clause has been the subject of a multitudinous collection of decisions, not all consistent, where common connecting phrases have been considered in a variety of contractual contexts. See the discussion in *Walter Rau Neusser Oel und Fett v Cross Pacific Trading Ltd* [2005] FCA 1102; BC200505922; and in *Comandate Marine Corp v Pan Australia Shipping Pty Ltd* (2006) 157 FCR 45; 238 ALR 457; [2006] FCAFC 192; BC200610833. Numerous authorities have considered the scope of connecting phrases such as "arising under", "arising out of" and "in connection with", with ample authority for the view that the former has a narrower scope and equally for the view that they all have the same scope: an observation made by the court in *WesTrac Pty Ltd v Eastcoast OTR Tyres Pty Ltd* (2008) 219 FLR 461; [2008] NSWSC 894; BC200807689 at [24].

Nevertheless, in approaching this task the current view is that there is a "clear tide of judicial opinion" as to arbitration clauses where the fair reading of them is not confined, which is "to give width, flexibility and amplitude to them" (*Incitec Ltd v Alkimos Shipping Corp* (2004) 138 FCR 496; 206 ALR 558; [2004] FCA 698; BC200403193) and that "as a matter of general principle, it is the duty of the court to give effect to the purpose which lies behind an arbitration agreement and to respect the intention of the parties as expressed in that agreement" (*Ansett Australia Ltd v Malaysian Airline System Berhad* (2008) 217 FLR 376; [2008] VSC 109; BC200802403 at [36]).

This approach is reflective of a relatively recent, but an oft repeated, observation that:

> When the parties to a commercial contract agree, at the time of making the contract, and before any disputes have yet arisen, to refer to arbitration any dispute or difference arising out of the agreement, their agreement should not be construed narrowly. They are unlikely to have intended that different disputes should be resolved before different tribunals, or that the appropriate tribunal should be determined by fine shades of difference in the legal character of individual issues, or by the ingenuity of lawyers in developing points of argument." (*Francis Travel Marketing Pty Ltd v Virgin Atlantic Airways Ltd* (1996) 39 NSWLR 160 at 165D (Gleeson CJ, with whom Meagher JA and Sheller JA agreed)).

A similar point was made in *Premium Nafta Products Ltd v Fili Shipping Company Ltd* [2007] All ER (D) 233 (Oct); [2007] 4 All ER 951; [2008] 1 Lloyd's Rep 254; [2007] UKHL 40, also known as *Fiona Trust & Holding Corp v Privalov* [2007] 4 All ER 951; [2008] 1 Lloyd's Rep 254; [2007] All ER (D) 233 (Oct); [2007] UKHL 40 at [11]–[12] (Lord Hoffmann), and [27], where Lord Hope, who cited *Comandate Marine Corp v Pan Australia Shipping Pty Ltd* (2006) 157 FCR 45; 238 ALR 457; [2006] FCAFC 192; BC200610833 on this point, said "arbitration may be chosen as a one-stop method of adjudication for the determination of all disputes"; and a similar view was expressed in Singapore in *Larsen Oil and Gas Pte Ltd v Petroprod Ltd* [2011] SGCA 21 at [13]–[19].

This approach (sometimes referred to as a "liberal approach") to construction of the dispute resolution clause "is not to depart from the meaning of the words chosen by the parties. Rather, it is to give effect to a coherent business purpose through an assumption commercial courts around the world will make that parties are unlikely to have intended multiple venues or occasions for the resolution of their disputes unless they say so" (*Lipman Pty Ltd v Emergency Services Superannuation Board* [2011] NSWCA 163; BC201104482 (*Lipman*) at [8] (Allsop P, with whom Young JA and Tobias AJA agreed)). This approach "can now . . . be seen as part of the law of international commerce" (in *Lipman* at [6], Allsop P adopted the statement of Lord Hope in *Fiona Trust & Holding Corp v Privalov* [2007] 4 All ER 951; [2008] 1 Lloyd's Rep 254; [2007] All ER (D) 233 (Oct); [2007] UKHL 40 at [31]). See also *Barclays Bank PLC v Nylon Capital LLP* [2011] EWCA Civ 826 at [25], Thomas LJ with whom Etherton LJ and Lord Neuberger MR agreed, and *Larsen Oil and Gas Pte Ltd v Petroprod Ltd* [2011] SGCA 21 at [12]–[19].

Only those matters that are the subject of the arbitration agreement can give rise to a stay. A claim may be derived from the agreement between the parties or it may have a different legal basis. Only those matters that are covered by the scope of the agreement can be arbitrated. The distinction is seen in *Tanning Research Laboratories Inc v O'Brien* (1990) 169 CLR 332; 91 ALR 180; 64 ALJR 211; BC9002954 (*Tanning*). A claim such as interest due under the contract to which the company in liquidation was a party, considered in the *Tanning* case, would be within the scope of the arbitration clause and must be referred to arbitration. But in contrast, if it were assumed that the liquidator had processed the claim of the creditor in such a dilatory way as to give rise to a claim for interest, then that type of claim would not fall within the scope of the arbitration agreement (*Tanning* at CLR 344 (Brennan and Dawson JJ)). Similarly, the decision of the liquidator ultimately to accept or reject the claim would be beyond the scope of the arbitration clause because the matter to be referred to arbitration cannot extend to issues which could not arise in the proceedings between the company in liquidation and the creditor, or which are unrelated to the contract containing the arbitration clause.

In *Seeley International Pty Ltd v Electra Air Conditioning BV* (2008) 246 ALR 589; [2008] FCA 29; BC200800246, the arbitration agreement contained a clause which stated: "Nothing in this [clause] prevents a party seeking injunctive or declaratory relief in the case of material breach or threatened breach of this Agreement." The applicant commenced proceedings seeking declarations, including a declaration that the defendant's conduct was in breach of s 52 of the Trade Practices Act 1974 (Cth), and orders under s 87. An application for a stay under s 7 was refused. The court held at [32] that as a matter of the proper construction of the arbitration agreement, "the parties' agreement [was] to treat disputes to which [the clause] refers differently from the regime for arbitration" (leave to appeal from this decision was refused; see *Electra Air Conditioning BV v Seeley International Pty Ltd ACN 054 687 035* [2008] FCAFC 169; BC200808797; and also *Paharpur Cooling Towers Ltd v Paramount (WA) Ltd* [2008] WASCA 110 at [45]–[47]). If the disputes have been, as a matter of construction, "carved out" of the arbitration agreement in the sense of being excluded from the scope of the arbitration clause, or if the disputes are discrete and intended to be the subject of a different regime under a different contract between the parties, then there is no agreement to refer the disputes to arbitration so as to attract a mandatory stay (*PT Thiess Contractors Indonesia v PT Kaltim Prima Coal* [2011] EWHC 1842 at [41]–[44]).

The decision in *Transfield Philippines Inc v Pacific Hydro Ltd* [2006] VSC 175; BC200609991 considered some interesting arguments put forward as to why the matter was not capable of settlement by arbitration. The proceedings were brought in Australia in the Federal Court and included claims under s 52 of the Trade Practices Act 1974 (Cth) for misleading conduct. There had been two previous arbitration proceedings between the same parties under an arbitration agreement where the seat of the arbitration was in Singapore and the substantive law governing the determination of the dispute was Philippines law. The first arbitration panel had declined to deal with the same s 52 claims when they were advanced in the earlier arbitration. This arbitral panel had delivered several awards and the arbitration had terminated. There had been a settlement of a second arbitration between the same parties. It was argued that because the settlement had taken place and there was no extant arbitration to which the court could refer the parties, the matter was not therefore capable of settlement by arbitration and the requirements in s 7(2) could not be met. The case was decided on the basis that service on the defendant should be set aside for other reasons, but the court nonetheless considered the case for a stay under s 7(2).

The argument that the matter was not capable of settlement by arbitration was rejected as:

(1) there is no express or implicit requirement in s 7(2) "that there be an extant arbitration before a stay can be ordered. The concluding words of the section merely require an ability on the part of the court to refer the parties to arbitration": at [74];

(2) the settlement of the second arbitration did not purport to foreclose the reference of future disputes to an arbitral tribunal: at [75];

(3) if there was an issue as to whether or not the arbitral tribunal was functus officio or willing to consider a claim, then that was a matter which the tribunal itself, not the court, should decide: at [76]–[77]. (A similar situation arose in *Doshion Ltd v Sembawang Engineers and Constructors Pte Ltd* [2011] SGHC 46, where the claim that the dispute to be arbitrated between the parties had been settled, was referred by the court back to the arbitrator appointed to determine the initial dispute.);

(4) even if the arbitral tribunal took the view that it was unable or unwilling to consider those matters then that does not necessarily lead to the conclusion that they are not capable of referring the matters to arbitration before "another tribunal": at [78]. The court noted that this conclusion was "entirely consistent with the importance of holding parties to their bargain in relation to arbitrations, which is part of the important public policy to which the International Arbitration Act gives effect": at [79].

In contrast, the court considered other claims in the proceedings for misrepresentation, which had been raised in the second arbitration and were within the terms of the settlement agreement reached in that second arbitration, with the parties agreeing to mutual releases of the claims made. As a result the court held that such claims and any alleged dispute were no longer capable of settlement by arbitration and no stay was granted in relation to those claims: at [80]–[83].

The requirement that the matter be "capable of settlement" may not be satisfied if, on the proper construction of the parties' agreement, the arbitrator is prevented from exercising a power necessarily involved in the determination of the claim. If the agreement expressly said that the arbitrator cannot vary or set aside the terms of the contractual relationship between the parties, a statutory claim to vary the contract would not be "capable of settlement" by arbitration (see *Nicola v Ideal Image Development Corp Inc* (2009) 261 ALR 1; [2009] FCA 1177; BC200909461 at [47]–[55]).

The arbitration clause may refer any dispute which may arise between the parties to be arbitrated by a named arbitration institution. If at the time the dispute arises that body has ceased to exist, the clause may still be enforceable if there is a legal successor to the named institution or, if the "the language used by the parties, reasonably interpreted, is capable of referring disputes" to another institution (*Dalimpex Ltd v Janicki* (2003) 64 OR (3d) 737; 228 DLR (4th) 179; 2003 CanLII 34234 (*Dalimpex*) at [27] and [37]). "Where an arbitration clause is capable of bearing two interpretations, and one of those interpretations fairly provides for arbitration, the courts should lean towards that option" (*Dalimpex* at [37]).

[s 7-12] Arbitrability of matters in dispute The second question that arises is whether matters in dispute can be arbitrated. This question is raised at the outset of the arbitration process to reflect the view that "arbitrability" is an issue to be determined by the application of domestic legal principles and law. Raising it at the outset reduces the possibility that any award which is ultimately made in the arbitration may be unenforceable because of Art V(2)(a) of the New York Convention which allows a court to refuse enforcement where "the subject matter of the difference is not capable of settlement by arbitration under the law of" the country in which enforcement is sought. There is no single international view of what disputes are "arbitrable" and what disputes must be determined by a judicial process.

The enforcement of an award may be refused by a court under s 8(7)(a) of the Act if the court finds that the "subject matter of the difference ... is not capable of settlement by arbitration" under the law in force in the State or Territory in which the court is sitting. This view that the arbitrability is a matter for domestic law is also reflected in Art 1(5) of the Model Law which provides that the Model Law "shall not affect any other [national] law ... by virtue of which certain disputes may not be submitted to arbitration". It is repeated in Art 34(2)(b)(i) of the Model Law, which allows a court to set aside an award if it finds that the "subject matter of the dispute is not capable of settlement by arbitration under the law of this State" (see also Art 36(2)(b)(i) of the Model Law).

The subject matter of the dispute must be arbitrable in the sense that it must not be a matter which cannot be arbitrated, such as a matter "relating to rights which are ... required to be determined exclusively by the exercise of judicial power" (*Tanning Research Laboratories Inc v O'Brien* (1990) 169 CLR 332 at 351; 91 ALR 180; 64 ALJR 211; BC9002954 (Deane and Gaudron JJ)). The powers of an arbitrator are limited by considerations of public policy and by the fact that the arbitrator is appointed by parties and not by the State.

Some disputes are required to be determined exclusively by the exercise of judicial power, eg, *Metrocall Inc v Electronic Tracking Systems Pty Ltd* (2000) 52 NSWLR 1; 101 IR 66; [2000] NSWIRComm 136 (*Metrocall*) at [63]–[80], where it was held that the power to decide issues in a proceeding under s 106 of the Industrial Arbitration Act 1996 (NSW) could not be conferred by agreement on an arbitrator. "What normally distinguishes this class of case is the existence of some legitimate public interest in seeing that disputes of the type in question are resolved by public institutions or in accordance with structures that are established by parliament rather than institutions established by the parties" (*Seimens Ltd v Origin Energy Uranquinty Power Pty Ltd* (2011) 279 ALR 759; [2011] NSWSC 195; BC201102144 at [38]; and see also *Larkden Pty Ltd v Lloyd Energy Systems Pty Ltd* (2011) 279 ALR 772; [2011] NSWSC 268; BC201102191 at [63]).

There are matters which may not be exercised by private individuals appointed by the parties, such as imposing a fine or term of imprisonment, making an award that binds the public at large, such as a divorce decree, a judgment *in rem* against a ship (*ACD Tridon Inc v Tridon Australia Pty Ltd* [2002] NSWSC 896; BC200206142 at [189] (*ACD Tridon*) or a winding-up order (*A Best Floor Sanding Pty Ltd v Skyer Australia Pty Ltd* [1999] VSC 170; BC9903185 at [18]), and "disputes arising from the operation of the statutory provisions of the insolvency regime [should be treated *per se*] as non-arbitrable even if the parties expressly included them within the scope of the arbitration agreement" (*Larsen Oil and Gas Pte Ltd v Petroprod Ltd* [2011] SGCA 21 at [46]). Yet a dispute involving questions under a statutory scheme may be arbitrable notwithstanding a statutorily imposed limitation on the scope of the relief obtainable in the arbitral proceedings. There may be resort to arbitration in respect of the dispute between shareholders or the company which forms the grounds upon which such relief may be sought (*Fulham Football Club (1987) Ltd v Richards* [2011] EWCA Civ 855 (*Fulham Football Club*) at [76]–[83], following *ACD Tridon* at [191]–[194]).

Disputes which affect the rights of third parties (*Allergan Pharmaceuticals Inc v Bausch & Lomb Inc* (1985) AIPC 90-262; (1985) ATPR 40-636; 3 BCL 61 at [35]) or where the third parties are necessary parties, may be non-arbitrable (*Paharpur Cooling Towers Ltd v Paramount (WA) Ltd* [2008] WASCA 110; BC200803347 at [43]; *Comandate Marine Corp v Pan Australia Shipping Pty Ltd* (2006) 157 FCR 45 at 98; 238 ALR 457; [2006] FCAFC 192; BC200610833 at [200]; *Nicola v Ideal Image Development Corp Inc* (2009) 261 ALR 1; [2009] FCA 1177; BC200909461 (*Nicola*) at [56]–[58]). However, "the limitation which the contractual basis of arbitration necessarily imposes on the power of the arbitrator to make orders affecting non-parties is not necessarily determinative of whether the subject matter of the dispute is itself arbitrable. It is necessary to consider in relation to the matters in dispute in each case whether they engage third-party rights or represent an attempt to delegate to the arbitrators what is a matter of public interest which cannot be determined within the limits of a private contractual process" (*Fulham Football Club* at [40] (Patten LJ)).

In those disputes that are in the exclusive domain of a national court or other tribunal, there is said to be a sufficient element of legitimate public interest in the subject matter of the dispute, making its private resolution outside the national court system inappropriate (*Larkden Pty Ltd v Lloyd Energy Systems Pty Ltd* (2011) 279 ALR 772; [2011] NSWSC 268; BC201102191 (*Larkden*) at [63]). Examples of such disputes include the determination of status, such as bankruptcy, the winding up of corporations in insolvency and whether or not a patent or trade mark should be granted (*Larkden* at [63]–[64]).

The modern trend both domestically and internationally (as also evidenced by the amendments to the Act made by the International Arbitration Amendment Act

2010 (Cth)) is to facilitate the promotion and use of arbitration and to minimise judicial intervention in the arbitration process. The court in *Larkden* noted (at [65]) evidence of this trend in Canada, eg, *Desputeaux v Editions Chouette* (1987) Inc 2003 SCC 17 at [38] and in Singapore, eg, *Tjong Very Sumito v Antig Investments* [2009] 4 SLR (R) 732 at 745, [28].

Some types of remedies that an arbitrator can award are limited by considerations of public policy and the fact that the arbitrator is appointed by the parties and not by the State. Equally there is no impediment to the parties investing in the arbitrator's power to resolve a dispute between themselves as to their rights in and entitlements to a patent application or an invention (*Larkden* at [67]).

Matters which are not arbitrable in this sense are diminishing, as there is a greater public and legislative acceptance of matters being resolved by alternate dispute resolution mechanisms. In *Petersville Ltd v Peters (WA) Ltd* (1997) ATPR 41-566 at 43–847; BC9702661, the court held that questions of market definition, competition within relevant markets and anti-competitive behaviour were not the types of questions contemplated by parties for private arbitration (contrast *Nicola* at [56]–[61]). In *Metrocall* at [71]–[80], the court refused to allow the matter to be arbitrated on the grounds that the specialist nature of the jurisdiction and the powers of the Commission in Court Session exercised in the proceedings, as well as the nature of the matters to be taken into account, removed the claim from the scope of powers which may be exercised by an arbitrator. On the other hand, court processes and judicial attitudes have become more supportive of alternative dispute resolution generally and it is possible that if this issue arose for reconsideration, the matter considered by these cases may be held to be arbitrable. In *AED Oil Ltd v Puffin FPSO Ltd (No 2)* [2009] VSC 534; BC200910755, the court rejected a claim that the contractual dispute was not arbitrable because it involved public policy considerations relating to tax issues and third-party interests (at [60]–[64]); this aspect of the decision was not reversed on appeal (see *AED Oil Ltd v Puffin FPSO Ltd (No 2)* (2010) 27 VR 22; 265 ALR 415; [2010] VSCA 37; BC201001025). Arguments such as a matter not being capable of being arbitrated "because [the proceedings involve serious allegations of fraud against the plaintiff and, accordingly, are not capable of settlement by arbitration" are unlikely to succeed (*Conagra International Fertiliser Co v Lief Investments Pty Ltd* (1997) 141 FLR 124 at 156; BC9705443, affirmed on appeal at *Lief Investments Pty Ltd v Conagra International Fertiliser Co* [1998] NSWCA 481; BC9803166).

[s 7-13] **"on the application of a party" (s 7(2)(b))** The right to seek a stay is expressed in s 7 as the private right of a party (ie, "on the application of a party") and the court cannot exercise the power in s 7 of its own motion. As the applicant is seeking to enforce a right, "the applicant for the stay, bears the onus of establishing that the requirements of the section are satisfied" (*Ansett Australia Ltd v Malaysian Airline System Berhad* (2008) 217 FLR 376; [2008] VSC 109; BC200802403 at [6]; *Tanning Research Laboratories Inc v O'Brien* (1990) 169 CLR 332 at 353; 91 ALR 180; 64 ALJR 211; BC9002954 (Deane and Gaudron JJ); *Recyclers of Australia Pty Ltd v Hettinga Equipment Inc* (2000) 100 FCR 420; 175 ALR 725; [2000] FCA 547; BC200002851 at [22]).

As a private right conferred by s 7 of the Act, "the parties to a foreign arbitration agreement within the meaning of the Act can, by agreement, exclude the operation of the Act" (*Abigroup Contractors Pty Ltd v Transfield Pty Ltd* (1998) 217 ALR 435; [1998] VSC 103; BC9805944 at [112]). In *Incitec Ltd v Alkimos Shipping Corp* (2004) 138 FCR 496; 206 ALR 558; [2004] FCA 698; BC200403193 (*Incitec*) the court noted the effect of the parties' agreement to replace an arbitration clause with an exclusive jurisdiction clause, which avoided the possibility of "a mandatory stay" under the Act (see *Incitec* at [64]).

A party can waive its rights to seek a stay. The right to arbitration, being a private one, may be waived and that waiver renders the arbitration agreement "inoperative" for the purpose of s 7(5) (discussed below at [s 7-21]).

Alternatively, "a party could so conduct itself as to become subject to a procedural estoppel precluding an application for a stay" (*Stericorp Ltd v Stericycle Inc* [2005] VSC 203; BC200504017 at [17]).

[s 7-14] "a person claiming through or under a party" (s 7(4)) The right to apply for a stay is not confined to a party to the arbitration agreement. The references in s 7(2) to "a party to an arbitration agreement" and to "proceedings instituted by a party" are extended by s 7(4) to include a reference to a person "claiming through or under a party". This subsection mirrors the extended definition of a "party" which was found in s 4(1) of the uniform Commercial Arbitration legislation in the States and Territories at the time of the enactment of s 7 and which stated that a party "in relation to an arbitration agreement, includes any person claiming through or under a party to the arbitration agreement".

This phrase, extending the definition of "a party", was considered by the High Court in *Tanning Research Laboratories Inc v O'Brien* (1990) 169 CLR 332; 91 ALR 180; 64 ALJR 211; BC9002954 (*Tanning*) at CLR 341–3 (Brennan and Dawson JJ) and at CLR 353 (Deane and Gaudron JJ). The High Court held that a liquidator of a company which had been a party to an arbitration agreement (where a creditor had commenced proceedings challenging the liquidator's rejection of the creditor's proof of debt) was a person claiming through or under a party, namely the liquidated company, to the arbitration agreement where the creditor was the other party to the arbitration agreement. This phrase was only established in relation to the liquidator's rejection of the proof of debt upon causes of action or grounds of defence, which were vested in or exercisable by the company in liquidation. Had the liquidator rejected the creditor's claims for reasons which were not available to the company that was a party to the agreement, then the extension in s 7(4) would not have been satisfied. The court held that the words "through" and "under" conveyed "the notion of a derivative cause of action or ground of defence . . . derived from the party. In other words an essential element of the cause of action or defence must be or must have been vested in or exercisable by the party before the person claiming through or under the party can rely on the cause of action or ground of defence" (*Tanning* at CLR 342 (Brennan and Dawson JJ)). Contrast the reasons of Deane and Gaudron JJ (at CLR 353) where the question of whether a person is claiming through or under a party is to "be answered by reference to the subject matter in controversy rather than the formal nature of the proceedings or the precise legal character of the person initiating or defending the proceedings" and, following this approach, the "liquidator stands precisely in the position in which [the company] would have stood if it were in a position to require and did require a determination of the amount, if any, of its enforceable indebtedness".

As was noted in *Tanning* (at CLR 341–2 (Brennan and Dawson JJ)) the phrase "through or under a party" or its equivalent has been construed to apply to:
 (i) a trustee of a bankrupt's estate;
 (ii) an assignee of a debt arising out of a contract containing an arbitration clause (see also *Heller Financial Services Ltd v Thiess Contractors Pty Ltd* [2000] FCA 802; BC200003220 at [11]–[14]);
 (iii) a company being a subsidiary of a parent company which is party to an arbitration agreement (although "it is not the fact of the existence of the parent–subsidiary relationship which alone satisfies the condition making the subsidiary a party to an arbitration agreement" (*McHutchinson v Western Research and Development Ltd* [2004] FCA 1234; BC200406153 at [15]); and
 (iv) a company being a parent of a subsidiary company which is party to an arbitration agreement when claims are brought against both companies based on the same facts (followed in *AED Oil Ltd v Puffin FPSO Ltd (No 2)* [2009] VSC 534; BC200910755 at [71]–[74] and upheld on appeal; see *AED Oil Ltd v Puffin FPSO Ltd (No 2)* (2010) 27 VR 22; 265 ALR 415; [2010] VSCA 37; BC201001025 at [38]).

Finkelstein J considered *Tanning* and other authorities bearing upon the nature of the relationship necessary to support derivative claims in *BHPB Freight Pty Ltd v Cosco Oceania Chartering Pty Ltd* (2008) 168 FCR 169; 247 ALR 369; [2008] FCA 551; BC200802869. Finkelstein J held (at [15]) that:

> these cases show that there are two somewhat overlapping criteria that must be met to trigger the operation of s 7(4). The first is that there is a relationship of sufficient proximity between the party to the arbitration agreement and the person claiming to prosecute or defend an action through or under that party. The second is that the claim or defence is derived from the party to the arbitration agreement.

This reasoning was applied in *AED Oil Ltd v Puffin FPSO Ltd (No 2)* [2009] VSC 534; BC200910755 at [73], and upheld on appeal: *AED Oil Ltd v Puffin FPSO Ltd (No 2)* (2010) 27 VR 22; 265 ALR 415; [2010] VSCA 37; BC201001025 at [38]. In *AED Oil Ltd (No 2)*, the company which was the ultimate owner of a contracting party to the arbitration agreement and which had guaranteed "to ensure performance by" its subsidiary of its obligations under the transaction containing the arbitration agreement, had also received identical demands as had been made upon its subsidiary. In the circumstances the parent was held to be entitled to claim "through or under" its subsidiary within the meaning of s 7(4).

[s 7-15] "the court shall" (s 7(2)) In the Explanatory Memorandum to the Bill which became the Arbitration (Foreign Awards and Agreements) Act 1974 (Cth), it was said that the Bill "will go further than the existing State and Territory legislation under which the question of whether a stay should be granted is left to the court's discretion" (at [6]), and on proof of the matters set out in s 7(2), "a court must grant a stay" (at [22]). There was discretion in relation to domestic arbitration agreements under the uniform Commercial Arbitration legislation but there was no discretion under the legislation in NSW, which had implemented the New York Convention. Section 4(4) of the Arbitration (Foreign Awards and Agreements) Act 1973 (NSW) stated that a court, upon being satisfied of the requirements in that section, "shall make an order staying the proceedings and referring the matter to arbitration".

It has been repeatedly noted by the courts that once the requirements of s 7 are satisfied, "a stay is mandatory" and there is no discretion, eg, *Flakt Australia Ltd v Wilkins and Davies Construction Co Ltd* [1979] 2 NSWLR 243 at 245; 25 ALR 605; 39 FLR 267; *Tanning Research Laboratories Inc v O'Brien* (1990) 169 CLR 332 at 350; 91 ALR 180; 64 ALJR 211; BC9002954 (Deane and Gaudron JJ); *Abigroup Contractors Pty Ltd v Transfield Pty Ltd* (1998) 217 ALR 435; [1998] VSC 103; BC9805944 at [79]–[80]; *Origin Energy Resources Ltd v Benaris International NV* [2002] TASSC 50; BC200204520 at [20]; *Transfield Philippines Inc v Pacific Hydro Ltd* [2006] VSC 175; BC200609991 at [55]; *Zhang v Shanghai Wool and Jute Textile Co Ltd* (2006) 201 FLR 178; [2006] VSCA 133; BC200604594 at [12] (Chernov JA); *Comandate Marine Corp v Pan Australia Shipping Pty Ltd* (2006) 157 FCR 45; 238 ALR 457; [2006] FCAFC 192; BC200610833 at [35]; *WesTrac Pty Ltd v Eastcoast OTR Tyres Pty Ltd* (2008) 219 FLR 461; [2008] NSWSC 894; BC200807689 at [7]; and *Ansett Australia Ltd v Malaysian Airline System Berhad* (2008) 217 FLR 376; [2008] VSC 109; BC200802403 at [4].

Procedural difficulties will arise if some parties to the litigation are entitled to a mandatory stay and others are not. The case of *Abigroup Contractors Pty Ltd v Transfield Pty Ltd* (1998) 217 ALR 435; [1998] VSC 103; BC9805944 involved multiple parties and multiple issues. The court noted that s 7 was satisfied in relation to the first and second defendants and the court was obliged to refer those parties and only those parties to arbitration. The result was said to be "unpractical, is likely to lead to a multiplicity of proceedings with attendant increases in legal costs and the real risk of inconsistent findings" (at [173]). The court accepted that the right to apply for a stay was given to a party and the parties could make an agreement not to apply for a stay, which would be enforced. However, in the particular circumstances of the case, there was no effective agreement excluding an application under s 7.

The problems of duplicated hearings and possibility of inconsistent findings were sought to be addressed in the case of *Aerospatiale Holdings Australia v Elspan International Ltd* (1992) 28 NSWLR 321 by the court granting a stay in respect of the defendant, which was bound by the arbitration agreement, and in relation to the claims against the other defendants, the court exercised its power of referral to order that the proceedings be referred to the person who had been appointed arbitrator but as a court-appointed referee. A single hearing was maintained through what was in substance, a consolidation, or concurrent hearings, of all claims before the same person (acting as both arbitrator and referee). Concurrent arbitrations using the powers conferred by s 38 of the Civil Procedure Act 2005 (NSW) were considered by the court in *WesTrac Pty Ltd v Eastcoast OTR Tyres Pty Ltd* (2008) 219 FLR 461; [2008] NSWSC 894; BC200807689 at [32]–[39] but rejected, as the court lacked the power to shape an arbitration under s 38 "so as to cause it to correspond or fit with the form of arbitration" envisaged by the parties' agreement which had given rise to the stay.

[s 7-16] An order under s 7 is interlocutory An order under s 7 granting a stay of proceedings and referring the parties to arbitration is interlocutory in character within the meaning of the Federal Court of Australia Act 1976 (Cth)

(*Hi-Fert Pty Ltd v Kiukiang Maritime Carriers Inc* (1998) 155 ALR 94; [1998] FCA 558).

[s 7-17]   "upon such conditions (if any) as it thinks fit" (s 7(2))   The power of a court to impose conditions on the mandatory stay does not appear in the New York Convention. The power to impose conditions was considered when the constitutional validity of the section was upheld by the Federal Court in *Hi-Fert Pty Ltd v Kiukiang Maritime Carriers Inc (No 5)* (1998) 90 FCR 1; 159 ALR 142; [1999] 2 Lloyd's Rep 782; BC9806222. Beaumont J expressed the view that such interference with the judicial process as does occur was kept within permissible limits and this "was achieved by the reservation to the Court of a power to impose appropriate conditions upon the grant of a stay" (at FCR 5).

Although the power is expressed in apparently wide terms, the power to impose conditions must be seen as incidental and ancillary to the achievement of the main purpose of s 7(2), which is to hold the parties to international commercial agreements to their agreement to arbitrate. This would not include conditions which effectively distorted the agreement initially entered between the parties. "The 'conditions' which s 7(2) of the Act contemplates are machinery conditions. They relate to hearing and the like procedures and not to conditions which determine, in effect, the substantive rights of the parties" (*O'Brien v Tanning Research Laboratories Inc* (1988) 14 NSWLR 601 at 622; 84 ALR 221; 93 FLR 270; (1989) 7 ACLC 182 (Kirby P)). "It is not open to the court to impose conditions upon a s 7 stay which will detract from the integrity of the arbitration process [which the Act] mandates" (*WesTrac Pty Ltd v Eastcoast OTR Tyres Pty Ltd* (2008) 219 FLR 461; [2008] NSWSC 894; BC200807689 at [30]).

A common form of condition is one which requires the applicant to act promptly if necessary to enable the arbitration to commence and to proceed with reasonable expedition (*Flakt Australia Ltd v Wilkins and Davies Construction Co Ltd* [1979] 2 NSWLR 243 at 251; 25 ALR 605; 39 FLR 267; *White Industries Ltd v Trammel* (1983) 51 ALR 779 at 786; 76 FLR 48; (1983) ATPR 40-429; *Allergan Pharmaceuticals Inc v Bausch & Lomb Inc* (1985) AIPC 90-262; (1985) ATPR 40-636 at 47,174; 3 BCL 61; *Recyclers of Australia Pty Ltd v Hettinga Equipment Inc* (2000) 100 FCR 420; 175 ALR 725; [2000] FCA 547; BC200002851 at [73]). Such a condition is designed to ensure that the party with the benefit of the stay does not unduly delay the arbitration.

In *Ansett Australia Ltd v Malaysian Airline System Berhad* (2008) 217 FLR 376; [2008] VSC 109; BC200802403 at [38]–[45], it was held that one of the conditions that may be imposed is the determination of the venue of arbitration. Although in the circumstances of that case, the court declined to impose such a condition.

Where not all matters raised in the litigation are capable of settlement by arbitration, the mandatory nature of the stay of only those matters capable of settlement by arbitration, gives rise to the possibility of inconsistent concurrent findings and duplication of effort and expense. This is a situation the courts strive to avoid. The imposition of conditions is but one means to mitigate the compulsory separation of the claims to be arbitrated, eg, *WesTrac Pty Ltd v Eastcoast OTR Tyres Pty Ltd* (2008) 219 FLR 461; [2008] NSWSC 894; BC200807689 at [40]–[44]; *Murrumbidgee Irrigation Ltd v Goodwood Services Pty Ltd* [2010] NSWSC 914; BC201006113 at [30]–[32].

It has been held that s 7(2) does accommodate a condition of the stay of proceedings and a compulsory referral to arbitration that postpones the arbitration until some other proceeding has been determined, eg, *Hi-Fert Pty Ltd v Kiukiang Maritime Carriers Inc (No 5)* (1998) 90 FCR 1 at 29; 159 ALR 142; [1999] 2 Lloyd's Rep 782; BC9806222 (Emmett J); *WesTrac Pty Ltd v Eastcoast OTR Tyres Pty Ltd* (2008) 219 FLR 461; [2008] NSWSC 894; BC200807689 at [43].

In some cases a decision arises as to whether to stay the whole or part of the proceedings. The section clearly contemplates that there may be issues in the proceedings which cannot be referred to arbitration yet the whole of the proceedings may be stayed. In *Tanning Research Laboratories Inc v O'Brien* (1990) 169 CLR 332; 91 ALR 180; 64 ALJR 211; BC9002954 the residual issues relating to the winding up were stayed because they were dependent upon the determination of the matters falling within the arbitration clause.

In Australia this additional power to impose conditions on the grant of a stay (a power not found in the New York Convention) has been a source of controversy because some conditions have been imposed which appear to negate the obligatory order which the court must issue referring the parties to arbitration. This is best illustrated by the decision of *Walter Rau Neusser Oel und Fett v Cross Pacific Trading Ltd* [2005] FCA 1102; BC200505922 (*Walter Rau*). There the court granted a stay of proceedings involving the matters which properly fell within the arbitration agreement, but other matters which were the subject of litigation were outside the scope of the arbitration clause. In respect of those matters the court was not prepared to grant a stay of the proceedings. It then proceeded, however, to impose two conditions on the stay of the matters within the arbitration clause. First, the court imposed a condition that the "reference to arbitration not proceed until after determination of proceedings in the Federal Court". Second, the court imposed a condition upon the parties to the arbitration "to consent to all aspects of any Trade Practices Act claims, which would have been justiciable in this court, being litigated in the arbitration irrespective of any conclusion as to the proper law" (*Walter Rau* at [111]).

With due respect, it is submitted that both conditions are beyond the power of the court. First, as was stated by the court, the first condition is that the "reference to arbitration" not proceed until after the determination of proceedings in the Federal Court. Section 7(2) only allows a condition to be imposed on the order staying the court proceedings. The court is required to refer the parties to arbitration in respect of that matter and the effect of the Federal Court's decision is to rewrite s 7(2) so that the phrase "upon such conditions" where it appears after the words "by order" has been moved to later in the paragraph where it follows and qualifies both "order" and "refer".

The second condition was imposed by the court because had the matter been arbitrated in accordance with the parties' arbitration agreement, the hearing would take place in London and then, in accordance with existing authority, the arbitral panel would not have, as a matter of construction of the arbitration agreement and the application of English law (excluding its conflicts of laws rules), any authority or power to arbitrate any of the Trade Practices Act 1974 (Cth) claims. This condition, which was imposed, in substance, required the parties as a matter of obtaining enforcement of their arbitration agreement, to consent to a variation of that very arbitration agreement before the arbitration under it could continue. It cannot have been contemplated by the legislature that the court could dictate to the parties what form their arbitration agreement should take as a condition to allowing them to arbitrate in accordance with their original agreement (see also *Elders CED Ltd v Dravo Corp* (1984) 59 ALR 206 at 210; 2 BCL 68).

The conditions in *Walter Rau* were considered and suggested by the court without argument. Subsequently, having had the benefit of argument in *Comandate Marine Corp v Pan Australia Shipping Pty Ltd* (2006) 157 FCR 45; 238 ALR 457; [2006] FCAFC 192; BC200610833 at [245], Allsop J stated that he would not have imposed the second condition in *Walter Rau* (the first does not seem to have been the subject of further consideration) as it would "pre-empt the decision of the arbitrator and the operation of the arbitration clause". Although the court in *In the matter of: ACN 103 753 484 Pty Ltd (in liq) formerly Blue Chip Development Corp Pty Ltd* [2011] QSC 64; BC201108440 at [24] indicated that it would grant a stay subject to conditions which would have varied the terms of the arbitration agreement by requiring that any person appointed to act as an arbitrator be legally qualified and admitted to practice as a legal practitioner.

[s 7-18] **"may, for the purpose of preserving the rights of the parties, make such interim or supplementary orders . . . in relation to any property that is the subject of the matter" (s 7(3))** This power does not appear to have been exercised by a court. Nonetheless, a court, "when it makes a stay order, may make supplementary orders to preserve property which is the subject matter of the dispute" (Explanatory Memorandum to the Arbitration (Foreign Awards and Agreements) Bill 1974 (Cth) at [23]).

[s 7-19] **"null and void, inoperative or incapable of being performed" (s 7(5))** Under s 7(5) the court shall not make an order staying the proceedings if the arbitration agreement is "null and void, inoperative or incapable of being performed". The phrase "null and void, inoperative or incapable of being performed" is taken from Art II(3) of the New York Convention and also appears in Art 8 of the Model Law. The meaning of each of these concepts is considered separately, although the reasoning applicable to the different concepts overlaps to some extent.

The question whether there was in effect an arbitration agreement or one which was null and void, inoperative or incapable of being performed is to be answered by looking at the state of affairs as it exists when the application for a stay is made (*Bakri Navigation Co Ltd v Owners of Ship 'Golden Glory' Glorious Shipping SA* (1991) 217 ALR 152 at 167; BC9103216).

[s 7-20] **"null and void"** As noted in *Comandate Marine Corp v Pan Australia Shipping Pty Ltd* (2006) 157 FCR 45; 238 ALR 457; [2006] FCAFC 192; BC200610833 at [209] by Allsop J, the phrase "null and void" is seen by the major text writers on the New York Convention as referring to situations where the arbitration agreement is affected by some invalidity right from the beginning and would cover such matters as the lack of consent due to misrepresentation, duress, fraud or undue influence, or where a party lacked a capacity to enter the arbitration agreement. The court noted the views of the leading English text writers concerning the phrase "null and void" (at [210]–[211]). Professor Merkin, *Arbitration Law*, LLP, London, 2004, at [8.32], expressed the view that an arbitration agreement is not null and void if it is merely voidable, at least until it has been avoided. Michael Mustill and Stewart Boyd (*Commercial Arbitration*, Butterworths, London, 1989, p 464), expressed the view that it includes circumstances not only where the arbitration agreement has never come into existence, such as when there was no concluded bargain, but also where an arbitration agreement has come into existence but has become void ab initio, eg, by rescission on the ground of misrepresentation.

[s 7-21] **"inoperative"** The word inoperative refers to the situation where the arbitration agreement, even though existing, has no relevant effect or has ceased to have an effect. In *Bakri Navigation Co Ltd v Owners of Ship 'Golden Glory' Glorious Shipping SA* (1991) 217 ALR 152; BC9103216 (*Bakri Navigation*), the parties were involved in a dispute arising out of negotiations for the sale of a ship. The plaintiff sought a declaration that there was a binding contract for the sale of the ship and obtained the arrest of the vessel. After the initiation of the court proceedings and before the application for a stay under s 7 was made, the parties entered into a further agreement which allowed for the release of the vessel that was the subject of the action and which resolved certain claims in the proceedings then before the court. The court found that there was a concluded contract for sale, which contained an arbitration clause requiring disputes to be arbitrated in London. The court then considered the terms of the subsequent undertaking to the court and the agreement which had been reached between the parties that allowed for the release of the vessel. The court found that the subject matter of this later agreement "was the whole of the proceeding" (at 168) before the court and not merely the release of the ship. In the circumstances, the subsequent agreement effected a variation of the arbitration agreement, which rendered it "inoperative or ineffective in respect of the claims involved in the . . . proceedings before the court" (at 168). The court (at 169) adopted the view that "inoperative" describes an arbitration agreement, which, although not void ab initio, has for some reason ceased to have effect for the future. This may be the result of a court order, it may arise out of the common law doctrines of frustration and discharge by breach and also, the arbitration agreement may have ceased to operate by reason of some further agreement between the parties. Thus, the "settlement of an arbitrable dispute rendered the arbitration agreement otherwise applicable 'inoperative'" (*Shanghai Foreign Trade Corp v Sigma Metallurgical Co Pty Ltd* (1996) 133 FLR 417 at 446; BC9603441, referring to the decision in *Bakri Navigation*), although as there was a dispute as to whether or not there had in fact been a settlement, that matter was ordered to be determined by the court first.

Although it should be noted that the fact that the main contract between the parties has been purportedly terminated or repudiated, does not result in the arbitration clause being inoperative within the meaning of s 7(5). A contract containing an arbitration clause may be held to have been terminated by repudiation or for frustration, but nevertheless the arbitration clause remains operative (*Codelfa Construction Pty Ltd v State Rail Authority* (1982) 149 CLR 337 at 363–6; 41 ALR 367; 56 ALJR 459; BC8200083 (Mason J)). See also the discussion of the principle of separability or severability in relation to Art 16 of the Model Law below.

An arbitration agreement may not be enforceable and therefore "inoperative" for the purposes of s 7(5) because the party seeking a stay has waived its rights under the agreement or has elected to abandon the arbitration agreement (*ACD Tridon*

Inc v Tridon Australia Pty Ltd [2002] NSWSC 896; BC200206142 at [53]–[63]; and *BHP Freight Pty Ltd v Cosco Oceania Chartering Pty Ltd* (2008) 168 FCR 169; 247 ALR 369; [2008] FCA 551; BC200802869 at [52]–[55]). In the present context, waiver is constituted by the deliberate, intentional and unequivocal release or abandonment of the right which is later sought to be enforced (*Zhang v Shanghai Wool and Jute Textile Co Ltd* (2006) 201 FLR 178; [2006] VSCA 133; BC200604594 at [14] (Chernov JA)). Waiver "must always be an intentional act with knowledge" (*AED Oil Ltd v Puffin FPSO Ltd (No 2)* [2009] VSC 534; BC200910755 at [78]; upheld on appeal: see *AED Oil Ltd v Puffin FPSO Ltd (No 2)* (2010) 27 VR 22; 265 ALR 415; [2010] VSCA 37; BC201001025 at [39]; see also *Stericorp Ltd v Stericycle Inc* [2005] VSC 203; BC200504017 at [9]–[18]).

An analysis of what is required to establish that a party had waived its rights under an arbitration agreement, or had elected not to pursue them, is found in *Comandate Marine Corp v Pan Australia Shipping Pty Ltd* (2006) 157 FCR 45; 238 ALR 457; [2006] FCAFC 192; BC200610833 at [235] (Allsop J). The party that was seeking to enforce an arbitration agreement had also commenced an action in rem seeking to arrest a vessel in connection with the disputes between the parties. The full court held that there was no waiver of the right to arbitrate or election not to arbitrate. To establish a binding waiver or an election requires two mutually inconsistent rights, where the exercise of one was inconsistent with the continued existence of the other. The "rights are inconsistent if neither may be enjoyed without the extinction of the other" (at [62], Allsop J, with whom Finn and Finkelstein JJ agreed). The full court held that the filing of the writ *in rem* by one party was not the exercise of a right to litigate, which was inconsistent with the continued existence of a right to arbitrate. The mere commencement of the proceedings by the writ *in rem* seeking the arrest of a vessel did not cause or presuppose the extinction of the rights under the parties' arbitration agreement.

The full court also distinguished the Victorian decision by Whelan J in *La Donna Pty Ltd v Wolford AG* (2005) 194 FLR 26; [2005] VSC 359; BC200506609, where it had been held that the defendant's conduct in the litigation did amount to a waiver of any rights to arbitrate the dispute before the court and amounted to an election not to arbitrate. The conduct of the defendant in that case was the making of an application for security of costs, which was unsuccessful. That conduct did amount to a waiver of a right to arbitrate because such an application was "based on the explicit premise" that the matter would proceed to a hearing and that the dispute "would be determined by the court" and not in arbitration.

The Victorian Court of Appeal expressed a similar view of waiver in *Zhang v Shanghai Wool and Jute Textile Co Ltd* (2006) 201 FLR 178; [2006] VSCA 133; BC200604594 at [15] (Chernov JA) that "waiver by election may be established by demonstrating that the party in question had elected to pursue a substantive right that is inconsistent with that which it is now seeking to press". There the court held that the participation in the litigation did not amount to a waiver of the arbitration agreement since at all times the party had "made it plain to the court that they wanted the dispute to be arbitrated" (at [16], Chernov JA).

An arbitration agreement may become inoperative because of the operation of statute; see, eg, *HIH Casualty & General Insurance Ltd (in liq) v Wallace* (2006) 68 NSWLR 603 at 619-20; 204 FLR 297; [2006] NSWSC 1150; BC200608859, where the effect of the operation of the Insurance Act 1987 (NSW) was considered; and also *Hi-Fert Pty Ltd v Kiukiang Maritime Carriers Inc (No 5)* (1998) 90 FCR 1 at 12.C; 159 ALR 142; [1999] 2 Lloyd's Rep 782; BC9806222 (Emmett J), where the Carriage of Goods by Sea Act 1991 (Cth) was considered. See also the commentary on s 2C above.

On one view, the circumstances where an arbitration agreement may become "inoperative" include "a case where the dispute is not arbitrable" (Professor R Merkin, *Arbitration Law*, Lloyd's Commercial Law Library, London, 2010) noted in *Fulham Football Club (1987) Ltd v Richards* [2011] EWCA Civ 855 at [35]; *Seimens Ltd v Origin Energy Uranquinty Power Pty Ltd* (2011) 279 ALR 759; [2011] NSWSC 195; BC201102144 at [36], and see the discussion on arbitrability above at [s 7-12].

[s 7-22] "incapable of being performed" The words "incapable of being performed" are "a strong expression, in my judgment denoting impossibility, or practical impossibility, and certainly not mere inconvenience or difficulty. A mere change of circumstances rendering arbitration a less attractive mode of resolving a dispute or rendering the forum or procedural rules chosen for any reason unattractive, could never be enough. For a party who has agreed to resolve any dispute by arbitration to be freed from his obligation . . . it is, in my judgment, necessary for him to show that his arbitration agreement simply cannot, with the best will in the world, be performed" (Lord Bingham, as quoted by the Hong Kong High Court in *Klöckner Pentaplast GmbH & Co v Advance Technology (H.K.) Co Ltd* [2011] HKCFI 48 at [19]).

The court in *Bakri Navigation Co Ltd v Owners of Ship 'Golden Glory' Glorious Shipping SA* (1991) 217 ALR 152; BC9103216 adopted the view of the court in *Paczy v Haendler & Natermann GmbH* [1981] 1 Lloyd's Rep 302 at 307 that an arbitration agreement "becomes incapable of performance . . . if the circumstances are such that it could no longer be performed, even if both parties were ready, able and willing to perform it". Such a situation may arise where the arbitration agreement refers to an unknown individual as arbitrator or to a specific arbitral institution that had ceased to exist.

An unusual and, with respect, questionable view of the concept of "inoperative or incapable of being performed" was taken by the court in *Lightsource Technologies Australia Pty Ltd v Pointsec Mobile Technologies AB* (2011) 250 FLR 63; [2011] ACTSC 59; BC201102227, where the arbitration clause prohibited claims being made more than six months after the party "knew or should have known of the basis for the action or claim". The court held that as the action was brought more than six months after that date, the arbitration agreement was "inoperative or incapable of performance" but that the action could be maintained in the court. The court took the view that the time limit in the clause had a "remedy-barring" effect and the party lost the right to arbitrate but not to litigate. See also *Grimaldi SpA v Sckihyo Lones Ltd* [1990] 1 WLR 708 at 715; *Nanjing Tianshun Shipbuilding Co Ltd v Orchard Tankers PTE Ltd* [2011] EWHC 164; and contrast *Tommy CP Sze & Co v Li & Fung (Trading) Ltd* [2002] HKCFI 682, where the court said at [42]: "The existence of a time bar has never been regarded as rendering an arbitration agreement incapable of being performed. The thinking behind this is that the arbitration agreement can of course proceed, only that the claim is at risk of being dismissed."

The inability of one party to meet its financial obligations under the agreed procedural rules of the arbitration institution chosen by the parties does not render the arbitration agreement inoperative or incapable of being performed (*El Nasharty v J Sainsbury PLC* [2007] EWHC 2618 (Comm) at [4]). The court does not attempt to assess the financial resources of a party when considering whether an agreement is inoperative or incapable of being performed.

[s 7-23] Time for making application In the initial New South Wales legislation implementing the New York Convention, the Arbitration (Foreign Awards and Agreements) Act 1973 (NSW), there was a requirement in s 4(3) that the application be made before delivering any pleadings or taking any other steps in the proceedings. There is also a requirement under Art 8(1) of the Model Law that an application for similar relief under the Model Law be made "not later than when submitting [a party's] statement on the substance of the dispute".

In contrast, no time limit was adopted, or is specified, in Pt II of the Act. The court in *Flakt Australia Ltd v Wilkins and Davies Construction Co Ltd* [1979] 2 NSWLR 243 at 250; 25 ALR 605; 39 FLR 267, saw no reason to read into s 7(2) an "unexpressed qualification as to the time when an application thereunder can be made".

[s 7-24] "the court" A limitation on the remedy is available under s 7(2) in that it only allows a stay of proceedings instituted in a court in Australia. A "court" is defined in s 3(1) as meaning "any court in Australia, including, but not limited to, the Federal Court of Australia, and a court of a State or Territory". If the proceedings are instituted in a court located in a jurisdiction outside of Australia then the party seeking to insist on the arbitration rather than litigation in the foreign court, may still do so — not using the jurisdiction conferred by s 7, but by seeking an anti-suit injunction from an Australian court, subject to the defendant being amenable to its jurisdiction.

[s 8] Recognition of foreign awards

8 (1) Subject to this Part, a foreign award is binding by virtue of this Act for all purposes on the parties to the arbitration agreement in pursuance of which it was made.

(2) Subject to this Part, a foreign award may be enforced in a court of a State or Territory as if the award were a judgment or order of that court.

(3) Subject to this Part, a foreign award may be enforced in the Federal Court of Australia as if the award were a judgment or order of that court.

(3A) The court may only refuse to enforce the foreign award in the circumstances mentioned in subsections (5) and (7).

(4) Where:
   (a) at any time, a person seeks the enforcement of a foreign award by virtue of this Part; and
   (b) the country in which the award was made is not, at that time, a Convention country;
this section does not have effect in relation to the award unless that person is, at that time, domiciled or ordinarily resident in Australia or in a Convention country.

(5) Subject to subsection (6), in any proceedings in which the enforcement of a foreign award by virtue of this Part is sought, the court may, at the request of the party against whom it is invoked, refuse to enforce the award if that party proves to the satisfaction of the court that:
  (a) that party, being a party to the arbitration agreement in pursuance of which the award was made, was, under the law applicable to him or her, under some incapacity at the time when the agreement was made;
  (b) the arbitration agreement is not valid under the law expressed in the agreement to be applicable to it or, where no law is so expressed to be applicable, under the law of the country where the award was made;
  (c) that party was not given proper notice of the appointment of the arbitrator or of the arbitration proceedings or was otherwise unable to present his or her case in the arbitration proceedings;
  (d) the award deals with a difference not contemplated by, or not falling within the terms of, the submission to arbitration, or contains a decision on a matter beyond the scope of the submission to arbitration;
  (e) the composition of the arbitral authority or the arbitral procedure was not in accordance with the agreement of the parties or, failing such agreement, was not in accordance with the law of the country where the arbitration took place; or
  (f) the award has not yet become binding on the parties to the arbitration agreement or has been set aside or suspended by a competent authority of the country in which, or under the law of which, the award was made.

(6) Where an award to which paragraph (5)(d) applies contains decisions on matters submitted to arbitration and those decisions can be separated from decisions on matters not so submitted, that part of the award which contains decisions on matters so submitted may be enforced.

(7) In any proceedings in which the enforcement of a foreign award by virtue of this Part is sought, the court may refuse to enforce the award if it finds that:
  (a) the subject matter of the difference between the parties to the award is not capable of settlement by arbitration under the laws in force in the State or Territory in which the court is sitting; or
  (b) to enforce the award would be contrary to public policy.

(7A) To avoid doubt and without limiting paragraph (7)(b), the enforcement of a foreign award would be contrary to public policy if:
  (a) the making of the award was induced or affected by fraud or corruption; or
  (b) a breach of the rules of natural justice occurred in connection with the making of the award.

(8) Where, in any proceedings in which the enforcement of a foreign award by virtue of this Part is sought, the court is satisfied that an application for the setting aside or suspension of the award has been made to a competent authority of the country in which, or under the law of which, the award was made, the court may, if it considers it proper to do so, adjourn the proceedings, or so much of the proceedings as relates to the award, as the case may be, and may also, on the application of the party claiming enforcement of the award, order the other party to give suitable security.

(9) A court may, if satisfied of any of the matters mentioned in subsection (10), make an order for one or more of the following:
  (a) for proceedings that have been adjourned, or that part of the proceedings that has been adjourned, under subsection (8) to be resumed;

(b) for costs against the person who made the application for the setting aside or suspension of the foreign award;
(c) for any other order appropriate in the circumstances.

(10) The matters are:
(a) the application for the setting aside or suspension of the award is not being pursued in good faith; and
(b) the application for the setting aside or suspension of the award is not being pursued with reasonable diligence; and
(c) the application for the setting aside or suspension of the award has been withdrawn or dismissed; and
(d) the continued adjournment of the proceedings is, for any reason, not justified.

(11) An order under subsection (9) may only be made on the application of a party to the proceedings that have, or a part of which has, been adjourned.

COMMENTARY ON SECTION 8

History of section	[s 8-1]
Procedure	[s 8-2]
"enforced . . . as if . . . a judgment" (s 8(2) and (3))	[s 8-3]
Form of Court Order	[s 8-4]
Enforcement of an award	[s 8-5]
Enforcement of a declaratory award	[s 8-6]
"court may *only* refuse to enforce" (s 8(3A))	[s 8-7]
"may be enforced" (s 8(2) and (3))	[s 8-8]
Reciprocity reservation (s 8(4))	[s 8-9]
Onus of proof	[s 8-10]
Estoppel, waiver and election may prevent a party from resisting enforcement	[s 8-11]
"that party . . . was, under the law applicable to him or her, under some incapacity . . ." (s 8(5)(a); Art V(1)(a) of the New York Convention; Arts 34(2)(a)(i) and 36(1)(a)(i) of the Model Law)	[s 8-12]
"the arbitration agreement is not valid under the law . . ." (s 8(5)(b); Art V(1)(a) of the New York Convention; Arts 34(2)(a)(i) and 36(1)(a)(i) of the Model Law)	[s 8-13]
"that party was not given proper notice" or "otherwise unable to present . . . case" (s 8(5)(c); Art V(1)(b) of the New York Convention; Arts 18, 34(2)(a)(ii) and 36(1)(a)(ii) of the Model Law)	[s 8-14]
"award deals with a difference not contemplated by . . . the submission to arbitration" or "contains a decision on a matter beyond the scope of the submission to arbitration" (s 8(5)(d); Art V(1)(c) of the New York Convention; Arts 34(2)(a)(iii) and 36(1)(a)(iii) of the Model Law)	[s 8-15]

"composition of the arbitral authority or the arbitral procedure" was not in accordance with arbitration agreement or applicable law (s 8(5)(e); Art V(1)(d) of

the New York Convention; Arts 34(2)(a)(iv) and
36(1)(a)(iv) of the Model Law) .... [s 8-16]
"the award has not yet become binding", "set aside" or
"suspended" (s 8(5)(f); Art V(1)(e) of the New York
Convention; Arts 34(2)(a)(v) and 36(1)(a)(v) of the
Model Law) .... [s 8-17]
Partial enforcement .... [s 8-18]
Grounds relating to laws of place of enforcement
(s 8(7)) .... [s 8-19]
"not capable of settlement by arbitration" (s 8(7)(a)) ... [s 8-20]
"public policy" of the forum (s 8(7)(b)) .... [s 8-21]
Public policy of the forum .... [s 8-22]
Matters which are deemed contrary to public policy (s
8(7A)) .... [s 8-23]
"the court may, if it considers proper, adjourn the
proceedings" for enforcement of an award (s 8(8)) ... [s 8-24]
"and may also ... order the other party to give suitable
security" (s 8(8)) .... [s 8-25]
Resumption of enforcement proceedings (s 8(9), (10)
and (11)) .... [s 8-26]
Interest on award and/or on judgment enforcing the
award .... [s 8-27]
Currency .... [s 8-28]
Limitation statutes .... [s 8-29]
Security for costs of an application for enforcement .... [s 8-30]
Common law enforcement of an award .... [s 8-31]
Enforcement of an award by issue estoppel .... [s 8-32]
Asset preservation orders (*Mareva* relief) .... [s 8-33]

[s 8-1] History of section Section 8 was enacted by the Arbitration (Foreign Awards and Agreements) Act 1974 (Cth) to give effect to the New York Convention.

Under the original terms of s 8(2) a foreign award "may be enforced in a court of a State or Territory as if the award had been made in the State or Territory in accordance with the law of that State or Territory".

In anticipation of a new federal court being created, s 8(3), when enacted in 1974, stated that "if a Court by the name of the Superior Court of Australia is established by an Act, a foreign award may, on or after the date on which that Court commences to exercise its jurisdiction, be enforced, by leave of that Court, as if the award were a judgment of that Court". This potential jurisdiction was removed in 1979, when following the establishment of the Federal Court of Australia in 1976, the Jurisdiction of Courts (Miscellaneous Amendments) Act 1979 (Cth) was passed, which repealed s 8(3) and removed the references to s 8(3) in s 8(4)(b). The legislative policy in 1979 was stated to be "that the Federal Court of Australia will have jurisdiction only in those matters where, for historical or special policy reasons, it is desirable that jurisdiction be exercised by a federal court" (Senator Durack, Second Reading Speech, 28 September 1978, Senate, Hansard, p 1060).

The wording in s 8 was again revised in 1989 and in 2008 by the International Arbitration Amendment Act 1989 (Cth) and the Statute Law Revision Act 2008 (Cth) respectively. The former substituted the word "Part" for "Act" and the latter added the words "or her" after "him" where it appears in the section.

On 21 November 2008 the Attorney-General announced a review of the Act and released a Discussion Paper which suggested a number of possible amendments to the legislation and invited comment. However, the legislative policy had again changed and the Discussion Paper raised the possibility of conferring exclusive jurisdiction under the Act on the Federal Court of Australia. Before the time for comment had expired, this possibility had in part been implemented when the Federal Justice System Amendment (Efficiency Measures) Bill (No 1) 2008 (Cth) was introduced into the Parliament. This Bill became the Federal Justice System Amendment (Efficiency Measures) Act (No 1) 2009 (Cth) and the legislation conferred on the Federal Court the jurisdiction contemplated by s 8(3). The then wording of s 8(3) as introduced in 2009 provided: "Subject to this Part, a foreign award, may with the leave of the Federal Court of Australia, be enforced in the Federal Court of Australia as if the award were a judgment or order of the Federal Court."

The review of the Act, which followed the release of the Discussion Paper, resulted in the International Arbitration Amendment Bill 2009 (Cth) which was the subject of an Explanatory Memorandum. The Government proposed some changes to this Bill in 2010 which were the subject of a Supplementary Explanatory Memorandum. The Bill was then replaced by the International Arbitration Amendment Bill 2010 (Cth). This last mentioned Bill was the subject of a Revised Explanatory Memorandum and became the International Arbitration Amendment Act 2010 (Cth). This Act repealed and replaced both s 8(2) and the newly inserted s 8(3). The Act also amended s 8(4) by omitting the words "subsections (1) and (2) do" and substituting "this section does" and added new subsections 8(3A), (7A), (9), (10) and (11). For a more detailed discussion of the passage of this legislation see L Nottage and R Garnett (eds), *International Arbitration in Australia*, Federation Press, Sydney, 2010, pp 14–18.

[s 8-2] Procedure The procedure followed by the Supreme Court of Victoria in relation to an application for enforcement of an award involves a two-stage process. This process was the subject of detailed analysis by the Court of Appeal in *IMC Aviation Solutions Pty Ltd v Altain Khuder LLC* [2011] VSCA 248; BC201106268 (*IMC Aviation Solutions*), where the members of the court described the process in slightly different terms. Section 8(1) provides that, subject to Pt II of the Act, a foreign award "is binding by virtue of this Act for all purposes on the parties to an arbitration agreement in pursuance of which it was made" and then s 8(2) provides that, subject to Pt II, a foreign award "may be enforced in a court . . . as if the award were a judgment or order of that court."

Section 9(1) requires the applicant to produce both the award and the arbitration agreement (or certified copies). Such documents once received by the court are "prima facie evidence". Thus s 9 assists the applicant award creditor to establish the necessary elements of s 8(1), namely who are the parties to the arbitration agreement.

In the view of Warren CJ, the words "arbitration agreement" in s 8(1) mean "purported or apparent arbitration agreement" (*IMC Aviation Solutions* at [43]). The applicant award creditor must establish these facts before the respondent award debtor is liable under s 8(1). The affect of the deeming provision in s 9(5) is "that the mere production of the original arbitration agreement and the original award (or duly certified copies of these documents) will normally be sufficient to discharge the burden that the Act places on the award creditor", such as in the situation where the arbitration agreement names the award debtor (at [43]). The applicant award creditor bears the onus of showing on the balance of probabilities that the award debtor is a party to the apparent or purported arbitration agreement under which the award purports to have been made. Once this threshold legal burden in s 8(1) has been satisfied, the award debtor may then only resist enforcement of the award by relying on one of the grounds in s 8(5) and (7). On this view, the "party-hood" of the award debtor is a threshold issue, and the claim by the award debtor that it is not a party to the arbitration agreement is dealt with at this stage. On this view, the claim by the respondent that it was not a party to the arbitration agreement is not treated as falling within the invalidity defence in s 8(5)(b), as it "would be to seriously strain the language" of the provision (at [47], Warren CJ). Thus a claim by an award debtor that it is not a party to the arbitration agreement places an onus on the award creditor to prove, on the balance of probabilities, that the award debtor is a party, whereas the award debtor bears the onus of making out one of the specified grounds for resisting enforcement (at [49], Warren CJ).

This approach emphasises the wording of s 8(1), which makes a foreign award "binding . . . on the parties to the arbitration agreement" and which contrasts with the alternative approach followed in England, where the equivalent section, s 101(1) of the Arbitration Act 1996 (Eng, W & NI), provides that "a New York Convention award shall be recognised as binding on the persons as between whom it was made".

The alternative approach favoured by Hansen JA and Kyrou AJA (at [132]) involves a two-stage process in accordance with the procedures set out in Order 9 of the Supreme Court (Miscellaneous Civil Proceedings) Rules 2008 (Vic) and Practice Note No 2 of 2010, Arbitration Business. This approach requires at stage one that the award creditor satisfies the enforcing court "on a prima facie basis" (at [135]) that:

(a) an award has been made by a foreign arbitral tribunal granting relief to the applicant award creditor against the respondent award debtor;
(b) the award was made pursuant to an arbitration agreement; and
(c) the award creditor and the award debtor are parties to the arbitration agreement.

Where, as in *IMC Aviation Solutions*, the required production under s 9(1) does not provide prima facie evidence of these three matters, the application should not proceed ex parte at stage one. The award creditor should be required "to give notice of the proceeding to the award debtor and the proceeding should continue on an inter partes basis" (at [140]). At this stage, the "evidential onus would be on the award creditor to adduce evidence, in addition to the arbitration agreement and the award, to satisfy the Court of those prima facie evidential requirements" (at [144]). Once "the award creditor discharges the evidential onus of adducing prima facie evidence of the [three] matters" at stage one, the matter proceeds to stage two and "the legal onus will immediately be on the award debtor to prove one of the matters set out in s 8(5) or (7)" (at [146]).

In propounding the alternative view, Hansen JA and Kyrou AJA held (at [171]) that s 8(5)(b) "extends to the ground that the award debtor was not a party to the arbitration agreement" following the approach of Lord Collins JSC in *Dallah Real Estate and Tourism Holding Company v Govt of Pakistan* [2010] All ER (D) 36 (Nov); [2011] 1 AC 763; [2011] 1 All ER 485; [2010] UKSC 46 at [77]; and Mance LJ in *Dardana Ltd v Yukos Oil Co* [2002] All ER (D) 126 (Apr); [2002] 1 All ER (Comm) 819 at 825[8]; [2002] 2 Lloyd's Rep 326; [2002] EWCA Civ 543. In this respect, Hansen JA and Kyrou AJA, whilst recognising (at [159]) that the terms of s 8(5)(b) "may be inapt to accommodate the ground that a person is not a party to the arbitration agreement", took a contrary view to that taken by Warren CJ (at [41] and [47]).

An application under s 8 is solely concerned with the award and agreement and the specified defences. As was noted in relation to the Arbitration Act 1996 (Eng, W & NI), "the presence of assets in the jurisdiction is not a precondition under the statute to the enforcement of the award" (*Rosseel NV v Oriental Commercial & Shipping Co (UK) Ltd* [1991] 2 Lloyd's Rep 625 at 629).

In the case of *ML Ubase Holdings Co Ltd v Trigem Computer Inc* [2005] NSWSC 224; BC200501412, the court required a plaintiff seeking enforcement of a foreign arbitral award in undefended proceedings, to satisfy three requirements (at [35]):

1. there is a written Arbitral Award;
2. each party to the Arbitral Award is a party to the [New York] Convention;
3. the Arbitral Award was handed down outside Australia.

However, the Act does not require that each party to the Award be a national of a party to the New York Convention. The New York Convention applies to an Award made in a State other than that in which enforcement is sought (see Art 1(1)). Whilst Art 1(3) allows a State to declare that it will only be applied to awards made in another Convention country, Australia has not made any such declaration: see the discussion of the reciprocity reservation in [s 8-9] below. Further, the wording of s 8(4) of the Act envisages the enforcement of awards made in a non-convention country, if the person seeking enforcement is domiciled or ordinarily resident in Australia or in a Convention country.

[s 8-3] "enforced . . . as if . . . a judgment" (s 8(2) and (3)) As noted above, the 2008 Discussion Paper first resulted in the International Arbitration Amendment Bill 2009 (Cth). This Bill proposed new wording for s 8(2) which provided: "Subject to this Part, a foreign award may be enforced in a court of a State or Territory with leave of that court as if the award were a judgment or order of that court." The proposed wording of the accompanying s 8(3) in the Bill was in identical terms but related to the Federal Court of Australia.

Following the Review, the Government proposed some changes to this Bill in 2010, which were the subject of a Supplementary Explanatory Memorandum including the removal of the phrase "with leave of that court". This phrase was removed as "the inclusion of this phrase may, inadvertently, result in a two-step enforcement process that involves the court considering an application for leave against the grounds in s 8(5) and (7) of the Act and then considering the substance of the application against unspecified criteria" (Supplementary Explanatory Memorandum, Notes on Amendments at [1] and [2]). The phrase "by leave of the court", when used in relation to the enforcement of domestic awards in s 33 of the now repealed Commercial Arbitration Act 1984 (NSW), had been held by the NSW Court of Appeal in *Tridon Australia Pty Ltd v ACD Tridon Inc* (2004) 20 BCL 413; [2004] NSWCA 146; BC200402458, to confer a general discretion in the court to refuse enforcement in circumstances such as where there was no apparent utility in making the order.

Subsequently, the International Arbitration Amendment Act 2010 (Cth) repealed and replaced both s 8(2) and (3) in terms different to those previously proposed.

The reference to State and Territory law was also removed from s 8(2) as it "might be seen to provide a Court with a basis to decline to enforce the award on any ground contained in that law in addition to those set out in the Act" (Revised Explanatory Memorandum to the International Arbitration Amendment Bill 2010 (Cth) at [25]).

Section 8(3) was also rewritten in 2010 "to ensure consistent phraseology with the" amendment to s 8(2) (Revised Explanatory Memorandum to the International Arbitration Amendment Bill 2010 (Cth) at [30]).

The terms of the repealed version of s 8(2) had been held to make "the foreign award completely analogous to a domestic award with respect to its enforcement" (*Brali v Hyundai Corp* (1988) 15 NSWLR 734 at 743.C; 84 ALR 176). Accordingly, where there had been a misnomer in the name of the defendant in the foreign award, the court on the enforcement application could, under the previous terms of the section, correct the misnomer using the power to correct the award found in the uniform Commercial Arbitration legislation which applied to domestic awards (*Lkt v Chun* [2004] NSWSC 820; BC200406102 at [27]). The procedure followed to enforce a foreign award at that time was to consider the application as if it was an application to enforce a domestic award, eg, *ACN 006 397 413 Pty Ltd v International Movie Group (Canada) Inc* [1997] 2 VR 31 at 32; BC9604108. This reasoning is no longer applicable in view of the new s 21, which provides that the Model Law covers the field.

[s 8-4] Form of Court Order A foreign arbitral award "does not have to be and cannot be registered under the [Act] before it can be enforced" (*Uganda Telecom Ltd v Hi-Tech Telecom Pty Ltd (No 2)* (2011) 277 ALR 441; [2011] FCA 206; BC201101086 at [5]). The court should treat the foreign arbitral award as if it were a judgment or order. That is, once this court has decided to enforce the award, it should give full effect to that decision by directing the entry of an appropriate money judgment or by making an appropriate order for payment. The words "as if" in s 8(2) and (3) do not contemplate something less than an actual judgment or order (*Uganda (No 2)* at [10] and [13]).

[s 8-5] Enforcement of an award In *Resort Condominiums Inc v Bolwell* [1995] 1 Qd R 406; (1993) 118 ALR 655; BC9303445, the court held that s 8 required a final award which determines the rights of the parties and that did not include a "pretrial order of a procedural or interlocutory nature". A similar view was expressed by Lord Mance in *Dallah Real Estate and Tourism Holding Company v Govt of Pakistan* [2010] All ER (D) 36 (Nov); [2011] 1 AC 763; [2011] 1 All ER

485; [2010] UKSC 46 at [77], when he said (at [22]): "I do not regard the New York Convention as concerned with preliminary awards on jurisdiction." See also the discussion of the meaning of a "binding" award as used in Art V.1(e) of the New York Convention in L Nottage and R Garnett (eds), *International Arbitration in Australia*, Federation Press, Sydney, 2010, pp 73–4.

[s 8-6] Enforcement of a declaratory award A foreign award which is a purely declaratory award may be enforced under s 8 (see the discussion in *AED Oil Ltd v Puffin FPSO Ltd* (2010) 27 VR 22; 265 ALR 415; [2010] VSCA 37; BC201001025 at [18]–[20]). Nevertheless, it could be strongly argued that there is no utility in asking another court to make the same declarations between the same parties as were made by the arbitral panel in a final award. The English Court of Appeal in *Margulies Brothers Ltd v Dafnis Thomaides & Co (UK) Ltd* [1958] 1 Lloyd's Rep 205 at 207 (Lord Evershed) held that a declaratory award, which did not specify a monetary amount, was not "capable of enforcement". In a domestic context, an application to make orders enforcing a declaratory award was refused in *Tridon Australia Pty Ltd v ACD Tridon Inc (Incorporated in Ontario)* (2004) 20 BCL 413; [2004] NSWCA 146; BC200402458 at [11], where Giles JA, Handley JA and Santow J agreeing, said:

> Enforcement is a plain word, and means something quite different from a restatement of the effect of the award in the form of a judgment. The summary procedure provided by s 33 of the [Commercial Arbitration] Act is a procedure with a purpose, the purpose of enabling a victorious party in an arbitration to obtain the material benefit of the award in its favour in an easier manner than having to sue on the award. There has been nothing put forward in this case to suggest any occasion for enforcement of the declarations made in the interim award. They are binding on the parties, and bind them for the balance of the arbitration and beyond that.

Enforcement requires more than merely repeating the declaration contained in the award. A judgment on a declaratory award will be made where entry of the judgment makes a positive contribution to securing the benefit of the award (*West Tankers Inc v Allianz SpA* [2011] EWHC 829 (Comm) at [28]–[29] and *African Fertilizers and Chemicals Nig Ltd (Nigeria) v BD Shipsnavo GmbH & Co* [2011] EWHC 2452 (Comm) at [24]-[26]). In a different context, see also *Momcilovic v R* (2011) 280 ALR 221; [2011] HCA 34; BC201106881 at [88] where French CJ noted the view that a declaration cannot be made if it will produce no foreseeable consequences for the parties by a federal court because it does not involve the exercise of judicial power.

A foreign binding declaratory award may establish an issue estoppel between the parties. Unlike the case with a monetary award, the successful party with the benefit of an issue estoppel does not usually require the added assistance of a further judgment or order from a foreign enforcing court. Whereas, in the case of a monetary award: "Unless the foreign arbitral award is reflected in a judgment or order of the Australian court in which recognition and enforcement is claimed, the party seeking to enforce that award will not be able to avail itself of the execution and recovery mechanisms available in that court" (*Uganda Telecom Ltd v Hi-Tech Telecom Pty Ltd (No 2)* (2011) 277 ALR 441; [2011] FCA 206; BC201101086 at [5]).

[s 8-7] "court may *only* refuse to enforce" (s 8(3A)) The Revised Explanatory Memorandum to the International Arbitration Amendment Bill 2010 (Cth) stated (at [37]–[40]) that:

> 37. The grounds set out in Article V of the New York Convention are intended to be exhaustive. In other words, enforcement of an award may only be refused if one of the grounds in Article V is made out.
>
> 38. Subsections 8(5) and 8(7) set out the grounds on which a court can refuse to enforce a foreign arbitral award under the Act. These grounds mirror those in Article V of the New York Convention.
>
> 39. During the Review of the Act, concern was expressed that courts do not always treat the grounds for refusal in subsections 8(5) and 8(7) as exhaustive. For example, in *Resort Condominiums Inc v Bolwell* [1995] 1 Qd R 406, the Supreme Court of Queensland found that the court retains a discretion to refuse to enforce a foreign arbitral award even if none of the grounds in section 8 of the Act are made out. Such an approach is inconsistent with the intention of the Convention.
>
> 40. Accordingly ... section 8 [is amended] to insert a new subsection 8(3A) that states that a court may only refuse to enforce a foreign award in the circumstances mentioned in subsections 8(5) and 8(7)." [emphasis in original]

Thus it can be seen that s 8(3A) removes the suggestion that the enforcing court has a residual discretion to refuse enforcement and "simply circumscribes the defences on which the award debtor can rely to resist enforcement once the award creditor has discharged" the preliminary burden to establish the elements of s 8(1) (*IMC Aviation Solutions Pty Ltd v Altain Khuder LLC* [2011] VSCA 248; BC201106268 at [40] (Warren CJ)).

[s 8-8] "may be enforced" (s 8(2) and (3)) The courts in Canada, Hong Kong and England have held that the use of the word "may" in Art V.1 of the New York Convention (the provision on which s 8 was modelled) confers a discretion to enforce an award even though one of the specified grounds for refusal has been established (*Dallah Real Estate and Tourism Holding Company v Govt of Pakistan* [2010] All ER (D) 36 (Nov); [2011] 1 AC 763; [2011] 1 All ER 485; [2010] UKSC 46 at [67]–[69] (Lord Mance) and [126]–[131] (Lord Collins); and see the discussion of the discretion in Arts 34 and 36 of the Model Law; *Europcar Italia SpA v Alba Tours International Inc* [1997] OJ, No 133 (Gen Div) para 12; *Brunswick Bowling & Billiards Corp v Shanghai Zhonglu Industrial Co Ltd* [2009] HKCFI 94 at [29]–[45]; *Pacific China Holdings Ltd v Grand Pacific Holdings Ltd* [2011] HKCFI 424 at [55]–[63]). The discretion is narrow and limited and a court is unlikely to allow enforcement of an award if it is satisfied that its integrity is fundamentally unsound. Although the court in an enforcing State retains a discretion to enforce an award even if one of the grounds for resisting enforcement have been made out, "the discretion will be exercised sparingly" (*Dowan Holding SA v Tanzania Electric Supply Co Ltd* [2011] EWHC 1957 (Comm) at [28]), such as "where the award had been set aside upon grounds which a court subsequently asked to enforce the award notwithstanding, would deprecate" (*Dowan* at [41]).

Section 8(2) of the Act also uses the word "may" and did confer a discretion: see the discussion of the residual discretion in s 8 not to enforce an award which existed prior to the amendments made to the Act in 2010, in L Nottage and R Garnett (eds), *International Arbitration in Australia*, Federation Press, Sydney, 2010, pp 67–70. No residual general discretion is now possible following the express legislative direction in s 8(3A) (which was introduced in 2010) that the court "may only refuse to enforce the award" in the circumstances mentioned in s 8(5) and (7). The word "may" is also found in similar provisions, eg, Arts 34 and 36 of the Model Law, which are also based on Art V.1 of the New York Convention where this residual discretion continues to exist. See the discussion of the discretion in Arts 34 and 36 of the Model Law below.

It has been held that the removal of the requirement for leave by the amendments made to the Act in 2010 brought about the same result as the introduction of s 8(3A). In *Uganda Telecom Ltd v Hi-Tech Telecom Pty Ltd* (2011) 277 ALR 415; [2011] FCA 131; BC201100586 at [23], it was submitted that the "requirement for leave [then found in s 8(3)] gave the Court a broad general discretion to refuse to enforce a foreign award". The case was commenced and argued before the amendments were made to the Act in 2010. As the judgment in the case was delivered after the amendments removed the requirement for "leave to enforce," the court rejected the submission saying (at [24]): "As the requirement for leave has now been removed from the Act, this point falls away." Section 8(3A) did not apply in that case, as this provision only applies to proceedings which were brought on or after 6 July 2011.

[s 8-9] Reciprocity reservation (s 8(4)) Section 8(4) has only had one minor change since its enactment in 1974, made by the International Arbitration Amendment Act 2010 (Cth), which amended the subsection by deleting "subsections (1) and (2) do" and substituting "this section does". This provision addresses the question of whether there is any need for reciprocity when seeking to enforce foreign awards. Contracting States may accede to the New York Convention subject to either the reciprocity reservation or the commercial reservation under Art I(3). Under the reciprocity reservation, a Contracting State may agree to apply the Convention but limited only to the recognition and enforcement of awards which are made in the territory of another Contracting State. Under the commercial reservation, a Contracting State may agree to apply the Convention but limited only to differences arising out of legal relationships, whether contractual or not, which are regarded as "commercial" under the law of that Contracting State. Even though Australia acceded to the New York Convention without either of these reservations, it did put a limited restriction in the terms of s 8(4) on those foreign awards which would be recognised and enforced where the particular award was made in a country which was not a Contracting State to the New York Convention.

There is no power under Pt II of the Act to enforce a foreign award made in a country which is not a Contracting State to the New York Convention, at the time of the application for enforcement, unless the applicant is domiciled or ordinarily resident in Australia or in another Contracting State. See also the discussion of the meaning of "ordinarily resident" or "domiciled" when used in s 7 above at [s 7-8]. An application to enforce a foreign award of this type may be made under the common law as discussed below at [s 8-31].

[s 8-10] Onus of proof Two views were expressed in *IMC Aviation Solutions Pty Ltd v Altain Khuder LLC* [2011] VSCA 248; BC201106268. Warren CJ, at [52]–[53], preferred the approach in *Briginshaw v Briginshaw* (1938) 60 CLR

336; [1938] ALR 334; (1938) 12 ALJR 100; BC3800027 (*Briginshaw*) at 362 (Dixon J), stating that the "enforcing court should treat allegations of vitiating irregularity as serious . . . [and a] correspondingly heavy onus falls upon the award debtor if it wishes to establish such an allegation on the balance of probabilities". This was similar to the approach taken by the judge at first instance (see *Altain Khuder LLC v IMC Mining Inc* (2011) 276 ALR 733; 246 FLR 47; [2011] VSC 1; BC201100150 at [88]). On the other hand, the majority view on appeal in *IMC Aviation Solutions Pty Ltd v Altain Khuder LLC* [2011] VSCA 248; BC201106268 at [192], held that what may be required, in a particular case, to produce proof on the balance of probabilities will depend on the nature and seriousness of that sought to be proved. The qualifications made by the first instance judge to the language in s 8(5) and (7) were held to impermissibly "raise the barrier to an evidentiary higher level of satisfaction than" the Act requires. Further, the majority held (at [194]) that whilst the judge's language may have been appropriate in a case of fraud, the use of language requiring "clear, cogent and strict" proof to satisfy s 8(5) and (7) "seemingly pitched the level of proof even higher".

Under the equivalent provision in England, the "burden rests squarely on [the resisting party] to prove one of the grounds of refusal . . . That burden must be discharged on a balance of probabilities" (*Rosseel NV v Oriental Commercial & Shipping Co (UK) Ltd* [1991] 2 Lloyd's Rep 625 at 628).

[s 8-11] Estoppel, waiver and election may prevent a party from resisting enforcement There is nothing in the Act which excludes the application of the ordinary principles of estoppel being relied upon in proceedings to enforce a foreign award (*IMC Aviation Solutions Pty Ltd v Altain Khuder LLC* [2011] VSCA 248; BC201106268 at [26] (Warren CJ)). Where a party wishes to raise an estoppel based on facts, it is necessary that that party prove by admissible evidence or otherwise the existence of the facts giving rise to the estoppel (at [23]–[24], Warren CJ). The manner in which estoppel may have been used to preclude an award debtor from resisting enforcement in other jurisdictions may not be determinative in proceedings concerning the same award debtor, as Australian principles of estoppel are not necessarily identical to those applicable in other jurisdictions (at [27], Warren CJ).

When there is an issue concerning the initial consent to arbitration, the enforcement court is not bound by the arbitral tribunal's ruling on the issue and must determine for itself whether or not the objecting party consented (*Dallah Real Estate and Tourism Holding Company v Govt of Pakistan* [2011] 1 AC 763; [2010] All ER (D) 36 (Nov); [2011] 1 All ER 485; [2010] UKSC 46 at [28], [98]–[104] and [161]–[162]).

A party seeking to resist enforcement of a foreign award may be estopped from raising one of the specified grounds. As Sir Anthony Mason NPJ noted in *Hebei Import & Export Corp v Polytek Engineering Co Ltd* [1991] 1 HKLRD 665 (CFA) at 689D–E: "What I have said does not exclude the possibility that a party may be precluded by his failure to raise a point before the court of supervisory jurisdiction from raising that point before the court of enforcement. Failure to raise such a point may amount to an estoppel or want of bona fides such as to justify the court of enforcement in enforcing an award . . . Obviously an injustice may arise if an award remains afoot but cannot be enforced on a ground which, if taken, would have resulted in the award being set aside."

The options of challenging an award in the supervising courts of the seat of arbitration and resisting enforcement of an award in the enforcing court are not mutually exclusive, although in some cases "a determination by the court of the seat may give rise to an issue estoppel or other preclusive effect in the court in which enforcement is sought. The fact that jurisdiction can no longer be challenged in the courts of the seat does not preclude consideration of the tribunal's jurisdiction by the enforcing court" (*Dallah Real Estate and Tourism Holding Company v Govt of Pakistan* [2010] All ER (D) 36 (Nov); [2011] 1 AC 763; [2011] 1 All ER 485; [2010] UKSC 46 (*Dallah Real Estate*) at [98] (Lord Collins)).

A person "who denies being a party to any relevant arbitration agreement has no obligation to participate in the arbitration or to take any steps in the country of the seat of what he maintains to be an invalid arbitration leading to an invalid award against him. The party initiating the arbitration must try to enforce the award where it can. Only then is it incumbent on the defendant denying the existence of any valid award to resist enforcement" (*Dallah Real Estate* at [23]–[24] and [28] (Lord Mance)). This view was endorsed by Hansen JA and Kyrou AJA in *IMC Aviation Solutions Pty Ltd v Altain Khuder LLC* [2011] VSCA 248; BC201106268 at [320].

A party who contests the jurisdiction of an arbitral tribunal may submit to the jurisdiction of that tribunal by actively taking on the role of a party to the arbitration and by seeking a ruling on jurisdiction: see the discussion in *Sovarex SA v Alvarez SA* [2011] EWHC 1661 (Comm) at [30], where there was "an assertion of non-jurisdiction rather than a participation in its exercise". The question "of submission to the jurisdiction of the arbitrators depends on whether, on an objective analysis, the [third party] intended to take any part in" the arbitration process (*Excalibur Ventures LLC v Texas Keystone Inc* [2011] EWHC 1624 (Comm) at [61]).

The High Court of Singapore in *Galsworthy Ltd v Glory Wealth Shipping Pte Ltd* [2011] 1 SLR 727; [2010] SGHC 304 (*Galsworthy*) held that a party was not entitled to resist enforcement in Singapore under the equivalent provisions of the International Arbitration Act on grounds which it had relied upon in challenging the award before the courts at the seat of arbitration. Such action was said to amount to an election and having "had the opportunity in choosing either, the supervisory or enforcement court to mount its challenge[, it] elected to proceed on the former" (*Galsworthy* at [8]). It is doubtful that this was a true case of an election. The two options were not mutually exclusive and the pursuit of one was not necessarily inconsistent with the other. A party has a separate and independent right to defend proceedings brought in an enforcement court. It is in the enforcement proceedings that it is then necessary to consider whether the particular issues that arise in the proceedings before the enforcement court, have already been finally determined between the parties in another competent court.

[s 8-12] "that party ... was, under the law applicable to him or her, under some incapacity ..." (s 8(5)(a); Art V(1)(a) of the New York Convention; Arts 34(2)(a)(i) and 36(1)(a)(i) of the Model Law) Section 8(5)(a) reproduces the first ground for resisting enforcement contained in Art V(1)(a) of the New York Convention. For a general discussion of this ground, see J Lew, L Mistelis and S Kröll, *Comparative International Arbitration*, Kluwer Law International, The Hague, 2003, pp 707–10, and GB Born,

International Commercial Arbitration, Wolters Kluwer, The Netherlands, 2009, pp 2777–97. The equivalent provision in the Arbitration Act 1996 (Eng, W & NI) was satisfied in award enforcement proceedings where there was "medical evidence [which showed that the respondent] was seriously ill and suffering from a life threatening cancer at the relevant time which was followed by clinical depression [which was not disputed]. It was ... realistically impossible for [the respondent] to concentrate on [the arbitration] so as to instruct counsel or solicitors in a meaningful way to appear for him ... and present the defence that, on the pleadings and on the basis of the Award, was obviously available to him ..." (*Kanoria v Guiness*, decision of Gloster 18 July 2005, unreported, as quoted in *Kanoria v Guiness* [2006] 2 All ER (Comm) 413; [2006] 1 Lloyd's Rep 701; [2006] EWCA Civ 222 at [18]).

[s 8-13] "the arbitration agreement is not valid under the law ..." (s 8(5)(b); Art V(1)(a) of the New York Convention; Arts 34(2)(a)(i) and 36(1)(a)(i) of the Model Law) Section 8(5)(b) reproduces the second ground for resisting enforcement contained in Art V(1)(a) of the New York Convention.

The enforcement court may be required to consider whether the arbitration agreement is void for uncertainty and not binding, eg, *Uganda Telecom Ltd v Hi-Tech Telecom Pty Ltd* (2011) 277 ALR 415; [2011] FCA 131; BC201100586 at [63]–[84]. Attempts to resist enforcement of a foreign award under this ground on the basis that the defendant was not a party to the arbitration agreement (and the award was thus not binding) failed in *Lkt v Chun* [2004] NSWSC 820; BC200406102 and, after a review of the evidence on appeal, succeeded in *IMC Aviation Solutions Pty Ltd v Altain Khuder LLC* [2011] VSCA 248; BC201106268 (*IMC Aviation Solutions*) at [201] (Hansen JA and Kyrou AJA).

The "validity" of the arbitration agreement under Art V(1)(a) includes the issue of whether there is any arbitration agreement between the parties at all (*Dallah Real Estate and Tourism Holding Company v Govt of Pakistan* [2010] All ER (D) 36 (Nov); [2011] 1 AC 763; [2011] 1 All ER 485; [2010] UKSC 46 (*Dallah Real Estate*) at [77] (Lord Collins); *IMC Aviation Solutions* at [171] (Hansen AJA and Kyrou AJA, with Warren CJ dissenting on this point at [41] and [47])).

In *Dallah Real Estate*, the UK Supreme Court upheld a decision under the equivalent provision in the Arbitration Act 1996 (Eng, W & NI), which was based on evidence in the enforcement proceedings, that under the law of the place where the award was made, there was no arbitration agreement between the parties, and refused enforcement.

Article V(1)(a) establishes that the parties could choose the law which governed the validity of the arbitration agreement and if there was no such agreement on the applicable law, the law which determined the validity of the agreement was the substantive law of the country where it was made and not its conflicts of laws rules (*Dallah Real Estate* at [123] (Lord Collins)).

[s 8-14] "that party was not given proper notice" or "otherwise unable to present ... case" (s 8(5)(c); Art V(1)(b) of the New York Convention; Arts 18, 34(2)(a)(ii) and 36(1)(a)(ii) of the Model Law) Section 8(5)(c) reproduces the grounds on which a court can refuse to enforce an award in Art V(1)(b) of the New York Convention and reflects the situation where there has been a failure by an arbitral tribunal to give each party a reasonable opportunity to present its case as required by Art 18 of the Model Law (as modified by s 18C of the Act).

Examples of failed attempts to establish the lack of notice referred to in s 8(5)(c) are *Lkt v Chun* [2004] NSWSC 820; BC200406102 at [29]–[76]; and *Uganda Telecom Ltd v Hi-Tech Telecom Pty Ltd* (2011) 277 ALR 415; [2011] FCA 131; BC201100586 at [92]–[118]. After a review of the evidence, this defence succeeded on appeal (*IMC Aviation Solutions Pty Ltd v Altain Khuder LLC* [2011] VSCA 248; BC201106268 at [261] and [305]–[306] (Hansen JA and Kyrou AJA)), where the evidence established that the resisting party was not a party to the agreement and was given no notice of the arbitration proceeding.

Under the equivalent provision of the Arbitration Act 1996 (Eng, W & NI), s 103(2)(c), it was held that "a party to an arbitration is unable to present his case if he is never informed of the case that he is called upon to meet" (*Kanoria v Guiness* [2006] 2 All ER (Comm) 413; [2006] 1 Lloyd's Rep 701; [2006] EWCA Civ 222 at [22] (Lord Phillips)). This will normally cover the case where the procedure adopted has been operated in a manner contrary to the rules of natural justice. The provision has been described as one which "protects the requirements of natural justice reflected in the audi alterem partem rule" (*Minmetals Germany v Ferco Steel* [1999] 1 All ER (Comm) 315 at 326) and "contemplates at least that the enforcee has been prevented from presenting his case by matters outside his control" (at 327).

The Hong Kong High Court considered the equivalent provision in Art 34(2)(a)(ii) of the Model Law in *Pacific China Holdings Ltd v Grand Pacific Holdings Ltd* [2011] HKCFI 424. The court held, at [121], that a procedural order made by the arbitral tribunal "was not in accordance with the agreement of the parties, and that [the party seeking to set aside the award] was thereby unable to present its case". Further, the court found, at [129], that in the particular circumstances of the case, the "Tribunal's refusal to receive and consider the additional authorities sought to be cited by [a party] prevented [that party] from presenting its case". The court also found that in the particular circumstances of the case "the failure of the Tribunal to give [a party] the opportunity to respond to [the other party's] submissions on [a particular legal issue] rendered [the first party] unable to present its case". A similar view was expressed in *Methanex Motunui Ltd v Spellman* [2004] 1 NZLR 95 at 131–2, [139], where the court said: "it is implicit in art 18 [of the Model Law] that each party has not only the right to present its case in relation to issues known at the outset but also to respond to such evidence and argument as may emanate from the other parties in the course of the hearing."

A contrary result is likely if the parties and the arbitral tribunal have agreed on a procedure which does not involve reply submissions in circumstances where both cases were already covered in pre-hearing memoranda and were known in advance; see, eg, *Margulead Ltd v Exide Technologies* [2004] All ER (D) 94 (May); [2004] 2 All ER (Comm) 727; [2004] EWHC 1019 at [28]: "There was no provision for [the resisting party] to have the last word as would have been the case under English court procedure. But it must or ought to have been clear to all concerned that the arbitrator was following an order of speeches combined with written submissions which did not correspond to this Court."

There is no assumption of a "right to an oral hearing" in arbitration and, absent a statutory right (such as found in Art 24(1) of the Model Law) or contractual right to an oral hearing, if both parties have a reasonable opportunity to present their cases in writing to the arbitral panel, there is no breach of Arts 18 and 34(2)(a)(ii) of the Model Law (*PT Asuransi Jasa Indonesia (Persero) v Dexia Bank SA* [2006] SGCA 41 at [22]).

If an arbitrator adopts an argument that was never put to the arbitrator and upon which the resisting party had no opportunity to address the arbitrator, this ground may be established. As expressed by Lord Bingham J in *Zermalt Holdings SA v Nu Life Upholstery Repairs Ltd* [1985] 2 EGLR 14 at 15, and applied by Colman J in *Vee Networks Ltd v Econonet Wireless International Ltd* [2004] EWHC 2909 (Comm) at [83]:

> If an arbitrator is impressed by a point that has never been raised by either side then it is his duty to put it to them so that they have an opportunity to comment. If he feels that the proper approach is one that has not been explored or advanced in evidence or submission, then again it is his duty to give the parties a chance to comment ...

It is not necessary that the enforcing court form the view that the arbitrator would have reached the same or a different result. It is enough to show that the arbitrator "might well never have reached" the result sought to be enforced (*Vee Networks Ltd v Econonet Wireless International Ltd* [2004] EWHC 2909 (Comm) at [90]).

The requirement that a party have an opportunity to present its case means that the arbitrator must confine him or herself to the material put before the arbitrator by the parties, unless the contrary is agreed (*Trustees of Rotoaira Forest Trust v Attorney-General* [1999] 2 NZLR 452 (*Rotoaira Forest Trust*) at 460). An arbitrator cannot use his or her own knowledge to derogate from the evidence led by a party without giving that party an opportunity to respond to his view (see the discussion in *Rotoaira Forest Trust* at 460–3). On the other hand, arbitrators chosen for their expertise in the subject matter of the dispute may draw on their knowledge and experience for general matters; "that is to say facts which form part of the general body of knowledge within their area of expertise as distinct from facts that are specific to the particular dispute" (*Methanex Motunui Ltd v Spellman* [2004] 1 NZLR 95 at 135, [156] (*Methanex*); and see generally *Brunswick Bowling & Billiards Corp v Shanghai Zhonglu Industrial Co Ltd* [2009] HKCFI 94 at [23]–[28]; *Paklito Investment Ltd v Klockner East Asia Ltd* [1993] 2 HKLR 39; *The Pamphilos* [2002] 2 Lloyd's Rep 681 at 686–7; *Fox v Welfair Ltd* [1981] 2 Lloyd's Rep 514.

One approach is to consider whether a reasonable party standing in the shoes of the parties in the subject circumstances would have foreseen the possibility of the reasoning in the award "and hence had the opportunity to present evidence and argument in anticipation of it" (*Methanex* at 136, [160]). If it is a new source of information bearing on the facts in issue, it should be put to the parties. See also the commentary in relation to Art 18 of the Model Law below.

An arbitral tribunal should not act upon evidence received by it secretly without giving parties an opportunity to deal with it. See also the commentary to Art 24 of the Model Law.

[s 8-15] "award deals with a difference not contemplated by . . . the submission to arbitration" or "contains a decision on a matter beyond the scope of the submission to arbitration" (s 8(5)(d); Art V(1)(c) of the New York Convention; Arts 34(2)(a)(iii) and 36(1)(a)(iii) of the Model Law) Section 8(5)(d) reproduces the grounds specified in Art V(1)(c) of the New York Convention. Article V(1)(c) also permits partial enforcement of a foreign award if this ground is only applicable to part of the award. Where s 8(5)(d) applies, the remainder of the award may be enforced under s 8(6), which is discussed below. The word "dispute" is used in Arts 34(2)(a)(iii) and 36(1)(a)(iii) of the Model Law in place of the word "difference".

The concept of the scope of the submission to arbitration is discussed above in relation to s 7(2)(b). Where the parties have used pleadings in an arbitration "to determine whether matters in an award were within or outside the scope of submission to arbitration, a reference to the pleadings would usually have to be made" (*Kempinski Hotels SA v PT Prima International Development* [2011] SGHC 171 at [55]; and, in another context, see also *Discovery Beach Project Pty Ltd v Northbuild Construction Pty Ltd* [2011] QSC 306; BC201108127 at [78]).

Article 34(2)(a)(iii) applies "where the arbitral tribunal improperly decided matters that had not been submitted to it or failed to decide matters that had been submitted to it" (*CRW Joint Operation v PT Perusahaan Gas Negara (Persero) TBK* [2011] SGCA 33 at [31]). The provision addresses the situation where the arbitral tribunal exceeded, or failed to exercise, the authority conferred by the parties.

The function of the equivalent provision in England has been described as "to exclude from enforcement awards made on issues falling outside those which were referred for decision to the arbitrators" (*Minmetals Germany v Ferco Steel* [1999] 1 All ER (Comm) 315 at 325) and not cases where evidence relied upon by the arbitrators was not provided to one party.

The standard of review which is applied by a court when considering an Application under Art 34(2)(a)(iii) was considered by the Court of Appeal for Ontario in *Mexico Inc v Cargill Inc* 2011 ONCA 622 (CanLII). The court held (at [42]) that the standard to apply is, "correctness, in the sense that the [arbitral] tribunal had to be correct in its determination that it had the ability to make the decision it made". The power conferred by Art 34(2)(a)(iii) does not give a court a broad scope for intervention and does not involve any questions of reasonableness or any review of the merits. The intervention by a court "is limited to true jurisdictional errors" (at [46]) and in assessing whether the arbitral tribunal exceeded the scope of the terms of jurisdiction, "the court is to avoid a review of the merits" (at [53]).

[s 8-16] "composition of the arbitral authority or the arbitral procedure" was not in accordance with arbitration agreement or applicable law (s 8(5)(e); Art V(1)(d) of the New York Convention; Arts 34(2)(a)(iv) and 36(1)(a)(iv) of the Model Law) Section 8(5)(e) reproduces the ground specified in Art V(1)(d) of the New York Convention. For a discussion of this ground, see J Lew, L Mistelis and S Kröll, *Comparative International Arbitration*, Kluwer Law International, The Hague, 2003, pp 715–16, and GB Born, *International Commercial Arbitration*, Wolters Kluwer, The Netherlands, 2009, pp 2764–77.

[s 8-17] "the award has not yet become binding", "set aside" or "suspended" (s 8(5)(f); Art V(1)(e) of the New York Convention; Arts 34(2)(a)(v) and 36(1)(a)(v) of the Model Law) Section 8(5)(f) reproduces the ground specified in Art V(1)(e) of the New York Convention.

The phrase "not yet binding" arose out of the Geneva Convention 1927, where the word "final" had been used in relation to the place where the award had been made. This meant that the award had to be declared as "final" by the court of the place of arbitration, and this gave rise to the problem of the *double exequatur*. In practice it was only possible to prove that the award had become "final" in the country in which the award was made by producing an exequatur (leave for enforcement or the like) issued in that country. As the party had also to acquire leave for enforcement in the country in which enforcement was sought, this amounted to a system of "double exequatur" (see the discussion of the observations of Albert Jan van den Berg, *The New York Arbitration Convention of 1958 — Towards a Uniform Judicial Interpretation* at 266, in *Dowan Holding SA v Tanzania Electric Supply Co Ltd* [2011] EWHC 1957 (Comm) (*Dowan Holding*) at [10]). The word "final" in the Geneva Convention 1927 was replaced by the word "binding" in the New York Convention (Art V(1)(e)) in order to indicate that there is no need to obtain an exequatur in the country of origin. Further, the party seeking enforcement of the award does not have to prove that the award has become binding in the country in which the award was made; rather, the party against whom the enforcement is sought has to prove that the award has not become binding.

An award is "binding" if it is no longer open to an appeal on the merits, either internally (within the relevant rules of arbitration) or by an application to the court (see the discussion in *Société Nationale d'Opérations Petrolières de la Cote d'Ivoire — Holding v Keen Lloyd Resources Ltd* [2001] HKCFI 173; and *Dowan Holding* at [12]–[27]).

The phrase "set aside" was considered in *TermioRio SA ESP v Electranta SP* 487 F 3d 928 at 934 (DC Cir 2007), cert denied, 128 SCt 650 (2007), where it was noted that to require a court to enforce awards that had been set aside by the competent authority of the country in and under the law of which the award was made, "would seriously undermine a principal precept of the New York Convention: an arbitration award does not exist to be enforced in other Contracting States if it has been lawfully 'set aside' by a competent authority in the State in which the award was made" (at F 3d 936). The court followed the decision in *Baker Marine (Nigeria) Ltd v Chevron (Nigeria) Ltd* 191 F 3d 194 at 196 (2d Cir 1999), where the US Court refused to enforce an award set aside by the courts of the seat in Nigeria notwithstanding that the award had been set aside on grounds not available in the US.

[s 8-18] Partial enforcement Section 8(6) relates to the consequences of s 8(5)(d) applying to part of an award. Section 8(6) enacts the latter part of Art V(1)(c) of the New York Convention, which recognises that a court has a discretion to enforce part of an award where decisions on matters submitted to arbitration can be separated from those matters which were not so submitted. The English Court of Appeal held that partial enforcement of an award is not confined to the limited circumstances stated in Art V(1)(c) and that enforcement is permissible in respect of those parts where there was "no credible challenge" under the equivalent provisions of the Arbitration Act 1996 (Eng, W & NI) (*IPCO (Nigeria) Ltd v Nigeria National Petroleum Corp* [2008] EWHC 797 (Comm) at [94], affirmed on appeal in *Nigerian National Petroleum Corp v IPCO (Nigeria) Ltd* [2008] All ER (D) 197 (Oct); [2009] 1 All ER (Comm) 611; [2009] 1 Lloyd's Rep 89; [2008] EWCA Civ 1157; see also the discussion of the analogous circumstances where separation is possible under the general law in *ACN 006 397 413 Pty Ltd v International Movie Group (Canada) Inc* [1997] 2 VR 31 at 38–47; BC9604108).

[s 8-19] Grounds relating to laws of place of enforcement (s 8(7)) Section 8(7) reproduces the two grounds specified in Art V(2) of the New York Convention, which relate to the laws of the place of enforcement.

[s 8-20] "not capable of settlement by arbitration" (s 8(7)(a)) Section 8(7)(a) reproduces the ground specified in Art V(2)(a) of the New York Convention. The meaning of the phrase "not capable of settlement by arbitration" in the sense of arbitrability is discussed in detail above in relation to s 7(2)(b) of the Act. The issue also arises in relation to Art 1(5) (scope of application), Art 34(2)(b)(i) (setting aside an award) and Art 36(2)(b)(i) (enforcement of an award) of the Model Law.

[s 8-21] "public policy" of the forum (s 8(7)(b)) Section 8(7)(b) reproduces the ground specified in Art V(2)(b) of the New York Convention and which is also found in Arts 34(2)(b)(ii) and 36(1)(b)(ii) of the Model Law. The public policy in the context of s 8(7)(b) "is the public policy of the country in which an award is sought to be enforced" (*IMC Aviation Solutions Pty Ltd v Altain Khuder LLC* [2011] VSCA 248; BC201106268 at [346], footnote 203 (Hansen JA and Kyrou AJA)). In that case, the Court of Appeal, after reviewing the evidence, concluded (at [346]) that the arbitral tribunal made the award "without giving prior notice to [the award debtor/resisting party] that it proposed to make any order against it. In these circumstances, the Tribunal breached the rules of natural justice and, accordingly, enforcement of the Award in Australia would be contrary to public policy".

A foreign award which is not in the form of a judgment usually made by the forum court may be contrary to public policy under s 8(7)(b), such as an order for the payment of money which does not specify the sum due (see the discussion in *AED Oil Ltd v Puffin FPSO Ltd* (2010) 27 VR 22; 265 ALR 415; [2010] VSCA 37; BC201001025 at [18]–[20]). The court in *Resort Condominiums Inc v Bolwell* [1995] 1 Qd R 406; (1993) 118 ALR 655; BC9303445, considered that some terms of the foreign award amounted to an interlocutory mandatory injunction which would not have been granted in Queensland without an undertaking as to damages and security. In these circumstances the court held that it would be contrary to public policy within the meaning of s 8(7)(b) to enforce the award.

A wide view of the purpose of s 8(7)(b) was taken in *Corvetina Technology Ltd v Clough Engineering Ltd* (2004) 183 FLR 317 at 322; [2004] NSWSC 700; BC200404900 at [18], where the court said that the purpose was "to preserve to the court in which enforcement is sought, the right to apply its own standards of public policy". A narrower view was taken by the Federal Court in *Uganda Telecom Ltd v Hi-Tech Telecom Pty Ltd* (2011) 277 ALR 415; [2011] FCA 131; BC201100586 in a decision handed down following the amendments made to the

Act in 2010. The Federal Court, at [132], said "the exception in s 8(7)(b) should be narrowly interpreted" and consistent with the approach that the enforcement of foreign awards may be denied on this ground only, where enforcement would violate the forum state's most basic notions of morality and justice.

A similar view had been expressed by Sir Anthony Mason, when sitting as a Non Permanent Judge on the Court of Final Appeal in Hong Kong in *Hebei Import & Export Corp v Polytek Engineering Co Ltd* [1999] 2 HKC 205 at 242, when he noted: "It has generally been accepted that the expression 'contrary to public policy of that country' in art V(2)(b) [of the New York Convention] means 'contrary to fundamental conceptions of morality and justice' of the forum." See also the discussion in *Stern v National Australia Bank* [1999] FCA 1421; BC9907269 at [133]–[177] of the analogous obligation on a party resisting the enforcement of a foreign judgment on the ground that it is contrary to public policy to establish that the foreign judgment is "against fundamental Australian public policy".

In New Zealand, an application was made under Art 34(2)(b)(ii) to set aside an award on the basis the relief granted amounted to a penalty, which was contrary to equitable notions of public policy. This was refused with the court adopting the view that something more was required, such as, enforcement of the award would be "wholly offensive to the ordinary reasonable and fully informed member of the public on whose behalf the powers of the state are exercised" (*Amaltal Corp Ltd v Maruha (NZ) Corp Ltd* [2003] 2 NZLR 92 at 100, [32]). The court found (at [43]) that an award based on "[p]enal provisions in a lawful and valid contract do[es] not approach" the required standard of an award which is clearly injurious to the public good or offensive to those on whose behalf the state's powers are exercised.

The same approach to public policy was taken by the Singapore Court of Appeal in the case of *PT Asuransi Jasa Indonesia (Persero) v Dexia Bank SA* [2006] SGCA 41 at [59], where the court stated (authorities omitted):

> Although the concept of public policy of the State is not defined in the Act or the Model Law, the general consensus of judicial and expert opinion is that public policy under the Act encompasses a narrow scope. In our view, it should only operate in instances where the upholding of an arbitral award would 'shock the conscience'. . . or is 'clearly injurious to the public good or . . . wholly offensive to the ordinary reasonable and fully informed member of the public'. . . or where it violates the forum's most basic notion of morality and justice . . . This would be consistent with the concept of public policy that can be ascertained from the preparatory materials to the Model Law. As was highlighted in the Commission Report (A/40/17), at para 297 . . . : In discussing the term 'public policy', it was understood that it was not equivalent to the political stance or international policies of a State but comprised the *fundamental notions and principles of justice* . . . It was understood that the term 'public policy', which was used in the 1958 New York Convention and many other treaties, covered fundamental principles of law and justice in substantive as well as procedural respects. Thus, instances such as *corruption, bribery or fraud* and similar serious cases would constitute a ground for setting aside.

A similar view has been adopted in New Zealand; see *Downer-Hill Joint Venture v Government of Fiji* [2005] 1 NZLR 554 at 569–70, [80]–[81], where the court endorsed the view that to establish that enforcement is contrary to public policy, which requires the suggestion that enforcement would "shock the conscience".

The US courts have also construed the public policy exception narrowly and the defence is applied "only where enforcement would violate our 'most basic notions of morality and justice'" (*Europcar Italia v Maiellano Tours*, 156 F 3d 310 at 315 (2d Cir 1998)).

In the case of *Gao Haiyan v Keeneye Holdings Ltd* [2011] HKCFI 767 (*Gao Haiyan*) at [97]–[102], enforcement of an award was refused because enforcement would be "contrary to the public policy" of the enforcement court in Hong Kong under the local equivalent of Art V(2)(b) of the New York Convention. During the arbitration a form of mediation occurred which involved a member of the arbitral panel and a third party. The enforcing court refused to enforce the award, as it found that the procedure at the mediation was not in accordance with that contemplated by the applicable arbitration rules, and was such as give rise to a "real risk of bias" on the part of the arbitral tribunal as discussed in *Porter v Magill* [2002] 2 AC 357; [2002] 1 All ER 465; [2002] 2 WLR 37; [2001] UKHL 67, and now enacted in s 18A of the Act for the purposes of Art 12 of the Model Law. The court had previously noted that "the basic notions of morality and justice in Hong Kong would not permit ex parte communication between a member of a tribunal and a party once an arbitration process had commenced" (*Gao Haiyan* at [16]). See also the discussion in relation to s 18A and Art 12 below.

Where the public policy relied on to resist enforcement of the award concerns an allegation of illegality which taints the main transaction; difficult questions of competing public interest arise particularly where the claim of illegality is within the scope of the arbitration agreement and was the subject of a ruling by the arbitrator rejecting the claim. Attempts are sometimes made to "seek to use the public policy doctrine to conduct a re-trial on the basis of additional evidence of illegality when it was open to . . . adduce that evidence before the arbitrators" (*Westacre Investments Inc v Jugoimport-SPDR Ltd* [1999] QB 740 at 771; [1998] 4 All ER 570; [1998] 3 WLR 770; [1998] 2 Lloyd's Rep 111 (*Westacre Investments*)). This situation requires the delicate balancing on the one hand of the public policy of sustaining the finality of awards in international arbitration and on the other hand the public policy of discouraging illegal or corrupt transactions.

The authorities were reviewed and the relevant principles summarised by Colman J in *Westacre Investments* at QB 767 and he refused leave to retry the issue of illegality on the application to enforce the foreign award in England. An appeal to the Court of Appeal in *Westacre Investments* was dismissed by a majority (*Westacre Investments Inc v Jugoimport-SPDR Holding Co Ltd* [2000] 1 QB 288; [1999] 3 All ER 864; [1999] 3 WLR 811, Mantell LJ and Sir David Hurst, with Waller LJ dissenting). The approach taken by Colman J and the majority in the Court of Appeal in *Westacre Investments* is seen as one of "two divergent approaches [adopted by the English courts] vis-à-vis the circumstances in which the [enforcing] court may reopen an arbitral tribunal's decision that an underlying contract is legal" (*AJU v AJT* [2011] SGCA 41 at [58]). The other, and a more liberal and interventionist, approach which would favour the enforcing court re-examining the merits of the claim of illegality, was taken by the Court of Appeal in *Soleimany v Soleimany* [1999] QB 785; [1999] 3 All ER 847; [1998] 3 WLR 811 and by Waller LJ in *Westacre Investments* in the Court of Appeal. The Singapore Court of Appeal in *AJU v AJT* preferred the approach taken by Colman J and by the majority in *Westacre Investments* as it is "consonant with the legislative policy of . . . giving primacy to the autonomy of arbitral proceedings and upholding the finality of arbitral awards . . ." (at [60]).

This issue was noted by the NSW Supreme Court in *Corvetina Technology Ltd v Clough Engineering Ltd* (2004) 183 FLR 317; [2004] NSWSC 700; BC200404900 where the court noted (at [10]) that "the discretion that is conferred (in Australia) by s 8(7)(b) of the Act is wide . . . [and it appeared that there] may also be . . . in addition, a general discretion". The issue was not finally addressed as the decision concerned a procedural motion. The decision was made prior to the 2010 amendments, which may be seen as reinforcing the finality of arbitral awards (eg, s 39(2)(b)(ii)).

For comparative consideration of "public policy" as a ground for refusing enforcement of foreign arbitral awards, see especially International Law Association Committee on International Commercial Arbitration, "Final Report on Public Policy as a Bar to Enforcement of International Arbitral Awards", in International Law Association, *Seventieth Report: New Delhi Conference* (2002); and International Law Association Committee on International Commercial Arbitration, "Interim Report on Public Policy as a Bar to Enforcement of International Arbitral Awards", in International Law Association, *Sixty-ninth Report: London Conference* (2000).

[s 8-22] **Public policy of the forum** When the court is considering an application to enforce the award, the public policy of the forum is in issue. Accordingly, the fact that the supervising court (the court of the seat) has refused to set aside an award as contrary to that court's public policy, does not give rise to an estoppel when it is the public policy of the enforcing court which is considered, eg, *Gao Haiyan v Keeneye Holdings Ltd* [2011] HKCFI 240 at [92], applying *Hebei Import & Export Corp v Polytek Engineering Co Ltd* [1991] 1 HKLRD 665 (CFA) at 688–9, [81]–[88] (Sir Anthony Mason NPJ).

[s 8-23] **Matters which are deemed contrary to public policy (s 8(7A))** Section 8(7A) was inserted by the International Arbitration Amendment Act 2010 (Cth) to replicate the terms of s 19 of the Act, which had been inserted in 1989. Section 19 states that, for the purposes of Arts 34(2)(b)(ii) and 36(1)(b)(ii) of the Model Law, "an award is in conflict with, or is contrary to, the public policy of Australia" if: (a) the making of the award was induced or affected by fraud or corruption; or (b) a breach of the rules of natural justice occurred in the making of the award.

Section 8(7A) (as with s 19) was introduced "so as to avoid any possible inference that the term 'public policy', which is referred to in the New York Convention, does not contain those elements" stated in s 8(7A) (Revised Explanatory Memorandum to the International Arbitration Amendment Bill 2010 (Cth) at [49], quoting from a similar statement made in relation to s 19 contained in the Explanatory Memorandum to the 1989 Bill).

The enforcing court in *IMC Aviation Solutions Pty Ltd v Altain Khuder LLC* [2011] VSCA 248; BC201106268 at [346] (Hansen JA and Kyrou AJA), found that the resisting party had established that it had been denied natural justice and refused to enforce the award.

An allegation that there has been a breach of the rules of natural justice raises similar considerations to those raised by an allegation under s 8(5)(c) that a party has not been afforded an "opportunity" of presenting its case contrary to Art 18 of the Model Law and that not all information and documents supplied to the arbitrator has been "communicated to the other party" contrary to Art 24(3) of the Model Law; see, eg, *Methanex Motunui Ltd v Spellman* [2004] 1 NZLR 95 at 131–43.

[s 8-24] **"the court may, if it considers proper, adjourn the proceedings" for enforcement of an award (s 8(8))** Section 8(8) gives effect to Art VI of the New York Convention and provides a mechanism for adjourning proceedings in circumstances where the award is being challenged in the country where it was made, so as to ensure that enforcement of an award does not occur where that award, in time, may be unenforceable. Article 36(2) of the Model Law provides the same mechanism for an adjournment of enforcement proceedings brought under the Model Law. Those drafting the article recommended its adoption "in order to permit the enforcement authority to adjourn its decision if it was satisfied that an application for annulment of the award or for its suspension was made for a good reason in the country where the award was given. At the same time, to prevent an abuse of that provision by the losing party which may have started annulment proceedings without a valid reason purely to delay or frustrate the enforcement of the award, the enforcement authority should in such a case have the right either to enforce the award forthwith or to adjourn its enforcement only on condition that the party opposing enforcement deposits a suitable security" (Summary Record of the 17th Meeting of the UN conference on International Commercial Arbitration E/CONF.26/SR.17 (3 June 1958)). The provision "can be used to avoid concurrent judicial review of the same grounds and possibly conflicting decisions, where this risk is not already excluded by the fact that the same court is seized with the application for setting aside and the other party's application for enforcement" (Secretary-General of UNCITRAL in *Analytical Commentary on Draft Text of a Model Law on International Commercial Arbitration*, UN Doc No A/CN.9/264, p 79, para 5).

In *ESCO Corp v Bradken Resources Pty Ltd* [2011] FCA 905; BC201105961 (*ESCO Corp*) at [55], the Federal Court suggested that s 8(8) was "not the only source of power which would enable [the] Court to adjourn" as the court has a "general power to control its own processes"; see, eg, *QH Tours Ltd v Ship Design and Management (Aust) Pty Ltd* (1991) 33 FCR 237 at 231.

As was noted in relation to the equivalent provision in England: "Pro-enforcement assumptions are sometimes outweighed by the respect due to the courts exercising jurisdiction in the country of origin — the venue chosen by the parties for their arbitration" (*IPCO (Nigeria) Ltd v Nigerian National Petroleum Corp* [2005] EWHC 726 (Comm) (*IPCO Nigeria*) at [14]).

An Australian court exercising this discretion after the amendments made to the Act in 2010 will have regard to the objects of the Act in s 2D and to the matters specified in s 39(2). As the court has the same discretion under Art 36(2) of the Model Law, it is arguable that regard may also be had to the matters specified in Art 2A of the Model Law.

The discretion contained in s 8(8) has been described as a "general discretion" to adjourn enforcement proceedings (*Hallen v Angledal* [1999] NSWSC 552; BC9903040 at [23]). The onus is on the party resisting enforcement to establish a case for an adjournment: at [20(d)]. In the absence of evidence that an application has been made to a "competent authority" and in a proper and timely manner and had, at least prima facie, some prospects of success, an adjournment will not be granted. The enforcing court's "assessment of the strength of the arguments in support of setting aside or suspending the award would ordinarily be undertaken on incomplete material and in circumstances where only the briefest consideration of the arguments would be appropriate" (*ESCO Corp* at [77]). An adjournment was granted in circumstances where the court could "not find" that the application which had been made to the competent authority was "unarguable" (*Toyo Engineering Corp v John Holland Pty Ltd* [2000] VSC 553; BC200007910 at [9]).

A similar approach was taken under the equivalent provision in Hong Kong in *Hebei Import & Export Corp v Polytek Engineering Co Ltd* [1996] 3 HKC 725, where the court (at 728) said: "It is for the defendant to show that it has some reasonably arguable grounds which afford some prospect of success . . . it is going too far to say that the defendant must show that he is likely to succeed."

The applicant for an adjournment needs to satisfy the court that its application to set aside or suspend the award has been made "bona fide" (*ESCO Corp* at [62], [66] and [86(a)]).

The discretion found in the equivalent section of the Arbitration Act 1996 (Eng, W & NI), s 103(5), was considered by the Court of Appeal in *Nigerian National Petroleum Corp v IPCO (Nigeria) Ltd* [2008] All ER (D) 197 (Oct); [2009] 1 All ER (Comm) 611; [2009] 1 Lloyd's Rep 89; [2008] EWCA Civ 1157, which noted (at [15]) that "the court may adjourn but only if it considers it 'proper' to do so. The enforcing court's role is not therefore entirely passive or mechanistic. The mere fact that a challenge has been made to the validity of an award in the home court does not prevent the enforcing court from enforcing the award if it considers the award to be manifestly valid".

In *Dardana Ltd v Yukos Oil Co* [2002] All ER (D) 126 (Apr); [2002] 1 All ER (Comm) 819 at 825[8]; [2002] 2 Lloyd's Rep 326; [2002] EWCA Civ 543, Mance LJ at [23]–[24] noted that a court could, of its own motion, consider that the determination of the application "would be an inappropriate use of Court time and/or contrary to comity or likely to give rise to conflict of laws problems which would be likely to resolve the issue in the country in which or under the law of which the award was made". Accordingly, even if the relevant principles of foreign law which were raised to challenge the award were agreed, it was preferable for the foreign court to apply them rather than the enforcing court and a stay was appropriate in that case.

In *IPCO Nigeria* at [15], Gross J, as he then was, said: "In my judgement, it would be wrong to read a fetter into this understandably wide discretion . . . Ordinarily, a number of considerations are likely to be relevant: (i) whether the application brought before the court in the country of origin is brought *bona fide* and not simply by way of delaying tactics; (ii) whether the application in the country of origin has at least a real (ie, realistic) prospect of success (the test in this jurisdiction for resisting summary judgement); (iii) the extent of the delay occasioned by an adjournment and any resulting prejudice. Beyond such matters, it is probably unwise to generalise; all must depend on the circumstances of the individual case."

The court in *ESCO Corp* (at [82]) followed the approach taken by these English authorities when considering whether to adjourn under s 8(8) of the Act.

Decisions on the equivalent legislation in the US recognise that an application for an adjournment under s 8(8) raises an inherent tension between competing concerns. On the one hand an adjournment of enforcement proceedings may be seen to impede the goals of arbitration — the expeditious resolution of disputes and the avoidance of protracted and expensive litigation — but on the other, where a parallel proceeding is ongoing in the originating country and there is a possibility that the award will be set aside, a court may be acting improvidently by enforcing the award prior to the completion of the foreign proceedings (*Europcar Italia v Maiellano Tours*, 156 F 3d 310 at 315 (2d Cir 1998)). In *Europcar*, at 317–18, the Court of Appeals for the Second Circuit said that a proper balancing of these concerns would involve a court considering a number of factors, including:

(1) the general objectives of arbitration — the expeditious resolution of disputes and the avoidance of protracted and expensive litigation;
(2) the status of the foreign proceedings and the estimated time for those proceedings to be resolved;
(3) whether the award sought to be enforced will receive greater scrutiny in the foreign proceedings under a less deferential standard of review;
(4) the characteristics of the foreign proceedings including:
  (i) whether they were brought to enforce an award (which would tend to weigh in favor of a stay) or to set the award aside (which would tend to weigh in favor of enforcement);
  (ii) whether they were initiated before the underlying enforcement proceeding so as to raise concerns of international comity;
  (iii) whether they were initiated by the party now seeking to enforce the award in federal court; and
  (iv) whether they were initiated under circumstances indicating an intent to hinder or delay resolution of the dispute;
(5) a balance of the possible hardships to each of the parties, keeping in mind that if enforcement is postponed under Article VI of the Convention, the party seeking enforcement may receive "suitable security" and that, under Article V of the Convention, an award should not be enforced if it is set aside or suspended in the originating country . . . ; and
(6) any other circumstances that could tend to shift the balance in favor of or against adjournment.

These principles have since been applied in the US in cases such as *GE Transportation SpA v Republic of Albania* 693 F Supp 2d 132 (2010); *Continental Transfert Technique Ltd v Federal Government of Nigeria* 697 F Supp 2d 46 at 60–1 (2010); and *DRC Inc v Republic of Honduras* 28 March 2011 (DDC 2011); and in Canada in cases such as *Powerex Corp v Alcan Inc* [2004] BCCA 504 (CanLII); and *Wires Jolley LLP v Wong* [2010] BCSC 391 (CanLII) at [39].

The powers of a court acting under the equivalent provision in Ontario have been described as confined to "allow, adjourn or dismiss the application" (*Dalimpex Ltd v Janicki* (2003) 64 OR (3d) 737 (CA) at [55] and [61]). See also *Powerex Corp v Alcan Inc* [2004] BCCA 504 (CanLII).

Under the equivalent provision in British Columbia, it was held that a court may grant a stay if the court cannot find that the "application to set aside the award is apparently without merit" and can find that "there is an issue to be tried" (*Wires Jolley LLP v Wong* [2010] BCSC 391 (CanLII) at [39]).

If an adjournment is refused and subsequently the award is set aside at the place of arbitration, it has been stated in relation to the equivalent English provision that the party which had obtained enforcement, "would be under a duty to reimburse the amount paid" (*Minmetals Germany v Ferco Steel* [1999] 1 All ER 315 (Comm) at 333).

[s 8-25] **"and may also . . . order the other party to give suitable security" (s 8(8))** Under the equivalent legislation in England the amount of the security may range from nil to "modest" (*Yukos Oil Co v Dardana Ltd* [2001] EWCA Civ 1007 at [12]) up to the full amount of the award. The amount will reflect the court's "initial impression [of] the chances of persuading" the court of the place of arbitration to set aside the award and the enforcing court to refuse enforcement (*Minmetals Germany v Ferco Steel* [1999] 1 All ER (Comm) 315 at 323). The "right approach is that of a sliding scale" (*IPCO (Nigeria) Ltd v Nigerian National Petroleum Corp* [2005] EWHC 726 (Comm) (*IPCO Nigeria*) at [15]; *Dowans Holding SA v Tanzania Electric Supply Co Ltd* [2011] EWHC 1957 (Comm) at [43] and [49]). This approach developed out of the decision of the Court of Appeal in *Soleh Boneh v Uganda Govt* [1993] 2 Lloyd's Rep 208 at 212, where Staughton LJ said:

> two important factors must be considered on such an application, although I do not mean to say there may not be others. The first is the strength of the argument that the award is invalid, as perceived on a brief consideration by the Court which is asked to enforce the award while proceedings to set it aside are pending elsewhere. If the award is manifestly invalid, there should be an adjournment and no order for security; if it is manifestly valid, there should either be an order for immediate enforcement, or else an order for substantial security. In between there will be various degrees of plausibility in the argument for invalidity; and the Judge must be guided by his preliminary conclusion on the point.
>
> The second point is that the Court must consider the ease or difficulty of enforcement of the award, and whether it will be rendered more difficult, for example, by movement of assets or by improvident trading, if enforcement is delayed. If that is likely to occur, the case for security is stronger; if, on the other hand, there are and always will be insufficient [sic] assets within the jurisdiction, the case for security must necessarily be weakened.

As there may be prejudice occasioned by an adjournment, it has been said in relation to the equivalent provision in England that the enforcing court must seek to minimise any claimed prejudice so far as it is practicable and appropriate to do so (*IPCO Nigeria* at [52(v)]). Although as Staughton LJ "in *Soleh* was careful to point out that there might be other relevant factors besides the merits and any potential prejudice to enforcement" (*Yukos Oil Co v Dardana Ltd* [2002] All ER (D) 126 (Apr); [2002] 1 All ER (Comm) 819; [2002] 2 Lloyd's Rep 326; [2002] EWCA Civ 543 at [52(iv)] (Mance LJ)).

It has been held under the equivalent provision in the US that security is not necessary if the resisting party clearly has sufficient assets to meet the arbitral award and is unlikely not to comply with an order of the enforcing court (*DRC Inc v Republic of Honduras* 28 March 2011 (DDC 2011) at 28).

A similar approach was adopted under the equivalent provision in Hong Kong in *Hebei Import & Export Corp v Polytek Engineering Co Ltd* [1996] 3 HKC 725. Security was not ordered against a "substantial Hong Kong company with ample assets and there is no reason to suppose that there is any risk against which the plaintiff needs to be protected by means of an order for security".

Under the equivalent provision in British Columbia, security may be ordered even though there is no real threat of asset removal prior to enforcement of the judgment, if there is a "necessity of monitoring the status of that property so as to preserve the equity for execution" (*Wires Jolley LLP v Wong* [2010] BCSC 391 (CanLII) at [44]).

[s 8-26] Resumption of enforcement proceedings (s 8(9), (10) and (11)) Subsections 8(9), (10) and (11) were added in 2010 to ensure that any adjournment granted under s 8(8) is not used to frustrate the enforcement of a foreign award in Australia by a party opposing enforcement commencing an action in a country where the award was made "on spurious grounds or with the sole intention of delaying enforcement" (Revised Explanatory Memorandum to the International Arbitration Amendment Bill 2010 (Cth) at [54]). These provisions give the court a significant power to monitor and supervise the enforcement proceeding during any period of adjournment and "recognise the need for the Court to keep a close and active eye on the progress of the foreign proceedings which will have underpinned any adjournment" (*ESCO Corp v Bradken Resources Pty Ltd* [2011] FCA 905; BC201105961 at [56]–[57]).

[s 8-27] Interest on award and/or on judgment enforcing the award Interest may be referrable to the time between when the cause of action arose and the time of making the award ("pre-award interest"), or it may be interest to apply from the date of the award up until the award is satisfied ("post-award interest"). The post-award interest may be referrable, first, to the period from the date of the award up until a judgment of the enforcing court and second, to the period from the date of the judgment of the enforcing court up until payment.

An arbitrator may be empowered to award interest under the arbitration agreement or pursuant to a statutory power such as is found in ss 25 and 26 of the Act; see the discussion of ss 25 and 26 below.

An award does not become a judgment of the enforcing court until the application is determined by the court. As a result the statutory power to award interest on judgment debts found in provisions such as s 52(1) of the Federal Court of Australia Act 1976 (Cth) does not apply until the judgment is entered by the court. The power of the enforcing court to order post-award pre-judgment interest will depend on the existence of a statutory power to do so. If the arbitral panel has exercised a power to award post-award interest, that interest may be reflected in the judgment made by the enforcing court.

In *Uganda Telecom Ltd v Hi-Tech Telecom Pty Ltd (No 2)* (2011) 277 ALR 441; [2011] FCA 206; BC201101086, the arbitrator had awarded post-award interest from the time of making the award up until payment in full at the rate of 24 per cent per annum. An application was made to the enforcement court, the Federal

Court of Australia, to make an order for post-award interest calculated at the lower rates the court would order on one of its judgments "upon the basis that the Award was, in fact, or should be treated as though it were, a judgment of [the] Court from the date when the Award was made" (at [14]). The Federal Court rejected this application. "The Award is not reflected in a judgment of this Court until this Court gives judgment for the amount awarded. That judgment will not operate retrospectively. The amount awarded by the arbitrator does not become a judgment debt which carries interest pursuant to s 52 of the Federal Court Act until it has been entered. Once entered, interest will run on the amount of the judgment debt at the prescribed rate" (at [15]). The amount of the judgment made by the court included a sum for interest at the rate of 24 per cent from the date of the award up to the date of the judgment. The court was not asked to, and nor did it of its own motion as allowed under s 8 and the New York Convention, consider any issue of public policy under s 8(7) of the Act which may arguably have applied. Although it seems that the applicable post-judgment interest was at the rate prescribed by the court and not that agreed by the parties.

[s 8-28] **Currency** When a foreign award expressed in a foreign currency is enforced, a court where so authorised, may give a judgment in the foreign currency, eg, *ML Ubase Holdings Co Ltd v Trigem Computer Inc* (2007) 69 NSWLR 577; [2007] NSWSC 859; BC200706318; *Uganda Telecom Ltd v Hi-Tech Telecom Pty Ltd* (2011) 277 ALR 415; [2011] FCA 131; BC201100586; and *Uganda Telecom Ltd v Hi-Tech Telecom Pty Ltd (No 2)* (2011) 277 ALR 441; [2011] FCA 206; BC201101086 (*Uganda Telecom No 2*).

In *Uganda Telecom No 2*, the Federal Court stated (at [20]) that: "Although it was once considered inappropriate for an Australian court to give judgment in a foreign currency, that is no longer the law. Judgments are now routinely given in a foreign currency, if the circumstances warrant such an approach. One circumstance which is regarded as warranting such an approach is where the action in question is to enforce a foreign money obligation."

Alternatively, the court may need to consider the date for conversion into Australian currency. Possible dates for conversion include the date on which the foreign award was made, eg, *Transpac Capital Pte Ltd v Buntoro* [2008] NSWSC 671; BC200805307, and the date on which the order for enforcement was obtained in Australia, eg, *China Sichuan Changhong Electric Co Ltd v CTA International Pty Ltd* [2009] FCA 397; BC200903081 at [10]. See also the discussion of possible dates of conversion in *ACN 006 397 413 Pty Ltd v International Movie Group (Canada) Inc* [1997] 2 VR 31 at 48; BC9604108.

[s 8-29] **Limitation statutes** It may be possible to resist enforcement of a foreign arbitral award under the Act on the ground that enforcement is barred by a limitation statute. Article III of the New York Convention requires that recognition and enforcement shall be "in accordance with the rules of procedure of the territory where the award is relied upon". Thus, the "rules of procedure" of the jurisdiction in which enforcement is sought will apply, insofar as they do not conflict with the express requirements of the Convention.

The Supreme Court of Canada in *Yugraneft Corp v Rexx Management Corp* 2010 SCC 19; [2010] 1 SCR 649 (*Yugraneft*) at [18], held that Art III of the New York Convention "permits (although it does not require) Contracting States (or, in the case of a federal State, a sub-national territory with jurisdiction over the matter) to subject the recognition and enforcement of foreign arbitral awards to a time limit. Thus, notwithstanding art.V, which sets out an otherwise exhaustive list of grounds on which recognition and enforcement may be resisted, the courts of a Contracting State may refuse to recognize and enforce a foreign arbitral award on the basis that such proceedings are time-barred".

In *Yugraneft* the local limitation statute which was expressed to apply "to any proceeding commenced or sought to be commenced ... in which a claimant seeks a remedial order," was held to apply to an action to enforce a foreign award. The Supreme Court held that the local limitation statute was intended to create a comprehensive and exhaustive limitations scheme applicable to all causes of action including an action to enforce a foreign award. The Supreme Court also rejected an argument that the application of the limitation statute was contrary to Art 5 of the Model Law which provides that "no court shall intervene except where so provided in this Law". It had been argued that, in the absence of a clear derogation from this principle, local procedural rules including the limitation statute, which were not contained in the statute enacting the Model Law, should not apply.

[s 8-30] Security for costs of an application for enforcement Article III of the New York Convention imposes an obligation on Contracting States not to impose "substantially more onerous conditions or higher fees or charges" than are imposed on the recognition of "domestic arbitral awards". An example of equal treatment is seen in relation to an application for security for costs against an applicant seeking to enforce a foreign award in *Gater Assets Ltd v Nak Naftogaz Ukrainiy* [2008] All ER (D) 232 (Oct); [2008] 1 All ER (Comm) 209; [2007] 2 Lloyd's Rep 558; [2007] EWCA Civ 988. In this case, the English Court of Appeal, whilst it had jurisdiction to award security, decided as a matter of discretion against awarding security for costs in relation to an enforcement of a foreign award on the basis that generally, security for costs is not normally ordered against an applicant for the enforcement of a domestic award.

This decision was followed by the Hong Kong Court of Appeal in declining to order security for costs in *Shangdong Hongri Acron Chemical Joint Stock Co Ltd v Petrochina International (Hong Kong) Corp Ltd* [2011] HKCA 124 at [43]–[49].

[s 8-31] Common law enforcement of an award In contrast to the procedure under s 8 of the Act, a foreign award may be enforced at common law by an action on the award. This involves proof of the agreement to arbitrate, that the conduct of the arbitration was in accordance with the agreement and that the award was final and valid according to the law of the country where it was made.

The action is founded upon the implied promise in the arbitration agreement to abide by the award (see *Bremer Oeltransport GmbH v Drewry* [1933] 1 KB 753 at 765; *F J Bloemen Pty Ltd v City of Gold Coast Council* (1972) 26 LGRA 78; [1973] AC 115 at 126; (1972) 46 ALJR 366; and *AEGIS Ltd v European Reinsurance Co of Zurich* [2003] All ER (D) 308 (Jan); [2003] 1 WLR 1041 at 1046; [2003] 1 All ER (Comm) 253; [2003] UKPC 11) although in one case the court proceeded on the "hypothesis" that the implied promise was in the award itself (*Brali v Hyundai Corp* (1988) 15 NSWLR 734 at 743E; 84 ALR 176). The Court of Final Appeal of Hong Kong in *Eton Properties Ltd* [2011] HKCFA 31 at [4], adopted the view that: "Parties to an arbitration agreement impliedly promise to perform a valid award. If the award is not performed the successful claimant can proceed by action in the ordinary courts for breach of this implied promise and obtain a judgment giving effect to the award. The court may give judgment for the amount of the award, or damages for failure to perform the award. It may also, in appropriate cases, decree specific performance of the award, grant an injunction preventing the losing party from disobeying the award, or make a declaration that the award is valid, or as to its construction and effect."

Accordingly, any limitation period starts to run from the time of the breach "occasioned by the ... failure to honour the award" (*Agromet v Maulden Engineering Ltd* [1985] 1 WLR 762 at 773; *Antclizo Shipping Corp v The Food Corp of India* (SC of WA, BC9806040 at 5–6, unreported)). Nevertheless, if, in the course of attempting to enforce a foreign award, the foreign award had been entered as a judgment in a foreign country, the award does not merge in that judgment for the purposes of enforcement in Australia (*Brali v Hyundai Corp* (1988) 15 NSWLR 734 at 742B; 84 ALR 176; but cf, *Resort Condominiums Inc v Bolwell* [1995] 1 Qd R 406 at 416; (1993) 118 ALR 655; BC9303445, line 35).

[s 8-32] Enforcement of an award by issue estoppel A foreign award may also be enforced by a party pleading an issue estoppel. Where an arbitral tribunal has decided an issue, "that decision binds the parties and neither party can thereafter dispute that decision" (*Associated Electric & Gas Insurance Services Ltd v European Reinsurance Co of Zurich* [2003] 1 WLR 11; [2003] UKPC 11 at [15]).

A claim which is raised and which falls within the scope of the reference or submission to arbitration is deemed to be abandoned irrevocably if it is not pursued or repeated in the pleadings and the arbitration proceeds to a final award (*Discovery Beach Project Pty Ltd v Northbuild Construction Pty Ltd* [2011] QC 306; BC201108127 (*Discovery Beach*) at [70]) and thereby creates an estoppel (*Discovery Beach* at [91]) which prevents the claim being raised again between the parties to the award. If it is a partial final award, the court is entitled to look at the relevant documents such as any directions or pleadings to see what was substituted to arbitration (*Discovery Beach* at [78]) and was the subject matter of the award.

[s 8-33] Asset preservation orders (*Mareva* relief) Where proceedings are brought to enforce a foreign award, a court with jurisdiction may, in an appropriate case, also grant *Mareva* relief (orders for asset preservation which originated in *Mareva Companania Naviera SA v International Bulkcarriers SA* [1975] 2 Lloyd's Rep 509, and considered as asset preservation in *Cardile v LED Builders Pty Ltd* (1999) 198 CLR 380; 162 ALR 294; [1999] HCA 18; BC9902073). As the proceedings are pursuant to a request made under the New York Convention to enforce an award made in another jurisdiction, a court, save in an exceptional case, "should stop short of making orders which extend beyond its own jurisdiction" (*Rosseel NV v Oriental Shipping Ltd* [1990] 1 WLR 1386 at 1389 (Lord Donaldson MR) where a territorial limitation was placed on the orders by the court).

[s 9] Evidence of awards and arbitration agreements

9 (1) In any proceedings in which a person seeks the enforcement of a foreign award by virtue of this Part, he or she shall produce to the court:
   (a) the duly authenticated original award or a duly certified copy; and

(b) the original arbitration agreement under which the award purports to have been made or a duly certified copy.

(2) For the purposes of subsection (1), an award shall be deemed to have been duly authenticated, and a copy of an award or agreement shall be deemed to have been duly certified, if:
    (a) it purports to have been authenticated or certified, as the case may be, by the arbitrator or, where the arbitrator is a tribunal, by an officer of that tribunal, and it has not been shown to the court that it was not in fact so authenticated or certified; or
    (b) it has been otherwise authenticated or certified to the satisfaction of the court.

(3) If a document or part of a document produced under subsection (1) is written in a language other than English, there shall be produced with the document a translation, in the English language, of the document or that part, as the case may be, certified to be a correct translation.

(4) For the purposes of subsection (3), a translation shall be certified by a diplomatic or consular agent in Australia of the country in which the award was made or otherwise to the satisfaction of the court.

(5) A document produced to a court in accordance with this section is, upon mere production, receivable by the court as *prima facie* evidence of the matters to which it relates.

COMMENTARY ON SECTION 9

History of section .... [s 9-1]
Requirements of section .... [s 9-2]
Anomalous contrast to Model Law .... [s 9-3]

[s 9-1] History of section Section 9 was enacted in 1974 and drafting amendments were made by the International Arbitration Amendment Act 1989 (Cth), which substituted the word "Part" for "Act" and the Statute Law Revision Act 2008 (Cth), which added the words "or she" after the word "he".

[s 9-2] Requirements of section Subsection 9(1) gives effect to Art IV of the New York Convention. On an application to enforce an award the applicant award creditor must at least produce the documents required by s 9(1) and the award debtor can therefore "resist enforcement" by arguing that the documents produced by the award creditor do not meet the description set out in s 9(1) (*IMC Aviation Solutions Pty Ltd v Altain Khuder LLC* [2011] VSCA 248; BC201106268 (*IMC Aviation Solutions*) at [40] (Warren CJ)).

Examples of the type of evidence needed are seen in the cases of *ML Ubase Holdings Co Ltd v Trigem Computer Inc* [2005] NSWSC 224; BC200501412; *Transpac Capital Pte Ltd v Buntoro* [2008] NSWSC 671; BC200805307; and *IMC Aviation Solutions*.

The requirement that the award or agreement be "certified to the satisfaction of the court" of the foreign award or agreement in s 9(2)(b), and if necessary, a translation of a document or part of a document in s 9(3) and (4), should be construed consistently with Arts III and IV of the New York Convention (*Yang v S & L Consulting Pty Ltd* [2009] NSWSC 223; BC200902011 at [9]). In that case, a sworn translation given in accordance with the procedural rules of the forum for qualifying as an expert translator was accepted as certification to the satisfaction of the court.

The words "*prima facie* evidence" in s 9(5) mean that in the absence of any contrary evidence, prima facie evidence is conclusive proof of the relevant fact (*IMC Aviation Solutions* at [46] (Warren CJ) applying JD Heydon, *Cross on Evidence* [Service 135, April 2011], ¶ 1600).

[s 9-3] **Anomalous contrast to Model Law** The Model Law also has a provision in Art 35(2) which is similar to s 9 and which also gives effect to Art IV of the New York Convention when an application is made for the enforcement of an arbitral award. The language used in Art 35(2) of the 1985 version of the Model Law was similar to that used in s 9 of the Act. However, the changes to the Model Law in 2006 modified and eased the requirements of Art 35(2) when applying to enforce a foreign award. The 2006 changes included deleting the requirement to provide the "duly authenticated" original, or a "duly certified" copy, of the original award and original arbitration agreement (see the commentary to Art 35 below). Whilst the legislature in 2010 accepted these changes as part of the Act in the Model Law, the legislature did not consider whether the corresponding changes were equally appropriate to the equivalent requirements in s 9. This problem is highlighted by the operation of s 20 which provides that when enforcement proceedings under s 8 of the Act apply, Ch VIII of the Model Law including the revised Art 35 do not apply.

It was stated in the Revised Explanatory Memorandum to the International Arbitration Amendment Bill 2010 (Cth), when adopting the 2006 changes to the Model Law, that "[t]he 2006 amendments to Article 35 of the Model Law are intended to reduce formality when seeking the recognition and enforcement of an award. They are relatively minor changes and received broad support from stakeholders". There is no reason why the requirements of s 9 should not be modified and eased in the same manner as was made to Art 35(2) of the Model Law.

[s 10] **Evidence relating to Convention**

10 (1) For the purposes of this Part, a certificate purporting to be signed by the Secretary of the Foreign Affairs Department and stating that a country specified in the certificate is, or was at a time so specified, a Convention country is, upon mere production, receivable in any proceedings as *prima facie* evidence of that fact.

(2) For the purposes of this Part, a copy of the *Gazette* containing a Proclamation fixing a date under subsection 2(2) is, upon mere production, receivable in any proceedings as *prima facie* evidence of:
    (a) the fact that Australia has acceded to the Convention; and
    (b) the fact that the Convention entered into force for Australia on or before the date so fixed.

COMMENTARY ON SECTION 10

History of section .... [s 10-1]

[s 10-1] **History of section** Section 10 was introduced by the Arbitration (Foreign Awards and Agreements) Act 1974 (Cth). Minor drafting changes were

made by the International Arbitration Amendment Act 1989 (Cth), which substituted the word "Part" for "Act" in s 10(1) and (2), and the Law and Justice Legislation Amendment Act 2004 (Cth), which repealed s 4 and omitted a reference to that section in s 10. A further amendment was made in 2011 by the Statute Law Revision Act 2011 (Cth), which substituted the words "Secretary to" for "Secretary of".

[s 10A] Delegation by Secretary of the Foreign Affairs Department

10A (1) The Secretary may, either generally or as otherwise provided by the instrument of delegation, in writing, delegate to the person occupying a specified office in the Foreign Affairs Department and Trade all or any of the Secretary's powers under subsection 10(1).

(2) A power delegated under subsection (1) shall, when exercised by the delegate, be deemed to have been exercised by the Secretary.

(3) The delegate is, in the exercise of a power delegated under subsection (1), subject to the directions of the Secretary.

(4) The delegation of a power under subsection (1) does not prevent the exercise of the power by the Secretary.

(5) In this section, *Secretary* means the Secretary of the Foreign Affairs Department and Trade.

COMMENTARY ON SECTION 10A

History of section .... [s 10A-1]

[s 10A-1] History of section Section 10A was introduced by the Statute Law (Miscellaneous Provisions) Act 1987 (Cth). The section was amended in 2011 "to correct technical errors that have occurred in Acts as a result of drafting and clerical mistakes": Explanatory Memorandum (at [2]) to the Statute Law Revision Bill (No 2) 2010 (Cth), which became the Statute Law Revision Act 2011 (Cth). The Statute Law Revision Act 2011 (Cth) substituted the words "Secretary of" for "Secretary to" in s 10A(5) in the heading to s 10A.

NOTE: Section 11 "This Act subject to Sea-Carriage of Goods Act" was repealed by the International Arbitration Amendment Act 1989 (Cth) and has not been replaced.

[s 12] Effect of this Part on other laws

12 (1) This Part applies to the exclusion of any provisions made by a law of a State or Territory with respect to the recognition of arbitration agreements and the enforcement of foreign awards, being provisions that operate in whole or in part by reference to the Convention.

(2) Except as provided in subsection (1), nothing in this Part affects the right of any person to the enforcement of a foreign award otherwise than in pursuance of this Act.

COMMENTARY ON SECTION 12

History of section .... [s 12-1]

[s 12-1] History of section Section 12 was enacted by the Arbitration (Foreign Awards and Agreements) Act 1974 (Cth). Minor drafting changes were made by the International Arbitration Amendment Act 1989 (Cth), which substituted the word "Part" for "Act" in s 12(1) and (2).

[s 13] Judiciary Act

13 A matter arising under this Part, including a question of interpretation of the Convention for the purposes of this Act, shall, for the purposes of section 38 of the Judiciary Act 1903–1973, be deemed not to be a matter arising directly under a treaty.

COMMENTARY ON SECTION 13

History of section .... [s 13-1]
Operation of section .... [s 13-2]

[s 13-1] History of section Section 13 was introduced by the Arbitration (Foreign Awards and Agreements) Act 1974 (Cth). A minor inconsequential drafting change was made by the International Arbitration Amendment Act 1989 (Cth), which substituted the word "Part" for "Act".

[s 13-2] Operation of section Section 38 of the Judiciary Act 1903 (Cth) states that the High Court of Australia has exclusive jurisdiction over "matters arising directly under any treaty". The effect of s 13 is that any court which is seized of a matter under Pt II of the Act (which implements the New York Convention) can proceed to decide the matter notwithstanding that a question of treaty interpretation may be involved, without the need to refer the matter to the High Court of Australia. A corresponding provision, s 38, which is found in Pt IV of the Act, has the same operation in relation to the Convention on the Settlement of Investment Disputes between States and Nationals of Other States.

[s 14] Application of Part

14 The application of this Part extends to agreements and awards made before the date fixed under subsection 2(2), including agreements and awards made before the day referred to in subsection 2(1).

COMMENTARY ON SECTION 14

History of section .... [s 14-1]

[s 14-1] History of section Section 14 was enacted by the Arbitration (Foreign Awards and Agreements) Act 1974 (Cth). A minor drafting change was made by the International Arbitration Amendment Act 1989 (Cth), which substituted the word "Part" for "Act".

PART III — INTERNATIONAL COMMERCIAL ARBITRATION

DIVISION 1 — PRELIMINARY

[s 15] Interpretation

15 (1) In this Part:

confidential information, in relation to arbitral proceedings, means information that relates to the proceedings or to an award made in the proceedings and includes:
  (a) the statement of claim, statement of defence, and all other pleadings, submissions, statements, or other information supplied to the arbitral tribunal by a party to the proceedings; and
  (b) any evidence (whether documentary or other) supplied to the arbitral tribunal; and
  (c) any notes made by the arbitral tribunal of oral evidence or submissions given before the arbitral tribunal; and
  (d) any transcript of oral evidence or submissions given before the arbitral tribunal; and
  (e) any rulings of the arbitral tribunal; and
  (f) any award of the arbitral tribunal.

disclose, in relation to confidential information, includes giving or communicating the confidential information in any way.

Model Law means the UNCITRAL Model Law on International Commercial Arbitration adopted by the United Nations Commission on International Trade Law on 21 June 1985 and amended by the United Nations Commission on International Trade Law on 7 July 2006, the English text of which is set out in Schedule 2.

(2) Except so far as the contrary intention appears, a word or expression that is used both in this Part and in the Model Law (whether or not a particular meaning is given to it by the Model Law) has, in this Part, the same meaning as it has in the Model Law.

COMMENTARY ON SECTION 15

History of section .... [s 15-1]
Confidential information .... [s 15-2]

[s 15-1] History of section Section 15 was introduced by the International Arbitration Amendment Act 1989 (Cth). The International Arbitration Amendment Act 2010 (Cth) repealed s 15(1), which had defined the reference to the Model Law in the Act to mean the 1985 UNCITRAL Model Law on International Commercial Arbitration, and inserted a new s 15(1), which defined the Model Law as the 2006 UNCITRAL Model Law and inserted definitions for "confidential information" and "disclose".

[s 15-2] Confidential information See the discussion of the optional confidentiality regime introduced by ss 23C to 23G of the Act which, together with the definition of "confidential information" in s 15(1), were added in 2010.

DIVISION 2 — MODEL LAW

[s 16] Model Law to have force of law

16 (1) Subject to this Part, the Model Law has the force of law in Australia.

(2) In the Model Law:

arbitration agreement has the meaning given in Option 1 of Article 7 of the Model Law.

State means Australia (including the external Territories) and any foreign country.

this State means Australia (including the external Territories).

COMMENTARY ON SECTION 16

History of section .... [s 16-1]
Force of law .... [s 16-2]

[s 16-1] History of section Section 16 was introduced by the International Arbitration Amendment Act 1989 (Cth).

[s 16-2] Force of law This provision gives the provisions set out in the Model Law the same legal effect as any other statutory provisions in the Act. The Model Law "has the force of domestic law" (*Comandate Marine Corp v Pan Australia Shipping Pty Ltd* (2006) 157 FCR 45; 238 ALR 457; [2006] FCAFC 192; BC200610833 at [194] (Allsop J)).

[s 17] Interpretation of Model Law — use of extrinsic material

17 (1) For the purposes of interpreting the Model Law, reference may be made to the documents of:

(a) the United Nations Commission on International Trade Law; and
(b) its working group for the preparation of the Model Law;

relating to the Model Law.

(2) Subsection (1) does not affect the application of section 15AB of the Acts Interpretation Act 1901 for the purposes of interpreting this Part.

COMMENTARY ON SECTION 17

History of section .... [s 17-1]
Proper construction of the Act .... [s 17-2]
Documents .... [s 17-3]
Acts Interpretation Act 1901 (Cth) s 15AB .... [s 17-4]

[s 17-1] History of section Section 17 was introduced by the International Arbitration Amendment Act 1989 (Cth).

[s 17-2] Proper construction of the Act "The proper construction and interpretation of the *International Arbitration Act*, in respect of its implementation of the New York Convention and the Model Law requires an understanding of the context of those international instruments and an understanding of the subjects of concern and debate in the Working Groups, meetings and other discussion leading up to their formation. That is expressly called for by s 17 of the *International Arbitration Act* and the Australian common law of statutory interpretation" (*Comandate Marine Corp v Pan Australia Shipping Pty Ltd* (2006) 157 FCR 45; 238 ALR 457; [2006] FCAFC 192; BC200610833 at [191] (Allsop J)). See also the commentary in relation to s 2D and s 39 of the Act.

[s 17-3] Documents This section is intended to assist a court or an arbitral tribunal in construing the provisions of the Model Law. "These bodies should be able to have recourse to the relevant travaux preparatoires and, specifically, the documents of UNCITRAL and its working group in which the Model Law was discussed" (Explanatory Memorandum to the International Arbitration Amendment Bill 1988 (Cth) at [7]). These UNCITRAL documents may be accessed freely on the internet at www.uncitral.org. For an analysis of the principles of interpretation of statutes with an international background including the use of *travaux préparatoires*, see the paper presented to the NSW Bar Association on 18 March 2005, by Allsop J, as he then was, entitled *Statutes: Some Comments on Context and Meaning* at pp 8–14. Allsop J noted at p 13: "It is no doubt true that *travaux préparatoires* (or, indeed, any extrinsic material) should not be viewed as an open cut mine from which to extract helpful tonnage of verbiage. But the *travaux* can be an invaluable source of understanding the bargaining and the compromises which are incorporated in, often general, language. The *travaux* may not point directly to the answer; but they may clearly reveal the ebb and flow of debate which was compromised by the words in question. As such, they may not themselves point to a definite intention, but they may give depth to any understanding of the foundation of any compromise involved in the words of the convention ..."

[s 17-4] Acts Interpretation Act 1901 (Cth) s 15AB The use of extrinsic material in the interpretation of an Act, provides:

(1) Subject to subsection (3), in the interpretation of a provision of an Act, if any material not forming pArt of the Act is capable of assisting in the ascertainment of the meaning of the provision, consideration may be given to that material:
   (a) to confirm that the meaning of the provision is the ordinary meaning conveyed by the text of the provision taking into account its context in the Act and the purpose or object underlying the Act; or
   (b) to determine the meaning of the provision when:
      (i) the provision is ambiguous or obscure; or
      (ii) the ordinary meaning conveyed by the text of the provision taking into account its context in the Act and the purpose or object underlying the Act leads to a result that is manifestly absurd or is unreasonable.
(2) Without limiting the generality of subsection (1), the material that may be considered in accordance with that subsection in the interpretation of a provision of an Act includes:
   (a) all matters not forming part of the Act that are set out in the document containing the text of the Act as printed by the Government Printer;

(b) any relevant report of a Royal Commission, Law Reform Commission, committee of inquiry or other similar body that was laid before either House of the Parliament before the time when the provision was enacted;

(c) any relevant report of a committee of the Parliament or of either House of the Parliament that was made to the Parliament or that House of the Parliament before the time when the provision was enacted;

(d) any treaty or other international agreement that is referred to in the Act;

(e) any explanatory memorandum relating to the Bill containing the provision, or any other relevant document, that was laid before, or furnished to the members of, either House of the Parliament by a Minister before the time when the provision was enacted;

(f) the speech made to a House of the Parliament by a Minister on the occasion of the moving by that Minister of a motion that the Bill containing the provision be read a second time in that House;

(g) any document (whether or not a document to which a preceding paragraph applies) that is declared by the Act to be a relevant document for the purposes of this section; and

(h) any relevant material in the Journals of the Senate, in the Votes and Proceedings of the House of Representatives or in any official record of debates in the Parliament or either House of the Parliament.

(3) In determining whether consideration should be given to any material in accordance with subsection (1), or in considering the weight to be given to any such material, regard shall be had, in addition to any other relevant matters, to:

(a) the desirability of persons being able to rely on the ordinary meaning conveyed by the text of the provision taking into account its context in the Act and the purpose or object underlying the Act; and

(b) the need to avoid prolonging legal or other proceedings without compensating advantage.

For a detailed discussion of the operation of s 15AB, see DC Pearce and RS Geddes, *Statutory Interpretation in Australia*, LexisNexis, Sydney, 2011, pp 82–8.

[s 18] Court or authority taken to have been specified in Article 6 of the Model Law

18 (1) A court or authority prescribed for the purposes of this subsection is taken to have been specified in Article 6 of the Model Law as a court or authority competent to perform the functions referred to in Article 11(3) of the Model Law.

(2) A court or authority prescribed for the purposes of this subsection is taken to have been specified in Article 6 of the Model Law as a court or authority competent to perform the functions referred to in Article 11(4) of the Model Law.

(3) The following courts are taken to have been specified in Article 6 of the Model Law as courts competent to perform the functions referred to in Articles 13(3), 14, 16(3) and 34(2) of the Model Law:
  (a) if the place of arbitration is, or is to be, in a State — the Supreme Court of that State;
  (b) if the place of arbitration is, or is to be, in a Territory:
     (i) the Supreme Court of that Territory; or
     (ii) if there is no Supreme Court established in that Territory — the Supreme Court of the State or Territory that has jurisdiction in relation to that Territory;
  (c) in any case — the Federal Court of Australia.

COMMENTARY ON SECTION 18

"authority prescribed for the purposes of this subsection" .... [s 18-1]

[s 18-1] "authority prescribed for the purposes of this subsection"
The Australian Centre for International Commercial Arbitration (ACICA) has been prescribed for the purposes of s 18(1) and (2), pursuant to clause 4 of the International Arbitration Regulations 2011 (Cth), made under s 40 of the Act and ACICA now has authority to perform the functions found in Arts 11(3) and (4).

[s 18A] Article 12 — justifiable doubts as to the impartiality or independence of an arbitrator

18A (1) For the purposes of Article 12(1) of the Model Law, there are justifiable doubts as to the impartiality or independence of a person approached in connection with a possible appointment as arbitrator only if there is a real danger of bias on the part of that person in conducting the arbitration.

(2) For the purposes of Article 12(2) of the Model Law, there are justifiable doubts as to the impartiality or independence of an arbitrator only if there is a real danger of bias on the part of the arbitrator in conducting the arbitration.

COMMENTARY ON SECTION 18A

History of section .... [s 18A-1]
Test for apprehended bias .... [s 18A-2]
Test in *R v Gough* .... [s 18A-3]
Application to "Arb-Med" situations .... [s 18A-4]

[s 18A-1] History of section The International Arbitration Amendment Act 2010 (Cth) inserted s 18A into the Act to introduce the test in *R v Gough* [1993] AC 646; [1993] 2 All ER 724; [1993] 2 WLR 883; (1993) 97 Cr App Rep 188, discussed below.

[s 18A-2] Test for apprehended bias There is an obligation on arbitrators under Art 12(1) of the Model Law to disclose any circumstances likely to give rise to justifiable doubts as to the arbitrators' impartiality or independence. This obligation attaches from the moment an arbitrator is approached about an appointment and continues throughout the appointment. Article 12(2) provides that an arbitrator may be challenged "only if circumstances exist that give rise to justifiable doubts as to his impartiality or independence, or if he does not possess qualifications agreed to by the parties". In Australia, the test for bias that has traditionally been applied to arbitrators is the same as that applied to judges. That test is whether a fair minded lay observer might reasonably apprehend that the arbitrator might not bring an impartial mind to the resolution of the dispute; see, eg, in relation to arbitrators, *ICT Pty Ltd v Sea Containers Ltd* [2002] NSWSC 77; BC200200385 at [27], affirmed on appeal at [2002] NSWCA 84, and in relation to judges, *British American Tobacco Australia Services Ltd v Laurie* (2011) 242 CLR 283; 273 ALR 429; [2011] HCA 2; BC201100308 at [104] (Heydon, Kiefel and Bell JJ).

[s 18A-3] Test in *R v Gough* During the Review of the Act following the release of the Discussion Paper in late 2008 a suggestion was made to adopt the approach taken to bias in the United Kingdom (Revised Explanatory Memorandum to the International Arbitration Amendment Bill 2010 (Cth) at [83]–[91]). The test applied in *R v Gough* [1993] AC 646; [1993] 2 All ER 724; [1993] 2 WLR 883; (1993) 97 Cr App Rep 188 was, "having ascertained the relevant circumstances, the court should ask itself whether, having regard to those circumstances, there was a *real danger of bias* on the part of the relevant member of the tribunal in question, in the sense that he might unfairly regard (or have unfairly regarded) with favour, or disfavour, the case of a party to the issue under consideration by him"; see Lord Goff at AC 670 (emphasis added) where it was expressly stated that this approach should apply to arbitrators, although this was not at issue in the decision. This approach of a real danger of bias test has been applied subsequently in the UK, eg, in *Porter v Magill* [2002] 2 AC 357; [2002] 1 All ER 465; [2002] 2 WLR 37; [2001] UKHL 6; and *R v Abdroikov* [2008] 1 All ER 315; [2007] All ER (D) 226 (Oct); [2007] 1 WLR 2679; [2007] UKHL 37 at [15], but was "not accepted" by the High Court of Australia in *British American Tobacco Australia Services Ltd v Laurie* (2011) 242 CLR 283; 273 ALR 429; [2011] HCA 2; BC201100308 at [36] (French CJ), where the court was considering a challenge to a judge. See generally, S Lutteral, "Australia Adopts the 'Real Danger' Test for Arbitrator Bias", (2010) *Arbitration International*, Vol 26, Issue 4, p 625.

[s 18A-4] Application to "Arb-Med" situations In the case of *Gao Haiyan v Keeneye Holdings Ltd* [2011] HKCFI 240, the enforcement of an award was refused, as it would be "contrary to the public policy" of the enforcement court under the equivalent of Art V(2)(b) of the New York Convention. During the arbitration a form of mediation occurred which involved a member of the arbitral panel. The enforcing court refused to enforce the award as it found that the procedure at the mediation was not in accordance with that contemplated by the applicable arbitration rules and was such as give rise to a "real risk of bias" on the part of the arbitral tribunal, as discussed in *Porter v Magill* [2002] 2 AC 357; [2002] 1 All ER 465; [2002] 2 WLR 37; [2001] UKHL 6 and now enacted in s 18A of the Act for the purposes of Art 12 of the Model Law. See also the discussion of s 8(7) above.

[s 18B] Article 17B — preliminary orders

18B Despite Article 17B of the Model Law:
(a) no party to an arbitration agreement may make an application for a preliminary order directing another party not to frustrate the purpose of an interim measure requested; and
(b) no arbitral tribunal may grant such a preliminary order.

COMMENTARY ON SECTION 18B
History of section .... [s 18B-1]

[s 18B-1] History of section The International Arbitration Amendment Act 2010 (Cth) inserted s 18B into the Act. The 2006 amendments to the Model Law included the introduction of Art 17B, which conferred on the arbitral tribunal the power to make a preliminary order on the application of a party "without notice to any other party" (Art 17B(1)). During the review of the Act, objections were made primarily on the basis that "such measures are inconsistent with the consensual underpinning of arbitration" (Revised Explanatory Memorandum to the International Arbitration Amendment Bill 2010 (Cth) at [74]). Accordingly, as a result of this section, despite Art 17B of the Model Law, preliminary orders which are made ex parte are not available under the Act or the Model Law.

[s 18C] Article 18 — reasonable opportunity to present case

18C For the purposes of Article 18 of the Model Law, a party to arbitral proceedings is taken to have been given a full opportunity to present the party's case if the party is given a reasonable opportunity to present the party's case.

COMMENTARY ON SECTION 18C
History of section .... [s 18C-1]
Development of this principle in international arbitration .... [s 18C-2]

[s 18C-1] History of section The International Arbitration Amendment Act 2010 (Cth) inserted s 18C into the Act. This provision arose out of a need by arbitral tribunals to have "a wide degree of discretion to manage proceedings and even truncate them where this would be in the interests of the parties by achieving a speedy resolution of their dispute. The requirement in Article 18 that parties be given a 'full opportunity' to present their case poses a potential impediment to the effective management of the proceedings by the arbitral tribunal" (Revised Explanatory Memorandum to the International Arbitration Amendment Bill 2010 (Cth) at [95]). When the section was introduced it was noted that the proposed s 18C is consistent with, or similar to, approaches taken in other jurisdictions such as Mauritius, New Zealand, Singapore, the UK, Hong Kong and Malaysia (at [97]).

[s 18C-2] Development of this principle in international arbitration Article 18 of the Model Law embodies the twin fundamental principles of international commercial arbitration, which are that each party must be treated with equality and that each party must be given an opportunity to present its case. A consideration of the development of the latter principle that a party must be given an opportunity to present its case suggests that this amendment may not have been necessary.

Article V(1)(b) of the 1958 New York Convention introduced the principle that the enforcement of an award may be refused if the party against whom the award is invoked "was unable" to present its case before the arbitral tribunal. This language had changed by the time the 1985 UNCITRAL Model Law was written. In Art 18 of the Model Law the requirement had become that each party shall be given a "full opportunity" of presenting its case. The 1985 Model Law adopted the language of the 1976 UNICTRAL Arbitration Rules (r 15(1)), which required the arbitral tribunal to conduct the arbitration in such manner as it considers appropriate provided each party is given a "full opportunity" of presenting its case.

There was a change in emphasis adopted in 1996 by s 33(1)(a) of the Arbitration Act 1996 (Eng, W & NI) which requires the arbitral tribunal to give each party a "reasonable opportunity" of presenting its case and dealing with that of the opponent. This language was then adopted in Art 15(2) of the 1998 ICC Arbitration Rules, which required the arbitral tribunal to ensure that each party has a "reasonable opportunity" to present its case. When the UNCITRAL Model Law was being revised in 2006, the opportunity was not taken of changing the phrase in Art 18 from "full" opportunity of presenting a case to a "reasonable" opportunity of presenting a case. Nevertheless the opportunity passed and the language of the 2006 Model Law remains that of a "full opportunity" as used in the 1985 version of the Model Law. In contrast, UNCITRAL, when revising the UNCITRAL Arbitration Rules in 2010, did adopt the language of a "reasonable opportunity" and Art 17(1) of the 2010 UNCITRAL Arbitration Rules provides that "the arbitral tribunal may conduct the arbitration in such manner as it considers appropriate, provided that the parties are treated with equality and that at an appropriate stage of the proceedings each party is given a reasonable opportunity of presenting its case".

Against this background of international harmonisation and uniformity, it is perhaps understandable (although arguably not consistent with the ordinary meaning of the words) that the Hong Kong High Court in *Pacific China Holdings Ltd v Grand Pacific Holdings Ltd* [2011] HKHCFI 424 at [16], accepted a submission that the distinction between a "reasonable opportunity" under the 1998 ICC Arbitration Rules, and a "full opportunity" under the 2006 Model Law is "a distinction without a difference".

[s 19]   Articles 17I, 34 and 36 of Model Law — public policy

19 Without limiting the generality of Articles 17I(1)(b)(ii), 34(2)(b)(ii) and 36(1)(b)(ii) of the Model Law, it is declared, for the avoidance of any doubt, that, for the purposes of those Articles, an interim measure or award is in conflict with, or is contrary to, the public policy of Australia if:

(a) the making of the interim measure or award was induced or affected by fraud or corruption; or

(b) a breach of the rules of natural justice occurred in connection with the making of the interim measure or award.

COMMENTARY ON SECTION 19

History of section .... [s 19-1]
Cross-reference to s 8(7A) .... [s 19-2]

[s 19-1] History of section The International Arbitration Amendment Act 1989 (Cth) inserted s 19 into the Act when the Model Law was adopted in Australia. The section was confined to "awards" covered by Arts 34(2)(b)(ii) and 36(1)(b)(iii) of the Model Law. This provision was repealed and the present wording substituted by the International Arbitration Amendment Act 2010 (Cth), making two changes. First, it extended the reach of the section to include an interim measure covered by Art 17I(1)(b)(ii) of the Model Law. Second, it added the words "is in conflict with, or is contrary to" public policy in recognition that there is a corresponding slight difference in the wording between Arts 34(2)(b)(ii) and 36(1)(b)(ii).

The drafting of the public policy varies slightly as between Arts 34 and 36. Article 34 provides that a court may set aside an award if the award "is in conflict with" public policy. By way of contrast, Art 36 allows a court to refuse to recognise or enforce an award where it finds that to do so "would be contrary to" public policy. The 2010 amendment was made to ensure that s 19 applies to both situations (Revised Explanatory Memorandum to the International Arbitration Amendment Bill 2010 (Cth) at [104]–[105]).

[s 19-2] Cross-reference to s 8(7A) Note also the discussion above of s 8(7A) which has a similar operation in award enforcement proceedings brought under s 8.

[s 20] Chapter VIII of Model Law not to apply in certain cases

20 Where, but for this section, both Chapter VIII of the Model Law and Part II of this Act would apply in relation to an award, Chapter VIII of the Model Law does not apply in relation to the award.

COMMENTARY ON SECTION 20

History of section .... [s 20-1]

[s 20-1] History of section The International Arbitration Amendment Act 1989 (Cth) inserted s 20 into the Act when the Model Law was adopted in Australia. Section 8, which is found in Pt II of the Act, had established a regime for the recognition and enforcement of foreign arbitral awards based on the provisions of the New York Convention. Chapter VIII of the Model Law contains a similar regime based on almost identical provisions in Art 36. The possibility of the dual application of s 8 and Art 36 was avoided by the insertion of s 20. This provision "accords with Article 1(1) of the Model Law" which states that the provisions of the Model Law apply subject to any agreement in force between Australia and other States (Explanatory Memorandum to the International Arbitration Amendment Bill 1988 (Cth) at [10]). The New York Convention is such an agreement which had been implemented by the prior enactment of s 8 in 1974.

[s 21] Model Law covers the field

21 If the Model Law applies to an arbitration, the law of a State or Territory relating to arbitration does not apply to that arbitration.

COMMENTARY ON SECTION 21

History of section	[s 21-1]
Original terms of section	[s 21-2]
2010 change in approach	[s 21-3]

[s 21-1] History of section The International Arbitration Amendment Act 1989 (Cth) inserted s 21 into the Act. The International Arbitration Amendment Act 2010 (Cth) then repealed and replaced the section in its present terms.

[s 21-2] Original terms of section Section 21 as originally enacted in 1989 was headed "Settlement of dispute otherwise than in accordance with Model Law", and provided:

21. If the parties to an arbitration agreement have (whether in the agreement or in any other document in writing) agreed that any dispute that has arisen or may arise between them is to be settled otherwise than in accordance with the Model Law, the Model Law does not apply in relation to the settlement of that dispute.

[s 21-3] 2010 change in approach The Attorney-General's 2008 Discussion Paper (referred to above in [s 8-1]) noted that one of the objectives of the review was to ensure that the Act provided "a comprehensive and clear framework governing international arbitration in Australia". The operation of s 21 had caused considerable practical and interpretive problems. For example, in *Australian Granites Ltd v Eisenwerk Hensel Bayreuth Dipl-Ing Burkhardt GmbH* [2001] 1 Qd R 461; BC9904474, the Queensland Court of Appeal held that by adopting the International Chamber of Commerce Rules of Arbitration, the parties had opted out of the Model Law. This interpretation was seen as "unsatisfactory because parties nominating either the ICC Rules or the Australian Centre for International Commercial Arbitration Rules (which are both procedural rules) would then be taken to have opted out of the Model Law in its entirety and be unable to pursue certain avenues of relief provided for in the Model Law . . . The rationale for allowing the parties to choose their own procedural rules is that they may tailor the rules to suit their specific wishes. This should not amount to ousting the Model Law completely" (Revised Explanatory Memorandum to the International Arbitration Amendment Bill 2010 (Cth) at [113]).

The Revised Explanatory Memorandum also noted (at [116]) that a number of decisions had undermined the "exclusivity" of the Act in governing international commercial arbitration in Australia. In *American Diagnostica Inc v Gradipore Ltd* (1998) 44 NSWLR 312; BC9800877, the court held that international arbitrations in Australia continued to be regulated by State and Territory laws governing commercial arbitration. A similar view was expressed in *Raguz v Sullivan* (2000) 50 NSWLR 236 at 249; [2000] NSWCA 240; BC200005212 (Spigelman CJ and Mason P), where it was said that State courts retained the power to remove the arbitrator in an international arbitration and to exercise "supervisory jurisdiction to police arbitrators' misconduct" under provisions such as ss 42 and 44 of the now repealed Commercial Arbitration Act 1984 (NSW). The uncertainty caused by the various State and Territory laws on arbitration being applicable to an international arbitration in addition to the Act (and with it the Model Law), was compounded by the debate then taking place as to whether these decisions were being correctly decided. On 16 August 2008 the Hon Justice RV Gyles AO, when speaking at the New Zealand Bar Association Conference in Sydney, said " . . . [i]t seems to have been assumed that [the State and Territory uniform commercial arbitration Acts] apply to international commercial arbitrations conducted in Australia, at least those with the seat of the arbitration being in Australia. In my opinion, that is debatable in view of the operation of s 109 of the Australian Constitution, which provides that Commonwealth law prevails in the event of an inconsistency between Commonwealth law and State law . . . The decision in *American Diagnostica Inc v Gradipore Ltd* (1998) 44 NSWLR 312; BC9800877 found that the [State legislation] applied, but the s 109 point was not argued". This uncertainty and debate provided a disincentive for international commercial arbitration taking place in Australia. The regulation of international commercial arbitration has evolved and developed as a product of international conferences (eg, the 1958 New York Convention) and of the work of international organisations such as UNCITRAL (eg, the Model Law) and the International Bar Association (eg, the IBA Rules on the Taking of Evidence in International Arbitration, and the IBA Guidelines on Conflict of Interest in International Arbitration). This evolutionary process involves continual public discussion and examination of the features of national arbitration laws and the consequences of those laws applying to international arbitrations taking place in a particular country. National laws are often compared to the Model Law, which is regarded as being the benchmark of arbitration laws applicable to an international commercial arbitration. The "suitability", or otherwise, of different arbitration laws is frequently raised in these discussions and conferences. An examination of the suitability of national arbitration laws, which are potentially applicable to an international arbitration, is seen as critical in determining the venue for the arbitration. The importance of this consideration is evidenced in the UNCITRAL 1996 publication, "Notes on Organising Arbitral Proceedings," which provides in para 22 the following:

> Various factual and legal factors influence the choice of the place of arbitration, and their relative importance varies from case to case. Among the more prominent factors are:
> (a) *suitability of the law on arbitral procedure of the place of arbitration* . . . [emphasis added]

The uncertainty as to which laws apply to international arbitrations in Australia and the possible overlapping operation of the State and Federal laws cast some doubt on the "suitability" of the state of the law then applicable to arbitral procedure for international arbitrations in Australia. This uncertainty provided a positive disincentive for those parties involved in international arbitrations to agree to their arbitrations taking place wholly or partly in Australia.

It was noted in the Revised Explanatory Memorandum to the International Arbitration Amendment Bill 2010 (Cth) that "there was strong support from stakeholders for making the Act the exclusive law governing international arbitration in Australia" (at [117]). As a result s 21 was rewritten and the ability to opt out of the Model Law was removed, and the laws of a State or Territory relating to arbitration no longer apply to an arbitration governed by the Model Law.

It should be noted that the uncertainty created by *Australian Granites Ltd v Eisenwerk Hensel Bayreuth Dipl-Ing Burkhardt GmbH* [2001] 1 Qd R 461; BC9904474, was both removed by the decisions in *Wagners Nouvelle Caledonie Sarl v Vale Inco Nouvelle Caledonie SAS* [2010] QCA 219; BC201005964 and *Cargill International SA v Peabody Australia Mining Ltd* [2010] NSWSC 887; BC201005660, and revived by the ACT Supreme Court in *Lightsource Technologies Australia Pty Ltd v Pointsec Mobile Technologies AB* (2011) 250 FLR 63; [2011] ACTSC 59; BC201102227 at [108]–[112] which, it is submitted, was wrongly decided. See the discussion above at [s 7-5].

DIVISION 3 — ADDITIONAL PROVISIONS

[s 22] Application of additional provisions

22 (1) **Application to arbitration under Model Law** This Division applies to any arbitration to which the Model Law applies.

(2) **Application of sections 23, 23A, 23B, 23J, 23K, 25, 26 and 27** Each of the following sections applies to arbitral proceedings commenced in reliance on an arbitration agreement unless the parties to the agreement agree (whether in the agreement or otherwise in writing) that it will not apply:

 (a) section 23;
 (b) section 23A;
 (c) section 23B;
 (d) section 23J;
 (e) section 23K;
 (f) section 25;
 (g) section 26;
 (h) section 27.

(3) **Application of sections 23C, 23D, 23E, 23F and 23G** The following sections apply to arbitral proceedings commenced in reliance on an arbitration agreement if the parties to the agreement agree (whether in the agreement or otherwise in writing) that they will apply:

 (a) section 23C;
 (b) section 23D;
 (c) section 23E;
 (d) section 23F;
 (e) section 23G.

(4) **Application of section 23H** Section 23H applies on the death of a party to an arbitration agreement unless the parties to the agreement agree (whether in the agreement or otherwise in writing) that it will not apply.

(5) **Application of section 24** Section 24 applies to arbitral proceedings commenced in reliance on an arbitration agreement if the parties to the agreement agree (whether in the agreement or otherwise in writing) that it will apply.

COMMENTARY ON SECTION 22

History of section .... [s 22-1]

Additional provisions .... [s 22-2]
New approach .... [s 22-3]

[s 22-1] History of section The International Arbitration Amendment Act 1989 (Cth) inserted s 22 into the Act. As introduced the section provided that ss 23–27, which governed matters such as consolidation of arbitral proceedings, costs, interest up to the making of an award and interest on a debt under an award, would only apply if the parties "opt in" to those provisions by agreement in writing. The International Arbitration Amendment Act 2010 (Cth) repealed s 22 and inserted the replacement s 22, which defines the operation of the additional provisions in Pt III Div 3 as either applicable unless the parties agree that the provisions will not apply (the opt-out provisions) or applicable if the parties agree that the provisions will apply (the opt-in provisions). As the Model Law now covers the field as a result of s 21, parties to an arbitration governed by the Model Law no longer have access to the supportive provisions in State or Territory arbitration laws relating to matters such as subpoenas; the additional provisions were supplemented to meet this need.

[s 22-2] Additional provisions Part III Div 3 now includes a range of provisions which supplement the provisions of the Model Law. "A number of these provisions have been identified as fundamental tools that should be available by default in any arbitral proceedings unless expressly excluded — these provisions include those concerning court assistance in taking evidence, interest and costs. Others, such as the provisions concerning consolidation of arbitral proceedings and confidentiality, are matters to which the parties should expressly turn their minds before they apply" (Revised Explanatory Memorandum to the International Arbitration Amendment Bill 2010 (Cth) at [127]).

[s 22-3] New approach The following table, taken from the Explanatory Memorandum to the International Arbitration Amendment Bill 2010 (Cth), shows a summary of the effect of s 22:

Section	Description	Opt in/Opt out
23	Parties may obtain subpoenas	Opt out
23A	Failure to assist arbitral tribunal	Opt out
23B	Default by party to an arbitration agreement	Opt out
23C	Disclosure of confidential information	Opt in
23D	Circumstances in which confidential information may be disclosed	Opt in
23E	Arbitral tribunal may allow disclosure in certain circumstances	Opt in
23F	Court may prohibit disclosure in certain circumstances	Opt in
23G	Court may allow disclosure in certain circumstances	Opt in
23H	Death of a party to an arbitration agreement	Opt out
23J	Evidence	Opt out
23K	Security for costs	Opt out
24	Consolidation of arbitral proceedings	Opt in
25	Interest up to making of award	Opt out

Section	Description	Opt in/Opt out
26	Interest on debt under award	Opt out
27	Costs	Opt out

[s 22A] Interpretation

22A In this Division:

court means:
  (a) in relation to arbitral proceedings that are, or are to be, conducted in a State — the Supreme Court of that State; and
  (b) in relation to arbitral proceedings that are, or are to be, conducted in a Territory:
      (i) the Supreme Court of the Territory; or
      (ii) if there is no Supreme Court established in that Territory — the Supreme Court of the State or Territory that has jurisdiction in relation to that Territory; and
  (c) in any case — the Federal Court of Australia.

COMMENTARY ON SECTION 22A

History of section .... [s 22A-1]

[s 22A-1] History of section The International Arbitration Amendment Act 2010 (Cth) inserted s 22A into the Act.

[s 23] Parties may obtain subpoenas

23 (1) A party to arbitral proceedings commenced in reliance on an arbitration agreement may apply to a court to issue a subpoena under subsection (3).

(2) However, this may only be done with the permission of the arbitral tribunal conducting the arbitral proceedings.

(3) The court may, for the purposes of the arbitral proceedings, issue a subpoena requiring a person to do either or both of the following:
  (a) to attend for examination before the arbitral tribunal;
  (b) to produce to the arbitral tribunal the documents specified in the subpoena.

(4) A person must not be compelled under a subpoena issued under subsection (3) to answer any question or produce any document which that person could not be compelled to answer or produce in a proceeding before that court.

(5) The court must not issue a subpoena under subsection (3) to a person who is not a party to the arbitral proceedings unless the court is satisfied that it is reasonable in all the circumstances to issue it to the person.

(6) Nothing in this section limits Article 27 of the Model Law.

COMMENTARY ON SECTION 23

History of section .... [s 23-1]
Subpoenas .... [s 23-2]

Safeguards .... [s 23-3]

[s 23-1] History of section The International Arbitration Amendment Act 2010 (Cth) inserted s 23 into the Act.

[s 23-2] Subpoenas Prior to the amendments made in 2010, a party to an arbitration that wanted to subpoena a third party to attend and give evidence or produce documents, was required to make an application for a subpoena under the arbitration law of the particular State or Territory. As s 21 now provides that such laws do not operate if the Model Law applies to the arbitration it was necessary to expressly confer a power to seek this assistance from a court.

[s 23-3] Safeguards Section 23 contains "four important safeguards" (Revised Explanatory Memorandum to the International Arbitration Amendment Bill 2010 (Cth) at [138]). First, the party may only approach the court with the permission of the arbitral tribunal. Second, the court may only issue a subpoena "for the purposes of the arbitral proceedings". Third, before issuing a subpoena with respect to a person who is not a party to the arbitral proceedings, the court must be satisfied that "it is reasonable in all the circumstances". Fourth, a person must not be compelled to answer any question or produce any documents which that person could not be compelled to answer or produce "in a proceeding before a court".

[s 23A] Failure to assist arbitral tribunal

23A (1) A party to arbitral proceedings commenced in reliance on an arbitration agreement may apply to a court for an order under subsection (3) if a person:
  (a) refuses or fails to attend before the arbitral tribunal conducting the arbitral proceedings for examination when required to do so under a subpoena issued under subsection 23(3); or
  (b) refuses or fails to attend before the arbitral tribunal when required to do so by the arbitral tribunal; or
  (c) refuses or fails to produce a document that the person is required to produce under a subpoena issued under subsection 23(3); or
  (d) refuses or fails to produce a document that the person is required to produce by the arbitral tribunal; or
  (e) appearing as a witness before the arbitral tribunal:
    (i) refuses or fails to take an oath or to make an affirmation or affidavit when required by the arbitral tribunal to do so; or
    (ii) refuses or fails to answer a question that the witness is required by the arbitral tribunal to answer; or
  (f) refuses or fails to do any other thing which the arbitral tribunal may require to assist the arbitral tribunal in the performance of its functions.

(2) However, an application may only be made under paragraph (1)(b), (d), (e) or (f) with the permission of the arbitral tribunal.

(3) The court may, for the purposes of the arbitral proceedings, order:
  (a) the person to attend before the court for examination or to produce to the court the relevant document or to do the relevant thing; and

(b) the person, or any other person, to transmit to the arbitral tribunal one or more of the following:
  (i) a record of any evidence given in compliance with the order;
  (ii) any document produced in compliance with the order, or a copy of the document;
  (iii) particulars of any other thing done in compliance with the order.

(4) A person must not be compelled under an order made under subsection (3) to answer any question or produce any document which that person could not be compelled to answer or produce in a proceeding before that court.

(5) The court must not make an order under subsection (3) in relation to a person who is not a party to the arbitral proceedings unless:
  (a) before the order is made, the person is given an opportunity to make representations to the court; and
  (b) the court is satisfied that it is reasonable in all the circumstances to make the order in relation to the person.

(6) Nothing in this section limits Article 27 of the Model Law.

COMMENTARY ON SECTION 23A

History of section .... [s 23A-1]
Operation of section .... [s 23A-2]

[s 23A-1] History of section The International Arbitration Amendment Act 2010 (Cth) inserted s 23A into the Act.

[s 23A-2] Operation of section Section 23A allows a court to issue a range of orders where a person has failed to cooperate with an arbitral tribunal or has not complied with a subpoena issued under the new s 23 — this section contains three of the four safeguards that apply to s 23. There is no requirement to seek the consent of the arbitral tribunal in relation to an order concerning a subpoena, as the permission of the tribunal is required before an application for a subpoena can be made under s 23 (Revised Explanatory Memorandum to the International Arbitration Amendment Bill 2010 (Cth) at [145]).

[s 23B] Default by party to an arbitration agreement

23B (1) This section applies if a party to arbitral proceedings commenced in reliance on an arbitration agreement:
  (a) refuses or fails to attend before an arbitral tribunal for examination when required to do so under a subpoena issued under subsection 23(3) (regardless of whether an application is made for an order under subsection 23A(3)); or
  (b) refuses or fails to produce a document to an arbitral tribunal when required to do so under a subpoena issued under subsection 23(3) (regardless of whether an application is made for an order under subsection 23A(3)); or
  (c) refuses or fails to comply with an order made by a court under subsection 23A(3); or
  (d) fails within the time specified by an arbitral tribunal, or if no time is specified within a reasonable time, to comply with any other requirement made by the arbitral tribunal to assist it in the performance of its functions.

(2) The arbitral tribunal may continue with the arbitration proceedings in default of appearance or of the other act and make an award on the evidence before it.

(3) Nothing in this provision affects any other power which the arbitral tribunal or a court may have in relation to the refusal or failure.

COMMENTARY ON SECTION 23B
History of section .... [s 23B-1]
Operation of section .... [s 23B-2]

[s 23B-1] History of section The International Arbitration Amendment Act 2010 (Cth) inserted s 23B into the Act.

[s 23B-2] Operation of section Section 23B sets out the consequences of failing to comply with a subpoena, an order from the court or a requirement of the arbitral tribunal. The section supplements Art 25 of the Model Law, which also addresses the failure of a party to communicate a statement of claim, or a statement of defence or to appear at a hearing or produce documentary evidence.

[s 23C] Disclosure of confidential information

23C (1) The parties to arbitral proceedings commenced in reliance on an arbitration agreement must not disclose confidential information in relation to the arbitral proceedings unless:
    (a) the disclosure is allowed under section 23D; or
    (b) the disclosure is allowed under an order made under section 23E and no order is in force under section 23F prohibiting that disclosure; or
    (c) the disclosure is allowed under an order made under section 23G.

(2) An arbitral tribunal must not disclose confidential information in relation to arbitral proceedings commenced in reliance on an arbitration agreement unless:
    (a) the disclosure is allowed under section 23D; or
    (b) the disclosure is allowed under an order made under section 23E and no order is in force under section 23F prohibiting that disclosure; or
    (c) the disclosure is allowed under an order made under section 23G.

COMMENTARY ON SECTION 23C
History of section .... [s 23C-1]
Confidentiality .... [s 23C-2]
New Zealand position .... [s 23C-3]
Sections only apply if parties agree they will apply ..... [s 23C-4]

[s 23C-1] History of section The International Arbitration Amendment Act 2010 (Cth) inserted s 23C into the Act, as well as the related provisions dealing with confidentiality — the definition of "confidential information" in s 15(1) and ss 23D, 23E, 23F and 23G.

[s 23C-2] Confidentiality In Australia the common law recognises the private nature of arbitration proceedings. On the other hand, accepting that the hearing is private, and that strangers may be excluded, does not mean that an arbitration hearing is confidential in the sense that there is a power to prohibit disclosure or publication of the hearing, or an obligation to keep the proceedings and matters disclosed in the proceedings confidential.

In *Esso Australia Resources Ltd v Plowman* (1995) 183 CLR 10 at 28–9; 128 ALR 391; 69 ALJR 404; BC9506416, Mason CJ noted that "for various reasons, complete confidentiality of the proceedings in an arbitration cannot be achieved". These reasons included:
  (i) no obligation of confidence attaches to witnesses who are free to disclose their knowledge of the process;
  (ii) there are various circumstances when the award may come before a public court, such as on an application for enforcement;
  (iii) an arbitrating party must be entitled to disclose to third parties the existence of the proceedings and the award, for example under an insurance policy, or under an obligation to disclose assets and liabilities such as disclosure by corporations to shareholders and regulatory authorities.

Accordingly, the High Court held that there is no implied term in an arbitration agreement imposing an obligation of confidentiality on parties.

In contrast, in England, confidentiality is recognised "in the sense of an implied agreement that documents disclosed or generated in arbitration can only be used for the purposes of the arbitration" (*Emmott v Michael Wilson & Partners Ltd* [2008] 2 All ER (Comm) 193; [2008] All ER (D) 162 (Mar); [2008] 1 Lloyd's Rep 616; [2008] EWCA Civ 184 at [79] (Lawrence Collins LJ)). English law does recognise exceptions to this principle (which to some extent mirror the reasons for the lack of any general principle of confidentiality in Australia). These exceptions (discussed at [93]–[107]) include:
  (i) "compulsion of law";
  (ii) "duty to the public requiring disclosure";
  (iii) "disclosure . . . permissible when, and to the extent to which, it was reasonably necessary for the establishment or protection of an arbitrating party's legal rights vis-à-vis a third party in order to found a cause of action against that third party or to defend a claim, or counterclaim"; and
  (iv) "circumstances where there has been express or implied consent".

The exception relating to the public duty may be alternatively expressed as: that disclosure is permissible "where the interests of justice require disclosure" (Lawrence Collins LJ at [107]). The Court of Appeal emphasised that the limits of this obligation of confidentiality "are still in the process of development on a case-by-case basis" (at [107] and see Thomas LJ at [117]).

[s 23C-3] New Zealand position Following the decision of the High Court in *Esso Australia Resources Ltd v Plowman* (1995) 183 CLR 10; 128 ALR 391; 69 ALJR 404; BC9506416, New Zealand introduced s 14 into the Arbitration Act 1996 (NZ), "which gave blanket confidentiality to arbitral proceedings as of rights . . . to negative the *Esso* decision" (A Willy, *Arbitration*, Thomson Reuters, Wellington, 2010, pp 128–9). Section 14 provided that an arbitration agreement, unless otherwise agreed by the parties, is deemed to provide that the parties shall not publish, disclose, or communicate any information relating to arbitral proceedings under the agreement or to an award made in those proceedings. This statutory "cloak of confidentiality" did not extend to enforcement proceedings

(*Television New Zealand Ltd v Langley Productions Ltd* [2000] 2 NZLR 250 at 255). This section was later revised, in 2007, following a report by the New Zealand Law Commission: Improving the Arbitration Act 1996, NZLC R83, 2003. These New Zealand provisions were used as the basis for the drafting of the optional confidentiality regime now found in ss 23C–23E of the Act (Revised Explanatory Memorandum to the International Arbitration Amendment Bill 2010 (Cth) at [153]).

The optional nature of this confidentiality regime is unusual in that the arbitration rules of most international arbitration institutions include extensive confidentiality regimes, which apply as a matter of contract to arbitrations conducted under those rules. See, for example, Art 18 of the Australian Centre for International Commercial Arbitration Rules, and see generally, M Hwang SC and K Chung, "Defining the Indefinable: Practical Problems of Confidentiality in Arbitration", 2009 *Journal of International Arbitration* 26(5), pp 609–45.

[s 23C-4] **Sections only apply if parties agree they will apply**   It should be noted that s 22(3) provides that ss 23C–23G apply to an arbitration "if the parties . . . agree . . . that they will apply".

[s 23D] Circumstances in which confidential information may be disclosed

23D   (1) This section sets out the circumstances in which confidential information in relation to arbitral proceedings may be disclosed by:

    (a) a party to the arbitral proceedings; or

    (b) an arbitral tribunal.

(2) The information may be disclosed with the consent of all of the parties to the arbitral proceedings.

(3) The information may be disclosed to a professional or other adviser of any of the parties to the arbitral proceedings.

(4) The information may be disclosed if it is necessary to ensure that a party to the arbitral proceedings has a full opportunity to present the party's case and the disclosure is no more than reasonable for that purpose.

(5) The information may be disclosed if it is necessary for the establishment or protection of the legal rights of a party to the arbitral proceedings in relation to a third party and the disclosure is no more than reasonable for that purpose.

(6) The information may be disclosed if it is necessary for the purpose of enforcing an arbitral award and the disclosure is no more than reasonable for that purpose.

(7) The information may be disclosed if it is necessary for the purposes of this Act, or the Model Law as in force under subsection 16(1) of this Act, and the disclosure is no more than reasonable for that purpose.

(8) The information may be disclosed if the disclosure is in accordance with an order made or a subpoena issued by a court.

(9) The information may be disclosed if the disclosure is authorised or required by another relevant law, or required by a competent regulatory body, and the person making the disclosure gives written details of the disclosure including an explanation of reasons for the disclosure to:

    (a) if the person is a party to the arbitral proceedings — the other parties to the proceedings and the arbitral tribunal; and

(b) if the arbitral tribunal is making the disclosure — all the parties to the proceedings.

(10) In subsection (9):

another relevant law means:
  (a) a law of the Commonwealth, other than this Act; and
  (b) a law of a State or Territory; and
  (c) a law of a foreign country, or of a part of a foreign country:
    (i) in which a party to the arbitration agreement has its principal place of business; or
    (ii) in which a substantial part of the obligations of the commercial relationship are to be performed; or
    (iii) to which the subject matter of the dispute is most commonly connected.

COMMENTARY ON SECTION 23D

History of section .... [s 23D-1]

[s 23D-1] History of section The International Arbitration Amendment Act 2010 (Cth) introduced s 23D into the Act as part of the optional regime of confidentiality; see the commentary to s 23C above.

[s 23E] Arbitral tribunal may allow disclosure in certain circumstances

23E (1) An arbitral tribunal may make an order allowing a party to arbitral proceedings to disclose confidential information in relation to the proceedings in circumstances other than those mentioned in section 23D.

(2) An order under subsection (1) may only be made at the request of one of the parties to the arbitral proceedings and after giving each of the parties to the arbitral proceedings the opportunity to be heard.

COMMENTARY ON SECTION 23E

History of section .... [s 23E-1]

[s 23E-1] History of section The International Arbitration Amendment Act 2010 (Cth) introduced s 23E into the Act as part of the optional regime of confidentiality; see the commentary to s 23C above.

[s 23F] Court may prohibit disclosure in certain circumstances

23F (1) A court may make an order prohibiting a party to arbitral proceedings from disclosing confidential information in relation to the arbitral proceedings if:
  (a) the court is satisfied in the circumstances of the particular case that the public interest in preserving the confidentiality of arbitral proceedings is not outweighed by other considerations that render it desirable in the public interest for the information to be disclosed; or
  (b) the disclosure is more than is reasonable for that purpose.

(2) An order under subsection (1) may only be made on the application of a party to the arbitral proceedings and after giving each of the parties to the arbitral proceedings the opportunity to be heard.

(3) A party to arbitral proceedings may only apply for an order under subsection (1) if the arbitral tribunal has made an order under subsection 23E(1) allowing the disclosure of the information.

(4) The court may order that the confidential information not be disclosed pending the outcome of the application under subsection (2).

(5) An order under this section is final.

COMMENTARY ON SECTION 23F
History of section .... [s 23F-1]

[s 23F-1] History of section The International Arbitration Amendment Act 2010 (Cth) introduced s 23F into the Act as part of the optional regime of confidentiality; see the commentary to s 23C above.

[s 23G] Court may allow disclosure in certain circumstances

23G (1) A court may make an order allowing a party to arbitral proceedings to disclose confidential information in relation to the arbitral proceedings in circumstances other than those mentioned in section 23D if:
    (a) the court is satisfied, in the circumstances of the particular case, that the public interest in preserving the confidentiality of arbitral proceedings is outweighed by other considerations that render it desirable in the public interest for the information to be disclosed; and
    (b) the disclosure is not more than is reasonable for that purpose.

(2) An order under subsection (1) may only be made on the application of a person who is or was a party to the arbitral proceedings and after giving each person who is or was a party to the arbitral proceedings the opportunity to be heard.

(3) A party to arbitral proceedings may only apply for an order under subsection (1) if:
    (a) the mandate of the arbitral tribunal has been terminated under Article 32 of the Model Law; or
    (b) a request by the party to the arbitral tribunal to make an order under subsection 23E(1) allowing the disclosure has been refused.

(4) An order under this section is final.

COMMENTARY ON SECTION 23G
History of section .... [s 23G-1]

[s 23G-1] History of section The International Arbitration Amendment Act 2010 (Cth) introduced s 23G into the Act as part of the optional regime of confidentiality; see the commentary to s 23C above.

[s 23H] Death of a party to an arbitration agreement

23H (1) If a party to an arbitration agreement dies:
    (a) the agreement is not discharged (either in respect of the deceased or any other party); and

(b) the authority of an arbitral tribunal is not revoked; and
(c) the arbitration agreement is enforceable by or against the personal representative of the deceased.

(2) Nothing in subsection (1) is taken to affect the operation of any enactment or rule of law by virtue of which a right of action is extinguished by the death of a person.

COMMENTARY ON SECTION 23H
History of section .... [s 23H-1]
Section applies unless parties agree otherwise .... [s 23H-2]

[s 23H-1] History of section The International Arbitration Amendment Act 2010 (Cth) introduced s 23H into the Act. Prior to the amendments made in 2010, both the Act and the Model Law did not address the consequences of the death of a party to an arbitration agreement. The effect of this provision is to provide that the death of a party does not discharge the arbitration agreement or revoke the authority of the arbitral tribunal.

[s 23H-2] Section applies unless parties agree otherwise Section 23H applies unless the parties agree, in the arbitration agreement or otherwise "in writing", that it will not apply (s 22(4)).

[s 23J] Evidence

23J (1) An arbitral tribunal may, at any time before the award is issued by which a dispute that is arbitrated by the tribunal is finally decided, make an order:
(a) allowing the tribunal or a person specified in the order to inspect, photograph, observe or conduct experiments on evidence that is in the possession of a party to the arbitral proceedings and that may be relevant to those proceedings (the *relevant evidence*); and
(b) allowing a sample of the relevant evidence to be taken by the tribunal or a person specified in the order.

(2) The tribunal may only specify a person in the order if the person is:
(a) a party to the proceedings; or
(b) an expert appointed by the tribunal under Article 26 of the Model Law; or
(c) an expert appointed by a party to the proceedings with the permission of the tribunal.

(3) The provisions of the Model Law apply in relation to an order under this section in the same way as they would apply to an interim measure under the Model Law.

COMMENTARY ON SECTION 23J
History of section .... [s 23J-1]
Evidence .... [s 23J-2]
Section applies unless parties agree otherwise .... [s 23J-3]

[s 23J-1] History of section The International Arbitration Amendment Act 2010 (Cth) introduced s 23J into the Act and inserted a "cover the field" provision in s 21 of the Act, which removed the parties' ability to have recourse to the provisions of State and Territory arbitration legislation for judicial assistance and support, eg, s 47 of the uniform Commercial Arbitration legislation. Section 23J was inserted into the Act to "compensate" for this removal, as the Model Law is not a complete law on arbitration (Revised Explanatory Memorandum to the International Arbitration Amendment Bill 2010 (Cth) at [164]–[168]).

[s 23J-2] **Evidence** Section 23J deals with orders with respect to evidence and confers power on an arbitral tribunal to order various matters such as allowing the tribunal or a person to inspect, photograph, observe or conduct experiments on evidence in the possession of a party to the proceedings and allowing the tribunal or a person to take a sample of such evidence.

[s 23J-3] **Section applies unless parties agree otherwise** Section 23J applies to arbitral proceedings unless the parties agree, in the arbitration agreement or otherwise "in writing", that it will not apply (s 22(2)(d)).

[s 23K] Security for costs

23K (1) An arbitral tribunal may, at any time before the award is issued by which a dispute that is arbitrated by the tribunal is finally decided, order a party to the arbitral proceedings to pay security for costs.

(2) However, the tribunal must not make such an order solely on the basis that:
   (a) the party is not ordinarily resident in Australia; or
   (b) the party is a corporation incorporated or an association formed under the law of a foreign country; or
   (c) the party is a corporation or association the central management or control of which is exercised in a foreign country.

(3) The provisions of the Model Law apply in relation to an order under this section in the same way as they would apply to an interim measure under the Model Law.

COMMENTARY ON SECTION 23K

History of section .... [s 23K-1]
Security for costs .... [s 23K-2]
Section applies unless parties agree otherwise .... [s 23K-3]

[s 23K-1] **History of section** The International Arbitration Amendment Act 2010 (Cth) inserted s 23K into the Act.

[s 23K-2] **Security for costs** Section 23K confers discretion on an arbitral tribunal to order a party to pay security for costs. This provision "protects parties that are the subject of ill-considered actions . . . and where the ability of a party taking a matter to arbitration to pay for the costs of the other party is in doubt. Whether security for costs is payable [is] entirely at the discretion of the tribunal" (Revised Explanatory Memorandum to the International Arbitration Amendment Bill 2010 (Cth) at [169]–[173]). See also the discussion on security for costs in award enforcement proceedings above at [s 8-30].

[s 23K-3] **Section applies unless parties agree otherwise** Section 23K applies unless the parties agree, in the arbitration agreement or otherwise "in writing", that it will not apply (s 22(2)(e)). See also the discussion on security for costs in the context of award enforcement in s 8 above.

[s 24] Consolidation of arbitral proceedings

24 (1) A party to arbitral proceedings before an arbitral tribunal may apply to the tribunal for an order under this section in relation to those proceedings and other arbitral proceedings (whether before that tribunal or another tribunal or other tribunals) on the ground that:
- (a) a common question of law or fact arises in all those proceedings;
- (b) the rights to relief claimed in all those proceedings are in respect of, or arise out of, the same transaction or series of transactions; or
- (c) for some other reason specified in the application, it is desirable that an order be made under this section.

(2) The following orders may be made under this section in relation to 2 or more arbitral proceedings:
- (a) that the proceedings be consolidated on terms specified in the order;
- (b) that the proceedings be heard at the same time or in a sequence specified in the order;
- (c) that any of the proceedings be stayed pending the determination of any other of the proceedings.

(3) Where an application has been made under subsection (1) in relation to 2 or more arbitral proceedings (in this section called the *related proceedings*), the following provisions have effect.

(4) If all the related proceedings are being heard by the same tribunal, the tribunal may make such order under this section as it thinks fit in relation to those proceedings and, if such an order is made, the proceedings shall be dealt with in accordance with the order.

(5) If 2 or more arbitral tribunals are hearing the related proceedings:
- (a) the tribunal that received the application shall communicate the substance of the application to the other tribunals concerned; and
- (b) the tribunals shall, as soon as practicable, deliberate jointly on the application.

(6) Where the tribunals agree, after deliberation on the application, that a particular order under this section should be made in relation to the related proceedings:
- (a) the tribunals shall jointly make the order;
- (b) the related proceedings shall be dealt with in accordance with the order; and
- (c) if the order is that the related proceedings be consolidated — the arbitrator or arbitrators for the purposes of the consolidated proceedings shall be appointed, in accordance with Articles 10 and 11 of the Model Law, from the members of the tribunals.

(7) If the tribunals are unable to make an order under subsection (6), the related proceedings shall proceed as if no application has been made under subsection (1).

(8) This section does not prevent the parties to related proceedings from agreeing to consolidate them and taking such steps as are necessary to effect that consolidation.

COMMENTARY ON SECTION 24

History of section .... [s 24-1]
Difficulties with consolidation .... [s 24-2]

Consolidation under institutional rules .... [s 24-3]
Optional provision .... [s 24-4]
Operation of section .... [s 24-5]

[s 24-1] History of section   The International Arbitration Amendment Act 1989 (Cth) inserted s 24 into the Act.

[s 24-2] Difficulties with consolidation   In order to allow a joinder where one party objects to another being joined, there must be present "a positive conferment of jurisdiction to add a claimant who is not a party to the arbitration agreement and to whose joinder a party to that agreement objects" (*The Bay Hotel and Resort Ltd v Cavalier Construction Co Ltd* [2001] All ER (D) 229 (Jul); [2001] 5 LRC 376; [2001] UKPC 34 at 47). "It would amount to a negation of the principle of party autonomy to give the tribunal or the Court the power to order consolidation or concurrent hearings. Indeed it would to our minds go far towards frustrating the agreement of the parties to have their own tribunal for their own purposes. Further difficulties could well arise, such as the disclosure of documents from one arbitration to the other" (at UKPC 44, quoting the Report of the UK Departmental Advisory Committee on Arbitration Law (February 1996) at [180]).

[s 24-3] Consolidation under institutional rules   A rule of an arbitration institution may, by incorporation, amount to express or implied consent to an extension of the arbitrators' jurisdiction. The basic criterion remains consent. The operation of this principle is seen in *Lafarge Redland Aggregates Ltd v Shepherd Hill Civil Engineering Ltd* [2001] 1 All ER 34; [2000] 1 WLR 1621; [2000] UKHL 46; and Art 10 of the ICC Arbitration Rules (2012).

[s 24-4] Optional provision   Section 24 applies to arbitral proceedings if the parties agree, whether in the arbitration agreement or otherwise "in writing", that it will apply (s 22(5)).

[s 24-5] Operation of section   Section 24 is not intended to prevent parties from agreeing to consolidate if they so wish. Where an application for consolidation is made in relation to two or more arbitral proceedings being heard by the same tribunal, the tribunal can determine the application as it thinks fit. However, where more than one tribunal is involved, the tribunal is required to consult the other tribunal concerned. After deliberation, if the tribunals agree, a joint order is issued as to how the proceedings are to be consolidated. If the tribunals are unable to agree, the application fails and the proceedings continue as if no application had been made (see the Explanatory Memorandum to the International Arbitration Amendment Bill 1988 (Cth) at [14]–[16]). No recourse to the court is available to the parties in relation to consolidation.

[s 25]   Interest up to making of award

25   (1) Where an arbitral tribunal determines to make an award for the payment of money (whether on a claim for a liquidated or an unliquidated amount), the tribunal may, subject to subsection (2), include in the sum for which the award is made interest, at such reasonable rate as the tribunal determines on the whole or any part of the money, for the whole or any part of the period between the date on which the cause of action arose and the date on which the award is made.

(2) Subsection (1) does not:
  (a) authorise the awarding of interest upon interest;
  (b) apply in relation to any amount upon which interest is payable as of right whether by virtue of an agreement or otherwise; or
  (c) affect the damages recoverable for the dishonour of a bill of exchange.

COMMENTARY ON SECTION 25

History of section .... [s 25-1]
Power of arbitral tribunal to award interest is implied in
  Australia .... [s 25-2]
Revised wording of section .... [s 25-3]
Interest up to date of award .... [s 25-4]
Compound interest .... [s 25-5]
Section applies unless parties agree that it shall not apply . [s 25-6]

[s 25-1] History of section The International Arbitration Amendment Act 1989 (Cth) inserted s 25 into the Act. When the provision conferring a statutory power to award pre-award interest was introduced into the Act, it was seen as an opt-in provision (see the Explanatory Memorandum to the International Arbitration Amendment Bill 1988 (Cth) at [17]–[19], and the placement of ss 25 and 26 in "Division 3 — Optional Provisions" of Pt III of the Act).

The 2010 Amendment Act deleted the following opening words in s 25(1): "Unless the parties to an arbitration agreement have (whether in the agreement or in any other document in writing) otherwise agreed, where", and substituted the word "Where". As a result of this change and the new s 22(2), this provision applies unless the parties opt out.

[s 25-2] Power of arbitral tribunal to award interest is implied in Australia The fact that this power to award interest was seen as an optional power and not a general incident of the arbitration process was unusual. It was generally accepted that although there may not have been express adoption of these provisions, under Australian law an arbitrator may award interest between the time of suffering the loss and the determination or assessment of that loss as part of the damages which need to be awarded to give proper compensation to such party for having been deprived of the use of the money from the time of the loss in the same manner as if the issue had been determined in a court of law. "What lies behind that principle is that arbitrators must determine disputes according to the law of the land" (*Codelfa Construction Pty Ltd v State Rail Authority of NSW* (1982) 149 CLR 337; 41 ALR 367; 56 ALJR 459; (1982) NSW ConvR 55-070; BC8200083 (*Codelfa*) at ALR 388, Mason J quoting Stephen J in *Government Insurance Office of New South Wales v Atkinson-Leighton Joint Venture* (1981) 146 CLR 206 at 235; 55 ALJR 212; 1 ANZ Ins Cas 60-425; BC8000098). Accordingly, interest may be awarded in international arbitrations which are subject to Australian procedural law, up to the date of the award, on the basis that "there is an implied authority" to award pre-award interest (*Codelfa* at ALR 389).

[s 25-3] Revised wording of section There was an apparent contradiction in the terms of s 22 and ss 25–27 before the amendments were made in 2010.

Section 22 originally provided that all or any of ss 25–27 applied, only if the parties to an arbitration agreement had agreed that they would apply. In other words, s 22 provided that these provisions would apply on an "opt-in" basis. However, ss 25–27 were all prefaced by the words unless the parties to an arbitration "have ... otherwise agreed". These prefatory words suggested that ss 25–27 applied on an "opt-out" basis in contradiction to s 22 (Revised Explanatory Memorandum to the International Arbitration Amendment Bill 2010 (Cth) at [179]). The 2010 change was intended to and, it is submitted notwithstanding the contrary statements in the Revised Explanatory Memorandum, does remove this apparent contradiction and makes the provision an opt-out provision.

[s 25-4] **Interest up to date of award** Section 25 confers power on an arbitral tribunal to award interest for the whole or any part of the period between the date on which the cause of action arose and the date on which the award is made. This is consistent with the requirement in Art 31(4) of the Model Law that an award shall state the date of the award.

[s 25-5] **Compound interest** Section 25(1) does not authorise an arbitral tribunal to award compound interest up to the date of the award. If the parties have authorised the arbitral tribunal to award compound interest by their agreement, the section does not prevent an arbitral tribunal from awarding compound interest.

[s 25-6] **Section applies unless parties agree that it shall not apply** Section 25 applies to arbitral proceedings unless the parties agree, in the arbitration agreement or otherwise "in writing", that it does not apply (s 22(2)(f)). This clearly results in a provision which applies unless the parties opt out. This approach is understandable given the common law position noted above. The confusion and contradiction in the language used in the Act before 2010 may have been removed, but has been retained in the Revised Explanatory Memorandum to the International Arbitration Amendment Bill 2010 (Cth). At [180], it states that the result of the proposed amendment in 2010 to s 25(1) "means the application of the provision is now governed exclusively by section 22 and applies on an 'opt in' basis".

[s 26] Interest on debt under award

26 (1) This section applies if:
   (a) an arbitral tribunal makes an award for the payment of an amount of money; and
   (b) under the award, the amount is to be paid by a particular day (the ***due date***).

(2) The arbitral tribunal may direct that interest, including compound interest, is payable if the amount is not paid on or before the due date.

(3) The arbitral tribunal may set a reasonable rate of interest.

(4) The interest is payable:
   (a) from the day immediately following the due date; and
   (b) on so much of the amount as remains unpaid.

(5) The direction is taken to form part of the award.

COMMENTARY ON SECTION 26

History of section .... [s 26-1]
Opt-out provision .... [s 26-2]
Compound interest .... [s 26-3]

[s 26-1] History of section The International Arbitration Amendment Act 1989 (Cth) inserted s 26 into the Act. When the provision conferring a statutory power to award post-award interest on an unpaid award was introduced into the Act, it was seen as an opt-in provision (see Explanatory Memorandum to the International Arbitration Amendment Bill 1988 (Cth) at [17]–[19], and also note the placement of ss 25 and 26 in "Division 3 — Optional Provisions" of Pt III of the Act).

The International Arbitration Amendment Act 2010 (Cth) substituted s 26 with a redrafted provision to overcome the same inconsistency in the language which had been used in the Act discussed above in relation to s 25.

[s 26-2] Opt-out provision Section 22(2)(g) relevantly states that s 26 "applies . . . unless the parties to the agreement agree . . . that it will not apply". This is understandable for the reasons discussed above in relation to s 25. The revised s 26 clearly applies on an opt-out basis. It is thus surprising for the Revised Explanatory Memorandum to the International Arbitration Amendment Bill 2010 (Cth) to state (at [185]) that this "redrafted provision" makes "three significant changes. First, as with [the proposed changes to ss 24 and 26], the words 'unless the parties to an arbitration agreement have (whether in the agreement or in any other document in writing) otherwise agreed' have been omitted so that the application of the provision is now governed exclusively by section 22 and applies on an 'opt in' basis. Secondly, the provision now allows the tribunal to direct the payment of compound interest. Thirdly, the provision has been restructured in the interests of clarity."

[s 26-3] Compound interest Section 26(2) confers power on an arbitral tribunal to award compound interest from the date the award is due up to the date of payment.

[s 27] Costs

27 (1) The costs of an arbitration (including the fees and expenses of the arbitrator or arbitrators) shall be in the discretion of the arbitral tribunal.
　(2) An arbitral tribunal may in making an award:
　　(a) direct to whom, by whom, and in what manner, the whole or any part of the costs that it awards shall be paid;
　　(b) tax or settle the amount of costs to be so paid or any part of those costs; and
　　(c) award costs to be taxed or settled as between party and party or as between solicitor and client; and
　　(d) limit the amount of costs that a party is to pay to a specified amount.
　(2A) An arbitral tribunal must, if it intends to make a direction under paragraph (2)(d), give the parties to the arbitration agreement notice of that intention sufficiently in advance of the incurring of costs to which it relates, or the taking of any steps in the arbitral proceedings which may be affected by it, for the limit to be taken into account.

(3) Any costs of an arbitration (other than the fees or expenses of an arbitrator) that are directed to be paid by an award are, to the extent that they have not been taxed or settled by the arbitral tribunal, taxable in the Court having jurisdiction under Article 34 of the Model Law to hear applications for setting aside the award.

(4) If no provision is made by an award with respect to the costs of the arbitration, a party to the arbitration agreement may, within 14 days after receiving the award, apply to the arbitral tribunal for directions as to the payment of those costs, and thereupon the tribunal shall, after hearing any party who wishes to be heard, amend the award by adding to it such directions as the tribunal thinks proper with respect to the payment of the costs of the arbitration.

COMMENTARY ON SECTION 27

History of section .... [s 27-1]
Section applies unless parties agree that it shall not apply . [s 27-2]
Additional power of an arbitral tribunal to limit costs .. [s 27-3]

[s 27-1] **History of section** The International Arbitration Amendment Act 1989 (Cth) inserted s 27 into the Act. When the provision was introduced into the Act, it was seen as an opt-in provision (see Explanatory Memorandum to the International Arbitration Amendment Bill 1988 (Cth) at [20]–[21], and note the placement of s 27 in "Division 3 — Optional Provisions" of Pt III of the Act).

The International Arbitration Amendment Act 2010 (Cth) deleted the opening words in s 27(1): "Unless the parties to an arbitration agreement have (whether in the agreement or in any other document in writing) otherwise agreed, the", and substituted the word "The". In addition, s 27(2)(d) and (2A) were added to enable the arbitral tribunal to limit costs as discussed below.

[s 27-2] **Section applies unless parties agree that it shall not apply** Section 27 applies to arbitral proceedings unless the parties agree, in the arbitration agreement or otherwise "in writing", that it does not apply (s 22(2)(h)). This clearly results in a provision which applies unless the parties opt out. This approach is understandable given the general position that costs normally follow the event in Australia. The confusion and contradiction in the language used in the Act before 2010 may have been removed but has been retained in the Revised Explanatory Memorandum to the International Arbitration Amendment Bill 2010 (Cth). At [188], it states that the result of the proposed amendment in 2010 to s 27(1) "means the application of the provision is now governed exclusively by section 22 and applies on an 'opt in' basis".

[s 27-3] **Additional power of an arbitral tribunal to limit costs** The 2010 amendments to the section included a power to limit costs in s 27(2)(d) subject to the arbitral tribunal giving advance notice to the parties (s 27(2A)). This provision was derived from s 65 of the Arbitration Act 1996 (Eng, W & NI) (Revised Explanatory Memorandum to the International Arbitration Amendment Bill 2010 (Cth) at [194]).

DIVISION 4 — MISCELLANEOUS

[s 28] Immunity

28 (1) An arbitrator is not liable for anything done or omitted to be done by the arbitrator in good faith in his or her capacity as arbitrator.

(2) An entity that appoints, or fails or refuses to appoint, a person as arbitrator is not liable in relation to the appointment, failure or refusal if it was done in good faith.

COMMENTARY ON SECTION 28

History of section	[s 28-1]
Onus	[s 28-2]
Appointing authority	[s 28-3]
Common law immunity	[s 28-4]
Possible contractual release and indemnity	[s 28-5]
Contrast with immunity conferred by ICSID Convention	[s 28-6]

[s 28-1] History of section The International Arbitration Amendment Act 1989 (Cth) introduced s 28 into the Act and the section was repealed and replaced by the International Arbitration Amendment Act 2010 (Cth). The original s 28 was one of a number of "minor additional provisions to facilitate arbitral proceedings" which were introduced into the Act when the Model Law was adopted in Australia (*Hansard*, Second Reading Speech, 3 November 1988, Lionel Bowen, Attorney-General, p 2399). In its original form, the section provided that "[a]n arbitrator is not liable for negligence in respect of anything done or omitted to be done in the capacity of arbitrator, but is liable for fraud in respect of anything done or omitted to be done in that capacity". The immunity was in the same terms as that then conferred upon an arbitrator by the uniform State and Territory commercial arbitration legislation, eg, Commercial Arbitration Act 1984 (NSW), s 50.

The Discussion Paper issued by the Attorney-General in 2009 and the resulting International Arbitration Amendment Bill 2009 (Cth) did not include any proposal to amend s 28. The present provision was inserted into the Bill in May 2010 following further submissions in response to the Discussion Paper and following the proposal to increase the immunity to be conferred on arbitrators by cl 39 of the new uniform Commercial Arbitration Bill 2009 (NSW).

The new wording of the provision confers "a broader immunity" (Revised Explanatory Memorandum to the International Arbitration Amendment Bill 2010 (Cth) at [198]) and widens the potential application of the section by providing that an arbitrator is "not liable" for anything done or omitted to be done as arbitrator and not confining the immunity to liability in negligence.

The new wording also limits the application of the section by adding a requirement of acting "in good faith" before the immunity arises. "This would provide a more appropriate balance of rights and interests as between arbitrators and parties" (Revised Explanatory Memorandum to the International Arbitration Amendment Bill 2010 (Cth) at [52] and [199]). This requirement may have been derived from s 29(1) of the Arbitration Act 1996 (Eng, W & NI) which provides:

"An arbitrator is not liable for anything done or omitted in the discharge or purported discharge of his functions as arbitrator unless the act or omission is shown to have been in bad faith."

Finally, the new wording extends the immunity to cover an entity charged with appointing arbitrators to an arbitral tribunal in terms of the new s 28(2). Arbitrators may be called upon to appoint or choose a third arbitrator under Art 11(3) of the Model Law. A court or other appointing authority such as ACICA may make the appointment under Art 11(4). Both the courts and arbitrators have an existing immunity. Accordingly, the extension of the immunity complements new s 18, which allows for an appointing authority to perform this function.

Part of the genesis for the amendment may also be the 2010 UNCITRAL Arbitration Rules. The Revised Explanatory Memorandum refers to the new provision as being "drafted in a more contemporary manner" (at [198]). The three elements in the new s 28 are also present in the exclusion of liability conferred on international arbitrators and institutions by Art 16 of the 2010 UNCITRAL Arbitration Rules. Article 16, which is headed "Exclusion of Liability", provides: "[s]ave for intentional wrongdoing, the parties waive, to the fullest extent permitted under the applicable law, any claim against the arbitrators, the appointing authority and any person appointed by the arbitral tribunal based on any act or omission in connection with the arbitration".

[s 28-2] **Onus** Section 28 places the onus of showing good faith on the arbitrator. This may be contrasted with s 29 of the Arbitration Act 1996 (Eng, W & NI), which, as noted above, places the onus on the plaintiff to demonstrate bad faith on the part of the arbitrator.

[s 28-3] **Appointing authority** The immunity conferred by s 28 on appointing authorities applies to any entity involved in the appointment process that acts in good faith. Although the new provision is said to complement the new s 18, the immunity is not confined to those appointing authorities that may be prescribed as an appointing authority under s 18(1) and (2) of the Act as being competent to perform the functions of an appointing authority under Art 11(3) and (4) of the Model Law.

The decision in *Road Regenerating and Repair Services v Mitchell Water Board* (Supreme Court of Victoria, Nathan J, 2261 of 1990, 15 June 1990, BC9000777, unreported) raised the potential liability of an appointing arbitration institution, where although the appointing body was not a party to the proceedings, the court said (at 4) that it "would expect [that body] to bear the costs of all parties to the dispute". Most international arbitration institutions also include provisions in their arbitration rules which confer a contractual-based immunity from suit on the arbitrator, the institution and its employees save in the case of fraud, eg, rr 43(4) and 44 of the ACICA Arbitration Rules. For an example of statutory immunity for an arbitral organisation (and an arbitrator), see Uniform Arbitration Act, Nevada, US, considered in *Slaughter v American Arbitration Association*, US D.Ct. Nevada, 2 June 2011, Dawson J, Case No 2: 10-CV-01437.

[s 28-4] **Common law immunity** It has been held that the statutory immunity in its more limited original form, and the immunity stated in similarly limited terms in the domestic uniform commercial arbitration legislation, "express

the pre-existing common law. The rationale for the immunity seems to have several strands. Perhaps the dominant one is that the parties to an arbitration impliedly agree to accept the arbitrator's decision as final and conclusive and to be bound by the award, each taking the risk that the award may be touched by error" (*Meshlawn Pty Ltd v Queensland* [2010] QCA 181; BC201005136 at [110] (Chesterman JA)).

The other bases for immunity were stated to include the inconveniences that would arise if an arbitrator were liable to an action for negligence, the nature of the discretionary judgment required of an arbitrator means that the exercise of the power is unsuitable for judicial scrutiny, and the fact that the nature of the arbitral function does not lend itself to the imposition of a duty of care to the parties to the arbitration because it is incompatible with the obligation to decide the conflict with strict impartiality; see also *Najjar v Haines* (1991) 25 NSWLR 224 at 232–4 and 269–74; 10 BCL 272; 11 BCL 315; and *Sinclair & Lindsay Sinclair Pty Ltd v Bayly & Earle* (1994) 11 BCL 439 at 441–2; BC9401256. Other bases may include the special status of an arbitrator as discussed by the Supreme Court in *Jivraj v Hashwani* [2011] All ER (D) 246 (Jul); [2011] 1 WLR 1872; [2011] UKSC 40 at [41]: Lord Clarke "is in effect a quasi-judicial adjudicator" although, at [44], "in a very different position from a judge", and the suggestion that arbitrators may be expected to give reasons for their award to a standard expected of a judge (*Oil Basins Ltd v BHP Billiton Ltd* (2007) 18 VR 346; [2007] VSCA 255; BC200709808 discussed below at [Sch 2 Art 31-3] in relation to Art 31(2) of the Model Law).

The common law immunity may not protect an arbitrator from liability under a costs order where the arbitrator adopts an adversarial role in an application to set aside the award (*Du Toit v Vale* (1993) 9 WAR 138 at 148–9; and *Mond v Berger* (2005) 21 BCL 125; [2004] VSC 150; BC200402294 at [56]–[71]).

[s 28-5] Possible contractual release and indemnity It has been accepted as common practice in Victoria, notwithstanding provisions such as the original s 28 of the Act, s 51 of the Commercial Arbitration Act 1984 (Vic) and s 27A of the Supreme Court Act 1986 (Vic), for arbitrators, mediators and experts to require a written retainer which includes a release and indemnity from suit before undertaking the task for which they were appointed (see *114 Nepean Highway Pty Ltd v Abnote Australasia Pty Ltd* [2009] VSCA 317 at [28] and [32]). In the absence of a contractual immunity, an arbitrator remains potentially liable where the arbitrator is unable to demonstrate that the arbitrator acted or omitted to act in good faith (see generally GB Born, *International Commercial Arbitration*, Wolters Kluwer, The Netherlands, 2009, pp 1652–60). The arbitrator may be liable for the costs of a successful challenge to an award if an arbitrator does not act in good faith and the arbitrator adopts an adversarial role in the proceedings challenging the award, eg, *Mond v Berger* (2005) 21 BCL 125; [2004] VSC 150; BC200402294 at [59]–[67] and [103]–[111].

[s 28-6] Contrast with immunity conferred by ICSID Convention The immunity conferred under s 28 of the Act or under a private contract, may be contrasted with the broader immunity from suit, which is conferred under the ICSID Convention, on a wide range of persons involved in an arbitration conducted under the ICSID Convention. See commentary to Arts 19–24 of the ICSID Convention in Sch 3 to the Act.

[s 29] Representation in proceedings

29 (1) Where, in accordance with the Model Law, with the agreement of the parties or at the request of a party, as the case may be, the arbitral tribunal holds oral hearings for the presentation of evidence or for oral argument, or conducts proceedings on the basis of documents or other materials, the following provisions shall, without prejudice to the Model Law, apply.

(2) A party may appear in person before an arbitral tribunal and may be represented:
  (a) by himself or herself;
  (b) by a duly qualified legal practitioner from any legal jurisdiction of that party's choice; or
  (c) by any other person of that party's choice.

(3) A legal practitioner or a person, referred to in paragraphs (2)(b) or (c) respectively, while acting on behalf of a party to an arbitral proceeding to which Part III applies, including appearing before an arbitral tribunal, shall not thereby be taken to have breached any law regulating admission to, or the practice of, the profession of the law within the legal jurisdiction in which the arbitral proceedings are conducted.

(4) Where, subject to the agreement of the parties, an arbitral tribunal conducts proceedings on the basis of documents and other materials, such documents and materials may be prepared and submitted by any legal practitioner or person who would, under subsection (2), be entitled to appear before the tribunal, and, in such a case, subsection (3) shall apply with the same force and effect to such a legal practitioner or person.

COMMENTARY ON SECTION 29

History of section .... [s 29-1]
Legal representation in international arbitration in Australia .... [s 29-2]

[s 29-1] History of section The International Arbitration Amendment Act 1989 (Cth) inserted s 29 into the Act.

[s 29-2] Legal representation in international arbitration in Australia In order to overcome potential difficulty for advocates appearing in international arbitrations taking place in Australia, the legislature also introduced a measure which supported a party's right to be represented by any person of that party's choosing. Section 29 provides that a person acting on behalf of a party in an international arbitration, whether legally qualified or not, is not to be thereby taken to have breached any law regulating the practice of the profession of law within the legal jurisdiction in which the arbitral proceedings are conducted. Accordingly, overseas lawyers and non-lawyers can appear in an arbitration without any fear of breaching any local laws restricting the right of practice to legal practitioners in Australia.

[s 30] Application of Part

30 This Part does not apply in relation to an international commercial arbitration between parties to an arbitration agreement that was concluded before the commencement of this Part unless the parties have (whether in the agreement or in any other document in writing) otherwise agreed.

COMMENTARY ON SECTION 30

History of section .... [s 30-1]
Operation of section .... [s 30-2]

[s 30-1] History of section The International Arbitration Amendment Act 1989 (Cth) inserted s 30 into the Act when the Model Law was adopted and the section has remained unaltered.

[s 30-2] Operation of section Section 7 of the International Arbitration Amendment Act 1989 (Cth) inserted, after s 14, a new Pt III comprising ss 15–30. The provisions of Pt III, including the Model Law, do not apply to an arbitration agreement made before 12 June 1989. An issue has arisen as to whether s 30 "render[s] the new amendments applicable to arbitration agreements entered into after 12 June 1989 but before 6 July 2010, or only agreements concluded on or after 6 July 2010?" It has been suggested "that the effect of s 30 is that the old s 21 will continue to apply in respect of agreements made before 6 July 2010" (L Nottage and R Garnett (eds), *International Arbitration in Australia*, Federation Press, Sydney, 2010, p 59). The basis put forward for this view is both the operation and effect of s 30 and also (at p 60) the "general presumption against legislation having retrospective impact". The advocates of this view also appear to suggest (at p 60) that "all of the new provisions in Part III . . . would only apply to arbitration agreements concluded after 6 July 2010". The first ground is contrary to the text of s 30. The legislative intent in s 30 is clear and as from its enactment in 1989, the section has had the single meaning that "this Part" does not apply to agreements made before 12 June 1989. That date, once ascertained in accordance with the commencement provisions of the International Arbitration Amendment Act 1989 (Cth), does not change, and has not been changed. Each of the amendments made to the provisions in Pt III of the International Arbitration Amendment Act 2010 (Cth) (only some were amended, not all) had a specific commencement date (see the table of dates in s 2). Section 30 was not altered. The second ground appears to have some considerable force, and has been further addressed in L Nottage and R Garnett, "The 2010 Amendments to the International Arbitration Act: A New Dawn for Australia?" (2011) 7 *Asian International Arbitration Journal* 29.

[s 30A] Severability

30A Without limiting its effect apart from this section, this Part also has the effect it would have if it were confined, by express provision, to arbitrations involving:
  (a) places, persons, matters or things external to Australia; or
  (b) disputes arising in the course of trade or commerce with another country, or between the States; or
  (c) disputes between parties at least one of which is a corporation to which paragraph 51(xx) of the Constitution applies; or
  (d) disputes arising in the course of trade or commerce in a Territory.

COMMENTARY ON SECTION 30A

History of section .... [s 30A-1]
Operation of section .... [s 30A-2]

[s 30A-1] History of section The International Arbitration Amendment Act 2010 (Cth) introduced s 30A into the Act. The Discussion Paper issued by the Attorney-General in 2008 and the resulting International Arbitration Amendment Bill 2009 (Cth) did not include any proposal to insert a new section along the lines of s 30A. The first such proposal was raised on 13 May 2010 as one of the Government's changes to the International Arbitration Amendment Bill 2009 (Cth).

[s 30A-2] Operation of section Part III of the Act is given an extended operation under s 30A. The new section sets out the various constitutional heads of power upon which Pt III can draw if its operation were expressly confined "to arbitrations involving":
  (a) places, persons, matters or things external to Australia [s 51(xxix)]; or
  (b) disputes arising in the course of trade or commerce with another country, or between the States [s 51(i)]; or
  (c) disputes between parties, at least one of which is a corporation ... [s 51(xx)]; or
  (d) disputes arising in the course of trade or commerce in a Territory [s 122].

PART IV — APPLICATION OF THE CONVENTION ON THE SETTLEMENT OF INVESTMENT DISPUTES BETWEEN STATES AND NATIONALS OF OTHER STATES

DIVISION 1 — PRELIMINARY

[s 31] Interpretation

31 (1) In this Part:

award includes:
   (a) an interpretation of an award under Article 50; and
   (b) a revision of an award under Article 51; and
   (c) an annulment of an award under Article 52.

Department means the Department of the Commonwealth primarily responsible for matters relating to foreign affairs.

Investment Convention means the Convention on the Settlement of Investment Disputes between States and Nationals of Other States signed by Australia on 24 March 1975, the English text of which is set out in Schedule 3.

Secretary means the Secretary of the Department.

(2) Except so far as the contrary intention appears, a word or expression used in this Part and in the Investment Convention (whether or not a particular meaning is given to it in the Investment Convention) has, in this Part, the same meaning as it has in the Investment Convention.

(3) A reference in this Part to a numbered Article is a reference to the Article so numbered in the Investment Convention.

COMMENTARY ON SECTION 31

History of section	[s 31-1]
"award"	[s 31-2]
Power of interpretation	[s 31-3]
Power of revision	[s 31-4]
Power of annulment	[s 31-5]
Commentary to Sch 3	[s 31-6]
"Department"	[s 31-7]
"Secretary"	[s 31-8]
"Investment Convention"	[s 31-9]
Interpret Pt IV consistently with ICSID Convention	[s 31-10]
Articles of ICSID Convention	[s 31-11]

[s 31-1] History of section The ICSID Implementation Act 1990 (Cth) introduced s 31 into the Act. The ICSID Implementation Act was an Act to amend the International Arbitration Act 1974 (Cth) and the International Organisations (Privileges and Immunities) Act 1963 (Cth) in order to fulfil Australia's obligations under the Convention on the Settlement of Investment Disputes between States and Nationals of other States (opened for signature 18 March 1965, 575 UNTS 159; entered into force 14 October 1966) (the ICSID Convention).

The effect of the ICSID Implementation Act 1990 (Cth) was, inter alia, to insert Pt IV into the International Arbitration Act 1974 (Cth), comprising ss 31–38, and include the ICSID Convention as Sch 3 to the Act. These provisions have remained unamended since they were introduced, with the exception of s 31, which was amended by the Statute Law Revision Act 2011 (Cth), and s 35, which was amended by the International Arbitration Amendment Act 2010 (Cth), both of which are described below.

[s 31-2] **"award"** Section 31(1) contains definitions, which are reasonably self-explanatory. The definition of "award" is stated as including an "interpretation" of an award, as may be issued under Art 50 of the ICSID Convention; a "revision" of an award, as may be rendered under Art 51 of the ICSID Convention; and an "annulment" of an award, which may be rendered under Art 52 of the ICSID Convention. These are post-award procedures which are commonly available in judicial and arbitral proceedings for the settlement of international disputes. On the power of interpretation, see, eg, *Statute of the International Court of Justice*, Art 60; *Statute of the International Tribunal for the Law of the Sea*, Art 33(3); and *American Convention on Human Rights*, Art 67. On the power of revision, see, eg, *Convention for the Pacific Settlement of International Disputes* (1899), Art 55; *Convention for the Pacific Settlement of International Disputes* (1907), Art 83; *Statute of the International Court of Justice*, Art 61; and *Rome Statute of the International Criminal Court*, Art 84. Examples can also be found in the rules of arbitration of some other arbitral institutions; see eg, ICC Arbitration Rules, r 29 (powers of correction and interpretation); LCIA Arbitration Rules, Art 27 (power of correction and power to issue an additional award); SIAC Arbitration Rules, Art 29 (power of correction and power to issue an additional award); and HKIAC Administered Arbitration Rules, Art 33 (power of interpretation), Art 34 (power of correction), and Art 35 (power to issue an additional award).

[s 31-3] **Power of interpretation** The power of "interpretation" typically enables an international court or tribunal to clarify any ambiguity, obscurity or apparent contradiction in the judgment or award, and in the context of an application made under Art 50 of the ICSID Convention, results in the tribunal publishing a separate "Decision on Interpretation". See eg, *Wena Hotels v Arab Republic of Egypt* (ICSID Case No ARB/98/4, Decision of 31 October 2005 on the Claimant's Application for Interpretation of the Award); and *ATA Construction, Industrial and Trading Co v Jordan* (ICSID Case No ARB/08/2, Decision of 7 March 2011 on Interpretation and on the Request for Provisional Measures).

[s 31-4] **Power of revision** The power of "revision" under Art 51 of the ICSID Convention enables an international court or tribunal to alter a judgment or award in order to take account of a decisive new fact unknown to the party and the court at the time of the judgment. Like an application for interpretation, this results in the publication of a new "Decision on Revision" (see further C Schreuer et al, *The ICSID Convention: A Commentary*, 2nd ed, Cambridge University Press, Cambridge, 2009, pp 878–89). There has, to date, been only one such decision rendered by an ICSID tribunal — *Victor Pey Casado and President Allende Foundation v Chile* (ICSID Case No ARB98/2, Decision of 18 November 2009 on the Application for the Revision of the Award) — although at least four other

applications for revision have been made, with two cases being settled by the parties (*American Manufacturing and Trading Inc v Democratic Republic of the Congo* (ICSID Case No ARB/93/1); and *Siemens AG v Argentina* (ICSID Case No ARB/02/8)). At the time of writing, the applications for revision in *Kardassopoulos v Georgia* (ICSID Case No ARB/05/18) and *Ron Fuchs v Georgia* (ICSID Case No ARB/07/15) remain pending.

[s 31-5] **Power of annulment** Finally, the power of "annulment" under Art 52 of the ICSID Convention enables a party to apply that the award be set aside in part or in full. Many applications for annulment have been made under the ICSID Convention: see further C Schreuer et al, *The ICSID Convention: A Commentary*, 2nd ed, Cambridge University Press, Cambridge, 2009, pp 890–1095.

[s 31-6] **Commentary to Sch 3** For further commentary on Arts 50–52 of the ICSID Convention, see Sch 3 of the Act.

[s 31-7] **"Department"** "Department" is defined in s 31(1) as meaning "the Department of the Commonwealth primarily responsible for matters relating to foreign affairs", which is self-evidently a reference to the Department of Foreign Affairs and Trade. The Statute Law Revision Act 2011 (Cth) had the effect of amending other references to the Department (in ss 10(1), 10A(1), and 10A(5)), by omitting the term "Department of Foreign Affairs" and replacing it with "Foreign Affairs Department". In addition, a definition of the term "Foreign Affairs Department" was inserted in s 3(1), which is defined as meaning "the Department administered by the Minister administering the Diplomatic Privileges and Immunities Act 1967". This would seem to create an inconsistency in how the "Department" is defined throughout the Act, but this does not appear to be problematic.

[s 31-8] **"Secretary"** The term "Secretary" is defined as meaning the "Secretary of the Department", ie, the most senior public servant. Sections 77–79 of the Statute Law Revision Act 2011 (Cth) also amended this definition, such that the definition was changed from "Secretary to the Department" to "Secretary of the Department". The Secretary of the Department of Foreign Affairs and Trade is presently Mr Dennis Richardson AO.

[s 31-9] **"Investment Convention"** The "Investment Convention" is defined as meaning the ICSID Convention.

[s 31-10] **Interpret Pt IV consistently with ICSID Convention** Section 31(2) provides that, unless stated otherwise, a word or expression in Pt IV of the Act has the same meaning as it does in the ICSID Convention (whether or not a particular meaning is given to it in the ICSID Convention). This is a reflection of the principle that legislation which is enacted in order to give effect to international obligations should be interpreted, unless the contrary intention appears, consistently with the relevant international instrument; see, eg, *Chu Kheng Lim v Minister for Immigration Local Government & Ethnic Affairs* (1992) 176 CLR 1 at 38; 110 ALR 97; 67 ALJR 125; BC9202669; *Minister for Immigration and Ethnic Affairs v Teoh* (1995) 39 ALD 206; 183 CLR 273; 128 ALR 353; BC9506417; and see also Acts Interpretation Act 1901 (Cth) s 15AB.

[s 31-11] Articles of ICSID Convention Finally, s 31(3) makes it clear that a reference to a numbered "Article" in Pt IV of the Act is a reference to an "Article", as so numbered, in the ICSID Convention.

DIVISION 2 — INVESTMENT CONVENTION

[s 32] Application of Investment Convention to Australia

32 Subject to this Part, Chapters II to VII (inclusive) of the Investment Convention have the force of law in Australia.

COMMENTARY ON SECTION 32

History of section	[s 32-1]
ICSID Convention generally has force of law	[s 32-2]
Chapter I of ICSID Convention excluded	[s 32-3]

[s 32-1] History of section The ICSID Implementation Act 1990 (Cth) introduced s 32 into the Act.

[s 32-2] ICSID Convention generally has force of law Section 32 provides that the ICSID Convention has the force of law in Australia, although this excludes Ch I of the Convention. The Explanatory Memorandum to the ICSID Implementation Bill 1990 (Cth) simply states that the section "gives Chapters II to VII (inclusive) of the [ICSID] Convention the force of law in Australia" (p 7).

[s 32-3] Chapter I of ICSID Convention excluded Chapter I of the ICSID Convention, which is excluded from having the force of law by s 32 of the Act, contains Arts 1–24, namely the provisions on the establishment and organisation of ICSID, the ICSID Administrative Council, the ICSID Secretariat, the Panels of Arbitrators and Conciliators, the financing of ICSID, and the legal status of ICSID, as well as the privileges and immunities that apply to it and certain persons who are officers of ICSID or are involved in ICSID proceedings. Amendments to the International Organisations (Privileges and Immunities) Act 1963 (Cth) give provisions on privileges the force of law in Australia. See the discussion of the relevant provisions of the ICSID Convention in Sch 3.

[s 33] Award is binding

33 (1) An award is binding on a party to the investment dispute to which the award relates.

(2) An award is not subject to any appeal or to any other remedy, otherwise than in accordance with the Investment Convention.

COMMENTARY ON SECTION 33

History of section	[s 33-1]
Award is binding and not subject to appeal	[s 33-2]

[s 33-1] History of section The ICSID Implementation Act 1990 (Cth) introduced s 33 into the Act.

[s 33-2] Award is binding and not subject to appeal Section 33 restates the principle contained in Art 53(1) of the ICSID Convention that "the Award shall be binding on the parties and shall not be subject to any appeal or to any other remedy except those provided for in this Convention". The Explanatory Memorandum to the ICSID Convention Bill 1990 (Cth) states that the purpose of this provision is to ensure "that the objectives of the [ICSID] Convention will not be able to be frustrated through ancillary litigation" (p 7).

[s 34] Investment Convention awards to prevail over other laws

34   Other laws relating to the recognition and enforcement of arbitral awards, including the provisions of Parts II and III, do not apply to:
  (a) a dispute within the jurisdiction of the Centre; or
  (b) an award under this Part.

COMMENTARY ON SECTION 34
History of section .... [s 34-1]
Other laws do not apply to ICSID disputes or awards . [s 34-2]

[s 34-1] History of section   The ICSID Implementation Act 1990 (Cth) introduced s 34 into the Act.

[s 34-2] Other laws do not apply to ICSID disputes or awards   The rationale behind this provision, as noted in the Explanatory Memorandum, is that "once parties to an investment dispute consent to arbitration under the [ICSID] Convention, such arbitration is to the exclusion of any other remedy". This is reflected in Art 26 of the ICSID Convention (Explanatory Memorandum to the ICSID Implementation Bill 1990 (Cth), p 7). Section 34 therefore provides that "Parts II and III of the International Arbitration Act 1974 (which deal with other means of enforcing arbitral awards) do not apply to an investment dispute or an award under the [ICSID] Convention" (p 7). This means that the provisions of the Act, which give effect to the relevant provisions of the New York Convention and the UNCITRAL Model Law, do not apply to disputes within the jurisdiction of ICSID and awards made under the ICSID Convention.

[s 35] Recognition of awards

35   (1) The Supreme Court of each State and Territory is designated for the purposes of Article 54.

(2) An award may be enforced in the Supreme Court of a State or Territory with the leave of that court as if the award were a judgment or order of that court.

(3) The Federal Court of Australia is designated for the purposes of Article 54.

(4) An award may be enforced in the Federal Court of Australia with the leave of that court as if the award were a judgment or order of that court.

COMMENTARY ON SECTION 35
History of section .... [s 35-1]
Amendments in 2009 and 2010 .... [s 35-2]

[s 35-1] History of section   The ICSID Implementation Act 1990 (Cth) introduced s 35 into the Act. As originally enacted, s 35 consisted only of s 35(1):

"The Supreme Court of each State and Territory is designated for the purposes of Article 54"; and s 35(2): "An award may be enforced in the Supreme Court of a State or Territory as if the award had been made in that State or Territory in accordance with the law of the State or Territory." The Explanatory Memorandum to the ICSID Implementation Bill 1990 (Cth) simply observed that this provision "designates the Supreme Courts of the States and Territories to be the courts which may enforce awards made under the [ICSID] Convention in conformity with Article 54 of the Convention" (p 8).

[s 35-2] **Amendments in 2009 and 2010** Section 35 was subsequently amended by the Federal Justice System Amendment (Efficiency Measures) Act (No 1) 2009 (Cth), which added subss (3) and (4), which designate the Federal Court of Australia for the purposes of Art 54 of the Act, and also provide that an award may be enforced in the Federal Court with the leave of that court as if the award were a judgment or order of that court (Sch 2). Section 35(2) was further amended by the International Arbitration Amendment Act 2010 (Cth), which added the proviso that an ICSID award may be enforced in the Supreme Court of a State or Territory, "with the leave of that court", as if the award were a judgment or order of that court (ss 24–25). It also amended s 35(4) to ensure that the wording matched that in s 35(2) (Explanatory Memorandum to the International Arbitration Amendment Bill 2010 (Cth), p 22).

DIVISION 3 — MISCELLANEOUS

[s 36] Evidence relating to Investment Convention

36 (1) A certificate purporting to be signed by the Secretary and stating that a country specified in the certificate is, or was at a time so specified, a Contracting State is, upon mere production, receivable in any proceedings as *prima facie* evidence of that fact.

(2) The Secretary may, by signed instrument, delegate the power to sign a certificate under subsection (1) to the holder of a specified office in the Department.

COMMENTARY ON SECTION 36

History of section .... [s 36-1]
Certificate by Secretary that a country is a State party to
    ICSID Convention .... [s 36-2]
Similar practice in other legislation .... [s 36-3]

[s 36-1] **History of section** The ICSID Implementation Act 1990 (Cth) introduced s 36 into the Act.

[s 36-2] **Certificate by Secretary that a country is a State party to ICSID Convention** According to the Explanatory Memorandum to the ICSID Implementation Bill 1990 (Cth), this provision "allows the Secretary to the Department of the Commonwealth primarily responsible for foreign affairs, or the Secretary's delegate, to sign a certificate which can be used as prima facie evidence that a particular country is a party to the [ICSID] Convention" (p 8).

[s 36-3] Similar practice in other legislation Similar provisions granting the power on a Commonwealth Minister or other official to issue a certificate for the purposes of evidence can be found in other legislation, relating to State immunity. Under s 40(1) of the Foreign States Immunities Act 1985 (Cth), the Minister for Foreign Affairs may certify various issues in writing, including that:

(a) a specified country is, or was on a specified day, a foreign State;
(b) a specified territory is or is not, or was or was not on a specified day, part of a foreign State;
(c) a specified person is, or was at a specified time, the head of, or the government or part of the government of, a foreign State or a former foreign State.

Other examples can be found in s 14 of the Diplomatic Privileges and Immunities Act 1967 (Cth) and s 12 of the Consular Privileges and Immunities Act 1972 (Cth).

[s 37] Representation in proceedings

37 (1) A party appearing in conciliation or arbitration proceedings may appear in person and may be represented:
(a) by himself or herself; or
(b) by a duly qualified legal practitioner from any legal jurisdiction of the party's choice; or
(c) by any other person of the party's choice.

(2) A legal practitioner or a person referred to in paragraph (1)(b) or (c) respectively, while acting on behalf of a party to conciliation or arbitration proceedings, is not thereby to be taken to have breached any law regulating admission to, or the practice of, the profession of the law within the legal jurisdiction in which the proceedings are being conducted.

(3) Where conciliation or arbitration proceedings are conducted on the basis of documents and other materials, the documents and materials may be prepared and submitted by any legal practitioner or person who would, under subsection (1), be entitled to appear in those proceedings, and, in such a case, subsection (2) applies with the same force and effect to such a legal practitioner or person.

COMMENTARY ON SECTION 37

History of section .... [s 37-1]
Right to representation of choice in arbitration proceedings .... [s 37-2]

[s 37-1] History of section The ICSID Implementation Act 1990 (Cth) introduced s 37 into the Act.

[s 37-2] Right to representation of choice in arbitration proceedings Section 37(1) ensures that a party to conciliation or arbitration proceedings under the ICSID Convention can be "represented and assisted by a duly qualified legal practitioner or any other person" (Explanatory Memorandum to the ICSID Implementation Bill 1990 (Cth), p 8). The duly qualified legal practitioner can be "from any legal jurisdiction of the party's choice" (s 37(1)(b)). Section 37(1) therefore reflects the provisions of s 29(2) of the Act, pursuant to which a party to an international arbitration may appear in person before an arbitral tribunal and may be represented by him or herself, by a duly qualified legal practitioner from any legal jurisdiction of that party's choice, or by any other person of that party's choice. This is consistent with, eg, s 36 of the Arbitration Act 1996 (Eng, W & NI), which provides that "[u]nless otherwise agreed by the parties, a party to arbitral proceedings may be represented in the proceedings by a lawyer or other person chosen by him" (Explanatory Memorandum to the ICSID Implementation Bill 1990 (Cth), p 8).

Section 37(2) ensures that "any such legal practitioner who appears for a party under this provision will not thereby be taken to have breached any law regulating admission to or practice by the legal profession in Australia within the State or Territory in which the conciliation or arbitration proceedings are conducted" (p 8). This provision therefore permits representation by foreign lawyers in conciliation or arbitration proceedings under the ICSID Convention.

[s 38] Judiciary Act

38 A matter arising under this Part, including a question of interpretation of the Investment Convention for the purposes of this Part, is not taken to be a matter arising directly under a treaty for the purposes of section 38 of the Judiciary Act 1903.

COMMENTARY ON SECTION 38

History of section	[s 38-1]
No exclusive jurisdiction for High Court of Australia over ICSID issues	[s 38-2]
Provision reflects s 13 of the Act	[s 38-3]

[s 38-1] History of section The ICSID Implementation Act 1990 (Cth) introduced s 38 into the Act.

[s 38-2] No exclusive jurisdiction for High Court of Australia over ICSID issues Section 38 provides that a matter arising under Pt IV of the Act (including a question of treaty interpretation) is not a matter "arising directly under any treaty" within the meaning of s 38 of the Judiciary Act 1903 (Cth). That provision states, in turn, that the High Court of Australia has exclusive jurisdiction over "matters arising directly under any treaty". The effect of this provision is that the relevant Supreme Court of a State or Territory which is seized of a matter under, eg, s 35 of the Act, can proceed to decide a question of treaty interpretation, should the need arise, without the need to refer the matter to the High Court of Australia.

[s 38-3] Provision reflects s 13 of the Act Section 38 reflects s 13 of the Act, which makes it clear that a question of interpretation of the New York Convention is not deemed to be a matter "arising directly under a treaty" for the purposes of s 38 of the Judiciary Act 1903 (Cth).

PART V — GENERAL MATTERS

[s 39] Matters to which court must have regard
39 (1) This section applies where:
  (a) a court is considering:
    (i) exercising a power under section 8 to enforce a foreign award; or
    (ii) exercising the power under section 8 to refuse to enforce a foreign award, including a refusal because the enforcement of the award would be contrary to public policy; or
    (iii) exercising a power under Article 35 of the Model Law, as in force under subsection 16(1) of this Act, to recognise or enforce an arbitral award; or
    (iv) exercising a power under Article 36 of the Model Law, as in force under subsection 16(1) of this Act, to refuse to recognise or enforce an arbitral award, including a refusal under Article 36(1)(b)(ii) because the recognition or enforcement of the arbitral award would be contrary to the public policy of Australia; or
    (v) if, under section 18, the court is taken to have been specified in Article 6 of the Model Law as a court competent to perform the functions referred to in that article — performing one or more of those functions; or
    (vi) performing any other functions or exercising any other powers under this Act, or the Model Law as in force under subsection 16(1) of this Act; or
    (vii) performing any function or exercising any power under an agreement or award to which this Act applies; or
  (b) a court is interpreting this Act, or the Model Law as in force under subsection 16(1) of this Act; or
  (c) a court is interpreting an agreement or award to which this Act applies; or
  (d) if, under section 18, an authority is taken to have been specified in Article 6 of the Model Law as an authority competent to perform the functions referred to in Articles 11(3) or 11(4) of the Model Law — the authority is considering performing one or more of those functions.

(2) The court or authority must, in doing so, have regard to:
  (a) the objects of the Act; and
  (b) the fact that:
    (i) arbitration is an efficient, impartial, enforceable and timely method by which to resolve commercial disputes; and
    (ii) awards are intended to provide certainty and finality.

(3) In this section:

arbitral award has the same meaning as in the Model Law.

foreign award has the same meaning as in Part II.

Model Law has the same meaning as in Part III.

COMMENTARY ON SECTION 39

History of section .... [s 39-1]
Matters giving rise to s 39 .... [s 39-2]

[s 39-1] History of section The International Arbitration Amendment Act 2010 (Cth) introduced s 39 into the Act.

[s 39-2] Matters giving rise to s 39 The Revised Explanatory Memorandum to the International Arbitration Amendment Bill 2010 (Cth) stated that a "concern raised consistently during the Review of the Act was that courts did not have sufficient guidance when interpreting the Act — particularly with regard to the principles that underpin arbitration and the international aspect of the operation of the Act" (at [210]). It explained: "The intention of this provision is to assist the courts in carrying out the important protective role they play with respect to international commercial arbitration while ensuring that this role is minimised to what is necessary in the circumstances" (at [213]).

[s 40] Regulations

40 The Governor-General may make regulations prescribing matters:
   (a) required or permitted by this Act to be prescribed; or
   (b) necessary or convenient to be prescribed for carrying out or giving effect to this Act.

COMMENTARY ON SECTION 40

History of section .... [s 40-1]
Regulations .... [s 40-2]
International Arbitration Regulations 2011 (Cth) .... [s 40-3]

[s 40-1] History of section The International Arbitration Amendment Act 2010 (Cth) introduced s 40 into the Act.

[s 40-2] Regulations Prior to 2010, the Act did not contain a regulation-making power. Section 18 allows the nomination of a court or other body to act as an appointing authority for arbitrators under the Model Law. This nomination may be made by exercise of the regulation making power in s 40. The Australian Centre for International Commercial Arbitration has been prescribed as an appointing authority to perform the functions referred to in Arts 11(3) and (4) of the Model Law.

[s 40-3] International Arbitration Regulations 2011 (Cth) Clause 4 of the International Arbitration Regulations 2011 (Cth) provides: "For subsections 18(1) and 18(2) of the Act, the Australian Centre for International Commercial Arbitration is prescribed."

[Sch 1] SCHEDULE 1 — UNITED NATIONS CONFERENCE ON INTERNATIONAL COMMERCIAL ARBITRATION CONVENTION ON THE RECOGNITION AND ENFORCEMENT OF FOREIGN ARBITRAL AWARDS

Section 3

ARTICLE I

1. This Convention shall apply to the recognition and enforcement of arbitral awards made in the territory of a State other than the State where the recognition and enforcement of such awards are sought, and arising out of differences between persons, whether physical or legal. It shall also apply to arbitral awards not considered as domestic awards in the State where their recognition and enforcement are sought.

2. The term "arbitral awards" shall include not only awards made by arbitrators appointed for each case but also those made by permanent arbitral bodies to which the parties have submitted.

3. When signing, ratifying or acceding to this Convention, or notifying extensions under article X hereof, any State may on the basis of reciprocity declare that it will apply the Convention to the recognition and enforcement of awards made only in the territory of another Contracting State. It may also declare that it will apply the Convention only to differences arising out of legal relationships, whether contractual or not, which are considered as commercial under the national law of the State making such declaration.

ARTICLE II

1. Each Contracting State shall recognize an agreement in writing under which the parties undertake to submit to arbitration all or any differences which have arisen or which may arise between them in respect of a defined legal relationship, whether contractual or not, concerning a subject matter capable of settlement by arbitration.

2. The term "agreement in writing" shall include an arbitral clause in a contract or an arbitration agreement, signed by the parties or contained in an exchange of letters or telegrams.

3. The court of a Contracting State, when seized of an action in a matter in respect of which the parties have made an agreement within the meaning of this article, shall, at the request of one of the parties, refer the parties to arbitration, unless it finds that the said agreement is null and void, inoperative or incapable of being performed.

ARTICLE III

Each Contracting State shall recognize arbitral awards as binding and enforce them in accordance with the rules of procedure of the territory where the award is relied upon, under the conditions laid down in the following articles. There shall not be imposed substantially more onerous conditions or higher fees or charges on the recognition or enforcement of arbitral awards to which this Convention applies than are imposed on the recognition or enforcement of domestic arbitral awards.

ARTICLE IV

1. To obtain the recognition and enforcement mentioned in the preceding article, the party applying for recognition and enforcement shall, at the time of the application, supply:

   (a) The duly authenticated original award or a duly certified copy thereof;

(b) The original agreement referred to in article II or a duly certified copy thereof.

2. If the said award or agreement is not made in an official language of the country in which the award is relied upon, the party applying for recognition and enforcement of the award shall produce a translation of these documents into such language. The translation shall be certified by an official or sworn translator or by a diplomatic or consular agent.

ARTICLE V

1. Recognition and enforcement of the award may be refused, at the request of the party against whom it is invoked, only if that party furnishes to the competent authority where the recognition and enforcement is sought, proof that:
    (a) The parties to the agreement referred to in article II were, under the law applicable to them, under some incapacity, or the said agreement is not valid under the law to which the parties have subjected it or, failing any indication thereon, under the law of the country where the award was made; or
    (b) The party against whom the award is invoked was not given proper notice of the appointment of the arbitrator or of the arbitration proceedings or was otherwise unable to present his case; or
    (c) The award deals with a difference not contemplated by or not falling within the terms of the submission to arbitration, or it contains decisions on matters beyond the scope of the submission to arbitration, provided that, if the decisions on matters submitted to arbitration can be separated from those not so submitted, that part of the award which contains decisions on matters submitted to arbitration may be recognized and enforced; or
    (d) The composition of the arbitral authority or the arbitral procedure was not in accordance with the agreement of the parties, or, failing such agreement, was not in accordance with the law of the country where the arbitration took place; or
    (e) The award has not yet become binding on the parties, or has been set aside or suspended by a competent authority of the country in which, or under the law of which, that award was made.

2. Recognition and enforcement of an arbitral award may also be refused if the competent authority in the country where recognition and enforcement is sought finds that:
    (a) The subject matter of the difference is not capable of settlement by arbitration under the law of that country; or
    (b) The recognition or enforcement of the award would be contrary to the public policy of that country.

ARTICLE VI

If an application for the setting aside or suspension of the award has been made to a competent authority referred to in article V(1)(e), the authority before which the award is sought to be relied upon may, if it considers it proper, adjourn the decision on the enforcement of the award and may also, on the application of the party claiming enforcement of the award, order the other party to give suitable security.

ARTICLE VII

1. The provisions of the present Convention shall not affect the validity of multilateral or bilateral agreements concerning the recognition and enforcement of arbitral awards entered into by the Contracting States nor deprive any interested party of any right he

may have to avail himself of an arbitral award in the manner and to the extent allowed by the law or the treaties of the country where such award is sought to be relied upon.

2. The Geneva Protocol on Arbitration Clauses of 1923 and the Geneva Convention on the Execution of Foreign Arbitral Awards of 1927 shall cease to have effect between Contracting States on their becoming bound and to the extent that they become bound, by this Convention.

ARTICLE VIII

1. This Convention shall be open until 31 December 1958 for signature on behalf of any Member of the United Nations and also on behalf of any other State which is or hereafter becomes a member of any specialized agency of the United Nations, or which is or hereafter becomes a party to the Statute of the International Court of Justice, or any other State to which an invitation has been addressed by the General Assembly of the United Nations.

2. This Convention shall be ratified and the instrument of ratification shall be deposited with the Secretary-General of the United Nations.

ARTICLE IX

1. This Convention shall be open for accession to all States referred to in article VIII.

2. Accession shall be effected by the deposit of an instrument of accession with the Secretary-General of the United Nations.

ARTICLE X

1. Any State may, at the time of signature, ratification or accession, declare that this Convention shall extend to all or any of the territories for the international relations of which it is responsible. Such a declaration shall take effect when the Convention enters into force for the State concerned.

2. At any time thereafter any such extensions shall be made by notification addressed to the Secretary-General of the United Nations and shall take effect as from the ninetieth day after the day of receipt by the Secretary-General of the United Nations of this notification, or as from the date of entry into force of the Convention for the State concerned, whichever is the later.

3. With respect to those territories to which this Convention is not extended at the time of signature, ratification or accession, each State concerned shall consider the possibility of taking the necessary steps in order to extend the application of this Convention to such territories, subject, where necessary for constitutional reasons, to the consent of the Governments of such territories.

ARTICLE XI

In the case of a federal or non-unitary State, the following provisions shall apply:
  (a) With respect to those articles of this Convention that come within the legislative jurisdiction of the federal authority, the obligations of the federal Government shall to this extent be the same as those of Contracting States which are not federal States;
  (b) With respect to those articles of this Convention that come within the legislative jurisdiction of constituent states or provinces which are not, under the constitutional system of the federation, bound to take legislative action, the federal Government shall bring such articles with a favourable recommendation to the notice of the appropriate authorities of constituent states or provinces at the earliest possible moment;

(c) A federal State party to this Convention shall, at the request of any other Contracting State transmitted through the Secretary-General of the United Nations, supply a statement of the law and practice of the federation and its constituent units in regard to any particular provision of this Convention, showing the extent to which effect has been given to that provision by legislative or other action.

ARTICLE XII

1. This Convention shall come into force on the ninetieth day following the date of deposit of the third instrument of ratification or accession.

2. For each State ratifying or acceding to this Convention after the deposit of the third instrument of ratification or accession, this Convention shall enter into force on the ninetieth day after deposit by such State of its instrument of ratification or accession.

ARTICLE XIII

1. Any Contracting State may denounce this Convention by a written notification to the Secretary-General of the United Nations. Denunciation shall take effect one year after the date of receipt of the notification by the Secretary-General.

2. Any State which has made a declaration or notification under article X may, at any time thereafter, by notification to the Secretary-General of the United Nations, declare that this Convention shall cease to extend to the territory concerned one year after the date of the receipt of the notification by the Secretary-General.

3. This Convention shall continue to be applicable to arbitral awards in respect of which recognition or enforcement proceedings have been instituted before the denunciation takes effect.

ARTICLE XIV

A Contracting State shall not be entitled to avail itself of the present Convention against other Contracting States except to the extent that it is itself bound to apply the Convention.

ARTICLE XV

The Secretary-General of the United Nations shall notify the States contemplated in article VIII of the following:

(a) Signatures and ratifications in accordance with article VIII;
(b) Accessions in accordance with article IX;
(c) Declarations and notifications under articles I, X and XI;
(d) The date upon which this Convention enters into force in accordance with article XII;
(e) Denunciations and notifications in accordance with article XIII.

ARTICLE XVI

1. This Convention, of which the Chinese, English, French, Russian and Spanish texts shall be equally authentic, shall be deposited in the archives of the United Nations.

2. The Secretary-General of the United Nations shall transmit a certified copy of this Convention to the States contemplated in article VIII.

[Sch 2] SCHEDULE 2 — UNCITRAL MODEL LAW ON INTERNATIONAL COMMERCIAL ARBITRATION (AS ADOPTED BY THE UNITED NATIONS COMMISSION ON INTERNATIONAL TRADE LAW ON 21 JUNE 1985, AND AS AMENDED BY THE UNITED NATIONS COMMISSION ON INTERNATIONAL TRADE LAW ON 7 JULY 2006)

Note: See subsection 15(1).

CHAPTER I. GENERAL PROVISIONS

Article 1. Scope of application[1]

(1) This Law applies to international commercial[2] arbitration, subject to any agreement in force between this State and any other State or States.

(2) The provisions of this Law, except articles 8, 9, 17 H, 17 I, 17 J, 35 and 36, apply only if the place of arbitration is in the territory of this State.

(Article 1(2) has been amended by the Commission at its thirty-ninth session, in 2006)

(3) An arbitration is international if:
 (a) the parties to an arbitration agreement have, at the time of the conclusion of that agreement, their places of business in different States; or
 (b) one of the following places is situated outside the State in which the parties have their places of business:
  (i) the place of arbitration if determined in, or pursuant to, the arbitration agreement;
  (ii) any place where a substantial part of the obligations of the commercial relationship is to be performed or the place with which the subject-matter of the dispute is most closely connected; or
 (c) the parties have expressly agreed that the subject matter of the arbitration agreement relates to more than one country.

(4) For the purposes of paragraph (3) of this article:
 (a) if a party has more than one place of business, the place of business is that which has the closest relationship to the arbitration agreement;
 (b) if a party does not have a place of business, reference is to be made to his habitual residence.

(5) This Law shall not affect any other law of this State by virtue of which certain disputes may not be submitted to arbitration or may be submitted to arbitration only according to provisions other than those of this Law.

---

[1] Article headings are for reference purposes only and are not to be used for purposes of interpretation.

[2] The term "commercial" should be given a wide interpretation so as to cover matters arising from all relationships of a commercial nature, whether contractual or not. Relationships of a commercial nature include, but are not limited to, the following transactions: any trade transaction for the supply or exchange of goods or services; distribution agreement; commercial representation or agency; factoring; leasing; construction of works; consulting; engineering; licensing; investment; financing; banking; insurance; exploitation agreement or concession; joint venture and other forms of industrial or business cooperation; carriage of goods or passengers by air, sea, rail or road.

COMMENTARY ON SCH 2 ART 1

Introduction	[Sch 2 Art 1-1]
Substantive scope of Model Law	[Sch 2 Art 1-2]
"international"	[Sch 2 Art 1-3]
"commercial"	[Sch 2 Art 1-4]
"arbitration"	[Sch 2 Art 1-5]
2006 amendment	[Sch 2 Art 1-6]
"subject to" any agreements between States (Art 1(1))	[Sch 2 Art 1-7]
Territorial approach; provisions "only apply" if place of arbitration is in this State (Art 1(2))	[Sch 2 Art 1-8]
Non arbitrable disputes (Art 1(5))	[Sch 2 Art 1-9]

[Sch 2 Art 1-1] Introduction Those responsible for drafting the Model Law considered the necessary connecting factor which would determine the applicability of the Model Law. Ultimately it was decided to adopt the "strict territorial criterion" whereby the law would apply only if the place of arbitration was in the State which had enacted the Model Law (*Report of UNCITRAL*, Yearbook, 1985, Vol XVI, UN Doc No A/40/17 at paras 73 and 80). As a result Art 1(2) provides that the law applies "only" if the place of arbitration is in Australia. It was recognised, however, that the courts of the adopting State would need to perform certain functions under the Model Law irrespective of the location of arbitration. Hence the exclusion in the 1985 Model Law in Art 1(2) of those functions described in Arts 8, 9, 35 and 36. Articles 17H to 17J were added to this list in the 2006 revisions to the Model Law.

[Sch 2 Art 1-2] Substantive scope of Model Law The substantive scope of the application of the Model Law is confined to "international commercial arbitration" which were the terms of the initial mandate given by UNCITRAL to the working group to draft the Model Law. UNCITRAL agreed that the text "should be geared to and only cover international arbitration" (*Report of UNCITRAL*, Yearbook, 1985, Vol XVI, UN Doc No A/40/17 at para 18).

[Sch 2 Art 1-3] "international" The Model Law was designed to establish a special regime for international cases, "in these cases the interests of a State in maintaining its traditional concepts and familiar rules is less strong than in a strictly domestic setting" (Report of the Secretary-General, International Commercial Arbitration: Analytical Commentary on Draft Text of a Model Law on International Commercial Arbitration, UN Doc No A/CN.9/264 at p 10, para 22 (UNCITRAL Analytical Commentary)). Presciently, the Secretary-General went on to state: "However, despite this design and legislative self-restraint, any State is free to take the model law, whether immediately or at a later stage, as a model for legislation on domestic arbitration and, thus, avoid a dichotomy within its arbitration law." The new uniform commercial arbitration legislation for Australian States and Territories is based on the Model Law. At the time of writing, the new uniform legislation has been enacted in New South Wales with the Commercial Arbitration Act 2010 (NSW), in South Australia with the Commercial Arbitration Act 2011 (SA), in Victoria with the Commercial Arbitration Act 2011 (Vic), and in the Northern Territory with the Commercial

Arbitration (National Uniform Legislation) Act 2011 (NT). Bills to enact the new uniform legislation have also been introduced into the Parliaments of Tasmania and Western Australia.

Under Art 1(3)(a), an arbitration is international if the parties have their places of business in different states. The terms of Art 1(3)(a) were seen as covering "the bulk of cases encountered in international commercial arbitration" (*Report of UNCITRAL*, Yearbook, 1985, Vol XVI, UN Doc No A/40/17 at para 27).

Article 1(4) clarified the place of business. If a party has more than one place of business then the place of business is that "which has the closest relationship to the arbitration agreement and if a party has no place of business then it is that party's habitual residence". These provisions relating to the place of business correspond with the test contained in Arts 1(1) and 10 of the 1980 *UN Convention on Contracts for the International Sale of Goods* (Vienna, 1980, United Nations, *Treaty Series*, Vol 1489, No. 25567, also known as the "CISG" or the "Vienna Sales Convention").

As it was the intention of the drafters of the Model Law that the definition be as wide as possible (*1979 Commission Report*, UN Doc No A/34/17 at paras 79–81), the scope of the concept of "international" is extended, first, by Art 1(3)(b)(i) which refers to the place of arbitration. The phrase "place of arbitration" is a reference to the "juridical seat" of the arbitration and is discussed below in relation to Art 20. Whilst it was recognised by UNCITRAL that this provision may allow a purely domestic relationship to qualify as international "simply because a foreign place of arbitration was chosen" by the parties, UNCITRAL "thought that party autonomy should extend to the question" of internationality (*Report of UNCITRAL*, Yearbook, 1985, Vol XVI, UN Doc No A/40/17 at paras 28 and 29).

Second, the scope of the concept of international is extended by Art 1(3)(b)(ii), which refers to the place of performance of the obligations under the contract, and to the place with which the subject matter of the dispute is most closely connected. It is possible for two Australian parties to enter into a contract in Australia, under Australian law and still find themselves in an international arbitration, if substantial performance of the commercial relationship is outside Australia. See an example of an analogous situation of two Hong Kong parties in *Fung Sang Trading Ltd v Kai Sun Sea Products & Food Co Ltd* [1991] HKCFI 190 at [17]–[18].

The final extension of the definition of "international" is found in Art 1(3)(c) where an arbitration will be deemed to be "international" if the parties have expressly agreed upon that consequence. The "opt-in party autonomy provided by . . . Article 1(3)(c) is merely the power to select, for the sake of certainty, either of two systems adopted by the State's legislature in cases in which the parties wish to arbitrate in their home State": H Holtzmann and J Neuhaus, *A Guide to the UNCITRAL Model Law on International Commercial Arbitration*, Kluwer Law International, The Hague, 1989, p 32.

[Sch 2 Art 1-4] "commercial" The word commercial is undefined, as the drafters could not agree upon a precise line between commercial and non-commercial relationships. However, it was seen as "undesirable" to leave the matter to individual States, and as an intermediate solution, some guidance for a uniform interpretation was provided by means of a footnote (UNCITRAL

Analytical Commentary at p 10, para 16). The content of the footnote reflects the legislative intent to construe the term "commercial" in a wide manner. As apparent from the terms of the footnote, it depends on the objective circumstances of the relationship between the parties and not their subjective intention.

This is in contrast to the approach taken to the concept of "commercial" under the New York Convention where, under Art I(3), Contracting States were entitled to declare that the Convention will only be applied to differences arising out of a legal relationship which is "considered as commercial under the national law" of the Contracting State. It was a conscious decision by UNCITRAL to take a different approach and that the Model Law should be interpreted "autonomously" in order to achieve the aim of a wide interpretation": UNCITRAL Analytical Commentary at p 11, para 19: "it would be wrong to apply national concepts which define commercial".

The term "commercial" was not intended to cover consumer claims: see *Second Working Group Report*, UN Doc No A/CN.9/232, at para 32. The meaning of the word "commercial" as used in the Model Law was considered by the Supreme Court of British Columbia in *United Mexican States v Metalclad Corp* (2001) BCSC 664 (CanLII); 14 BLR (3d) 285 at [40]–[48]. The court held that as the arbitration arose out of "a relationship of investing", it was a commercial relationship within the meaning used in the Model Law.

[Sch 2 Art 1-5] **"arbitration"** The Model Law, as with most conventions and national laws on arbitration, does not define the term "arbitration". It merely clarifies in Art 2(a) that the law applies to ad hoc arbitration and to any type of tion (UNCITRAL Analytical Commentary at p 9, para 13).

An early definition of arbitration was that "[if] it appears from the terms of the agreement by which a matter is submitted to a person's decision, that the intention of the parties was that he should hold an inquiry in the nature of a judicial inquiry, and hear the respective cases of the parties and decide upon evidence laid before him, then the case is one of arbitration" (*Re Carus-Wilson and Greene* (1887) 18 QBD 7 at 9, per Lord Esher MR). This is a definition which "has stood the test of time" (*Queensland Power Trading Corp v Xstrata Queensland Ltd* [2005] QCA 477; BC200510862 (*Queensland Power Trading Corp*) (per Williams JA at [9] and [10]); and see also *Australia Pacific Airports (Melbourne) Pty Ltd v Nuance Group (Australia) Pty Ltd* [2005] VSCA 133; BC200503467 (Callaway JA at [43]); and *Shoalhaven City Council v Firedam Civil Engineering Pty Ltd* [2011] HCA 38; BC201107576 (French CJ, Crennan and Kiefel JJ at [25])). The question is not whether the parties intended arbitration but whether there "is a subject matter in the nature of a judicial inquiry" (Debelle J in *Santos Ltd v Pipelines Authority of South Australia* (1996) 66 SASR 38 at 48; BC9601565, quoted with approval in *Queensland Power Trading Corp* at [10]).

[Sch 2 Art 1-6] **2006 amendment** The 2006 amendments to the Model Law involved a consequential amendment to Art 1(2). The 1985 Model Law had provided in Art 1(2) that "the provisions of this Law, except Articles 8, 9, 35 and 36, apply only if the place of arbitration is in the territory of this State". Consequent upon the introduction to the Model Law in 2006 of provisions relating to interim orders in Arts 17H–17J, a reference to these new articles was inserted into Art 1(2). The new articles relate to the recognition and enforcement of interim measures made by an arbitral tribunal (Art 17H) and interim measures made by a court (Art 17J). Such recognition and enforcement may be necessary irrespective of the location where such measures were made. These excluded provisions "apply without regard to the place of arbitration or any choice of procedural law" (UNCITRAL Analytical Commentary at p 12, para 25).

[Sch 2 Art 1-7] "subject to" any agreements between States (Art 1(1)) The proviso in Art 1(1) is intended to reflect the usual priority of treaty law in the hierarchy of sources of law found in most legal systems. The legislative intent is not to affect the operation of any bilateral or multilateral treaties in force in Australia, such as the New York Convention and the Washington Convention, which contain provisions on arbitration (UNCITRAL Analytical Commentary at p 8, paras 9 and 10). This provision was given as the reason for enacting s 20 of the Act (see the discussion above at [s 20-1]).

[Sch 2 Art 1-8] Territorial approach; provisions "only apply" if place of arbitration is in this State (Art 1(2)) As noted above, those drafting the Model Law adopted the territorial approach found in most national laws. Thus the connecting factor which determines the applicability of the Model Law is the territorial criterion. The territorial limitation of Art 1(2) is reflected in s 16(1) of the Act, which defines the phrase "this State" to mean Australia including the external territories. Exceptions to the territorial principle are found in Arts 8, 9, 17H–17J, 35 and 36.

The territorial approach is extended by the concept of the place or "juridical seat" of the arbitration which may be chosen by the parties and may be a different location to that where the arbitration physically takes place. The Article recognises "the freedom of the parties to submit a dispute to the legal regime established pursuant to the Model Law" (Explanatory Note by the UNCITRAL Secretariat on the 1985 Model Law on International Commercial Arbitration as Amended in 2006) (UNCITRAL Explanatory Note 2006 at para 11). Confusingly, the phrase "place of arbitration" means, depending on its context, either, or both of, the physical location where the arbitral process is undertaken, and the juridical seat of the arbitration. See the discussion of the place of arbitration below in relation to Art 20 of the Model Law.

In this context, the reference to the "place of arbitration" is a reference to the juridical seat of the arbitration (*PT Garuda Indonesia v Birgen Air* [2002] 1 SLR(R) 401 at [19]–[22]). Thus, if the parties to an arbitration which has a juridical seat outside Australia choose a venue for the hearing in Australia, the Model Law will not apply to the arbitration (Art 1(2)), unless the parties have in fact agreed to change the place of arbitration to a place within Australia (see *PT Garuda Indonesia* at [34]).

[Sch 2 Art 1-9] Non arbitrable disputes (Art 1(5)) Those drafting the Model Law agreed to defer the issue of whether a dispute may be submitted to arbitration, to the national law of the country adopting the Model Law. There is a widespread view that certain matters affecting status, such as aspects of bankruptcy law, patent law and trademark law, are not capable of settlement by arbitration. This issue of arbitrability is discussed above at [s 7-12] in relation to s 7(2)(b) of the Act. The issue also arises on an application to set aside an award under Art 34(2)(b)(i) of the Model Law and also arises when the enforcement of an award is resisted on a ground under Art 36(2)(b)(i) of the Model Law.

Article 2. Definitions and rules of interpretation

For the purposes of this Law:
(a) "arbitration" means any arbitration whether or not administered by a permanent arbitral institution;
(b) "arbitral tribunal" means a sole arbitrator or a panel of arbitrators;
(c) "court" means a body or organ of the judicial system of a State;
(d) where a provision of this Law, except article 28, leaves the parties free to determine a certain issue, such freedom includes the right of the parties to authorize a third party, including an institution, to make that determination;
(e) where a provision of this Law refers to the fact that the parties have agreed or that they may agree or in any other way refers to an agreement of the parties, such agreement includes any arbitration rules referred to in that agreement;
(f) where a provision of this Law, other than in articles 25*(a)* and 32(2)*(a)*, refers to a claim, it also applies to a counter-claim, and where it refers to a defence, it also applies to a defence to such counter-claim.

COMMENTARY ON SCH 2 ART 2

"arbitration" (Art 2(a))	[Sch 2 Art 2-1]
"arbitral tribunal" and "court" (Art 2(b) and (c))	[Sch 2 Art 2-2]
"the right of the parties to authorise a third party"(Art 2(d))	[Sch 2 Art 2-3]
"agreement includes any arbitration rules referred to in that agreement" (Art 2(e))	[Sch 2 Art 2-4]

[Sch 2 Art 2-1] "arbitration" (Art 2(a)) The Model Law does not define what is meant by the word "arbitration" although the provision removes any doubt that it is intended to cover both institutional and ad hoc arbitrations. The Model Law was intended to apply only to consensual arbitration, ie, arbitration based on the parties' agreement to submit their disputes to arbitration. There must be agreement to arbitrate. The Model Law was not intended to apply to "compulsory arbitration", nor to "free arbitration" such as the German "Schiedsgutachten" — translation: "expert determination" (UNCITRAL Analytical Commentary at p 10, para 5). See also the discussion above at [Sch 2 Art 1-5].

[Sch 2 Art 2-2] "arbitral tribunal" and "court" (Art 2(b) and (c)) These definitions are intended to avoid any misunderstandings arising from the use of words such as "tribunal", which may describe both judicial or arbitral bodies, and from the common use of the word "court" by arbitration bodies such as the International Chamber of Commerce International Court of Arbitration, or the London Court of International Arbitration (UNCITRAL Analytical Commentary at p 15, para 1).

[Sch 2 Art 2-3] "the right of the parties to authorise a third party" (Art 2(d)) The parties' "freedom" to make decisions and right to authorise a third party, such as an arbitration institution, to determine issues arising under the

Model Law, are subject to an important qualification. Under Art 28 the parties have a greater freedom when choosing the basis on which the merits of their substantive dispute shall be determined. The parties are free not to choose a national "law" and may choose "rules of law" to determine their dispute. The parties may agree to use non-national substantive rules to determine their dispute. An example of non-national substantive rules of law is the UNIDROIT Principles of International Commercial Contracts 2010 (UNIDROIT Principles 2010), which may be accessed at www.unidroit.org. Failing agreement, the arbitral tribunal has less freedom and may only choose a "law" as the basis on which the parties' substantive dispute shall be determined.

[Sch 2 Art 2-4] **"agreement includes any arbitration rules referred to in that agreement" (Art 2(e))** The Model Law recognises that many arbitration agreements incorporate by reference the arbitration rules of an arbitral institution, such as ACICA, ICC, LCIA, SIAC, HKIAC, and CIETAC. See also the commentary on the operation of s 3(5) of the Act on incorporation by reference, and the commentary on the operation of Art 7(6) of the Model Law.

Article 2A. International origin and general principles
(As adopted by the Commission at its thirty-ninth session, in 2006)

(1) In the interpretation of this Law, regard is to be had to its international origin and to the need to promote uniformity in its application and the observance of good faith.

(2) Questions concerning matters governed by this Law which are not expressly settled in it are to be settled in conformity with the general principles on which this Law is based.

COMMENTARY ON SCH 2 ART 2A
Introduction .... [Sch 2 Art 2A-1]
Origin of Article .... [Sch 2 Art 2A-2]

[Sch 2 Art 2A-1] **Introduction** The amendments made to the Model Law in 2006 included the addition of Art 2A. When the revised Model Law with Art 2A was introduced into the Act in 2010, it was said that Art 2A was "designed to facilitate interpretation by reference to internationally accepted principles and is aimed at promoting a uniform understanding of the Model Law" (Revised Explanatory Memorandum to the International Arbitration Amendment Bill 2010 (Cth) at [64]). It was noted that "it is important that the Model Law is interpreted in a way that is consistent with approaches taken overseas. Novel or perverse interpretations by Australian courts have the potential to undermine confidence in Australia as a venue for conducting arbitration" (at [65]). Further, it was said that Australian courts "must have regard to Article 2A" (at [214]) including "to the need to promote . . . the observance of good faith" (see Art 2A(1)).

[Sch 2 Art 2A-2] **Origin of Article** The origin of Art 2A is seen in the *travaux préparatoires* to the amendments adopted by UNCITRAL in 2006. UNCITRAL considered whether the Model Law should include a provision along the lines of Art 7 of the *UN Convention on Contracts for the International Sale* *of Goods* (Vienna, 1980, United Nations, Treaty Series, Vol 1489, No 25567, also known as the "CISG" or the "Vienna Sales Convention"), which was designed to facilitate interpretation by reference to internationally accepted principles. UNCITRAL observed that similar provisions were included in other model laws prepared by the Commission, including Art 3 of the *UNCITRAL Model Law on Electronic Commerce*. UNCITRAL agreed that the inclusion of such a provision would be useful and desirable because it would promote a more uniform understanding of the Model Law (*Report of UNCITRAL on the Work of its 39th Session*, UN Doc No A/61/17 at paras 174 and 175).

Article 3. Receipt of written communications

(1) Unless otherwise agreed by the parties:
(a) any written communication is deemed to have been received if it is delivered to the addressee personally or if it is delivered at his place of business, habitual residence or mailing address; if none of these can be found after making a reasonable inquiry, a written communication is deemed to have been received if it is sent to the addressee's last-known place of business, habitual residence or mailing address by registered letter or any other means which provides a record of the attempt to deliver it;
(b) the communication is deemed to have been received on the day it is so delivered.

(2) The provisions of this article do not apply to communications in court proceedings.

COMMENTARY ON SCH 2 ART 3

Introduction .... [Sch 2 Art 3-1]
Does not apply to court proceedings .... [Sch 2 Art 3-2]
Subject matter .... [Sch 2 Art 3-3]
Application to appointing authorities .... [Sch 2 Art 3-4]

[Sch 2 Art 3-1] Introduction Article 3 was "modelled" on Art 2(1) of the 1976 UNCITRAL Arbitration Rules (UNCITRAL Analytical Commentary at p 16, para 6). Article 2(1) of the 1976 UNCITRAL Arbitration Rules provided:

> For the purposes of these Rules, any notice, including a notification, communication or proposal, is deemed to have been received if it is physically delivered to the addressee or if it is delivered at his habitual residence, place of business or mailing address, or, if none of these can be found after making reasonable inquiry, then at the addressee's last-known residence or place of business. Notice shall be deemed to have been received on the day it is so delivered.

[Sch 2 Art 3-2] Does not apply to court proceedings UNCITRAL, in adopting Art 3, "decided to clarify that the provision on receipt of communications did not apply to court proceedings or measures but only to the arbitral proceedings proper, including any steps in the appointment process by a party, an arbitrator or an appointing authority" (see *Report of UNCITRAL*, Yearbook, 1985, Vol XVI, UN Doc No A/40/17 at para 106).

[Sch 2 Art 3-3] Subject matter Article 3 establishes both the fact and the date of receipt of written communications in the arbitration. The phrase "written communication" applies to communications between the parties.

The question of notice and receipt of written communications is mainly relevant at the commencement stage of the arbitration, although it is also relevant in relation to:
  (i) Article 11, the written communications by the parties, by arbitrators and by the appointing authority in the appointment process;
  (ii) Article 21, the date of commencement of arbitral proceedings;
  (iii) Article 23, service of the statements of claim and defence.

[Sch 2 Art 3-4] Application to appointing authorities Some functions under the Model Law, such as the appointment of the arbitrators under Art 11(4), may be performed by a "court or other authority specified in Article 6". The exclusion in Art 3(2) only applies to the court and not the "other authority specified" unless it falls within the definition of the word "court" in Art 2(c) to mean a body or organ of the judicial system of a State. As a result if there is an arbitration institution specified to act as an appointing authority then Art 3 will also apply to communications to and from that appointing authority.

Article 4. Waiver of right to object

A party who knows that any provision of this Law from which the parties may derogate or any requirement under the arbitration agreement has not been complied with and yet proceeds with the arbitration without stating his objection to such non-compliance without undue delay or, if a time-limit is provided therefor, within such period of time, shall be deemed to have waived his right to object.

COMMENTARY ON SCH 2 ART 4

Introduction	[Sch 2 Art 4-1]
"any provision of [the Model Law] from which the parties may derogate"	[Sch 2 Art 4-2]
"any requirement under the arbitration agreement"	[Sch 2 Art 4-3]
"knows"	[Sch 2 Art 4-4]
"without undue delay"	[Sch 2 Art 4-5]
"within [the] time-limit"	[Sch 2 Art 4-6]
"proceeds with the arbitration"	[Sch 2 Art 4-7]
"deemed to have waived"	[Sch 2 Art 4-8]

[Sch 2 Art 4-1] Introduction Article 4 addresses similar issues to that addressed by Art 30 of the 1976 UNCITRAL Arbitration Rules: "A party who knows that any provision of, or requirement under, these Rules has not been complied with and yet proceeds with the arbitration without promptly stating his objection to such non-compliance, shall be deemed to have waived his right to object." Where a procedural requirement under the arbitration agreement or the Model Law is not complied with a party may have a right to object. Article 4 implies a waiver of this right in particular conditions, based on general principles such as waiver, "estoppel" or *"venire contra factum proprium"* (UNCITRAL Analytical Commentary at p 17, para 1).

[Sch 2 Art 4-2] "any provision of [the Model Law] from which the parties may derogate" This article only operates in relation to non-compliance with a non-mandatory provision of the Model Law. There is a debate as to precisely which provisions fall within this description (see S Greenberg, C Kee and R Weeramantry, *International Commercial Arbitration: An Asia-Pacific Perspective*, Cambridge University Press, Melbourne, 2011, pp 88–95). The provisions of the Model Law which may be classed as mandatory include:

(i) Article 18: each party shall be treated with equality and shall be afforded a full opportunity to present its case;
(ii) Article 23(1): the claimant shall state the facts supporting the claim and the respondent shall state its defence;
(iii) Article 24(2): the parties shall be given sufficient notice of any hearing or meeting;
(iv) Article 24(3): all statements, documents or other information supplied to the tribunal shall be communicated to the other party;
(v) Article 27: the arbitral tribunal or a party, with the approval of the tribunal may request from a competent court, assistance in taking evidence;
(vi) Article 30(2): an award on agreed terms shall be made in accordance with Art 31 and shall state that it is an award;
(vii) Article 31(1): the award shall be made in writing;
(viii) Article 31(3): the award shall state its date and the place of arbitration;
(ix) Article 31(4): the award shall be delivered to each party;
(x) Article 32: the arbitral proceedings are terminated by a final award;
(xi) Article 33(1): if a justified request is made, the tribunal shall make a correction to, or an interpretation of, the award;
(xii) Article 33(2): the tribunal, on its own initiative, may correct an error in the award within thirty days of the award;
(xiii) Article 33(4): the tribunal may extend the time within which it shall make a correction or interpretation or additional award;
(xiv) Article 33(5): the correction or interpretation or additional award shall be made in accordance with Art 31.

[Sch 2 Art 4-3] "any requirement under the arbitration agreement" The requirement under the agreement must be valid and not in conflict with a mandatory provision of the Model Law. The Article assumes the validity of arbitration agreement and does not apply to questions such as the validity of the arbitration agreement itself.

[Sch 2 Art 4-4] "knows" The provision requires actual knowledge. The words "or ought to have known" were in the draft of this provision which was the subject of the UNCITRAL Analytical Commentary, prepared by the Secretary-General, but those words were subsequently omitted from the final version. See *Report of UNCITRAL*, Yearbook, 1985, Vol XVI, UN Doc No A/40/17 at para 64: "Noting that these words ["or ought to have known"] were not contained in the corresponding provision in the UNCITRAL Arbitration Rules (article 30), the Commission decided to delete them since they might create more problems than they solved."

[Sch 2 Art 4-5] "without undue delay" A party to an arbitration that wishes to rely on non-compliance with the rules governing an arbitration should do so promptly and should not proceed with the arbitration as if there has been compliance with a relevant rule, keeping the point of non-compliance up one's sleeve for later use; see, eg, *Hebei Import & Export Corp v Polytek Engineering Co Ltd* [1991] 1 HKLRD 665 (CFA) at 690b (Sir Anthony Mason NPJ); and *Gao Haiyan v Keeneye Holdings Ltd* [2011] HKCFI 240 at [81].

[Sch 2 Art 4-6] "within [the] time-limit" The requirement in Art 4 that "if a time-limit is provided therefor, within such period of time" does not allow any possible extensions of time, as was available under the previous uniform domestic commercial arbitration legislation, and is available under s 12 of the Arbitration Act 1996 (Eng, W & NI) notwithstanding any agreement between the parties to the contrary; see, eg, *SOS Corporación Alimentaria SA v Inerco Trade SA* [2010] 2 Lloyd's Rep 345; [2010] EWHC 162 (Comm).

[Sch 2 Art 4-7] "proceeds with the arbitration" Silence or inaction is not sufficient. The provision takes effect when the party takes a step in the arbitration and not where there is inaction by a party.

[Sch 2 Art 4-8] "deemed to have waived" Article 4 prevents the matter being raised not only before the arbitral tribunal during the arbitration but subsequently before a court hearing a challenge to, or an application for enforcement of, the award under Arts 34 and 36 of the Model Law.

Article 5. Extent of court intervention

In matters governed by this Law, no court shall intervene except where so provided in this Law.

COMMENTARY ON SCH 2 ART 5

Introduction .... [Sch 2 Art 5-1]
Limited scope of Art 5 .... [Sch 2 Art 5-2]
Limited extent of court intervention .... [Sch 2 Art 5-3]
No inherent jurisdiction to intervene .... [Sch 2 Art 5-4]
Limitation period does not constitute intervention .... [Sch 2 Art 5-5]

[Sch 2 Art 5-1] Introduction The principle of non-intervention in Art 5 is a fundamental tenet of the Model Law. It is recognition that those parties that have chosen international arbitration under the Model Law to resolve their disputes have done so in the knowledge that no court will intrude or intervene in their chosen process except where stated in the Model Law. A similar observation was made by the UNCITRAL Secretariat in the UNCITRAL Explanatory Note 2006 at para 15, where it stated: "Recent amendments to arbitration laws reveal a trend in favour of limiting and clearly defining court involvement in international commercial arbitration. This is justified in view of the fact that the parties to an arbitration agreement make a conscious decision to exclude court jurisdiction and prefer the finality and expediency of the arbitral process." The UNCITRAL Secretariat also observed (at para 17) that "protecting the arbitral process from unpredictable or disruptive court interference is essential to parties who choose arbitration (in particular foreign parties)".

[Sch 2 Art 5-2] Limited scope of Art 5 The Model Law is not a comprehensive law on arbitration. It does not regulate matters such as party costs and arbitrators' fees, security and consolidation of arbitrations. The scope of Art 5 is narrower than the substantive scope of the Model Law, which is international commercial arbitration as defined in Art 1, in that Art 5 is limited to those issues and matters which are regulated, expressly or impliedly, by the Model Law (*Carter Holt Harvey Ltd v Genesis Power Ltd* [2006] 3 NZLR 794 (*Carter Holt Harvey*) at [40]–[44]). The effect of Art 5 is that where the court is permitted to intervene it may only do so in the manner provided by the Model Law (*Carter Holt Harvey* at [54]). In *Mitsui Engineering and Shipbuilding Co Ltd v Easton Graham Rush* (2004) SLR 14, the High Court of Singapore declined an application to restrain an arbitrator from taking further steps in the arbitration pending a challenge under Arts 12 and 13, and an application to set aside the award under Art 34 of the Model Law. As these articles applied, Art 5 precluded further intervention by the court.

[Sch 2 Art 5-3] Limited extent of court intervention The Model Law provides for court intervention only under:
  (i) Article 8(1) where, if a party so requests, the court shall refer the parties to arbitration;
  (ii) Article 11(3) and (4) where the court (or other authority) may appoint an arbitrator where the appointment procedure fails;
  (iii) Article 13(3) where the court (or other authority) may decide on a challenge of an arbitrator;
  (iv) Article 14(1) where the court (or other authority) may decide on the termination of an arbitrator's mandate;
  (v) Article 16(3) where the court may make a decision on the preliminary question whether the tribunal has jurisdiction;
  (vi) Article 27 where the court may provide assistance in taking evidence;
  (vii) Article 34 where the court may decide an application to set aside an award; and
  (viii) Article 36 where the court may decide whether to enforce or recognise an award.

[Sch 2 Art 5-4] No inherent jurisdiction to intervene There is no inherent jurisdiction for a court to interfere in an entirely private system of adjudication (*Imperial Leatherware Co Pty Ltd v Macri & Marcellino Pty Ltd* (1991) NSWLR 653 at 662–5; *Resort Condominiums International Inc v Bolwell* [1995] 1 Qd R 406 at 421; (1993) 118 ALR 655; BC9303445; and *Coppee Lavalin v Ken-Ren* [1995] 1 AC 38 at 48; [1994] 2 All ER 449; [1994] 2 Lloyd's Rep 109; [1994] 2 WLR 631, where Lord Mustill observed that the English High Court "has no inherent jurisdiction to intervene in a pending arbitration").

[Sch 2 Art 5-5] Limitation period does not constitute intervention An argument based on Art 5 was considered by the Supreme Court of Canada in *Yugraneft Corp v Rexx Management Corp* 2010 SCC 19; [2010] 1 SCR 649. The local limitation statute, which was expressed to apply "to any proceeding commenced or sought to be commenced . . . in which a claimant seeks a remedial order", was held to apply to an action to enforce a foreign award. The Supreme

Court held that the local limitation Act was intended to create a comprehensive and exhaustive limitations scheme applicable to all causes of action including an action to enforce a foreign award. The Supreme Court rejected an argument that the application of the limitation statute amounted to a judicial intervention which was contrary to Art 5 of the Model Law.

Article 6. Court or other authority for certain functions of arbitration assistance and supervision

The functions referred to in articles 11(3), 11(4), 13(3), 14, 16(3) and 34(2) shall be performed by ... [Each State enacting this model law specifies the court, courts or, where referred to therein, other authority competent to perform these functions.]

COMMENTARY ON SCH 2 ART 6

Introduction .... [Sch 2 Art 6-1]
The specified courts .... [Sch 2 Art 6-2]
Australian Centre for International Commercial Arbitration (ACICA) is specified authority ..... [Sch 2 Art 6-3]
ACICA Rules .... [Sch 2 Art 6-4]
Agreed procedural rules .... [Sch 2 Art 6-5]

[Sch 2 Art 6-1] Introduction The Model Law envisages court or other outside involvement in a limited number of instances. The first group comprises issues of appointment, challenge and termination of the mandate of the arbitrator (Arts 11, 13 and 14) and of the setting aside of the arbitral award (Art 34). These are functions "that should be entrusted, for the sake of centralisation, specialisation and efficiency, to a specially designated court" (UNCITRAL Explanatory Note 2006 at para 16). The second group comprises issues of court assistance in taking evidence (Art 27), recognition of the arbitration agreement, including its compatibility with court-ordered interim measures (Art 8), court-ordered interim measures (Art 17J), and recognition and enforcement of interim measures (Arts 17H and 17I) and of arbitral awards (Arts 35 and 36).

[Sch 2 Art 6-2] The specified courts Under s 18 of the Act, the Federal Court of Australia is a specified court for the purposes of Art 6. Additionally, where the place of arbitration is in a State or Territory, the Supreme Court of that State or Territory is also a specified court.

[Sch 2 Art 6-3] Australian Centre for International Commercial Arbitration (ACICA) is specified authority On 2 March 2011, the International Arbitration Regulations 2011 (Cth) (Regulations) came into force, prescribing the Australian Centre for International Commercial Arbitration Limited ACN 006 404 664 (ACICA) as the sole competent authority to perform the functions set out in Art 11(3) and (4) of the Model Law. ACICA is the peak body for international commercial arbitration in Australia. By prescribing ACICA as the sole appointing authority, parties are not required to resort to the courts where disputes arise over the appointment function. The Regulations provide a means of appointing arbitrators where the parties, arbitrators or an arbitral institution fail to do so or are otherwise unable to do so. Pursuant to Art 11(5), any appointment made by ACICA is unreviewable by a court.

However, it is possible that the High Court's original jurisdiction found in s 75 of the Constitution would nonetheless entitle it to review any decision made by ACICA as a specified authority.

[Sch 2 Art 6-4] ACICA Rules For arbitrations governed by analogous provisions of the ACICA Arbitration Rules, r 9.3 provides that, in appointing a sole arbitrator, ACICA shall have regard to such considerations as are likely to secure the appointment of an independent and impartial arbitrator and shall take into account as well the advisability of appointing an arbitrator of a nationality other than the nationalities of the parties. ACICA can also require such information from the parties as it deems necessary prior to making an appointment (ACICA Arbitration Rules, r 12.2).

[Sch 2 Art 6-5] Agreed procedural rules For arbitrations not governed by the ACICA Arbitration Rules, the chosen rules of arbitration may similarly provide for relevant considerations which ACICA is required to take into account when appointing an arbitrator. Where such rules are silent (or where the parties have chosen no rules), Art 11(5) of the Model Law requires ACICA to nonetheless have due regard to any qualifications required of the arbitrator by the agreement of the parties and to such considerations as are likely to secure the appointment of an independent and impartial arbitrator, as well as the advisability of appointing an arbitrator of a nationality other than that or those of the parties.

CHAPTER II. ARBITRATION AGREEMENT

Option I

Article 7. Definition and form of arbitration agreement
(As adopted by the Commission at its thirty-ninth session, in 2006)

(1) "Arbitration agreement" is an agreement by the parties to submit to arbitration all or certain disputes which have arisen or which may arise between them in respect of a defined legal relationship, whether contractual or not. An arbitration agreement may be in the form of an arbitration clause in a contract or in the form of a separate agreement.

(2) The arbitration agreement shall be in writing.

(3) An arbitration agreement is in writing if its content is recorded in any form, whether or not the arbitration agreement or contract has been concluded orally, by conduct, or by other means.

(4) The requirement that an arbitration agreement be in writing is met by an electronic communication if the information contained therein is accessible so as to be useable for subsequent reference; "electronic communication" means any communication that the parties make by means of data messages; "data message" means information generated, sent, received or stored by electronic, magnetic, optical or similar means, including, but not limited to, electronic data interchange (EDI), electronic mail, telegram, telexor telecopy.

(5) Furthermore, an arbitration agreement is in writing if it is contained in an exchange of statements of claim and defence in which the existence of an agreement is alleged by one party and not denied by the other.

(6) The reference in a contract to any document containing an arbitration clause constitutes an arbitration agreement in writing, provided that the reference is such as to make that clause part of the contract.

Option II

Article 7. Definition of arbitration agreement
(As adopted by the Commission at its thirty-ninth session, in 2006)

"Arbitration agreement" is an agreement by the parties to submit to arbitration all or certain disputes which have arisen or which may arise between them in respect of a defined legal relationship, whether contractual or not.

COMMENTARY ON SCH 2 ART 7

Introduction	[Sch 2 Art 7-1]
1985 definition of "arbitration agreement"	[Sch 2 Art 7-2]
2006 definition of "arbitration agreement": Options I and II	[Sch 2 Art 7-3]
Option I adopted in Australia	[Sch 2 Art 7-4]
Option I	[Sch 2 Art 7-5]
Arbitration agreement is in writing "if its content is recorded in any form" (Art 7(3))	[Sch 2 Art 7-6]
Arbitration agreement is in writing "if it is contained in an exchange of statements of claim and defence" (Art 7(5))	[Sch 2 Art 7-7]
"reference to any document containing an arbitration clause" (Art 7(6))	[Sch 2 Art 7-8]
Recommendation by UNCITRAL and UN	[Sch 2 Art 7-9]

[Sch 2 Art 7-1] Introduction The wording of the original 1985 definition of an arbitration agreement in Art 7 was "similar, but not the same as, that in Article II sub-articles 1 and 2" of the New York Convention (*Comandate Marine Corp v Pan Australia Shipping Pty Ltd* (2006) 157 FCR 45; 238 ALR 457; [2006] FCAFC 192; BC200610833 (*Comandate Marine Corp*) at [159] (Allsop J)). The definition required that an arbitration agreement be in writing and used language reflecting the available means of communication in 1985. The court in *Comandate Marine Corp* at [159], noted that the words "which provide a record of the agreement" appearing in Art 7(2) of the 1985 version of the Model Law do not appear in the New York Convention. Some uncertainty was thereby created for a court considering a request for a stay under Art 8. Article 1(2) provided that the provisions of the Model Law (except relevantly Art 8) applied only if the seat of the arbitration is in Australia. Thus, it could be argued that if the arbitration has a foreign seat, Art 7 does not apply (is not picked up) and cannot be used to ascertain the meaning of "arbitration agreement" in Art 8, which does apply in the case of a foreign-seated arbitration. The court expressed the view (at [160]) that "in order to give efficacy and content to Article 8, such parts of Articles 1, 2, 3 and 7 as are necessary for Article 8 to operate according to its terms would be picked up by the express reference to Article 8 by Article 1(2) of the Model Law".

In 2006 Art 7 was amended "to better conform to international contract practices" (UNCITRAL Explanatory Note 2006 at para 19) and two definitions were included as alternative options for States to consider. No preference was expressed by UNCITRAL in favour of either Option I or II. As discussed below, Australia adopted Option I.

[Sch 2 Art 7-2] 1985 definition of "arbitration agreement" The definition of an arbitration agreement in Art 7 of the 1985 Model Law was:

Article 7. Definition and form of arbitration agreement
(1) "Arbitration agreement" is an agreement by the parties to submit to arbitration all or certain disputes which have arisen or which may arise between them in respect of a defined legal relationship, whether contractual or not. An arbitration agreement may be in the form of an arbitration clause in a contract or in the form of a separate agreement.
(2) The arbitration agreement shall be in writing. An agreement is in writing if it is contained in a document signed by the parties or in an exchange of letters, telex, telegrams or other means of telecommunication which provide a record of the agreement, or in an exchange of statements of claim and defence in which the existence of an agreement is alleged by one party and not denied by another. The reference in a contract to a document containing an arbitration clause constitutes an arbitration agreement provided that the contract is in writing and the reference is such as to make that clause part of the contract.

[Sch 2 Art 7-3] 2006 definition of "arbitration agreement": Options I and II The 2006 amendments to the Model Law offer States alternative versions of Art 7. States must choose which version of Art 7 they wish to incorporate into their laws. Option I is in substantially the same terms as the 1985 iteration of Art 7, although there are two significant changes. First, Option I clarifies that an agreement may be concluded orally, through conduct or other means, provided that its content is recorded in some form. Second, the provision reflects the use of electronic communications to conclude commercial arrangements. Option II is less prescriptive than both the original iteration of Art 7 and Option I. It includes a definition of "arbitration agreement" but excludes any formal requirements, including the requirement that an agreement be in writing (Revised Explanatory Memorandum to the International Arbitration Amendment Bill 2010 (Cth) at [67]).

[Sch 2 Art 7-4] Option I adopted in Australia During consultations conducted as part of the Review of the Act, following the release by the Attorney-General in late 2008 of a Discussion Paper which suggested possible amendments to the legislation, "there was widespread support for adopting Option I . . . [whereas] Option II [was seen as involving] a substantial departure from current practice in Australia" (Revised Explanatory Memorandum to the International Arbitration Amendment Bill 2010 (Cth) at [68]). Option I is also more reflective of the writing requirement in the New York Convention. Accordingly, s 16 of the Act was amended to provide that "arbitration agreement" has the same meaning as in Option I.

[Sch 2 Art 7-5] Option I Option I follows the structure of the original 1985 text and also follows the New York Convention in requiring the written form of the arbitration agreement, but recognises a record of the "contents" of the agreement "in any form" as equivalent to traditional "writing". The agreement to arbitrate may be entered into in any form (including orally) as long as the content of the agreement is recorded. It no longer requires signatures of the parties or an exchange of messages between the parties. It modernises the language by adopting wording from the 1996 UNCITRAL Model Law on Electronic Commerce and the *2005 United Nations Convention on the Use of Electronic Communications in International Contracts*. It also covers the situation where there has been "an exchange of statements of claim and defence in which the existence of the agreement is alleged by one party and not denied by another". It covers the situation where there is a reference in a contract to a document, such as general conditions, which contains an arbitration clause "provided that the reference is such as to make that clause part of the contract".

[Sch 2 Art 7-6] Arbitration agreement is in writing "if its content is recorded in any form" (Art 7(3)) Article 7(3) includes the situation previously covered in Art 7(2) of the 1985 definition, which provided that an arbitration agreement is an "agreement ... in writing if it is contained ... in an exchange of letters ... which provide a record of the agreement". An example of a situation where one party did not sign the agreement but it was nonetheless held that Art 7(2) was satisfied because "there are ample exchanges of letters which provide a record of the agreement" is seen in *Gay Constructions Pty Ltd v Caledonian Techmore (Building) Ltd* [1995] 2 HKLR 35 at 39.

[Sch 2 Art 7-7] Arbitration agreement is in writing "if it is contained in an exchange of statements of claim and defence" (Art 7(5)) Article 7(5) includes the situation previously covered by Art 7(2) of the 1985 definition, which provided that an arbitration agreement is an "agreement ... in writing if it is contained ... in an exchange of statements of claim and defence in which the existence of an agreement is alleged by one party and not denied by another". In *Gay Constructions Pty Ltd v Caledonian Techmore (Building) Ltd* [1995] 2 HKLR 35, the court noted, at 39, that "the phrase 'statements of claim and defence' in Article 7(2) of the 1985 Model Law was not defined and [the court could] see no reason why they should be read as referring only to pleadings in the formal sense". In that case, a detailed contractual document outlining the claim for loss and expense was held to satisfy Art 7(2).

[Sch 2 Art 7-8] "reference to any document containing an arbitration clause" (Art 7(6)) The last sentence of Art 7(2) of the 1985 definition relating to the issue of incorporation by reference, is now found in the 2006 definition in Art 7(6) subject to the minor change from "a document" to "any document". There are conflicting views internationally as to the nature of the reference required before an arbitration clause is incorporated into an agreement. See the discussion in A Tweedale and K Tweedale, "Incorporation of Arbitration Clauses Revisited" (2010) 76(4) *Arbitration* 656–60; and Rebecca James and Michael Schoenberg, "Incorporating an Arbitration Clause 'by reference': Reconciling Model Law Article VII and Australian Common Law in Light of Recent Developments" (2011) 77(1) *Arbitration* 84–98.

In some cases, express reference is required to the arbitration agreement before it can be incorporated, which is derived in part from the view that "distinct and specific words" are needed before the courts' jurisdiction is ousted (*TW Thomas & Co v Portsea Steamship Co* [1912] AC 1 at 6 (Lord Atkinson)).

A contrasting approach is seen in *Habas Sinai VE Tibbi Gazlar Isthisal Endustri AS v Sometal SAL* [2010] All ER (D) 99 (Jan); [2010] 1 All ER (Comm) 1143; [2010] 1 Lloyd's Rep 661; [2010] EWHC 29 (Comm) (*Habas Sinai*) at [51], where it was said: "But a businessman would have no difficulty in regarding the arbitration clause (as he would call it) as part of a contract and as capable of incorporation, by appropriate wording, as any other term of such a contract; and it is, as it seems to me to a businessman's understanding that the court should be disposed to give effect. A businessman who had agreed with his counterparty a contract with 10 specific terms under various headings and then agreed with the same counterparty terms 1–5 under the same headings as before and, as to the rest, that all the terms of the previous contract should apply, would, I think, be surprised to find that '*all*' should be interpreted so as to mean '*all but the arbitration clause*' [emphasis in original]".

The reasons put forward for the restrictive approach to the incorporation of arbitration clauses followed by the English courts were recently summarised in *Habas Sinai* at [34] as (authorities omitted):

(a) Arbitration clauses are not "germane" or "directly" relevant to, nor part of the subject matter of, the main contract, and general words must generally be taken to cover only those contractual provisions that are germane to the subject matter of the bill of lading contract (eg, provisions as to carriage and discharge) and are capable of being operated in conjunction with that subject matter because the court cannot confidently infer that the parties intended to incorporate any more than that . . . .

(b) Arbitration clauses are ancillary provisions by way of dispute resolution essentially personal to the parties which agree them so that general words of incorporation are insufficient . . . an arbitration clause is, thus, not incorporated by language which refers to all terms . . . or all conditions . . .

(c) Arbitration clauses oust the jurisdiction of the courts and clear words are need for that purpose . . . . Section 7 of the Arbitration Act 1979 requires an arbitration agreement to be in writing and shows the need for a conscious and deliberate relinquishment of a right to go to court . . .

(d) Bills of lading may come into the hands of those who will, or may, neither know, nor have the means of knowing, the arbitration clause in the charterparty which they will not have seen and to which they would be unlikely to assent. They will not therefore appreciate that by becoming a party to the bill they became parties to a contact precluding access to the courts . . . although the fact that a contract is not contained in a negotiable instrument does not mean that general words of incorporation are in general capable of incorporating arbitration clauses . . .

(e) The terms of a charterparty arbitration clause may not be applicable to disputes between the bill of lading holder and the shipowner . . . and on that account are not to be regarded as incorporated by a general reference;

(f) The need for certainty in the law.

The position in Australia under s 3(5) and Art 7(6) of the Model Law has yet to be the subject of judicial consideration. (For the position under the common law in Australia see *Lief Investments Pty Ltd v Conagra International Fertiliser Co* [1998] NSWCA 481; BC9803166.)

The English courts have noted that if the Model Law applied in England, the English authorities could be put to "one side" as "it appears that the function of the last 14 words [in Art 7(2) of the Model Law] was to exclude incorporation where the reference was by way of mention rather than by way of incorporation" (*Trygg Hansa Insurance Co Ltd v Equitas Ltd* [1998] 2 Lloyd's Rep 439 at 447).

The operation of Art 7 in the 1985 Model Law was considered in *Astel-Peiniger Joint Venture v Argos Engineering & Heavy Industries Co Ltd* [1995] 1 HKLR 300; [1994] 3 HKC 328. The court rejected a submission that the document containing the arbitration clause which was referred to had to be a contract between the same parties and held it was possible to incorporate an arbitration clause contained in a contract between other parties or by reference to an unsigned standard form of contract. The court held (at 306–7) that the "language adopted [in Art 7(2)] appears to mean that the general conditions, prior contract or other document must have been intended to be incorporated into the contract, and not merely referred to in, for example, a 'whereas' clause or as background to the agreement". The court distinguished *Thomas v Portsea* [1912] AC 1 noting that the decision in that case was based on the particular context of a negotiable instrument and on reservations about ousting the jurisdiction of the court. The court held (at 311) that the task required by Art 7 in determining whether or not there has been incorporation of a document by reference "is one of construction; namely, to ascertain the parties' intentions when they entered into the contract by reference to the words that they used". The court endorsed the view of Sir John Donaldson in the Court of Appeal in *Skips Nordheim v Syrian Petroleum* [1984] 1 QB 599 at 616 that the "operative words of incorporation may be precise or general, narrow or wide . . . what must be sought is incorporation, not notice of the existence or terms of another which is not incorporated [emphasis in original]". The same approach to Art 7(2) was taken in *Gay Constructions Pty Ltd v Caledonian Techmore (Building) Ltd* [1995] 2 HKLR 35. See also the discussion of incorporation by reference found in S Greenberg, C Kee and R Weeramantry, *International Commercial Arbitration: An Asia-Pacific Perspective*, Cambridge University Press, Melbourne, 2011, pp 151–5.

[Sch 2 Art 7-9] Recommendation by UNCITRAL and UN As noted in relation to s 3 of the Act, a further attempt to expand the definition was made by UNCITRAL in its Report (A/61/17) of 14 July 2006. UNCITRAL adopted a recommendation "that article II, paragraph (2) of the Convention be applied recognising that the circumstances described therein are not exhaustive". The General Assembly of the United Nations adopted the recommendation, which in its resolution 61/33 of 4 December 2006 noted that "in connection with the modernisation of articles of the Model Law, the promotion of a uniform interpretation and application of the [New York Convention] is particularly timely". The recommendation encourages States to apply Art II(2) of the New York Convention "recognising that the circumstances described therein are not exhaustive".

Article 8. Arbitration agreement and substantive claim before court

(1) A court before which an action is brought in a matter which is the subject of an arbitration agreement shall, if a party so requests not later than when submitting his first statement on the substance of the dispute, refer the parties to arbitration unless it finds that the agreement is null and void, inoperative or incapable of being performed.

(2) Where an action referred to in paragraph (1) of this article has been brought, arbitral proceedings may nevertheless be commenced or continued, and an award may be made, while the issue is pending before the court.

COMMENTARY ON SCH 2 ART 8

Introduction	[Sch 2 Art 8-1]
Place of arbitration	[Sch 2 Art 8-2]
Relationship between Art 8 and Art 7	[Sch 2 Art 8-3]
Relationship between Art 8 and Art 16	[Sch 2 Art 8-4]
Requirements for a stay	[Sch 2 Art 8-5]
"first statement on the substance of the dispute"	[Sch 2 Art 8-6]
Arbitration proceedings may continue	[Sch 2 Art 8-7]

[Sch 2 Art 8-1] Introduction Article 8 operates independently from, but in a similar manner to, s 7 of the Act. Both s 7 and Art 8 are based on Art II(3) of the New York Convention. Section 7 and Art 8 are mandatory provisions, and are by their nature binding on the courts of the State when a party makes such a request in the circumstances outlined in the article. The mere fact that there may be some connection between the court proceeding and the matter which is the subject of the arbitration agreement is not sufficient to engage Art 8(1). There must be a direct relationship between the matter before the court and the matter which is the subject of the arbitration agreement (*Carter Holt Harvey Ltd v Genesis Power Ltd* [2006] 3 NZLR 794 at [58]).

[Sch 2 Art 8-2] Place of arbitration Article 8 is not confined to agreements providing for arbitration within Australia. This provision also applies in the case of a foreign-seated arbitration. Accordingly, if the required circumstances exist, a court is required to refer the parties to arbitration whether or not the arbitration is to take place in Australia.

[Sch 2 Art 8-3] Relationship between Art 8 and Art 7 As discussed above in relation to Art 8, it was noted in *Comandate Marine Corp v Pan Australia Shipping Pty Ltd* (2006) 157 FCR 45; 238 ALR 457; [2006] FCAFC 192; BC200610833 at [159] (Allsop J) that the words "which provide a record of the agreement" appearing in Art 7(2) of the 1985 version of the Model Law do not appear in the New York Convention. Some uncertainty was thereby created for a court considering a request for a stay under Art 8. Article 1(2) provided that the provisions of the Model Law (except relevantly Art 8) applied only if the seat of the arbitration is in Australia. Thus it could be argued that if the arbitration has a foreign seat, Art 7 does not apply (is not picked up) and could not be used to ascertain the meaning of "arbitration agreement" in Art 8, which does apply in the case of a foreign-seated arbitration. The court expressed the view (at [160]) that "in order to give efficacy and content to Article 8, such parts of Articles 1, 2, 3 and 7 as are necessary for Article 8 to operate according to its terms would be picked up by the express reference to Article 8 by Article 1(2) of the Model Law".

[Sch 2 Art 8-4] Relationship between Art 8 and Art 16 When an application for a stay is made under Art 8, an issue may arise as to the jurisdiction of the arbitrator to hear the dispute. The question then arises as to whether it is the role of the court, in cases where the arbitral tribunal has the power to rule on its own jurisdiction under Art 16, to make a definitive pronouncement on the jurisdiction of the arbitrator on the application for a stay, or whether the preferable approach is to leave the matter to the arbitrator as decision-maker of first instance.

One view is that only where it is clear that there is no jurisdiction to grant a stay, will the court consider on an application under Art 8, an issue related to the existence or validity of the arbitration agreement; see, eg, *Gulf Canada Resources v Arochem International* [1992] CanLII 4033 (BC CA); (1992) 43 CPR (3d) 390 at 397. Article 8 does not obligate a court to deal with a claim that an arbitration agreement is "inoperative or null and void" (*ABN Amro Bank v Krupp Mak Maschinenbau GmbH* (1996) 135 DLR (4th) 130 at 133 (Adams J, Dunnet J concurring)). On this view, it is not for the court on an application for a stay of proceedings under Art 8 to reach any final determination as to the scope of the arbitration agreement, or whether a particular party to the legal proceedings is a party to the arbitration agreement, because those are matters within the jurisdiction of the arbitral tribunal under Art 16. Only where it is clear that the dispute is outside the terms of the arbitration agreement, or that a party is not a party to the arbitration agreement, or that the application is out of time, should the court reach any final determination in respect of such matters on an application for a stay of proceedings. Thus, where an issue arises on an application for a stay under Art 8 as to whether the agreement is: (a) null and void; (b) inoperative; or (c) incapable of being performed, and where it is clear that one of these situations exists, the court will make a determinative finding to that effect and dismiss the motion for referral, eg, *Dalimpex Ltd v Janicki* (2003) 64 OR (3d) 737; 228 DLR (4th) 179; [2003] CanLII 34234 at [21]–[22]; and *Tommy CP Sze & Co v Li & Fung (Trading) Ltd* [2002] HKCFI 682 at [18]–[24].

Even where it is not clear whether one of the situations exists, the court when considering an application under Art 8, may order that the issue "be determined separately and in advance of any other issues" in the proceedings, eg, *Shanghai Foreign Trade Corp v Sigma Metallurgical Co Pty Ltd* (1996) 133 FLR 417 at 446; BC9603441, which concerned an application brought under Art 8 and s 7, following the approach taken by the court in *Bakri Navigation Co Ltd v Owners of Ship 'Golden Glory' Glorious Shipping SA* (1991) 217 ALR 152; BC9103216.

[Sch 2 Art 8-5] Requirements for a stay The application must be made by a party — the court cannot act on its own motion — and must be made before that party submits its "first statement on the substance of the dispute". Unlike the terms of s 7 of the Act, there is no extension which confers a right to apply for a stay on a person claiming through or under a party bound by the arbitration agreement. Indeed, no extension of time is possible, therefore, the application must be made within time. The arbitration agreement must not be "null, void, inoperative or incapable of being performed"; see the discussion of the meaning of these words in relation to s 7 above. Once the elements of Art 8 are established, a stay is mandatory, eg, *Marnell Corrao Associates Inc v Sensation Yachts Ltd* (High Court of New Zealand, Wild J, 22 August 2000, unreported, at [73]).

[Sch 2 Art 8-6] **"first statement on the substance of the dispute"** In the UNCITRAL Analytical Commentary, contained in the report of the Secretary-General to the 18th Session of UNCITRAL, it was stated (at para 3) in respect of Art 8 that: "A time element has been added that the request be made at the latest with or in the first statement on the substance of the dispute. It is submitted that this point of time should be taken literally and applied uniformly in all legal systems, including those which normally regard such a request as a procedural plea to be raised at an earlier stage than any pleadings on substance" (as noted by the court in *ABN Amro Bank v Krupp Mak Maschinenbau GmbH* (1996) 135 DLR (4th) 130 at 135 (Adams J, Dunnet J concurring)). Accordingly, a request for a stay contained in the pleadings (ie, the statement of defence) was made "with or in the first statement on the substance of the dispute" (*ABN Amro Bank v Krupp Mak Maschinenbau GmbH* (Ontario Supreme Court, Then J, 7 June 1995, unreported, at [7]), affirmed on appeal at (1996) 135 DLR (4th) 130 at 133 (Adams J, Dunnet J concurring)). If a defence is filed without a prior or concurrent application for a stay, a court cannot grant a stay under Art 8, eg, *429545 BC Ltd v Joseph B Herlihy* (Supreme Court of British Columbia, Hood J, 28 July 1998, 1998 CanLII 887 (BC SC) at [21] and [23]).

As the court noted in *Louis Dreyfus Trading Ltd v Bonarich International (Group) Ltd* (1997) HKCFI 312 at [21], "it is not the intention of the Model Law to take away the strong new right of a Mandatory Stay easily by any casual act of the Defendant [and that Art 8 provides for] some formal document (probably first in a series) specially submitted by a party to the court which contains what that party says on the substance of the dispute". This view is reflected in the decision reached in *The Property People Ltd v Housing New Zealand Ltd* (1999) 14 PRNZ 66, where the court was hearing an application for an interim injunction. The defendant filed a notice of opposition and "substantive" affidavits in opposing the application (at [23]). The court (at [24]) held that these documents constituted a statement on the substance of the dispute. In *Pathak v Tourism Transport Ltd* [2002] 3 NZLR 681 (*Pathak*) at [47], the court noted that a plaintiff who initiates interim injunction proceedings without reference to an arbitration agreement is not protected by Art 9, and has submitted a statement on the substance of the dispute and is prevented from applying for a stay under Art 8. "Similarly a defendant who opposes interim relief and fails to seek a stay (or protest jurisdiction) in respect of the substantive dispute will also be prevented from seeking a stay" (under Art 8, *Pathak* at [47]).

[Sch 2 Art 8-7] **Arbitration proceedings may continue** Article 8(2) gives an arbitral tribunal express power to continue with the arbitration proceedings. This power is not found in Art II(3) of the New York Convention and is not expressly stated in s 7 of the Act.

Article 9. Arbitration agreement and interim measures by court

It is not incompatible with an arbitration agreement for a party to request, before or during arbitral proceedings, from a court an interim measure of protection and for a court to grant such measure.

COMMENTARY ON SCH 2 ART 9

Introduction	[Sch 2 Art 9-1]
Place of arbitration	[Sch 2 Art 9-2]
Art 9 does not confer jurisdiction on a court	[Sch 2 Art 9-3]
Waiver at common law	[Sch 2 Art 9-4]

[Sch 2 Art 9-1] Introduction Article 9 allows the parties to seek the assistance of the court without affecting their rights to arbitrate the dispute under the arbitration agreement. "Wherever a request for interim measures may be made to a court, it may not be relied upon, under the Model Law, as a waiver or an objection against the existence or effect of the arbitration agreement" (UNCITRAL Explanatory Note 2006 at para 22).

[Sch 2 Art 9-2] Place of arbitration Article 9 is not confined to agreements providing for arbitration within Australia. This provision also applies in the case of a foreign-seated arbitration. Accordingly, if the court has jurisdiction to grant interim measures, a request for such assistance and the grant of such assistance, does not affect the parties' rights and obligations under the arbitration agreement even if the arbitration is to take place in Australia or elsewhere.

[Sch 2 Art 9-3] Art 9 does not confer jurisdiction on a court Article 9 is addressed to the courts and ensures that interim measures issued by a court are not incompatible with the continued operation of the arbitration agreement, irrespective of the place of arbitration. Article 9 "is permissive in nature and merely means that parties to international arbitrations may apply to a domestic court for interim measures where the court has power to grant such measures ... [and] Article 9 in itself does not make them available" (*Swift-Fortune Ltd v Magnifica Marine SA* [2006] SGCA 42 at [25]). In New Zealand, where interim measures of protection are granted under the "jurisdiction" conferred by Art 9 however, the Model Law article has been supplemented by Art 9(2) and (3), which specifically confer express power to make various orders described in those provisions; see, eg, *Marnell Corrao Associates Inc v Sensation Yachts Ltd* (High Court of New Zealand, Wild J, 22 August 2000, unreported, at [74] and [98]) where the orders were made; and *Lindow v Barton McGill Marine Ltd* (2002) 16 PRNZ 796 at [10]–[15], where an application for an order for security for costs was refused, as it did not fall within the terms of Art 9(2) and (3).

[Sch 2 Art 9-4] Waiver at common law As discussed above in relation to s 7 of the Act, to establish a binding waiver at common law requires two mutually inconsistent rights, where the exercise of one is inconsistent with the continued existence of the other. The "rights are inconsistent if neither may be enjoyed without the extinction of the other" (*Comandate Marine Corp v Pan Australia Shipping Pty Ltd* (2006) 157 FCR 45; 238 ALR 457; [2006] FCAFC 192; BC200610833 at [62] (Allsop J)). In this case, the full court held that the filing of the writ *in rem* by one party was not the exercise of a right to litigate, which was inconsistent with the continued existence of a right to arbitrate. The mere commencement of the proceedings by the writ *in rem* seeking the arrest of a vessel did not cause or pre-suppose the extinction of the rights under the parties' arbitration agreement. The same approach was taken by the English High Court in

Ispat Industries Ltd v Western Bulk Pte Ltd [2011] EWHC 93 (Comm). Here, the court noted (at [46]) that it "is well established that ancillary applications for security are not a breach of an arbitration clause so long as there is no attempt to have the merits of the dispute heard other than by the agreed arbitral tribunal".

CHAPTER III. COMPOSITION OF ARBITRAL TRIBUNAL

Article 10. Number of arbitrators

(1) The parties are free to determine the number of arbitrators.
(2) Failing such determination, the number of arbitrators shall be three.

COMMENTARY ON SCH 2 ART 10

Introduction	[Sch 2 Art 10-1]
Party autonomy in determining number of arbitrators	[Sch 2 Art 10-2]
Supplementary rule	[Sch 2 Art 10-3]

[Sch 2 Art 10-1] Introduction Article 10 caused little controversy when it was drafted, notwithstanding the fact that it introduced a significant change for many countries whose legislation required the number of arbitrators to be uneven; see, eg, H Holtzmann and J Neuhaus, *A Guide to the UNCITRAL Model Law on International Commercial Arbitration*, Kluwer Law International, The Hague, 1989, p 348. As Aron Broches observed: "There is a great variety on this point among national laws. Some require that the tribunal be composed of an odd number of arbitrators, while others either leave the parties free to deviate by agreement from that requirement or contain no provisions on the subject": A Broches, *Commentary on the UNCITRAL Model Law on International Commercial Arbitration*, Kluwer Law International, Deventer, 1990, p 53.

The UNCITRAL Working Group agreed that requiring that the number of arbitrators must be uneven would be overprotective. As such, it was decided that the parties would be free to determine the number of arbitrators (Holtzmann and Neuhaus, pp 348–51, citing First Secretariat Note, UN Doc No A/CN.9/207, 14 May 1981, para 67 and First Working Group Report, UN Doc No A/CN.9/216, 23 March 1982, para 46).

[Sch 2 Art 10-2] Party autonomy in determining number of arbitrators Article 10(1) provides that the parties are free to determine the number of arbitrators, and thus embodies the principle of complete party autonomy: P Sanders, *The Work of UNCITRAL on Arbitration and Conciliation*, Kluwer Law International, The Hague, 2001, p 34. As UNCITRAL's Analytical Commentary states at p 26:

> Paragraph (1) recognises the parties' freedom to determine the number of arbitrators. Thus, the choice of any number would be given effect, even in those legal systems which at present require an uneven number. As generally stated in Article 2(c), the freedom of the parties is not limited to determining the issue themselves but includes the right to authorise a third party to make that determination.

[Sch 2 Art 10-3] Supplementary rule Under Art 10(2), where the parties have not agreed on the number of arbitrators, that number shall be three. This was argued by the Working Group to be the best option because: a tribunal of three arbitrators was more likely to guarantee equal understanding of the positions of the parties; three-person arbitral tribunals were the most common configuration in international commercial arbitration; and Art 5 of the UNCITRAL Arbitration Rules provides for three arbitrators, in the absence of a contrary agreement by the parties: H Holtzmann and J Neuhaus, *A Guide to the UNCITRAL Model Law on International Commercial Arbitration*, Kluwer Law International, The Hague, 1989, p 349, citing Second Working Group Report, UN Doc No A/CN.9/232, para 81; see also A Broches, *Commentary on the UNCITRAL Model Law on International Commercial Arbitration*, Kluwer Law International, Deventer, 1990, p 54.

Article 11. Appointment of arbitrators

(1) No person shall be precluded by reason of his nationality from acting as an arbitrator, unless otherwise agreed by the parties.

(2) The parties are free to agree on a procedure of appointing the arbitrator or arbitrators, subject to the provisions of paragraphs (4) and (5) of this article.

(3) Failing such agreement,
   (a) in an arbitration with three arbitrators, each party shall appoint one arbitrator, and the two arbitrators thus appointed shall appoint the third arbitrator; if a party fails to appoint the arbitrator within thirty days of receipt of a request to do so from the other party, or if the two arbitrators fail to agree on the third arbitrator within thirty days of their appointment, the appointment shall be made, upon request of a party, by the court or other authority specified in article 6;
   (b) in an arbitration with a sole arbitrator, if the parties are unable to agree on the arbitrator, he shall be appointed, upon request of a party, by the court or other authority specified in article 6.

(4) Where, under an appointment procedure agreed upon by the parties,
   (a) a party fails to act as required under such procedure, or
   (b) the parties, or two arbitrators, are unable to reach an agreement expected of them under such procedure, or
   (c) a third party, including an institution, fails to perform any function entrusted to it under such procedure,
any party may request the court or other authority specified in article 6 to take the necessary measure, unless the agreement on the appointment procedure provides other means for securing the appointment.

(5) A decision on a matter entrusted by paragraph (3) or (4) of this article to the court or other authority specified in article 6 shall be subject to no appeal. The court or other authority, in appointing an arbitrator, shall have due regard to any qualifications required of the arbitrator by the agreement of the parties and to such considerations as are likely to secure the appointment of an independent and impartial arbitrator and, in the case of a sole or third arbitrator, shall take into account as well the advisability of appointing an arbitrator of a nationality other than those of the parties.

COMMENTARY ON SCH 2 ART 11

No discrimination of foreign nationals .... [Sch 2 Art 11-1]
Parties can agree on procedure for appointment of
    arbitrators .... [Sch 2 Art 11-2]
Limitations on parties' freedom .... [Sch 2 Art 11-3]
Failure to follow appointment procedure in parties'
    agreement can lead to award being set aside ... [Sch 2 Art 11-4]
Default appointment procedure .... [Sch 2 Art 11-5]
Court or other authority prescribed under the Act . [Sch 2 Art 11-6]
Waiting period before applying to the court ...... [Sch 2 Art 11-7]
Appointment procedure for tribunal of other than
    one or three arbitrators .... [Sch 2 Art 11-8]
Appointment by court or other authority .... [Sch 2 Art 11-9]
Decision of court or other authority subject to no
    appeal .... [Sch 2 Art 11-10]
Possibility of appeal if issue relates to, eg, existence
    of arbitration agreemen .... [Sch 2 Art 11-11]
Considerations of court or other authority in
    making appointments .... [Sch 2 Art 11-12]
Important to ensure that "no grievance is felt" in
    making such appointments .... [Sch 2 Art 11-13]
Court may seek to put parties in position they
    would have been in .... [Sch 2 Art 11-14]

[Sch 2 Art 11-1] No discrimination of foreign nationals An important factor in establishing "truly international arbitration" is the requirement that no person be precluded by virtue of their nationality from serving as an arbitrator (H Holtzmann and J Neuhaus, *A Guide to the UNCITRAL Model Law on International Commercial Arbitration*, Kluwer Law International, The Hague, 1989, p 359).

Article 11(1) removes the restrictions in those national laws that prevent foreigners from serving as arbitrators (see also *Hashwani v Jivraj* [2011] All ER (D) 246 (Jul); 1 WLR 1872; [2011] UKSC 40). However, as observed in UNCITRAL Analytical Commentary, this must give way to the principle of party autonomy; in other words, it is not intended "to preclude parties from specifying that nationals of certain States may, or may not, be appointed as arbitrators" (UNCITRAL Analytical Commentary, p 28, para 1). In adopting this provision, however, the UNCITRAL Working Group noted that States could not be prevented from altering the Model Law on this point to reflect their particular policies (Fourth Working Group Report, UN Doc No A/CN.9/245, 22 September 1983, para 193, cited in Holtzmann and Neuhaus at p 376; see also UNCITRAL Analytical Commentary, p 28, para 1, n 41).

[Sch 2 Art 11-2] Parties can agree on procedure for appointment of arbitrators Article 11(2) does not restrict the parties' ability to agree on a procedure for the appointment of arbitrators except to the extent set out in Art 11(4) and (5). As is noted in the UNCITRAL Analytical Commentary: "Parties may not exclude, in their agreement on the appointment, the right of a party under paragraph (4) to resort to the Court specified in Article 6 in any of the situations described in that paragraph, or exclude the finality of the Court's decision provided for in paragraph (5)" (UNCITRAL Analytical Commentary, p 28, para 3; see further H Holtzmann and J Neuhaus, *A Guide to the UNCITRAL Model Law on International Commercial Arbitration*, Kluwer Law International, The Hague, 1989, p 359; and A Broches, *Commentary on the UNCITRAL Model Law on International Commercial Arbitration*, Kluwer Law International, The Hague, 1990, p 56).

[Sch 2 Art 11-3] Limitations on parties' freedom In drafting Art 11(2), the UNCITRAL Working Group recognised that "the Model Law as a whole implied certain restrictions on the parties' agreement regarding appointment of arbitrators" (H Holtzmann and J Neuhaus, *A Guide to the UNCITRAL Model Law on International Commercial Arbitration*, Kluwer Law International, The Hague, 1989, p 360). The Third Working Group Report cited as examples two articles that give rise to such restrictions: Art 12, concerning the grounds for challenging arbitrators, and Art 34, concerning the courts' power to set aside arbitral awards (Holtzmann and Neuhaus, p 373, citing Third Working Group Report, UN Doc No A/CN.9/233, 28 March 1983, para 90). For example, "if the procedure agreed by the parties results in the constitution of an arbitral tribunal that fails to meet the standards of impartiality and independence required under Article 12" of the Model Law, the arbitrator(s) in question would be subject to challenge (Holtzmann and Neuhaus, p 360). Likewise, "if an appointment procedure results in a party not receiving 'proper notice of the appointment of an arbitrator', an award may be set aside and refused recognition or enforcement under Articles 34(2)(a)(ii) and 36(1)(a)(ii)" (Holtzmann and Neuhaus, p 360, referring to Third Working Group Report, UN Doc No A/CN.9/233, 28 March 1983, para 90).

The UNCITRAL Working Group considered adding to Art 11 a limitation on the parties' freedom to determine the appointment procedure by stating that "a procedure agreed upon by the parties would be invalid if, or to the extent that, it gave one party a 'predominant position', or in the words of an alternative draft, a 'manifestly unfair advantage', with regard to the appointment of arbitrators" (Holtzmann and Neuhaus, p 360). This proposal was not adopted for various reasons, including the infrequency with which the problem arose; the possibility of the problem being addressed by other provisions of the Model Law (such as Arts 12 and 34); and, in addition, the proposed wording was regarded as "too vague", meaning that it could give rise to "controversy, dilatory tactics, and, potentially, invalidation of 'well-established and recognised appointment practices'" (Holtzmann and Neuhaus, p 360, citing Third Working Group Report, para 90).

[Sch 2 Art 11-4] Failure to follow appointment procedure in parties' agreement can lead to award being set aside In *Donald Fleming, Florence Fleming and Donna Moran v Space Homes Ltd* [1985] CanLII 1458 (AB QB) (Queen's Bench of Alberta, Cormack J, 15 January 1985), the issue before the court was whether the award had been "improperly procured" within the meaning of s 11 of the Arbitration Act R.S.A. 1980 because the composition of the arbitral tribunal was not in accordance with the agreement of the parties (contrary to Art 34(2)(a)(iv) of the Model Law). Two arbitrators had been appointed by the parties, but before the third appointment could be made, the applicant's arbitrator died. A person later claimed to have taken over the deceased's practice and to have been appointed as arbitrator for the applicants. Rather than appoint a third arbitrator, the two purported party-appointed arbitrators simply agreed that the third arbitrator determine the dispute (at [27]). The court held that only the parties could have varied the arbitration agreement, but not the arbitrators themselves, without explicit authority (at [37]). It also observed that "it must be assumed that [the two party-appointed arbitrators] were aware of the authorities which make it clear that where three arbitrators are appointed they may not delegate their collective authority to a sole arbitrator and similarly where a decision is to be made by a committee of three it must be unanimous" (at [43]). The court concluded that the purported third arbitrator had "acted without authority to render his decision as sole arbitrator and hence the arbitration award is set aside" (at [48]).

[Sch 2 Art 11-5] **Default appointment procedure** Article 11(3) sets out the default procedure for the appointment of arbitrators where the parties have failed to agree on that procedure. That procedure, which involves an application being made to the court or other authority specified under Art 6 of the Model Law, is relatively self-explanatory. As the UNCITRAL Analytical Commentary states at p 29, para 5:

> Paragraph (3) supplies those parties that have not agreed on a procedure for the appointment with a system for appointing either three arbitrators or one arbitrator, these numbers being the two most common ones in international cases. Sub-paragraph (a) lays down the rules for the appointment of three arbitrators, whether this number has been agreed upon by the parties under Article 10(1) or whether it follows from Article 10(2). Sub-paragraph (b) lays down the method of appointing a sole arbitrator for those cases where the parties have made no provision for the appointment, except to agree on the number (ie, one).

The provisions of Art 11(3)(a) for the appointment of three arbitrators are similar to the applicable procedure under the UNCITRAL Arbitration Rules (Art 7 of the 1976 Rules and Art 9 of the 2010 Rules) and provide for the same time limits.

[Sch 2 Art 11-6] **Court or other authority prescribed under the Act** The Australian Centre for International Commercial Arbitration (ACICA) has been prescribed as an appointing authority competent to perform the functions under Art 11(3) and (4) of the Model Law. See the discussion above of the meaning of "court or other authority" prescribed under the Act in relation to ss 18 and 40 of the Act and Art 6 of the Model Law.

[Sch 2 Art 11-7] **Waiting period before applying to the court** In the case of a three-person arbitral tribunal, Art 11(3)(a) provides that the party wishing to keep the appointment process moving must wait 30 days before applying to the court for either: (i) the appointment of the other party's party-appointed arbitrator; or (ii) the appointment of the third arbitrator by the two party-appointed arbitrators. However, in the situation where the tribunal is to consist of a sole arbitrator, Art 11(3)(b) does not prescribe a "waiting period within which the parties must attempt to reach agreement before course is had to the court": A Broches, *Commentary on the UNCITRAL Model Law on International*

Commercial Arbitration, Kluwer Law International, The Hague, 1990, p 57. According to UNCITRAL: "This general wording seems acceptable . . . since the persons expected to agree are the parties and their inability to do so becomes apparent from the request to the Court by one of them" (UNCITRAL Analytical Commentary, p 29, para 6).

[Sch 2 Art 11-8] Appointment procedure for tribunal of other than one or three arbitrators There is "an intentional gap" in the UNCITRAL Model Law, where "the parties have agreed on a number of arbitrators other than one or three, but have failed to reach agreement on a method of appointing them" (H Holtzmann and J Neuhaus, *A Guide to the UNCITRAL Model Law on International Commercial Arbitration*, Kluwer Law International, The Hague, 1989, p 361). It follows from this that "the appointment of arbitrators in such situations can probably be considered a matter not governed by the Model Law". Parties to such arbitration agreements must instead have recourse to other provisions of domestic law and to intervention by the courts (Holtzmann and Neuhaus, p 361).

[Sch 2 Art 11-9] Appointment by court or other authority Article 11(4) provides that where there is a breakdown in the appointment procedure agreed upon by the parties — either because: a party fails to appoint an arbitrator or agree on the appointment of an arbitrator; the parties, or two arbitrators, are unable to reach an agreement expected of them; or a third party fails to perform any function entrusted to it — any party may request the court or other authority to "take the necessary measure" in order to secure the appointment. The UNCITRAL Working Group explained that the words "to take the necessary measure" to secure the appointment were intended to mean "that the court should make the appointment itself and not merely order the recalcitrant party or appointing authority to act" (H Holtzmann and J Neuhaus, *A Guide to the UNCITRAL Model Law on International Commercial Arbitration*, Kluwer Law International, The Hague, 1989, p 362, citing Fifth Working Group Report, UN Doc No A/CN.9/246, 6 March 1984, para 32). UNCITRAL further explained that the assistance of the court is not necessary "if the parties themselves have, in their agreement on the appointment procedure, provided other means for securing the appointment" (UNCITRAL Analytical Commentary, p 29, para 4).

[Sch 2 Art 11-10] Decision of court or other authority subject to no appeal Article 11(5) provides that where a court or other authority is entrusted with a decision under Art 11(3) or (4), that decision shall be "subject to no appeal". UNCITRAL adopted this language as a clearer term than the word "final", which had appeared in the Working Group's draft of the provision; see, eg, UNCITRAL Analytical Commentary, p 28; Fifth Draft, UN Doc No A/CN.9/246 (Annex), Art 11(5), 6 March 1984.

[Sch 2 Art 11-11] Possibility of appeal if issue relates to, eg, existence of arbitration agreemen In *Private Company "Triple V" Inc v Star (Universal) Co Ltd* [1995] 3 HKC 129 (Hong Kong Court of Appeal, Litton VP, Liu JA and Keith J, 7 July 1995), the plaintiff had applied to the High Court for the appointment of an arbitrator under Art 11(3) of the Model Law. The defendant appealed the decision of the High Court, and the question was whether an appeal could be made, in light of Art 11(5). The Court of Appeal noted "[t]he UNCITRAL Model Law confers a wide jurisdiction on an arbitrator duly appointed under Article 11(3)", and referred in particular to "Article 16(1) which says that the arbitral tribunal may rule on its own jurisdiction, including any objections to the existence or validity of the arbitration agreement" (Litton VP, p 3). At first instance, Leonard J had held that evidence of the nature of the contractual disputes did give rise to a prima facie dispute and that the matter should go to arbitration and be decided by the arbitrator. The Court of Appeal agreed. However, the Court of Appeal held that Art 11(3) was "only engaged where the failure to agree the appointment of the arbitrator is because the parties have not agreed on a procedure for his appointment. It is not engaged where the failure to agree is because the parties do not agree that there should be an arbitration at all, or that the arbitration should involve a particular party" (Keith J, p 8). It therefore followed that the orders made by the judge relating to the appointment of the arbitrator were not decisions to which Art 11(3) related, and thus the appeal was not excluded by Art 11(5) of the Model Law (Keith J, p 9).

[Sch 2 Art 11-12] **Considerations of court or other authority in making appointments** Under Art 11(5), the court or other authority "is required to have regard for the qualifications required of the arbitrator by the parties' agreement, and to such considerations as are likely to secure the appointment of an independent and impartial arbitrator" (H Holtzmann and J Neuhaus, *A Guide to the UNCITRAL Model Law on International Commercial Arbitration*, Kluwer Law International, The Hague, 1989, p 362). In the case of the appointment of a sole arbitrator or a presiding arbitrator, the court or other authority is to take into account "the advisability of appointing an arbitrator of a nationality other than those of the parties". These considerations are modelled on Art 6(4) of the UNCITRAL Arbitration Rules (1976), though it should be noted that this language was abandoned in the 2010 version of the UNCITRAL Arbitration Rules in favour of a list procedure (see Art 8 of the 2010 Rules).

[Sch 2 Art 11-13] **Important to ensure that "no grievance is felt" in making such appointments** In a judgment of the High Court of Hong Kong, *Fung Sang Trading Ltd v Kai Sun Sea Products and Food Co Ltd* [1991] HKCFI 190, the court made an order under Art 11(5). In doing so, Kaplan J held (at [73]) that: "it is important that when the court is appointing on behalf of the defaulting appointing party, it should go out of its way to ensure that no sense of grievance is felt, however unreasonable that attitude might appear to others".

[Sch 2 Art 11-14] **Court may seek to put parties in position they would have been in** In another Hong Kong case, *China Ocean Shipping Co v Mitrans Maritime Panama SA* [1994] 2 HKC 614 (High Court of Hong Kong, Leonard J, 28 September 1993), the plaintiffs made an application to the High Court for the appointment of an arbitrator on behalf of the defendants where the defendants had failed to make an appointment. The plaintiffs also applied for costs, as it was "constantly finding itself driven to come to [the] court in order to obtain the appointment of arbitrators on behalf of defendants who have failed to honour agreements freely entered into by them to refer disputes to arbitration" (p 2). Leonard J held that, taking into account the particular facts of this case, he considered that "the conduct of the defendants was such that it [was] proper that the plaintiffs should be placed in the position in which they would have been in if the defendants had honoured their obligation under the arbitration agreement to appoint an arbitrator without recourse to this court" (p 3) and made an order for costs. Although indemnity costs may be ordered where the non-complying party has acted in "flagrant breach of its contractual obligations to arbitrate" (*Safond Shipping Sdn Bhd v East Asia Sawmill Corp* [1993] HKCFI 151 at [19]).

Article 12. Grounds for challenge

(1) When a person is approached in connection with his possible appointment as an arbitrator, he shall disclose any circumstances likely to give rise to justifiable doubts as to his impartiality or independence. An arbitrator, from the time of his appointment and throughout the arbitral proceedings, shall without delay disclose any such circumstances to the parties unless they have already been informed of them by him.

(2) An arbitrator may be challenged only if circumstances exist that give rise to justifiable doubts as to his impartiality or independence, or if he does not possess qualifications agreed to by the parties. A party may challenge an arbitrator appointed by him, or in whose appointment he has participated, only for reasons of which he becomes aware after the appointment has been made.

COMMENTARY ON SCH 2 ART 12

Grounds for challenge	[Sch 2 Art 12-1]
Two ways of implementing principle of impartiality and independence	[Sch 2 Art 12-2]
Obligation of disclosure is a continuing obligation	[Sch 2 Art 12-3]
Duty to disclose triggered only by justifiable doubts as to arbitrator's impartiality or independence	[Sch 2 Art 12-4]
Article 12 imposes an affirmative duty on arbitrators to investigate possible conflicts of interest	[Sch 2 Art 12-5]
Test for challenges	[Sch 2 Art 12-6]
"real danger of bias"	[Sch 2 Art 12-7]
Relevance of arbitrator's nationality	[Sch 2 Art 12-8]

[Sch 2 Art 12-1] Grounds for challenge Article 12 provides for the grounds on which an arbitrator may be challenged. The UNCITRAL Working Group decided that it would not attempt to list "all possible connections to the parties or other circumstances that might justify a challenge" (H Holtzmann and J Neuhaus, *A Guide to the UNCITRAL Model Law on International Commercial Arbitration*, Kluwer Law International, The Hague, 1989, p 388, referring to First Working Group Report, UN Doc No A/CN.9/216, 23 March 1982, para 43). The Secretariat had observed that the general test contained in Art 12 is appropriate for a Model Law, as it was likely to be more widely accepted than any single list of specific criteria (First Secretariat Note, UN Doc No A/CN.9/207, 14 May 1981, para 65; see also UNCITRAL Analytical Commentary, pp 30–1, para 4). Article 12 is loosely based on Arts 9 and 10 of the UNCITRAL Arbitration Rules (1976) (Holtzmann and Neuhaus, p 389).

[Sch 2 Art 12-2] Two ways of implementing principle of impartiality and independence Article 12 "implements in two ways the principle that arbitrators shall be impartial and independent". UNCITRAL explains that: "Paragraph (1) requires any prospective or appointed arbitrator to disclose promptly any circumstances likely to cast doubt on his impartiality or independence. Paragraph (2) lays the basis for securing impartiality and independence by recognising those circumstances which give rise to justifiable doubts in this respect as reasons for a challenge" (UNCITRAL Analytical Commentary, p 30, para 1).

[Sch 2 Art 12-3] Obligation of disclosure is a continuing obligation Under Art 12(1), the prospective or appointed arbitrator's duty of disclosure is expressly stated as being an obligation that continues throughout the arbitral proceedings (UNCITRAL Analytical Commentary, p 30, paras 2–3).

[Sch 2 Art 12-4] Duty to disclose triggered only by justifiable doubts as to arbitrator's impartiality or independence In *Gascor v Ellicott* [1996] VR 332, the appellant had sought to remove one of the arbitrators on the grounds of possible bias due to a previous contact or relationship between the arbitrator and one of the parties. The arbitrator did not withdraw, and a judge refused to order his removal. The Court of Appeal upheld the judge's decision. In his judgment, Ormiston JA cited Art 12(1) of the Model Law, and held that "a precept should be accepted for arbitrators under the Commercial Arbitration Act that they advise the parties as soon as possible of any disqualifying facts or circumstances, if they choose not to disqualify themselves" (at 357, Ormiston JA). However, Ormiston JA (at 361) stated that he could not accept that an arbitrator is obliged to provide "a detailed history of his or her professional business life for the purpose of allowing one party or the other to create claims of potential bias which do not exist".

[Sch 2 Art 12-5] Article 12 imposes an affirmative duty on arbitrators to investigate possible conflicts of interest In *HSMV Corp v Australian Defence Industries Ltd* 72 FSupp 2d 1122 at 1199 US Dist LEXIS 18712 (US District Court for the Central District of California, Collins J, 8 November 1999), two companies entered into an agreement concerning the manufacture and delivery of military vehicles. Two arbitrations took place in 1999, both with the same person as sole arbitrator. The US company, the Californian HSMV Corp, learned that the arbitrator's law firm had, since 1998, been representing the Commonwealth of Australia in its efforts to privatise the Australian company involved in the arbitration. The arbitrator said he was unaware that his law firm had been representing the Commonwealth of Australia (at 1125). HSMV Corp challenged the second award. The court held that "[the arbitrator's] law firm's contemporaneous representation of ADI's owner clearly presented a conflict of interest. The question is whether [the arbitrator] had a duty to investigate ... the Court concludes that such a duty existed under applicable California and Australian arbitration rules" (at 1128). The court held that the California International Arbitration and Conciliation Act "imposes a duty upon arbitrators to disclose conflicts of interest" (at 1129) and that "the United Nations Commission on International Trade Law's Model Law on International Commercial Arbitration (Model Law), which Australia has adopted, imposes the same duty" (at 1129). The court held that: "[W]hile neither the [Californian] Act nor the Model Law expressly provides that the arbitrator must 'investigate' whether he has any of the questionable relationships and/or interests, the Court concludes that the disclosure requirement imposed by both rules necessarily implicates a duty to investigate whether instances of potential conflict exist. Under either rule, an arbitrator is obligated to conduct a conflicts check to see if he must disclose any circumstances that might cause his impartiality to be questioned. It is undisputed that [the arbitrator] failed to do so" (at 1129). The court vacated the award.

[Sch 2 Art 12-6] **Test for challenges** Article 12(2) provides that the test to be applied in challenges to arbitrators is whether "circumstances exist that give rise to justifiable doubts as to his impartiality or independence, or if he does not possess qualifications agreed to by the parties". Article 12(2) further states that these are the "only" circumstances that are relevant in considering a challenge. These grounds are therefore exhaustive (UNCITRAL Analytical Commentary, pp 30–1, para 4; A Broches, *Commentary on the UNCITRAL Model Law on International Commercial Arbitration*, Kluwer Law International, The Hague, 1990, p 60).

The 2004 *IBA Guidelines on the Conflicts of Interest in International Arbitration* outline a practical test to determine whether a conflict of interest exists. These guidelines have been used by courts in a range of jurisdictions which historically host many international arbitration proceedings, such as Switzerland, England, USA, Sweden, The Netherlands and Austria; see generally "The IBA Guidelines on Conflicts of Interest in International Arbitration: The First Five Years 2004–2009" published in *Dispute Resolution International*, Vol 4, No 1, May 2010, pp 5–53.

[Sch 2 Art 12-7] **"real danger of bias"** Since amendments to the Act became operational on 17 June 2010, Art 12 of the UNCITRAL Model Law must, in Australia, be read together with s 18A of the Act, which provides that:

18A Article 12 — justifiable doubts as to the impartiality or independence of an arbitrator

(1) For the purposes of Article 12(1) of the Model Law, there are justifiable doubts as to the impartiality or independence of a person approached in connection with a possible appointment as arbitrator only if there is a real danger of bias on the part of that person in conducting the arbitration.

(2) For the purposes of Article 12(2) of the Model Law, there are justifiable doubts as to the impartiality or independence of an arbitrator only if there is a real danger on the part of the arbitrator in conducting the arbitration.

Section 18A of the Act enacts the "real danger of bias" test applied by the House of Lords in *R v Gough* [1993] AC 646; [1993] 2 All ER 724; [1993] 2 WLR 883; (1993) 97 Cr App Rep 188. It appears to have been adopted following a submission to the Attorney-General's Department (N Brown QC and S Luttrell, Submissions on Review of International Arbitration Act 1974 (Cth), pp 11–15; see further L Nottage and R Garnett (eds), *International Arbitration in Australia*, Federation Press, Sydney, 2010, p 27; and S Luttrell, "Australia Adopts the 'Real Danger' Test for Arbitrator Bias" (2010) 26 *Arbitration International* 625).

[Sch 2 Art 12-8] **Relevance of arbitrator's nationality** UNCITRAL considered whether an arbitrator's nationality might in certain circumstances give rise to justifiable doubts as to his or her impartiality or independence

(H Holtzmann and J Neuhaus, *A Guide to the UNCITRAL Model Law on International Commercial Arbitration*, Kluwer Law International, The Hague, 1989, p 389). An arbitrator's nationality might give rise to such doubts, though such circumstances would be exceptional, for otherwise, Art 11, which states that "no person shall be precluded by reason of his nationality from acting as arbitrator", would be devoid of meaning (Holtzmann and Neuhaus, p 389).

Article 13. Challenge procedure

(1) The parties are free to agree on a procedure for challenging an arbitrator, subject to the provisions of paragraph (3) of this article.

(2) Failing such agreement, a party who intends to challenge an arbitrator shall, within fifteen days after becoming aware of the constitution of the arbitral tribunal or after becoming aware of any circumstance referred to in article 12(2), send a written statement of the reasons for the challenge to the arbitral tribunal. Unless the challenged arbitrator withdraws from his office or the other party agrees to the challenge, the arbitral tribunal shall decide on the challenge.

(3) If a challenge under any procedure agreed upon by the parties or under the procedure of paragraph (2) of this article is not successful, the challenging party may request, within thirty days after having received notice of the decision rejecting the challenge, the court or other authority specified in article 6 to decide on the challenge, which decision shall be subject to no appeal; while such a request is pending, the arbitral tribunal, including the challenged arbitrator, may continue the arbitral proceedings and make an award.

COMMENTARY ON SCH 2 ART 13

Introduction	[Sch 2 Art 13-1]
Freedom of parties to agree on challenge procedure	[Sch 2 Art 13-2]
Procedure agreed by parties subject to Art 13(3)	[Sch 2 Art 13-3]
Applicable procedure where parties have not reached agreement	[Sch 2 Art 13-4]
Arbitral tribunal to decide if challenged arbitrator does not withdraw or other party does not agree to challenge	[Sch 2 Art 13-5]
Court or other authority to make ultimate decision on challenge	[Sch 2 Art 13-6]

[Sch 2 Art 13-1] Introduction This provision gave rise to "widely divergent views and repeated redrafts" at the UNCITRAL Working Group (A Broches, *Commentary on the UNCITRAL Model Law on International Commercial Arbitration*, Kluwer Law International, The Hague, 1990, p 62). At the outset, there was only agreement on the principle that the parties should be able to agree on a challenge procedure, but it was not agreed that such a procedure could exclude resort to the courts (Broches, pp 62–3).

[Sch 2 Art 13-2] Freedom of parties to agree on challenge procedure Article 13(1) recognises the principle that the parties are free to agree on a procedure for challenging an arbitrator. The reasons for such challenges are set forth in Art 12(2) of the Model Law (UNCITRAL Analytical Commentary, p 32, para 1). As has been noted in the context of Art 12, it is clear that those grounds are exhaustive.

[Sch 2 Art 13-3] Procedure agreed by parties subject to Art 13(3) Although the parties are free to agree on a procedure for challenging an arbitrator, Art 13(1) provides they may not exclude a challenge to the court or other authority specified in Art 6 of the UNCITRAL Model Law to decide a challenge in accordance with the procedure stipulated in Art 13(3).

[Sch 2 Art 13-4] Applicable procedure where parties have not reached agreement Article 13(2) provides that parties "who have not agreed on a challenge procedure with a system of challenge by specifying the time and the form for bringing a challenge and the mode of deciding thereon, [are] subject to ultimate judicial control" (UNCITRAL Analytical Commentary, p 32, para 3). It was decided at an early stage to provide such a supplementary procedure in case the parties failed to agree (H Holtzmann and J Neuhaus, *A Guide to the UNCITRAL Model Law on International Commercial Arbitration*, Kluwer Law International, The Hague, 1989, p 406). There was general agreement that under the Art 13(2) procedure, the arbitral tribunal (including the challenged arbitrator), should initially decide the challenge (Holtzmann and Neuhaus, p 406). It has been noted that "the challenge procedure in Article 13 is designed to deal with those situations where the arbitrator has a possible disqualifying conflict of interest [and] is not designed to encompass challenges to the arbitrator's conduct during the course of the proceedings" (DAR Williams, "Arbitration and Dispute Resolution", [2004] *New Zealand Law Review* 87 at 96). Any concern regarding the arbitrator's conduct during the proceedings may give rise to grounds to set aside the award under Art 34(2)(b)(ii) which include a denial of natural justice (s 19).

[Sch 2 Art 13-5] Arbitral tribunal to decide if challenged arbitrator does not withdraw or other party does not agree to challenge Article 13(2) makes it clear that the arbitral tribunal is to decide the challenge only if a decision is needed, ie, where the challenged arbitrator does not withdraw or the other party does not agree to the challenge. Where the challenge is not "frivolous or obviously unfounded", there is an advantage in the tribunal first considering the challenge, as this would make "the last resort to the Court unnecessary" (UNCITRAL Analytical Commentary, p 32, para 4).

[Sch 2 Art 13-6] Court or other authority to make ultimate decision on challenge Under Art 13(3), a challenging party who has been unsuccessful in a challenge under the procedure agreed by the parties (under Art 13(1)) or before the arbitral tribunal (under Art 13(2)) has a "last resort" of bringing the challenge before the "court or other authority" specified under Art 6 of the Model Law (UNCITRAL Analytical Commentary, p 33, para 5). (For the relevant "court or other authority" in Australia; see s 18 of the Act and Art 6.) Article 13(3) was the most controversial of the provisions in the challenge procedure (H Holtzmann and J Neuhaus, *A Guide to the UNCITRAL Model Law on International Commercial Arbitration*, Kluwer Law International, The Hague, 1989, pp 407–8). The solution finally adopted permits court intervention during the arbitration proceedings, but it includes "three features designed to minimise the risk and adverse effects of dilatory tactics":

> The first element is the short period of time of fifteen days for requesting the Court to overrule the negative decision of the arbitral tribunal or any other body agreed upon by

the parties. The second feature is that the decision by the Court shall be final; in addition to excluding appeal, other measures relating to the organisation of the Court specified in Article 6 may accelerate matters. The third feature is that the arbitral tribunal, including the challenged arbitrator, may continue the arbitral proceedings while the request is pending with the Court; it would certainly do so, if it regards the challenge as totally unfounded and serving merely dilatory purposes [UNCITRAL Analytical Commentary, p 33, para 6].

Article 14. Failure or impossibility to act

(1) If an arbitrator becomes *de jure* or *de facto* unable to perform his functions or for other reasons fails to act without undue delay, his mandate terminates if he withdraws from his office or if the parties agree on the termination. Otherwise, if a controversy remains concerning any of these grounds, any party may request the court or other authority specified in article 6 to decide on the termination of the mandate, which decision shall be subject to no appeal.

(2) If, under this article or article 13(2), an arbitrator withdraws from his office or a party agrees to the termination of the mandate of an arbitrator, this does not imply acceptance of the validity of any ground referred to in this article or article 12(2).

COMMENTARY ON SCH 2 ART 14

Introduction .... [Sch 2 Art 14-1]
Meaning of "fails to act" .... [Sch 2 Art 14-2]
Failure to act "without undue delay" .... [Sch 2 Art 14-3]
Manner of termination .... [Sch 2 Art 14-4]
Subject to no appeal .... [Sch 2 Art 14-5]
Withdrawal of arbitrator not to be deemed to be
 acceptance of validity of challenge .... [Sch 2 Art 14-6]

[Sch 2 Art 14-1] Introduction This provision deals with the termination of an arbitrator's mandate who becomes *de jure* or *de facto* unable to perform his functions, or otherwise "fails to act without undue delay". These grounds were taken from Art 13(2) of the UNCITRAL Arbitration Rules (1976) (H Holtzmann and J Neuhaus, *A Guide to the UNCITRAL Model Law on International Commercial Arbitration*, Kluwer Law International, The Hague, 1989, p 439; though see now the UNCITRAL Arbitration Rules (2010), Art 12(3)).

[Sch 2 Art 14-2] Meaning of "fails to act" On the meaning of the term "fails to act", the UNCITRAL Analytical Commentary suggests (p 34, para 4) that:

> [I]n judging whether an arbitrator failed to act the following considerations may be relevant: Which action was expected or required of him in the light of the arbitration agreement and the specific procedural situation? If he has not done anything in this regard, has the delay been so inordinate as to be unacceptable in the light of the circumstances, including technical difficulties and the complexity of the case? If he has done something and acted in a certain way, did his conduct fall clearly below the standard of what may reasonably be expected from an arbitrator? Amongst the factors influencing the level of expectations are the ability to function efficiently and expeditiously and any special competence or other qualifications required of the arbitrator by agreement of the parties.

[Sch 2 Art 14-3] Failure to act "without undue delay" Article 14 differs from Art 13(2) of the UNCITRAL Arbitration Rules (1976) by the addition of the words "without undue delay" to the term "fails to act" (H Holtzmann and J Neuhaus, *A Guide to the UNCITRAL Model Law on International Commercial Arbitration*, Kluwer Law International, The Hague, 1989, p 439). As is pointed out in the UNCITRAL Analytical Commentary, there is an "(undefined) time element inherent in the term 'failure'" (p 34, para 3) and UNCITRAL decided to make this element explicit, partly in view of the many national laws and arbitral rules which make express reference to the speed of arbitration (Holtzmann and Neuhaus, p 439).

[Sch 2 Art 14-4] Manner of termination It is uncontroversial that an arbitrator's mandate will terminate if he or she withdraws from office, but it is also possible for the parties to agree on the termination of the arbitrator's mandate under Art 14(1). If there is a dispute about the grounds for termination being made out, any party may request the court specified in Art 6 to decide on the termination of the mandate. This is inconsistent with the UNCITRAL Arbitration Rules (1976), pursuant to which the parties may agree that a third party shall determine this issue (H Holtzmann and J Neuhaus, *A Guide to the UNCITRAL Model Law on International Commercial Arbitration*, Kluwer Law International, The Hague, 1989, pp 440–1). It is also inconsistent with Art 11 of the Model Law, which provides that parties can agree on their own method of appointing arbitrators, and Art 13, which provides that parties can agree on their own method of challenging arbitrators (A Broches, *Commentary on the UNCITRAL Model Law on International Commercial Arbitration*, Kluwer Law International, The Hague, 1990, p 68). It appears to be accepted that, because Art 2(d) of the Model Law provides that parties are free to determine certain issues, and because Art 14(1) provides that the parties can agree on the termination of an arbitrator's mandate, this means that Art 14(1) can be interpreted as meaning that the parties can agree that a third party shall decide on the issue of termination of an arbitrator's mandate (Holtzmann and Neuhaus, pp 440–1).

[Sch 2 Art 14-5] Subject to no appeal The decision of the court or other authority identified in Art 6 on the termination of an arbitrator's mandate is "subject to no appeal". Contrast this with the term "final", which is the expression which had been proposed by the UNCITRAL Working Group (UNCITRAL Analytical Commentary, p 33, Article 14).

[Sch 2 Art 14-6] Withdrawal of arbitrator not to be deemed to be acceptance of validity of challenge Article 14(2), in providing that if an arbitrator withdraws, or the parties agree on the termination of an arbitrator's mandate, does not imply acceptance of the validity of any ground referred to in Arts 14(2) or 12(2). This provision therefore facilitates the withdrawal of the arbitrator "in order to prevent lengthy controversies" (UNCITRAL Analytical Commentary, p 35, para 1; P Sanders, *The Work of UNCITRAL on Arbitration and Conciliation*, Kluwer Law International, The Hague, 2001, p 38).

Article 15. Appointment of substitute arbitrator

Where the mandate of an arbitrator terminates under article 13 or 14 or because of his withdrawal from office for any other reason or because of the revocation of his mandate by agreement of the parties or in any other case of termination of his mandate, a substitute arbitrator shall be appointed according to the rules that were applicable to the appointment of the arbitrator being replaced.

COMMENTARY ON SCH 2 ART 15

Introduction .... [Sch 2 Art 15-1]
Comprehensive approach .... [Sch 2 Art 15-2]
Ability of an arbitrator to withdraw from office .. [Sch 2 Art 15-3]
Procedure for appointment of substitute arbitrator . [Sch 2 Art 15-4]

[Sch 2 Art 15-1] Introduction The first draft of this provision, modelled on Arts 12(2) and 13(1) of the UNICTRAL Arbitration Rules (1976), provided for the appointment of a substitute where the arbitrator's mandate had terminated, where the arbitrator had died, or where the arbitrator had resigned. This approach did not change substantially until later sessions of the UNCITRAL Working Group, when it considered the situation where parties had "unlimited freedom to terminate the mandate of an arbitrator" and the arbitrator had "unlimited freedom to resign" (H Holtzmann and J Neuhaus, *A Guide to the UNCITRAL Model Law on International Commercial Arbitration*, Kluwer Law International, The Hague, 1989, p 464).

[Sch 2 Art 15-2] Comprehensive approach As finally adopted, Art 15 deals with the question of "how a substitute arbitrator might be appointed" and with "all possible cases where such a need may arise"; ie, not only where a vacancy arises due to an arbitrator being challenged under Art 13, or failing to act under Art 14 (UNCITRAL Analytical Commentary, pp 35–6, paras 1–2).

[Sch 2 Art 15-3] Ability of an arbitrator to withdraw from office There was some resistance during the drafting of this provision from delegates who considered that an arbitrator should be barred from resigning "for capricious reasons" (H Holtzmann and J Neuhaus, *A Guide to the UNCITRAL Model Law on International Commercial Arbitration*, Kluwer Law International, The Hague, 1989, pp 464–5). As Pieter Sanders argues (in *The Work of UNCITRAL on Arbitration and Conciliation*, Kluwer Law International, The Hague, 2001, p 38):

> An arbitrator, once appointed, cannot freely withdraw. He has to fulfil his task until the final award, in some cases (inter alia an additional award) even thereafter. He cannot withdraw on his own initiative. The arbitrator should have a just cause for withdrawal on his own initiative.

[Sch 2 Art 15-4] Procedure for appointment of substitute arbitrator The text as finally adopted does not expressly state that the parties may agree on a different method of appointing substitute arbitrators, but since Art 15 refers to "the rules that were applicable to the appointment of the arbitrator being replaced", this is understood as incorporating the parties' autonomy regarding the appointment procedures that are provided in Art 11(2) of the Model Law (Holtzmann and Neuhaus, pp 465–6).

CHAPTER IV. JURISDICTION OF ARBITRAL TRIBUNAL

Article 16. Competence of arbitral tribunal to rule on its jurisdiction

(1) The arbitral tribunal may rule on its own jurisdiction, including any objections with respect to the existence or validity of the arbitration agreement. For that purpose, an arbitration clause which forms part of a contract shall be treated as an agreement independent of the other terms of the contract. A decision by the arbitral tribunal that the contract is null and void shall not entail *ipso jure* the invalidity of the arbitration clause.

(2) A plea that the arbitral tribunal does not have jurisdiction shall be raised not later than the submission of the statement of defence. A party is not precluded from raising such a plea by the fact that he has appointed, or participated in the appointment of, an arbitrator. A plea that the arbitral tribunal is exceeding the scope of its authority shall be raised as soon as the matter alleged to be beyond the scope of its authority is raised during the arbitral proceedings. The arbitral tribunal may, in either case, admit a later plea if it considers the delay justified.

(3) The arbitral tribunal may rule on a plea referred to in paragraph (2) of this article either as a preliminary question or in an award on the merits. If the arbitral tribunal rules as a preliminary question that it has jurisdiction, any party may request, within thirty days after having received notice of that ruling, the court specified in article 6 to decide the matter, which decision shall be subject to no appeal; while such a request is pending, the arbitral tribunal may continue the arbitral proceedings and make an award.

COMMENTARY ON SCH 2 ART 16

Introduction	[Sch 2 Art 16-1]
Principle of separability	[Sch 2 Art 16-2]
Principle of *"kompetenz-kompetenz"*	[Sch 2 Art 16-3]
Discretionary power to rule on its own jurisdiction (Art 16(1))	[Sch 2 Art 16-4]
Tribunal to apply law	[Sch 2 Art 16-5]
Procedural options after ruling on jurisdiction (Art 16(2))	[Sch 2 Art 16-6]
Procedural constraints upon jurisdictional challenges (Art 16(3))	[Sch 2 Art 16-7]
Preliminary jurisdictional issues	[Sch 2 Art 16-8]
Nature of hearing by court on jurisdiction	[Sch 2 Art 16-9]
Jurisdiction may be created by estoppel	[Sch 2 Art 16-10]

[Sch 2 Art 16-1] Introduction Article 16(1) adopts two important but connected principles: First, the principle of "separability" (or "severability" or "autonomy of the arbitration clause") and second, the principle of "*kompetenz-kompetenz*" (or "*compétence de la compétence*"). Separability means that an arbitration clause is treated as an agreement independent of the other terms of the contract. The principle of *kompetenz-kompetenz* means that the arbitral tribunal may independently rule on the question of whether it has jurisdiction, including any objections with respect to the existence or validity of the arbitration agreement, without having to resort to a court (UNCITRAL Explanatory Note 2006, para 25; and for a more detailed discussion on these terms, see J Crawford, "Continuity and Discontinuity in International Dispute Settlement", *Journal of International Dispute Settlement*, (2009) 1 at 13–18, and J Lew, L Mistelis and S Kröll, *Comparative International Arbitration*, Kluwer Law International, The Hague, 2003, at 332–5).

[Sch 2 Art 16-2] Principle of separability "Article 16(1) enshrines the principle of separability" (*Fung Sang Trading Ltd v Kai Sun Sea Products & Food Co Ltd* [1991] HKCFI 190 at [57]). In Australia, the principle of separability has been recognised as part of the common law. Accordingly, an arbitration clause is to be regarded as separate and severable from the main contract (*Comandate Marine Corp v Pan Australia Shipping Pty Ltd* (2006) 157 FCR 45; 238 ALR 457; [2006] FCAFC 192; BC200610833 (*Comandate Marine Corp*) at [224]; and see *IBM Australia v National Distribution Services* (1991) 22 NSWLR 466; 100 ALR 361; 20 IPR 95; ATPR 41-094; *QH Tours Ltd v Ship Design & Management (Aust) Pty Ltd* (1991) 33 FCR 227; 105 ALR 371; 22 IPR 447; BC9103569; and *Ferris v Plaister* (1994) 34 NSWLR 474; 11 BCL 417; BC9404937). This principle is also established in English law (see *Harbour Assurance Co (UK) Ltd v Kansa General International Insurance Co Ltd* [1993] QB 701; [1993] 3 All ER 897; [1993] 3 WLR 42; [1993] 1 Lloyd's Rep 455) and has been enacted in s 7 of the Arbitration Act 1996 (Eng, W & NI). The arbitration agreement "must be treated as a 'distinct agreement' and can be void or voidable only on the grounds which relate directly to the arbitration agreement" (*Premium Nafta Products v Fili Shipping Co* [2007] UKHL 40 (*Premium Nafta Products*) (Lord Hoffman at [17])). The principle does not apply in the case where the main agreement and the arbitration clause were in the one document, and one of the parties claims that there was never any agreement, and the signature of that party is forged (*Premium Nafta Products* at [17] (Lord Hoffmann) and [34] (Lord Hope)).

The principle of separability gives an arbitrator jurisdiction to determine whether the main contract is void *ab initio*, for example on the grounds of fraud or illegality, or is voidable, for example for misrepresentation or repudiatory breach, provided always that there was a binding agreement to arbitrate (*Vee Networks Ltd v Econet Wireless International Ltd* [2004] All ER (D) 209 (Dec); [2004] EWHC 2909 (Comm); [2005] 1 All ER (Comm) 303; [2005] 1 Lloyd's Rep 192 (*Vee Networks*) at 197, [19]). Unless the agreement to arbitrate is independently void or invalid, the separability principle means that that agreement remains in effect and the arbitrator can determine conclusively whether the main contract was enforceable. Thus if the arbitrator finds the main contract void, the tribunal can continue to exercise such jurisdiction under the arbitration agreement as its scope permits. For example, if there was an alternative claim in tort or restitution which was within the scope of the clause, the tribunal would continue to have jurisdiction conclusively to determine that claim (*Vee Networks* at 198, [21]). If the issue is not only whether the main contract is void or otherwise non-existent but also whether the arbitration agreement is independently void or non-existent, that issue of jurisdiction can be determined by the arbitrator, but not conclusively. This is where the principle of *kompetenz-kompetenz* comes into play. The arbitrator nonetheless remains competent to rule on the question of jurisdiction.

The common law doctrine of separability has two principal and important aspects: First, the arbitrator has a clear basis of jurisdiction to decide whether the substantive contract is void, or voidable, or should be rescinded, without destroying his or her own authority or jurisdiction to arbitrate; second, the invalidity of the substantive contract does not necessarily entail the invalidity of the arbitration clause (*Comandate Marine Corp* at [219]).

[Sch 2 Art 16-3] Principle of *"kompetenz-kompetenz"* As discussed above, this principle empowers the arbitral tribunal to rule on the tribunal's jurisdiction, but it does not, of itself, prevent a competent court from reviewing that decision (*Dallah Real Estate and Tourism Holding Co* [2011] UKSC 46 at [28], [98]–[104] and [161]–[162]). This principle is enacted in s 30 of the Arbitration Act 1996 (Eng, W & NI).

[Sch 2 Art 16-4] Discretionary power to rule on its own jurisdiction (Art 16(1)) The first sentence of Art 16(1) confers discretionary power upon the arbitral tribunal to rule on its own jurisdiction. The tribunal may rule on jurisdiction of its own motion. The use of the word "including" has been said "to enlarge the discretionary power of the arbitral tribunal to rule on the specified matters, which are 'any objections with respect to the existence or validity of the arbitration agreement'" (*Christian Mutual Life Insurance Co v ACE Bermuda Insurance Ltd* [2002] Bda LR 1 at 13). The second sentence requires that an arbitration clause is to be treated as an independent agreement in the case where the arbitral tribunal is exercising its discretionary power to rule on its own jurisdiction, including the matters specified in the first sentence.

[Sch 2 Art 16-5] Tribunal to apply law The applicable law which should be applied by the tribunal when ruling on jurisdiction is the law "which the Court specified in article 6 would apply in setting aside proceedings under article 34, since these proceedings constitute the ultimate court control over the arbitral tribunal's decision (Article 16(3))" (UNCITRAL Analytical Commentary, p 38, para 3).

[Sch 2 Art 16-6] Procedural options after ruling on jurisdiction (Art 16(2)) Article 16(2) deals with the procedures for raising a plea of lack of jurisdiction or authority and the relevant time limits for raising it. The tribunal has discretion to extend the time within which a plea must be raised if it considers the delay justified. If a party fails to object, the waiver provision in Art 4 of the Model Law does not apply because Art 16 is not a provision "from which the parties may derogate".

The court in *Christian Mutual Life Insurance Co v ACE Bermuda Insurance Ltd* [2002] Bda LR 1 at 19, held that Art 16(2) contemplates that an arbitral tribunal faced with jurisdictional objections may do any of the following:

(1) give a preliminary ruling that it has jurisdiction;
(2) give a preliminary ruling that it does not have jurisdiction;
(3) give a preliminary ruling that it is exceeding the scope of its authority;
(4) give a preliminary ruling that it is not exceeding the scope of its authority; or
(5) defer making any ruling until making an award.

[Sch 2 Art 16-7] Procedural constraints upon jurisdictional challenges (Art 16(3)) Where the arbitral tribunal rules as a preliminary question that it has jurisdiction, Art 16(3) allows for immediate court control in order to avoid waste of time and money. Critically, it enables an aggrieved party only to seek from a court "a preliminary ruling given by an arbitral tribunal that it has jurisdiction" (*Christian Mutual Life Insurance Co v ACE Bermuda Insurance Ltd* [2002] Bda LR 1 at 19) "but not when it rules that it does not have jurisdiction" (*PT Asuransi Jasa Indonesia (Persero) v Dexia Bank SA* [2006] SGCA 41 (*PT Asuransi*) at [45]). A contrary, and, it is submitted, questionable view, was taken in New Zealand, where the court said that "if [a party] wished to challenge [a] finding [that the arbitrator did not have jurisdiction], the appropriate step would have been to challenge the jurisdiction under article 16" (*Attorney-General v Feary* [2007] NZHC 112 at [10]).

Michael Wilson & Partners Ltd v Emmott [2008] EWHC 2684 (Comm) at [18] accepted that the question of whether or not a ruling as to jurisdiction is an award, "is a question of substance and not of form". The court noted a decision in *Ranko Group v Antarctic Maritime SA* (Commercial Court, Toulson J, 12 June 1998, unreported), where the court considered a letter written by an arbitrator in which he stated that he made certain "rulings" concerning his jurisdiction. The court held that the letter was an award as to the arbitrator's jurisdiction notwithstanding that the letter was not described in terms as an award.

If the ruling as to jurisdiction is an award for the purposes of the Model Law, then an application to set aside the award may be brought under Art 34 in the case of a negative ruling on jurisdiction. In Singapore the legislature has adopted a narrow definition of an award as meaning "a decision on the substance of the dispute" (International Arbitration Act (Singapore), s 2(1)) which has resulted in a court finding that a ruling on jurisdiction under Art 16 cannot be challenged under Art 34 of the Model Law (*PT Asuransi* at [62]–[66]).

Article 16 contains three procedural safeguards to reduce the risk and effect of dilatory tactics in the arbitration: (a) a short time period for resort to court (30 days); (b) the court's decision is not appealable (in some Model Law jurisdictions such as Singapore, an appeal is available by leave, see International Arbitration Act (Singapore) s 10); and (c) the arbitral tribunal has a discretion to continue the proceedings and to make an award while the matter is pending before the court. In those cases where the arbitral tribunal decides to combine its decision on jurisdiction with an award on the merits, judicial review on the question of jurisdiction is available in setting aside proceedings under Art 34 or in enforcement proceedings under Art 36. An advantage may be gained by allowing the supervisory courts of the seat to make a ruling on jurisdiction under Art 16(3) since such a ruling may find an estoppel and prevent jurisdiction being raised subsequently before the enforcing courts (see the discussion above in relation to s 8(8) of the Act).

[Sch 2 Art 16-8] Preliminary jurisdictional issues The matter of the arbitrability of the dispute may be raised as a preliminary issue, eg, *Larkden Pty Ltd v Lloyd Energy Systems Pty Ltd* (2011) 279 ALR 772; [2011] NSWSC 268; BC201102191. Whether or not the dispute was one which had been settled in a prior arbitration between the same parties may be raised as a preliminary issue, eg, *Doshion Ltd v Sembawang Engineers and Constructors Pte Ltd* [2011] SGHC 46.

[Sch 2 Art 16-9] Nature of hearing by court on jurisdiction A challenge under Art 16(3) may be brought before a court and the court's decision is not subject to an appeal. A similar limitation on any further appeal is found in proceedings challenging any decision of "the court or other authority" made under Arts 11(3) and 13(3).

The court hearing the appeal does not conduct a review but may conduct a complete re-hearing, including if necessary the calling of witnesses heard by the arbitral tribunal. Under Art 16(3), "the court's jurisdiction to decide on the jurisdiction of an arbitral tribunal is an original jurisdiction and not an appellate one" (*Insigma Technology Co Ltd v Alstom Technology Ltd* [2008] SGHC 134 at [21], affirmed on appeal at [2009] SGCA 24).

[Sch 2 Art 16-10] Jurisdiction may be created by estoppel   A party who contests the jurisdiction of an arbitral tribunal may find that it has submitted to the jurisdiction of the arbitral tribunal by actively taking on the role of a party to the arbitration and by seeking a ruling on jurisdiction (see discussion in *Sovarex SA v Alvarez SA* [2011] EWHC 1661 (Comm) at [30]), where there was no such estoppel, as there was "an assertion of non-jurisdiction rather than a participation in its exercise". The question "of submission to the jurisdiction of the arbitrators depends on whether, on an objective analysis, the [third party] intended to take any part in" the arbitration process (*Excalibur Ventures LLC v Texas Keystone Inc* [2011] EWHC 1624 (Comm) at [61]).

CHAPTER IVA.   INTERIM MEASURES AND PRELIMINARY ORDERS

(As adopted by the Commission at its thirty-ninth session, in 2006)

Section 1.   Interim measures

Article 17.   Power of arbitral tribunal to order interim measures

(1) Unless otherwise agreed by the parties, the arbitral tribunal may, at the request of a party, grant interim measures.

(2) An interim measure is any temporary measure, whether in the form of an award or in another form, by which, at any time prior to the issuance of the award by which the dispute is finally decided, the arbitral tribunal orders a party to:
   (a) Maintain or restore the status quo pending determination of the dispute;
   (b) Take action that would prevent, or refrain from taking action that is likely to cause, current or imminent harm or prejudice to the arbitral process itself;
   (c) Provide a means of preserving assets out of which a subsequent award may be satisfied; or
   (d) Preserve evidence that may be relevant and material to the resolution of the dispute.

COMMENTARY ON SCH 2 ART 17
Introduction .... [Sch 2 Art 17-1]
Power commonly found in statutes and rules of
   international courts and tribunals .... [Sch 2 Art 17-2]
Power considered an inherent power .... [Sch 2 Art 17-3]
Power is of arbitral tribunal, not of domestic
   courts .... [Sch 2 Art 17-4]

Purpose of power .... [Sch 2 Art 17-5]
Legislative history .... [Sch 2 Art 17-6]
Revision of Model Law's regime on interim
 measures .... [Sch 2 Art 17-7]
Characteristics of interim measures .... [Sch 2 Art 17-8]
Scope of interim measures .... [Sch 2 Art 17-9]
Anti-suit injunctions .... [Sch 2 Art 17-10]
Form of interim measures .... [Sch 2 Art 17-11]
Further provisions adopted in 2006 revisions ..... [Sch 2 Art 17-12]

[Sch 2 Art 17-1] Introduction Article 17 of the UNCITRAL Model Law confers the power of the tribunal to grant interim measures, which are also referred to as "provisional" measures, or "conservatory" measures; see, eg, Report of the Secretary-General, "Preparation of Uniform Provisions on: Written Form for Arbitration Agreements, Interim Measures of Protection, and Conciliation", UN Doc No A/CN.9/WG.II/WP.113, 23 March 2001, paras 17–18, fn 21.

[Sch 2 Art 17-2] Power commonly found in statutes and rules of international courts and tribunals See, eg, Statute of the International Court of Justice, Art 41; United Nations Convention on the Law of the Sea, Art 290; European Court of Human Rights Rules of Court, r 39; American Convention on Human Rights, Art 63(2). This common power is also widely available to international arbitral tribunals, including those constituted under the ICSID Convention (Convention on the Settlement of Investment Disputes between States and Nationals of other States, Art 47), the UNCITRAL Arbitration Rules (see Art 26 of the 1976 and 2010 Rules), the ICC Arbitration Rules (Art 23), the LCIA Arbitration Rules (Art 25), the SIAC Arbitration Rules (Art 24(f), (g), (j), (l), (m) and (n)), the HKIAC Arbitration Rules (Art 24) and the ACICA Arbitration Rules (Art 28).

[Sch 2 Art 17-3] Power considered an inherent power There is substantial authority for the proposition that the power to award interim measures is an "inherent power" available to international dispute settlement bodies; see, eg, *Grammophone Co Ltd v Deutsche Grammophone AG* 1 TAM 857 (Anglo-German MAT, 1922); *Trail Smelter Case* 3 RIAA 1911 (US-Canada, 1938); *E-Systems, Inc v Iran* 2 Ir-USCTR 51 at 57 (Iran-United States Claims Tribunal, 1983); *Ford Aerospace and Communications Corp v Air Force of Iran* 6 Ir-USCTR 104 at 108–9 (Iran-United States Claims Tribunal, 1984); *Veerman v Germany* 25 ILR 522 at 523 (Arbitral Tribunal on Property, Rights and Interests in Germany, 1957); *Velásquez Rodríguez (Merits)* 95 ILR 259 at 268 (Inter-American Court on Human Rights, 1988).

[Sch 2 Art 17-4] Power is of arbitral tribunal, not of domestic courts It is important to note that the power conferred by Art 17 is the power of the arbitral tribunal to grant interim measures, rather than the power of the domestic court having supervisory jurisdiction over the arbitration. Article 9 of the UNCITRAL Model Law, as noted above, provides that: "[i]t is not incompatible with an arbitration agreement for a party to request, before or during arbitral proceedings, from a court an interim measure of protection and for a court to grant such measure". When considering making a request for interim measures, a party thus has the choice of requesting the arbitral tribunal, or a court of competent jurisdiction. Naturally, a party will have to apply to the court for interim measures if the arbitral tribunal has not yet been constituted and no emergency relief is available under the agreed arbitration rules. Emergency relief is available under the ACICA Arbitration Rules (2011) and the SIAC Arbitration Rules (2010), both of which provide for the appointment of an "emergency arbitrator". On relief from the courts, see generally P Sanders, *The Work of UNCITRAL on Arbitration and Conciliation*, Kluwer Law International, The Hague, 2001, p 40.

[Sch 2 Art 17-5] **Purpose of power** The purpose of the power to grant interim measures is the preservation of the respective rights of the parties pending the decision on the merits of the case, and the safeguarding of the jurisdiction of the arbitral tribunal to render an award which is effective. The need for international arbitral tribunals to be able to grant interim relief stems from the fact that once a notice of arbitration is filed commencing arbitration proceedings, the arbitral tribunal (once constituted) might not be in a position to determine the merits of the dispute for some time. In the intervening period, the rights of the parties might be prejudiced by events which would prevent the tribunal from being able to render an effective award.

[Sch 2 Art 17-6] **Legislative history** As originally adopted in 1985, the text of Art 17 (UNCITRAL Model Law on International Commercial Arbitration) was as follows:

> Unless otherwise agreed by the parties, the arbitral tribunal may, at the request of a party, order any party to take such interim measures of protection as the arbitral tribunal may consider necessary in respect of the subject-matter of the dispute. The arbitral tribunal may require any party to provide appropriate security in connection with such measure.

Article 17 was modelled on Art 26 of the UNCITRAL Arbitration Rules (1976) (H Holtzmann and J Neuhaus, *A Guide to the UNCITRAL Model Law on International Commercial Arbitration*, Kluwer Law International, The Hague, 1989, p 531). A number of changes were made to the text of Art 26 (see Holtzmann and Neuhaus, pp 531–2), as follows:

> First, the provision in the Model Law omits the non-exclusive list of examples provided by the Rule: 'including measures for the conservation of the goods forming the subject-matter in dispute, such as ordering their deposit with a third person or the sale of perishable goods.' . . .

> A second change from the UNCITRAL Arbitration Rule provision was that the sentence regarding security in Article 17 uses more general language — 'appropriate security in connection with such measure' instead of 'security for the costs of such measure.' . . .

> Third, the provision in the Model Law is explicitly limited to orders directed to the parties, not to third parties. . . .

> Finally, the Model Law provision is limited to measures that the arbitral tribunal can order, excluding any measures that the arbitral tribunal might itself take.

Under the original terms of Art 17, the interim measures of protection were confined by the requirement that the interim measure be "in relation to the subject matter of the dispute". As a result of this requirement in Art 17, it was held in *David Lindow v Barton McGill Marine Ltd* (2002) 16 PRNZ 796 at [9], that the court did not have jurisdiction to make orders for security for costs.

[Sch 2 Art 17-7] Revision of Model Law's regime on interim measures At the 32nd session of UNCITRAL in 1999, the Commission had before it a note entitled "Possible future work in the area of international commercial arbitration" (UN Doc No A/CN.4/460). UNCITRAL welcomed the opportunity to assess the experience of States with, for example, the enactment of the UNCITRAL Model Law on International Commercial Arbitration, and also "to evaluate in the universal forum of the Commission the acceptability of ideas and proposals for improvement of arbitration laws, rules and practices" (*Report of the Working Group on Arbitration on the Work of its 36th Session*, New York, 4–8 March 2002, UN Doc No A/CN.9/508, 12 April 2002, para 1). UNCITRAL entrusted this work to a "Working Group on Arbitration" and decided on certain priority items for the Working Group. These were conciliation, the "in writing" requirement for the arbitration agreement (as found in Art 7, as discussed above), the enforceability of interim measures of protection, and the possible enforcement of an award that had been set aside in the State of origin (*Report on the 36th Session*, para 2).

During the early work of the Working Group, the view was expressed that the text of Art 17 was satisfactory and should be maintained, as it permitted arbitral tribunals to issue a broad range of interim measures. But according to another view, the words "in respect of the subject-matter of the dispute" restricted "the scope of the interim measures that the arbitral tribunal might issue". The Working Group considered that as the provision contained the power to grant interim measures, "it was necessary to consider how that power should be most appropriately expressed" (*Report of the Working Group on Arbitration on the Work of its 34th Session*, New York, 21 May–1 June 2001, UN Doc A/CN.9/487, 15 June 2001, para 65).

It was also suggested that the Working Group draft "language that would address the conditions or the criteria for the issuance of those measures", and also that any new provision "should set out in a generic way the types of interim measures that were intended to be covered" (*Report on the 34th Session*, para 66).

In addition to considering amendments to Art 17 as it was originally drafted, the Working Group also considered other provisions, including one permitting an arbitral tribunal to make a temporary interim measure on an ex parte basis, and one on the enforcement of interim measures of protection (*Report on the 34th Session*, paras 69–74). Those amendments are considered below.

[Sch 2 Art 17-8] Characteristics of interim measures Interim measures have certain characteristics, including that the measures be given at the request of one party; that they be made in the form of an order or interim award; and that they are intended to be temporary, pending a final outcome of the arbitration (Report of the Secretary-General, "Preparation of Uniform Provisions on: Written Form for Arbitration Agreements, Interim Measures of Protection, and Conciliation", UN Doc No A/CN.9/WG.II/WP.113, 23 March 2001, fn 21).

[Sch 2 Art 17-9] Scope of interim measures During the drafting of the original version of Art 17, there was some support of the Model Law for the idea that the scope of interim measures should be specifically limited to "measures for the conserving, or maintaining the value of, the goods forming the subject-matter in dispute" (H Holtzmann and J Neuhaus, *A Guide to the UNCITRAL Model Law on International Commercial Arbitration*, Kluwer Law International, The Hague, 1989, p 530). However, the Working Group considered that a list of examples was "too much geared to only one type of transaction, ie, sale of goods", and it was ultimately decided that the power should be cast in broader terms so as to encompass "any measures of protection in respect of the subject-matter of the dispute" (Holtzmann and Neuhaus, pp 530–2). Other examples of situations where interim measures might be sought by parties include requests for the preservation of evidence; measures to preserve goods, such as depositing them with a third party, or selling perishable items; opening bank letters of credit; using or maintaining equipment, or completing phases of construction in order to prevent irreparable harm; and the preservation of assets, in order to avoid one party dissipating funds or assets which might later be needed to satisfy a final award (Holtzmann and Neuhaus, p 531).

In 2001, during the revision process, a Report of the Secretary-General to UNCITRAL identified three situations in which parties might seek interim measures of protection:

(a) *Measures aimed at facilitating the conduct of arbitral proceedings*, such as orders requiring a party to allow certain evidence to be taken (eg to allow access to premises to inspect particular goods, property or documents); orders for a party to preserve evidence (e.g. not to make certain alterations at a site); orders to the parties and other participants in arbitral proceedings to protect the privacy of the proceedings (e.g. to keep files in a certain place under lock or not to disclose the time and place of hearings);

(b) *Measures to avoid loss or damage and measures aimed at preserving a certain state of affairs until the dispute is resolved*, such as orders to continue performing a contract during the arbitral proceedings (eg an order to a contractor to continue construction works despite its claim that it is entitled to suspend the works); orders to refrain from taking an action until the award is made; orders to safeguard goods (eg to take specific safety measures, to sell perishable goods or to appoint an administrator of assets); orders to take the appropriate action to avoid the loss of a right (eg to pay the fees needed to extend the validity of an intellectual property right); orders relating to the clean-up of a polluted site;

(c) *Measures to facilitate later enforcement of the award*, such as attachments of assets and similar acts that seek to preserve assets in the jurisdiction where enforcement of the award will be sought (attachments may concern, for example, physical property, bank accounts or payment claims); orders not to move assets or the subject-matter of the dispute out of a jurisdiction; orders for depositing in a joint account the amount in dispute or for depositing movable property in dispute with a third person; orders to a party or parties to provide security (eg a guarantee) for costs of arbitration or orders to provide security for all or part of the amount claimed from the party.

See Report of the Secretary-General, "Possible Uniform Rules on Certain Issues concerning Settlement of Commercial Disputes: Conciliation, Interim Measures of Protection, Written Form for Arbitration Agreement", UN Commission on International Trade Law, Working Group on Arbitration, 32nd Session, Vienna, UN Doc No A/CN.9/WG.II/WP.108, 20–31 March 2000, para 63.

The Report of the Secretary-General noted that this "enumeration of possible interim measures of protection" was "not exhaustive": para 65. The Working Group ultimately agreed on the terms of Art 17(2), which sets out the scope of the power to order interim measures. The Working Group agreed that "to the extent that all the purposes for interim measures were generically covered by the revised list contained in [Art 17(2)], the list could be expressed as an exhaustive one" (Note by the Secretariat, "Settlement of Commercial Disputes — Interim Measures", UN Doc No A/CN.9/605, 25 April 2006, para 6).

[Sch 2 Art 17-10] **Anti-suit injunctions** During UNCITRAL's final consideration of the text of the revised Art 17, a question was raised as to whether the words "or prejudice to the arbitral process itself" should be retained at the end of Art 17(2)(b). UNCITRAL recalled "that the purpose of those words was to clarify that an arbitral tribunal had the power to prevent obstruction or delay of the arbitral process, including by issuing anti-suit injunctions". UNCITRAL also recalled that "the words in question should not be understood as merely covering anti-suit injunctions but rather as more broadly covering injunctions against the large variety of actions that existed and were used in practice to obstruct the arbitral process" (*Report of UNCITRAL on the Work of its 39th Session, 17 June–7 July 2006*, UN Doc No A/61/17, p 16, paras 92–4).

[Sch 2 Art 17-11] **Form of interim measures** As can be seen from the text above, the original version of Art 17 merely provided that interim measures would be in the form of an "order". This gave rise to difficulties with enforcement, as the legislation of most countries did not normally contain rules for the enforcement of orders of the arbitral tribunal (P Sanders, *The Work of UNCITRAL on Arbitration and Conciliation*, Kluwer Law International, The Hague, 2001, p 40). These concerns over enforcement led to parties to arbitration proceedings choosing to apply to the court with supervisory jurisdiction over the arbitration for interim measures. The amendment to the text of Art 17, stating that the interim measures may be granted in the form of an award, was intended to alleviate such concerns. In the revision process, Art 17 was amended to incorporate Art 26(2) of the 1976 UNCITRAL Arbitration Rules, which provides in part that: "Such interim measures may be established in the form of an interim award." However, the UNCITRAL Working Group did not wish to be "overly prescriptive in respect of the form that an interim measure should take" (Note by the Secretariat, "Settlement of Commercial Disputes — Interim Measures", UN Doc No A/CN.9/605, 25 April 2006, para 5).

[Sch 2 Art 17-12] **Further provisions adopted in 2006 revisions** UNCITRAL also adopted further provisions relating to interim measures in the process of the 2006 revisions, being Arts 17A–17J. These additional provisions provide useful guidance on the Model Law regime concerning requests for interim measures.

Article 17A. Conditions for granting interim measures

(1) The party requesting an interim measure under article 17(2)*(a)*, *(b)* and *(c)* shall satisfy the arbitral tribunal that:
  (a) Harm not adequately reparable by an award of damages is likely to result if the measure is not ordered, and such harm substantially outweighs the harm that is likely to result to the party against whom the measure is directed if the measure is granted; and
  (b) There is a reasonable possibility that the requesting party will succeed on the merits of the claim. The determination on this possibility shall not affect the discretion of the arbitral tribunal in making any subsequent determination.

(2) With regard to a request for an interim measure under article 17(2)*(d)*, the requirements in paragraphs (1)*(a)* and *(b)* of this article shall apply only to the extent the arbitral tribunal considers appropriate.

COMMENTARY ON SCH 2 ART 17A

Introduction .... [Sch 2 Art 17A-1]
Conditions generally applicable to requests for
  interim measures .... [Sch 2 Art 17A-2]
"Harm not adequately reparable" .... [Sch 2 Art 17A-3]
"substantially outweighs" .... [Sch 2 Art 17A-4]
"urgency" not a necessary condition .... [Sch 2 Art 17A-5]
"reasonable possibility that the requesting party will
  succeed on the merits of the claim" .... [Sch 2 Art 17A-6]
Interim measures to preserve evidence .... [Sch 2 Art 17A-7]

[Sch 2 Art 17A-1] Introduction Article 17A, introduced in the 2006 amendments adopted by UNCITRAL, sets out the conditions for granting interim measures under Art 17. These conditions were not previously set out in the Model Law.

[Sch 2 Art 17A-2] Conditions generally applicable to requests for interim measures Where a request for interim measures is made in order to: (a) maintain or restore the status quo pending determination of the dispute; (b) take action that would prevent, or refrain from taking action that is likely to cause, current or imminent harm or prejudice to the arbitral process itself; or provide a means of preserving assets out of which a subsequent award may be satisfied (ie, a request which falls within Art 17(2)(a), (b) or (c)), the party must satisfy the arbitral tribunal that: "(a) [h]arm not adequately reparable by an award of damages is likely to result if the measure is not ordered, and such harm substantially outweighs the harm that is likely to result to the party against whom the measure is directed if the measure is granted; and (b) [t]here is a reasonable possibility that the requesting party will succeed on the merits of the claim. . ." (Art 17A(1)). Further, any determination of the tribunal that the requesting party will succeed on the merits of the claim does not prejudice any subsequent determination by the arbitral tribunal (Art 17A(1)(b)).

[Sch 2 Art 17A-3] "Harm not adequately reparable" The UNCITRAL Working Group decided to include the word "adequately" in Art 17A(1) and clarified that this provision should "be interpreted in a flexible manner by balancing the degree of harm suffered by the applicant if the interim measure was not granted against the degree of harm suffered by the party opposing the measure if that measure was granted" (Note by the Secretariat, "Settlement of Commercial Disputes — Interim Measures", UN Doc No A/CN.9/605, 25 April 2006, p 7, para 7).

[Sch 2 Art 17A-4] "substantially outweighs" UNCITRAL considered deleting the term "substantially" from the text of Art 17A(1)(a), on the basis that it was an "unnecessary and unclear requirement, making it more difficult for the arbitral tribunal to issue an interim measure (*Report of UNCITRAL on the Work of its 39th Session, 17 June–7 July 2006*, UN Doc No A/61/17, p 17, para 98). However, it was ultimately adopted as proposed by the Working Group, given that the text of Art 17A(1)(a), "including the word 'substantially'" was "consistent with existing standards in many judicial systems for the granting of an interim measure" (*Report on the 39th Session*, p 17, paras 98–100).

[Sch 2 Art 17A-5] "urgency" not a necessary condition The UNCITRAL Working Group decided that the need for "urgency" should "not be a general feature of interim measures", and was therefore not included in the list of conditions (Note by the Secretariat, "Settlement of Commercial Disputes — Interim Measures", UN Doc No A/CN.9/605, 25 April 2006, p 7, para 9). Contrast this with the case law of many international courts and tribunals, for which urgency is a necessary condition for the granting of provisional measures. The International Court of Justice, for instance, will only indicate provisional measures if there is "urgency", in the sense that the order cannot await a decision on the merits (*Passage through the Great Belt* [1991] ICJ Rep 12 at 17). For instance, in *Convention on the Elimination of All Forms of Racial Discrimination* (*Georgia v Russia*), Order of 15 October 2008 at para 129, the International Court of Justice held that:

> [T]he power of the Court to indicate provisional measures will be exercised only if there is urgency in the sense that there is a real risk that action prejudicial to the rights of either party might be taken before the Court has given its final decision...

However, it is clear that the concept of "urgency" impacts on the conditions listed in Art 17A, as acknowledged by UNCITRAL (*Report of UNCITRAL on the Work of its 39th Session, 17 June–7 July 2006*, UN Doc No A/61/17, p 17, para 97).

[Sch 2 Art 17A-6] "reasonable possibility that the requesting party will succeed on the merits of the claim" In UNCITRAL, a proposal was made to delete Art 17A(1)(b) on the basis that "interim measures might need to be granted as a matter of urgency" — thus acknowledging the role of "urgency", as noted above — and it was argued that "a requirement for an arbitral tribunal to make a determination as to the possibility of success on the merits of the claim might unnecessarily delay matters or appear as a prejudgement of the case". However, this proposal was not supported, as Art 17A(1)(b) was considered to be "a necessary safeguard for the granting of interim measures", and the intention was that "the arbitral tribunal would make a preliminary judgement based on the information available to it at the time of its determination" (*Report of UNCITRAL on the Work of its 39th Session, 17 June–7 July 2006*, UN Doc No A/61/17, p 18, para 101).

[Sch 2 Art 17A-7] Interim measures to preserve evidence Where a request for interim measures is made to "preserve evidence that may be relevant and material to the resolution of the dispute", within the meaning of Art 17(2)(d), the conditions set forth in Art 17A(1)(a) and (b) only apply "to the extent the arbitral tribunal considers appropriate". This would appear to suggest that in the context of requests for an order to preserve evidence, the arbitral tribunal may apply a lower standard in determining whether to order such interim measures.

Section 2. Preliminary orders

Article 17B. Applications for preliminary orders and conditions for granting preliminary orders

(1) Unless otherwise agreed by the parties, a party may, without notice to any other party, make a request for an interim measure together with an application for a preliminary order directing a party not to frustrate the purpose of the interim measure requested.

(2) The arbitral tribunal may grant a preliminary order provided it considers that prior disclosure of the request for the interim measure to the party against whom it is directed risks frustrating the purpose of the measure.

(3) The conditions defined under article 17A apply to any preliminary order, provided that the harm to be assessed under article 17A(1)*(a)*, is the harm likely to result from the order being granted or not.

COMMENTARY ON SCH 2 ART 17B

Introduction .... [Sch 2 Art 17B-1]
Status in Australian law .... [Sch 2 Art 17B-2]

[Sch 2 Art 17B-1] Introduction UNCITRAL also adopted Art 17B of the Model Law as part of the 2006 amendments. Article 17B was the product of a detailed review of the provisions regarding the power of an arbitral tribunal to grant interim relief on an ex parte basis, which took place at the forty-first (13–17 September 2004) and forty-second (10–14 January 2005) sessions of the UNCITRAL Working Group. The UNCITRAL Secretariat explains, in the UNCITRAL Explanatory Note 2006, p 31, para 28, that:

> Preliminary orders provide a means for preserving the status quo until the arbitral tribunal issues an interim measure adopting or modifying the preliminary order.

The term "preliminary order" is used, rather than the term "interim measure", to describe "a measure issued on an *ex parte* basis". This term emphasises the "temporary and extraordinary nature of the order, as well as its distinct scope and purpose" (Note by the Secretariat, "Settlement of Commercial Disputes — Interim Measures", UN Doc No A/CN.9/605, 25 April 2006, para 10).

[Sch 2 Art 17B-2] Status in Australian law Article 17B of the Model Law must be read together with s 18B of the Act, which provides that:

Despite Article 17B of the Model Law:
  (a) no party to an arbitration agreement may make an application for a preliminary order directing another party not to frustrate the purpose of an interim measure requested; and
  (b) no arbitral tribunal may grant such a preliminary order.

The Explanatory Memorandum to the International Arbitration Amendment Bill 2009 (Cth) explained that:

> 74. ... Articles 17B and 17C of the Model Law establish a regime for preliminary orders. These are the equivalent of ex parte orders made by a court in circumstances where there is a perceived risk that a party will attempt to frustrate interim measures. While this proposal received some support from stakeholders, it was extremely controversial when considered by UNCITRAL and was opposed by key stakeholders in Australia during the Review.
>
> 75. The primary objection to the provisions allowing for preliminary measures [sic] is that such measures are inconsistent with the consensual underpinning of arbitration. Accordingly, Item 14 amends the Act to provide that, despite Article 17B of the Model Law, preliminary orders are not available under the Act or the Model Law.

See the Explanatory Memorandum to the International Arbitration Amendment Bill 2009 (Cth), p 11, [74]–[75]; and also the Revised Explanatory Memorandum to the International Arbitration Amendment Bill 2010 (Cth), p 11, [72]–[73].

The regime for "preliminary orders" under Arts 17B and 17C of the Model Law does not, accordingly, form part of the law of Australia.

Article 17C. Specific regime for preliminary orders

(1) Immediately after the arbitral tribunal has made a determination in respect of an application for a preliminary order, the arbitral tribunal shall give notice to all parties of the request for the interim measure, the application for the preliminary order, the preliminary order, if any, and all other communications, including by indicating the content of any oral communication, between any party and the arbitral tribunal in relation thereto.

(2) At the same time, the arbitral tribunal shall give an opportunity to any party against whom a preliminary order is directed to present its case at the earliest practicable time.

(3) The arbitral tribunal shall decide promptly on any objection to the preliminary order.

(4) A preliminary order shall expire after twenty days from the date on which it was issued by the arbitral tribunal. However, the arbitral tribunal may issue an interim measure adopting or modifying the preliminary order, after the party against whom the preliminary order is directed has been given notice and an opportunity to present its case.

(5) A preliminary order shall be binding on the parties but shall not be subject to enforcement by a court. Such a preliminary order does not constitute an award.

COMMENTARY ON SCH 2 ART 17C
Status in Australian law .... [Sch 2 Art 17C-1]

[Sch 2 Art 17C-1] **Status in Australian law** As noted in relation to Art 17B, Art 17C does not form part of the law of Australia.

Section 3. Provisions applicable to interim measures and preliminary orders

Article 17D. Modification, suspension, termination

The arbitral tribunal may modify, suspend or terminate an interim measure or a preliminary order it has granted, upon application of any party or, in exceptional circumstances and upon prior notice to the parties, on the arbitral tribunal's own initiative.

COMMENTARY ON SCH 2 ART 17D

Introduction .... [Sch 2 Art 17D-1]
Provisions applicable to interim measures and
 preliminary orders .... [Sch 2 Art 17D-2]
Purpose of Article .... [Sch 2 Art 17D-3]
History of Article .... [Sch 2 Art 17D-4]
Arbitral tribunal may only modify, suspend or
 revoke interim measure or preliminary order "it
 has granted" .... [Sch 2 Art 17D-5]

[Sch 2 Art 17D-1] **Introduction** Article 17D was introduced in the 2006 amendments adopted by UNCITRAL.

[Sch 2 Art 17D-2] **Provisions applicable to interim measures and preliminary orders** Section 3 of Ch IVA of the UNCITRAL Model Law (which contains Arts 17D, 17E, 17F and 17G) sets forth provisions that are applicable to interim measures ordered under Arts 17 and 17A, as well as preliminary orders made under Arts 17B and 17C.

[Sch 2 Art 17D-3] **Purpose of Article** Article 17D generally provides that the arbitral tribunal may modify, suspend or terminate an interim measure or preliminary order that it has granted. It may do so upon the application of any party, and in exceptional circumstances and upon giving notice to the parties, it may do so on the arbitral tribunal's own initiative.

[Sch 2 Art 17D-4] **History of Article** Article 17D was included as Draft Art 17(6) in a revised version of Art 17 of the Model Law prepared by the Secretariat on the basis of discussions and decisions made by the UNCITRAL Working Group at its fortieth session (*Report of the Working Group on the Work of its 40th Session (New York, 23–27 February 2004)*, pp 17–31, UN Doc No A/CN.9/547, paras 68–116). The Secretariat's proposed version of Draft Art 17(6) read as follows:

> The arbitral tribunal may modify, suspend or terminate an interim measure of protection it has granted, at any time, upon application of any party or, in exceptional circumstances, on the arbitral tribunal's own initiative, upon prior notice to the parties. [UNCITRAL Secretariat, "Settlement of Commercial Disputes — Interim Measures of Protection", UN Doc No A/CN.9/WG.II/WP.131, 26 July 2004, pp 2–4, para 4.]

Before its adoption as Art 17D, Draft Art 17(6) was ultimately amended so that it also included "preliminary orders".

[Sch 2 Art 17D-5] Arbitral tribunal may only modify, suspend or revoke interim measure or preliminary order "it has granted" The words "it has granted" in Art 17D were inserted to reflect the decision of the Working Group that the arbitral tribunal could only modify, suspend or revoke an interim measure or preliminary order issued by that tribunal (*Report of the Working Group on the Work of its 40th Session (New York, 23–27 February 2004)*, UN Doc No A/CN.9/547, 16 April 2004, p 27, para 102; *Report of the Working Group on the Work of its 39th Session (Vienna 10–14 November 2003)*, UN Doc No A/CN.9/545, 8 December 2003, p 14, para 41). In particular, the Working Group stressed that an arbitral tribunal was not permitted to modify, suspend or revoke interim measures or ex parte orders that might be issued by a State court:

> It was noted that the issue of allowing an arbitral tribunal to review a court-ordered interim measure was a contentious matter and raised sensitive issues regarding the role of courts and balancing the role of private arbitral bodies against that of courts, which had sovereign powers and an appellate regime. The Working Group noted that Article 9 of the Model Law appropriately addressed the concurrent jurisdiction of the arbitral tribunal and the courts and unambiguously provided for the right of the parties to request an interim measure of protection from a court, before or during the arbitral proceedings. The Working Group agreed that that issue of possible review of a court-ordered interim measure by an arbitral tribunal should not be dealt with in the Model Law. In that connection, it was pointed out that there existed various techniques to address the issue. For example, parties could, of their own initiative, revert to the court that had issued the measure to seek review of that measure, or the parties could ask the court to include within the interim measure, the right for the arbitral tribunal to modify that measure once it was established. In addition, it was always open to the arbitral tribunal to require the parties to revert to the court with the decision made by the arbitral tribunal. [*Report of the Working Group on the Work of its 40th Session (New York, 23–27 February 2004)*, UN Doc No A/CN.9/547, 16 April 2004, p 27, para 104.]

Article 17E. Provision of security

(1) The arbitral tribunal may require the party requesting an interim measure to provide appropriate security in connection with the measure.

(2) The arbitral tribunal shall require the party applying for a preliminary order to provide security in connection with the order unless the arbitral tribunal considers it inappropriate or unnecessary to do so.

COMMENTARY ON SCH 2 ART 17E
Introduction .... [Sch 2 Art 17E-1]
Article 17E makes different provisions for interim
    measures and preliminary orders .... [Sch 2 Art 17E-2]
History of Article .... [Sch 2 Art 17E-3]
Security for interim measures and preliminary
    orders .... [Sch 2 Art 17E-4]

[Sch 2 Art 17E-1] Introduction Article 17E, introduced in the 2006 amendments adopted by UNCITRAL, confers power on the arbitral tribunal to require the provision of security (such as, eg, security for costs) in connection with requests for interim measures or applications for preliminary orders. Article 17E confers power on the arbitral tribunal to order that the applicant for the interim measure provide appropriate security to meet any liability for damages which might arise under Art 17C of the Model Law in the event that the arbitral tribunal later determines that the measure should not have been granted in the first place.

[Sch 2 Art 17E-2] **Article 17E makes different provisions for interim measures and preliminary orders** Like Art 17D, Art 17E applies to interim measures and preliminary orders. However, it should be noted that Art 17E(1) applies specifically to interim measures, whereas Art 17E(2) applies specifically to preliminary orders.

[Sch 2 Art 17E-3] **History of Article** In discussions in the Working Group, the general view emerged that "the granting of security should not be a condition precedent to the granting of an interim measure". In this context, it was pointed out that "Article 17 of the Model Law as well as Article 26(2) of the UNCITRAL Arbitration Rules did not include such a requirement" (*Report of the Working Group on the Work of its 40th Session (New York, 23–27 February 2004)*, UN Doc No A/CN.9/547, p 25, para 92). The proposal was made that the arbitral tribunal should have the power to require any party (ie, not just the party requesting the interim measure) to provide an appropriate security (*Report of the Working Group on the Work of its 40th Session (New York, 23–27 February 2004)*, UN Doc No A/CN.9/547, p 25, paras 93–6).

This was reflected in an early version of Draft Art 17(4) by the Secretariat, which read as follows:

> The arbitral tribunal may require the requesting party or any other party to provide appropriate security in connection with such interim measure of protection. [UNCITRAL Secretariat, "Settlement of Commercial Disputes — Interim Measures of Protection", UN Doc No A/CN.9/WG.II/WP.131, 26 July 2004, pp 2–4, para 4.]

Ultimately, the proposed power of the arbitral tribunal to require "any other party" to provide appropriate security was not retained.

[Sch 2 Art 17E-4] **Security for interim measures and preliminary orders** Article 17E(1) provides that the arbitral tribunal "may require the party requesting an interim measure to provide appropriate security in connection with the measure". This is, accordingly, discretionary. In contrast, under Art 17E(2), the arbitral tribunal shall require a party "applying for a preliminary order to provide security in connection with the order unless the arbitral tribunal considers it inappropriate or unnecessary to do so". The provision of security for preliminary orders is, accordingly, mandatory, unless the tribunal exercises its discretion, which it may do if it considers it "inappropriate or unnecessary" to require the provision of security. Given that preliminary orders are not available under the Act, only Art 17E(1) is relevant in Australia.

Article 17F. Disclosure

(1) The arbitral tribunal may require any party promptly to disclose any material change in the circumstances on the basis of which the measure was requested or granted.

(2) The party applying for a preliminary order shall disclose to the arbitral tribunal all circumstances that are likely to be relevant to the arbitral tribunal's determination whether to grant or maintain the order, and such obligation shall continue until the party against whom the order has been requested has had an opportunity to present its case. Thereafter, paragraph (1) of this article shall apply.

COMMENTARY ON SCH 2 ART 17F

Introduction .... [Sch 2 Art 17F-1]
Article 17F makes different provisions for interim
   measures and preliminary orders .... [Sch 2 Art 17F-2]
History of Article .... [Sch 2 Art 17F-3]
No specific sanction for non-compliance .... [Sch 2 Art 17F-4]

[Sch 2 Art 17F-1] Introduction Article 17F, introduced in the 2006 amendments adopted by UNCITRAL, makes provision for an obligation on the party requesting an interim measure, or applying for a preliminary order, generally to make disclosure of any change in circumstances relevant to the request or application.

[Sch 2 Art 17F-2] Article 17F makes different provisions for interim measures and preliminary orders Like Arts 17D and 17E, Art 17F applies to interim measures and preliminary orders. However, also like Art 17E, Art 17F makes different provisions for the two "types" of interim measure. Article 17F(1) applies specifically to interim measures and Art 17F(2) applies specifically to preliminary orders. In the case of interim measures, Art 17F(1) relevantly provides that the arbitral tribunal "may require" any party to disclose any "material change in the circumstances on the basis of which the measure was requested or granted". In contrast, in the case of preliminary orders, Art 17F(2) provides that the party applying for the preliminary order "shall disclose" to the tribunal "all circumstances that are likely to be relevant to the arbitral tribunal's determination" on the application for the preliminary order. Thus, not only is the obligation of disclosure mandatory in the case of preliminary orders, but it is also a more onerous obligation than in the case of interim measures.

[Sch 2 Art 17F-3] History of Article In an earlier version prepared by the Secretariat, Draft Art 17(5) (as it then was) provided that:

> The requesting party shall promptly make disclosure of any material change in the circumstances on the basis of which the party made the request for, or the arbitral tribunal granted, the interim measure of protection. [UNCITRAL Secretariat, "Settlement of Commercial Disputes — Interim Measures of Protection", UN Doc No A/CN.9/WG.II/WP.131, 26 July 2004, pp 2–4, para 4.]

The Secretariat explained that the draft provision reflected the decision of the Working Group that "the obligation to inform be expressed in a more neutral way and avoided any inference being drawn that the paragraph excluded the obligation under Article 24(3) of the Model Law [ie, the obligation to communicate all statements, documents or other information supplied by one party to the tribunal to the other party]" (UNCITRAL Secretariat, "Settlement of Commercial Disputes — Interim Measures of Protection", UN Doc No A/CN.9/WG.II/WP.131, 26 July 2004, p 7, para 21).

[Sch 2 Art 17F-4] No specific sanction for non-compliance The Secretariat also observed that the Working Group had agreed that there was no need to include a sanction for non-compliance with the obligation of disclosure contained in Draft Art 17(5). As the Secretariat explained:

> [T]he express inclusion of a sanction under paragraph (5) in case of non-compliance with the obligation to disclose any material change in the circumstances ... was not necessary, as in any case the usual sanction for non-compliance with that obligation was either the suspension or termination of the measure, or the award of damages. [UNCITRAL Secretariat, "Settlement of Commercial Disputes — Interim Measures of Protection", UN Doc No A/CN.9/WG.II/WP.131, 26 July 2004, p 7, para 22, referring to *Report of the Working Group on the Work of its 40th Session (New York, 23–27 February 2004)*, UN Doc No A/CN.9/547, A/CN.9/547, p 26, paras 99–100].

Article 17G. Costs and damages

The party requesting an interim measure or applying for a preliminary order shall be liable for any costs and damages caused by the measure or the order to any party if the arbitral tribunal later determines that, in the circumstances, the measure or the order should not have been granted. The arbitral tribunal may award such costs and damages at any point during the proceedings.

COMMENTARY ON SCH 2 ART 17G

Introduction .... [Sch 2 Art 17G-1]
History of Article .... [Sch 2 Art 17G-2]

[Sch 2 Art 17G-1] Introduction Article 17G, introduced in the 2006 amendments adopted by UNCITRAL, generally provides that a party requesting an interim measure or applying for a preliminary order shall be liable for any costs or damages caused by the interim measure or preliminary order to any party, if the tribunal later determines that the interim measure or preliminary order should not have been granted.

[Sch 2 Art 17G-2] History of Article At the thirty-seventh session of the UNCITRAL Working Group (Vienna, 7–11 October 2002), it was agreed that the revised draft of Art 17 of the Model Law should ensure that "the requesting party be considered strictly liable for damages caused to the responding party by an unjustified measure" (*Report of the Working Group on the Work of its 37th Session (Vienna, 7–11 October 2002)*, UN Doc No A/CN.9/523, p 11, para 31). In a version of Art 17G prepared by the Secretariat in 2004, Draft Art 17(6*bis*) (as it then was) provided that:

> The requesting party shall be liable for any costs and damages caused by the interim measure of protection to the party against whom it is directed, if the arbitral tribunal later determines that, in the circumstances, the interim measure should not have been granted. The arbitral tribunal may order an award of costs and damages at any point during the proceedings. [UNCITRAL Secretariat, "Settlement of Commercial Disputes — Interim Measures of Protection", UN Doc No A/CN.9/WG.II/WP.131, 26 July 2004, pp 2–4, para 4.]

This version was later amended such that it also applied to preliminary orders. This had been the intention in early drafts of the regime for preliminary orders (see, eg, Draft Art 17(7)(b) of the Secretariat's draft text of 26 July 2004, which provided that Draft Art 17(6*bis*) should also apply to applications for preliminary orders (UNCITRAL Secretariat, "Settlement of Commercial Disputes — Interim Measures of Protection", UN Doc No A/CN.9/WG.II/WP.131, 26 July 2004, pp 2–4, para 4)).

Section 4. Recognition and enforcement of interim measures

Article 17H. Recognition and enforcement

(1) An interim measure issued by an arbitral tribunal shall be recognized as binding and, unless otherwise provided by the arbitral tribunal, enforced upon application to the competent court, irrespective of the country in which it was issued, subject to the provisions of article 17I.

(2) The party who is seeking or has obtained recognition or enforcement of an interim measure shall promptly inform the court of any termination, suspension or modification of that interim measure.

(3) The court of the State where recognition or enforcement is sought may, if it considers it proper, order the requesting party to provide appropriate security if the arbitral tribunal has not already made a determination with respect to security or where such a decision is necessary to protect the rights of third parties.

COMMENTARY ON SCH 2 ART 17H

Introduction .... [Sch 2 Art 17H-1]
Purpose of s 4 of Ch IV(A) of the Model Law ... [Sch 2 Art 17H-2]
Scope of application of s 4 of Ch IV(A) of the
 Model Law .... [Sch 2 Art 17H-3]
History of Article .... [Sch 2 Art 17H-4]
"Shall be recognised as binding" .... [Sch 2 Art 17H-5]
Relationship between s 4 of Ch IV(A) and Arts 35
 and 36 of the Model Law .... [Sch 2 Art 17H-6]
Obligation of disclosure .... [Sch 2 Art 17H-7]
Appropriate security .... [Sch 2 Art 17H-8]

[Sch 2 Art 17H-1] Introduction Section 4 of Ch IV(A) of the Model Law was considered an "important innovation" of the 2006 amendments. It creates a regime for the recognition and enforcement of interim measures, and the UNCITRAL Secretariat reports that it was "modelled, as appropriate, on the regime for the recognition and enforcement of arbitral awards under Articles 35 and 36 of the Model Law" (UNCITRAL Explanatory Note 2006, p 31, para 27). Article 17H has the force of law in Australia by virtue of s 16(1) of the Act.

[Sch 2 Art 17H-2] Purpose of s 4 of Ch IV(A) of the Model Law The issue of recognition and enforcement had been one of the key issues which led to the reconsideration by UNCITRAL of the Model Law's regime for interim measures. As the Secretariat observes in its Explanatory Note to the UNICTRAL Model Law, the revision of Art 17 "includes an enforcement regime for such measures in recognition of the fact that the effectiveness of arbitration frequently depends upon the possibility of enforcing interim measures" (UNCITRAL Explanatory Note 2006, p 23, para 4).

[Sch 2 Art 17H-3] Scope of application of s 4 of Ch IV(A) of the Model Law It is recalled that Art 1(2) of the Model Law, which has the force of law by virtue of s 16(1) of the Act, provides that the provisions of the Model Law "except. . . Articles 17H, 17I, [and] 17J . . . apply only if the place of arbitration is in the territory of this State [ie, Australia]." In other words, the provisions of section 4 of Ch IV(A) of the Model Law apply to an interim measure irrespective of where the relevant arbitral tribunal has its seat.

[Sch 2 Art 17H-4] History of Article An earlier version of the regime for the recognition and enforcement of interim measures was contained in Draft Art 17*bis*. As formulated by the Secretariat in July 2004, this provided that:

(1) An interim measure of protection issued by an arbitral tribunal shall be recognized as binding and, unless otherwise provided by the arbitral tribunal, enforced upon application to the competent court, irrespective of the country in which it was issued, subject to the provisions of this article.

(2) The court may refuse to recognize or enforce an interim measure of protection, only:
  (a) At the request of the party against whom it is invoked, if the court is satisfied that:
    (i) [There is a substantial question relating to any grounds for refusal] [Such refusal is warranted on the grounds] set forth in article 36, paragraphs (1)(a)(i), (iii) or (iv); or
    (ii) Such refusal is warranted on the grounds set forth in article 36, paragraph (1)(a)(ii); or
    [(iii) The requirement to provide appropriate security in connection with the interim measure issued by the arbitral tribunal has not been complied with;] or
    (iv) The interim measure has been terminated or suspended by the arbitral tribunal or, where so empowered, by the court of the State in which, [or under the law of which, that interim measure was granted] [the arbitration takes place]; or
  (b) if the court finds that:
    (i) The interim measure is incompatible with the powers conferred upon the court by the law, unless the court decides to reformulate the interim measure to the extent necessary to adapt it to its own powers and procedures for the purposes of enforcing that interim measure and without modifying its substance; or
    (ii) Any of the grounds set forth in article 36, paragraphs (1)(b)(i) or (ii) apply to the recognition and enforcement of the interim measure.

(3) Any determination made by the court on any ground in paragraph (2) of this article shall be effective only for the purposes of the application to recognize and enforce the interim measure of protection. The court where recognition or enforcement is sought shall not, in exercising that power, undertake a review of the substance of the interim measure.

(4) The party who is seeking or has obtained recognition or enforcement of an interim measure of protection shall promptly inform the court of any termination, suspension or modification of that interim measure.

(5) The court where recognition or enforcement is sought may, if it considers it proper, order the requesting party to provide appropriate security, unless the arbitral tribunal has already made a determination with respect to security, or where such an order is necessary to protect the rights of third parties.

(6) An interim measure issued by an arbitral tribunal under standards substantially equivalent to those set forth in paragraph (7) of article 17 shall not be denied enforcement pursuant to paragraph 2(a)(ii) of this article because of the measure's ex parte status, provided that any court action to enforce such measure must be issued within twenty (20) days after the date on which the arbitral tribunal issued the measure. [UNCITRAL Secretariat, "Settlement of Commercial Disputes — Interim Measures of Protection", UN Doc No A/CN.9/WG.II/WP.131, 26 July 2004, pp 12–13, para 46.]

As can be seen from this version of Draft Art 17*bis*, only paras (1), (4) and (5) were retained in Art 17H. Paragraphs (2) and (3) were ultimately included (in amended form) as Art 17I and para (6) was considered (but ultimately not adopted) as part of the provisions in s 2 of Ch IV(A) of the UNCITRAL Model Law, being the regime for preliminary orders. (See, on this point, Art 17C(5), which provides that: "A preliminary order . . . shall not be subject to enforcement by a court.")

[Sch 2 Art 17H-5] **"Shall be recognised as binding"** During the drafting of Art 17H, a proposal that the provision should indicate that an interim measure was binding "on the parties" was rejected, on the basis that Art 35(1), on which Art 17H was based, did not include any reference to the parties (*Report of the Working Group on the Work of its 43rd Session (Vienna, 3–7 October 2005)*, UN Doc No A/CN.9/589, 12 October 2005, p 16, para 76).

[Sch 2 Art 17H-6] **Relationship between s 4 of Ch IV(A) and Arts 35 and 36 of the Model Law** In the drafting of s 4 (which contains Arts 17H and 17I of the Model Law), a proposal was made to clarify the relationship between its recognition and enforcement regime and that set out in Arts 35 and 36 of the Model Law (*Report of the Working Group on the Work of its 43rd Session (Vienna, 3–7 October 2005)*, UN Doc No A/CN.9/589, 12 October 2005, p 17, para 77). But this was ultimately not pursued, for "Articles 35 and 36 dealt with recognition and enforcement of awards whereas Article 17*bis* dealt expressly with recognition and enforcement of interim measures and adding the proposed words might create further ambiguity" (*Report of the Working Group on the Work of its 43rd Session (Vienna, 3–7 October 2005)*, UN Doc No A/CN.9/589, 12 October 2005, p 17, para 79).

[Sch 2 Art 17H-7] **Obligation of disclosure** Under Art 17H(2), the party seeking (or having obtained) recognition or enforcement of an interim measure is obliged promptly to "inform the court of any termination, suspension or modification of that interim measure". This is similar to the power of the arbitral tribunal to require "any party promptly to disclose any material change in the circumstances on the basis of which the measure was requested or granted" under Art 17F(1), although where a party is seeking or has obtained recognition and enforcement of an interim measure, that party has an *obligation* to inform the court of any termination, suspension or modification of the measure in question.

[Sch 2 Art 17H-8] **Appropriate security** Under Art 17H(3), the court of the State where recognition or enforcement is sought may, if it considers it proper, order the requesting party to provide appropriate security. The court may take this step in circumstances where "the arbitral tribunal has not already made a determination with respect to security or where such a decision is necessary to protect the rights of third parties". This merely ensures that the court has the same power as regards the provision of security as the arbitral tribunal has under Art 17E(1).

Article 17I. Grounds for refusing recognition or enforcement[3]

(1) Recognition or enforcement of an interim measure may be refused only:
(a) At the request of the party against whom it is invoked if the court is satisfied that:
  (i) Such refusal is warranted on the grounds set forth in article 36(1)(*a*)(i), (ii), (iii) or (iv); or
  (ii) The arbitral tribunal's decision with respect to the provision of security in connection with the interim measure issued by the arbitral tribunal has not been complied with; or
  (iii) The interim measure has been terminated or suspended by the arbitral tribunal or, where so empowered, by the court of the State in which the arbitration takes place or under the law of which that interim measure was granted; or
(b) If the court finds that:
  (i) The interim measure is incompatible with the powers conferred upon the court unless the court decides to reformulate the interim measure to the extent necessary to adapt it to its own powers and procedures for the purposes of enforcing that interim measure and without modifying its substance; or
  (ii) Any of the grounds set forth in article 36(1)(*b*)(i) or (ii), apply to the recognition and enforcement of the interim measure.

(2) Any determination made by the court on any ground in paragraph (1) of this article shall be effective only for the purposes of the application to recognize and enforce the interim measure. The court where recognition or enforcement is sought shall not, in making that determination, undertake a review of the substance of the interim measure.

---

[3] The conditions set forth in article 17I are intended to limit the number of circumstances in which the court may refuse to enforce an interim measure. It would not be contrary to the level of harmonization sought to be achieved by these model provisions if a State were to adopt fewer circumstances in which enforcement may be refused.

COMMENTARY ON SCH 2 ART 17I

Introduction .... [Sch 2 Art 17I-1]
Relationship with Art 36 of the Model Law ...... [Sch 2 Art 17I-2]
Differences from grounds for refusing recognition
 and enforcement of arbitral awards .... [Sch 2 Art 17I-3]
Decision on recognition and enforcement effective
 only for application to recognise and enforce .. [Sch 2 Art 17I-4]
Footnote to Art 17I .... [Sch 2 Art 17I-5]
Section 19 of the Act .... [Sch 2 Art 17I-6]

[Sch 2 Art 17I-1] Introduction Article 17I, introduced in the 2006 amendments adopted by UNCITRAL, sets out the grounds on which recognition and enforcement of an interim measure, ordered in accordance with Ch IV(A) of the UNCITRAL Model Law, may be refused.

[Sch 2 Art 17I-2] Relationship with Art 36 of the Model Law Article 17I essentially reflects the provisions of Art 36 of the UNCITRAL Model Law, which sets out the grounds on which recognition or enforcement of an arbitral award may be refused. Reference is therefore made to the commentary on Art 36 of the UNCITRAL Model Law in this text, as well as to the commentary on s 8 of the Act.

[Sch 2 Art 17I-3] Differences from grounds for refusing recognition and enforcement of arbitral awards However, a number of differences can be noted from the grounds set forth in Art 36 on which the recognition and enforcement of an arbitral award may be refused. First, Art 17I(1) does not provide that recognition or enforcement of an interim measure may be refused if such refusal is warranted on the grounds set forth in Art 36(1)(a)(v) (namely, that "the award has not yet become binding on the parties or has been set aside or suspended by a court of the country in which, or under the law of which, that award was made"). It had been proposed to reflect the terms of Art 36(1)(a)(v) in an earlier version of Art 17I (see Art 17*bis*(2)(iv), as set out above (UNCITRAL Secretariat, "Settlement of Commercial Disputes — Interim Measures of Protection", UN Doc No A/CN.9/WG.II/WP.131, 26 July 2004, pp 12–13, para 46), but this was not adopted. Second, recognition or enforcement of an interim measure may be refused under Art 17I(1)(ii) if "[t]he arbitral tribunal's decision with respect to the provision of security in connection with the interim measure issued by the arbitral tribunal has not been complied with". Third, recognition or enforcement of an interim measure may be refused under Art 17I(1)(iii) if "[t]he interim measure has been terminated or suspended by the arbitral tribunal or, where so empowered, by the court of the State in which the arbitration takes place or under the law of which that interim measure was granted". And fourth, recognition or enforcement of an interim measure may be refused under Art 17I(1)(b)(i) if it is "incompatible with the powers conferred upon the court unless the court decides to reformulate the interim measure to the extent necessary to adapt it to its own powers and procedures for the purposes of enforcing that interim measure and without modifying its substance".

[Sch 2 Art 17I-4] Decision on recognition and enforcement effective only for application to recognise and enforce Under Art 17I(2), any determination by a court on an application for the recognition and enforcement of an interim measure is only effective for the purposes of that application. Further, the court is not to undertake "a review of the substance of the interim measure".

[Sch 2 Art 17I-5] Footnote to Art 17I A footnote to Art 17I in the Model Law states that: "The conditions set forth in Article 17I are intended to limit the number of circumstances in which the court may refuse to enforce an interim measure. It would not be contrary to the level of harmonization sought to be achieved by these model provisions if a State were to adopt fewer circumstances in which enforcement may be refused."

[Sch 2 Art 17I-6] Section 19 of the Act Although Art 17I has the force of law in Australia by virtue of s 16(1) of the Act, Art 17I must be read together with s 19, which provides that:

> Without limiting the generality of Articles 17I(1)(b)(ii), 34(2)(b)(ii) and 36(1)(b)(ii) of the Model Law, it is declared, for the avoidance of any doubt, that, for the purposes of those Articles, an interim measure or award is in conflict with, or is contrary to, the public policy of Australia if:
> (a) the making of the interim measure or award was induced or affected by fraud or corruption; or
> (b) a breach of the rules of natural justice occurred in connection with the making of the interim measure or award.

Section 5. Court-ordered interim measures

Article 17J. Court-ordered interim measures

A court shall have the same power of issuing an interim measure in relation to arbitration proceedings, irrespective of whether their place is in the territory of this State, as it has in relation to proceedings in courts. The court shall exercise such power in accordance with its own procedures in consideration of the specific features of international arbitration.

COMMENTARY ON SCH 2 ART 17J

Introduction	[Sch 2 Art 17J-1]
History of Article	[Sch 2 Art 17J-2]
Interaction between power of courts and power of arbitral tribunals to grant interim measures	[Sch 2 Art 17J-3]
Power of courts to order interim measures under own procedures	[Sch 2 Art 17J-4]

[Sch 2 Art 17J-1] Introduction Article 17J was introduced in the 2006 amendments adopted by UNCITRAL and according to the UNCITRAL Secretariat, was added "to put it beyond any doubt that the existence of an arbitration agreement does not infringe on the powers of the competent court to issue interim measures and that the party to such an arbitration agreement is free to approach the court with a request to order interim measures" (UNCITRAL Explanatory Note 2006, p 31, para 30).

[Sch 2 Art 17J-2] History of Article A draft provision expressing "the power of State courts to order interim measures of protection in support of arbitration" was first discussed at the forty-second session of the UNCITRAL Working Group, which was held in New York from 10–14 January 2005 (Note by the Secretariat, "Settlement of Commercial Disputes — Interim Measures of Protection", UN Doc No A/CN.9/WG.II/WP.138, 8 August 2005, p 3, para 3). An early version of Art 17J, which was adopted as Draft Art 17*ter*, provided that:

> The court shall have the same power of issuing interim measures of protection for the purposes of and in relation to arbitration proceedings as it has for the purposes of and in relation to proceedings in the courts and shall exercise that power in accordance with its own rules and procedures insofar as these are relevant to the specific features of an international arbitration. [Note by the Secretariat, Settlement of Commercial Disputes — Interim Measures of Protection', UN Doc No A/CN.9/WG.II/WP.138, 8 August 2005, p 17, para 63.]

During the discussions in the Working Group, the view was expressed that it was unclear whether the powers of arbitral tribunals and State courts to grant interim measures were "coextensive", or whether the "exercise of the State court power overrode the power of the arbitral tribunal". It was said that this "uncertainty could allow parties to defeat the power of arbitral tribunals to issue interim measures by seeking such measures from the State courts" (*Report of the Working Group on the Work of its 43rd Session (Vienna, 3–7 October 2005)*, UN Doc No A/CN.9/589, 12 October 2005, p 21, para 103). There, it was suggested that:

> to better delineate the interaction of these powers, Article 17*ter* could provide that a State court could only act in circumstances where, and to the extent that, the arbitral tribunal did not have the power to so act or was unable to act effectively, for example, if an interim measure was needed to bind a third party or the arbitral tribunal was not yet constituted or the arbitral tribunal had only made a preliminary order.

This proposal received some support, but it was ultimately not adopted, as it had "far-reaching legal and practical implications and raised complex issues" (*Report on the 43rd Session*, p 21, para 103).

[Sch 2 Art 17J-3] Interaction between power of courts and power of arbitral tribunals to grant interim measures In *Trade Fortune Incorporated v Amalgamated Mill Supplies Ltd* (1994) 89 BCLR (2d) 132; 113 DLR (4th) 116, prior to the adoption of Art 17J, Bouck J of the Supreme Court of British Columbia held (at [16]) that: "Section 9 [ie, Art 9 of the Model Law] prevails over section 17 [ie, Art 17 of the Model Law] since section 9 clearly states that it is not incompatible with the arbitral proceedings for the plaintiffs to seek an order for protection in this court."

[Sch 2 Art 17J-4] Power of courts to order interim measures under own procedures Under Art 17J, the court is to exercise its powers to order interim measures in accordance with its own procedures, taking into account "the specific features of international arbitration".

CHAPTER V. CONDUCT OF ARBITRAL PROCEEDINGS

Article 18. Equal treatment of parties

The parties shall be treated with equality and each party shall be given a full opportunity of presenting his case.

COMMENTARY ON SCH 2 ART 18

Introduction	[Sch 2 Art 18-1]
Further illustrations of principles	[Sch 2 Art 18-2]
History of Article	[Sch 2 Art 18-3]
Article 18 and "natural justice"	[Sch 2 Art 18-4]
"Full opportunity" of presenting a party's case	[Sch 2 Art 18-5]
Where a party has not had a reasonable opportunity to present its case	[Sch 2 Art 18-6]

[Sch 2 Art 18-1] Introduction In providing that the parties are to be treated equally and that each party shall be given "a full opportunity of presenting [its] case", Art 18 embodies the fundamental procedural rights of the parties. The right of equal treatment is a general principle of law known as "*audi alteram partem*" (Bin Cheng, *General Principles of Law as Applied by International Courts and Tribunals*, first published 1953, 1987 ed, p 291); as Holtzmann and Neuhaus put it: "Although Article 18 is only one sentence long, it is the heart of the law's regulation of arbitral proceedings — other Articles provide the detailed mechanisms by which the goals of equality and fair procedure are to be achieved. For this reason, Article 18 has been rightly described as a key element of the 'Magna Carta of Arbitral Procedure'. Likewise, it might well be called the 'due process' clause of arbitration, akin to similar provisions in national constitutions that establish the requirement of procedural fairness as the indispensable foundation of a system of justice" (H Holtzmann and J Neuhaus, *A Guide to the UNCITRAL Model Law on International Commercial Arbitration*, Kluwer Law International, The Hague, 1989, p 550 (footnote omitted), and noted by the court in *Methanex Motunui Ltd v Spellman* [2004] 1 NZLR 95 at 139).

[Sch 2 Art 18-2] Further illustrations of principles The UNCITRAL Secretariat observes that these fundamental procedural rights are illustrated in a number of provisions, including Art 24(1) (on the right of either party to demand a hearing), Art 24(2) (on the provision to the parties of sufficient notice of any hearing), Art 24(3) (on the provision of all statements, documents and other information to the arbitral tribunal and to the other party) and Art 26(2) (on the participation of expert witnesses appointed by the arbitral tribunal at the hearing to be cross-examined by the parties) (UNCITRAL Explanatory Note 2006, p 32, paras 32–3).

[Sch 2 Art 18-3] History of Article Article 18 was modelled on Art 15(1) of the UNCITRAL Arbitration Rules (1976). The text of Art 18 was originally included as para 3 in Art 19; see, eg, UNCITRAL Analytical Commentary, p 44. UNCITRAL provided no authoritative guidance on the interpretation of the terms "treated with equality" and "full opportunity of presenting his case". The Working Group reports are similarly devoid of clear guidance (H Holtzmann and

J Neuhaus, *A Guide to the UNCITRAL Model Law on International Commercial Arbitration*, Kluwer Law International, The Hague, 1989, p 551). These authors suggested (at p 551, footnotes omitted), that:

> [T]he terms 'equality' and 'full opportunity' are to be interpreted reasonably in regulating the procedural aspects of the arbitration. While, on the one hand, the arbitral tribunal must provide reasonable opportunities to each party, this does not mean that it must sacrifice all efficiency in order to accommodate unreasonable procedural demands by a party.

As UNCITRAL noted, the right of the party to have "a full opportunity" of presenting its case "does not entitle a party to obstruct the proceedings by dilatory tactics and, for example, present any objections, amendments, or evidence on the eve of the award" (UNCITRAL Analytical Commentary, p 46, para 8).

[Sch 2 Art 18-4]   Article 18 and "natural justice"   The court in *Trustees of Rotoaira Forest Trust v Attorney-General* [1999] 2 NZLR 452 at 459, expressed the view that "art 18 reflects the pre-existing common law" rules on natural justice and adopted a summary of the basic requirements in an arbitration in M Mustill and S Boyd, *The Law and Practice of Commercial Arbitration in England*, 2nd ed, Butterworths, London, 1989, at 302:

1 Each party must have notice that the hearing is to take place.
2 Each party must have a reasonable opportunity to be present at the hearing, together with his advisors and witnesses.
3 Each party must have the opportunity to be present throughout the hearing.
4 Each party must have a reasonable opportunity to present evidence and argument in support of his own case.
5 Each party must have a reasonable opportunity to test his opponent's case by cross-examining his witnesses, presenting rebutting evidence and addressing oral argument.
6 The hearing must, unless the contrary is expressly agreed, be the occasion on which the parties present the whole of their evidence and argument.

To this list the court added (at 460) that "the arbitrator must confine himself to the material put before him by the parties" otherwise the arbitrator would deprive a party of the opportunity of presenting its case on such material.

[Sch 2 Art 18-5]   "Full opportunity" of presenting a party's case   As noted above, the court in *Trustees of Rotoaira Forest Trust v Attorney-General* [1999] 2 NZLR 452 at 459, saw no clash between "full opportunity" in Art 18 and a "reasonable opportunity" at common law. There is a basis for treating any distinction between these phrases as a distinction without a difference as discussed above in relation to s 18C of the Act. Nonetheless, in Australia, Art 18 must be read together with s 18C of the Act, which provides that for the purposes of Art 18 of the Model Law, a party to arbitral proceedings is taken to have been given a full opportunity to present the party's case if the party is given a reasonable opportunity to present the party's case.

The Revised Explanatory Memorandum to the International Arbitration Bill 2010 (Cth) (at p 14, [95]–[96]) explained that:

95. One of the key purposes of arbitration is to provide an effective alternative to judicial consideration. To ensure that this is the case, tribunals need a wide degree of discretion to manage proceedings and even truncate them where this would be in the interests of the parties by achieving a speedy resolution of their dispute. The requirement in Article 18 [of the Model Law] that parties be given a 'full opportunity' to present their case poses a potential impediment to the effective management of the proceedings by the arbitral tribunal.

96. This item will also insert a new section 18C into the Act that provides that if a party has been given a 'reasonable opportunity' to present their case then this would satisfy the requirement in Article 18 of the Model Law that they be given a 'full opportunity' to present their case. This section is intended to give arbitral tribunals a wider degree of flexibility in controlling arbitral proceedings without removing requirements for the parties to be treated with equality and have an appropriate opportunity to make out their case.

The UNCITRAL Arbitration Rules (2010) now also provide in Art 17(1) that "the arbitral tribunal may conduct the arbitration in such manner as it considers appropriate, provided that the parties are treated with equality and that at an appropriate stage of the proceedings each party is given a reasonable opportunity of presenting its case".

[Sch 2 Art 18-6] Where a party has not had a reasonable opportunity to present its case If a party is not given a reasonable opportunity to present its case, that party has a right under Art 34(2)(a)(ii) of the Model Law to apply to set aside the award. An enforcement court may also refuse to enforce the award on the same grounds set out in s 8(5)(c) of the Act and Art 36(1)(a)(ii) of the Model Law. See also the discussion at s 8(5)(c) and Art 36(1)(a)(ii).

Article 19. Determination of rules of procedure

(1) Subject to the provisions of this Law, the parties are free to agree on the procedure to be followed by the arbitral tribunal in conducting the proceedings.

(2) Failing such agreement, the arbitral tribunal may, subject to the provisions of this Law, conduct the arbitration in such manner as it considers appropriate. The power conferred upon the arbitral tribunal includes the power to determine the admissibility, relevance, materiality and weight of any evidence.

COMMENTARY ON SCH 2 ART 19

Introduction	[Sch 2 Art 19-1]
Freedom of parties to agree on procedure	[Sch 2 Art 19-2]
Residual power of arbitral tribunal to determine procedure	[Sch 2 Art 19-3]
Admissibility, relevance, materiality and weight of evidence	[Sch 2 Art 19-4]
Burden of proof	[Sch 2 Art 19-5]

[Sch 2 Art 19-1] Introduction As the UNCITRAL Secretariat noted in the context of both Arts 18 and 19 (as they were originally part of the same provision), this is the "Magna Carta of Arbitral Procedure". As the Secretariat observed, the provision "goes a long way towards establishing procedural autonomy by recognising the parties' freedom to lay down the rules of procedure (paragraph (1)) and by granting the arbitral tribunal, failing agreement of the parties, wide discretion as to how to conduct the proceedings (paragraph (2))" (UNCITRAL Analytical Commentary, p 44, para 1).

[Sch 2 Art 19-2] Freedom of parties to agree on procedure Under Art 19(1), the parties are free to determine the procedure that will apply to the arbitration proceedings. They may do so by preparing their own set of rules, or by adopting one of the institutional sets of arbitration rules for either administered or ad hoc arbitration (UNCITRAL Analytical Commentary, p 44, para 2). They may also agree on a procedure which is found in a national or sub-national legal system, such as, eg, "the law of England and Wales", or "the law of New York". The parties' freedom to agree on the applicable procedure is however subject to the mandatory provisions of the Model Law, which UNCITRAL identifies as including Arts 18, 23(1), 24(2) and (3), 27, 30(2), 31(1), (3) and (4), 32 and 33(1), (2), (4) and (5) (UNCITRAL Analytical Commentary, p 45, para 3). (For a detailed consideration of the provisions of the UNCITRAL Model Law which may be considered as mandatory, see especially S Greenberg, C Kee and R Weeramantry, *International Commercial Arbitration: An Asia-Pacific Perspective*, Cambridge University Press, Melbourne, 2011, pp 88–95.

In *Brunswick Bowling & Billiards Corp v Zhonglu Industrial Co Ltd* [2009] HKCFI 84 at [84]–[90], the court considered that the freedom of the parties in agreeing to arbitral procedures in Art 19(1) is subject to the overriding objectives of Art 18. The court held (at [88]) that "if the arbitrators were of the view that the procedure agreed by the parties would result in a breach of Article 18, they should take steps to conduct the arbitration in such a manner that could redress the problem instead of being constrained by an unworkable agreement of the parties".

[Sch 2 Art 19-3] Residual power of arbitral tribunal to determine procedure Under Art 19(2), the arbitral tribunal has the power to conduct the arbitration "in such manner as it considers appropriate" where the parties have not agreed on any procedure. This is consistent with the inherent power of international courts and tribunals to decide on issues of procedure. For instance, the Permanent Court of International Justice observed that:

> Neither the Statute nor the Rules of Court contain any rule regarding the procedure to be followed in the event of an objection being taken *in limine litis* to the Court's jurisdiction. The Court therefore is at liberty to adopt the principle which it considers best calculated to ensure the administration of justice, most suited to procedure before an international tribunal and most in conformity with the fundamental principles of international law. [*Mavrommatis Palestine Concessions (Greece v United Kingdom)* PCIJ Rep, Series A (No 2), p 1 and 16 (1924).]

The power of the arbitral tribunal to conduct the arbitration "in such manner as it considers appropriate" is however subject to the provisions of the Model Law which provide for special features of the discretionary powers of the arbitral tribunal (UNCITRAL Analytical Commentary, p 45, para 4). But the discretionary powers of the arbitral tribunal remain "considerable", particularly as the Model Law provides a liberal framework which "enables the arbitral tribunal to meet the needs of the particular case and to select the most suitable procedure when organising the arbitration, conducting individual hearings or other meetings and determining the important specifics of taking and evaluating evidence" (UNCITRAL Analytical Commentary, p 45, para 5). The flexibility of Art 19 also means that the arbitral tribunal can adopt (and adapt) procedures from common law, civil law or mixed legal systems, depending on the origin of the parties to the dispute (UNCITRAL Analytical Commentary, p 46, para 6).

[Sch 2 Art 19-4] **Admissibility, relevance, materiality and weight of evidence** Article 19(2) provides that the arbitral tribunal's power includes "the power to determine the admissibility, relevance, materiality and weight of any evidence". This was modelled on Art 25(6) of the UNCITRAL Arbitration Rules (1976) (and see now Art 27(4) of the UNCITRAL Arbitration Rules (2010)). This provision should be regarded as non-mandatory, as it refers to "the 'power' conferred directly by the Model Law in the first sentence of paragraph 2, and not the 'power' conferred by the parties' agreement under paragraph 1" (H Holtzmann and J Neuhaus, *A Guide to the UNCITRAL Model Law on International Commercial Arbitration*, Kluwer Law International, The Hague, 1989, p 566). This means that if parties agree that certain evidence should be excluded, or should be regarded as the only evidence to be considered, the arbitral tribunal should respect that agreement (see especially Holtzmann and Neuhaus, pp 566–7).

[Sch 2 Art 19-5] **Burden of proof** The Model Law is silent on the issue of the burden of proof, though proposals were made to include a provision making it clear that each party was to bear the burden "of proving the facts relied on to support its claim or defence" (H Holtzmann and J Neuhaus, *A Guide to the UNCITRAL Model Law on International Commercial Arbitration*, Kluwer Law International, The Hague, 1989, p 568). The UNCITRAL Arbitration Rules contain such a provision (see Art 24(1) of the 1976 Rules and Art 27(1) of the 2010 Rules), which provide in near identical terms: "Each party shall have the burden of proving the facts relied on to support its claim or defence." A provision on the burden of proof was not included as it was considered that such a provision may interfere with the provision on the choice of law (Art 28) and the parties' (and arbitral tribunal's) freedom in the conduct of the arbitration under Art 19 (Holtzmann and Neuhaus, p 568; and see also A Broches, *Commentary on the UNCITRAL Model Law on International Commercial Arbitration*, Kluwer Law International, The Hague, 1990, p 100).

Article 20. Place of arbitration

(1) The parties are free to agree on the place of arbitration. Failing such agreement, the place of arbitration shall be determined by the arbitral tribunal having regard to the circumstances of the case, including the convenience of the parties.

(2) Notwithstanding the provisions of paragraph (1) of this article, the arbitral tribunal may, unless otherwise agreed by the parties, meet at any place it considers appropriate for consultation among its members, for hearing witnesses, experts or the parties, or for inspection of goods, other property or documents.

COMMENTARY ON SCH 2 ART 20

Introduction	[Sch 2 Art 20-1]
Place or juridical seat of arbitration	[Sch 2 Art 20-2]
Laws of the seat	[Sch 2 Art 20-3]
Agreement as to seat of arbitration	[Sch 2 Art 20-4]
Identification of place or seat of arbitration	[Sch 2 Art 20-5]
A seat in federal State	[Sch 2 Art 20-6]
Anti-suit injunction	[Sch 2 Art 20-7]
Common law	[Sch 2 Art 20-8]
Award is made at place of arbitration	[Sch 2 Art 20-9]
Arbitral tribunal may determine place of arbitration	[Sch 2 Art 20-10]

[Sch 2 Art 20-1] Introduction The phrase "the place of the arbitration", as used in Art 20 (and Arts 1(2) and (3), 17I(1)(a), 17J, 31 and 36(1)(a)(iv) of the Model Law and ss 8(5)(e) and 18 of the Act) involves two distinct concepts. There is a "distinction between the legal localization of an arbitration on the one hand and the appropriate or convenient geographical locality for hearings of the arbitration on the other" (*Naviera Amazonica Peruana SA v Compania International De Seguros Del Peru* [1988] 2 Lloyd's Rep 116 at 117 (Kerr LJ)). The place or legal localisation of the arbitration "does not change even though the tribunal may meet to hear witnesses or do any other things in relation to the arbitration at a location other than the place of the arbitration" (*PT Garuda Indonesia v Birgen Air* [2002] 1 SLR(R) 401 at 407). "The legal place of the arbitration remains the same even if the physical place changes from time to time, unless of course the parties agree to change it" (*Union of India v McDonnell Douglas Corp* [1993] 2 Lloyd's Rep 48, Saville J at 50). The mere fact that an arbitral panel may choose to sit in a particular location may be "for many reasons or be purely accidental; a choice so made should not affect the parties' rights" (*James Miller & Partners Ltd v Whitworth Street Estates (Manchester) Ltd* [1970] AC 583; [1970] 1 All ER 796; [1970] 2 WLR 728; [1970] 1 Lloyd's Rep 269, Lord Wilberforce at 616).

[Sch 2 Art 20-2] Place or juridical seat of arbitration An international arbitration is not the natural extension of the judicial process of any one particular country and in that sense may be seen as legally unattached. However, the common law "does not recognize the concept of arbitral procedures floating in the transnational firmament unconnected with any municipal system of law" (*Bank Mellat v Helliniki Techniki SA* [1984] QB 291; [1983] 3 All ER 428; (1983) 133 NLJ 597; [1983] 3 WLR 783, Kerr LJ at 301). Every international arbitration must be localised in the sense of having a juridical base or home which is generally where the arbitration is deemed to be located, although physically the arbitration process may involve venues and participants in a number of different jurisdictions. The arbitration hearing may take place in a number of jurisdictions either sequentially or even concurrently, as may occur when teleconferencing or videoconferencing is used, with the parties and each of the members of the arbitral panel being located in different countries. In the case of an international arbitration, there may be no natural law of the forum to regulate the procedure to be followed should disputes arise. The parties must therefore choose a place where their arbitration is to be located legally. This place so identified is referred to variously as the juridical seat or home of the arbitration, the place of the arbitration, the legal situs of the arbitration and, most commonly, the seat of the arbitration.

As noted by the Singapore Court of Appeal, "the English concept of 'seat of arbitration' is the same as 'place of arbitration' under the Model Law (*PT Garuda Indonesia v Birgen Air* [2002] 1 SLR(R) 401 at 407).

[Sch 2 Art 20-3] Laws of the seat The choice of a juridical seat for the arbitration carries with it the choice of the laws of that place as the laws to govern the arbitration process from start to finish (cf, S Greenberg, C Kee and R Weeramantry, *International Commercial Arbitration: An Asia-Pacific Perspective*, Cambridge University Press, Melbourne, 2011, pp 60–1).

The use of the word "juridical" in qualifying the seat of arbitration is deliberate, as the word "means and connotes the administration of justice so far as the arbitration is concerned. It implies that there must be a country whose job it is to administer, control or decide what control there is to be over an arbitration" (*Braes of Doune Wind Farm (Scotland) Ltd v Alfred McAlpine Business Services Ltd* [2008] All ER (D) 222 (Mar); [2008] BLR 321; [2008] 1 Lloyd's Rep 608; [2008] EWHC 426 (TCC) at [15]). Thus selecting the juridical seat, whilst it does involve choosing a physical location, is concerned with selecting a legal system as distinct from choosing a venue for any hearing. Thus the choice of the seat involves the parties choosing the arbitration law of the seat. This law so selected is variously referred to as the *lex arbitri*, the curial law of the arbitration or procedural law. This law was discussed above in relation to the meaning of the phrase "the procedure in relation to arbitration ... is governed ... by the law of" where it appears in s 7(1)(a) and (b) of the Act. Nevertheless, to describe this law as the "procedural" law is misleading, because it is concerned with not only procedural matters but also with the substantive rights of the parties such as possible rights of appeal or rights to challenge to the award.

[Sch 2 Art 20-4] Agreement as to seat of arbitration A choice of seat for the arbitration is a choice of forum for remedies seeking to attack the award. An agreement as to the seat of arbitration is analogous to an exclusive jurisdiction clause. Any claim for a remedy going to the existence or scope of the arbitrator's jurisdiction or as to the validity of an existing interim or final award is agreed to be made only in the courts of the place designated as the seat of the arbitration (*C v D* [2007] EWCA 1282, Longmore LJ at [17]). The parties' choice of the seat is an agreement that the courts of the seat will have exclusive supervisory jurisdiction over the arbitration. Thus, any challenge to the award should be made under the laws of the seat absent an express agreement between the parties to the contrary and except where the challenge arises on an application for enforcement of the award under the New York Convention. The law of the seat is the curial law which governs the validity of the award and challenges to it. The "principle is that a party should not generally bring proceedings in relation to an arbitration except in the courts of the jurisdiction of the seat of the arbitration" (*Chalbury McCouat International Ltd v PG Foils Ltd* [2011] 1 All ER (Comm) 435; [2010] BLR 593; [2011] 1 Lloyd's Rep 23; [2010] EWHC 2050 (TCC) at [21], except of course enforcement proceedings in those jurisdictions where the assets may be located).

[Sch 2 Art 20-5] Identification of place or seat of arbitration As the choice of the seat is dependent upon the parties' agreement, it is necessary to ascertain the proper construction of the parties' agreement to identify the seat. Arbitration agreements embedded in the main contract sometimes cause problems when the parties have not made their intentions clear or have failed to take into account the impact of other clauses in their agreement.

One distinctive approach is seen in *Braes of Doune Wind Farm (Scotland) Ltd v Alfred McAlpine Business Services Ltd* [2008] All ER (D) 222 (Mar); [2008] BLR 321; [2008] 1 Lloyd's Rep 608; [2008] EWHC 426 (TCC) — notwithstanding that the parties had expressly agreed that the "seat" of arbitration was to be Glasgow, Scotland, the court construed the clause as merely referring only to the place in which the parties agreed that the hearings should take place. The court reasoned that by all the other references, the parties were agreeing that the curial law or law which governed the arbitral proceedings was that of England and Wales and that, where in substance the parties had agreed that the laws of one country will govern and control a given arbitration, the place where the arbitration is to be heard will not dictate what the governing or controlling law will be. Thus the supervisory court was the English court even though the parties had stated that the seat of their arbitration was in Glasgow.

In contrast, in the case of *Union of India v McDonnell Douglas* [1993] 2 Lloyd's Rep 48, the arbitration clause relevantly said on the one hand, "the arbitration shall be conducted in accordance with the procedure provided in the Indian Arbitration Act of 1940 or any reenactment or modification thereof" and on the other, it said "the seat shall be London, United Kingdom". The UK High Court found as a matter of the proper construction of the clause, that the arbitration and any award "was subject to the supervisory jurisdiction of" the English courts and not the Indian courts.

[Sch 2 Art 20-6] **A seat in federal State** The choice of the seat is directed at ascertaining the particular system of law to regulate and support the arbitration process and the award. This does not cause problems for states having a unitary system of law but, if the seat is located in a federal State such as Australia or Switzerland, it is necessary to specify a city such as Sydney or, as occurred in *Raguz v Sullivan* (2000) 50 NSWLR 236; [2000] NSWCA 240; BC200005212, Lausanne, as the seat. Otherwise merely specifying Australia or Switzerland would not have identified the particular applicable system of law. This is the unstated premise for the form of the recommended clause in Guideline 4 of the *IBA Guidelines for Drafting International Arbitration Clauses*. Guideline 4 states: "The parties should select the place of arbitration. This selection should be based on both practical and juridical considerations." The recommended clause reads: "The place of the arbitration shall be [city, country]."

[Sch 2 Art 20-7] **Anti-suit injunction** There is an implied term in the parties' agreement on the seat and the curial law, that the courts of the seat of arbitration will have exclusive supervisory jurisdiction (*C v D* [2007] All ER (D) 365 (Jun); [2007] 2 All ER (Comm) 557; [2007] EWHC 1541 (Comm) at [52], affirmed on appeal *C v D* [2007] All ER (D) 61 (Dec); [2008] 1 All ER (Comm) 1001; [2008] 1 Lloyd's Rep 239; [2007] EWCA Civ 1282). Accordingly an attempt to invoke the courts of another jurisdiction to set aside the award is in breach of the parties' contractual rights and may be restrained by an anti-suit injunction (*Shashoua v Sharma* [2009] All ER (D) 64 (May); [2009] 2 All ER (Comm) 477; [2009] EWHC 957 (Comm) Ramsey J at [23]).

[Sch 2 Art 20-8] **Common law** The common law recognises this distinction between the physical location of the process and the juridical seat of the arbitration (see *American Diagnostica Inc v Gradipore Ltd* (1998) 44 NSWLR 312 at 324;

BC9800877; *Raguz v Sullivan* (2000) 50 NSWLR 236; [2000] NSWCA 240; BC200005212 at [93]–[110] (Spigelman CJ and Mason P); and *Union of India v McDonnell Douglas Corp* [1993] 2 Lloyd's Rep 48).

[Sch 2 Art 20-9]   Award is made at place of arbitration   The seat of the arbitration is also the place where the award is usually made following the conclusion of the hearing (Art 31(3) of the Model Law). This provision (and provisions to a similar effect found in most procedural rules eg, Art 16(4) of the UNCITRAL Arbitration Rules (1976) and Art 18(2) of the UNCITRAL Arbitration Rules (2010)) overcomes the problem identified in *Hiscox v Outhwaite* [1992] 1 AC 562; [1991] 3 All ER 124; [1991] 2 Lloyd's Rep 1; [1991] 2 WLR 1321, that absent such a provision, an award as a written instrument is made when it is perfected. In other words it is made when, and where, it is signed by the arbitral panel. The place of signing may be fortuitous and may, as it did in that case, cause problems for the parties by inadvertently changing the law applicable to the award. These provisions also overcome the practical problem of an award being signed by the members of a three-member panel, each being located in different jurisdictions.

[Sch 2 Art 20-10]   Arbitral tribunal may determine place of arbitration   Where the parties have not chosen the seat or place of arbitration, either expressly or impliedly, the arbitral tribunal may make the determination (Art 20(1) of the Model Law). To assist in making this determination UNCITRAL in 1996 published *Notes on Organizing Arbitral Proceedings* which stated (at para 25):

> Various factual and legal factors influence the choice of the place of arbitration, and their relative importance varies from case to case. Among the more prominent factors are: (a) suitability of the law on arbitral procedure of the place of arbitration; (b) whether there is a multilateral or bilateral treaty on enforcement of arbitral awards between the State where the arbitration takes place and the State or States where the award may have to be enforced; (c) convenience of the parties and the arbitrators, including the travel distances; (d) availability and cost of support services needed; and (e) location of the subject matter in dispute and proximity of evidence.

Article 21.   Commencement of arbitral proceedings

Unless otherwise agreed by the parties, the arbitral proceedings in respect of a particular dispute commence on the date on which a request for that dispute to be referred to arbitration is received by the respondent.

COMMENTARY ON SCH 2 ART 21
Introduction .... [Sch 2 Art 21-1]
Diverse approach among national legal systems ... [Sch 2 Art 21-2]
Rule as agreed .... [Sch 2 Art 21-3]
Parties may derogate .... [Sch 2 Art 21-4]

[Sch 2 Art 21-1]   Introduction   This provision was considered necessary because the time or manner of commencing the arbitration may be important in interpreting other provisions of the Model Law (see, eg, Art 8(b), which refers to arbitral proceedings being "commenced", or Art 30(1), which refers to the settlement of the dispute "during arbitral proceedings": H Holtzmann and J Neuhaus, *A Guide to the UNCITRAL Model Law on International Commercial Arbitration*, Kluwer Law International, The Hague, 1989, p 610). In addition, as the Model Law aims to provide a set of rules for parties who have not adopted a comprehensive set of arbitration rules (such as the ICC Arbitration Rules, or the ACICA Arbitration Rules), it was considered that the Model Law should make provision for "every significant step of the proceedings" (Holtzmann and Neuhaus, p 610).

[Sch 2 Art 21-2] **Diverse approach among national legal systems** In drafting Art 21, the UNCITRAL Working Group was concerned with the issue of defining the point in time when the limitation period for bringing a legal action is interrupted by the commencement of arbitral proceedings, which is an issue otherwise not addressed in the Model Law (H Holtzmann and J Neuhaus, *A Guide to the UNCITRAL Model Law on International Commercial Arbitration*, Kluwer Law International, The Hague, 1989, p 610). Not all national arbitration laws provide that commencing arbitral proceedings will affect the applicable limitation period (Holtzmann and Neuhaus, p 611).

[Sch 2 Art 21-3] **Rule as agreed** As finally adopted, Art 21 provides a rule "for determining the point in time at which the arbitral proceedings in respect of a particular dispute commence" (UNCITRAL Analytical Commentary, p 49, para 1). The arbitral proceedings are deemed to commence on the date on which the respondent receives a request for the dispute to be referred to arbitration. This is consistent with the approach in Art 3(2) of the UNCITRAL Arbitration Rules (2010), and also Art 3(2) of the UNCITRAL Arbitration Rules (1976). The rule leaves open the question of the effect of the commencement of arbitral proceedings on the limitation period to the relevant applicable law (H Holtzmann and J Neuhaus, *A Guide to the UNCITRAL Model Law on International Commercial Arbitration*, Kluwer Law International, The Hague, 1989, p 612).

[Sch 2 Art 21-4] **Parties may derogate** The parties to an arbitration are free to derogate from this provision and choose a different point in time (UNCITRAL Analytical Commentary, p 49, para 3). In the context of an arbitration administered by an institution, the parties "may agree, by reference to the institutional rules, that the relevant date is the one on which the request for arbitration is received by the arbitral institution" (UNCITRAL Analytical Commentary, p 49, para 3).

Article 22. Language

(1) The parties are free to agree on the language or languages to be used in the arbitral proceedings. Failing such agreement, the arbitral tribunal shall determine the language or languages to be used in the proceedings. This agreement or determination, unless otherwise specified therein, shall apply to any written statement by a party, any hearing and any award, decision or other communication by the arbitral tribunal.

(2) The arbitral tribunal may order that any documentary evidence shall be accompanied by a translation into the language or languages agreed upon by the parties or determined by the arbitral tribunal.

COMMENTARY ON SCH 2 ART 22

Introduction .... [Sch 2 Art 22-1]
Party autonomy .... [Sch 2 Art 22-2]
If parties do not reach agreement .... [Sch 2 Art 22-3]
Timing for agreement or determination on
  language .... [Sch 2 Art 22-4]
Language to apply to written submissions, hearing,
  communications and decisions/awards .... [Sch 2 Art 22-5]
Documentary evidence .... [Sch 2 Art 22-6]

[Sch 2 Art 22-1] Introduction As the issue of the applicable language is not usually addressed in national legislation on international arbitration, the UNCITRAL Working Group considered it prudent to make express provision that the parties are free to agree on the language governing the arbitration (H Holtzmann and J Neuhaus, *A Guide to the UNCITRAL Model Law on International Commercial Arbitration*, Kluwer Law International, The Hague, 1989, p 628). Article 22 is modelled on Art 17 of the UNCITRAL Arbitration Rules (1976) (now Art 19 of the UNCITRAL Arbitration Rules (2010)).

[Sch 2 Art 22-2] Party autonomy It is clear from Art 22 that "the arbitral proceedings are not subject to any local language requirement, for example, any 'official' language or languages for court proceedings at the place of arbitration" (UNCITRAL Analytical Commentary, pp 49–50, para 1). It was considered important for party autonomy to prevail on this issue, as the decision on language "affects their position in the proceedings and the expediency and costs of the arbitration" (UNCITRAL Analytical Commentary, p 50, para 2).

[Sch 2 Art 22-3] If parties do not reach agreement Article 22(1) provides that if the parties are not able to reach agreement the arbitral tribunal shall determine the "language or languages to be used". If called upon to decide, the tribunal should consider: whether a single language would be acceptable, or whether more than one language should be used; the effect of such a decision on the expediency and costs of the arbitration; and of course the tribunal's own language capabilities (UNCITRAL Analytical Commentary, p 50, paras 2–3).

[Sch 2 Art 22-4] Timing for agreement or determination on language Article 22 does not make clear when the agreement on the applicable language, or the tribunal's determination on this issue, should be made. But "the exigencies of arbitral procedure would suggest ... that any agreement or determination should be made early" (H Holtzmann and J Neuhaus, *A Guide to the UNCITRAL Model Law on International Commercial Arbitration*, Kluwer Law International, The Hague, 1989, p 629).

[Sch 2 Art 22-5] Language to apply to written submissions, hearing, communications and decisions/awards The third sentence of Art 22(1) provides that the language of the arbitration, as agreed by the parties, or as determined by the tribunal, shall apply to "any written statement by a party, any hearing and any award, decision or communication by the arbitral tribunal", unless agreed or determined otherwise. However, this does not mean that a party is not able to use its own language at any hearing; rather that "[t]hat party may, in fact, use his language in any hearing or other meeting but he must arrange, or at least pay, for the interpretation into the language of the proceedings" (UNCITRAL Analytical Commentary, p 50, para 4).

[Sch 2 Art 22-6] **Documentary evidence** Article 22(2) makes it clear that it is up to the arbitral tribunal to order that any documentary evidence be accompanied by a translation into the language or languages of the arbitration. The tribunal has discretion to make such an order, which reflects the possibility that "such documents may be voluminous and only in part truly relevant to the dispute" (UNCITRAL Analytical Commentary, p 50, para 5).

Article 23. Statements of claim and defence

(1) Within the period of time agreed by the parties or determined by the arbitral tribunal, the claimant shall state the facts supporting his claim, the points at issue and the relief or remedy sought, and the respondent shall state his defence in respect of these particulars, unless the parties have otherwise agreed as to the required elements of such statements. The parties may submit with their statements all documents they consider to be relevant or may add a reference to the documents or other evidence they will submit.

(2) Unless otherwise agreed by the parties, either party may amend or supplement his claim or defence during the course of the arbitral proceedings, unless the arbitral tribunal considers it inappropriate to allow such amendment having regard to the delay in making it.

COMMENTARY ON SCH 2 ART 23

History of Article	[Sch 2 Art 23-1]
Content of Art 23(1)	[Sch 2 Art 23-2]
Article 23(1) not mandatory	[Sch 2 Art 23-3]
Amending or supplementing statement of claim or defence	[Sch 2 Art 23-4]
Article 23(2) not mandatory	[Sch 2 Art 23-5]
Counter-claims and set-off	[Sch 2 Art 23-6]

[Sch 2 Art 23-1] **History of Article** In drafting Art 23(1), the UNCITRAL Working Group considered two approaches: the first would be a mandatory rule "in order to ensure certainty" concerning the scope of the submission to arbitration; and the second, to provide more comprehensive rules for the commencement of the arbitration, which might be modelled on Arts 18–20 of the UNCITRAL Arbitration Rules (1976) (H Holtzmann and J Neuhaus, *A Guide to the UNCITRAL Model Law on International Commercial Arbitration*, Kluwer Law International, The Hague, 1989, pp 646–7). The UNCITRAL Working Group preferred the first approach, because "such a rule should only deal with those elements of initial pleadings which were essential for defining the dispute on which the arbitral tribunal is to give decision" (Third Working Group Report, cited in Holtzmann and Neuhaus, p 647). As ultimately adopted, Art 23(1) "sets forth those elements of the initial pleadings which are essential for defining the dispute on which the arbitral tribunal is to give a decision" (UNCITRAL Analytical Commentary, p 51, para 1), and these elements are drawn from Arts 18(2) and 19(2) of the UNCITRAL Arbitration Rules (1976) (Holtzmann and Neuhaus, p 647).

[Sch 2 Art 23-2] Content of Art 23(1) As UNCITRAL notes, "[t]he required contents of the initial statement of claim and of the respondent's reply may be regarded as so basic and necessary so as to conform with all established arbitration systems and rules" (UNCITRAL Analytical Commentary, p 51, para 1).

[Sch 2 Art 23-3] Article 23(1) not mandatory According to UNCITRAL, the rule should be considered as non-mandatory: "For example, arbitration rules may describe these essential contents in slightly different form or may require their inclusion already in the initial request for arbitration" (UNCITRAL Analytical Commentary, p 51, para 2). The solution adopted was a requirement that some statement from each party is mandatory, but the parties can agree to vary the elements of the statement (H Holtzmann and J Neuhaus, *A Guide to the UNCITRAL Model Law on International Commercial Arbitration*, Kluwer Law International, The Hague, 1989, p 647).

[Sch 2 Art 23-4] Amending or supplementing statement of claim or defence Under Art 23(2), the arbitral tribunal has the discretion to decide whether the parties may amend or supplement their statement of claim or defence. In making this decision, the arbitral tribunal is to have regard to the appropriateness of the statement of claim being amended or supplemented, having regard to the delay in the amendment or supplement being made. In an earlier formulation, which was modelled on Art 20 of the UNCITRAL Arbitration Rules (1976) (and see now Art 22 of the UNCITRAL Arbitration Rules (2010)), the arbitral tribunal was also to consider whether such amendment or supplement would be inappropriate having regard to any "prejudice to the other party or any other circumstances" (UNCITRAL Analytical Commentary, p 51, draft Art 23(3)), which was not included in the version as finally adopted.

[Sch 2 Art 23-5] Article 23(2) not mandatory Article 23(2) is clearly not mandatory, so the parties can derogate from the terms of this provision and agree, eg, that amendments are prohibited or that they are allowed "as a matter of right" (UNCITRAL Analytical Commentary, p 52, para 6).

[Sch 2 Art 23-6] Counter-claims and set-off This provision is considered to apply *mutatis mutandis* to counter-claims and set-off (UNCITRAL Analytical Commentary, p 52, paras 7–8).

Article 24. Hearings and written proceedings

(1) Subject to any contrary agreement by the parties, the arbitral tribunal shall decide whether to hold oral hearings for the presentation of evidence or for oral argument, or whether the proceedings shall be conducted on the basis of documents and other materials. However, unless the parties have agreed that no hearings shall be held, the arbitral tribunal shall hold such hearings at an appropriate stage of the proceedings, if so requested by a party.

(2) The parties shall be given sufficient advance notice of any hearing and of any meeting of the arbitral tribunal for the purposes of inspection of goods, other property or documents.

(3) All statements, documents or other information supplied to the arbitral tribunal by one party shall be communicated to the other party. Also any expert report or evidentiary document on which the arbitral tribunal may rely in making its decision shall be communicated to the parties.

COMMENTARY ON SCH 2 ART 24

Introduction	[Sch 2 Art 24-1]
Unless agreed otherwise, party has right to demand hearing	[Sch 2 Art 24-2]
Arbitral tribunal has control over hearing	[Sch 2 Art 24-3]
Sufficient advance notice of hearing	[Sch 2 Art 24-4]
Communication of documents, etc	[Sch 2 Art 24-5]
Expert report or evidentiary document relied upon by arbitral tribunal	[Sch 2 Art 24-6]

[Sch 2 Art 24-1] Introduction This provision was modelled on Art 15(2) of the UNCITRAL Arbitration Rules (1976) (and see now Arts 17(3) and 28 of the UNCITRAL Arbitration Rules (2010)) (H Holtzmann and J Neuhaus, *A Guide to the UNCITRAL Model Law on International Commercial Arbitration*, Kluwer Law International, The Hague, 1989, p 670).

[Sch 2 Art 24-2] Unless agreed otherwise, party has right to demand hearing Article 24(1) provides that, subject to the agreement of the parties, the arbitral tribunal should have the power to decide whether to hold oral hearings or to decide the dispute on the basis of documents. However, it also states that, unless the parties had agreed that no hearings be held, a party should have the right to demand a hearing (see further UNCITRAL Analytical Commentary, pp 53–4, paras 1–5; H Holtzmann and J Neuhaus, *A Guide to the UNCITRAL Model Law on International Commercial Arbitration*, Kluwer Law International, The Hague, 1989, pp 671–4).

[Sch 2 Art 24-3] Arbitral tribunal has control over hearing In the event that a hearing is held, the arbitral tribunal has considerable control over the timing and length of the hearing, as well as other aspects of the procedure. This is of course subject to the limitations in Arts 18 and 19 of the UNCITRAL Model Law, which provide that the parties are to be treated equally and that the tribunal shall determine the rules of procedure in the absence of any agreement by the parties (H Holtzmann and J Neuhaus, *A Guide to the UNCITRAL Model Law on International Commercial Arbitration*, Kluwer Law International, The Hague, 1989, p 674).

[Sch 2 Art 24-4] Sufficient advance notice of hearing Article 25(2) implements the provisions of Art 18, by providing "that the parties shall be notified sufficiently in advance of any hearing and of any meeting of the arbitral tribunal for the purpose of inspecting goods, property, or documents" (UNCITRAL Analytical Commentary, p 55, para 6). This is a mandatory provision, so even if the parties agree "to dispense with notice or to provide for a shorter than 'sufficient' period of notice, such an agreement would be ineffective" (H Holtzmann and J Neuhaus, *A Guide to the UNCITRAL Model Law on International Commercial Arbitration*, Kluwer Law International, The Hague, 1989, p 674). This is also a "fundamental provision", as it is essential for the operation of Art 25(c), which permits the arbitral tribunal to proceed with the hearing even if a party fails to appear before it (Holtzmann and Neuhaus, p 674). The term "sufficient" to define the amount of notice to be given was based on Art 16(3) of the UNCITRAL Arbitration Rules (1976). The inclusion of a requirement that notice be given at least 40 days in advance was rejected, because this was considered inappropriate "in view of the great variety of cases" that would be subject to the Model Law (Holtzmann and Neuhaus, p 674).

[Sch 2 Art 24-5] **Communication of documents, etc** Article 24(3) covers the same ground as Art 15(3) of the UNCITRAL Arbitration Rules (1976), which requires that "all documents and information supplied to the arbitral tribunal by one party shall at the same time, be communicated by that party to the other party" (see now, in slightly amended form, Art 17(4) of the UNCITRAL Arbitration Rules (2010), which refers to "communications" of the parties). The requirement that such "statements, documents or other information" be provided to the other party "at the same time" was not retained in order to accommodate the practices of some arbitral institutions "under which documents are sent first to the institution or the tribunal, which then transmits them to the arbitrators and the other party" (H Holtzmann and J Neuhaus, *A Guide to the UNCITRAL Model Law on International Commercial Arbitration*, Kluwer Law International, The Hague, 1989, p 674).

[Sch 2 Art 24-6] **Expert report or evidentiary document relied upon by arbitral tribunal** The second sentence of Art 24(3) provides that the arbitral tribunal must communicate or make available any "expert report or evidentiary document" on which it relies in making its decision. It initially required that any report "or other document" relied upon by the arbitral tribunal had to be communicated or made available to the parties. This suggests that the arbitral tribunal is permitted to carry out its own research in reaching its decision and is not bound to the submissions of the parties (in application of the principle *jura novit curia*), so long as the parties are provided with access to such expert reports or evidentiary documents. In an earlier draft, the term "evidentiary document" was not included, but the much broader term "other document" was to be found. This broader term was replaced by the term "evidentiary document" so to ensure that "research material prepared or collected by the arbitral tribunal did not have to be communicated to the parties" (H Holtzmann and J Neuhaus, *A Guide to the UNCITRAL Model Law on International Commercial Arbitration*, Kluwer Law International, The Hague, 1989, p 675; cf UNCITRAL Analytical Commentary, p 55, para 8). To the extent that Art 24(3) requires disclosure of any "new material presented to or relied upon by, the independent expert . . . [the parties have] an implied right to present evidence and argument in response to it" (*Methanex Motunui Ltd v Spellman* [2004] 1 NZLR 95 at 132, [141]). This arises out of a linkage with Art 18, as there would be little point in communicating the material unless the parties were given the opportunity to present their case in response to it before any decision was made.

Article 25. Default of a party

Unless otherwise agreed by the parties, if, without showing sufficient cause,
(a) the claimant fails to communicate his statement of claim in accordance with article 23(1), the arbitral tribunal shall terminate the proceedings;
(b) the respondent fails to communicate his statement of defence in accordance with article 23(1), the arbitral tribunal shall continue the proceedings without treating such failure in itself as an admission of the claimant's allegations;
(c) any party fails to appear at a hearing or to produce documentary evidence, the arbitral tribunal may continue the proceedings and make the award on the evidence before it.

COMMENTARY ON SCH 2 ART 25

Introduction	[Sch 2 Art 25-1]
Safeguards	[Sch 2 Art 25-2]
"without showing sufficient cause"	[Sch 2 Art 25-3]
Failure to communicate statement of claim	[Sch 2 Art 25-4]
Failure to communicate statement of defence	[Sch 2 Art 25-5]
Failure to appear at hearing or produce documentary evidence	[Sch 2 Art 25-6]

[Sch 2 Art 25-1] Introduction The imperative behind Art 25 is to ensure that an international arbitration can continue to an award in circumstances where a party to an arbitration agreement is in default (H Holtzmann and J Neuhaus, *A Guide to the UNCITRAL Model Law on International Commercial Arbitration*, Kluwer Law International, The Hague, 1989, p 698). This provision is based on Art 28 of the UNCITRAL Arbitration Rules (1976) (and see now Art 30 of the UNCITRAL Arbitration Rules (2010)). Article 25 sets out consequences of such default and ensures the effectiveness of arbitration agreements (UNCITRAL Analytical Commentary, p 56, para 1).

[Sch 2 Art 25-2] Safeguards In drafting the provision, UNCITRAL was concerned that there had to be "safeguards to ensure the fair exercise of the arbitral tribunal's power to terminate or continue the proceedings upon default" (First Secretariat Note, UN Doc No A/CN.9/207, para 80, cited in H Holtzmann and J Neuhaus, *A Guide to the UNCITRAL Model Law on International Commercial Arbitration*, Kluwer Law International, The Hague, 1989, p 698). Much of the drafting of Art 25 was concerned with these safeguards. Holtzmann and Neuhaus identify these three safeguards (at p 699) as follows:

> First, the defaulting party must have been duly notified in advance of the requirement that was not fulfilled. Second, that party must have defaulted without showing sufficient cause for the failure to comply. Third, in the case of a failure by the respondent to communicate its statement of defence — that is, if it refuses to participate in the proceedings at all — the failure in itself will not be treated as an admission of the claimant's allegations.

[Sch 2 Art 25-3] "without showing sufficient cause" The phrase "without showing sufficient cause" was taken from Art 28 of the 1976 UNCITRAL Arbitration Rules. This forms the second of the procedural safeguards, namely that the defaulting party must have been notified sufficiently in advance and "that he defaulted without showing sufficient cause therefor" (UNCITRAL Analytical Commentary, p 56, para 2).

[Sch 2 Art 25-4] Failure to communicate statement of claim Article 25(a) provides that the arbitral tribunal shall terminate the proceedings if the claimant fails to communicate its statement of claim. Of the three situations of default under consideration, this would be a relatively rare occurrence and was included for the sake of completeness (UNCITRAL Analytical Commentary, p 56, para 3).

[Sch 2 Art 25-5] Failure to communicate statement of defence Article 25(b) provides for the third of the three safeguards, namely that failure to communicate a statement of defence is not to be considered "an admission of the claimant's allegations". UNCITRAL observed that: "This rule concerning the assessment of the respondent's failure seems useful in view of the fact that under many national laws on civil procedure default of the defendant in court proceedings is treated as an admission of the claimant's allegations" (UNCITRAL Analytical Commentary, p 56, para 4). This particular formulation was chosen as it provided the arbitral tribunal with "certain discretion" (Fifth Working Group Report, UN Doc No A/CN.9/246, para 83, cited in H Holtzmann and J Neuhaus, *A Guide to the UNCITRAL Model Law on International Commercial Arbitration*, Kluwer Law International, The Hague, 1989, p 700). For instance, the arbitral tribunal would not be "bound to treat the [default] as a full denial of the claim and all supporting facts" (UNCITRAL Analytical Commentary, p 56, para 4); presumably it could instead require proof only of the principal allegations of the claim (Holtzmann and Neuhaus, p 700).

[Sch 2 Art 25-6] Failure to appear at hearing or produce documentary evidence Article 25(c) empowers the arbitral tribunal to continue the proceedings and make the award on the basis of the evidence before it where a party fails to appear at the hearing, or fails to produce documentary evidence. Importantly, "[t]he arbitral tribunal is not precluded from drawing inferences from a party's failure to produce any evidence as requested" (UNCITRAL Analytical Commentary, p 56, para 5).

Article 26. Expert appointed by arbitral tribunal

(1) Unless otherwise agreed by the parties, the arbitral tribunal
 (a) may appoint one or more experts to report to it on specific issues to be determined by the arbitral tribunal;
 (b) may require a party to give the expert any relevant information or to produce, or to provide access to, any relevant documents, goods or other property for his inspection.

(2) Unless otherwise agreed by the parties, if a party so requests or if the arbitral tribunal considers it necessary, the expert shall, after delivery of his written or oral report, participate in a hearing where the parties have the opportunity to put questions to him and to present expert witnesses in order to testify on the points at issue.

COMMENTARY ON SCH 2 ART 26

Introduction .... [Sch 2 Art 26-1]
Scope of power .... [Sch 2 Art 26-2]
Experts appointed by tribunal .... [Sch 2 Art 26-3]
Participation of experts in hearing .... [Sch 2 Art 26-4]

[Sch 2 Art 26-1] Introduction This provision was originally modelled on Art 27 of the UNICTRAL Arbitration Rules (1976) (see now Art 29 of the UNCITRAL Arbitration Rules (2010)). The power to appoint experts is usually expressly conferred on international courts and tribunals (see, eg, Statute of the International Court of Justice, Article 50, and Dispute Settlement Understanding of the WTO, Article 13(1)), and is also regarded as an "inherent power" (eg, G White, *The Use of Experts by International Tribunals*, Syracuse University Press, New York, 1965, p 73).

[Sch 2 Art 26-2] Scope of power Article 26(1) confers power on the arbitral tribunal not only to appoint its own experts, but also to require a party to provide that expert with "any relevant information" and access to "documents, goods or other property for his inspection". Holtzmann and Neuhaus state that this is an "implied power that the parties may alter by agreement", which is, therefore, non-mandatory (H Holtzmann and J Neuhaus, *A Guide to the UNCITRAL Model Law on International Commercial Arbitration*, Kluwer Law International, The Hague, 1989, p 718). It was ultimately decided that the provision should not be mandatory and that party autonomy should prevail, because: (a) the parties are in the best position to know how to settle the dispute; (b) the parties would have to bear the costs of any experts; (c) the parties might not accept or have confidence in any expert appointed by the tribunal; and (d) the parties would bear the cost of wasted time and effort if an arbitrator resigned because of any late decision by the parties to disallow experts (Holtzmann and Neuhaus, p 719).

[Sch 2 Art 26-3] Experts appointed by tribunal Notably, Art 26(1) is only concerned with the tribunal's appointment of its own expert. It does not deal with expert witnesses that may be presented by a party (UNCITRAL Analytical Commentary, p 57, para 1).

[Sch 2 Art 26-4] Participation of experts in hearing Article 26(2) guarantees "a fundamental procedural right", namely that the parties "are given the opportunity to interrogate the expert, after he has delivered his written or oral report, and to present expert witnesses in order to testify on the points in issue" (UNCITRAL Analytical Commentary, p 58, para 3).

Article 27. *Court assistance in taking evidence*

The arbitral tribunal or a party with the approval of the arbitral tribunal may request from a competent court of this State assistance in taking evidence. The court may execute the request within its competence and according to its rules on taking evidence.

COMMENTARY ON SCH 2 ART 27

Introduction .... [Sch 2 Art 27-1]
"A competent court of this State" .... [Sch 2 Art 27-2]
Includes subpoenas to produce documents .... [Sch 2 Art 27-3]

Ensuring integration with existing court
procedures .... [Sch 2 Art 27-4]
Role of the court .... [Sch 2 Art 27-5]
Assistance of courts of other countries .... [Sch 2 Art 27-6]

[Sch 2 Art 27-1] Introduction Article 27 provides that either the arbitral tribunal or a party with the approval of the arbitral tribunal may request the courts to provide assistance in taking evidence, by, eg, "compelling the attendance of a witness, production of a document or access to a property for inspection" (UNCITRAL Analytical Commentary, p 59, para 1). A number of concerns were raised during the drafting of this provision, such as the question of integration with existing court procedures; the possibility of abuse of such requests; and the question of securing the assistance of courts in other countries (H Holtzmann and J Neuhaus, *A Guide to the UNCITRAL Model Law on International Commercial Arbitration*, Kluwer Law International, The Hague, 1989, p 734).

[Sch 2 Art 27-2] "A competent court of this State" Article 27 is limited to arbitrations taking place "in this State". As UNCITRAL notes, "it envisages neither assistance to foreign arbitrations nor requests to foreign courts in arbitral proceedings held under the Model Law" (UNCITRAL Analytical Commentary, pp 59–60, para 4).

[Sch 2 Art 27-3] Includes subpoenas to produce documents In *Vibroflotation AG v Express Builders Co Ltd* (High Court of Hong Kong, Kaplan J, 15 August 1994, unreported), Kaplan J held (at 6) that:

[T]he granting of a subpoena is expressly covered by Article 27 and in my judgment it is perfectly plain and, indeed, it is not argued to the contrary that Article 27 is the governing article in relation to the issue of a subpoena. Provided the Court has jurisdiction to grant a subpoena, that is, provided the domestic law makes provision for the grant of such an order, then the Court can make an order if otherwise within the terms of Article 27.

[Sch 2 Art 27-4] Ensuring integration with existing court procedures To minimise the impact of the Model Law on existing court procedures, the UNCITRAL Working Group reduced the provision to one that gave the court the power to decide between two ways of taking evidence, namely that "the court may, within its competence and according to its rules on taking evidence, execute the request either by taking the evidence itself or by ordering that the evidence be provided directly to the arbitral tribunal" (Fifth Draft, UN Doc No A/CN.9/246 (Annex), Art 27(2), cited in H Holtzmann and J Neuhaus, *A Guide to the UNCITRAL Model Law on International Commercial Arbitration*, Kluwer Law International, The Hague, 1989, p 735). But ultimately UNCITRAL simplified the provision even further, deciding that "there was no need to indicate the manner in which the court should execute the request" and that "in some countries it would be difficult to imagine the court ordering that the evidence be provided directly to the arbitral tribunal" (Commission Report, UN Doc No A/40/17, para 228, cited in Holtzmann and Neuhaus, p 735). The final version merely provides that "[t]he court may execute the request within its competence and according to its rules on taking evidence".

[Sch 2 Art 27-5] Role of the court As finally adopted, Art 27 includes the requirement that the request for assistance be made by the arbitral tribunal or by a party (provided in the latter case that the arbitral tribunal supports the request) (H Holtzmann and J Neuhaus, *A Guide to the UNCITRAL Model Law on International Commercial Arbitration*, Kluwer Law International, The Hague, 1989, p 736). In *Delphi Petroleum Inc v Derin Shipping and Training Ltd* 24 Admin LR (2d) 94; 73 FTR 241 (Federal Court Trial Division, Denault J, 3 December 1993), the Federal Court noted that under Art 27 of the Model Law, it was mandated to provide assistance with regard to matters of evidence, and observed that "an inquiry into the reasons for the request is likely not necessary because the request issues from the arbitral tribunal itself or has the approval of the arbitral tribunal, and the role of the court is merely to exercise for the arbitral tribunal the compulsion power which the arbitral tribunal may not have" (at [10]).

[Sch 2 Art 27-6] Assistance of courts of other countries The UNCITRAL Working Group recognised the problem that "[a]n acceptable system of international court assistance could not be established unilaterally through a model law since the principle of reciprocity and bilaterally or multilaterally accepted procedural rules were essential conditions for the functioning of such a system" (Fourth Working Group Report, UN Doc No A/CN.9/245, para 43, cited in H Holtzmann and J Neuhaus, *A Guide to the UNCITRAL Model Law on International Commercial Arbitration*, Kluwer Law International, The Hague, 1989, p 737). As finally adopted, however, Art 27 does not address the issue of international court assistance in taking evidence in arbitral proceedings, so that any other applicable provisions of law on the question (such as may be found in, eg, bilateral treaties on mutual legal assistance) continue to apply (Holtzmann and Neuhaus, p 738).

CHAPTER VI. MAKING OF AWARD AND TERMINATION OF PROCEEDINGS

Article 28. Rules applicable to substance of dispute

(1) The arbitral tribunal shall decide the dispute in accordance with such rules of law as are chosen by the parties as applicable to the substance of the dispute. Any designation of the law or legal system of a given State shall be construed, unless otherwise expressed, as directly referring to the substantive law of that State and not to its conflict of laws rules.

(2) Failing any designation by the parties, the arbitral tribunal shall apply the law determined by the conflict of laws rules which it considers applicable.

(3) The arbitral tribunal shall decide *ex aequo et bono* or as *amiable compositeur* only if the parties have expressly authorized it to do so.

(4) In all cases, the arbitral tribunal shall decide in accordance with the terms of the contract and shall take into account the usages of the trade applicable to the transaction.

COMMENTARY ON SCH 2 ART 28
Introduction .... [Sch 2 Art 28-1]
Parties' choice of "rules of law" .... [Sch 2 Art 28-2]

Tribunal's choice of "law" .... [Sch 2 Art 28-3]
"*ex aequo et bono*" and "*amiable compositeur*" .... [Sch 2 Art 28-4]
"terms of the contract" and "usages of the trade" . [Sch 2 Art 28-5]

[Sch 2 Art 28-1] Introduction There is an important distinction between the arbitral law which regulates the process by which a dispute is arbitrated, and the substantive law which is applied to determine the merits of the dispute. Article 28 contemplates party choice as to the latter. For example, in an arbitration between a party from Australia and a party from New Zealand, the parties may select the law of a third country as the applicable law to determine the substance of the dispute.

[Sch 2 Art 28-2] Parties' choice of "rules of law" Article 28(1) grants the parties full autonomy to choose the "rules of law" to be applied when deciding their dispute. The phrase "rules of law" had been used in the ICSID Convention found in Sch 3 to the Act (see Art 42(1)). The parties are thus free to contract out of national laws and to agree to use non-national substantive rules to determine their dispute. Examples of non-national substantive rules of law include the *lex mercatoria*, the *UNIDROIT Principles of International Commercial Contracts* or "such general principles of international trade law as have been applied by national and international tribunals", a description used by the parties in their contract noted in *Channel Tunnel Group Ltd v Balfour Beatty Construction Ltd* [1993] AC 334; [1993] 1 All ER 664; [1993] 2 WLR 262; [1993] 1 Lloyd's Rep 291 at 347.

[Sch 2 Art 28-3] Tribunal's choice of "law" If the parties have failed to designate the applicable substantive law, the tribunal is empowered to determine the applicable substantive law using the conflict of laws rules which it considers applicable. Significantly, the tribunal can only choose a "law" and unlike the parties may not designate "rules of law". The tribunal is unable to determine that it will apply non-national substantive rules of law. This approach was modelled on Art 33(1) of the UNCITRAL Arbitration Rules (1976) which provided:

> The arbitral tribunal shall apply the law designated by the parties as applicable to the substance of the dispute. Failing such designation by the parties, the arbitral tribunal shall apply the law determined by the conflict of laws rules which it considers applicable.

For further consideration of the applicable law in international commercial arbitration, see International Arbitration Committee of the International Law Association, "Report and Recommendations on Ascertaining the Contents of the Applicable Law in International Commercial Arbitration" (2010) 26 *Arbitration International* 193.

[Sch 2 Art 28-4] "*ex aequo et bono*" and "*amiable compositeur*" The arbitral tribunal may apply the non-legal rules of "*ex aequo et bono*" and "*amiable compositeur*", but only if the parties have expressly agreed to confer this power on the tribunal. The Model Law does not make any attempt to define these terms or to distinguish between them. For a detailed discussion on these terms see J Lew, L Mistelis and S Kröll, *Comparative International Arbitration*, Kluwer Law International, The Hague, 2003, at 470–4 and S Greenberg, C Kee and R

Weeramantry, *International Commercial Arbitration: An Asia-Pacific Perspective*, Cambridge University Press, Melbourne, 2011, pp 138–43.

The Model Law simply calls the parties' attention to the need to provide clarification in the arbitration agreement and specifically to empower the arbitral tribunal to use these rules if that is their choice. However, Art 28(4) makes it clear that in all cases where the dispute relates to a contract (including arbitrations in which the principles of *ex aequo et bono* and *amiable compositeur* are applicable) the arbitral tribunal must decide in accordance with the terms of the contract and shall take into account the usages of the trade applicable to the transaction.

In the case of *Liberty Re-insurance Canada v QBE Insurance and Re-insurance (Europe) Ltd* (2002) 42 CCLI (3d) 249; 2002 CanLII 6636 (ONSC) (Ont.S.C.J.) it was held that a reference to "an honourable agreement" in the arbitration agreement was an express request for the arbitrators to decide the dispute *ex aequo et bono*. The use of this concept, which involves the tribunal deciding the substance of the dispute based on general considerations of fairness and equity, rather than on specific legal rules, is mainly found in re-insurance treaties.

[Sch 2 Art 28-5] "terms of the contract" and "usages of the trade" Article 28(4) relates to contractual terms and trade usages. The provision repeats the terms of Art 33(3) of the UNCITRAL Arbitration Rules (1976). As noted, the tribunal, although deciding on the basis of equity and fairness in accordance with Art 33(3), cannot make a determination that is contrary to the contractual terms of the parties. Nonetheless, there is a different emphasis in that in the reference to "the usages of the trade applicable to the transaction", the operative requirement is to "take into account" this matter as opposed to the operative requirement to "decide in accordance with" the contractual terms. This would allow a tribunal to take into account an agreed matter such as the *lex mercatoria* provided it was consistent with the parties' contract.

Article 29. Decision-making by panel of arbitrators

In arbitral proceedings with more than one arbitrator, any decision of the arbitral tribunal shall be made, unless otherwise agreed by the parties, by a majority of all its members. However, questions of procedure may be decided by a presiding arbitrator, if so authorized by the parties or all members of the arbitral tribunal.

COMMENTARY ON SCH 2 ART 29
Introduction .... [Sch 2 Art 29-1]
Dissenting arbitrator .... [Sch 2 Art 29-2]
Signing the award .... [Sch 2 Art 29-3]
When making decisions .... [Sch 2 Art 29-4]

[Sch 2 Art 29-1] Introduction Article 29 is modelled on Art 31 of the UNCITRAL Arbitration Rules (1976) which allowed an award or other decision to be made by a majority of arbitrators. It is not a mandatory provision and the parties are free to agree on a requirement that any decisions must be made unanimously by the members of the arbitral tribunal. A different regime is provided for questions of procedure, although there is no definition provided in the Model Law as to what constitutes a question of procedure.

[Sch 2 Art 29-2] Dissenting arbitrator The Model Law neither requires nor prohibits dissenting reasons or opinions. Further, it has recently been observed in England that the majority are "under no obligation" to refer to the concerns of a dissenting arbitrator but are under an obligation to deal with and to decide the issues raised by the parties (*Industries Ltd v Western Bulk Ltd* [2011] EWHC 93 (Comm) at [16]).

[Sch 2 Art 29-3] Signing the award The majority principle applies also to the signing of the award, provided that the reason for any omitted signature is stated (see Art 31(1)).

[Sch 2 Art 29-4] When making decisions When the Model Law was inserted into the Act in 1989, the accompanying Explanatory Memorandum stated (at [66]) that it "is implicit in [Art 29] that the arbitrators may make decisions without being present at the same place".

Article 30. Settlement

(1) If, during arbitral proceedings, the parties settle the dispute, the arbitral tribunal shall terminate the proceedings and, if requested by the parties and not objected to by the arbitral tribunal, record the settlement in the form of an arbitral award on agreed terms.

(2) An award on agreed terms shall be made in accordance with the provisions of article 31 and shall state that it is an award. Such an award has the same status and effect as any other award on the merits of the case.

COMMENTARY ON SCH 2 ART 30
Introduction .... [Sch 2 Art 30-1]
Form of agreed award (Art 30(2)) .... [Sch 2 Art 30-2]

[Sch 2 Art 30-1] Introduction Article 30 of the Model Law is modelled on Art 34(1) of the UNCITRAL Arbitration Rules (1976). It allows for a consent award with full force and effect to be made on the request of all the parties. As a result of a concern of arbitral tribunals being involved in possible fraudulent or money laundering activities, or violations of income tax legislation, the provision gives the arbitral tribunal a power to object and decline to make an award on agreed terms (see UNCITRAL Analytical Commentary, p 65, para 2). Further, an award on agreed terms, if it is later found to be fraudulent, is not automatically void. It would need to be set aside under Art 34.

[Sch 2 Art 30-2] Form of agreed award (Art 30(2)) If an award on agreed terms is made, the requirements of Art 31 need to be complied with.

Article 31. Form and contents of award

(1) The award shall be made in writing and shall be signed by the arbitrator or arbitrators. In arbitral proceedings with more than one arbitrator, the signatures of the majority of all members of the arbitral tribunal shall suffice, provided that the reason for any omitted signature is stated.

(2) The award shall state the reasons upon which it is based, unless the parties have agreed that no reasons are to be given or the award is an award on agreed terms under article 30.

(3) The award shall state its date and the place of arbitration as determined in accordance with article 20(1). The award shall be deemed to have been made at that place.

(4) After the award is made, a copy signed by the arbitrators in accordance with paragraph (1) of this article shall be delivered to each party.

COMMENTARY ON SCH 2 ART 31

Introduction	[Sch 2 Art 31-1]
Statement of reasons	[Sch 2 Art 31-2]
Nature and extent of reasons required	[Sch 2 Art 31-3]
Dissenting reasons	[Sch 2 Art 31-4]
Parties may agree to dispense with reasons (Art 31(2))	[Sch 2 Art 31-5]
Date and place of arbitration (Art 31(3))	[Sch 2 Art 31-6]
Delivery of award to parties (Art 31(4))	[Sch 2 Art 31-7]

[Sch 2 Art 31-1] Introduction Article 31(1) uses the language of Art 32(3) of the UNCITRAL Arbitration Rules (1976). The award must be signed by the arbitrators in accordance with Art 31(1) and cannot be signed by anyone on behalf of the members of the tribunal such as the Secretary or Presiding Member. Article 32(3) of the Rules provided: "The arbitral tribunal shall state the reasons upon which the award was based, unless the parties have agreed that no reasons are to be given."

[Sch 2 Art 31-2] Statement of reasons Article 31(2) requires that the award state the reasons upon which it is based, and is in the same terms as Art 32(3) of the UNCITRAL Arbitration Rules (1976). The parties may dispense with the requirements for reasons, which are not required if the award is an award of agreed terms.

[Sch 2 Art 31-3] Nature and extent of reasons required The Model Law does not require specific qualifications of a person before he or she can act as an arbitrator. Where the arbitrator does not have legal qualifications, the arbitrator cannot be criticised for expressing him or herself as a businessperson rather than as a lawyer.

In *The Bay Hotel and Resort Ltd v Cavalier Construction Co Ltd* [2001] All ER (D) 229 (Jul); [2001] 5 LRC 376; [2001] UKPC 34 (at [40]–[42]), the Privy Council considered the requirements for the reasons for an award in the Arbitration Act 1996 (Eng, W & NI), which was stated as being a "similar provision to that in Article 31(2) of the Model Law". The Privy Council endorsed the approach in *Bremer Handelsgellschaft v Westzucker (No 2)* [1981] 2 Lloyd's Rep 130 (*Bremer Handelsgellschaft*) (at 132–3), where, when considering the obligation under the Arbitration Act 1979 (UK), Donaldson LJ had said: "All that is necessary is that the arbitrators should set out what, on their view of the evidence, did or did not happen and should explain succinctly why, in the light of what happened, they have reached their decision and what that decision is."

The nature and content of the statutory requirement for an arbitrator to state the reasons for making the award is informed by the legislative context in which the obligation is found. In contrast to the context in which the obligation is found in the Model Law, where there was a statutory right to appeal an award on a question of law, it has been said that an arbitrator's "reasons must not be so economical that a party is deprived of having an issue of law dealt with by a court" (*Menna v HD Building Pty Ltd* (NSW Supreme Court, Smart J, 1 December 1986, unreported), quoted in *Imperial Leatherware Co Pty Ltd v Macri & Marcellino Pty Ltd* (1991) 22 NSWLR 653 at 657).

The same reasoning was used to determine the standard, nature and extent of the requirements for reasons in the Arbitration Act 1979 (UK), which referred to but did not define a "reasoned award". Section 1(5) of the 1979 Act enabled a party to an arbitration, where "it appear[ed] to the High Court that the award d[id] not or d[id] not sufficiently set out the reasons for the award", to apply for an order directing "the arbitrator or umpire concerned to state the reasons for his award in sufficient detail to enable the court, should an appeal be brought under this section, to consider any question of law arising out of the award". In this context, a "reasoned award" was held to mean "one which states the reasons for the award in sufficient detail for the court to consider any question of law arising therefrom, if, of course, [the court] were to give leave to appeal" (*Trave Schiffahrtsgesellschaft mbH & Co KG v Ninemia Maritime Corp* [1986] QB 802; [1986] 2 All ER 244; [1986] 2 WLR 773; [1986] 1 Lloyd's Rep 393, Sir Donaldson MR at 807D).

There was a conflict of opinion as to the nature and extent of reasons required by an arbitral tribunal in Australia between the Courts of Appeal in New South Wales and Victoria, although in neither case did the Model Law apply to the arbitration and the award. The Victorian Court of Appeal in *Oil Basins Ltd v BHP Billiton Ltd* (2007) 18 VR 346; [2007] VSCA 255; BC200709808 (*Oil Basins*) upheld a decision that held that an arbitral tribunal in Victoria was, in the particular circumstances of the arbitration, "under a duty to give reasons of a standard which was equivalent to the reasons to be expected from a judge deciding a commercial case" (*BHP Billiton Ltd v Oil Basins Ltd* [2006] VSC 402; BC200608700 at [23]). The comparison was an unusual one since the content of the judicial obligation to give reasons depends on the public nature of the judicial office and the function to be served by the judicial reasons. The nature and extent of the obligation will be measured by matters such as whether they allow the parties to consider any rights of appeal and whether they allow an appeal court to perform its appellate functions.

In contrast, the New South Wales Court of Appeal in *Gordian Runoff Ltd v Westport Insurance Corp* (2010) 267 ALR 74; [2010] NSWCA 57; BC201001877 (*Gordian v Westport*) disapproved of the reasoning in *Oil Basins*. Allsop P, with whom Spigelman CJ and Macfarlan JA agreed, noted (at [207]) that the expression in Art 31(2) of the Model Law was based on the UNCITRAL Arbitration Rules (1976) (Art 32(3)) and expressed the opinion that it should be viewed against the context of the compromise embodied in the Model Law and the background of international commercial arbitration. This compromise was not between those who thought arbitrators' reasons should reach the standard of detail of a judge in the common law system and those who thought some lesser standard was called for; rather, it was a compromise between national laws requiring reasons and those not requiring any reasons. Allsop P reasoned (at [208]) that there was no national law which could be identified leading up to the agreement on the Model Law in which arbitrators were required to give reasons commensurate with a judge in a common law system. Allsop P adopted (at [220]) the statement of principle of Donaldson LJ in *Bremer Handelsgellschaft* (at 132–3, [25]) "as a crisp summary of what is required" by Art 31(2) of the Model Law and by s 29(1)(c) of the now repealed Commercial Arbitration Act 1984 (NSW). As noted above, the statement of Donaldson LJ was: "All that is necessary is that the arbitrators should set out what, on their view of the evidence, did or did not happen and should explain succinctly why, in the light of what happened, they have reached their decision and what that decision is. That is all that is meant by a 'reasoned award'."

In view of the inconsistency between intermediate appellate courts, the High Court granted leave to appeal from the decision in *Gordian v Westport* and the matter was argued in the High Court on 3 and 4 February 2011. There had been no decision at the time of writing (22 August 2011) although an attempt to reconcile the decisions was made in *Thoroughvision Pty Ltd v Sky Channel Pty Ltd* [2010] VSC 139; BC201002353. The Queensland Supreme Court in *Northbuild Construction Pty Ltd v Discovery Beach Project Pty Ltd* [2010] QSC 94; BC201002049 at [40] noted the disagreement and followed the earlier decision by the Queensland Court of Appeal in *Cypressvale Pty Ltd v Retail Shop Leases Tribunal* [1996] 2 Qd R 462 at 485; [1995] QCA 187; BC9505854.

On 5 October 2011 the High Court delivered its judgment in *Westport Insurance Corp v Gordian Runoff Ltd* [2011] HCA 37; BC2011075079. In the judgment of the plurality, French CJ and Gummow, Crenin and Bell JJ, at [23], it was expressly stated that the "proper construction of the federal Act and the Model Law may be left for determination on another occasion. The provisions of the federal scheme may be put to one side in construing the (now repealed domestic arbitration legislation) upon which this litigation turns".

Both the judgment of French CJ, Gummow, Crennary and Bell JJ and the separate judgment of Kiefel J, were critical of the reference in *Oil Basins* to "the judicial standard". In the plurality judgment at [53], it was referred to as "an unfortunate gloss". Kiefel J went further and stated at [169]: "There is nothing in (the now repealed domestic arbitration legislation) ... which suggests as necessary that [the arbitrator's] reasons be to a judicial standard".

In the High Court it was noted (at [54]) that both the appellant and the respondent were "content ... to rest, like Allsop P, upon what was set out" in the reasons of Donaldson LJ in *Bremer Handelsgellschaft* quoted above. The majority then applied the agreed test in *Bremer Handelsgellschaft* but in their application they came to a different result to that reached by the Court of Appeal. Kiefel J went further and held that Allsop P had "considered, *correctly in my view* that, a statement in *Bremer* is apt to apply to" the requirement for reasons in the now repealed domestic arbitration legislation (see [169], emphasis added).

[Sch 2 Art 31-4] Dissenting reasons A dissenting member of the arbitral tribunal is under no obligation to give reasons and, as noted in relation to Art 29 above, where there is an award by a majority, there is generally "no obligation" to refer to the reasons, if expressed, or concerns, of the dissenting arbitrator (*Ispat Industries Ltd v Western Bulk PTE Ltd* [2011] EWHC 93 (Comm) at [16]).

[Sch 2 Art 31-5] **Parties may agree to dispense with reasons (Art 31(2))** Article 31(2) allows the parties to completely dispense with reasons. "Given that art 31(2) expressly authorises agreement to completely dispense with reasons it is implied that the parties can agree to truncation of reasons" (*Methanex Motunui Ltd v Spellman* [2004] 1 NZLR 95 at 143, [196])."There can be no doubt that at common law the parties are free to agree on a form of award which would constitute something less than a reasoned award in the eyes of English common lawyers" (*The Bay Hotel and Resort Ltd v Cavalier Construction Co Ltd* [2001] UKPC 34 at [41]).

[Sch 2 Art 31-6] **Date and place of arbitration (Art 31(3))** Under Art 31(3) the award must state the date and place of arbitration. The arbitrators have no discretion to state any place other than the one determined in accordance with Art 20(1). The place where the actual hearings took place is irrelevant to the place of the award. Article 31(3) deems the award to be made at the curial seat of the arbitration. This overcomes the problem identified in *Hiscox v Outhwaite* [1992] 1 AC 562; [1991] 3 All ER 641; [1991] 3 WLR 297; [1991] 2 Lloyd's Rep 435, which held that the award, as a written instrument, was made when it was perfected, and that it was perfected when it was signed by the arbitrator. Article 31(3) "also recognises that the making of the award is a legal act, but not necessarily a single act: deliberations may occur in various places, by telephone or by correspondence" (Explanatory Memorandum to the International Arbitration Amendment Bill 1988 (Cth) at [70]).

[Sch 2 Art 31-7] **Delivery of award to parties (Art 31(4))** Article 31(4) requires a copy of the award to be delivered to each party. This mandatory provision must be complied with, and the date of delivery is significant because it sets time running for proceedings to be commenced to set aside the award. Any such proceedings must be commenced within three months from the date on which the party making the application received the award (Art 34(3)).

Article 32. Termination of proceedings

(1) The arbitral proceedings are terminated by the final award or by an order of the arbitral tribunal in accordance with paragraph (2) of this article.

(2) The arbitral tribunal shall issue an order for the termination of the arbitral proceedings when:
- (a) the claimant withdraws his claim, unless the respondent objects thereto and the arbitral tribunal recognizes a legitimate interest on his part in obtaining a final settlement of the dispute;
- (b) the parties agree on the termination of the proceedings;
- (c) the arbitral tribunal finds that the continuation of the proceedings has for any other reason become unnecessary or impossible.

(3) The mandate of the arbitral tribunal terminates with the termination of the arbitral proceedings, subject to the provisions of articles 33 and 34(4).

COMMENTARY ON SCH 2 ART 32

Introduction .... [Sch 2 Art 32-1]
Termination .... [Sch 2 Art 32-2]

[Sch 2 Art 32-1] Introduction Article 32(1) gives recognition to the principle of "functus officio". An arbitrator is appointed by the parties to perform a task, namely to make a final award determining the dispute between the parties in accordance with their agreement and any applicable law. Once this mandate has been fulfilled it is of no further effect. For a discussion of the origin and rationale for the doctrine see *Leung v Minister for Immigration and Multicultural Affairs* (1997) 74 FCR 430; 46 ALD 519; 25 AAR 113; BC9701664 at 409–10. A final award is one that addresses all substantive issues, including costs, between the parties to the proceedings (*Tan Boon Jek Jeffrey v Tan Poh Lang Stanley* [2001] 3 SLR 237). Once "an arbitrator has issued a decision on an issue referred to him an issue estoppel arises and the arbitrator is powerless to revisit it" (*Opotiki Packing v Opotiki Fruitgrowers* [2003] 1 NZLR 205 at 213, [24]) and once the final award is made and published to the parties, the arbitrator is functus officio. An arbitral tribunal once having finally disposed of an issue is functus officio in respect of that issue (*Kempinski Hotels SA v PT Prima International Development* [2011] SGHC 171 at [30]–[43]; and see also *ABB Service Pty Ltd v Pyrmont Light Rail Company Ltd* (2010) 77 NSWLR 321 at 336–7; [2010] NSWSC 831; BC201005359 at [62]–[70]; and *Discovery Beach Project Pty Ltd v Northbuild Construction Pty Ltd* [2011] QSC 306; BC201108127 at [68]).

[Sch 2 Art 32-2] Termination The parties can bring the arbitral proceedings to an end by making an agreement that terminates the proceedings (Art 32(2)(b)). Equally, the tribunal can terminate proceedings by finding that the continuation has become "unnecessary or impossible". This phrase was adopted from Art 34 of the UNCITRAL Arbitration Rules (1976).

Article 33. Correction and interpretation of award; additional award

(1) Within thirty days of receipt of the award, unless another period of time has been agreed upon by the parties:
  (a) a party, with notice to the other party, may request the arbitral tribunal to correct in the award any errors in computation, any clerical or typographical errors or any errors of similar nature;
  (b) if so agreed by the parties, a party, with notice to the other party, may request the arbitral tribunal to give an interpretation of a specific point or part of the award.

If the arbitral tribunal considers the request to be justified, it shall make the correction or give the interpretation within thirty days of receipt of the request. The interpretation shall form part of the award.

(2) The arbitral tribunal may correct any error of the type referred to in paragraph (1)*(a)* of this article on its own initiative within thirty days of the date of the award.

(3) Unless otherwise agreed by the parties, a party, with notice to the other party, may request, within thirty days of receipt of the award, the arbitral tribunal to make an additional award as to claims presented in the arbitral proceedings but omitted from the award. If the arbitral tribunal considers the request to be justified, it shall make the additional award within sixty days.

(4) The arbitral tribunal may extend, if necessary, the period of time within which it shall make a correction, interpretation or an additional award under paragraph (1) or (3) of this article.

(5) The provisions of article 31 shall apply to a correction or interpretation of the award or to an additional award.

COMMENTARY ON SCH 2 ART 33

Introduction .... [Sch 2 Art 33-1]
Claims presented in proceedings but omitted from award .... [Sch 2 Art 33-2]
Form and contents .... [Sch 2 Art 33-3]

[Sch 2 Art 33-1] Introduction Article 33 confers power of correction for any computation, clerical or typographical errors or any other errors of a similar nature, and a power of interpretation. Article 33 therefore extends the mandate of the arbitral tribunal beyond the making of the award. This power is modelled on a similar power conferred by the UNCITRAL Arbitration Rules (1976) (Arts 35(1) and 36(1)). Absent a specific provision, any mandate of the arbitral tribunal would come to an end on delivery of the final award and the arbitral tribunal would have no power to correct or interpret the award or to make an additional award. Article 33 confers a "limited residual power" for a tribunal to correct or interpret an arbitral award after it has been issued, but this cannot be used to raise "new issues" for determination (*Kempinski Hotels SA v PT Prima International Development* [2011] SGHC 171 at [63]). Note that whilst a correction may be made on the application of a party, the request for interpretation may be made "only if agreed by the parties" (*Opotiki Packing v Opotiki Fruitgrowers* [2003] 1 NZLR 205 at 220, [26]).

[Sch 2 Art 33-2] Claims presented in proceedings but omitted from award Where an arbitrator has not dealt with claims presented in the arbitral proceedings and has omitted any determination in the award, such an omission could not be corrected by making a request under Arts 35 and 36 of the UNCITRAL Arbitration Rules (1976) (see, eg, *Margulead Ltd v Exide Technologies* [2004] All ER (D) 94 (May); [2004] EWHC 1019 (Comm); [2004] 2 All ER (Comm) 727 at [21]–[23], for an arbitrator's decision to this effect under Arts 35 and 36 of the UNCITRAL Arbitration Rules (1976)), as any such request would amount to a request to "re-address" a claim rather than to correct an error of a computational, clerical or typographical nature. On the other hand, the Model Law specifically added this additional power in relation to "claims presented" but "omitted from" the award, in Art 33(3). An additional award is only available where the parties have not agreed otherwise, and where any such request for an additional award is made within 30 days of the receipt of the award. In addition, the arbitral tribunal may also be given an opportunity to cure significant defects listed in Art 34(2) of the Model Law if the court, in the course of proceedings to set aside the award, decides to remit the case back to the tribunal in accordance with Art 34(4).

[Sch 2 Art 33-3] Form and contents Any correction or interpretation or any additional award made under Art 33(3) must comply with Art 31. It must be signed by all the arbitrators or contain an explanation as to why it is not signed. It must include a statement of reasons unless the parties have agreed otherwise and it must state the date and place of arbitration and be delivered to the parties.

CHAPTER VII. RECOURSE AGAINST AWARD

Article 34. Application for setting aside as exclusive recourse against arbitral award

(1) Recourse to a court against an arbitral award may be made only by an application for setting aside in accordance with paragraphs (2) and (3) of this article.

(2) An arbitral award may be set aside by the court specified in article 6 only if:
  (a) the party making the application furnishes proof that:
    (i) a party to the arbitration agreement referred to in article 7 was under some incapacity; or the said agreement is not valid under the law to which the parties have subjected it or, failing any indication thereon, under the law of this State; or
    (ii) the party making the application was not given proper notice of the appointment of an arbitrator or of the arbitral proceedings or was otherwise unable to present his case; or
    (iii) the award deals with a dispute not contemplated by or not falling within the terms of the submission to arbitration, or contains decisions on matters beyond the scope of the submission to arbitration, provided that, if the decisions on matters submitted to arbitration can be separated from those not so submitted, only that part of the award which contains decisions on matters not submitted to arbitration may be set aside; or
    (iv) the composition of the arbitral tribunal or the arbitral procedure was not in accordance with the agreement of the parties, unless such agreement was in conflict with a provision of this Law from which the parties cannot derogate, or, failing such agreement, was not in accordance with this Law; or
  (b) the court finds that:
    (i) the subject-matter of the dispute is not capable of settlement by arbitration under the law of this State; or
    (ii) the award is in conflict with the public policy of this State.

(3) An application for setting aside may not be made after three months have elapsed from the date on which the party making that application had received the award or, if a request had been made under article 33, from the date on which that request had been disposed of by the arbitral tribunal.

(4) The court, when asked to set aside an award, may, where appropriate and so requested by a party, suspend the setting aside proceedings for a period of time determined by it in order to give the arbitral tribunal an opportunity to resume the arbitral proceedings or to take such other action as in the arbitral tribunal's opinion will eliminate the grounds for setting aside.

COMMENTARY ON SCH 2 ART 34

Introduction: exclusive recourse .... [Sch 2 Art 34-1]
Only a party may make application and only if place of arbitration is in Australia .... [Sch 2 Art 34-2]

Grounds to set aside award	[Sch 2 Art 34-3]
Public policy and application of s 19 of the Act to Art 34	[Sch 2 Art 34-4]
Contracting out of Art 34	[Sch 2 Art 34-5]
Discretionary remedy	[Sch 2 Art 34-6]
Limitation period (Art 34(3))	[Sch 2 Art 34-7]
Cross-references	[Sch 2 Art 34-8]
Remission to arbitral tribunal	[Sch 2 Art 34-9]

[Sch 2 Art 34-1] Introduction: exclusive recourse The different approaches found in national arbitration laws relating to appeals from, and challenges to, awards and the arbitration process were seen as presenting a major difficulty in harmonising international arbitration legislation. The varying delays occasioned by these processes were also a matter of concern (UNCITRAL Explanatory Note 2006, para 44). Article 34 was introduced to provide uniform grounds upon which (and clear time periods within which) recourse against an arbitral award may be made.

Article 34 allows "only" one type of recourse, to the exclusion of any other recourse regulated in any procedural law. Article 34(1) is mandatory and provides that the sole recourse against an arbitral award is by application for setting aside. In regulating "recourse" (ie, the means through which a party may actively "attack" the award), Art 34 does not preclude a party from seeking court control by way of defence in enforcement proceedings. Article 34 is limited to action before a court (ie, an organ of the judicial system of a State). However, a party is not precluded from appealing to an arbitral tribunal of second instance if the parties have agreed on such a possibility (as is common in certain commodity trades) (UNCITRAL Explanatory Note 2006, para 45, and see the discussion of the AMINZ Appeal Tribunal in Anthony Wily, *Arbitration*, Thomson Reuters, Wellington, 2010, p 134).

[Sch 2 Art 34-2] Only a party may make application and only if place of arbitration is in Australia The court in *Methanex Motunui v Spellman* [2004] 1 NZLR 95 at 114–6, [55]–[59] rejected a submission that a person who was not a party to the arbitration could make an application to set aside the award.

As a result of the operation of Arts 1(2), 20(1) and 31(3), a court in Australia may only set aside an award under Art 34 if the place of arbitration is within Australia. See *PT Garuda Indonesia v Birgen Air* [2002] 1 SLR(R) 401 at [21].

[Sch 2 Art 34-3] Grounds to set aside award The bases on which an award may be challenged are strictly limited to the grounds specified. There is no basis for a challenge based on an error of law and a review of the merits. The reasons for setting aside the award in Art 34(1) "are essentially the same as those set out in the New York Convention" (Explanatory Memorandum to the International Arbitration Amendment Bill 1988 (Cth) at [75]) and are in almost the same terms in Art 36(1). This was seen as desirable in view of the policy of the Model Law to reduce the impact of the place of arbitration. It recognises the fact that both provisions, with their different purposes, form part of the alternative defence system which provides a party with the option of attacking the award or invoking the grounds when recognition or enforcement is sought; it also recognises the fact that these provisions do not operate in isolation. The effect of traditional concepts and rules familiar and peculiar to the legal system ruling at the place of arbitration is not limited to the State where the arbitration takes place but extends to many other States by virtue of Art 36(1)(a)(v) of the Model Law or Art V(1)(e) of the New York Convention (UNCITRAL Analytical Commentary, p 72, para 8).

Although the grounds for setting aside as set out in Art 34(2) are almost identical to those for refusing recognition or enforcement as set out in Art 36(1), one practical difference is that an application for setting aside under Art 34(2) may only be made to a court in the State where the award was rendered, whereas an application for enforcement might be made in a court in any State. For that reason, the grounds relating to public policy and non-arbitrability may vary in substance with the different law being applied by the court in the State of setting aside or in the State of enforcement.

Although the grounds reflect those contained in Art V(1)(a) of the New York Convention, which provides that recognition and enforcement may be refused if "the parties to the arbitration agreement were, under the law applicable to them, under some incapacity", they were modified in both Arts 34 and 36, "since it was viewed as containing an incomplete and potentially misleading conflict-of-laws rule" and accordingly, the words "under the law applicable to them" were deleted (UNCITRAL Explanatory Note 2006, para 54).

[Sch 2 Art 34-4] Public policy and application of s 19 of the Act to Art 34 The International Arbitration Amendment Act 2010 (Cth) made a minor, but related, technical change to s 19 to include the words "or is contrary to" after the words "conflict with". Section 19 of the Act is an interpretative provision that clarifies that for the purposes of Arts 34 and 36 of the Model Law, an award is in conflict with the public policy of Australia if: (a) the making of the award was induced or affected by fraud or corruption; or (b) a breach of the rules of natural justice occurred in connection with the making of the award. The drafting of the public policy ground varies slightly as between Arts 34 and 36. Article 34 provides that a court may set aside an award if the award "is in conflict with" public policy. By way of contrast, Art 36 allows a court to refuse to recognise or enforce an award where it finds that to do so "would be contrary to" public policy. The 2010 amendment was made to ensure that s 19 applies to both situations (Revised Explanatory Memorandum to the International Arbitration Amendment Bill 2010 (Cth) at [104] and [105]).

It has been suggested that there is a difference in the scope of public policy and the approach of the court under Arts 34 and 36. On this view the "supervisory jurisdiction under Article 34 is broader, with the court having more scope for intervening to set aside than it has in refusing to grant enforcement" (DAR Williams, "Arbitration and Dispute Resolution", [2004] *New Zealand Law Review* 87 at 110). See also the approach of the Indian courts in this regard, which have also held that the scope of "public policy" is broader in the context of a challenge to an award, when compared with an application to refuse enforcement of an award: *ONGC Ltd v Saw Pipes Ltd* (2003) 5 SCC 705 at 727–8; although this has been subjected to criticism; see, eg, A Stephenson, L Carroll and J DeBoos, "Interference by a Local Court and a Failure to Enforce: Actionable under a Bilateral Investment Treaty?" in C Brown and K Miles (eds), *Evolution in Investment Treaty Law and Arbitration*, Cambridge University Press, Cambridge, 2011. On the content of "public policy", for a comparative view see International Law

Association Committee on International Commercial Arbitration, "Final Report on Public Policy as a Bar to Enforcement of International Arbitral Awards", in International Law Association, *Seventieth Report: New Delhi Conference* (2002); and International Law Association Committee on International Commercial Arbitration, "Interim Report on Public Policy as a Bar to Enforcement of International Arbitral Awards", in International Law Association, *Sixty-ninth Report: London Conference* (2000).

[Sch 2 Art 34-5] Contracting out of Art 34 Under Art 28.6 of the ICC Arbitration Rules (1998), it is provided that "the parties undertake to carry out any Award without delay, and shall be deemed to have waived their right to any form of recourse insofar as any waiver can validly be made". Thus, any parties in an arbitration bound by the ICC Rules are unable to appeal on a question of law under s 69 of the Arbitration Act 1996 (Eng, W & NI) as they have "otherwise agreed" (see, eg, *Lesotho Highlands Development Authority v Impregilio SpA* [2006] 1 AC 221; [2005] All ER (D) 363 (Jun); [2005] 3 All ER 789; [2005] UKHL 43 at [5], where it was acknowledged that the ICC Rule was "an effective exclusion agreement of the right of appeal on a point of law under section 69").

In New Zealand where the Model Law has been adopted, the view was expressed in *Downer-Hill Joint Venture v Government of Fiji* [2005] 1 NZLR 554 at 566, [68] that parties "could not contract out of Article 34" by agreeing to an arbitration under the ICC Rules. It was also held in *Methanex Motunui Ltd v Spellman* [2004] 1 NZLR 95 at 129–30, [127]–[132] that a party could not contract out of its rights to review or challenge under Art 34 for breach of natural justice. The court noted the provisions of Arts 18 and 24(3) and found (at 130, [132]) that "where the dominant intention of the parties is to have their dispute determined by arbitration, attempts to contractually exclude the right to review for breach of natural justice must be regarded as incompatible with that intention and therefore ineffective".

[Sch 2 Art 34-6] Discretionary remedy The use of the word "may" in Art 34(2) was considered by the Hong Kong High Court to confer a discretion on the court considering the application not to set aside the award even if one of the specified grounds had been established (*Pacific China Holdings Ltd v Grand Pacific Holdings Ltd* [2011] HKCFI 424 at [62]). The court held (at [88]) that "consistently with the pro-enforcement bias of the legislation, in my view, the onus in establishing the basis for the appropriate exercise of the discretion will be on the party seeking to attack the award". However, once the court finds that one of the grounds has been established, the award will be set aside unless the court is satisfied "that it can exclude the possibility that if the violation established had not occurred, the outcome of the award would not have been different" (at [90]; see also *Brunswick Bowling & Billiards Corp v Shanghai Zhonglu Industrial Co Ltd* [2009] HKCFI 94 at [29]–[45]; and *Paklito Investment Ltd v Klockner East Asia Ltd* [1993] 2 HKLR 39 at 49). Thus, only if it is beyond doubt that the decision would have been the same, would the court be justified in overriding a serious violation (at [97]). The possibility of a court having a similar residual discretion in award enforcement proceedings under Pt II of the Act arising out of the use of the word "may" in s 8(2) and (3) of the Act (which uses the same language taken from the New York Convention) was removed by the International Arbitration Amendment

Act 2010 (Cth), which inserted s 8(3A) into the Act. See the discussion in relation to the discretion which previously existed under s 8, at [s 8-8] above, and which exists in relation to Art 36.

[Sch 2 Art 34-7] **Limitation period (Art 34(3))** An application to set aside the award must be made within three months from the date on which the applicant received the award or, if a request had been made under Art 33, from the date on which that request was dealt with by the arbitral tribunal. No extension is possible. It is a question of considering three months from the date of receipt of the "award" (eg, *Opotiki Packing v Opotiki Fruitgrowers* [2003] 1 NZLR 205 at 220, [13]). No amendment that essentially introduces new areas and new grounds of challenge made after the three-month time limit is permissible. It is a strict three-month "limitation" period (*Downer-Hill Joint Venture v Government of Fiji* [2005] 1 NZLR 554 at 560, [31]) and the "whole tenor of the [provisions] is to restrict Court review of arbitration awards both with respect to grounds and time" (at 565, [62]).

[Sch 2 Art 34-8] **Cross-references** For a discussion of each of the grounds for setting aside an award as found in Art 34(2), see the discussion of the corresponding text as it is found in s 8 above. It should be noted that the relevant subsections in s 8 deal with the grounds for refusing enforcement of an award, but they are substantively identical to the grounds upon which an arbitral award can be challenged:

> Art 34(2)(a)(i) = s 8(5)(a) and (b);
> Art 34(2)(a)(ii) = s 8(5)(c);
> Art 34(2)(a)(iii) = s 8(5)(d) and (6);
> Art 34(2)(a)(iv) = s 8(5)(e);
> Art 34(2)(b)(i) = s 8(7)(a); and
> Art 34(2)(b)(ii) = s 8(7)(b).

[Sch 2 Art 34-9] **Remission to arbitral tribunal** Article 34(4) empowers a court to stay the proceedings, not indefinitely, and to remit an award to the arbitral tribunal in order to give the tribunal the opportunity to eliminate a potential reason or reasons for setting aside the award. If the award is not remitted but set aside, it is suggested that the position does not revert to the position which existed immediately before the arbitrator published the award (see the discussion in *Hussmann (Europe) Ltd v Ahmed Pharaon* [2003] All ER (D) 17 (Mar); [2003] 1 All ER (Comm) 879; [2003] EWCA Civ 266 at [78]–[81]; and cf *Kempinski Hotels SA v PT Prima International Development* [2011] SGHC 171 at [115]–[117]).

CHAPTER VIII. RECOGNITION AND ENFORCEMENT OF AWARDS

Article 35. Recognition and enforcement

(1) An arbitral award, irrespective of the country in which it was made, shall be recognized as binding and, upon application in writing to the competent court, shall be enforced subject to the provisions of this article and of article 36.

(2) The party relying on an award or applying for its enforcement shall supply the original award or a copy thereof. If the award is not made in an official language of this State, the court may request the party to supply a translation thereof into such language.[4]

(Article 35(2) has been amended by the Commission at its thirty-ninth session, in 2006)

COMMENTARY ON SCH 2 ART 35

Introduction	[Sch 2 Art 35-1]
2006 amendments	[Sch 2 Art 35-2]
Anomalous contrast to s 9 of the Act	[Sch 2 Art 35-3]
Recognition	[Sch 2 Art 35-4]
Award is binding	[Sch 2 Art 35-5]

[Sch 2 Art 35-1] Introduction Chapter VIII of the Model Law deals with the recognition and enforcement of awards. Its provisions reflect the significant policy decision that the same rules should apply to international arbitral awards whether made in the country of enforcement or abroad, and that those rules should follow closely the New York Convention. By treating awards rendered in international commercial arbitration in a uniform manner irrespective of where they were made, the Model Law distinguishes between "international" and "non-international" awards instead of relying on the traditional distinction between "foreign" and "domestic" awards which is found in Pt II of the Act. By modelling the recognition and enforcement rules on the relevant provisions of the New York Convention, the Model Law supplements, without conflicting with, the regime of recognition and enforcement created by the New York Convention (UNCITRAL Explanatory Note 2006, paras 49–54). Although it should be noted that the provisions of Ch VIII of the Model Law do not supplement the provisions of the Act, as s 20 of the Act renders them inapplicable.

[Sch 2 Art 35-2] 2006 amendments The Model Law sets certain procedural requirements for obtaining enforcement in Art 35(2) which are based on Art IV of the New York Convention. Article 35(2) was amended in 2006 to liberalise formal requirements and to reflect the amendment made to Art 7 on the form of the arbitration agreement. Presentation of a copy of the arbitration agreement is no longer required under Art 35(2).

The 2006 changes were to delete the requirements that the applicant supply a "duly authenticated" original award, or a "duly certified" copy thereof, or "the original arbitration agreement referred to in Article 7 or a duly certified copy thereof". The requirement to produce a translation of the arbitration agreement was also deleted, and, if the award was in a foreign language, it was no longer necessary to "supply a duly certified translation thereof".

[Sch 2 Art 35-3] Anomalous contrast to s 9 of the Act The Act also has a provision in s 9 which is similar to Art 35(2) and which also gives effect to Art IV of the New York Convention when an application is made for the enforcement of an arbitral award. The language used in the 1985 version of the Model Law was similar to that used by s 9. However, the changes to the Model Law in 2006 modified and eased the requirements needed when applying to enforce a foreign

---

[4] The conditions set forth in this paragraph are intended to set maximum standards. It would, thus, not be contrary to the harmonization to be achieved by the model law if a State retained even less onerous conditions.

award. Whilst these changes were accepted in the Model Law, they appear to have overlooked the fact that similar changes were needed to the equivalent requirements in s 9. Also, it should be noted that the revised provisions do not apply, as s 20 of the Act renders them inapplicable.

[Sch 2 Art 35-4] Recognition Article 35 distinguishes recognition from enforcement, the former constituting only the necessary precondition for enforcement. "Recognition may also be important in the context of other proceedings where a particular award may be relied on. Recognition of an award as binding means that it will be binding between the parties as from the date of the award" (Explanatory Memorandum to the International Arbitration Amendment Bill 1988 (Cth) at [77]).

[Sch 2 Art 35-5] Award is binding Article 35(1) of the Model Law provides that an arbitral award shall be recognised as "binding" subject to the provisions of Arts 35 and 36 of the Model Law. Accordingly, an arbitral award creates a *res judicata* (see generally International Arbitration Committee of the International Law Association, "Interim Report: *Res Judicata* and Arbitration", in International Law Association, *Report of the Seventy-first Conference of the International Law Association: Berlin* (2004), p 826).

Article 36. Grounds for refusing recognition or enforcement

(1) Recognition or enforcement of an arbitral award, irrespective of the country in which it was made, may be refused only:
  (a) at the request of the party against whom it is invoked, if that party furnishes to the competent court where recognition or enforcement is sought proof that:
    (i) a party to the arbitration agreement referred to in article 7 was under some incapacity; or the said agreement is not valid under the law to which the parties have subjected it or, failing any indication thereon, under the law of the country where the award was made; or
    (ii) the party against whom the award is invoked was not given proper notice of the appointment of an arbitrator or of the arbitral proceedings or was otherwise unable to present his case; or
    (iii) the award deals with a dispute not contemplated by or not falling within the terms of the submission to arbitration, or it contains decisions on matters beyond the scope of the submission to arbitration, provided that, if the decisions on matters submitted to arbitration can be separated from those not so submitted, that part of the award which contains decisions on matters submitted to arbitration may be recognized and enforced; or
    (iv) the composition of the arbitral tribunal or the arbitral procedure was not in accordance with the agreement of the parties or, failing such agreement, was not in accordance with the law of the country where the arbitration took place; or
    (v) the award has not yet become binding on the parties or has been set aside or suspended by a court of the country in which, or under the law of which, that award was made; or
  (b) if the court finds that:
    (i) the subject-matter of the dispute is not capable of settlement by arbitration under the law of this State; or

(ii) the recognition or enforcement of the award would be contrary to the public policy of this State.

(2) If an application for setting aside or suspension of an award has been made to a court referred to in paragraph (1)(a)(v) of this article, the court where recognition or enforcement is sought may, if it considers it proper, adjourn its decision and may also, on the application of the party claiming recognition or enforcement of the award, order the other party to provide appropriate security.

COMMENTARY ON SCH 2 ART 36

Introduction .... [Sch 2 Art 36-1]
"irrespective of the country in which it was made"
    (Art 36(1)) .... [Sch 2 Art 36-2]
Grounds on which recognition may be refused ... [Sch 2 Art 36-3]
Discretionary power .... [Sch 2 Art 36-4]
Public policy and application of s 19 of the Act to
    Art 36 .... [Sch 2 Art 36-5]
Cross-references .... [Sch 2 Art 36-6]

[Sch 2 Art 36-1] Introduction Article 36 "is an almost literal adoption of Article V of the New York Convention" (Explanatory Memorandum to the International Arbitration Amendment Bill 1988 (Cth) at [79]). Article V was first implemented in Australia in 1974 with the enactment of s 8. When the 1985 Model Law was subsequently adopted in the Act in 1989 with a similar right to seek recognition and enforcement of an award conferred by Ch VIII, the dual application of s 8 and Ch VIII (including Art 36) was avoided by the insertion of s 20 into the Act. Where both sets of provisions potentially apply, s 20 states that Ch VIII of the Model Law does not apply in relation to the award.

[Sch 2 Art 36-2] "irrespective of the country in which it was made" (Art 36(1)) The terms of Art 36(1) are wider in scope than Art V of the New York Convention (and its counterpart in the Act, s 8) in that Ch VIII and Art 36 apply to an international arbitral award "irrespective of the country in which it was made".

[Sch 2 Art 36-3] Grounds on which recognition may be refused Although the grounds on which recognition or enforcement may be refused under the Model Law are, with one exception, identical to those listed in Art V of the New York Convention, the grounds listed in the Model Law are relevant not only to foreign awards but to all international awards irrespective of where they were made. Generally, it was deemed desirable to adopt, for the sake of harmony, the same approach and wording as the Convention. However, the first ground contained in the New York Convention (Art V(1)(a) which provides that recognition and enforcement may be refused if "the parties to the arbitration agreement were, under the law applicable to them, under some incapacity") was modified "since it was viewed as containing an incomplete and potentially misleading conflict-of-laws rule" and the words "under the law applicable to them" were deleted (UNCITRAL Explanatory Note 2006, para 54).

[Sch 2 Art 36-4] Discretionary power The use of the word "may" in Art 36(1) confers residual discretion on a court to enforce an award even if one of the specified grounds has been established. (For a decision on the equivalent provision in Hong Kong, see *Nanjing Cereals, Oils and Foodstuffs Import & Export Corp v Luckmate Commodities Trading Ltd* [1994] HKCFI 140 at [3]; and in Canada, see *Michel Rhéaume v Société d'Investissements l'Excellence Inc* 2010 QCCA 2269 (CanLII) at [51]–[64], where special leave to appeal to the Supreme Court was refused (2011) CanLII 36002 (SCC)). The word "may" is taken from Art V of the New York Convention. See the discussion above of the similar discretion which exists arising out of the use of the word "may" in Art 34(2) and which previously existed in s 8(2) and (3), although the insertion of s 8(3A) in 2010 removed the discretion where the court is proceeding under s 8.

[Sch 2 Art 36-5] Public policy and application of s 19 of the Act to Art 36 The International Arbitration Amendment Act 2010 (Cth) made a minor, but related, technical change to s 19 to include the words "or is contrary to" after the words "conflict with". Section 19 of the Act is an interpretative provision that clarifies that for the purposes of Arts 34 and 36 of the Model Law, an award is in conflict with the public policy of Australia if: (a) the making of the award was induced or affected by fraud or corruption; or (b) a breach of the rules of natural justice occurred in connection with the making of the award. The drafting of the public policy ground varies slightly as between Arts 34 and 36. Article 34 provides that a court may set aside an award if the award "is in conflict with" public policy. By way of contrast, Art 36 allows a court to refuse to recognise or enforce an award where it finds that to do so "would be contrary to" public policy. The 2010 amendment was made to ensure that s 19 applies to both situations (Revised Explanatory Memorandum to the International Arbitration Amendment Bill 2010 (Cth) at [104] and [105]) and does not distinguish between the two provisions. For a comparative consideration on the content of "public policy", see International Law Association Committee on International Commercial Arbitration, "Final Report on Public Policy as a Bar to Enforcement of International Arbitral Awards", in International Law Association, *Seventieth Report: New Delhi Conference* (2002); and International Law Association Committee on International Commercial Arbitration, "Interim Report on Public Policy as a Bar to Enforcement of International Arbitral Awards", in International Law Association, *Sixty-ninth Report: London Conference* (2000).

[Sch 2 Art 36-6] Cross-references For a discussion of each of the grounds for refusing recognition or enforcement, and the power of a court to adjourn enforcement proceedings, found in Art 36, see the discussion of the corresponding provisions where found in the Act:

- Art 36(1)(a)(i) = s 8(5)(a) and (b);
- Art 36(1)(a)(ii) = s 8(5)(c);
- Art 36(1)(a)(iii) = s 8(5)(d) and (6);
- Art 36(1)(a)(iv) = s 8(5)(e);
- Art 36(1)(a)(v) = s 8(5)(f);
- Art 36(1)(b)(i) = s 8(7)(a);
- Art 36(1)(b)(ii) = s 8(7)(b); and
- Art 36(2) = s 8(8).

[Sch 3] SCHEDULE 3 — CONVENTION ON THE SETTLEMENT OF INVESTMENT DISPUTES BETWEEN STATES AND NATIONALS OF OTHER STATES

Subsection 31(1)

PREAMBLE

The Contracting States

Considering the need for international cooperation for economic development, and the role of private international investment therein;

Bearing in mind the possibility that from time to time disputes may arise in connection with such investment between Contracting States and nationals of other Contracting States;

Recognizing that while such disputes would usually be subject to national legal processes, international methods of settlement may be appropriate in certain cases;

Attaching particular importance to the availability of facilities for international conciliation or arbitration to which Contracting States and nationals of other Contracting States may submit such disputes if they so desire;

Desiring to establish such facilities under the auspices of the International Bank for Reconstruction and Development;

Recognizing that mutual consent by the parties to submit such disputes to conciliation or to arbitration through such facilities constitutes a binding agreement which requires in particular that due consideration be given to any recommendation of conciliators, and that any arbitral award be complied with; and

Declaring that no Contracting State shall by the mere fact of its ratification, acceptance or approval of this Convention and without its consent be deemed to be under any obligation to submit any particular dispute to conciliation or arbitration,

Have agreed as follows:

COMMENTARY ON SCH 3 PREAMBLE
Preamble relevant for interpretation of ICSID
Convention ....[Sch 3 Preamble-1]

[Sch 3 Preamble-1] Preamble relevant for interpretation of ICSID Convention The Preamble to the Convention on the Settlement of Investment Disputes between States and Nationals of other States (opened for signature 18 March 1965, 575 UNTS 159 (entered into force 14 October 1966), which is also known as the "ICSID Convention", or the "Washington Convention", and in the Act as the "Investment Convention"), is not specifically given the force of law in Australia. Section 32 of the Act provides that: "Subject to this Part, Chapters II to VII (inclusive) of the Investment Convention have the force of law in

Australia." Chapters II to VII embrace the provisions of Arts 25–63 of the ICSID Convention.

Nevertheless, the preamble is important for the interpretation of the provisions of the ICSID Convention. Under Art 31(1) of the Vienna Convention on the Law of Treaties (opened for signature 23 May 1969, 1155 UNTS 311 (entered into force 27 January 1980)): "A treaty shall be interpreted in good faith in accordance with the ordinary meaning to be given to the terms of the treaty in their context and in the light of its object and purpose." Article 31(2) of the Vienna Convention on the Law of Treaties provides that "[t]he context for the purpose of the interpretation of a treaty" includes "its preamble".

The preamble to the ICSID Convention has been relevant in the interpretation of various of its provisions (see especially C Schreuer et al, *The ICSID Convention: A Commentary*, 2nd ed, Cambridge University Press, Cambridge, 2009, pp 1–9), but it has proved particularly relevant in the context of the issue concerning the nature of an "investment" for the purposes of the jurisdiction of ICSID under Art 25, and the question of whether a transaction or project should contribute to the economic development of the host State in order to constitute an "investment" under the ICSID Convention. Such arguments have referred specifically to the preambular phrase "*[c]onsidering* the need for international cooperation for economic development, and the role of private international investment therein" (emphasis in original) (see, eg, *Malaysian Historical Salvors Sdn Bhd v Malaysia* (ICSID Case No ARB/05/10, Decision on Annulment of 16 April 2009, Diss Op Judge Shahabuddeen), paras 14–32; see also D Williams QC and S Foote, "Recent Developments in the Approach to Identifying an 'Investment' pursuant to Article 25 of the ICSID Convention", in C Brown and K Miles (eds), *Evolution in Investment Treaty Law and Arbitration*, Cambridge University Press, Cambridge, 2011, p 42).

CHAPTER I
International Centre for Settlement of Investment Disputes
SECTION 1
Establishment and Organization

Article 1

(1) There is hereby established the International Centre for Settlement of Investment Disputes (hereinafter called the Centre).

(2) The purpose of the Centre shall be to provide facilities for conciliation and arbitration of investment disputes between Contracting States and nationals of other Contracting States in accordance with the provisions of this Convention.

COMMENTARY ON SCH 3 ART 1
Establishment of ICSID .... [Sch 3 Art 1-1]
Name of ICSID .... [Sch 3 Art 1-2]
Purpose and functions of ICSID .... [Sch 3 Art 1-3]

Settlement of investment disputes to be done in
accordance with ICSID Convention .... [Sch 3 Art 1-4]

[Sch 3 Art 1-1] Establishment of ICSID The International Centre for Settlement of Investment Disputes (ICSID) was established by the ICSID Convention. The ICSID Convention was opened for signature on 18 March 1965, and entered into force on 14 October 1966, being 30 days after the date of deposit of the twentieth instrument of ratification in accordance with Art 68(2). Today, the ICSID Convention has 147 Member States (see www.worldbank.org/icsid (last accessed 21 September 2011)).

[Sch 3 Art 1-2] Name of ICSID An initial proposal for the name of the Centre was the "International Conciliation and Arbitration Center". This was changed to "International Center for the Settlement of Investment Disputes", before the spelling "Centre" was adopted, and the word "the" was deleted (C Schreuer et al, *The ICSID Convention: A Commentary*, 2nd ed, Cambridge University Press, Cambridge, 2009, p 10).

[Sch 3 Art 1-3] Purpose and functions of ICSID Article 1(2) provides that the purpose of ICSID is "to provide facilities" for the conciliation and arbitration of investment disputes between States which are parties to the ICSID Convention, and nationals of other States parties to the ICSID Convention. It is important to note that what ICSID does is to "provide facilities" for the settlement of such disputes. ICSID is not a standing tribunal or an international court with jurisdiction over all such disputes. Rather, ICSID provides physical facilities (ie, hearing and meeting rooms at its headquarters at the World Bank in Washington DC) which are available to parties to investment disputes. In addition, ICSID "provides facilities" for the resolution of investment disputes by providing for the creation of tribunals to settle disputes by conciliation (under Arts 28–35) and arbitration (under Arts 36–55).

ICSID's functions in "providing facilities" for the conciliation and arbitration of investment disputes have extended to its adopting "detailed rules and regulations"; "drafting model clauses for use in contracts"; maintaining "a panel of conciliators and a panel of arbitrators"; the screening of requests for conciliation and requests for arbitration, and the registration of such requests that are not manifestly outside ICSID's jurisdiction; assisting in the constitution of conciliation commissions and arbitral tribunals; providing "services and facilities for the conduct of proceedings"; and "communicating relevant documents and information to the parties" (C Schreuer et al, *The ICSID Convention: A Commentary*, 2nd ed, Cambridge University Press, Cambridge, 2009, p 11). Importantly, ICSID also maintains a website, at www.worldbank.org/icsid, which provides a wealth of information on ICSID's activities, including a list of pending and concluded ICSID cases, relevant information concerning those cases, such as the identities of the arbitrators, the procedural phase of the case, and, where the parties to the dispute have given their consent, decisions and awards. ICSID also publishes the *ICSID Review — Foreign Investment Law Journal*, a bi-annual academic publication which contains scholarly articles as well as decisions and awards of ICSID tribunals which ICSID considers worthy of dissemination into the public domain.

[Sch 3 Art 1-4] Settlement of investment disputes to be done in accordance with ICSID Convention Finally, Art 1(2) also specifies that the settlement of investment disputes by conciliation and arbitration must be done "in accordance with the provisions of this Convention".

Article 2

The seat of the Centre shall be at the principal office of the International Bank for Reconstruction and Development (hereinafter called the Bank). The seat may be moved to another place by decision of the Administrative Council adopted by a majority of two-thirds of its members.

COMMENTARY ON SCH 3 ART 2

History of provision .... [Sch 3 Art 2-1]
Creation of World Bank .... [Sch 3 Art 2-2]
Hearings need not be held at World Bank .... [Sch 3 Art 2-3]
Relationship between ICSID and World Bank .... [Sch 3 Art 2-4]

[Sch 3 Art 2-1] History of provision In the planning stages for the negotiation of the ICSID Convention, it was always foreseen that ICSID would be housed at the World Bank's headquarters in Washington DC. There was some discussion of the possibility of relocating ICSID, and this led to the inclusion of a provision empowering the ICSID Administrative Council to adopt such a decision. However, there has never been an attempt to move ICSID to a different location (C Schreuer et al, *The ICSID Convention: A Commentary*, 2nd ed, Cambridge University Press, Cambridge, 2009, p 13). The World Bank — and, accordingly, ICSID — is located at 1818 H Street, NW, MSN U3-301, Washington, DC, 20433, United States of America.

[Sch 3 Art 2-2] Creation of World Bank The official name of the World Bank is the "International Bank for Reconstruction and Development", which is one of the institutions established at the Bretton Woods conference in 1944. The conference established two permanent financial organisations, being the International Monetary Fund (IMF) and the World Bank. The purpose of the IMF was to "enable States to achieve financial stability with growth, by making its resources available to them for purposes consistent with the Articles of Agreement". In contrast, the World Bank was devoted to "long-term economic development, first to reconstruction of countries ravaged by war, then to development of countries not yet in the economic mainstream" (A Lowenfeld, *International Economic Law*, Oxford University Press, Oxford, 2002, p 502).

[Sch 3 Art 2-3] Hearings need not be held at World Bank Although ICSID has its "seat" at the World Bank, this does not mean that conciliation and arbitration proceedings must all take place there. Article 62 of the ICSID Convention provides that hearings shall take place at ICSID except as provided in Art 63; this, in turn, provides that the parties may agree to hold hearings at, for example, the Permanent Court of Arbitration, or any other appropriate institution with which ICSID may have made arrangements. According to the ICSID website, such arrangements have, in addition to the PCA, also been made with the Regional Arbitration Centres of the Asian-African Legal Consultative Committee at Cairo, Kuala Lumpur and Lagos; the Australian Commercial Disputes Centre and the Australian Centre for International Commercial Arbitration; the Singapore International Arbitration Centre; the Gulf Cooperation Council Commercial Arbitration Centre at Bahrain; the German Institution of Arbitration; and Maxwell Chambers, Singapore. Article 63 further provides that hearings may take place "at any other place" which is approved by the Conciliation Commission or Arbitral Tribunal after consulting with the ICSID Secretary-General. Occasionally, ICSID hearings take place at the Paris office of the World Bank.

[Sch 3 Art 2-4] Relationship between ICSID and World Bank The relationship between ICSID and the World Bank goes beyond the fact that they share the same premises. The President of the World Bank is *ex officio* the Chairman of the ICSID Administrative Council and the Governors of the World Bank are also *ex officio* members of the ICSID Administrative Council (C Schreuer et al, *The ICSID Convention: A Commentary*, 2nd ed, Cambridge University Press, Cambridge, 2009, p 14); the World Bank provides ICSID "with offices, services, and facilities" in accordance with the "Memorandum of Administrative Arrangements agreed between the International Bank for Reconstruction and Development and the International Centre for Settlement of Investment Disputes" which was agreed in 1967 (Schreuer et al, pp 14, 24); and finally, ICSID's administrative budget is covered by the World Bank. The Executive Directors of the World Bank noted in their Report that they had decided "that the Bank should be prepared to provide the Centre with office accommodation free of charge as long as the Centre has its seat at the Bank's headquarters and to underwrite, within reasonable limits, the basic overhead expenditure of the Centre for a period of years to be determined after the Centre is established" (Report of the Executive Directors on the Convention on the Settlement of Investment Disputes between States and Nationals of other States, reproduced in ICSID, *ICSID Convention, Regulations and Rules* (ICSID/15, April 2006) (hereafter referred to as the Report of the Executive Directors) p 38, para 17).

Article 3
　　The Centre shall have an Administrative Council and a Secretariat and shall maintain a Panel of Conciliators and a Panel of Arbitrators.

COMMENTARY ON SCH 3 ART 3
Structure of ICSID .... [Sch 3 Art 3-1]

[Sch 3 Art 3-1] Structure of ICSID ICSID has a very simple administrative structure consisting of an Administrative Council, a Secretariat and the Panels of Conciliators and Arbitrators. In their Report, the Executive Directors noted that "[s]implicity and economy consistent with the efficient discharge of the functions of the Centre characterise its structure" (Report of the Executive Directors, para 18). More detailed provision is made for the Administrative Council, the Secretariat and the Panels of Conciliators and Arbitrators in, respectively, Arts 4–8, Arts 9–11 and Arts 12–16 (see also C Schreuer et al, *The ICSID Convention: A Commentary*, 2nd ed, Cambridge University Press, Cambridge, 2009, p 15).

SECTION 2

The Administrative Council

Article 4

(1) The Administrative Council shall be composed of one representative of each Contracting State. An alternate may act as representative in case of his principal's absence from a meeting or inability to act.

(2) In the absence of a contrary designation, each governor and alternate governor of the Bank appointed by a Contracting State shall be *ex officio* its representative and its alternate respectively.

COMMENTARY ON SCH 3 ART 4
Composition of ICSID Administrative Council ... [Sch 3 Art 4-1]
ICSID Administrative Council essentially same as
   World Bank Board of Governors .... [Sch 3 Art 4-2]

[Sch 3 Art 4-1]   Composition of ICSID Administrative Council   The ICSID Administrative Council is composed of one representative of each Contracting State, who serves without being remunerated by ICSID (Report of the Executive Directors, para 18). Importantly, each Contracting State of the ICSID Convention has a representative on the Administrative Council, rather than each member State of the World Bank (C Schreuer et al, *The ICSID Convention: A Commentary*, 2nd ed, Cambridge University Press, Cambridge, 2009, p 16). Article 4(1) makes it clear that each Contracting State may have an alternate representative who can participate in activities of the Administrative Council if the principal representative is absent or unable to act.

[Sch 3 Art 4-2]   ICSID Administrative Council essentially same as World Bank Board of Governors   Under Art 4(2), the Administrative Council is composed of the same people who are on the Board of Governors of the World Bank, who are, typically, the ministers of finance or treasurers of each member State. (Contracting States of the ICSID Convention which are not member States of the World Bank have to make their own appointments to the ICSID Administrative Council.) This arrangement is convenient for most ICSID Contracting States, as the annual meeting of the Administrative Council can be held at the same time as the annual meeting of the World Bank (C Schreuer et al, *The ICSID Convention: A Commentary*, 2nd ed, Cambridge University Press, Cambridge, 2009, p 16).

Article 5

The President of the Bank shall be *ex officio* Chairman of the Administrative Council (hereinafter called the Chairman) but shall have no vote. During his absence or inability to act and during any vacancy in the office of President of the Bank, the person for the time being acting as President shall act as Chairman of the Administrative Council.

COMMENTARY ON SCH 3 ART 5

World Bank President is Chairman of ICSID
   Administrative Council .... [Sch 3 Art 5-1]
Acting President .... [Sch 3 Art 5-2]
Powers of Chairman .... [Sch 3 Art 5-3]

[Sch 3 Art 5-1] World Bank President is Chairman of ICSID Administrative Council Under Art 5, the President of the World Bank serves as the Chairman of the ICSID Administrative Council, but does not have the right to vote (Report of the Executive Directors, para 18). This was a compromise reached by the drafting of the ICSID Convention, as some States were concerned at the close links in the executive positions of the two institutions. The solution was to designate the President of the World Bank as the "Chairman" of ICSID's Administrative Council, but without voting power (C Schreuer et al, *The ICSID Convention: A Commentary*, 2nd ed, Cambridge University Press, Cambridge, 2009, p 18).

[Sch 3 Art 5-2] Acting President The second sentence of this provision envisages that the World Bank will have an acting President if the President is absent or unable to act, or if there is a vacancy in the office of President. There is no formal position of "Acting President" of the World Bank under its founding Articles of Agreement, but the President has always appointed an acting President "on an *ad hoc* basis" (C Schreuer et al, *The ICSID Convention: A Commentary*, 2nd ed, Cambridge University Press, Cambridge, 2009, p 18).

[Sch 3 Art 5-3] Powers of Chairman The Chairman of the Administrative Council has reasonably broad powers under the ICSID Convention, including chairing meetings of the Administrative Council (Art 7), the nomination of ICSID's Secretary-General and Deputy Secretary-General (who must then be elected by the Administrative Council) (Art 10(1)), the designation of persons to the Panels of Conciliators and Arbitrators (Art 13(2)), the appointment of conciliators and arbitrators in certain situations (Arts 30, 38, 52(3), 56(3)), and also deciding on proposals to disqualify conciliators and arbitrators (Art 58).

Article 6

(1) Without prejudice to the powers and functions vested in it by other provisions of this Convention, the Administrative Council shall
  (a) adopt the administrative and financial regulations of the Centre;
  (b) adopt the rules of procedure for the institution of conciliation and arbitration proceedings;
  (c) adopt the rules of procedure for conciliation and arbitration proceedings (hereinafter called the Conciliation Rules and the Arbitration Rules);
  (d) approve arrangements with the Bank for the use of the Bank's administrative facilities and services;
  (e) determine the conditions of service of the Secretary-General and of any Deputy Secretary-General;
  (f) adopt the annual budget of revenues and expenditures of the Centre;
  (g) approve the annual report on the operation of the Centre.

The decisions referred to in sub-paragraphs (a), (b), (c) and (f) above shall be adopted by a majority of two-thirds of the members of the Administrative Council.

(2) The Administrative Council may appoint such committees as it considers necessary.

(3) The Administrative Council shall also exercise such other powers and perform such other functions as it shall determine to be necessary for the implementation of the provisions of this Convention.

COMMENTARY ON SCH 3 ART 6

Powers and functions of Administrative Council ..	[Sch 3 Art 6-1]
Procedure for adopting decisions of Administrative Council	[Sch 3 Art 6-2]
Formation of committees	[Sch 3 Art 6-3]
Other powers	[Sch 3 Art 6-4]
Adoption of Additional Facility by ICSID Administrative Council	[Sch 3 Art 6-5]

[Sch 3 Art 6-1] Powers and functions of Administrative Council Article 6 spells out the powers and functions of the Administrative Council, but is stated as being "without prejudice" to any other functions vested in the Administrative Council.

The specific functions and powers enumerated in Art 6(1) are listed as being functions and powers that the Administrative Council "shall" perform, which suggests that it is mandatory for the Administrative Council to perform these functions. These include the adoption of ICSID's Administrative and Financial Regulations, which deal with the procedures and organisation of the Administrative Council and the Secretariat (C Schreuer et al, *The ICSID Convention: A Commentary*, 2nd ed, Cambridge University Press, Cambridge, 2009, p 22); the adoption of ICSID's Rules of Procedure for the Institution of Conciliation and Arbitration Proceedings, which make provision for the manner in which conciliation and arbitration proceedings are initiated (Schreuer et al, pp 22–3); the adoption of ICSID's Rules of Procedure for Conciliation Proceedings (Schreuer et al, p 23), and the adoption of ICSID's Rules of Procedure for Arbitration Proceedings (Schreuer et al, p 23). In addition, Art 6(1) provides that the Administrative Council shall approve arrangements with the World Bank for the use of the Bank's administrative services and facilities. These arrangements were agreed in the Memorandum of Administrative Arrangements Agreed between the International Bank for Reconstruction and Development and the International Centre for Settlement of Investment Disputes, which was agreed on 13 February 1967 (for the text of the Memorandum of Understanding, see Schreuer et al, pp 24–5). Further functions and powers of the Administrative Council are to "determine the conditions of service of the Secretary-General and of any Deputy Secretary-General", "adopt the annual budget of revenues and expenditures" of ICSID, and approve the annual report on ICSID's operations (ICSID Convention, Art 6(1)(e)–(g)).

[Sch 3 Art 6-2] Procedure for adopting decisions of Administrative Council Article 6(1) confirms that decisions taken in pursuance of the

Administrative Council's functions under subparas (a)–(g) are to be adopted by a two-thirds majority.

[Sch 3 Art 6-3] Formation of committees Article 6(2) provides that the Administrative Council can form committees, but in practice, this provision has not been invoked.

[Sch 3 Art 6-4] Other powers Article 6(3) is a type of "catch-all" provision which enables the Administrative Council to exercise such other powers as may be necessary, in its discretion, in order to implement the provisions of the ICSID Convention.

[Sch 3 Art 6-5] Adoption of Additional Facility by ICSID Administrative Council It is possible that Art 6(3) provided the power relied on by the Administrative Council to adopt the "Additional Facility" in 1978, which extends the availability of ICSID to certain types of proceedings between States and foreign nationals that fall outside the scope of the ICSID Convention. These additional types of proceedings are: (a) fact-finding proceedings; (b) conciliation or arbitration proceedings for the settlement of investment disputes between parties, one of which is not a Contracting State or a national of a Contracting State; and (c) conciliation and arbitration proceedings between parties, at least one of which is a Contracting State or a national of a Contracting State for the settlement of disputes that do not arise directly out of an investment, provided that the underlying transaction is not an ordinary commercial transaction (ICSID Rules Governing the Additional Facility for the Administration of Proceedings by the Secretariat of ICSID (ICSID/11, April 2006)).

Of these types of proceedings which may be brought under the ICSID Additional Facility Rules, the most relevant are the rules that extend ICSID's jurisdiction to cover investment disputes where only one of the States involved is a Contracting State. It is important to note that the provisions of the ICSID Convention do not apply to proceedings under the Additional Facility. Instead, such proceedings are simply governed by the Additional Facility Rules. This means that an award rendered under the ICSID Additional Facility should be treated as an ordinary international commercial arbitration award, such as those rendered under, for example, the Arbitration Rules of the United Nations Commission on International Trade Law (UNCITRAL). This is why, under Art 19 of the ICSID Additional Facility Rules, arbitral proceedings under the Additional Facility may only be held in States which are parties to the *Convention on the Recognition and Enforcement of Foreign Arbitral Awards* (opened for signature 10 June 1958, 330 UNTS 3 (entered into force 7 June 1959) ("New York Convention")), in order to ensure that the resulting awards can be enforced.

Article 7

(1) The Administrative Council shall hold an annual meeting and such other meetings as may be determined by the Council, or convened by the Chairman, or convened by the Secretary-General at the request of not less than five members of the Council.

(2) Each member of the Administrative Council shall have one vote and, except as otherwise herein provided, all matters before the Council shall be decided by a majority of the votes cast.

(3) A quorum for any meeting of the Administrative Council shall be a majority of its members.

(4) The Administrative Council may establish, by a majority of two-thirds of its members, a procedure whereby the Chairman may seek a vote of the Council without convening a meeting of the Council. The vote shall be considered valid only if the majority of the members of the Council cast their votes within the time limit fixed by the said procedure.

COMMENTARY ON SCH 3 ART 7

Meetings of Administrative Council	[Sch 3 Art 7-1]
Annual meeting	[Sch 3 Art 7-2]
Voting	[Sch 3 Art 7-3]
Quorum	[Sch 3 Art 7-4]
Voting without holding meeting	[Sch 3 Art 7-5]

[Sch 3 Art 7-1] Meetings of Administrative Council Article 7 deals with the frequency of meetings of the Administrative Council, votes at such meetings, the required quorum for meetings, and the procedures for voting.

[Sch 3 Art 7-2] Annual meeting As has been noted in connection with Art 4, the annual meeting of the Administrative Council is held at the same time as the annual meeting of the World Bank (see also ICSID Administrative and Financial Regulations, reg 1(1); and C Schreuer et al, *The ICSID Convention: A Commentary*, 2nd ed, Cambridge University Press, Cambridge, 2009, p 29). The Administrative Council can also hold additional meetings, as determined by the Administrative Council itself, or convened by the Chairman of the Administrative Council, or as convened by the ICSID Secretary-General at the request of no fewer than five members of the Council (ICSID Convention, Art 7(1)).

[Sch 3 Art 7-3] Voting Each member of the Administrative Council has one vote, which is weighted equally with other votes. With the exception of certain matters which are specifically provided for in the Convention, all matters are to be decided by a simple majority of the votes cast (Art 7(2)). The matters which require a two-thirds majority (which is a two-thirds majority of the entire membership of the Administrative Council, rather than of votes cast) are as follows: moving the seat of ICSID (Art 2), adopting the various rules and regulations, and the budget (Art 6), adopting a different voting procedure (Art 7(4)), electing the office bearers (Art 10(1)), amending the ICSID Convention (Art 66(1)), and inviting non-members of the World Bank to become Contracting States to the ICSID Convention (Art 67) (C Schreuer et al, *The ICSID Convention: A Commentary*, 2nd ed, Cambridge University Press, Cambridge, 2009, pp 29–30).

[Sch 3 Art 7-4] Quorum A simple majority of the Council's members must be present for there to be a quorum at meetings of the Administrative Council.

[Sch 3 Art 7-5] Voting without holding meeting Article 7(4) contemplates the Administrative Council establishing a procedure whereby decisions may be taken which require a vote without actually holding a meeting of the Council. This procedure has been established in reg 7(3) of the ICSID

Administrative and Financial Regulations (C Schreuer et al, *The ICSID Convention: A Commentary*, 2nd ed, Cambridge University Press, Cambridge, 2009, p 30).

Article 8

Members of the Administrative Council and the Chairman shall serve without remuneration from the Centre.

COMMENTARY ON SCH 3 ART 8

No remuneration for members of Administrative Council .... [Sch 3 Art 8-1]

[Sch 3 Art 8-1] No remuneration for members of Administrative Council As the members of the Administrative Council are usually people who are civil servants of the Contracting States, they are not entitled to any remuneration from ICSID for performing their functions as members of the Administrative Council. Likewise, as the Chairman of the Administrative Council is the President of the World Bank, he or she is not entitled to any additional remuneration (C Schreuer et al, *The ICSID Convention: A Commentary*, 2nd ed, Cambridge University Press, Cambridge, 2009, p 31).

SECTION 3

The Secretariat

Article 9

The Secretariat shall consist of a Secretary General, one or more Deputy Secretaries General and staff.

COMMENTARY ON SCH 3 ART 9

Composition of ICSID Secretariat .... [Sch 3 Art 9-1]
ICSID Secretary-General .... [Sch 3 Art 9-2]
Other members of Secretariat .... [Sch 3 Art 9-3]

[Sch 3 Art 9-1] Composition of ICSID Secretariat The Secretary-General of ICSID is the chief executive officer of the organisation. The Report of the Executive Directors explains (at para 18) that: "The Secretariat will consist of a Secretary-General, one or more Deputy Secretaries-General and staff. In the interest of flexibility the Convention provides for the possibility of there being more than one Deputy Secretary-General, but the Executive Directors do not now see foresee the need for more than one or two full time high officials of [ICSID]."

[Sch 3 Art 9-2] ICSID Secretary-General The first Secretary-General of ICSID was Mr Aron Broches (Dutch). The current Secretary-General is Meg Kinnear (Canadian).

[Sch 3 Art 9-3] Other members of Secretariat According to the ICSID website, the ICSID Secretariat has approximately 30 other staff members, including lawyers and financial and administrative staff.

Article 10

(1) The Secretary General and any Deputy Secretary General shall be elected by the Administrative Council by a majority of two thirds of its members upon the nomination of the Chairman for a term of service not exceeding six years and shall be eligible for re election. After consulting the members of the Administrative Council, the Chairman shall propose one or more candidates for each such office.

(2) The offices of Secretary General and Deputy Secretary General shall be incompatible with the exercise of any political function. Neither the Secretary General nor any Deputy Secretary General may hold any other employment or engage in any other occupation except with the approval of the Administrative Council.

(3) During the Secretary General's absence or inability to act, and during any vacancy of the office of Secretary General, the Deputy Secretary General shall act as Secretary General. If there shall be more than one Deputy Secretary General, the Administrative Council shall determine in advance the order in which they shall act as Secretary General.

COMMENTARY ON SCH 3 ART 10

Nomination of Secretary-General and Deputy
  Secretary-General .... [Sch 3 Art 10-1]
Independence .... [Sch 3 Art 10-2]
Separation from World Bank role .... [Sch 3 Art 10-3]
Role of Deputy Secretary-General .... [Sch 3 Art 10-4]

[Sch 3 Art 10-1] Nomination of Secretary-General and Deputy Secretary-General The Secretary-General and Deputy Secretary-General must be first nominated by the Chairman of the Administrative Council, and they then need to be elected by the Administrative Council by a two-thirds majority. The term of office is six years, and the Secretary-General and Deputy Secretary-General may be re-elected.

[Sch 3 Art 10-2] Independence Importantly, the two offices are stated as being "incompatible with the exercise of any political function". The Secretary-General or Deputy Secretary-General may not "hold other employment or engage in any other occupation except with the approval of the Administrative Council". This was regarded as being important to protect the independence of the two offices.

[Sch 3 Art 10-3] Separation from World Bank role Until 2008, the Secretary-General always held the office of General Counsel of the World Bank. The two functions were separated in 2008 (C Schreuer et al, *The ICSID Convention: A Commentary*, 2nd ed, Cambridge University Press, Cambridge, 2009, p 36).

[Sch 3 Art 10-4] Role of Deputy Secretary-General According to Art 10(3), the Deputy Secretary-General shall perform the functions of the

Secretary-General if the Secretary-General is absent, unable to act, or during any vacancy in the office of the Secretary-General. In recent years, the Deputy Secretary-General, Nassib Ziadé, was the Acting Secretary-General during the time between the resignation of Ana Palacio in April 2008 and the appointment of Meg Kinnear in June 2009. Article 10(3) also refers the situation of there being more than one Deputy Secretary-General, but this has never been the case (C Schreuer et al, *The ICSID Convention: A Commentary*, 2nd ed, Cambridge University Press, Cambridge, 2009, p 36).

Article 11
The Secretary-General shall be the legal representative and the principal officer of the Centre and shall be responsible for its administration, including the appointment of staff, in accordance with the provisions of this Convention and the rules adopted by the Administrative Council. He shall perform the function of registrar and shall have the power to authenticate arbitral awards rendered pursuant to this Convention, and to certify copies thereof.

COMMENTARY ON SCH 3 ART 11

Functions and role of Secretary-General	[Sch 3 Art 11-1]
Representative of ICSID	[Sch 3 Art 11-2]
Registrar	[Sch 3 Art 11-3]
Publications	[Sch 3 Art 11-4]
Functions under ICSID Additional Facility	[Sch 3 Art 11-5]
Appointing authority	[Sch 3 Art 11-6]

[Sch 3 Art 11-1] Functions and role of Secretary-General The Report of the Executive Directors states (at para 20) that the ICSID Convention "requires the Secretary-General to perform a variety of administrative functions as legal representative, registrar and principal officer of [ICSID]". Article 11 mentions some of the functions of the Secretary-General, but does not include an exhaustive list. The Secretary-General's functions are spelled out more fully in other provisions of the ICSID Convention, the ICSID Administrative and Financial Regulations, the ICSID Institutional Rules, the ICSID Arbitration Rules and the ICSID Conciliation Rules (C Schreuer et al, *The ICSID Convention: A Commentary*, 2nd ed, Cambridge University Press, Cambridge, 2009, pp 37–8).

[Sch 3 Art 11-2] Representative of ICSID The Secretary-General represents ICSID in its external relations with States and other international organisations and is responsible for its administrative affairs.

[Sch 3 Art 11-3] Registrar As registrar, the Secretary-General maintains records of information such as a list of the ICSID Convention's member States (ICSID Administrative and Financial Regulations, reg 20), and also receives and registers requests for conciliation and arbitration under Arts 28 and 36 of the ICSID Convention, in addition to other functions that the Secretary-General may perform in connection with such cases (C Schreuer et al, *The ICSID Convention: A Commentary*, 2nd ed, Cambridge University Press, Cambridge, 2009, p 39). The Secretary-General also provides administrative support in ICSID conciliation and arbitration proceedings, which includes providing a venue for the hearing, appointing a Tribunal Secretary and serving as "the official channel of communications between the parties, commissions, tribunals, ad hoc committees and the [ICSID] Chairman" (Schreuer et al, p 40).

[Sch 3 Art 11-4] Publications The Secretary-General also publishes information about ICSID's activities (ICSID Administrative and Financial Regulations, reg 22). These include the *ICSID Review — Foreign Investment Law Journal*, the *News from ICSID* newsletter, statistics on ICSID's caseload and various other items.

[Sch 3 Art 11-5] Functions under ICSID Additional Facility The Secretary-General also performs functions under the ICSID Additional Facility. In particular, Art 4(1) of the ICSID Additional Facility Rules stipulates that "[a]ny agreement providing for conciliation or arbitration proceedings under the Additional Facility in respect of existing or future disputes requires the approval of the Secretary-General". Other functions of the Secretary-General under the ICSID Additional Facility Rules are largely similar to those performed under, for example, the ICSID Convention and ICSID Arbitration Rules (C Schreuer et al, *The ICSID Convention: A Commentary*, 2nd ed, Cambridge University Press, Cambridge, 2009, pp 40–1).

[Sch 3 Art 11-6] Appointing authority Another function of the Secretary-General may arise in cases that are not brought under the ICSID Convention or the ICSID Additional Facility Rules, being that parties to arbitrations may designate the Secretary-General as the appointing authority in their arbitration agreement. Where this is the case, this does not mean that the arbitration becomes an arbitration under the ICSID Convention or ICSID Arbitration Rules (or the Additional Facility Rules) (C Schreuer et al, *The ICSID Convention: A Commentary*, 2nd ed, Cambridge University Press, Cambridge, 2009, p 41); it merely means that the parties have selected the Secretary-General to perform the function of the appointing authority (which may include, for instance, the appointment of an arbitrator where one party fails to do so within the stipulated time period).

SECTION 4
The Panels

Article 12

The Panel of Conciliators and the Panel of Arbitrators shall each consist of qualified persons, designated as hereinafter provided, who are willing to serve thereon.

COMMENTARY ON SCH 3 ART 12

Maintenance of Panels .... [Sch 3 Art 12-1]
Purpose of Panels .... [Sch 3 Art 12-2]
Qualities of members of Panels .... [Sch 3 Art 12-3]

[Sch 3 Art 12-1] Maintenance of Panels Article 3 of the ICSID Convention provides that ICSID shall "maintain a Panel of Conciliators and a Panel of Arbitrators". Article 12, and the subsequent provisions in s 4 of the ICSID

Convention, was based on Art 23 of the *Convention for the Pacific Settlement of International Disputes* of 1899 (opened for signature 29 July 1899, 1 Bevans 230 (entered into force 4 September 1900)) and Art 44 of the *Convention for the Pacific Settlement of International Disputes* of 1907 (opened for signature 18 October 1907, 1 Bevans 577 (entered into force 26 January 1910)).

[Sch 3 Art 12-2] Purpose of Panels The purpose of the "Panels", which are lists of persons who may be appointed as conciliator or arbitrator, is to assist parties to proceedings to find appropriate conciliators and arbitrators, although the parties are not restricted to selecting persons who are on these lists (see also ICSID Convention, Arts 31 and 40). However, if the Chairman of the ICSID Administrative Council is exercising his or her functions in making appointments, such appointments may only be made from these Panels (ICSID Convention, Arts 31(1), 40(1) and 52(3); see further C Schreuer et al, *The ICSID Convention: A Commentary*, 2nd ed, Cambridge University Press, Cambridge, 2009, p 44).

[Sch 3 Art 12-3] Qualities of members of Panels The persons included in the Panels have to be "qualified persons". Subsequent provisions of s 4 of the ICSID Convention set out the qualities required of persons on the Panels. Persons on the Panels must also be "willing to serve thereon", and this should be understood as meaning "willing to be on the Panel" as well as "willing to be appointed as arbitrator or conciliator", should the person be appointed to a conciliation commission, arbitral tribunal, or ad hoc committee (C Schreuer et al, *The ICSID Convention: A Commentary*, 2nd ed, Cambridge University Press, Cambridge, 2009, p 44).

Article 13

(1) Each Contracting State may designate to each Panel four persons who may but need not be its nationals.

(2) The Chairman may designate ten persons to each Panel. The persons so designated to a Panel shall each have a different nationality.

COMMENTARY ON SCH 3 ART 13

States to designate four persons to each Panel	[Sch 3 Art 13-1]
Membership of Panels may overlap	[Sch 3 Art 13-2]
States can appoint panellists of different nationality	[Sch 3 Art 13-3]
Australia's panellists	[Sch 3 Art 13-4]
Chairman of ICSID Administrative Council may appoint 10 panellists	[Sch 3 Art 13-5]

[Sch 3 Art 13-1] States to designate four persons to each Panel States that are parties to the ICSID Convention are permitted to nominate four persons to each of the Panel of Conciliators and Panel of Arbitrators. This model was always included in the various drafts leading to the adoption of the ICSID Convention and is consistent with the approach adopted by the States parties to the *Conventions for the Pacific Settlement of International Disputes* of 1899 and 1907, as noted above.

[Sch 3 Art 13-2] Membership of Panels may overlap It is possible for the membership of the two Panels to overlap. This is the case, for instance, with respect to the persons designated by Italy to the Panels, as their nominees, Professor Piero Bernardini, Professor Guido Carducci, Professor Andrea Giardina and Professor Giorgio Sacerdoti have all been designated to the Panel of Conciliators as well as the Panel of Arbitrators (Members of the Panels of Conciliators and of Arbitrators, Doc CSID/10 (November 2010), p 37). Other States, such as the United Kingdom, have designated different persons to the two Panels. The United Kingdom's designated members of the Panel of Conciliators are Sir Sydney Lipworth QC, Arthur Marriott QC, Francis Neate and the Rt Hon Sir Christopher Staughton; and its designated members on the Panel of Arbitrators are Sir Franklin Berman KCMG QC, Sir David Edward KCMG QC, Professor Sir Christopher Greenwood KB CMG QC and the Rt Hon Lord Michael Mustill (Members of the Panels of Conciliators and of Arbitrators, Doc ICSID/10 (November 2010), pp 62–3).

[Sch 3 Art 13-3] States can appoint panellists of different nationality States parties to the ICSID Convention may nominate persons of their own nationality, or persons of another nationality. For instance, Guyana has designated Professor Philippe Sands QC, who holds British and French nationality, to the Panel of Arbitrators (Members of the Panels of Conciliators and of Arbitrators, Doc ICSID/10 (November 2010), p 34).

[Sch 3 Art 13-4] Australia's panellists Australia's nominees to the ICSID Panels, as at November 2010, are as follows: the Hon Neil Brown QC, Ian Hanger QC, Henry Jolson QC and Sir Laurence Street AC KCMG are members of the Panel of Conciliators; and Dr Gavan Griffith AO QC, Professor Doug Jones, the Hon Michael Kirby and Professor Michael Pryles are members of the Panel of Arbitrators (Members of the Panels of Conciliators and of Arbitrators, Doc ICSID/10 (November 2010), pp 9–10).

Each of Australia's designated members will serve a term which is due to expire in July 2016.

[Sch 3 Art 13-5] Chairman of ICSID Administrative Council may appoint 10 panellists The Chairman of ICSID's Administrative Council may also designate ten persons to each Panel and the persons so designated must be of different nationalities. On 15 September 2011, the Chairman designated the following ten persons to the Panel of Arbitrators: Ms Teresa Chung SC (China), Mr Eduardo Zuleta (Colombia), Professor Alain Pellet (France), Dr Claus von Wobeser (Mexico), Professor Azzedine Kettani (Morocco), Professor Donald McRae (New Zealand/Canada), Mrs Tinuade Oyekunle (Nigeria), Mr Muhammad Makhdoom Ali Khan (Pakistan), Professor Pierre Tercier (Switzerland) and Ms Lucy Reed (USA). The persons designated by the Chairman to the Panel of Conciliators are: Professor Laurence Boulle (Australia/South Africa), Professor Luiz Olavo Baptista (Brazil), Mr Roberto Echandi (Costa Rica), Mrs Anna Joubin-Bret (France), Professor Dr Siegfried Elsing (Germany), Professor Nayla Comair-Obeid (Lebanon), Dr David J A Cairns (New Zealand/UK), Professor Lawrence Boo (Singapore), the Hon Justice James Ogoola

(Uganda) and Professor Jeswald W Salacuse (USA) (Members of the Panels of Conciliators and of Arbitrators, Doc ICSID/10 (September 2011), pp 7–10).

Article 14

(1) Persons designated to serve on the Panels shall be persons of high moral character and recognized competence in the fields of law, commerce, industry or finance, who may be relied upon to exercise independent judgment. Competence in the field of law shall be of particular importance in the case of persons on the Panel of Arbitrators.

(2) The Chairman, in designating persons to serve on the Panels, shall in addition pay due regard to the importance of assuring representation on the Panels of the principal legal systems of the world and of the main forms of economic activity.

COMMENTARY ON SCH 3 ART 14
Qualities of panellists .... [Sch 3 Art 14-1]
"high moral character" .... [Sch 3 Art 14-2]
"recognised competence" .... [Sch 3 Art 14-3]
Representation of principal legal systems of the
    world .... [Sch 3 Art 14-4]

[Sch 3 Art 14-1] Qualities of panellists Article 14(1) requires that persons designated to serve on the Panel of Conciliators and the Panel of Arbitrators be persons of "high moral character", and of "recognised competence in the fields of law, commerce, industry or finance", and that they be persons who may be "relied upon to exercise independent judgment".

[Sch 3 Art 14-2] "high moral character" The requirement that the persons be of "high moral character" was taken from the *Statute of the International Court of Justice* (opened for signature 26 June 1945, 3 Bevans 1153 (entered into force 24 October 1945), Art 2), which was, in turn, adopted from the *Conventions for the Pacific Settlement of International Disputes* of 1899 and 1907. The nominees must also be persons who can be relied upon to act independently. It is noteworthy that the term "impartiality" is not included in Art 14(1), but ICSID tribunals seem to interpret the phrase "independent judgment" as including a requirement of impartiality (see, eg, S Luttrell, "Bias Challenges in Investor-State Arbitration: Lessons from International Commercial Arbitration", in C Brown and K Miles (eds), *Evolution in Investment Treaty Law and Arbitration*, Cambridge University Press, Cambridge, 2011, p 445, fn 46, citing *Suez, Sociedad General de Aguas de Barcelona SA and InterAguas Servicios Integrales del Agua SA v The Argentine Republic* (ICSID Case No ARB/03/17, Decision on the Proposal for the Disqualification of a Member of an Arbitral Tribunal of 22 October 2007, para 42)). Similar language can be found in the constitutive instruments of a range of other international tribunals (see, eg, C Brown, "The Evolution and Application of Rules Concerning Independence of the 'International Judiciary'" (2003) 2 *Law and Practice of International Courts and Tribunals* 63).

[Sch 3 Art 14-3] "recognised competence" Article 14(1) also specifies that the members of the Panels shall have "recognised competence in the fields of law, commerce, industry or finance", and in the case of members of the Panel of Arbitrators, competence in the field of law is of "particular importance". This cannot be read as meaning that non-lawyers may not be designated to the Panel of Arbitrators, as the decision of who to appoint seems to be within each State party's discretion. Nonetheless, the addition of this sentence to Art 14(1) suggests to States that it would be prudent to designate qualified lawyers to the Panel of Arbitrators as opposed to non-lawyers.

[Sch 3 Art 14-4] Representation of principal legal systems of the world Article 14(2) provides that the Chairman, in designating persons to his or her list of nominees should, in addition to the qualities spelled out in Art 14(1), also take due regard of "the importance of assuring representation on the Panels of the principal legal systems of the world", and also of "the main forms of economic activity". The Chairman's list would appear to provide a reasonably broad representation of the principal legal systems of the world, although if one considers the geographical representation of the members, it is noteworthy that only one member of the Chairman's list is from Asia (Fali Nariman, from India).

Article 15

(1) Panel members shall serve for renewable periods of six years.

(2) In case of death or resignation of a member of a Panel, the authority which designated the member shall have the right to designate another person to serve for the remainder of that memberîs term.

(3) Panel members shall continue in office until their successors have been designated.

COMMENTARY ON SCH 3 ART 15

Term of Panel members .... [Sch 3 Art 15-1]
Vacancy due to death or resignation................ [Sch 3 Art 15-2]
Panellists to remain until successors designated .... [Sch 3 Art 15-3]

[Sch 3 Art 15-1] Term of Panel members Members of the Panel of Arbitrators and the Panel of Conciliators shall serve for a term of six years, which term may be renewed. There is, apparently, no limit to the number of times that this six-year term may be renewed. The term "shall serve" suggests that it is not open to the designating authority (whether it be the Chairman of the ICSID Administrative Council or a Contracting State) to appoint somebody for a shorter term than six years, or to remove them from the Panel before the expiry of the six-year term (C Schreuer et al, *The ICSID Convention: A Commentary*, 2nd ed, Cambridge University Press, Cambridge, 2009, p 52).

[Sch 3 Art 15-2] Vacancy due to death or resignation Article 15(2) also makes provision for the death or resignation of a member of a Panel. This provision was included in all drafts leading up to the adoption of the ICSID Convention (C Schreuer et al, *The ICSID Convention: A Commentary*, 2nd ed, Cambridge University Press, Cambridge, 2009, p 53).

[Sch 3 Art 15-3] Panellists to remain until successors designated Article 15(3) states that members of the Panel of Arbitrators and the Panel of Conciliators shall remain on the Panel until their successors have been designated. This means that, even though their six-year term may have expired, members of the Panels are not automatically removed from their Panel, but remain designated members until such time as they are replaced by the relevant designating authority (which may be one of the States parties to the ICSID Convention under Art 13(1), or the Chairman of the ICSID Administrative Council, under Art 13(2)) (C Schreuer et al, *The ICSID Convention: A Commentary*, 2nd ed, Cambridge University Press, Cambridge, 2009, pp 52–3).

Article 16

(1) A person may serve on both Panels.

(2) If a person shall have been designated to serve on the same Panel by more than one Contracting State, or by one or more Contracting States and the Chairman, he shall be deemed to have been designated by the authority which first designated him or, if one such authority is the State of which he is a national, by that State.

(3) All designations shall be notified to the Secretary-General and shall take effect from the date on which the notification is received.

COMMENTARY ON SCH 3 ART 16

Membership of both panels possible .... [Sch 3 Art 16-1]
Joint or multiple designations possible .... [Sch 3 Art 16-2]
Designations notified to Secretary-General of ICSID .... [Sch 3 Art 16-3]

[Sch 3 Art 16-1] Membership of both panels possible Under Art 16(1), it is possible for a person to serve on both the Panel of Conciliators and the Panel of Arbitrators; this has already been noted above, in the context of Art 13.

[Sch 3 Art 16-2] Joint or multiple designations possible It is possible for a person to be designated by more than one State, or by one State (or more than one State) and the Chairman of the ICSID Administrative Council. Where this occurs, Art 16(2) provides that that person is "deemed to have been designated by the authority which first designated him or, if one such authority is the State of which he is a national, by that State".

[Sch 3 Art 16-3] Designations notified to Secretary-General of ICSID Under Art 16(3), all designations are to be notified to the Secretary-General of ICSID, and under the ICSID Administrative and Financial Regulations, the Secretary-General publishes and circulates lists of the Panels (ICSID Administrative and Financial Regulations, reg 21; see also C Schreuer et al, *The ICSID Convention: A Commentary*, 2nd ed, Cambridge University Press, Cambridge, 2009, pp 54–5).

SECTION 5
Financing the Centre

Article 17

If the expenditure of the Centre cannot be met out of charges for the use of its facilities, or out of other receipts, the excess shall be borne by Contracting States which are members of the Bank in proportion to their respective subscriptions to the capital stock of the Bank, and by Contracting States which are not members of the Bank in accordance with rules adopted by the Administrative Council.

COMMENTARY ON SCH 3 ART 17

Financing of ICSID underwritten by Contracting
States which are members of World Bank ...... [Sch 3 Art 17-1]
Memorandum of Administrative Agreement ...... [Sch 3 Art 17-2]

[Sch 3 Art 17-1] Financing of ICSID underwritten by Contracting States which are members of World Bank Article 17 concerns the financing of ICSID (which is contrasted with the costs of individual arbitration and conciliation proceedings, which are to be met by the parties to such proceedings: ICSID Convention, Arts 60–61; see also C Schreuer et al, *The ICSID Convention: A Commentary*, 2nd ed, Cambridge University Press, Cambridge, 2009, p 56). The basic principle espoused in Art 17 is that the World Bank essentially underwrites the administrative expenses of ICSID, although provision is made for States parties to the ICSID Convention which are not members of the World Bank to make an appropriate contribution.

The formulation of Art 17 states that if the costs of ICSID cannot be met out of the charges levied for the use of its facilities (such as the costs charged to parties to proceedings) or out of "other receipts" (which was intended "as a reference to the possibility that the World Bank might finance the costs of [ICSID]": Schreuer et al, p 56), then any excess costs are to be met by the "Contracting States which are members of the Bank in proportion to their respective subscriptions to the capital stock of the Bank", and also "by Contracting States which are not members of the Bank in accordance with rules adopted by the Administrative Council" (ICSID Convention, Art 17). Further background on this provision is provided in the Report of the Executive Directors, which explains (at para 17) that the Executive Directors had decided:

> [T]hat the Bank should be prepared to provide [ICSID] with office accommodation free of charge as long as [ICSID] has its seat at the Bank's headquarters and to underwrite, within reasonable limits, the basic overhead expenditure of [ICSID] for a period of years to be determined after [ICSID] is established.

[Sch 3 Art 17-2] Memorandum of Administrative Agreement Further detail on the financial relationship is set out in the Memorandum of Administrative Arrangements of 13 February 1967, which states that the World Bank is to meet the costs of ICSID's staff, as well as its administrative costs. In this practical sense, the practice has been that the World Bank has met all of ICSID's administrative costs. This means that it has, to date, not been necessary to levy any further charges on members of the World Bank or on Contracting States to the ICSID Convention which are not members of the World Bank (C Schreuer et al, *The ICSID Convention: A Commentary*, 2nd ed, Cambridge University Press, Cambridge, 2009, p 57).

SECTION 6

Status, Immunities and Privileges

Article 18

The Centre shall have full international legal personality. The legal capacity of the Centre shall include the capacity
  (a) to contract;
  (b) to acquire and dispose of movable and immovable property;
  (c) to institute legal proceedings.

COMMENTARY ON SCH 3 ART 18

ICSID has international legal personality .... [Sch 3 Art 18-1]
"Full" international legal personality .... [Sch 3 Art 18-2]
Other international organisations .... [Sch 3 Art 18-3]

[Sch 3 Art 18-1] ICSID has international legal personality Although ICSID is physically located within the World Bank and has many institutional linkages to it, ICSID is, legally, a separate entity. The Report of the Executive Directors of the World Bank states (at para 15) that the ICSID Convention established ICSID "as an autonomous international institution".

[Sch 3 Art 18-2] "Full" international legal personality Article 18 makes it clear that ICSID has "full international legal personality", and further states that the capacities of ICSID include the capacity to enter into contracts, acquire and dispose of immovable property, and commence legal proceedings. The reference to ICSID having "full international legal personality" may well be a reference to the advisory opinion of the International Court of Justice in *Reparations for Injuries Suffered in the Service of the United Nations* [1949] ICJ Rep 174, in which the International Court of Justice held that the United Nations, being an international organisation, rather than a State, only had a "large measure of international personality", meaning that it lacked full international legal personality (at 179; see further P Sands and P Klein, *Bowett's Law of International Institutions*, 5th ed, Sweet & Maxwell, London, 2001, pp 469–85.) In practice, ICSID enters into publishing contracts, and it does not hold any property or have any financial resources. Nor has ICSID ever been a party in "legal proceedings before national courts" (C Schreuer et al, *The ICSID Convention: A Commentary*, 2nd ed, Cambridge University Press, Cambridge, 2009, p 59).

[Sch 3 Art 18-3] Other international organisations It is usual practice for the States parties to international organisations to conclude treaties in which they agree that the international organisation in question has legal personality, and that the organisation has separate privileges and immunities. For instance, the *Charter of the United Nations* (opened for signature 26 June 1945, 3 Bevans 1153 (entered into force 24 October 1945)) provides for the creation of certain specialised agencies of the United Nations (Art 57), and there is a separate treaty, the *Convention on the Privileges and Immunities of the Specialized Agencies* (opened for signature 21 November 1947, 33 UNTS 261 (entered into force 2 December 1948)), that makes this type of provision for those agencies. ICSID is an exception in that there is no separate treaty for these matters; all the relevant provisions are contained within the ICSID Convention itself (C Schreuer et al, *The ICSID Convention: A Commentary*, 2nd ed, Cambridge University Press, Cambridge, 2009, p 58).

Article 19
To enable the Centre to fulfil its functions, it shall enjoy in the territories of each Contracting State the immunities and privileges set forth in this Section.

COMMENTARY ON SCH 3 ART 19

ICSID's privileges and immunities .... [Sch 3 Art 19-1]
ICSID's privileges and immunities in Australian law .... [Sch 3 Art 19-2]

[Sch 3 Art 19-1] ICSID's privileges and immunities Article 19 sets out the general principle that ICSID shall enjoy the privileges and immunities set out in Arts 20–24 "in the territories of each Contracting State". The details of those privileges and immunities are set out in the subsequent provisions, Arts 20–24.

[Sch 3 Art 19-2] ICSID's privileges and immunities in Australian law Articles 20–24 have been implemented in Australia in the ICSID Implementation Act 1990 (Cth), which in part amended the International Organisations (Privileges and Immunities) Act 1963 (Cth). Section 8 of the ICSID Implementation Act 1990 (Cth) inserted s 9A of the International Organisations (Privileges and Immunities) Act 1963 (Cth). Section 9A provides that regulations could be adopted to confer upon certain persons the privileges and immunities contained in Arts 21, 22 and 24 of the ICSID Convention. The International Centre for Settlement of Investment Disputes (Privileges and Immunities) Regulations 1991 (Cth) were duly adopted to implement these provisions of the ICSID Convention in Australian law.

Article 20
The Centre, its property and assets shall enjoy immunity from all legal process, except when the Centre waives this immunity.

COMMENTARY ON SCH 3 ART 20

ICSID has immunity from legal process .... [Sch 3 Art 20-1]
Waiver of immunity .... [Sch 3 Art 20-2]
Implementation in Australian law .... [Sch 3 Art 20-3]

[Sch 3 Art 20-1] ICSID has immunity from legal process Article 20 provides that ICSID, its property and assets enjoy immunity from "all legal process", which should be interpreted expansively to cover both civil and criminal proceedings. This provision provides a wider immunity from legal process than is afforded to diplomatic agents under Art 31 of the *Vienna Convention on Diplomatic Relations* (opened for signature 18 April 1961, 500 UNTS 95 (entered into force 24 April 1964)), which has the force of law in Australia (by virtue of s 7 of the Diplomatic Privileges and Immunities Act 1967 (Cth)), and which provides for some limited exceptions to diplomatic agents' immunity from civil proceedings (*Vienna Convention on Diplomatic Relations*, Art 31; see, eg, E Denza, *Diplomatic Law*,

3rd ed, Oxford University Press, Oxford, 2008, pp 280–313). Due to the breadth of ICSID's immunity, any potential claims against ICSID are highly likely to be ineffective (C Schreuer et al, *The ICSID Convention: A Commentary*, 2nd ed, Cambridge University Press, Cambridge, 2009, p 61).

[Sch 3 Art 20-2] **Waiver of immunity** It is possible for ICSID to waive its immunity from legal process. A formal declaration was made at the time of the negotiation of the ICSID Convention that ICSID would waive its immunity in respect of "counterclaims directly connected with the principal claim in proceedings instituted by [ICSID]" (C Schreuer et al, *The ICSID Convention: A Commentary*, 2nd ed, Cambridge University Press, Cambridge, 2009, p 61).

[Sch 3 Art 20-3] **Implementation in Australian law** Article 20 is implemented in Australia by the International Centre for Settlement of Investment Disputes (Privileges and Immunities) Regulations 1991 (Cth). Regulation 6 provides that "[ICSID] shall have the privileges and immunities specified in paragraphs 1, 4, 6, 7, and 11 of the First Schedule to the [International Organisations (Privileges and Immunities) Act 1963 (Cth)]." These are as follows:

- "[i]mmunity of the organisation, and of the property and assets of, or in the custody of, or administered by, the organisation, from suit and from other legal process" (International Organisations (Privileges and Immunities) Act 1963 (Cth), First Schedule, para 1);
- "[i]nviolability of archives" (International Organisations (Privileges and Immunities) Act 1963 (Cth), First Schedule, para 4);
- "[e]xemption from duties on the importation or exportation of:
  (a) goods imported or exported by the organisation for its official use; and
  (b) publications of the organisation imported or exported by it" (International Organisations (Privileges and Immunities) Act 1963 (Cth), First Schedule, para 6);
- "[e]xemption of the organisation from the liability to pay or collect taxes other than duties on the importation or exportation of goods and of the income, property, assets and transactions of the organisation from such taxes" (International Organisations (Privileges and Immunities) Act 1963 (Cth), First Schedule, para 7); and
- "[a]bsence of censorship for official correspondence and other official communications" (International Organisations (Privileges and Immunities) Act 1963 (Cth), First Schedule, para 11).

It does not seem likely that this provision will come before Australian courts, as ICSID would not appear to have any property in Australia.

Article 21

The Chairman, the members of the Administrative Council, persons acting as conciliators or arbitrators or members of a Committee appointed pursuant to paragraph (3) of Article 52, and the officers and employees of the Secretariat
  (a) shall enjoy immunity from legal process with respect to acts performed by them in the exercise of their functions, except when the Centre waives this immunity;
  (b) not being local nationals, shall enjoy the same immunities from immigration restrictions, alien registration requirements and national service obligations, the

same facilities as regards exchange restrictions and the same treatment in respect of travelling facilities as are accorded by Contracting States to the representatives, officials and employees of comparable rank of other Contracting States.

COMMENTARY ON SCH 3 ART 21

Immunities for certain persons .... [Sch 3 Art 21-1]
Persons benefitting from immunities .... [Sch 3 Art 21-2]
Immunity from legal process a limited "functional" or "official act immunity" .... [Sch 3 Art 21-3]
Waiver of immunity .... [Sch 3 Art 21-4]
Other privileges and immunities .... [Sch 3 Art 21-5]
Implementation in Australian law .... [Sch 3 Art 21-6]

[Sch 3 Art 21-1] Immunities for certain persons Article 21 has two purposes: to confer immunity from legal process to certain listed persons (Art 21(a)); and to confer other privileges and immunities on those same persons (Art 21(b)) (C Schreuer et al, *The ICSID Convention: A Commentary*, 2nd ed, Cambridge University Press, Cambridge, 2009, pp 62–4).

[Sch 3 Art 21-2] Persons benefitting from immunities The persons to whom these privileges and immunities are conferred are "[t]he Chairman [and] members of the Administrative Council", arbitrators, conciliators, members of ad hoc annulment committees, and "officers and employees of the ICSID Secretariat". This raises the question of the position of legal assistants and secretaries to ICSID tribunals, conciliation commissions and ad hoc committees, whose situation is not explicitly addressed. If the person in question is drawn from the ICSID Secretariat, then he or she would clearly benefit from the relevant privileges and immunities, but other legal assistants to ICSID tribunals, commissions and ad hoc committees may fall outside the scope of Art 21, unless they can be regarded as "employees of the ICSID Secretariat".

[Sch 3 Art 21-3] Immunity from legal process a limited "functional" or "official act immunity" Article 21(a) confers immunity from legal process upon the listed persons. It is important to note, however, that the immunity is only conferred "with respect to acts performed by them in the exercise of their functions". This means that the persons are not conferred an absolute "personal immunity", but a more limited "official act immunity", which is also known as "functional immunity". This is, for instance, the same limited form of immunity conferred on a diplomatic agent who is "a national of or permanently resident in" the receiving State (*Vienna Convention on Diplomatic Relations*, opened for signature 18 April 1961, 500 UNTS 95 (entered into force 24 April 1964), Art 38(1)); this immunity does not extend to acts carried out in listed persons' private capacity. This "functional immunity" is consistent with the immunity granted to officials of other international organisations (see, eg, *Convention on the Privileges and Immunities of the Specialized Agencies*, opened for signature 21 November 1947, 33 UNTS 261 (entered into force 2 December 1948), ss 19 and 22; see also C Schreuer et al, *The ICSID Convention: A Commentary*, 2nd ed, Cambridge University Press, Cambridge, 2009, p 63).

[Sch 3 Art 21-4] **Waiver of immunity** The ICSID Secretary-General may waive the immunity of members of ICSID's staff; the Chairman of the Administrative Council may waive the immunity of the Secretary-General, Deputy Secretary-General and arbitrators, conciliators and members of an ad hoc committee; and the Administrative Council may waive the immunity of the Chairman and members of the Administrative Council (ICSID Administrative and Financial Regulations, reg 32).

[Sch 3 Art 21-5] **Other privileges and immunities** Article 21(b) confers other privileges and immunities on persons listed in Art 21, including immunities from "immigration restrictions, alien registration requirements and national service obligations", and also "the same facilities as regards exchange restrictions" and "the same treatment in respect of travelling facilities" as are accorded by Contracting States to the ICSID Convention to officials "of comparable rank" of other Contracting States. This provision aims to ensure that the persons listed in Art 21 are able to travel without hindrance to carry out ICSID business (for which purpose the ICSID Secretary-General issues certificates of official travel: ICSID Administrative and Financial Regulations, reg 31) (C Schreuer et al, *The ICSID Convention: A Commentary*, 2nd ed, Cambridge University Press, Cambridge, 2009, p 64) and are able to benefit from these additional relatively low-level privileges and immunities.

[Sch 3 Art 21-6] **Implementation in Australian law** Article 21 is implemented in Australian law by the International Centre for Settlement of Investment Disputes (Privileges and Immunities) Regulations 1991 (Cth). Under reg 7, "[a] person who is a Council member or an officer shall have the immunity specified in paragraph 1 of the Fourth Schedule to the Act, which is "[i]mmunity from suit and from other legal process in respect of acts and things done in his capacity as such an officer" (where "Council member" is defined in reg 3 as meaning "the Chairman or a member of the Administrative Council of [ICSID]", and "officer" is defined in reg 3 as meaning "a person, other than a Council member, who holds an office in the Secretariat"). Regulation 8 confers additional privileges and immunities on "Council members" and "officers" of ICSID (but only to persons who are not Australian citizens); these are that a Council member is "exempt from taxation on emoluments (other than salary) received from [ICSID]" (reg 8(2)); and an officer is "exempt from taxation on salary and other emoluments received from [ICSID]" (reg 8(3)). Further, under reg 8(4), a person who is a Council member or an officer benefits from the privileges and immunities specified in paras 3, 4, 5 and 6 of Pt 1 of the Fourth Schedule to the International Organisations (Privileges and Immunities) Act 1963 (Cth). These are:

3. Exemption (including exemption of a spouse and any dependent relatives) from the application of laws relating to immigration and the registration of aliens.
4. Exemption from the obligation to perform national service.
5. Exemption from currency or exchange restrictions to such extent as is accorded to an official, of comparable rank, forming part of a diplomatic mission.

6. The like repatriation facilities (including repatriation facilities for a spouse and any dependent relatives) in time of international crisis as are accorded to a diplomatic agent.

Article 21 also confers privileges and immunities on conciliators, arbitrators and members of ad hoc committees. These privileges and immunities are implemented in Australian law in reg 9 of the International Centre for Settlement of Investment Disputes (Privileges and Immunities) Regulations 1991 (Cth). Conciliators, arbitrators and members of ad hoc committees benefit from immunity from legal process with respect to acts performed by the person in the exercise of his or her functions (reg 9(1)); and the fees or expenses of conciliators, arbitrators and members of ad hoc committees are exempt from taxation (reg 9(2)). In addition, a person who is a conciliator, arbitrator or ad hoc committee member who is not an Australian citizen also benefits from the privileges and immunities contained in paras 3–6 of Pt 1 of the Fourth Schedule to the International Organisations (Privileges and Immunities) Act 1963 (Cth), which are set out above.

Article 22

The provisions of Article 21 shall apply to persons appearing in proceedings under this Convention as parties, agents, counsel, advocates, witnesses or experts; provided, however, that sub-paragraph (b) thereof shall apply only in connection with their travel to and from, and their stay at, the place where the proceedings are held.

COMMENTARY ON SCH 3 ART 22

Persons appearing in ICSID proceedings also to
  benefit from privileges and immunities .... [Sch 3 Art 22-1]
Implementation in Australian law .... [Sch 3 Art 22-2]

[Sch 3 Art 22-1] Persons appearing in ICSID proceedings also to benefit from privileges and immunities The purpose of Art 22 is to extend the limited privileges and immunities provided for in Art 21 to "persons appearing in [ICSID] proceedings", whether they be the parties, counsel, witnesses and experts. This provision was included "to ensure the proper functioning of proceedings" (C Schreuer et al, *The ICSID Convention: A Commentary*, 2nd ed, Cambridge University Press, Cambridge, 2009, p 65). However, Art 22 makes it clear that the additional privileges and immunities contained in Art 21(b) are only to apply in respect of travel to and from the place where the ICSID proceedings are held, and their stay at that place during the hearing.

[Sch 3 Art 22-2] Implementation in Australian law Article 22 is implemented in Australian law by reg 10 of the International Centre for Settlement of Investment Disputes (Privileges and Immunities) Regulations 1991 (Cth). Under reg 10(2), a person who is a "party, agent, counsel, advocate, witness or expert in proceedings" has "immunity from legal process with respect to acts performed by the person in the exercise of his or her function as a party, agent, counsel, advocate, witness or expert in proceedings". Under reg 10(3), such persons have, in connection with their travel to and from, and their stay at, the place where the proceedings are held, "the privileges and immunities specified in paragraphs 3, 4, 5 and 6 of Part 1 of the Fourth Schedule to the Act" (set out above at [Sch 3 Art 21-6]), although this only applies where the person concerned is not an Australian citizen, and their travel or stay "is undertaken in the exercise of his or her function as a party, agent, counsel, advocate, witness or expert in proceedings" (reg 10(4)).

Article 23

(1) The archives of the Centre shall be inviolable, wherever they may be.

(2) With regard to its official communications, the Centre shall be accorded by each Contracting State treatment not less favourable than that accorded to other international organizations.

COMMENTARY ON SCH 3 ART 23
Inviolability of ICSID's archives .... [Sch 3 Art 23-1]
Implementation in Australian law .... [Sch 3 Art 23-2]
Official communications of ICSID also protected . [Sch 3 Art 23-3]

[Sch 3 Art 23-1] Inviolability of ICSID's archives Article 23(1) corresponds with Art 24 of the *Vienna Convention on Diplomatic Relations*, which provides that the archives and documents of a diplomatic mission "shall be inviolable at any time and wherever they may be". There have apparently never been any problems "concerning the inviolability of [ICSID's] archives" (C Schreuer et al, *The ICSID Convention: A Commentary*, 2nd ed, Cambridge University Press, Cambridge, 2009, p 67). As ICSID does not have any archives located in Australia, this provision is unlikely to ever come before an Australian court.

[Sch 3 Art 23-2] Implementation in Australian law This provision is given the force of law in Australia by reg 6 of the International Centre for Settlement of Investment Disputes (Privileges and Immunities) Regulations 1991 (Cth), which provides that ICSID shall have the privileges and immunities set out in paras 1, 4, 6, 7 and 11 of the First Schedule to the International Organisations (Privileges and Immunities) Act 1963 (Cth); these include the "[i]nviolability of the archives" (para 4) and "[a]bsence of censorship for official correspondence and other official communications" (para 11).

[Sch 3 Art 23-3] Official communications of ICSID also protected Article 23(2) concerns the official communications of ICSID and provides that ICSID shall be accorded by each Contracting State "treatment not less favourable than that accorded to other international organisations". This formulation imposes a type of "most-favoured-nation" obligation on each State party to the ICSID Convention. Article 23(2) covers "issues such as priority of transmission, transmission rates and taxes as well as freedom from censorship and interception" (C Schreuer et al, *The ICSID Convention: A Commentary*, 2nd ed, Cambridge University Press, Cambridge, 2009, p 68). As explained above, this obligation is implemented in reg 6 of the International Centre for Settlement of Investment Disputes (Privileges and Immunities) Regulations 1991 (Cth).

Article 24

(1) The Centre, its assets, property and income, and its operations and transactions authorized by this Convention shall be exempt from all taxation and customs duties. The Centre shall also be exempt from liability for the collection or payment of any taxes or customs duties.

(2) Except in the case of local nationals, no tax shall be levied on or in respect of expense allowances paid by the Centre to the Chairman or members of the Administrative Council, or on or in respect of salaries, expense allowances or other emoluments paid by the Centre to officials or employees of the Secretariat.

(3) No tax shall be levied on or in respect of fees or expense allowances received by persons acting as conciliators, or arbitrators, or members of a Committee appointed pursuant to paragraph (3) of Article 52, in proceedings under this Convention, if the sole jurisdictional basis for such tax is the location of the Centre or the place where such proceedings are conducted or the place where such fees or allowances are paid.

COMMENTARY ON SCH 3 ART 24

ICSID, certain officers of ICSID and arbitrators, conciliators and members of Annulment Committees exempt from certain taxation and customs duties.	[Sch 3 Art 24-1]
ICSID's immunities and exemptions	[Sch 3 Art 24-2]
Implementation in Australian law	[Sch 3 Art 24-3]
Expense allowances, salaries and emoluments of certain ICSID officers exempt	[Sch 3 Art 24-4]
Implementation in Australian law	[Sch 3 Art 24-5]
Payments to arbitrators, conciliators and members of Annulment Committees	[Sch 3 Art 24-6]
Implementation in Australian law	[Sch 3 Art 24-7]

[Sch 3 Art 24-1] ICSID, certain officers of ICSID and arbitrators, conciliators and members of Annulment Committees exempt from certain taxation and customs duties Article 24 concerns taxation and the immunity from taxation of ICSID, ICSID officials and employees, and conciliators, arbitrators and members of ad hoc committees (see generally C Schreuer et al, *The ICSID Convention: A Commentary*, 2nd ed, Cambridge University Press, Cambridge, 2009, pp 69–70). It therefore deals with three different types of exemption, which are considered separately.

[Sch 3 Art 24-2] ICSID's immunities and exemptions Article 24(1) is based on the Articles of Agreement of the World Bank and the International Monetary Fund (C Schreuer et al, *The ICSID Convention: A Commentary*, 2nd ed, Cambridge University Press, Cambridge, 2009, p 69). The exemption from any liability "for the collection or payment of any taxes or customs duties" is aimed at legislation in some countries which imposes an obligation on employers to withhold and pay taxes (Schreuer et al, p 70).

[Sch 3 Art 24-3] Implementation in Australian law Article 24(1) is implemented in Australian law in reg 6 of the International Centre for Settlement of Investment Disputes (Privileges and Immunities) Regulations 1991 (Cth). Under paras 6 and 7 of the First Schedule to the International Organisations (Privileges and Immunities) Act 1963 (Cth), ICSID has the following privileges and immunities: "[e]xemption from duties on the importation or exportation of: (a) goods imported or exported by the organisation for its official use; and (b) publications of the organisation imported or exported by it" (para 6); and "[e]xemption of the organisation from the liability to pay or collect taxes other than duties on the importation or exportation of goods and of the income, property, assets and transactions of the organisation from such taxes" (para 7).

[Sch 3 Art 24-4]   Expense allowances, salaries and emoluments of certain ICSID officers exempt   Article 24(2) addresses expense allowances of the Chairman and members of the Administrative Council, and expense allowances, salaries and other emoluments paid to officials and employees of the ICSID Secretariat (including the Secretary-General and the Deputy Secretary-General). This provision stipulates that no taxes shall be levied on such payments "except in the case of local nationals".

[Sch 3 Art 24-5]   Implementation in Australian law   Article 24(2) is implemented in Australian law by regs 7, 8 and 9 of the International Centre for Settlement of Investment Disputes (Privileges and Immunities) Regulations 1991 (Cth).

[Sch 3 Art 24-6]   Payments to arbitrators, conciliators and members of Annulment Committees   Finally, Art 24(3) provides that payments made to arbitrators, conciliators, or members of ad hoc committees shall not be subject to tax "if the sole jurisdictional basis . . . is the location of [ICSID] or the place where such proceedings are conducted or the place where the fees or allowances are paid". This provision "does not affect the tax liability of conciliators, arbitrators and members of ad hoc committees in their countries of residence. . . Article 24(3) does not create a tax exemption but merely restricts the geographical basis for taxation" (C Schreuer et al, *The ICSID Convention: A Commentary*, 2nd ed, Cambridge University Press, Cambridge, 2009, p 70).

[Sch 3 Art 24-7]   Implementation in Australian law   Article 24(3) is implemented in reg 9(2) of the International Centre for Settlement of Investment Disputes (Privileges and Immunities) Regulations 1991 (Cth), which provides that:

> Where:
> (a) a person receives fees or expense allowances in his or her capacity as a conciliator or an arbitrator in proceedings; and
> (b) but for this sub-regulation, the person would be liable to taxation on the fees or allowances by reason only of the occurrence of either or both of the following circumstances:
> > (i) the proceedings (or part of the proceedings) were conducted in Australia;
> > (ii) the fees or expense allowances were paid in Australia;
> the person is exempt from that taxation.

CHAPTER II

Jurisdiction of the Centre

Article 25

(1) The jurisdiction of the Centre shall extend to any legal dispute arising directly out of an investment, between a Contracting State (or any constituent subdivision or agency of a Contracting State designated to the Centre by that State) and a national of another Contracting State, which the parties to the dispute consent in writing to submit to the Centre. When the parties have given their consent, no party may withdraw its consent unilaterally.

(2) "National of another Contracting State" means:
   (a) any natural person who had the nationality of a Contracting State other than the State party to the dispute on the date on which the parties consented to submit such dispute to conciliation or arbitration as well as on the date on which the request was registered pursuant to paragraph (3) of Article 28 or paragraph (3) of Article 36, but does not include any person who on either date also had the nationality of the Contracting State party to the dispute; and
   (b) any juridical person which had the nationality of a Contracting State other than the State party to the dispute on the date on which the parties consented to submit such dispute to conciliation or arbitration and any juridical person which had the nationality of the Contracting State party to the dispute on that date and which, because of foreign control, the parties have agreed should be treated as a national of another Contracting State for the purposes of this Convention.

(3) Consent by a constituent subdivision or agency of a Contracting State shall require the approval of that State unless that State notifies the Centre that no such approval is required.

(4) Any Contracting State may, at the time of ratification, acceptance or approval of this Convention or at any time thereafter, notify the Centre of the class or classes of disputes which it would or would not consider submitting to the jurisdiction of the Centre. The Secretary-General shall forthwith transmit such notification to all Contracting States. Such notification shall not constitute the consent required by paragraph (1).

COMMENTARY ON SCH 3 ART 25

Jurisdiction of ICSID	[Sch 3 Art 25-1]
Introduction	[Sch 3 Art 25-2]
Conditions for ICSID jurisdiction	[Sch 3 Art 25-3]
"legal dispute"	[Sch 3 Art 25-4]
Is there a "dispute"?	[Sch 3 Art 25-5]
Is the dispute a "legal dispute"?	[Sch 3 Art 25-6]
"arise directly" out of "an investment"	[Sch 3 Art 25-7]
"directly"	[Sch 3 Art 25-8]
"investment"	[Sch 3 Art 25-9]
Definition of "investment" may be contained in another instrument	[Sch 3 Art 25-10]

Parties do not have unlimited freedom in defining
"investment" .... [Sch 3 Art 25-11]
Characteristics of "investment" and so-called *Salini*
criteria .... [Sch 3 Art 25-12]
Dispute must be between "a Contracting State . . .
and a national of another Contracting State" .. [Sch 3 Art 25-13]
Nationality of legal persons .... [Sch 3 Art 25-14]
Consent to ICSID's jurisdiction must be "in
writing" .... [Sch 3 Art 25-15]
Consent may not be withdrawn .... [Sch 3 Art 25-16]
Consent by constituent subdivision or agency of a
State requires approval of that State .... [Sch 3 Art 25-17]
Notifications by States of class or classes of disputes
they would or would not consider submitting to
ICSID .... [Sch 3 Art 25-18]
Article 25(4) notifications are not reservations .... [Sch 3 Art 25-19]

[Sch 3 Art 25-1] Jurisdiction of ICSID Article 25 sets out the parameters of ICSID's jurisdiction (for an extensive discussion of Art 25, see especially C Schreuer et al, *The ICSID Convention: A Commentary*, 2nd ed, Cambridge University Press, Cambridge, 2009, pp 71–347). As it is contained within Ch II of the ICSID Convention, Art 25 (along with all of the other provisions in Chs II–VII of the ICSID Convention, subject to Pt IV of the Act) has the force of law in Australia under s 32 of the Act.

[Sch 3 Art 25-2] Introduction Unlike a typical commercial arbitration, where the parties can agree in their arbitral clause that whatever dispute they have can be referred to arbitration, ICSID has a number of independent jurisdictional requirements that have to be satisfied, in addition to having the parties' consent to refer the dispute to ICSID arbitration.

[Sch 3 Art 25-3] Conditions for ICSID jurisdiction In the opening paragraph of Art 25(1), the States parties agree that:

> The jurisdiction of the Centre shall extend to any legal dispute arising directly out of an investment, between a Contracting State (or any constituent subdivision or agency of a Contracting State designated to the Centre by that State) and a national of another Contracting State, which the parties to the dispute consent in writing to submit to the Centre. When the parties have given their consent, no party may withdraw its consent unilaterally.

Thus, in order for a dispute between an investor and a State to be eligible for ICSID arbitration, the following conditions must be met: (a) there must be a "legal dispute"; (b) the dispute must arise "directly out of an investment"; (c) the dispute must be between, on the one hand, either a Contracting State, or one of its subdivisions or agencies, and on the other hand, a national of another Contracting State; and (d) all parties to the dispute must consent in writing to having the investment dispute submitted to ICSID.

[Sch 3 Art 25-4] "legal dispute" The first requirement set forth in Art 25(1) is that there be a "legal dispute" (see further C Schreuer et al, *The ICSID*

Convention: A Commentary, 2nd ed, Cambridge University Press, Cambridge, 2009, pp 93–106). This requirement itself can be split into two questions; first, the requirement that there be a "dispute", and second, that the dispute be a "legal dispute".

[Sch 3 Art 25-5]   Is there a "dispute"?   The existence of a dispute may come about in several ways — but it must be a dispute. For instance, a mere difference of opinion may not be sufficiently concrete to amount to a dispute that is susceptible of arbitration (see, eg, J Collier and V Lowe, *The Settlement of Disputes in International Law: Institutions and Procedures*, Oxford University Press, Oxford, 1999, pp 10–14). And there may be a dispute that is hypothetical, or which has since become moot — this, too, is not a "dispute" (see especially *Northern Cameroons (Cameroon v United Kingdom)* [1963] ICJ Rep 15 at 97–9 (Sep Op of Sir Gerald Fitzmaurice); *Nuclear Tests (Australia v France)* [1974] ICJ Rep 253 at 267–72).

As Professor Schreuer has noted, "[t]he existence of a dispute presupposes that there be a minimum level of communication between the parties. The matter must have been taken up with the other party, which must have opposed the claimant's position if only indirectly" (C Schreuer et al, *The ICSID Convention: A Commentary*, 2nd ed, Cambridge University Press, Cambridge, 2009, p 94). Perhaps the best definition of what constitutes a "dispute" can be found in the judgment of the International Court of Justice in *South West Africa (Ethiopia v South Africa) (Liberia v South Africa)* [1962] ICJ 319, where it held (at 328) that:

> it is not sufficient for one party to a contentious case to assert that a dispute exists with the other party. A mere assertion is not sufficient to prove the existence of a dispute any more than a mere denial of the existence of the dispute proves its non-existence. Nor is it adequate to show that the interests of the two parties to such a case are in conflict. It must be shown that the claim of one party is positively opposed by the other.

This test for the existence of a dispute has been accepted in the jurisprudence of a range of other courts and tribunals.

[Sch 3 Art 25-6]   Is the dispute a "legal dispute"?   The second requirement in Art 25(1) is that the dispute must be a "legal dispute". The ICSID Convention does not define what is meant by this term. The Report of the World Bank Executive Directors states (at para 26) that this means that "[t]he dispute must concern the existence or scope of a legal right or obligation, or the nature or extent of the reparation to be made for the breach of a legal obligation". This is consistent with how ICSID tribunals have generally interpreted this phrase.

[Sch 3 Art 25-7]   "arise directly" out of "an investment"   The next element of the jurisdictional requirements of Art 25(1) is that the dispute must "arise directly" out of "an investment". Again, there are two separate elements.

[Sch 3 Art 25-8]   "directly"   The requirement of "directness" relates to the dispute in relation to the investment. It is one of the objective criteria for jurisdiction under Art 25(1) and is "independent of the parties' consent". This means that, no matter what the parties have agreed, the dispute must not only be connected to an investment, "but must also be reasonably closely connected" (C Schreuer et al, *The ICSID Convention: A Commentary*, 2nd ed, Cambridge

University Press, Cambridge, 2009, p 106). The question of the proper interpretation of the term "directly" arose in *Fedax NV v Venezuela* (ICSID Case No ARB/96/3, Decision on Jurisdiction of 11 July 1997). In this case, the respondent State argued that because the transaction in issue concerned debt instruments, the claimant had not made a "direct investment" which therefore could not be considered to be an investment within the meaning of Art 25(1). In its decision on jurisdiction, the tribunal held that the term "directly" in Art 25(1) related "to the 'dispute' and not to the 'investment'" (para 28). It followed, in the view of the tribunal, that "jurisdiction can exist even in respect of investments that are not direct, so long as the dispute arises directly from such transaction" (para 28).

[Sch 3 Art 25-9] **"investment"** As for the requirement that the dispute arise directly out of an "investment", there is no guidance in the ICSID Convention on what constitutes an "investment" (C Schreuer et al, *The ICSID Convention: A Commentary*, 2nd ed, Cambridge University Press, Cambridge, 2009, pp 114–34). This was a deliberate decision by the drafters, who recognised that, given the pivotal role of consent, a definition of the term could prove unhelpfully restrictive. In the words of the Executive Directors (at para 27, Report of the Executive Directors):

> No attempt was made to define the term 'investment' given the essential requirement of consent by the parties, and the mechanism through which Contracting States can make known in advance, if they so desire, the classes of disputes which they would or would not consider submitting to [ICSID].

[Sch 3 Art 25-10] **Definition of "investment" may be contained in another instrument** The Executive Directors' reference to the parties' consent refers to the possibility that another instrument may provide a definition. First, if the parties to a concession contract include a clause by which they consent to submit to ICSID, this will be a strong indication that they consider their transaction an "investment" for the purposes of the ICSID Convention. The parties might even include a specific statement in their contract that the planned transaction is an "investment". Second, if the claim is brought under a bilateral investment treaty (BIT) or multilateral investment treaty (MIT), that instrument may contain a definition of the term "investment". In modern BITs, these are typically drafted in broad terms — they are introduced by a broad general description followed by a non-exhaustive list of typical rights. The general description frequently refers to "any kind of asset". The list typically includes traditional property rights; participation in companies; money claims and rights to performance; intellectual and industrial property rights; and concession or similar rights.

For instance, the United Kingdom's Model BIT provides the following definition of "investment" in Art 1:

> "investment" means every kind of asset, owned or controlled directly or indirectly, and in particular, though not exclusively, includes:
> (i) movable and immovable property and any other property rights such as mortgages, liens or pledges;
> (ii) shares in and stock and debentures of a company and any other form of participation in a company;

(iii) claims to money or to any performance under contract having a financial value;
(iv) intellectual property rights, goodwill, technical processes and know-how;
(v) business concessions conferred by law or under contract, including concessions to search for, cultivate, extract or exploit natural resources.

The definition further provides that:

A change in the form in which assets are invested does not affect their character as investments and the term 'investment' includes all investments, whether made before or after the date of entry into force of this Agreement.

[Sch 3 Art 25-11] Parties do not have unlimited freedom in defining "investment" However, "[t]he reference to the essential requirement for consent in the Report of the Executive Directors . . . does not imply unlimited freedom for the parties' to define the term, as it is understood that the term 'investment' has 'an objective meaning independent of the parties' disposition" (C Schreuer et al, *The ICSID Convention: A Commentary*, 2nd ed, Cambridge University Press, Cambridge, 2009, p 117). It is, therefore, important to remember that the definition of "investment" under the ICSID Convention is an autonomous term — and an ICSID tribunal will have to consider carefully whether the transaction out of which the dispute arises meets both: (a) the objective criteria of an "investment" under Art 25(1) of the Convention; as well as (b) the definition in the instrument containing the parties' consent, whether it be a contract or a BIT. This has been referred to as the "double barrelled test" (*Malaysian Historical Salvors Sdn Bhd v Malaysia* (ICSID Case No ARB/05/10, Decision on Jurisdiction of 17 May 2007, para 55); and see D Williams QC and S Foote, "Recent Developments in the Approach to Identifying an 'Investment' pursuant to Article 25 of the ICSID Convention", in C Brown and K Miles (eds), *Evolution in Investment Treaty Law and Arbitration*, Cambridge University Press, Cambridge, 2011, p 42).

[Sch 3 Art 25-12] Characteristics of "investment" and so-called *Salini* criteria In the past, ICSID tribunals have found that in order for a project or transaction to qualify as an investment for the purposes of the ICSID Convention, the project or transaction must at a minimum: (a) be for a significant duration; (b) provide a measureable return to the investor; (c) involve an element of risk on both sides; (d) involve a substantial commitment on the part of the investor; and (e) be significant to the host State's development. These criteria were applied by the arbitral tribunal in *Fedax NV v Venezuela* (ICSID Case No ARB/96/3, Decision on Jurisdiction of 11 July 1997, para 43) in 1998, and they were then re-stated in various cases, including *Salini Costruttori SpA and Italstrade SpA v Morocco* (ICSID Case No ARB/00/04, Decision on Jurisdiction of 23 July 2001, para 52) in 2001, although the criterion relating to a regular profit and return for the investor was not included. Since then, these criteria have become known as the "*Salini* criteria" (C Schreuer et al, *The ICSID Convention: A Commentary*, 2nd ed, Cambridge University Press, Cambridge, 2009, p 129).

Although these criteria have become generally recognised as constituting the definition of an "investment" for the purposes of ICSID jurisdiction, it has not been fully clarified whether and to what extent each of the criteria have to be met in each case. A certain degree of flexibility has to be applied, and some decisions have been criticised for appearing to elevate these criteria into inflexible jurisdictional requirements (Schreuer et al, pp 129–34).

One case where the tribunal denied that there was an investment for the purposes of Art 25(1) is *Malaysian Historical Salvors Sdn Bhd v Malaysia* (ICSID Case No ARB/05/10, Decision on Jurisdiction of 17 May 2007). In that case, a British company had entered into a contract with Malaysia to salvage the shipwreck of a vessel called the "Diana" which had sunk in the Straits of Malacca in 1817. The claimant managed to recover 24,000 pieces from the sunken vessel, which were successfully sold by Christie's (the London-based auction house) for a total of US$3 million. The claimant alleged that, rather than pay it the 70 per cent that it was due, the Malaysian Government had only paid it US$1.2 million or 40 per cent of the proceeds of sale, and also that certain items had been withheld from sale by the Malaysian Government, which were worth around US$400,000 (see *Malaysian Historical Salvors Sdn Bhd v Malaysia* (ICSID Case No ARB/05/10, Decision on Jurisdiction of 17 May 2007, paras 7–14)). In its decision on jurisdiction, the tribunal held that although the claimant might have made an investment for the purposes of the United Kingdom–Malaysia BIT, the company had not made an "investment" within the meaning of the ICSID Convention. This was because, in the tribunal's view, the salvage contract did not make a "significant contribution" to the economic development of the host State (paras 123–4, 143–6). Accordingly, because this characteristic of the concept of investment was not satisfied, there was no jurisdiction under the ICSID Convention (paras 148, 151).

Since the decision on jurisdiction in *Malaysian Historical Salvors*, there has been a reaction to the strict application of the *Salini* criteria. This can be seen in the Award in *Biwater Gauff (Tanzania) Ltd v Tanzania* (ICSID Case No ARB/05/22, Award of 24 July 2008) where the tribunal held (at para 314) that:

> The strict application of the *Salini* test is problematic if the 'typical characteristics' of an investment as identified in that decision are elevated into a fixed and inflexible test, and if transactions are to be presumed excluded from the ICSID Convention unless each of the five criteria are satisfied. This risks the arbitrary exclusion of certain types of transaction from the scope of the Convention. It also leads to a definition that may contradict individual agreements . . . as well as a developing consensus in parts of the world as to the meaning of 'investment' (as expressed, eg, in bilateral investment treaties).

The tribunal referred to, inter alia, D Krishan, "A Notion of ICSID Investment", in T Weiler (ed), *Investment Treaty Arbitration and International Law*, Juris Publishing, New York, 2008.

The tribunal concluded (at para 316) that:

> a more flexible and pragmatic approach to the meaning of 'investment' is appropriate, which takes into account the features identified in *Salini*, but along with all the circumstances of the case, including the nature of the instrument containing the relevant consent to ICSID.

The ad hoc annulment committee in *Malaysian Historical Salvors Sdn Bhd v Malaysia* (ICSID Case No ARB/05/10, Decision on Annulment of 16 April 2009) adopted the same approach; see also J Ho, "The Meaning of 'Investment' in ICSID Arbitrations" (2010) 26 *Arbitration International* 633.

In contrast, the ICSID tribunal in *Phoenix Action v Czech Republic* (ICSID Case No ARB/06/5, Award of 15 April 2009) considered that, not only did the *Salini* criteria need to be satisfied, but an investment also had to be made in accordance with the laws of the host State, and also in good faith, thus adding another criterion to the test. The ICSID tribunal put the position (at para 114) as follows:

> To summarise all the requirements for an investment to benefit from the international protection of ICSID, the Tribunal considers that the following six elements have to be taken into account:
> 1. a contribution in money or other assets;
> 2. a certain duration;
> 3. an element of risk;
> 4. an operation made in order to develop an economic activity in the host State;
> 5. assets invested in accordance with the laws of the host State; and
> 6. assets invested bona fide.

Another view was provided by the ICSID tribunal in *Saba Fakes v Turkey* (ICSID Case No ARB/07/20, Award of 14 July 2010), which held that the relevant criteria were: (a) that there should be a contribution; (b) that the investment should be for a certain duration; and (c) that there should be an element of risk. In particular, the tribunal considered that it was irrelevant whether there was a contribution to the host State's economy and explained (at para 110) that "this approach reflects an objective definition of 'investment' that embodies specific criteria corresponding to the ordinary meaning of the term 'investment', without doing violence either to the text or the object and purpose of the ICSID Convention".

However, the view that a contribution to the development of the host State's economy is irrelevant can be contrasted with the strong dissent of Judge Shahabuddeen, a member of the Annulment Committee, in *Malaysian Historical Salvors Sdn Bhd v Malaysia* (ICSID Case No ARB/05/10, Decision on Annulment of 16 April 2009, Diss Op Judge Shahabuddeen), who argued forcefully that the economic development of the host State is a necessary condition for there to be an "investment" under the ICSID Convention. This proposition also has substantial academic support (M Sornarajah, "Evolution or Revolution in International Investment Arbitration? The Descent into Normlessness", in C Brown and K Miles (eds), *Evolution in Investment Treaty Law and Arbitration*, Cambridge University Press, Cambridge, 2011, p 631).

[Sch 3 Art 25-13] Dispute must be between "a Contracting State . . . and a national of another Contracting State" The next requirement of Art 25(1) is that the dispute be between "a Contracting State (or any constituent subdivision or agency of a Contracting State designated to the Centre by that State) and a national of another Contracting State". It is easy to identify a Contracting State if the contract which forms the basis of the consent (ie, which contains an ICSID arbitration clause), is with the State itself, or the claim under a BIT, which has an investor-State dispute settlement provision in favour of ICSID. But Art 25 refers to a Contracting State "or any constituent subdivision or agency of a Contracting State designated to the Centre by that State".

The ICSID Secretariat maintains a list of the "constituent subdivisions or agencies" of the ICSID Contracting States that have been designated to ICSID as capable of being a party to ICSID proceedings ("Designations by Contracting States Regarding Constituent Subdivisions or Agencies", ICSID Doc ICSID/8-C). Australia has done this with respect to the various States and Territories (although not, curiously, with respect to Western Australia). Other Contracting States have designated State-owned or State-controlled companies. In some cases, there will be a question of whether the State which is the respondent to the claim is actually responsible, as a matter of international law, for certain conduct. Such issues fall to be determined under the rules of attribution under customary international law (see especially J Crawford, *The International Law Commission's Articles on State Responsibility*, Cambridge University Press, Cambridge, 2002, pp 100–23 (Arts 5–11)).

The other party to the dispute must be "a national of another Contracting State" (ICSID Convention, Art 25(1)). Article 25(2) of the ICSID Convention sets out a detailed definition of the term "national of a Contracting State". In the case of natural persons, the criterion is that the national must hold the nationality of a Contracting State other than the State party to the dispute, on the date on which the parties consented to submit the dispute to arbitration, as well as on the date that the request (either for arbitration or conciliation) is registered. But, importantly, the claimant cannot also be a national of the State party to the dispute (ICSID Convention, Art 25(2)(a)). The Report of the Executive Directors makes this clear (at para 29):

> It should be noted that under clause (a) of Article 25(2) a natural person who was a national of the State party to the dispute would not be eligible to be a party in proceedings under the auspices of [ICSID], even if at the same time he had the nationality of another State. This ineligibility is absolute and cannot be cured even if the State party to the dispute had given its consent.

[Sch 3 Art 25-14] Nationality of legal persons In the case of legal persons, the legal entity must hold the nationality of the Contracting State other than the State party to the dispute on the date of the agreement to go to ICSID arbitration, meaning that for companies, the key is the country of incorporation or country where the company has its "seat", depending on which rule of corporate nationality that country applies (ICSID Convention, Art 25(2)(b); see further C Schreuer et al, *The ICSID Convention: A Commentary*, 2nd ed, Cambridge University Press, Cambridge, 2009, pp 279–83). However, the ICSID Convention recognises the realities of modern investment project structures and that even if the legal person does not have the requisite nationality on the date of consent, ICSID has jurisdiction if, "because of foreign control", that legal person should be treated as a national of another Contracting State (Schreuer et al, pp 296–337). There is no definition in the Convention as to what constitutes sufficient "foreign control", so this is a matter to be determined by tribunals on a case-by-case basis.

[Sch 3 Art 25-15] Consent to ICSID's jurisdiction must be "in writing" The next requirement of Art 25(1) is that consent of the parties to ICSID jurisdiction must be "in writing". This requirement is easily satisfied if there is an ICSID arbitral clause in a contract, or the claim is brought under a domestic investment law, or a bilateral investment treaty. However, there may be conditions attached to the consent. For instance, in *Gruslin v Malaysia* (ICSID Case

No ARB/99/3, Award of 27 November 2000), it was noted (at paras 9.2, 17 and 25.6–25.7) that the applicable BIT (the Belgium/Luxembourg Economic Union–Malaysia BIT) stipulated that the Belgian investment in Malaysia must have received the formal written approval of the relevant Malaysian department (which, on the evidence, it had not obtained) (Art 1(3)).

[Sch 3 Art 25-16] Consent may not be withdrawn The final stipulation in Art 25(1) is that once consent has been given, it may not be unilaterally withdrawn.

[Sch 3 Art 25-17] Consent by constituent subdivision or agency of a State requires approval of that State Under Art 25(3), the consent to ICSID jurisdiction "by a constituent subdivision or agency of a Contracting State shall require the approval of that State unless that State notifies [ICSID] that no such approval is required". The effect of this provision is that in order for a subdivision or agency of a Contracting State to consent to ICSID jurisdiction, it must first have been designated to ICSID by the relevant Contracting State under Art 25(1), and that consent to jurisdiction must also be specifically approved by the Contracting State under Art 25(3). However, it is open to the Contracting State in question to waive the second requirement under Art 25(3) (C Schreuer et al, *The ICSID Convention: A Commentary*, 2nd ed, Cambridge University Press, Cambridge, 2009, pp 338–41).

[Sch 3 Art 25-18] Notifications by States of class or classes of disputes they would or would not consider submitting to ICSID Article 25(4) provides that any Contracting State may "at the time of ratification, acceptance or approval of [the ICSID] Convention or at any time thereafter", notify ICSID of "the class or classes of disputes which it would or would not consider submitting" to the jurisdiction of ICSID. The Report of the Executive Directors explains this provision (at para 31) in the following terms:

> While no conciliation or arbitration proceedings could be brought against a Contracting State without its consent and while no Contracting State is under any obligation to give its consent to such proceedings, it was nevertheless felt that adherence to the Convention might be interpreted as holding out an expectation that Contracting States would give favourable consideration to requests by investors for the submission of a dispute to the Centre. It was pointed out in that connection that there might be classes of investment disputes which governments would consider unsuitable for submission to the Centre or which, under their own law, they were not permitted to submit to the Centre. In order to avoid any risk of misunderstanding on this score, Article 25(4) expressly permits Contracting States to make known to the Centre in advance, if they so desire, the classes of disputes which they would or would not consider submitting to the Centre. The provision makes clear that a statement by a Contracting State that it would consider submitting a certain class of dispute to the Centre would serve for purposes of information only and would not constitute the consent required to give the Centre jurisdiction. Of course, a statement excluding certain classes of disputes from consideration would not constitute a reservation to the Convention.

Various States have made notifications under Art 25(4) (see "Notifications Concerning Classes of Disputes Considered Suitable or Unsuitable for Submission to the Centre", ICSID Doc ICSID/8-D), although these States do not include Australia. For instance, China has stated that it "would only consider submitting to the jurisdiction of the International Centre for Settlement of Investment Disputes disputes over compensation resulting from expropriation and nationalization" (p 1). Saudi Arabia has stated that it "reserves the right of not submitting all questions pertaining to oil and pertaining to acts of sovereignty to the International Centre for the Settlement of Investment Disputes whether by way of conciliation or arbitration" (p 3).

[Sch 3 Art 25-19] **Article 25(4) notifications are not reservations** Based on these notifications, it seems that they may have the effect of narrowing the scope of a State's consent to ICSID jurisdiction. Yet "a notification under Article 25(4) does not amount to a reservation to the Convention", and such notifications "are for purposes of information only and are designed to avoid misunderstandings" (C Schreuer et al, *The ICSID Convention: A Commentary*, 2nd ed, Cambridge University Press, Cambridge, 2009, p 343).

When the issue arose in *PSEG Global Inc v Turkey* (ICSID Case No ARB/02/5, Decision on Jurisdiction of 4 June 2004, para 142), the tribunal essentially agreed with this interpretation, holding that although the notifications might, in theory, be regarded as unilateral acts which are capable of giving rise to legal obligations under international law, this was not the case as the notifications were not "autonomous acts" as they "depend on the [ICSID] Convention"; see also Schreuer et al, p 346. The tribunal concluded (at para 145) that in order for the notification under Art 25(4) to affect the relevant Contracting State's consent to ICSID jurisdiction:

> the contents of a notification will always have to be embodied in the consent that the Contracting Party will later give in its agreements or treaties. If, as in this case, consent was given in the Treaty before the notification, that treaty could have been supplemented by means of a Protocol to include the limitations of the notification into the State's consent. Otherwise the consent given in the Treaty stands unqualified by the notification.

Article 26

Consent of the parties to arbitration under this Convention shall, unless otherwise stated, be deemed consent to such arbitration to the exclusion of any other remedy. A Contracting State may require the exhaustion of local administrative or judicial remedies as a condition of its consent to arbitration under this Convention.

COMMENTARY ON SCH 3 ART 26

"Exclusive remedy" provision .... [Sch 3 Art 26-1]
States may require exhaustion of local remedies .. [Sch 3 Art 26-2]
Purpose of provision .... [Sch 3 Art 26-3]
Article 26 only applies to ICSID arbitration, not conciliation .... [Sch 3 Art 26-4]

[Sch 3 Art 26-1] **"Exclusive remedy" provision** Article 26 is known as the "exclusive remedy" provision. It essentially provides that once the parties to the dispute have given their consent to ICSID arbitration, this shall be understood as meaning that the parties have thereby chosen to exclude any other means of settling the dispute, "unless otherwise stated". In this regard, Art 26 has been referred to as "the clearest expression of the self-contained and autonomous nature of the arbitration procedure provided for by the Convention" (C Schreuer et al, *The ICSID Convention: A Commentary*, 2nd ed, Cambridge University Press, Cambridge, 2009, p 351).

[Sch 3 Art 26-2]   States may require exhaustion of local remedies   The second sentence of Art 26 provides that States parties to the ICSID Convention may require, as a condition of their consent to ICSID arbitration, that the claimant first exhaust local remedies. This may be done in the terms of an investment treaty, in domestic legislation providing for ICSID arbitration, or in an investment contract (C Schreuer et al, *The ICSID Convention: A Commentary*, 2nd ed, Cambridge University Press, Cambridge, 2009, pp 404–13).

[Sch 3 Art 26-3]   Purpose of provision   The purpose of the rule is "to provide an effective forum and to dispense with other proceedings which for a variety of reasons appear unattractive to the parties". Investors, for instance, are typically reluctant to commence litigation before the domestic courts of the host State of their investment, and host States will only rarely agree to the jurisdiction of foreign courts. The doctrine of State immunity can also create problems before domestic courts. These issues mean that Art 26 "meets a number of needs of the host States and of the foreign investors" (C Schreuer et al, *The ICSID Convention: A Commentary*, 2nd ed, Cambridge University Press, Cambridge, 2009, p 352).

The Executive Directors of the World Bank explain the provision (at para 32, Report of the Executive Directors) as follows:

> It may be presumed that when a State and an investor agree to have recourse to arbitration, and do not reserve the right to have recourse to other remedies or require the prior exhaustion of other remedies, the intention of the parties is to have recourse to arbitration to the exclusion of any other remedy. This rule of interpretation is embodied in the first sentence of Article 26. In order to make clear that it was not intended thereby to modify the rules of international law regarding the exhaustion of local remedies, the second sentence explicitly recognizes the right of a State to require the prior exhaustion of local remedies.

[Sch 3 Art 26-4]   Article 26 only applies to ICSID arbitration, not conciliation   It is noteworthy that Art 26 applies only to arbitration under the ICSID Convention, and not to conciliation.

Article 27

(1) No Contracting State shall give diplomatic protection, or bring an international claim, in respect of a dispute which one of its nationals and another Contracting State shall have consented to submit or shall have submitted to arbitration under this Convention, unless such other Contracting State shall have failed to abide by and comply with the award rendered in such dispute.

(2) Diplomatic protection, for the purposes of paragraph (1), shall not include informal diplomatic exchanges for the sole purpose of facilitating a settlement of the dispute.

COMMENTARY ON SCH 3 ART 27

No diplomatic protection where dispute has been submitted to ICSID arbitration .... [Sch 3 Art 27-1]
Tribunals have upheld exclusion of diplomatic protection .... [Sch 3 Art 27-2]
Informal diplomatic exchanges not excluded ..... [Sch 3 Art 27-3]

[Sch 3 Art 27-1] No diplomatic protection where dispute has been submitted to ICSID arbitration The ICSID Convention provides a framework for natural and legal persons to commence proceedings (in arbitration or conciliation) directly against the host State of their investment, provided that the jurisdictional requirements of Art 25 are met, including that of consent. Without that consent, if an investor considers that some wrong has been done to it by the host State of its investment for which it wants some redress, the investor would have to challenge the host State with action before the local courts; and if the investor did not obtain an appropriate remedy before those courts, it would then have to fall back on the rules provided by the law of diplomatic protection (on the rules relating to such claims, see, eg, I Brownlie, *Principles of Public International Law*, 7th ed, Oxford University Press, Oxford, 2008, pp 475–505; C Schreuer et al, *The ICSID Convention: A Commentary*, 2nd ed, Cambridge University Press, Cambridge, 2009, pp 415–7). Under the law of diplomatic protection, a State espouses the claim of one of its nationals against another State, and presents that claim in its own name. The national's home State would present the claim (either by way of communication through the diplomatic channels, or by formal submission of a claim to an international court, such as the International Court of Justice) because an individual has, generally speaking, no right to present a claim at the international level against a State; only States have been traditionally been regarded as possessing "international legal personality" (eg, Brownlie, pp 57–67).

Because the ICSID Convention makes provision for individuals to bring a claim directly, in their own name, against the host State of their investment, there is no need for States to give diplomatic protection to its nationals. As the Executive Directors noted in their Report (at para 33):

> When a host State consents to the submission of a dispute with an investor to the Centre, thereby giving the investor direct access to an international jurisdiction, the investor should not be in a position to ask his State to espouse his case and that State should not be permitted to do so. Accordingly, Article 27 expressly prohibits a Contracting State from giving diplomatic protection, or bringing an international claim, in respect of a dispute which one of its nationals and another Contracting State have consented to submit, or have submitted, to arbitration under the Convention, unless the State party to the dispute fails to honor the award rendered in that dispute.

[Sch 3 Art 27-2] Tribunals have upheld exclusion of diplomatic protection In *Banro American Resources, Inc v Democratic Republic of the Congo* (ICSID Case No ARB/98/7, Award of 1 September 2000), the US claimant commenced ICSID arbitration against the host State of its investment, and at the same time, the Government of Canada provided diplomatic protection to the Canadian company in the Banro group, Banro Resources, Inc. The ICSID tribunal held that it was not open to the Banro group to pursue diplomatic protection while at the same time commencing ICSID proceedings (C Schreuer et al, *The ICSID Convention: A Commentary*, 2nd ed, Cambridge University Press, Cambridge, 2009, pp 418–9). As the tribunal explained (at para 21):

> The exclusion of diplomatic protection is, we note, inherent in the system, of which it constitutes an essential element, and we thus understand that it precludes derogation by the parties. By consenting to ICSID arbitration, the host State knows that it will be protected from diplomatic intervention on the part of the State of which the investor is a national. Conversely, the State of which the investor is a national, by becoming a party to the ICSID Convention, knows that an investor who is a national and has consented to ICSID arbitration at the time of the investment in another Contracting State cannot seek assistance, and if such a request is made, it cannot grant it. Any method of combining diplomatic protection with ICSID arbitration is precluded. This principle is rigorously imposed by the logic of the system. Not only would the arbitration process run the risk of being hampered by current diplomatic *démarches*, but this would go against the essence of the ICSID system by leaving the host State open to arbitration proceedings initiated by a foreign investor and diplomatic pressure by the State of which this investor is a national.

[Sch 3 Art 27-3] Informal diplomatic exchanges not excluded However, Art 27(2) stipulates that diplomatic protection is not to be understood as including "informal diplomatic exchanges for the sole purpose of facilitating a settlement of the dispute". (For instances of where this has occurred, see C Schreuer et al, *The ICSID Convention: A Commentary*, 2nd ed, Cambridge University Press, Cambridge, 2009, pp 427–30.)

CHAPTER III
Conciliation
SECTION 1
Request for Conciliation

Article 28

(1) Any Contracting State or any national of a Contracting State wishing to institute conciliation proceedings shall address a request to that effect in writing to the Secretary-General who shall send a copy of the request to the other party.

(2) The request shall contain information concerning the issues in dispute, the identity of the parties and their consent to conciliation in accordance with the rules of procedure for the institution of conciliation and arbitration proceedings.

(3) The Secretary-General shall register the request unless he finds, on the basis of the information contained in the request, that the dispute is manifestly outside the jurisdiction of the Centre. He shall forthwith notify the parties of registration or refusal to register.

COMMENTARY ON SCH 3 ART 28

Procedure for commencement of conciliation proceedings .... [Sch 3 Art 28-1]
ICSID Conciliation not frequently utilised .... [Sch 3 Art 28-2]

[Sch 3 Art 28-1] Procedure for commencement of conciliation proceedings Article 28 provides for the procedure by which a Contracting

State to the ICSID Convention, or a national of a Contracting State, can initiate conciliation proceedings. It is in substance identical to Art 36, which sets out the procedure for the commencement of arbitration proceedings, but for the substitution of the word "conciliation" as appropriate. Article 28(2) sets out what information the request for conciliation should contain and further detail is provided in the ICSID Institution Rules. Under Art 28(3), the ICSID Secretary-General shall register the request for conciliation unless he or she finds, on the basis of the information contained in the request, that the dispute is "manifestly outside the jurisdiction of [ICSID]" (C Schreuer et al, *The ICSID Convention: A Commentary*, 2nd ed, Cambridge University Press, Cambridge, 2009, pp 431–2).

[Sch 3 Art 28-2] ICSID Conciliation not frequently utilised There have been relatively few conciliations under the ICSID Convention, with only seven requests for conciliation having been registered at the time of writing — *SEDITEX v Madagascar (No 1)* (ICSID Case No CONC/82/1); *Tesoro v Trinidad and Tobago* (ICSID Case No CONC/83/1); *SEDITEX v Madagascar (No 2)* (ICSID Case No CONC/94/1); *TG World Petroleum Ltd v Niger* (ICSID Case No CONC/03/1); *Togo Eléctricité v Togo* (ICSID Case No CONC/05/1); *SESAM v Central African Republic* (ICSID Case No CONC/07/1); and *RSM Production Corp v Cameroon* (ICSID Case No CONC/11/1).

SECTION 2

Constitution of the Conciliation Commission

Article 29

(1) The Conciliation Commission (hereinafter called the Commission) shall be constituted as soon as possible after registration of a request pursuant to Article 28.

(2) (a) The Commission shall consist of a sole conciliator or any uneven number of conciliators appointed as the parties shall agree.
    (b) Where the parties do not agree upon the number of conciliators and the method of their appointment, the Commission shall consist of three conciliators, one conciliator appointed by each party and the third, who shall be the president of the Commission, appointed by agreement of the parties.

COMMENTARY ON SCH 3 ART 29
Procedure for constitution of Conciliation
Commission .... [Sch 3 Art 29-1]

[Sch 3 Art 29-1] Procedure for constitution of Conciliation Commission Article 29 sets out the procedure for the constitution of the conciliation commission (the Commission), and like Art 28, it is essentially identical to its counterpart provision which deals with the constitution of arbitral tribunals (Art 37).

The Commission is to be established as soon as possible after the registration of a request for conciliation pursuant to Art 28(3). The Commission may consist of a sole conciliator, or any uneven number of conciliators, as the parties to the dispute may agree. In the event that the parties do not reach agreement on the number of conciliators, there shall be three conciliators; one appointed by each party, and the third conciliator to be appointed by agreement of the parties. Further details on the establishment of the Commission are provided in the ICSID Conciliation Rules (see also C Schreuer et al, *The ICSID Convention: A Commentary*, 2nd ed, Cambridge University Press, Cambridge, 2009, pp 433–4).

Article 30

If the Commission shall not have been constituted within 90 days after notice of registration of the request has been dispatched by the Secretary-General in accordance with paragraph (3) of Article 28, or such other period as the parties may agree, the Chairman shall, at the request of either party and after consulting both parties as far as possible, appoint the conciliator or conciliators not yet appointed.

COMMENTARY ON SCH 3 ART 30
Procedure for failure to constitute the Conciliation
Commission .... [Sch 3 Art 30-1]

[Sch 3 Art 30-1] Procedure for failure to constitute the Conciliation Commission Article 30 provides for a mechanism to break the deadlock in case one of the parties fails to appoint its conciliator, or if the parties fail to agree on the appointment of the presiding conciliator, pursuant to Art 29. The mechanism is for the Chairman of the ICSID Administrative Council to make the appointment(s). There are no nationality-based restrictions on the Chairman's power to make any such appointments (C Schreuer et al, *The ICSID Convention: A Commentary*, 2nd ed, Cambridge University Press, Cambridge, 2009, pp 436–7).

Article 31

(1) Conciliators may be appointed from outside the Panel of Conciliators, except in the case of appointments by the Chairman pursuant to Article 30.

(2) Conciliators appointed from outside the Panel of Conciliators shall possess the qualities stated in paragraph (1) of Article 14.

COMMENTARY ON SCH 3 ART 31
Conciliators need not be member of Panel of
Conciliators .... [Sch 3 Art 31-1]

[Sch 3 Art 31-1] Conciliators need not be member of Panel of Conciliators Under Art 31, there is no need for conciliators to be drawn from the Panel of Conciliators maintained by ICSID pursuant to Arts 12–16, unless the appointment is being made by the Chairman of the ICSID Administrative Council under Art 30. In all cases, conciliators must possess the qualities set forth in Art 14, namely that they be of "high moral character", and possess "recognised competence in the fields of law, commerce, industry or finance", and who may be relied upon to exercise "independent judgment" (C Schreuer et al, *The ICSID Convention: A Commentary*, 2nd ed, Cambridge University Press, Cambridge, 2009, pp 48–51, 438).

SECTION 3
Conciliation Proceedings

Article 32

(1) The Commission shall be the judge of its own competence.

(2) Any objection by a party to the dispute that that dispute is not within the jurisdiction of the Centre, or for other reasons is not within the competence of the Commission, shall be considered by the Commission which shall determine whether to deal with it as a preliminary question or to join it to the merits of the dispute.

COMMENTARY ON SCH 3 ART 32
Jurisdiction of Conciliation Commission .... [Sch 3 Art 32-1]

[Sch 3 Art 32-1] Jurisdiction of Conciliation Commission Article 32(1) states the generally accepted rule that the Commission established under the ICSID Convention has the power to determine the extent of its own jurisdiction. This is widely accepted as an inherent power of international courts and tribunals (see, eg, C Brown, "The Inherent Powers of International Courts and Tribunals" (2005) 76 *British Yearbook of International Law* 195). Under Art 32(2), if there is an objection to the Commission's jurisdiction, the Commission shall decide whether to consider it as a preliminary question, or whether the objection should be joined to the merits phase.

Further details on the Commission's power to determine its jurisdiction are set out in the ICSID Conciliation Rules (ICSID Conciliation Rules, r 29; see also C Schreuer et al, *The ICSID Convention: A Commentary*, 2nd ed, Cambridge University Press, Cambridge, 2009, pp 439–40).

Article 33

Any conciliation proceeding shall be conducted in accordance with the provisions of this Section and, except as the parties otherwise agree, in accordance with the Conciliation Rules in effect on the date on which the parties consented to conciliation. If any question of procedure arises which is not covered by this Section or the Conciliation Rules or any rules agreed by the parties, the Commission shall decide the question.

COMMENTARY ON SCH 3 ART 33
Procedure in ICSID Convention to apply .... [Sch 3 Art 33-1]

[Sch 3 Art 33-1] Procedure in ICSID Convention to apply Article 33 provides that the conciliation shall be carried out under the procedures contained in Arts 32–35 of the ICSID Convention, and, subject to the agreement of the parties to the dispute, in accordance with the ICSID Conciliation Rules. It also leaves a residual power to the Commission to decide any questions of procedure that are not covered by the ICSID Convention or the ICSID Conciliation Rules (see also C Schreuer et al, *The ICSID Convention: A Commentary*, 2nd ed, Cambridge University Press, Cambridge, 2009, pp 441–2).

Article 34

(1) It shall be the duty of the Commission to clarify the issues in dispute between the parties and to endeavour to bring about agreement between them upon mutually acceptable terms. To that end, the Commission may at any stage of the proceedings and from time to time recommend terms of settlement to the parties. The parties shall cooperate in good faith with the Commission in order to enable the Commission to carry out its functions, and shall give their most serious consideration to its recommendations.

(2) If the parties reach agreement, the Commission shall draw up a report noting the issues in dispute and recording that the parties have reached agreement. If, at any stage of the proceedings, it appears to the Commission that there is no likelihood of agreement between the parties, it shall close the proceedings and shall draw up a report noting the submission of the dispute and recording the failure of the parties to reach agreement. If one party fails to appear or participate in the proceedings, the Commission shall close the proceedings and shall draw up a report noting that partyîs failure to appear or participate.

COMMENTARY ON SCH 3 ART 34

Function of Conciliation Commission .... [Sch 3 Art 34-1]
Nature of conciliation .... [Sch 3 Art 34-2]
Conciliation Commission to produce report if dispute is not settled .... [Sch 3 Art 34-3]

[Sch 3 Art 34-1] Function of Conciliation Commission Article 34 is the central provision which deals with conciliation under the ICSID Convention.

[Sch 3 Art 34-2] Nature of conciliation As is well known, conciliation differs from arbitration in that it does not result in a binding decision for the parties, but rather aims to produce a recommendation that may be adopted by the parties as the terms of an agreed settlement. This is clear from Art 34(1), which states that the Commission has a "duty" to "clarify the issues in dispute between the parties", and to "endeavour to bring about agreement between them on mutually acceptable terms". The Commission may, at any stage of the proceedings, "recommend terms of settlement to the parties", to which they are to give "their most serious consideration". (On the functioning of the Commission, see C Schreuer et al, *The ICSID Convention: A Commentary*, 2nd ed, Cambridge University Press, Cambridge, 2009, pp 443–52; and see especially the view of Lord Wilberforce, the sole conciliator in *Tesoro v Trinidad and Tobago* (ICSID Case No CONC/83/1), as extracted in Schreuer et al, p 446).

[Sch 3 Art 34-3] Conciliation Commission to produce report if dispute is not settled If the parties succeed in settling the dispute, the Commission's work is not done, for under Art 34(2) it is to "draw up a report noting the issues in dispute and recording that the parties have reached agreement". However, the report should not publish the parties' terms of settlement, which may remain confidential; under the ICSID Conciliation Rules, the report shall only record the terms of settlement if this is requested by both parties (ICSID Conciliation Rules, r 31, note C). Article 34(2) also guides the Commission on how it is to proceed in the event that no settlement is reached, or if one of the parties fails to appear or participate in the proceedings. Should this occur, the Commission is to prepare a report noting the failure of the parties to settle the dispute, or the non-appearance of one of the parties, as the case may be.

Article 35

Except as the parties to the dispute shall otherwise agree, neither party to a conciliation proceeding shall be entitled in any other proceeding, whether before arbitrators or in a court of law or otherwise, to invoke or rely on any views expressed or statements or admissions or offers of settlement made by the other party in the conciliation proceedings, or the report or any recommendations made by the Commission.

COMMENTARY ON SCH 3 ART 35

Conciliation proceedings to be on "without prejudice" basis .... [Sch 3 Art 35-1]

[Sch 3 Art 35-1] Conciliation proceedings to be on "without prejudice" basis Article 35 states that, unless the parties agree otherwise, parties to conciliation proceedings are not entitled to invoke or rely on any statements made in the course of the conciliation before an arbitral tribunal or court. The purpose of this provision is to ensure that parties to conciliation proceedings can discuss their dispute candidly and flexibly, without the fear that any position adopted, or offer of settlement proposed, by them in the conciliation might later be used against them in subsequent proceedings, should the conciliation fail to result in an agreed settlement of the dispute (C Schreuer et al, *The ICSID Convention: A Commentary*, 2nd ed, Cambridge University Press, Cambridge, 2009, pp 453–4).

CHAPTER IV

Arbitration

SECTION 1

Request for Arbitration

Article 36

(1) Any Contracting State or any national of a Contracting State wishing to institute arbitration proceedings shall address a request to that effect in writing to the Secretary-General who shall send a copy of the request to the other party.

(2) The request shall contain information concerning the issues in dispute, the identity of the parties and their consent to arbitration in accordance with the rules of procedure for the institution of conciliation and arbitration proceedings.

(3) The Secretary-General shall register the request unless he finds, on the basis of the information contained in the request, that the dispute is manifestly outside the jurisdiction of the Centre. He shall forthwith notify the parties of registration or refusal to register.

COMMENTARY ON SCH 3 ART 36

Procedure for commencement of arbitration proceedings	[Sch 3 Art 36-1]
Either host State or investor can commence arbitration	[Sch 3 Art 36-2]
Information to be included in request for arbitration	[Sch 3 Art 36-3]
"Screening power" of ICSID Secretary-General ..	[Sch 3 Art 36-4]
Decision of Secretary-General is final	[Sch 3 Art 36-5]
Effect of registration by Secretary-General	[Sch 3 Art 36-6]

[Sch 3 Art 36-1] Procedure for commencement of arbitration proceedings Article 36 sets out the way in which any claimant in international arbitration proceedings under the ICSID Convention is to institute such proceedings, namely by way of a "request for arbitration". The counterpart of Art 36 in the context of ICSID conciliation proceedings is Art 28 of the ICSID Convention.

More detailed guidance on the applicable procedures in the early stages of ICSID arbitration proceedings are provided in the ICSID Rules of Procedure for the Institution of Conciliation and Arbitration Proceedings, which deal with the time period between the filing of the request for arbitration to the dispatch of the notice from the ICSID Secretariat to the parties confirming that the request for arbitration has been registered (C Schreuer et al, *The ICSID Convention: A Commentary*, 2nd ed, Cambridge University Press, Cambridge, 2009, p 456).

[Sch 3 Art 36-2] Either host State or investor can commence arbitration Under Art 36(1), either the host State or the investor can initiate the arbitration proceedings, although in practice it is almost always the investor which is the claimant in such proceedings (C Schreuer et al, *The ICSID Convention: A Commentary*, 2nd ed, Cambridge University Press, Cambridge, 2009, p 456). Details on the form of the request are contained in r 1 of the ICSID Rules of Procedure for the Institution of Conciliation and Arbitration Proceedings. Under r 1, the request for arbitration "shall be drawn up in an official language of [ICSID], shall be dated, and shall be signed by the requesting party or its duly authorised representative". Under r 4, the request for arbitration has to be accompanied by five additional signed copies. The claimant must also pay a non-refundable lodging fee of US$25,000 in accordance with reg 16 of the ICSID Administrative and Financial Regulations and the ICSID Schedule of Fees.

[Sch 3 Art 36-3] Information to be included in request for arbitration Article 36(2) states what information the claimant should include in the request for arbitration, which is namely "information concerning the issues in dispute, the identity of the parties and their consent to arbitration in accordance with the rules of procedure for the institution of conciliation and arbitration proceedings". Further guidance can be found in rr 2 and 3 of the ICSID Rules of Procedure on the Institution of Conciliation and Arbitration Proceedings.

[Sch 3 Art 36-4] "Screening power" of ICSID Secretary-General Importantly, Art 36(3) provides that the ICSID Secretary-General shall register the request "unless he finds, on the basis of the information contained in the request, that the dispute is manifestly outside the jurisdiction of [ICSID]". This is typically referred to as the "screening power" of the Secretary-General. Schreuer and his co-authors explain the reason for this power (C Schreuer et al, *The ICSID Convention: A Commentary*, 2nd ed, Cambridge University Press, Cambridge, 2009, p 468) as follows:

> The constitution of a tribunal involves time, effort and expense. The Secretary-General's screening power is designed to avoid a situation where a tribunal, once established, would almost certainly find itself without competence. In addition, the procedure should not be set in motion merely to pressure or embarrass a party, especially a host State, if it had not given its consent to jurisdiction.

[Sch 3 Art 36-5] Decision of Secretary-General is final A decision by the Secretary-General to register, or not to register, a request for arbitration is final and is not subject to any form of review (C Schreuer et al, *The ICSID Convention: A Commentary*, 2nd ed, Cambridge University Press, Cambridge, 2009, pp 471–2). However, it does not bind the arbitral tribunal, which has the power to find that the claim is outside its jurisdiction or that of ICSID in accordance with Art 41 of the ICSID Convention. The Secretary-General is required to notify the parties of the decision on registration by issuing a notice of registration in accordance with rr 6 and 7 of the ICSID Rules of Procedure for the Institution of Conciliation and Arbitration Proceedings.

[Sch 3 Art 36-6] Effect of registration by Secretary-General If the Secretary-General registers the request for arbitration, the request is entered into the Arbitration Register maintained in accordance with reg 23 of the ICSID Administrative and Financial Regulations (C Schreuer et al, *The ICSID Convention: A Commentary*, 2nd ed, Cambridge University Press, Cambridge, 2009, p 472).

SECTION 2
Constitution of the Tribunal

Article 37

(1) The Arbitral Tribunal (hereinafter called the Tribunal) shall be constituted as soon as possible after registration of a request pursuant to Article 36.

(2) (a) The Tribunal shall consist of a sole arbitrator or any uneven number of arbitrators appointed as the parties shall agree.

    (b) Where the parties do not agree upon the number of arbitrators and the method of their appointment, the Tribunal shall consist of three arbitrators, one arbitrator appointed by each party and the third, who shall be the president of the Tribunal, appointed by agreement of the parties.

COMMENTARY ON SCH 3 ART 37

Procedure for constitution of ICSID arbitral
  tribunals .... [Sch 3 Art 37-1]
Parties free to agree on appointment of arbitrators . [Sch 3 Art 37-2]
Appointment procedure if no agreement .... [Sch 3 Art 37-3]

[Sch 3 Art 37-1] Procedure for constitution of ICSID arbitral tribunals Article 37 provides for the constitution of the arbitral tribunal. Article 37(1) requires that the tribunal be constituted "as soon as possible" once the request for arbitration has been registered under Art 36. The ICSID Arbitration Rules restate this, providing in r 1 that "[u]pon notification of the registration of the request for arbitration, the parties shall, with all possible dispatch, proceed to constitute a Tribunal, with due regard to Section 2 of Chapter IV of the Convention".

[Sch 3 Art 37-2] Parties free to agree on appointment of arbitrators Article 37(2)(a) indicates that the parties are free to agree on the number of arbitrators and on the method of their appointment, provided that there be an uneven number of arbitrators (C Schreuer et al, *The ICSID Convention: A Commentary*, 2nd ed, Cambridge University Press, Cambridge, 2009, pp 477–85). This agreement may be a prior or an ad hoc agreement. Rule 2 of the ICSID Arbitration Rules sets out the procedure which should be followed for an ad hoc agreement on the number and method of appointment of the arbitrators. If no agreement is reached between the parties within 60 days from the date of registration of the request for arbitration, either party may inform the Secretary-General that it chooses the default method of constituting the tribunal, which is set out in Art 37(2)(b).

[Sch 3 Art 37-3] Appointment procedure if no agreement Where the parties have not reached an agreement on the number of arbitrators and the method of their appointment, Art 37(2)(b) states that the tribunal "shall consist of three arbitrators, one arbitrator appointed by each party and the third, who shall be president of the Tribunal, appointed by agreement of the parties". Rule 3 of the ICSID Arbitration Rules gives further guidance on this process (see also C Schreuer et al, *The ICSID Convention: A Commentary*, 2nd ed, Cambridge University Press, Cambridge, 2009, pp 486–8). In particular, r 3(1)(a) provides that the party-appointed arbitrators "shall not have the same nationality as or be a national of either party".

Article 38

If the Tribunal shall not have been constituted within 90 days after notice of registration of the request has been dispatched by the Secretary-General in accordance with paragraph (3) of Article 36, or such other period as the parties may agree, the Chairman shall, at the request of either party and after consulting both parties as far as possible, appoint the arbitrator or arbitrators not yet appointed. Arbitrators appointed by the Chairman pursuant to this Article shall not be nationals of the Contracting State party to the dispute or of the Contracting State whose national is a party to the dispute.

COMMENTARY ON SCH 3 ART 38

Default procedure for establishing arbitral tribunal	[Sch 3 Art 38-1]
Commencement of 90-day time limit	[Sch 3 Art 38-2]
Power may only be exercised at request of a party	[Sch 3 Art 38-3]
Chairman of ICSID Administrative Council is obliged to make appointments	[Sch 3 Art 38-4]
Nationality restriction on appointments by Chairman	[Sch 3 Art 38-5]

[Sch 3 Art 38-1] Default procedure for establishing arbitral tribunal Article 38 contains the default method of establishing the tribunal where it has not been constituted within 90 days of the registration of the request for arbitration by the ICSID Secretary-General. Article 38 is "the most important Article designed to safeguard the principle of non-frustration in the constitution of the tribunal", as it provides the parties with "a fallback procedure that may be initiated by either party". This deadlock-breaking provision is similar in content to other default provisions in the rules of arbitration of other arbitral institutions (C Schreuer et al, *The ICSID Convention: A Commentary*, 2nd ed, Cambridge University Press, Cambridge, 2009, pp 490–1).

[Sch 3 Art 38-2] Commencement of 90-day time limit The time limit of 90 days starts on the day the Secretary-General informs the parties of the registration of the request for arbitration. The parties may agree to extend the time period (or reduce it, although this is unlikely to occur in practice). As a practical matter, it can be difficult for parties to constitute the tribunal within 90 days, and so they may agree to extend the period in order to reach agreement on a President of the Tribunal (C Schreuer et al, *The ICSID Convention: A Commentary*, 2nd ed, Cambridge University Press, Cambridge, 2009, p 492).

[Sch 3 Art 38-3] Power may only be exercised at request of a party It is clear that the Chairman of the Administrative Council may only exercise his or her powers under Art 38 "at the request of [a] party", implying that this power may not be exercised *proprio motu*. Further, if asked to exercise his or her powers, the Chairman is required to consult "both parties as far as possible". The purpose of the consultation process is "to avoid appointments that are objectionable to one or both of the parties", even though the Chairman is, in theory, "free to disregard objections made by the parties" (C Schreuer et al, *The ICSID Convention: A Commentary*, 2nd ed, Cambridge University Press, Cambridge, 2009, p 493). Further guidance on the procedure to be followed is contained in r 4 of the ICSID Arbitration Rules.

[Sch 3 Art 38-4] Chairman of ICSID Administrative Council is obliged to make appointments Where a request is made under Art 38, the Chairman has an obligation, rather than a discretion, to make the relevant appointment(s) (C Schreuer et al, *The ICSID Convention: A Commentary*, 2nd ed, Cambridge University Press, Cambridge, 2009, pp 494–6). Under r 4 of the ICSID Arbitration Rules, "the Chairman shall use his best efforts to comply with that request within 30 days after its receipt".

[Sch 3 Art 38-5] Nationality restriction on appointments by Chairman Finally, any appointments made by the Chairman "shall not be nationals of the Contracting State party to the dispute or of the Contracting State whose national is a party to the dispute" (ICSID Convention, Art 38). However, this limitation only applies where the appointment is made "pursuant to this Article"; it does not apply, for instance, "where the Chairman is acting as appointing authority under an agreement between the parties" (C Schreuer et al, *The ICSID Convention: A Commentary*, 2nd ed, Cambridge University Press, Cambridge, 2009, p 496).

Article 39

The majority of the arbitrators shall be nationals of States other than the Contracting State party to the dispute and the Contracting State whose national is a party to the dispute; provided, however, that the foregoing provisions of this Article shall not apply if the sole arbitrator or each individual member of the Tribunal has been appointed by agreement of the parties.

COMMENTARY ON SCH 3 ART 39

Restriction on nationality of arbitrators .... [Sch 3 Art 39-1]
Restriction only applies in arbitration proceedings . [Sch 3 Art 39-2]
Consequences of non-compliance .... [Sch 3 Art 39-3]
Restriction does not apply if tribunal appointed by
   agreement of parties .... [Sch 3 Art 39-4]

[Sch 3 Art 39-1] Restriction on nationality of arbitrators Article 39 generally contains a restriction on the nationality of the arbitrators. The purpose of the provision is to "avoid a situation in which the third arbitrator, as the only one appointed by a neutral party, might find himself in the position of a sole arbitrator in having to maintain a balance between the two other arbitrators who were more inclined to act as advocates for the parties appointing them" (A Broches, "Convention on the Settlement of Investment Disputes between States and Nationals of other States of 1965: Explanatory Notes and Survey of its Application" (1993) 18 *Yearbook Commercial Arbitration* 627 at 662, cited in C Schreuer et al, *The ICSID Convention: A Commentary*, 2nd ed, Cambridge University Press, Cambridge, 2009, p 499).

Rule 1(3) of the ICSID Arbitration Rules gives further guidance on the application of Art 39. In particular, the provisions of r 1(3) prevent a situation arising in which one party appoints an arbitrator who has the same nationality as the appointing party, thereby leaving the respondent party to appoint an arbitrator of a different nationality, and also requiring the President of the Tribunal to be of a different nationality. It provides in part that "[w]here the Tribunal is to consist of three members, a national of either of these States may not be appointed as an arbitrator by a party without the agreement of the other party to the dispute. Where the Tribunal is to consist of five or more members, nationals of either of these States may not be appointed as arbitrators by a party if appointment by the other party of the same number of arbitrators of either of these nationalities would result in a majority of arbitrators of these nationalities" (it should be noted, however, that r 1(3) can be displaced by the agreement of the parties: ICSID Convention, Art 44).

[Sch 3 Art 39-2] Restriction only applies in arbitration proceedings Article 39 does not have a parallel provision which applies in the context of ICSID conciliation proceedings. As the Executive Directors explain (Report of the Executive Directors, para 39):

> While the Convention does not restrict the appointment of conciliators with reference to nationality, Article 39 lays down the rule that the majority of the members of an Arbitral Tribunal should not be nationals either of the State party to the dispute or of the State whose national is a party to the dispute. This rule is likely to have the effect of excluding persons having these nationalities from serving on a Tribunal composed of not more than three members. However, the rule will not apply where each and every arbitrator on the Tribunal has been appointed by agreement of the members.

[Sch 3 Art 39-3] Consequences of non-compliance If the tribunal is not constituted in accordance with the nationality requirements of Art 39, a number of consequences may follow, including the possible challenge of an arbitrator under Art 57, or an application for annulment under Art 52(1)(a) on the grounds that the tribunal was not properly constituted (C Schreuer et al, *The ICSID Convention: A Commentary*, 2nd ed, Cambridge University Press, Cambridge, 2009, p 500).

[Sch 3 Art 39-4] Restriction does not apply if tribunal appointed by agreement of parties Clearly, the restriction on nationality does not apply if the tribunal "has been appointed by agreement of the parties". So, for instance, in *IBM Word Trade Corp v Ecuador* (ICSID Case No ARB/02/10, Decision on Jurisdiction of 22 December 2003), the parties agreed on the appointment of three arbitrators, all of whom had Ecuadorian nationality (at para 4, noted in C Schreuer et al, *The ICSID Convention: A Commentary*, 2nd ed, Cambridge University Press, Cambridge, 2009, p 506.)

Article 40

(1) Arbitrators may be appointed from outside the Panel of Arbitrators, except in the case of appointments by the Chairman pursuant to Article 38.

(2) Arbitrators appointed from outside the Panel of Arbitrators shall possess the qualities stated in paragraph (1) of Article 14.

COMMENTARY ON SCH 3 ART 40

Party-appointed arbitrators need not be on ICSID
   Panel of Arbitrators .... [Sch 3 Art 40-1]
Qualities required of arbitrators .... [Sch 3 Art 40-2]

[Sch 3 Art 40-1] Party-appointed arbitrators need not be on ICSID Panel of Arbitrators Article 40 provides that parties may appoint arbitrators from outside the Panel of Arbitrators maintained by ICSID, but the Chairman of the ICSID Administrative Council is only permitted to appoint arbitrators from the Panel of Arbitrators, when called upon to make such appointments under Art 38. As the Executive Directors explain in their Report (at para 21):

> In keeping with the essentially flexible character of the proceedings, the Convention permits the parties to appoint conciliators and arbitrators from outside the Panels but requires (Articles 31(2) and 40(2)) that such appointees possess the qualities stated in

Article 14(1). The Chairman, when called upon to appoint a conciliator or arbitrator pursuant to Article 30 or 38, is restricted in his choice to Panel members.

[Sch 3 Art 40-2] Qualities required of arbitrators As has been noted above, the qualities stated in Art 14(1) are high moral character, recognised competence in the fields of law, commerce, industry or finance, and reliability to exercise independent judgment. Under Art 40(2), arbitrators appointed from outside the ICSID Panel of Arbitrators are also required to have these qualities (see further C Schreuer et al, *The ICSID Convention: A Commentary*, 2nd ed, Cambridge University Press, Cambridge, 2009, pp 507–15).

SECTION 3
Powers and Functions of the Tribunal

Article 41

(1) The Tribunal shall be the judge of its own competence.

(2) Any objection by a party to the dispute that that dispute is not within the jurisdiction of the Centre, or for other reasons is not within the competence of the Tribunal, shall be considered by the Tribunal which shall determine whether to deal with it as a preliminary question or to join it to the merits of the dispute.

COMMENTARY ON SCH 3 ART 41

Compétence de la compétence	[Sch 3 Art 41-1]
Power corresponds to that of conciliation commissions	[Sch 3 Art 41-2]
Purpose of power	[Sch 3 Art 41-3]
Power of arbitral tribunals to determine own jurisdiction is exclusive	[Sch 3 Art 41-4]
Objections to jurisdiction	[Sch 3 Art 41-5]
Tribunal can raise issues of jurisdiction of own motion	[Sch 3 Art 41-6]
Jurisdiction and admissibility	[Sch 3 Art 41-7]
Effect of jurisdictional objection being made	[Sch 3 Art 41-8]
Tribunal may consider jurisdictional objection separately or join it to merits of dispute	[Sch 3 Art 41-9]
Procedure for summary dismissal	[Sch 3 Art 41-10]

[Sch 3 Art 41-1] *Compétence de la compétence* Article 41 confirms the general principle of international adjudication that a judicial body has the power to determine the extent of its jurisdiction. The statutes of a range of other international courts and tribunals contain similar provisions (see, eg, Statute of the International Court of Justice, Art 36(6)), and this power also exists as an inherent power, as has been confirmed in arbitral and international judicial practice (see, eg, C Schreuer et al, *The ICSID Convention: A Commentary*, 2nd ed, Cambridge University Press, Cambridge, 2009, p 517; C Brown, "The Inherent Powers of International Courts and Tribunals" (2005) 76 *British Yearbook of International Law*

195; I Shihata, *The Power of the International Court to Determine its own Jurisdiction: Compétence de la Compétence*, Nijhoff, The Hague, 1965).

[Sch 3 Art 41-2] Power corresponds to that of conciliation commissions Article 41 is, in substance, identical to Art 32, which provides for an equivalent power for conciliation commissions. And under Art 52(4), Art 41 also applies to ad hoc committees (C Schreuer et al, *The ICSID Convention: A Commentary*, 2nd ed, Cambridge University Press, Cambridge, 2009, p 518).

[Sch 3 Art 41-3] Purpose of power The purpose of Art 41 is "to prevent a frustration of the arbitration proceedings through a unilateral denial of the tribunal's competence by one of the parties ... This power of the tribunal to determine its own competence has never been challenged seriously in ICSID proceedings" (C Schreuer et al, *The ICSID Convention: A Commentary*, 2nd ed, Cambridge University Press, Cambridge, 2009, p 518). As the tribunal found in *Inceysa Vallisoletana SL v El Salvador* (ICSID Case No ARB/03/26, Award of 2 August 2006, para 150):

> [T]he Arbitral Tribunal has an original and unquestionable competence, which arises from its own constitution and the ICSID Convention, and whose only object is to determine its competence to decide the substantive dispute presented by the parties. Only after the Arbitral Tribunal determines its own competence can it hear and decide the merits of the matter presented.

[Sch 3 Art 41-4] Power of arbitral tribunals to determine own jurisdiction is exclusive The tribunal's power to determine the extent of its jurisdiction under Art 41(1) is exclusive. The fact that the ICSID Secretary-General has registered the request for arbitration under Art 36(3) of the ICSID Convention is "purely preliminary" and the actual decision on jurisdiction is made by the Tribunal (see C Schreuer et al, *The ICSID Convention: A Commentary*, 2nd ed, Cambridge University Press, Cambridge, 2009, p 520). Indeed, the Secretary-General only declines to register the request for arbitration if it is "manifestly outside the jurisdiction of [ICSID]". As the Executive Directors noted in their Report (at para 38), "the power of the Secretary-General to refuse registration of a request for conciliation or arbitration ... is narrowly defined as not to encroach on the prerogative of Commissions and Tribunals to determine their own competence and, on the other hand, that registration of a request by the Secretary-General does not ... preclude a Commission or Tribunal from finding that the dispute is outside the jurisdiction of [ICSID]".

The exclusivity of the arbitral tribunal's power also means that it is not open to a party to apply to a national court for a stay of proceedings commenced under the ICSID Convention. So, in *Attorney-General v Mobil Oil New Zealand Ltd* (High Court, 1 July 1987, 4 ICSID Reports 117), after the registration of the request for arbitration, the Attorney-General instituted proceedings in the domestic courts, seeking an injunction to restrain Mobil Oil from continuing with the ICSID proceedings, arguing that the claim was outside the scope of ICSID's jurisdiction. Mobil Oil sought a stay of the domestic proceedings. The New Zealand High Court granted a stay of the High Court proceedings until the ICSID tribunal had determined its jurisdiction, and it based its decision, inter alia, on Art 41 of the

Convention (see further C Schreuer et al, *The ICSID Convention: A Commentary*, 2nd ed, Cambridge University Press, Cambridge, 2009, pp 521–2).

[Sch 3 Art 41-5] Objections to jurisdiction Article 41(2) provides that where a party makes an objection that the dispute is not within the jurisdiction of ICSID or is otherwise not within the competence of the tribunal, the tribunal may deal with that objection as a preliminary issue, or may join it to the merits of the dispute. It is common for respondents to ICSID arbitration proceedings to make objections to the tribunal's jurisdiction. Rule 41 of the ICSID Arbitration Rules provides further guidance on the making of such objections:

> Any objection that the dispute or any ancillary claim is not within the jurisdiction of [ICSID] or, for other reasons, is not within the competence of the Tribunal shall be made as early as possible. A party shall file the objection with the Secretary-General no later than the expiration of the time limit fixed for the filing of the counter-memorial, or, if the objection relates to an ancillary claim, for the filing of the rejoinder — unless the facts on which the objection is based are unknown to the party at that time.

Where parties have not complied with the direction to make jurisdictional objections "as early as possible", they have been the subject of censure by arbitral tribunals (see, eg, *Desert Line v Yemen* (ICSID Case No ARB/05/17, Award of 6 February 2008, para 97)).

[Sch 3 Art 41-6] Tribunal can raise issues of jurisdiction of own motion The tribunal is not required to wait for a party to make an objection to its jurisdiction, but it also has the power to raise questions concerning its jurisdiction of its own motion, in accordance with r 41(2) of the ICSID Arbitration Rules:

> The Tribunal may on its own initiative consider, at any stage of the proceeding, whether the dispute or any ancillary claim before it is within the jurisdiction of [ICSID] and within its own competence.

[Sch 3 Art 41-7] Jurisdiction and admissibility It is recalled that Art 41(2) refers to objections "that dispute is not within the jurisdiction of [ICSID], or for other reasons is not within the competence of the Tribunal". There are two distinct concepts here: "the jurisdiction of [ICSID]" refers to the conditions contained in Art 25 of the ICSID Convention; and "the competence of the Tribunal" is a broader concept which encompasses the issue of the admissibility of the claim (see, eg, J Paulsson, "Jurisdiction and Admissibility", in *Global Reflections on International Law, Commerce and Dispute Resolution: Liber Amicorum in Honour of Robert Briner*, ICC Publications, Paris, 2005, p 601; I Laird, "A Distinction without A Difference? An Examination of the Concepts of Admissibility and Jurisdiction", in T Weiler (ed), *Foreign Investment Law and Arbitration: Leading Cases from the ICSID, NAFTA, Bilateral Treaties and Customary International Law*, Cameron May, London, 2005, p 201; Sir G Fitzmaurice, *The Law and Procedure of the International Court of Justice*, vol II, Grotius Publications, Cambridge, 1986, p 439).

[Sch 3 Art 41-8] Effect of jurisdictional objection being made Where a jurisdictional objection is made, this may lead to the suspension of the proceedings on the merits. Rule 41(3) of the ICSID Arbitration Rules provides that:

Upon the formal raising of an objection relating to the dispute, the Tribunal may decide to suspend the proceedings on the merits. The President of the Tribunal, after consultation with its other members, shall fix a time limit within which the parties may file observations on the objection.

[Sch 3 Art 41-9] Tribunal may consider jurisdictional objection separately or join it to merits of dispute The tribunal may decide on the jurisdictional objection by: (a) deciding the question "by way of a separate preliminary decision"; (b) deciding the question "as part of the award on the merits"; and (c) finding "that it does not have jurisdiction, a decision that is final by definition and hence an award" (C Schreuer et al, *The ICSID Convention: A Commentary*, 2nd ed, Cambridge University Press, Cambridge, 2009, p 535). If the tribunal chooses to decide the issue of jurisdiction in a separate preliminary decision, that decision on jurisdiction is not subject to annulment proceedings until the tribunal has given its final award (Schreuer et al, p 524). As will be seen, Art 52 provides for the annulment of "awards", rather than interim "decisions". However, tribunals usually incorporate the content of interim decisions on issues of jurisdiction into their final awards (Schreuer et al, pp 523–4).

[Sch 3 Art 41-10] Procedure for summary dismissal Finally, it should be noted that the ICSID Arbitration Rules contain a summary dismissal procedure, which was included in the Rules in April 2006. Rule 41(5) provides that:

> Unless the parties have agreed to another expedited procedure for making preliminary objections, a party may, no longer than 30 days after the constitution of the Tribunal, and in any event before the first session of the Tribunal, file an objection that a claim is manifestly without legal merit. The party shall specify as precisely as possible the basis for the objection. The Tribunal, after giving the parties the opportunity to present their observations on the objection, shall, at its first session or promptly thereafter, notify the parties of its decision on the objection. The decision of the Tribunal shall be without prejudice to the right of a party to file an objection pursuant to paragraph (1) or to object, in the course of the proceeding, that the claim lacks legal merit.

It is clear from the terms of r 41(5) that this provides an additional way in which a party can object to a claim. One of the first tribunals which considered the application and interpretation of r 41(5) confirmed that the objections which can be made under this provision can include an objection that the claim is outside the jurisdiction of ICSID or the tribunal (*Brandes Investment Partners, LP v Venezuela* (ICSID Case No ARB/08/3, Decision on Objection under Rule 41(5) of 2 February 2009, paras 50–55); see further C Brown and S Puig, "The Power of ICSID Tribunals to Dismiss Proceedings Summarily: An Analysis of Rule 41(5) of the ICSID Arbitration Rules" (2011) 10 *Law and Practice of International Courts and Tribunals* 227).

Article 42

(1) The Tribunal shall decide a dispute in accordance with such rules of law as may be agreed by the parties. In the absence of such agreement, the Tribunal shall apply the law of the Contracting State party to the dispute (including its rules on the conflict of laws) and such rules of international law as may be applicable.

(2) The Tribunal may not bring in a finding of *non liquet* on the ground of silence or obscurity of the law.

(3) The provisions of paragraphs (1) and (2) shall not prejudice the power of the Tribunal to decide a dispute *ex aequo et bono* if the parties so agree.

COMMENTARY ON SCH 3 ART 42

Applicable law in ICSID arbitration	[Sch 3 Art 42-1]
Rules only apply to substantive law	[Sch 3 Art 42-2]
Parties free to choose "rules of law"	[Sch 3 Art 42-3]
Where no agreement by parties, tribunal shall apply law of Contracting State party and applicable rules of international law	[Sch 3 Art 42-4]
Some ICSID tribunals have given international law a "supplemental and corrective function"	[Sch 3 Art 42-5]
Other ICSID tribunals have held that international law can be applied directly	[Sch 3 Art 42-6]
Other ICSID tribunals have applied domestic and international law on an issue-by-issue basis	[Sch 3 Art 42-7]
No *non liquet*	[Sch 3 Art 42-8]
Parties can agree that tribunal will decide *ex aequo et bono*	[Sch 3 Art 42-9]

[Sch 3 Art 42-1] Applicable law in ICSID arbitration Article 42 contains the rules which ICSID tribunals are to apply in determining the applicable law. In this sense, it contains conflict of law rules which ICSID tribunals are to apply (C Schreuer et al, *The ICSID Convention: A Commentary*, 2nd ed, Cambridge University Press, Cambridge, 2009, pp 550–1).

[Sch 3 Art 42-2] Rules only apply to substantive law The rules set forth in Art 42 only apply to the substantive law to be applied, rather than the procedural law. It is clear from the terms of Art 44 that the ICSID Convention and the various rules adopted under the Convention regulate the procedure, subject to any agreement of the parties (C Schreuer et al, *The ICSID Convention: A Commentary*, 2nd ed, Cambridge University Press, Cambridge, 2009, pp 550–1). It is also accepted that Art 42 does not apply to the issue of whether the tribunal has jurisdiction under Art 25 of the Convention. This was confirmed by the tribunal in *CMS Gas Transmission Co v Argentina* (ICSID Case No ARB/01/8, Decision on Jurisdiction of 17 July 2003), which held (at para 88) that:

> Article 42 is mainly designed for the resolution of disputes on the merits and, as such, it is in principle independent from the decisions on jurisdiction, governed solely by Article 25 of the Convention and those other provisions of the consent instrument which might be applicable, in the instant case the Treaty provisions.

Similarly, Art 42 does not apply to determine the issue of the investor's nationality, which is to be decided in accordance with "the law of the State whose nationality is claimed" (Schreuer et al, pp 552–3; *Soufraki v United Arab Emirates* (ICSID Case No ARB/02/7, Award of 7 July 2004, para 55)).

[Sch 3 Art 42-3] Parties free to choose "rules of law" Article 42(1) confirms that the parties are free to choose the "rules of law" which are most appropriate to govern their relationship. This choice may be made in their arbitration agreement, or in any contractual agreement entered into between the investor and the host State, or in a provision of the host State's legislation, or in an investment treaty (C Schreuer et al, *The ICSID Convention: A Commentary*, 2nd ed, Cambridge University Press, Cambridge, 2009, p 558). It is noteworthy that the parties may choose "rules of law", rather than simply "law" or "system of law". This means that the parties have flexibility in choosing rules from different bodies of law. As the tribunal noted (at para 96) in *Autopista Concesionada de Venezuela, SA v Venezuela* (ICSID Case No ARB/00/5, Award of 23 September 2003):

> [T]he first sentence of Article 42(1) refers to 'rules of law' rather than to systems of law. It is generally accepted that this wording allows the parties to agree on a partial choice of law, and in particular to select specific rules from a specific system of law.

[Sch 3 Art 42-4] Where no agreement by parties, tribunal shall apply law of Contracting State party and applicable rules of international law Where no agreement has been made by the parties as to the law to be applied, the tribunal shall apply the law of the Contracting State party to the dispute (including its rules of private international law "and such rules of international law as may be applicable" (Art 42(1)). The Report of the Executive Directors indicates (at para 40) that the term "international law" as used in Art 42(1) "should be understood in the sense given to it by Article 38(1) of the Statute of the International Court of Justice".

[Sch 3 Art 42-5] Some ICSID tribunals have given international law a "supplemental and corrective function" In applying Art 42(1), some ICSID tribunals have given international law a supplemental and corrective function. For instance, the tribunal in *Liberian Eastern Timber Company (LETCO) v Liberia* (ICSID Case No ARB/83/2, Award of 31 March 1986); 2 ICSID Reps 358) held (at 372) that:

> This provision of the ICSID Convention envisages that, in the absence of any express choice of law by the parties, the Tribunal must apply a system of concurrent law. The law of the Contracting State is recognised as paramount within its own territory, but is nevertheless subjected to control by international law. The role of international law as a 'regulator' of national systems of law has been much discussed, with particular emphasis being focused on the problems likely to arise if there is divergence on a particular point between national and international law. No such problem arises in the present case; the Tribunal is satisfied that the rules and principles of Liberian law which it has taken into account are in conformity with generally accepted principles of public international law governing the validity of contracts and the remedies for their breach.

This approach has been followed in subsequent cases (C Schreuer et al, *The ICSID Convention: A Commentary*, 2nd ed, Cambridge University Press, Cambridge, 2009, pp 620–6; Z Douglas, *The International Law of Investment Claims*, Cambridge University Press, Cambridge, 2009, pp 130–3).

[Sch 3 Art 42-6] Other ICSID tribunals have held that international law can be applied directly Other ICSID tribunals have held that international law has more than merely a supplemental and corrective function. In *Wena Hotels Ltd v Egypt* (ICSID Case No ARB/98/4, Decision on Annulment of 5 February 2002, para 40), the ad hoc annulment committee held that "the sense and meaning of the negotiations leading to the second sentence of Article 42(1) allowed for both legal orders to have a role. The law of the host State can indeed be applied in conjunction with international law if this is justified. So too international law can be applied by itself if the appropriate rule is found in this other ambit". This has led eminent writers to argue that ICSID tribunals are able to decide whether international law is directly applicable to a dispute, "without any requirement of initial scrutiny into the law of the host State" (E Gaillard and Y Banifatemi, "The Meaning of 'and' in Article 42(1), Second Sentence, of the Washington Convention: The Role of International Law in the ICSID Choice of Law Process" (2003) 18 *ICSID Review — Foreign Investment Law Journal* 375, at p 409, cited in C Schreuer et al, *The ICSID Convention: A Commentary*, 2nd ed, Cambridge University Press, Cambridge, 2009, p 628; see also *LG&E v Argentina* (ICSID Case No ARB/02/1, Decision on Liability of 3 October 2006, para 96)).

[Sch 3 Art 42-7] Other ICSID tribunals have applied domestic and international law on an issue-by-issue basis Another approach followed by the ICSID tribunal in *Sempra Energy International v Argentina* (ICSID Case No ARB/02/16, Award of 28 September 2007, paras 235–6) is to give both legal systems simultaneous roles, depending on the nature of the legal issue to be decided. As Professor Schreuer sums up (in C Schreuer et al, *The ICSID Convention: A Commentary*, 2nd ed, Cambridge University Press, Cambridge, 2009, p 630) this more pragmatic, fact-specific approach:

> means that tribunals will have to identify the various legal issues before them in their proper legal contexts. Tribunals will then apply international law to some of these issues and domestic law to other issues. Tribunals will not have complete discretion in selecting international and domestic law. They will have to identify the questions to which the respective legal systems apply.

[Sch 3 Art 42-8] No *non liquet* Article 42(2) confirms the general principle of law that an international tribunal may not fail to decide an issue on the ground that there is no applicable legal rule.

[Sch 3 Art 42-9] Parties can agree that tribunal will decide *ex aequo et bono* Finally, Art 42(3) provides that the parties to a dispute can agree that the tribunal has the power to decide a dispute on the basis of equity, rather than the application of rules of law. The formulation of Art 42(3) is similar to Art 38(2) of the Statute of the International Court of Justice.

Article 43

Except as the parties otherwise agree, the Tribunal may, if it deems it necessary at any stage of the proceedings,
    (a) call upon the parties to produce documents or other evidence, and
    (b) visit the scene connected with the dispute, and conduct such inquiries there as it may deem appropriate.

COMMENTARY ON SCH 3 ART 43
Powers concerning evidence .... [Sch 3 Art 43-1]
Provision is non-mandatory .... [Sch 3 Art 43-2]
Nature of evidence-gathering powers .... [Sch 3 Art 43-3]

Other potentially relevant rules	[Sch 3 Art 43-4]
"If [the tribunal] deems it necessary"	[Sch 3 Art 43-5]
Non-application of national rules of evidence	[Sch 3 Art 43-6]

[Sch 3 Art 43-1] Powers concerning evidence Article 43 confers certain evidence-gathering powers on ICSID tribunals.

[Sch 3 Art 43-2] Provision is non-mandatory It is clear from the opening words of Art 43 that the parties to an ICSID arbitration may agree to vary its provisions. It is also clear that an ICSID tribunal may only exercise its evidence-gathering powers under Art 43 "if it deems it necessary", although this is solely within the subjective appreciation of the tribunal, which may also exercise these powers "at any stage of the proceedings".

[Sch 3 Art 43-3] Nature of evidence-gathering powers The first of the two powers conferred by Art 43 is the power to "call upon the parties to produce documents or other evidence" (Art 43(a)). This also encompasses the tribunal's power to call upon the parties to produce witnesses who may give testimony on the facts and circumstances of the dispute, as well as experts who may submit expert reports, and also attend the hearing to give oral evidence. However, ICSID tribunals have no power to subpoena witnesses (C Schreuer et al, *The ICSID Convention: A Commentary*, 2nd ed, Cambridge University Press, Cambridge, 2009, pp 661–6). The second is the power to "visit the scene connected with the dispute, and conduct such inquiries there as it may deem appropriate" (Art 43(b)). This power has only very rarely been exercised (Schreuer et al, pp 670–1).

Further provisions on the evidence-gathering process in an ICSID arbitration are contained in the ICSID Arbitration Rules. Rule 33 states that "each party shall . . . communicate to the Secretary-General . . . precise information regarding the evidence which it intends to produce and that which it intends to request the Tribunal to call for, together with an indication of the points to which such evidence will be directed". Under r 34, "[t]he Tribunal shall be the judge of the admissibility of any evidence adduced and of its probative value". As Schreuer notes (at p 643), these provisions make it clear that "Article 43 is supplementary in the sense that it is designed to close gaps left after the parties have adduced all the material that they deem relevant".

[Sch 3 Art 43-4] Other potentially relevant rules In addition to the provisions of the ICSID Convention and the ICSID Arbitration Rules, parties to ICSID arbitrations, and ICSID tribunals, often make reference to the IBA Rules on the Taking of Evidence in International Arbitration (which are not binding per se).

[Sch 3 Art 43-5] "If [the tribunal] deems it necessary" In determining whether it is "necessary" to exercise their powers under Art 43, ICSID tribunals have, by and large, adopted an approach largely consistent with the IBA Rules on the Taking of Evidence in International Arbitration. For instance, in *Aguas del Tunari SA v Bolivia* ((IC SID Case No ARB/02/3, Decision on Jurisdiction of 21 October 2005), citing Procedural Order No 1 of 8 April 2003, para 14), the tribunal indicated (at para 25) that it would take into account the following consideration in deciding whether to order the production of documents:

[T]he necessity of the requests made to the point the requesting party wishes to support, the relevance and likely merit of the point the requesting party wishes seeks to support, the cost and burden of the request on the Claimant and the question of how the request may be specified so as to both fulfil legitimate requests by a party while not allowing inquiries that are an abuse of process.

See C Schreuer et al, *The ICSID Convention: A Commentary*, 2nd ed, Cambridge University Press, Cambridge, 2009, p 644, where this case is cited.

[Sch 3 Art 43-6] Non-application of national rules of evidence Difficulties have arisen where parties have declined to produce documents, citing grounds under national law for their refusal to do so. But in *Biwater Gauff (Tanzania) Ltd v Tanzania* (ICSID Case No ARB/05/22, Procedural Order No 2 of 24 May 2006, p 8), the ICSID tribunal determined that it was not bound by rules of evidence applicable under domestic legal systems (see C Schreuer et al, *The ICSID Convention: A Commentary*, 2nd ed, Cambridge University Press, Cambridge, 2009, p 659). It held (at p 9) that the only exception which would justify non-disclosure is if the documents in question are "considered politically sensitive, as for example containing State secrets", and that even this would have to be determined by the tribunal, rather than by the disputing party itself.

Article 44

Any arbitration proceeding shall be conducted in accordance with the provisions of this Section and, except as the parties otherwise agree, in accordance with the Arbitration Rules in effect on the date on which the parties consented to arbitration. If any question of procedure arises which is not covered by this Section or the Arbitration Rules or any rules agreed by the parties, the Tribunal shall decide the question.

COMMENTARY ON SCH 3 ART 44

Rules of procedure applicable in ICSID arbitration .... [Sch 3 Art 44-1]
ICSID tribunals have power to decide other procedural issues .... [Sch 3 Art 44-2]

[Sch 3 Art 44-1] Rules of procedure applicable in ICSID arbitration Article 44 concerns the rules of procedure applicable in arbitration under the ICSID Convention. It provides that any arbitration proceeding under the ICSID Convention shall be conducted in accordance with: (a) the provisions of Arts 41–47 of the ICSID Convention; and (b) the ICSID Arbitration Rules. It is important to note that the ICSID Arbitration Rules may be amended from time to time, and it is the version of the ICSID Arbitration Rules that is in force on the date the parties consent to arbitration which is to apply. If the dispute arises out of a contract, that will be the version of the ICSID Arbitration Rules in force on the date of the contract; if the claim is brought under an investment treaty or national investment legislation, it will be the date of the request for arbitration (ICSID Rules of Procedure for the Institution of Conciliation and Arbitration Proceedings, r 2(3); C Schreuer et al, *The ICSID Convention: A Commentary*, 2nd ed, Cambridge University Press, Cambridge, 2009, pp 686–7). It is clear from the text of Art 44 that the parties may agree to use another version of the ICSID Arbitration Rules.

[Sch 3 Art 44-2] ICSID tribunals have power to decide other procedural issues In accordance with the second sentence of Art 44, the tribunal has the power to decide on procedural issues which are not addressed by the ICSID Convention, the ICSID Arbitration Rules, or where there is no agreement of the parties. This reflects the consistent practice of international courts and tribunals and conforms with the inherent powers of ICSID tribunals (see, eg, *RSM Production Corp v Grenada* (ICSID Case No ARB/05/14, Decision on RSM Production Corp's Application for a Preliminary Ruling of 7 December 2009, para 20); and *Hrvatska Elektroprivreda v Slovenia* (ICSID Case No ARB/05/24, Decision on the Participation of Counsel of 6 May 2008, para 33).

Article 45

(1) Failure of a party to appear or to present his case shall not be deemed an admission of the other party's assertions.

(2) If a party fails to appear or to present his case at any stage of the proceedings the other party may request the Tribunal to deal with the questions submitted to it and to render an award. Before rendering an award, the Tribunal shall notify, and grant a period of grace to, the party failing to appear or to present its case, unless it is satisfied that that party does not intend to do so.

COMMENTARY ON SCH 3 ART 45

Failure of party to appear or present its case ...... [Sch 3 Art 45-1]
Party which appears still required to prove its case . [Sch 3 Art 45-2]
ICSID tribunal to grant period of grace to
  non-appearing party .... [Sch 3 Art 45-3]
ICSID Rules contain further guidance .... [Sch 3 Art 45-4]

[Sch 3 Art 45-1] Failure of party to appear or present its case Article 45 provides guidance on the procedure to be followed should one party fail to appear or present its case. This provision is similar to Art 53 of the Statute of the International Court of Justice in dealing with the "phenomenon of non-cooperating parties" (C Schreuer et al, *The ICSID Convention: A Commentary*, 2nd ed, Cambridge University Press, Cambridge, 2009, p 709). It ensures that arbitration proceedings under the ICSID Convention are not frustrated by the recalcitrance of one of the parties in not appearing or presenting its case. It is worth clarifying that it is possible for a party to appear, but to fail to present its case; the two situations are not interchangeable. The provision also covers situations where one of the parties has failed to cooperate with the tribunal, or meet deadlines for the submission of pleadings and other documents (Schreuer et al, pp 714–21).

[Sch 3 Art 45-2] Party which appears still required to prove its case Article 45 should not be read as meaning that the party who appears is entitled to an award in its favour without more; it still remains for that party to prove its case, as the ICSID tribunal in *LETCO v Liberia* (ICSID Case

No ARB/83/2, Award of 31 March 1986); 2 ICSID Reps 358 confirmed:

> [T]he failure of the Government of Liberia to take part in the present arbitral proceedings does not entitle the claimant to an award in its favour as a matter of right. The onus is still upon the claimant to establish the claim which it has put forward in its Request for Arbitration and other documents.

Article 45 also has the effect that the appearing party still has to put forward the evidence on which it relies, as failure to appear to present its case does not mean that the party admits the other's assertions (Art 45(1)).

[Sch 3 Art 45-3] ICSID tribunal to grant period of grace to non-appearing party Further, if a party does not appear or present its case, an ICSID tribunal should "notify, and grant a period of grace to, the party failing to appear or to present its case", unless the tribunal "is satisfied that that party does not intend to do so" (Art 45(2)).

[Sch 3 Art 45-4] ICSID Rules contain further guidance Further guidance on the procedure to be adopted in the event that a party fails to appear or present its case can be found in the ICSID Arbitration Rules, rr 42–45 (C Schreuer et al, *The ICSID Convention: A Commentary*, 2nd ed, Cambridge University Press, Cambridge, 2009, pp 721–30).

Article 46

Except as the parties otherwise agree, the Tribunal shall, if requested by a party, determine any incidental or additional claims or counter-claims arising directly out of the subject-matter of the dispute provided that they are within the scope of the consent of the parties and are otherwise within the jurisdiction of the Centre.

COMMENTARY ON SCH 3 ART 46

Power of ICSID tribunals to determine incidental
or additional claims .... [Sch 3 Art 46-1]

[Sch 3 Art 46-1] Power of ICSID tribunals to determine incidental or additional claims Article 46 concerns the powers of ICSID tribunals to determine incidental or additional claims or counterclaims. The purpose of this provision is to ensure that related claims are dealt with in the same proceedings, unless the parties agree on a different procedure. "Incidental" and "additional" claims may include claims arising from, for example, "transactions between the claimant and a third party designed to facilitate the investment operation" (C Schreuer et al, *The ICSID Convention: A Commentary*, 2nd ed, Cambridge University Press, Cambridge, 2009, p 741); claims for interest on the amount of the award (Schreuer et al, pp 743–8); and procedural costs, such as costs incurred by a party in non-ICSID proceedings (Schreuer et al, pp 748–9). The incidental or additional claim or counterclaim must arise "directly out of the subject-matter of the dispute provided that they are within the scope of the consent of the parties and [must be] otherwise within the jurisdiction of the Centre" (Art 46).

Article 47

Except as the parties otherwise agree, the Tribunal may, if it considers that the circumstances so require, recommend any provisional measures which should be taken to preserve the respective rights of either party.

COMMENTARY ON SCH 3 ART 47

Power to recommend provisional measures	[Sch 3 Art 47-1]
Other international courts and tribunals have this power	[Sch 3 Art 47-2]
Purpose of power	[Sch 3 Art 47-3]
Provisional measures not an "award"	[Sch 3 Art 47-4]
Conditions for recommending provisional measures	[Sch 3 Art 47-5]
Provisional measures considered binding	[Sch 3 Art 47-6]

[Sch 3 Art 47-1] Power to recommend provisional measures Article 47 contains the power of ICSID tribunals to "recommend" provisional measures. Detailed guidance on the application of Art 47 is set out in r 39 of the ICSID Arbitration Rules.

[Sch 3 Art 47-2] Other international courts and tribunals have this power This power to grant provisional measures is one which is usually found in the statutes and rules of procedure of international courts and tribunals (see, eg, Statute of the International Court of Justice, Art 41; UN Convention on the Law of the Sea, Art 290; ITLOS Statute, Art 25(1); ECHR Rules of Court, r 39; American Convention on Human Rights, Art 63(2); Treaty on the Functioning of the European Union, Art 279; ECJ Rules of Procedure, Arts 83–90). It is also widely available to international arbitral tribunals, including those constituted under the UNCITRAL Arbitration Rules (Art 26), the ICC Arbitration Rules (Art 23), the LCIA Arbitration Rules (Art 25), the HKIAC Arbitration Rules (Art 24) and the ACICA Arbitration Rules (Art 28). There is also some authority for it being considered an "inherent power" available to international dispute settlement bodies (see, eg, *Grammophone Co Ltd v Deutsche Grammophone* AG 1 TAM 857 (Anglo-German MAT, 1922); *Trail Smelter Case* 3 RIAA 1911 (US-Canada, 1938); *E-Systems, Inc v Iran* 2 Ir-USCTR 51 at 57 (1983); *Ford Aerospace and Communications Corp v Air Force of Iran* 6 Ir-USCTR 104 at 108–9 (1984); *Veerman v Germany* 25 ILR 522 at 523 (Arbitral Tribunal on Property, Rights and Interests in Germany, 1957); and *Velásquez Rodríguez (Merits)* 95 ILR 259 at 268 (IACHR, 1988)).

[Sch 3 Art 47-3] Purpose of power The essential purpose of the power of international courts to grant provisional measures is to preserve the respective rights of the parties pending the decision on the merits and to safeguard the jurisdiction of the international court to render a judgment which is effective. In this regard, the International Court of Justice has stated that its power "has as its object to preserve the respective rights of the parties, and presupposes that irreparable prejudice should not be caused to rights which are the subject of dispute in judicial proceedings" (*Fisheries Jurisdiction (Interim Protection)* [1972] ICJ Rep 12 at 16, 30, 34).

[Sch 3 Art 47-4] Provisional measures not an "award" It bears emphasis that an order for provisional measures under Art 47 is to be distinguished from an award, which means that the provisions of the ICSID Convention on recognition and enforcement of awards do not apply to orders granting provisional measures (C Schreuer et al, *The ICSID Convention: A Commentary*, 2nd ed, Cambridge University Press, Cambridge, 2009, p 760).

[Sch 3 Art 47-5] Conditions for recommending provisional measures ICSID tribunals have accepted certain criteria that have to be satisfied before they will grant provisional measures under Art 47. These are that they will only do so if it is established that they have prima facie jurisdiction over the dispute (see, eg, *CEMEX Caracas Investments BV v Venezuela* (ICSID Case No ARB/08/15, Decision on Provisional Measures of 3 March 2010, paras 44–56); *Occidental Petroleum Corp and Occidental Exploration and Production Co v Ecuador* (ICSID Case No ARB/06/11, Decision on Provisional Measures of 17 August 2007, paras 59–62)); if provisional measures are necessary in order to prevent irreparable damage being done to the rights of the parties; and if the provisional measures are required as a matter of urgency (see especially C Schreuer et al, *The ICSID Convention: A Commentary*, 2nd ed, Cambridge University Press, Cambridge, 2009, pp 771–80).

[Sch 3 Art 47-6] Provisional measures considered binding Another important feature of Art 47 is that it is expressed in non-mandatory terms; it confers power on ICSID tribunals to "recommend" provisional measures, rather than a power to "order" or "prescribe" them. However, ICSID tribunals have in recent years consistently held that such "recommendations" are binding. In *Maffezini v Spain* (ICSID Case No ARB/97/7, Decision on Provisional Measures of 28 October 1999), the ICSID tribunal held (at para 9) that:

> While there is a semantic difference between the word 'recommend' as used in Rule 39 and the word 'order' as used elsewhere in the Rules to describe the Tribunal's ability to require a party to take a certain action, the difference is more apparent than real . . . The Tribunal does not believe that the parties to the Convention meant to create a substantial difference in the effect of these two words. The Tribunal's authority to rule on provisional measures is no less binding than that of a final award.

This approach has been adopted by a number of other ICSID tribunals (*Victor Pey Casado and President Allende Foundation v Chile* (ICSID Case No ARB/98/2, Decision on Provisional Measures of 25 September 2001); 16 *ICSID Review — Foreign Investment Law Journal* 567 at 577–80, which cited the decision in *Maffezini v Spain* with approval; see also *Tokios Tokeles v Ukraine* (ICSID Case No ARB/02/18, Procedural Order No 1 of 1 July 2003, para 4), which expressly adopted it; and see *Occidental Petroleum Corp and Occidental Exploration and Production Co v Ecuador* (ICSID Case No ARB/06/11, Decision on Provisional Measures of 17 August 2007, para 58)). Nonetheless, some controversy remains about the binding nature of provisional measures under the ICSID Convention (*Caratube International Oil Co LLP v Kazakhstan* (ICSID Case No ARB/08/12, Decision on Provisional Measures of 31 July 2009, para 67), which stressed that provisional measures could only be "recommended" under Art 47 of the ICSID Convention; see also C Schreuer et al, *The ICSID Convention: A Commentary*, 2nd ed, Cambridge University Press, Cambridge, 2009, pp 764–5).

SECTION 4
The Award

Article 48

(1) The Tribunal shall decide questions by a majority of the votes of all its members.

(2) The award of the Tribunal shall be in writing and shall be signed by the members of the Tribunal who voted for it.

(3) The award shall deal with every question submitted to the Tribunal, and shall state the reasons upon which it is based.

(4) Any member of the Tribunal may attach his individual opinion to the award, whether he dissents from the majority or not, or a statement of his dissent.

(5) The Centre shall not publish the award without the consent of the parties.

COMMENTARY ON SCH 3 ART 48

Award	[Sch 3 Art 48-1]
"Questions" to be taken by majority vote	[Sch 3 Art 48-2]
Award must be "in writing"	[Sch 3 Art 48-3]
Award to deal with all questions submitted to tribunal	[Sch 3 Art 48-4]
Separate and dissenting opinions permitted	[Sch 3 Art 48-5]
Publication of award by ICSID only with consent of parties	[Sch 3 Art 48-6]

[Sch 3 Art 48-1] **Award** Article 48 concerns the award and covers matters including the need for a majority, requirements of form and substance, the issues to be addressed in the award, the possibility of separate or dissenting opinions, and publication of the award (see especially C Schreuer et al, *The ICSID Convention: A Commentary*, 2nd ed, Cambridge University Press, Cambridge, 2009, pp 805–39).

[Sch 3 Art 48-2] **"Questions" to be taken by majority vote** Article 48(1) provides that the tribunal shall decide "questions" by a majority of votes of its members. This is expressed in broad terms, and includes preliminary and procedural issues that the tribunal will have to address prior to deciding the substantive issues which fall to be determined in the award. This provision is amplified in r 16(1) of the ICSID Arbitration Rules, which states that: "Decisions of the Tribunal shall be taken by a majority of the votes of all its members. Abstention shall count as a negative vote" (see also C Schreuer et al, *The ICSID Convention: A Commentary*, 2nd ed, Cambridge University Press, Cambridge, 2009, pp 807–9).

[Sch 3 Art 48-3] **Award must be "in writing"** Article 48(2) requires that the award be in writing and that it be signed by the members of the tribunal who voted for it. This is consistent with Art 31(1) of the UNCITRAL Model Law. Rule 47(1) of the ICSID Arbitration Rules sets out in more detail the information to be included in an award. This includes:

    (a) a precise designation of each party;

(b) a statement that the Tribunal was established under the Convention, and a description of its method of constitution;
(c) the name of each member of the Tribunal, and an identification of the appointing authority of each;
(d) the names of the agents, counsel and advocates of the parties;
(e) the dates and place of the sittings of the Tribunal;
(f) a summary of the procedure;
(g) a statement of the facts as found by the Tribunal;
(h) the submissions of the parties;
(i) the decision of the Tribunal on every question submitted to it, together with the reasons upon which the decision is based; and
(j) any decision of the Tribunal regarding the cost of the proceeding.

[Sch 3 Art 48-4] Award to deal with all questions submitted to tribunal Under Art 48(3), the award is to deal with every question submitted to the tribunal, and is to state the reasons on which it is based. This is also covered in r 47(1)(i), as has been noted above. Failure of the tribunal to state the reasons on which the award is based is a ground for annulment under Art 52(1)(e) (see C Schreuer et al, *The ICSID Convention: A Commentary*, 2nd ed, Cambridge University Press, Cambridge, 2009, pp 815–24).

[Sch 3 Art 48-5] Separate and dissenting opinions permitted Article 48(4) provides that any member may issue a separate opinion (whether dissenting or not). This is consistent with the rules of procedure of international courts and tribunals (see, eg, Statute of the International Court of Justice, Art 57), although the possibility of making a separate opinion is not made express in some rules of arbitration (see, eg, UNCITRAL Arbitration Rules (2010), Arts 33–34).

[Sch 3 Art 48-6] Publication of award by ICSID only with consent of parties Finally, under Art 48(5), ICSID is not permitted to publish the award without the consent of the parties to the dispute. However, r 48(4) of the ICSID Arbitration Rules states that ICSID shall "promptly include in its publications excerpts of the legal reasoning of the Tribunal". Those awards which ICSID has been permitted to publish are usually available on the ICSID website, at www.worldbank.org/icsid, or are published in the *ICSID Review — Foreign Investment Law Journal*. Many ICSID awards enter the public domain by other means, for example, where one of the parties releases it (as Art 48(5) only prevents ICSID, rather than the parties, from publishing the award).

Article 49

(1) The Secretary-General shall promptly dispatch certified copies of the award to the parties. The award shall be deemed to have been rendered on the date on which the certified copies were dispatched.

(2) The Tribunal upon the request of a party made within 45 days after the date on which the award was rendered may after notice to the other party decide any question which it had omitted to decide in the award, and shall rectify any clerical, arithmetical

or similar error in the award. Its decision shall become part of the award and shall be notified to the parties in the same manner as the award. The periods of time provided for under paragraph (2) of Article 51 and paragraph (2) of Article 52 shall run from the date on which the decision was rendered.

COMMENTARY ON SCH 3 ART 49

Dispatch of Award to parties	[Sch 3 Art 49-1]
Supplementary or additional award, and rectification of award	[Sch 3 Art 49-2]
Decision to become part of Award	[Sch 3 Art 49-3]
Running of time limit for further possible post-award procedures	[Sch 3 Art 49-4]

[Sch 3 Art 49-1] Dispatch of Award to parties Article 49 is the second provision in Ch IV which deals with "the award". Under Art 49(1), the ICSID Secretary-General, rather than the tribunal, dispatches the completed award to the parties. The date of dispatch is deemed to be the date on which the award was made.

[Sch 3 Art 49-2] Supplementary or additional award, and rectification of award Article 49(2) provides that, within 45 days of the date of the award, either party may request that the tribunal "decide any question which it had omitted to decide in the award" (ie, a supplementary or additional award), and also that the tribunal "rectify any clerical, arithmetical or similar error in the award" (ie, correction or rectification of the award). Article 49(2) is amplified by r 49 of the ICSID Arbitration Rules. This provision is not intended to "afford a substantive review or reconsideration of the decision but enables the tribunal to correct mistakes that may have occurred in the award's drafting in a non-bureaucratic and expeditious manner" (C Schreuer et al, *The ICSID Convention: A Commentary*, 2nd ed, Cambridge University Press, Cambridge, 2009, pp 849–50).

The rules of arbitration of various other arbitral institutions include similar provisions (see, eg, ICC Arbitration Rules, Art 29; LCIA Arbitration Rules, Art 27; SIAC Arbitration Rules, Art 29; ACICA Arbitration Rules, Arts 37–38, and UNCITRAL Arbitration Rules (2010), Arts 38–39). In the context of international dispute settlement, it is arguable that the power to correct any errors in the award is an inherent power (see, eg, *Application for Revision and Interpretation of the Judgment of 24 February 1982 in the Case Concerning the Continental Shelf (Tunisia/Libya) (Tunisia v Libya)* [1985] ICJ Rep 192 at 198). ICSID tribunals have been faced with a relatively small number of requests for a supplementary or additional award, or a correction or rectification of the award (Schreuer et al, pp 854–60).

[Sch 3 Art 49-3] Decision to become part of Award Article 49(2) further provides that any decision of the ICSID tribunal in response to the application for an additional award, or for correction, is to become "part of the award".

[Sch 3 Art 49-4] Running of time limit for further possible post-award procedures Finally, if either party wishes to make an application for revision of the award (under Art 51), or annulment of the award (under Art 52), the relevant time limit for the making of such an application is deemed to commence on the date on which the decision on the application for an additional award or rectification of the award is rendered (see further C Schreuer et al, *The ICSID Convention: A Commentary*, 2nd ed, Cambridge University Press, Cambridge, 2009, pp 864–5).

SECTION 5
Interpretation, Revision and Annulment of the Award

Article 50

(1) If any dispute shall arise between the parties as to the meaning or scope of an award, either party may request interpretation of the award by an application in writing addressed to the Secretary-General.

(2) The request shall, if possible, be submitted to the Tribunal which rendered the award. If this shall not be possible, a new Tribunal shall be constituted in accordance with Section 2 of this Chapter. The Tribunal may, if it considers that the circumstances so require, stay enforcement of the award pending its decision.

COMMENTARY ON SCH 3 ART 50

Power of interpretation .... [Sch 3 Art 50-1]
Other international courts and tribunals have this
  power .... [Sch 3 Art 50-2]
Must be dispute concerning issues decided with
  binding force .... [Sch 3 Art 50-3]
Power only available to ICSID arbitral tribunals .. [Sch 3 Art 50-4]
Stay of enforcement of award .... [Sch 3 Art 50-5]

[Sch 3 Art 50-1] Power of interpretation Pursuant to Art 50(1), if any dispute arises between the parties "as to the meaning or scope of an award, either party may request interpretation of the award". The request for interpretation is made to the ICSID Secretary-General who will, if possible, submit the request to the tribunal which rendered the award. If it is not possible for the original tribunal to consider the request for interpretation, a new tribunal is constituted.

[Sch 3 Art 50-2] Other international courts and tribunals have this power The power to give an interpretation of judgments and awards is commonly found in the statutes and rules of procedure of international courts and tribunals (see, eg, the Statute of the International Court of Justice, Art 60; Statute of the International Tribunal for the Law of the Sea, Art 33(3); American Convention on Human Rights, Art 67; and Rules of Procedure of the Iran-United States Claims Tribunal, Art 30). The rules of arbitration of various other arbitral institutions also include the power of interpretation (see, eg, ICC Arbitration Rules, Art 29(2); SIAC Arbitration Rules, Art 29(4); ACICA Arbitration Rules, Art 36; UNCITRAL Arbitration Rules (2010), Art 37). There is also authority for the proposition that this power is an inherent power (see, eg, ICC Case No 6233 (1992), in J-J Arnaldez, Y Derains, and D Hascher (eds), *Collection of ICC Arbitral Awards 1991–1995*, ICC Publishing, Paris, 1997, p 332).

[Sch 3 Art 50-3] **Must be dispute concerning issues decided with binding force** In *Wena Hotels v Egypt* (ICSID Case No ARB/98/4, Decision on Interpretation of 31 October 2005, para 82), a request was made for the interpretation of the award. In its decision on interpretation, the tribunal agreed with the dictum of the Permanent Court of International Justice in *Factory at Chorzow (Interpretation of Judgments Nos 7 and 8)*, PCIJ Ser A (No 13), p 11 (1927) that: "In order that a difference of opinion should become the subject of a request for interpretation under Article 60 of the Statute, there must therefore exist a difference of opinion between the Parties as to those points in the judgment in question which have been decided with binding force." In that case, the Permanent Court of Justice also clarified (at p 12) that: "A difference of opinion as to whether a particular point has or has not been decided with binding force also constitutes a case which comes within the terms of the provision in question [. . .]."

[Sch 3 Art 50-4] **Power only available to ICSID arbitral tribunals** The procedure of interpretation is not available to ad hoc committees established for the purpose of annulment proceedings (see C Schreuer et al, *The ICSID Convention: A Commentary*, 2nd ed, Cambridge University Press, Cambridge, 2009, p 870).

[Sch 3 Art 50-5] **Stay of enforcement of award** Under Art 50(2), the tribunal may stay the enforcement of the award pending its decision on the interpretation of the award. The possibility of a stay of enforcement of the award is available where an application has been made for the interpretation of the award under Art 50, revision of the award under Art 51, or annulment of the award under Art 52 (see ICSID Arbitration Rules, r 54; C Schreuer et al, *The ICSID Convention: A Commentary*, 2nd ed, Cambridge University Press, Cambridge, 2009, pp 876–7).

Article 51

(1) Either party may request revision of the award by an application in writing addressed to the Secretary-General on the ground of discovery of some fact of such a nature as decisively to affect the award, provided that when the award was rendered that fact was unknown to the Tribunal and to the applicant and that the applicant's ignorance of that fact was not due to negligence.

(2) The application shall be made within 90 days after the discovery of such fact and in any event within three years after the date on which the award was rendered.

(3) The request shall, if possible, be submitted to the Tribunal which rendered the award. If this shall not be possible, a new Tribunal shall be constituted in accordance with Section 2 of this Chapter.

(4) The Tribunal may, if it considers that the circumstances so require, stay enforcement of the award pending its decision. If the applicant requests a stay of enforcement of the award in his application, enforcement shall be stayed provisionally until the Tribunal rules on such request.

COMMENTARY ON SCH 3 ART 51

Power of revision .... [Sch 3 Art 51-1]
Other international courts and tribunals have this
  power .... [Sch 3 Art 51-2]
Conditions for power of revision to be exercised .. [Sch 3 Art 51-3]
Time limit for requesting revision .... [Sch 3 Art 51-4]
Original tribunal to consider request .... [Sch 3 Art 51-5]
Stay of enforcement of Award .... [Sch 3 Art 51-6]

[Sch 3 Art 51-1]   Power of revision   Article 51 provides generally that awards rendered under the ICSID Convention are subject to "revision", if the relevant conditions are met. The purpose of the power of revision is to alter an award to take account of a decisive new fact which was unknown to the party and the tribunal at the time of the award.

[Sch 3 Art 51-2]   Other international courts and tribunals have this power   Like the power of interpretation, the power of revision is often found in the statutes and rules of procedure of international courts and tribunals (see, eg, the Statute of the International Court of Justice, Art 61; Rules of the Tribunal of the International Tribunal for the Law of the Sea, Art 179; Rules of Court of the European Court of Human Rights, r 80; and Rome Statute of the International Criminal Court, Art 84). The rules of arbitration of other arbitral institutions do not tend to include the power of revision. There is, however, authority in international judicial practice for the proposition that the power of revision can be considered to be an inherent power (see, eg, *LeHigh Valley Railroad Co* 8 RIAA 160 at 188–90 (US-German Mixed Claims Commission, 1933; *Effect of Awards of Compensation of the United Nations Administrative Tribunal* [1954] ICJ Rep 47 at 53–5; *Biloune and Marine Drive Complex Ltd v Ghana Investments Centre and the Government of Ghana* 95 ILR 184 at 222 (1990); *Ram International Industries, Inc v Air Force of Iran* 29 Ir-USCTR 383 at 390–1 (1993); *Genie Lacayo (Judicial Review)*, Ser C (No 45) (IACHR, 1997)).

[Sch 3 Art 51-3]   Conditions for power of revision to be exercised   Article 51 sets out the conditions which have to be satisfied in order for a request for revision to be admissible. Under Art 51(1), the request for revision must be made on the basis of "discovery of some fact of such a nature as decisively to affect the award". This means that the fact must be "of such a nature that it would have led to a different decision had it been known to the tribunal" (C Schreuer et al, *The ICSID Convention: A Commentary*, 2nd ed, Cambridge University Press, Cambridge, 2009, p 883). If the fact in question would have been "decisive", there is a further requirement, at the time the award was rendered, that "that fact was unknown to the Tribunal and to the applicant and that the applicant's ignorance of that fact was not due to negligence". Here, "[o]nly the ignorance of the party making the application for revision is decisive" (Schreuer et al, p 884). Further, it is "for the Tribunal to decide whether the applicant's ignorance was due to negligence" (Schreuer et al, p 885).

[Sch 3 Art 51-4]   Time limit for requesting revision   Under Art 51(2), the request for revision must be made within 90 days of the discovery of that fact, and in any event within three years of the date of the award. The purpose of the three-year limitation period is to strike a balance between the imperatives of ensuring that awards are made based on all relevant facts, and also the need for finality in the settlement of disputes.

[Sch 3 Art 51-5] Original tribunal to consider request Under Art 51(3), the Secretary-General is to submit the request to the tribunal which rendered the award, but if this is not possible, a new tribunal is constituted.

[Sch 3 Art 51-6] Stay of enforcement of Award Article 51(4) provides that the tribunal has the discretion to stay the enforcement of the award pending its decision on the request for revision. If the applicant requests a stay of enforcement of the award, enforcement is stayed provisionally until the tribunal is able to decide on that request (see also ICSID Arbitration Rules, r 54).

Article 52

(1) Either party may request annulment of the award by an application in writing addressed to the Secretary-General on one or more of the following grounds:
   (a) that the Tribunal was not properly constituted;
   (b) that the Tribunal has manifestly exceeded its powers;
   (c) that there was corruption on the part of a member of the Tribunal;
   (d) that there has been a serious departure from a fundamental rule of procedure; or
   (e) that the award has failed to state the reasons on which it is based.

(2) The application shall be made within 120 days after the date on which the award was rendered except that when annulment is requested on the ground of corruption such application shall be made within 120 days after discovery of the corruption and in any event within three years after the date on which the award was rendered.

(3) On receipt of the request the Chairman shall forthwith appoint from the Panel of Arbitrators an *ad hoc* Committee of three persons. None of the members of the Committee shall have been a member of the Tribunal which rendered the award, shall be of the same nationality as any such member, shall be a national of the State party to the dispute or of the State whose national is a party to the dispute, shall have been designated to the Panel of Arbitrators by either of those States, or shall have acted as a conciliator in the same dispute. The Committee shall have the authority to annul the award or any part thereof on any of the grounds set forth in paragraph (1).

(4) The provisions of Articles 41–45, 48, 49, 53 and 54, and of Chapters VI and VII shall apply *mutatis mutandis* to proceedings before the Committee.

(5) The Committee may, if it considers that the circumstances so require, stay enforcement of the award pending its decision. If the applicant requests a stay of enforcement of the award in his application, enforcement shall be stayed provisionally until the Committee rules on such request.

(6) If the award is annulled the dispute shall, at the request of either party, be submitted to a new Tribunal constituted in accordance with Section 2 of this Chapter.

COMMENTARY ON SCH 3 ART 52
Power of annulment .... [Sch 3 Art 52-1]
Grounds for annulment superficially similar to
   grounds for setting aside arbitral awards .... [Sch 3 Art 52-2]

Tribunal not properly constituted .... [Sch 3 Art 52-3]
Tribunal has "manifestly exceeded its powers" .... [Sch 3 Art 52-4]
Meaning of "manifest" .... [Sch 3 Art 52-5]
Corruption on part of member of tribunal .... [Sch 3 Art 52-6]
"serious departure from a fundamental rule of procedure" .... [Sch 3 Art 52-7]
Failure to state reasons on which award is based .. [Sch 3 Art 52-8]
Procedural requirements for applications for annulment .... [Sch 3 Art 52-9]
Appointment of Annulment Committee by Chairman of ICSID Administrative Council ... [Sch 3 Art 52-10]
Procedure conducted under ICSID Arbitration Rules .... [Sch 3 Art 52-11]
Role of ad hoc Annulment Committee .... [Sch 3 Art 52-12]
Stay of enforcement of award pending application for annulment .... [Sch 3 Art 52-13]
Provision of security for stay of enforcement ..... [Sch 3 Art 52-14]
Effect of annulment .... [Sch 3 Art 52-15]

[Sch 3 Art 52-1] **Power of annulment** Under Art 52(1), either party may seek annulment of the award on any of five specified grounds: (a) that the tribunal was not properly constituted; (b) that the tribunal had manifestly exceeded its powers; (c) that there was corruption on the part of a member of the tribunal; (d) that there had been a serious departure from a fundamental rule of procedure; or (e) that the award had failed to state the reasons on which it was based (see especially C Schreuer et al, *The ICSID Convention: A Commentary*, 2nd ed, Cambridge University Press, Cambridge, 2009, pp 890–1095; R Dolzer and C Schreuer, *Principles of International Investment Law*, Oxford University Press, Oxford, 2008, pp 280–1).

[Sch 3 Art 52-2] **Grounds for annulment superficially similar to grounds for setting aside arbitral awards** On a superficial comparison, Art 52(1)(a)–(e) reflect conventional bases, whereby arbitration awards commonly may be challenged under national laws, such as Art 34 of the UNCITRAL Model Law. However, there are significant qualifications. For example, para (b) requires that the tribunal has "manifestly" exceeded its powers and para (d) requires that be a "serious" departure from a "fundamental" rule of procedure. Furthermore, the annulment regime established under Art 52 is self-contained, meaning that it is insulated from any interference by national courts.

[Sch 3 Art 52-3] **Tribunal not properly constituted** Under Art 52(1)(a), an application for annulment can be made on the ground that "the Tribunal was not properly constituted". This ground was invoked in the annulment proceedings in *Azurix Corp v Argentina* (ICSID Case No ARB/01/12, Decision on Annulment of 1 September 2009), on account of the claim that the President of the ICSID tribunal had conflicts of interest and that there was an appearance of bias. The committee found that the expression "properly constituted" meant proper compliance with the provisions of the ICSID Convention and ICSID Arbitration Rules dealing with the constitution of the tribunal. It noted that there were procedures under the ICSID Convention for challenging arbitrators before the proceedings on the merits before the tribunal, and considered that if these procedures were complied with, or were not invoked, it cannot be said that the tribunal was "not properly constituted". The committee held, in particular, that: "Article 52(1)(a) cannot be interpreted as providing the parties with a *de novo* opportunity to challenge members of the tribunal after the tribunal has already given its award" (para 280).

[Sch 3 Art 52-4]   Tribunal has "manifestly exceeded its powers"   Under Art 52(1)(b), an application for annulment can be made on the ground that "the Tribunal has manifestly exceeded its powers". This ground of annulment has been found to exist where the tribunal lacks jurisdiction because the dispute is not within the scope of the arbitration agreement, or because the tribunal has plainly gone beyond what the parties have submitted as their dispute (*Klöckner Industrie-Anlagen GmbH v Cameroon and Société Camerouaise des Engrais* (ICSID Case No ARB/81/2, Decision on Annulment of 3 May 1985, para 4)). This ground of annulment can also be made out where the ICSID tribunal fails to apply the applicable law, or bases the award on a law other than the applicable law under Art 42 of the ICSID Convention (see, eg, R Dolzer and C Schreuer, *Principles of International Investment Law*, Oxford University Press, Oxford, 2008, p 282; *Enron Creditors Recovery Corp v Argentina* (ICSID Case No ARB/01/3, Decision on Annulment of 30 July 2010, paras 67–9, 377, 393, 395)). For instance, in *Maritime International Nominees Establishment v Guinea* (ICSID Case No ARB/84/4, Decision on Annulment of 22 December 1989), the ad hoc committee held that: "Disregard of the applicable rules of law must be distinguished from erroneous application of those rules which, even if manifestly unwarranted, furnishes no ground for annulment" (para 5.04). There is a narrow dividing line between non-application of the applicable law (which is a ground for annulment), and the incorrect application of the applicable law (which is not a ground for annulment) (see especially *Enron Creditors Recovery Corp v Argentina* at paras 67–9).

[Sch 3 Art 52-5]   Meaning of "manifest"   The expression "manifestly" in this provision has been said to mean "obvious" rather than "grave", that is, whether the excess of power can be discerned with little effort and without deeper analysis. For example, in *Repsol YPF Ecuador SA v Empresa Estatal Petroleos del Ecuador* (ICSID Case No ARB/01/10, Decision on the Application for Annulment of 8 January 2007), the committee stated (at para 36) that: "It is generally understood that exceeding one's powers is '*manifest*' when it is '*obvious by itself*' simply by reading the Award, that is, even prior to a detailed examination of its contents" (emphasis in original). In *MTD Equity Sdn Bhd & MTD Chile SA v Chile* (ICSID Case No ARB/01/7, Decision on Annulment of 21 March 2007), the committee added (at para 47) that "the error must be 'manifest', not arguable, and a misapprehension (still less mere disagreement) as to the content of a particular rule is not enough".

[Sch 3 Art 52-6]   Corruption on part of member of tribunal   Under Art 52(1)(c), an application for annulment may be made on the ground that "there was corruption on the part of a member of the Tribunal". This ground has not featured in the annulment case law. As Professor Schreuer puts it, "Corruption of an arbitrator is an obvious ground for annulment", but "instances of corruption of members of arbitral tribunals seem to be so unusual that they are rarely contemplated" (C Schreuer et al, *The ICSID Convention: A Commentary*, 2nd ed, Cambridge University Press, Cambridge, 2009, p 978).

[Sch 3 Art 52-7] "**serious departure from a fundamental rule of procedure**"   Under Art 52(1)(d), an application for annulment may be made on the ground that "there has been a serious departure from a fundamental rule of procedure". There are two important qualifications for this ground of annulment to be made out. Not only must the departure from the rule of procedure be "serious", but the rule of procedure in question must be found to be "fundamental". The committee in *Maritime International Nominees Establishment v Guinea* (ICSID Case No ARB/84/4, Decision on Annulment of 22 December 1989) explained (at paras 5.05–5.06) that:

> A first comment on this provision concerns the term 'serious'. In order to constitute a ground for annulment the departure from a 'fundamental rule of procedure' must be serious. The Committee considers that this establishes both quantitative and qualitative criteria: the departure must be substantial and be such as to deprive a party of the benefit or protection which the rule was intended to provide. A second comment concerns the term 'fundamental': even a serious departure from a rule of procedure will not give rise to annulment, unless that rule is 'fundamental'. The Committee considers that a clear example of such a fundamental rule is to be found in Article 18 of the UNCITRAL Model Law on International Commercial Arbitration which provides: 'The parties shall be treated with equality and each party shall be given full opportunity of presenting his case.' The term 'fundamental rule of procedure' is not to be understood as necessarily including all of the Arbitration Rules adopted by the Centre.

As Professors Dolzer and Schreuer explain further: "The seriousness of the departure requires that it is more than minimal and that it must have had a material effect on a party" (R Dolzer and C Schreuer, *Principles of International Investment Law*, Oxford University Press, Oxford, 2008, p 283). In *Wena Hotels v Egypt* (ICSID Case No ARB/98/4, Decision on Annulment of 5 February 2002), the committee said (at para 48) that: "In order to be a 'serious' departure from a fundamental rule of procedure, the violation of such a rule must have caused the Tribunal to reach a result substantially different from what it would have awarded had such a rule been observed".

[Sch 3 Art 52-8]   Failure to state reasons on which award is based   Under Art 52(1)(e), an application for annulment may be made on the ground that the award has failed to state the reasons on which it is based. Ad hoc committees have typically adopted a forgiving approach to the requirement to state reasons. Accordingly, the ground will not be established unless the reasoning of the tribunal is clearly deficient, in the sense that the committee has failed to give any reasons, or has given clearly contradictory reasons, or such that inadequately explain the result. It is not enough that the tribunal has failed "to state correct or convincing reasons" (*MTD Equity Sdn Bhd & MTD Chile SA v Chile* (ICSID Case No ARB/01/7, Decision on Annulment of 21 March 2007, para 50)).

In a passage which has been frequently quoted, the ad hoc committee in *MINE Maritime International Nominees Establishment v Guinea* (ICSID Case No ARB/84/4, Decision on Annulment of 22 December 1989) said (at paras 5.08–5.09) that:

> [T]he requirement that an award has to be motivated implies that it must enable the reader to follow the reasoning of the Tribunal on points of fact and law. It implies that, and only that. The adequacy of the reasoning is not an appropriate standard of review under paragraph 1(e) . . . In the Committee's view, the requirement to state reasons is satisfied as long as the award enables one to follow how the tribunal proceeded from Point A to point B and eventually to its conclusion, even if it made an error of fact or of law. This minimum requirement is in particular not satisfied by either contradictory or frivolous reasons.

Further, the ad hoc committee in *Compagnia de Aguas del Aconquija SA and Vivendi Universal v Argentina* (ICSID Case No ARB/97/3, Decision on Annulment of 3 July 2002) explained (at paras 64 and 65) that:

> 64. . . . [I]t is well accepted both in the cases and the literature that Article 52(1)(e) concerns a failure to state any reasons with respect to all or part of an award, not the failure to state correct or convincing reasons . . . Provided that the reasons given by a tribunal can be followed and relate to the issues that were before the tribunal, their correctness is beside the point in terms of Article 52(1)(e). Moreover, reasons may be stated succinctly or at length, and different legal traditions differ in their modes of expressing reasons. Tribunals must be allowed a degree of discretion as to the way in which they express their reasoning.
> 65. In the Committee's view, annulment under Article (52)(1)(e) should only occur in a clear case. This entails two conditions: first, the failure to state reasons must leave the decision on a particular point essentially lacking in any expressed rationale; and second, that point must itself be necessary to the tribunal's decision.

[Sch 3 Art 52-9] Procedural requirements for applications for annulment The procedural requirements for an application for annulment are set out in Art 52(2) and ICSID Arbitration Rules, r 50(1). These provide that, in general, annulment proceedings must be commenced within 120 days after the date on which the award was rendered by an application for annulment made in writing to the Secretary-General, containing the information specified in r 50(1) of the ICSID Arbitration Rules, and accompanied by the relevant fee. In the case of an allegation that the award should be annulled because there was corruption on the part of a member of the tribunal within the meaning of Art 52(1)(c), the application for annulment must be made within 120 days of the discovery of the alleged corruption, and in any event within three years of the date of the award (Art 52(2)). The Secretary-General will thereupon register the application and transmit a copy of the application to the other party (r 50(2)), and will also request the Chairman of the Administrative Council to appoint an ad hoc committee (r 52).

[Sch 3 Art 52-10] Appointment of Annulment Committee by Chairman of ICSID Administrative Council In accordance with Art 52(3), the Chairman will appoint a committee of three persons, who must all be on the Panel of Arbitrators, none of whom shall have been a member of the original tribunal, and who must also meet certain nationality requirements. Once the committee is constituted, the party who is the applicant for annulment will be solely responsible for making the required advance payment on expenses to ICSID, without prejudice to the right of the committee under Art 61(2) (which is applicable in annulment proceedings by virtue of Art 52(4)) to award costs in its final decision (see, eg, *RSM Production Corp v Grenada* (ICSID Case No ARB/5/14, Order Discontinuing the Proceeding and Decision on Costs of 28 April 2011)).

[Sch 3 Art 52-11] Procedure conducted under ICSID Arbitration Rules Upon the ad hoc committee being constituted, proceedings before it are conducted in accordance with the same rules of arbitration that governed the original arbitration proceedings (ICSID Arbitration Rules, r 53). Article 52(4) also provides that "[t]he provisions of Articles 41–45, 48, 49, 53 and 54, and of Chapters VI and VII [of the ICSID Convention] shall apply *mutatis mutandis* to proceedings before the Committee".

[Sch 3 Art 52-12] Role of ad hoc Annulment Committee An ad hoc committee is not a court of appeal; it cannot consider the substance of the dispute, and may only determine whether the award should be annulled on one of the five grounds in Art 52(1). A committee may annul the award, but cannot substitute a new decision on the merits. In this regard, the ad hoc committee in *MCI Power Group LC and New Turbine, Inc v Ecuador* (ICSID Case No ARB/03/6, Decision on Annulment of 19 October 2009) commented (at para 24) that:

> [T]he role of an *ad hoc* committee is a limited one, restricted to assessing the legitimacy of the award and not its correctness . . . The annulment mechanism is not designed to bring about consistency in the interpretation and application of international investment law. The responsibility for ensuring consistency in the jurisprudence and for building a coherent body of law rests primarily with the investment tribunals. They are assisted in their task by the development of a common legal opinion and the progressive emergence of '*une jurisprudence constante*'.

[Sch 3 Art 52-13] Stay of enforcement of award pending application for annulment Under Art 52(5), a party may request a stay of the enforcement of the award pending the decision on its application for annulment. If this request is made, enforcement will automatically be stayed provisionally. In that event, the party requesting the stay must request the committee, within 30 days after it is constituted, to rule on whether the stay should be continued; otherwise the stay will automatically terminate. The committee has a broad discretion as to whether to continue the stay (*Enron Creditors Recovery Corp v Argentine Republic* (ICSID Case No ARB/01/3, Decision on the Argentine Republic's Request for a Continued Stay of Enforcement of the Award of 7 October 2008, para 26)), and a recent ad hoc committee has observed that "[s]tay of enforcement during the annulment proceeding is by no way automatic, quite to the contrary, a stay is contingent upon the existence of relevant circumstances which must be proven by the Applicant" (*Ron Fuchs v Georgia* (ICSID Case No AR/7/15, Decision of the ad hoc Committee on the Stay of Enforcement of Award of 12 November 2010, para 26)).

[Sch 3 Art 52-14] Provision of security for stay of enforcement The committee may order the applicant to provide security for the performance of the award in return for a stay. A stay, if ordered by a committee may be modified or terminated at any time by the committee, and will automatically terminate when the committee gives its final decision (ICSID Arbitration Rules, r 54(3)).

[Sch 3 Art 52-15] Effect of annulment At the end of the annulment proceedings, the committee renders its decision on the application for annulment, in which it may annul the award in whole, or in any part, if it finds any Art 52(1) grounds to be established. If the award is annulled, a party can request the dispute to be submitted to a new ICSID tribunal, and for the dispute to be re-arbitrated (or if the award is partially annulled, for the annulled portion to be re-arbitrated) (Art 52(6)). Thus, whether or not a claim succeeds on the merits following annulment would depend on the outcome in any resubmission proceeding.

SECTION 6
Recognition and Enforcement of the Award

Article 53

(1) The award shall be binding on the parties and shall not be subject to any appeal or to any other remedy except those provided for in this Convention. Each party shall abide by and comply with the terms of the award except to the extent that enforcement shall have been stayed pursuant to the relevant provisions of this Convention.

(2) For the purposes of this Section, "award" shall include any decision interpreting, revising or annulling such award pursuant to Articles 50, 51 or 52.

COMMENTARY ON SCH 3 ART 53

Award binding on parties and not subject to appeal	[Sch 3 Art 53-1]
Award has *res judicata* effect	[Sch 3 Art 53-2]
ICSID Convention is self-contained and insulated .	[Sch 3 Art 53-3]
Parties to comply with Award unless enforcement stayed	[Sch 3 Art 53-4]
"Award" includes decisions on interpretation, revision or annulment	[Sch 3 Art 53-5]

[Sch 3 Art 53-1] Award binding on parties and not subject to appeal Article 53 provides that the award is binding on the parties, and it also confirms the exhaustive and self-contained nature of the post-award procedures in the ICSID Convention (C Schreuer et al, *The ICSID Convention: A Commentary*, 2nd ed, Cambridge University Press, Cambridge, 2009, p 1097). In addition, s 33(1) of the Act confirms that "[a]n award is binding on a party to the investment dispute to which the award relates", and s 33(2) provides that "[a]n award is not subject to any appeal or to any other remedy, otherwise than in accordance with the Investment Convention".

[Sch 3 Art 53-2] Award has *res judicata* effect The binding nature of the award is a manifestation of the general principle of law of *res judicata*. The constitutive instruments of international courts and tribunals confirm the binding nature of judgments and awards which are rendered (see, eg, Statute of the International Court of Justice, Arts 59, 60; ICC Arbitration Rules, Art 28(6); ACICA Arbitration Rules, Art 33(2); and see also the UNCITRAL Model Law, Art 35(1)). It is noteworthy that the award is only binding on the parties to the arbitration, rather than non-parties (see also C Schreuer et al, *The ICSID Convention: A Commentary*, 2nd ed, Cambridge University Press, Cambridge, 2009, pp 1100–1).

[Sch 3 Art 53-3] ICSID Convention is self-contained and insulated The ICSID Convention contains a "self-contained system of review of awards" (C Schreuer et al, *The ICSID Convention: A Commentary*, 2nd ed, Cambridge University Press, Cambridge, 2009, p 1102). As the Executive Directors explained in their Report (at para 41):

> Article 53 declares that the parties are bound by the award and that it shall not be subject to appeal or to any other remedy except those provided for in the Convention. The remedies provided for are revision (Article 51) and annulment (Article 52). In addition, a party may ask a Tribunal which omitted to decide any question submitted to it, to supplement its award (Article 49(2)) and may request interpretation of the award (Article 50).

The self-contained system does not include an appeals mechanism or procedure, although this possibility has been the subject of much discussion (see, eg, C Tams, "Is there a Need for an ICSID Appellate Structure?", in R Hoffman and C Tams (eds), *The International Convention for the Settlement of Investment Disputes: Taking Stock after 40 Years*, Nomos, Baden-Baden, 2007, p 223; Schreuer et al, pp 1104–5).

[Sch 3 Art 53-4] Parties to comply with Award unless enforcement stayed Further, Art 53(1) clarifies that parties are obliged to comply with the award except to the extent that enforcement of the award has been stayed under the ICSID Convention.

[Sch 3 Art 53-5] "Award" includes decisions on interpretation, revision or annulment Under Art 53(2), "award" is to be understood as including "any decision interpreting, revising or annulling such award pursuant to Articles 50, 51 or 52". This clarifies that the obligation to comply with the award under Art 53(1) "relates to the award as interpreted or revised", as well as any decision on annulment (C Schreuer et al, *The ICSID Convention: A Commentary*, 2nd ed, Cambridge University Press, Cambridge, 2009, pp 1113–14).

Article 54

(1) Each Contracting State shall recognize an award rendered pursuant to this Convention as binding and enforce the pecuniary obligations imposed by that award within its territories as if it were a final judgment of a court in that State. A Contracting State with a federal constitution may enforce such an award in or through its federal courts and may provide that such courts shall treat the award as if it were a final judgment of the courts of a constituent state.

(2) A party seeking recognition or enforcement in the territories of a Contracting State shall furnish to a competent court or other authority which such State shall have

designated for this purpose a copy of the award certified by the Secretary-General. Each Contracting State shall notify the Secretary-General of the designation of the competent court or other authority for this purpose and of any subsequent change in such designation.

(3) Execution of the award shall be governed by the laws concerning the execution of judgments in force in the State in whose territories such execution is sought.

COMMENTARY ON SCH 3 ART 54

Introduction	[Sch 3 Art 54-1]
ICSID Convention has own regime for recognition and enforcement	[Sch 3 Art 54-2]
Contracting States to recognise ICSID Awards as "binding" and enforce "pecuniary obligations" .	[Sch 3 Art 54-3]
Federal States	[Sch 3 Art 54-4]
Procedure for recognition or enforcement of an ICSID Award	[Sch 3 Art 54-5]
Designation of "competent courts" by Australia ...	[Sch 3 Art 54-6]
Execution of award to be governed by domestic law in State of execution	[Sch 3 Art 54-7]

[Sch 3 Art 54-1] Introduction Article 54 is one of the most important provisions of the ICSID Convention, as it "provides for the recognition and enforcement of ICSID awards by the courts of all States parties to the Convention" (C Schreuer et al, *The ICSID Convention: A Commentary*, 2nd ed, Cambridge University Press, Cambridge, 2009, p 1117).

[Sch 3 Art 54-2] ICSID Convention has own regime for recognition and enforcement The ICSID Convention has its own regime for the recognition and enforcement of ICSID awards. In other words, awards made under the ICSID Convention are not subject to the recognition and enforcement procedures that are contained in the New York Convention (ie, the Convention on the Recognition and Enforcement of Foreign Arbitral Awards, signed 10 June 1958, 330 UNTS 38 (entered into force 7 June 1959)). This means that it is not open to a party to resist the enforcement of an ICSID award before the national courts in the country of enforcement on the ground that, for instance, the award is contrary to the public policy of that country, within the meaning of Art V(2)(b) of the New York Convention. The procedure for the recognition and enforcement of awards made under the ICSID Convention is emphasised in s 34 of the Act, which provides that: "Other laws relating to the recognition and enforcement of arbitral awards, including the provisions of Parts II and III, do not apply to: (a) a dispute within the jurisdiction of the Centre; or (b) an award under this Part."

[Sch 3 Art 54-3] Contracting States to recognise ICSID Awards as "binding" and enforce "pecuniary obligations" Under Art 54(1), "[e]ach Contracting State shall recognize an award rendered pursuant to this Convention as binding", and "shall enforce the pecuniary obligations imposed by that award within its territories as if it were a final judgment of a court in that State". The fact that only the "pecuniary obligations" imposed by an award are subject to enforcement has led to the suggestion that ICSID tribunals cannot order non-pecuniary remedies. However, the ICSID tribunal in *Enron Corp and Ponderosa Assets LP v Argentina* (ICSID Case No ARB/01/3, Decision on Jurisdiction of 14 January 2004, para 81) declared that it had "the power to order measures involving performance or injunction of certain acts". The power of ICSID tribunals to issue mandatory orders other than for the payment of monetary compensation has also been accepted by commentators (see, eg, C Schreuer et al, *The ICSID Convention: A Commentary*, 2nd ed, Cambridge University Press, Cambridge, 2009, pp 1136–9; C Schreuer, "Non-Pecuniary Remedies in ICSID Arbitration" (2004) 20 *Arbitration International* 325). The difficulty, however, is that any remedies such as an order for restitution, for example, or specific performance contained in an award rendered under the ICSID Convention, would not be enforceable in a national court.

Article 54(1) confirms that the obligation on States parties is to enforce the pecuniary obligations imposed by the award "as if it were a final judgment of a court in that State". This means that the role of the domestic court is limited to ascertaining the authenticity of the award (Schreuer et al, p 1139). There have been recent attempts by Argentina to ask its national courts to review ICSID awards made against it on constitutional grounds; this approach is contrary to Argentina's obligations under the ICSID Convention (Schreuer et al, p 1141).

[Sch 3 Art 54-4] Federal States Article 54(1) also provides that "[a] Contracting State with a federal constitution may enforce such an award in or through its federal courts and may provide that such courts shall treat the award as if it were a final judgment of the courts of a constituent state". This provision would seem to be duplicative of the possibility of States parties designating the competent court for the recognition and enforcement of ICSID awards under Art 54(2) (C Schreuer et al, *The ICSID Convention: A Commentary*, 2nd ed, Cambridge University Press, Cambridge, 2009, p 1143).

[Sch 3 Art 54-5] Procedure for recognition or enforcement of an ICSID Award Under Art 54(2), "[a] party seeking recognition or enforcement in the territories of a Contracting State shall furnish to a competent court or other authority which such State shall have designated for this purpose a copy of the award certified by the Secretary-General". The provision further stipulates that "[e]ach Contracting State shall notify the Secretary-General of the designation of the competent court or other authority for this purpose and of any subsequent change in such designation".

[Sch 3 Art 54-6] Designation of "competent courts" by Australia Australia has made the relevant designation of its "competent courts" as regards the recognition and enforcement of ICSID awards. These are the Supreme Courts of New South Wales, Victoria, Queensland, Western Australia, South Australia, Tasmania, the Northern Territory and the Australian Capital Territory (ICSID, *Contracting States and Measures Taken by them for the Purpose of the Convention* (April 2008), Doc ICSID 8/E, p 1, at www.worldbank.org/icsid).

Section 35 of the Act would seem to be inconsistent with the designation made by Australia to ICSID, in that it suggests that the Federal Court has also been designated under Art 54(2). Section 35(1) provides that "[t]he Supreme Court of each State and Territory is designated for the purposes of Article 54", and s 35(2) states that "[a]n award may be enforced in the Supreme Court of a State or Territory with the leave of that court as if the award were a judgment or order of that court" (which is consistent with the designations made by Australia); but s 35(3) provides that "[t]he Federal Court of Australia is designated for the purposes of Article 54", and s 35(4) stipulates that "[a]n award may be enforced in the Federal Court of Australia with the leave of that court as if the award were a judgment or order of that court".

[Sch 3 Art 54-7] Execution of award to be governed by domestic law in State of execution Article 54(3) provides that the execution of the award "shall be governed by the laws concerning the execution of judgments in force in the State in whose territories such execution is sought". The Executive Directors explain this provision (Report of the Executive Directors, para 42) as follows:

> Because of the different legal techniques followed in common law and civil law jurisdictions and the different judicial systems found in unitary and federal or other non-unitary States, Article 54 does not prescribe any particular method to be followed in its domestic implementation, but requires each Contracting State to meet the requirements of the Article in accordance with its own legal system.

This means that Art 54(3) does not negate the obligation of States parties to recognise ICSID awards as binding and enforce the pecuniary obligations imposed by the award as if it were a final judgment of a court in that State; it merely means that "States may carry out their obligation to enforce ICSID awards according to the modalities of their own laws concerning the execution of judgments" (C Schreuer et al, *The ICSID Convention: A Commentary*, 2nd ed, Cambridge University Press, Cambridge, 2009, p 1149).

Article 55
Nothing in Article 54 shall be construed as derogating from the law in force in any Contracting State relating to immunity of that State or of any foreign State from execution.

COMMENTARY ON SCH 3 ART 55

Continuing relevance of State immunity	[Sch 3 Art 55-1]
Article 55 only preserves immunity from execution	[Sch 3 Art 55-2]
State immunity in Australia	[Sch 3 Art 55-3]

[Sch 3 Art 55-1] Continuing relevance of State immunity Article 55 provides for the chief obstacle to the enforcement of ICSID awards in national courts — that the provisions of Art 54 are without prejudice to the law in force in any State party relating to State immunity from execution. In this sense, Art 55 must be read together with Art 54.

The Executive Directors explain the operation of Arts 54 and 55 (Report of the Executive Directors, para 43) as follows:

> The doctrine of sovereign immunity may prevent the forced execution in a State of judgments obtained against foreign States or against the State in which execution is sought. Article 54 requires Contracting States to equate an award rendered pursuant to

the Convention with a final judgment of its own courts. It does not require them to go beyond that and to undertake forced execution of awards rendered pursuant to the Convention in cases in which final judgments could not be executed. In order to leave no doubt on this point Article 55 provides that nothing in Article 54 shall be construed as derogating from the law in force in any Contracting State relating to immunity of that State or of any foreign State from execution.

[Sch 3 Art 55-2] **Article 55 only preserves immunity from execution** It bears emphasis that Art 55 only concerns immunity from execution, rather than immunity from jurisdiction (C Schreuer et al, *The ICSID Convention: A Commentary*, 2nd ed, Cambridge University Press, Cambridge, 2009, p 1153). This provision has been described as the "Achilles' heel of the Convention", for "[t]he otherwise effective machinery of arbitration has its weak point when it comes to the actual execution against States of pecuniary obligations under awards. The self-contained nature of the procedure ... does not extend to the stage of execution" (Schreuer et al, p 1154).

[Sch 3 Art 55-3] **State immunity in Australia** The relevant law of State immunity in Australia is provided by the Foreign States Immunities Act 1985 (Cth). Section 30 provides that:

> Except as provided by this Part, the property of a foreign State is not subject to any process or order (whether interim or final) of the courts of Australia for the satisfaction or enforcement of a judgment, order or arbitration award or, in Admiralty proceedings, for the arrest, detention or sale of the property.

There are, however, exceptions to the rule of immunity of foreign States from execution, including: where immunity from execution has been waived (Foreign States Immunities Act 1985 (Cth), s 31); where the property against which the award or judgment is sought to be executed is commercial property (s 32); and where the property is immovable property (s 33).

CHAPTER V

Replacement and Disqualification of Conciliators and Arbitrators

Article 56

(1) After a Commission or a Tribunal has been constituted and proceedings have begun, its composition shall remain unchanged; provided, however, that if a conciliator or an arbitrator should die, become incapacitated, or resign, the resulting vacancy shall be filled in accordance with the provisions of Section 2 of Chapter III or Section 2 of Chapter IV.

(2) A member of a Commission or Tribunal shall continue to serve in that capacity notwithstanding that he shall have ceased to be a member of the Panel.

(3) If a conciliator or arbitrator appointed by a party shall have resigned without the consent of the Commission or Tribunal of which he was a member, the Chairman shall appoint a person from the appropriate Panel to fill the resulting vacancy.

COMMENTARY ON SCH 3 ART 56

Replacement of conciliators or arbitrators in event of vacancy .... [Sch 3 Art 56-1]

Cessation of membership of Panel does not affect continuing service of conciliator or arbitrator .. [Sch 3 Art 56-2]

Different procedure if conciliator or arbitrator resigns without consent of Commission or Tribunal .... [Sch 3 Art 56-3]

[Sch 3 Art 56-1] Replacement of conciliators or arbitrators in event of vacancy Article 56 contains the procedure for the replacement of conciliators and arbitrators in the event that they die, become incapacitated, or resign. Once a commission or tribunal has been constituted and the proceedings have begun, the composition of that commission or tribunal shall in general remain unchanged. However, Art 56(1) envisages three situations where a vacancy in the commission or tribunal might be created: ie, if a conciliator or an arbitrator should die, become incapacitated (which covers the situation of a mental or physical inability to participate in the work of the commission or tribunal), or resign (C Schreuer et al, *The ICSID Convention: A Commentary*, 2nd ed, Cambridge University Press, Cambridge, 2009, pp 1188, 1191–3). If either of these three situations should arise, the resulting vacancy is to be filled in accordance with the procedure set out in Arts 29–31 (in the case of a conciliation), or Arts 37–40 (in the case of an arbitration). It is noteworthy that where a member resigns, the member concerned "must submit the resignation to the other members of the Commission or Tribunal and to the Secretary-General", and the resignation "must be accompanied by a statement of reasons" (Schreuer et al, p 1192). Where the member was appointed by one of the parties, "the Tribunal shall promptly consider the reasons for his resignation and decide whether it consents thereto" (ICSID Arbitration Rules, r 8(2)).

[Sch 3 Art 56-2] Cessation of membership of Panel does not affect continuing service of conciliator or arbitrator Under Art 56(2), the fact that a conciliator or an arbitrator is no longer a member of the Panel of Conciliators or the Panel of Arbitrators does not have the effect that they can no longer serve as a member of the commission or tribunal which has already been constituted (C Schreuer et al, *The ICSID Convention: A Commentary*, 2nd ed, Cambridge University Press, Cambridge, 2009, pp 1193–4).

[Sch 3 Art 56-3] Different procedure if conciliator or arbitrator resigns without consent of Commission or Tribunal Article 56(3) provides that where a conciliator or arbitrator appointed by a party has resigned without the consent of the commission or tribunal of which he or she was a member, the Chairman of the ICSID Administrative Council shall appoint a person from the relevant Panel to fill the vacancy. This is an exception to the usual position, as set out in Art 56(1), that the vacancy shall be filled by using "the same method that was used for the original appointment" (C Schreuer et al, *The ICSID Convention: A Commentary*, 2nd ed, Cambridge University Press, Cambridge, 2009, p 1194).

Article 57

A party may propose to a Commission or Tribunal the disqualification of any of its members on account of any fact indicating a manifest lack of the qualities required by paragraph (1) of Article 14. A party to arbitration proceedings may, in addition, propose the disqualification of an arbitrator on the ground that he was ineligible for appointment to the Tribunal under Section 2 of Chapter IV.

COMMENTARY ON SCH 3 ART 57

Challenges to conciliators and arbitrators .... [Sch 3 Art 57-1]
No specified time period .... [Sch 3 Art 57-2]
"manifest lack of the qualities" required by
    Art 14(1) .... [Sch 3 Art 57-3]

[Sch 3 Art 57-1] Challenges to conciliators and arbitrators Article 57 governs the process of challenging conciliators and arbitrators in ICSID proceedings. It allows for the challenge of any commission or tribunal member "on account of any fact indicating manifest lack of the qualities" required under Art 14(1) (ie, high moral character, recognised competence in the fields of law, commerce, industry or finance, and reliability to exercise independent judgment (C Schreuer et al, *The ICSID Convention: A Commentary*, 2nd ed, Cambridge University Press, Cambridge, 2009, p 1202)). Article 57 also provides that a party may propose the disqualification of an arbitrator on the ground that he or she was ineligible for appointment under the nationality requirements contained in Ch IV of the ICSID Convention.

[Sch 3 Art 57-2] No specified time period It is noteworthy that Art 57 does not stipulate a time period within which a proposal for disqualification must be made. Rule 9(1) of the ICSID Arbitration Rules makes further provision for the disqualification of arbitrators, and this states that a proposal for disqualification "shall be made promptly, and in any event before the proceeding is declared closed".

[Sch 3 Art 57-3] "manifest lack of the qualities" required by Art 14(1) Article 57 makes no reference to any objective or "reasonable third person" test. Dr Sam Luttrell explains that "[t]he ICSID test for bias is . . . unique: the inter-operation of Articles 14(1) and 57 produces a rule that an ICSID arbitrator may only be challenged for bias where he or she manifestly lacks the capacity to exercise independent judgment" (S Luttrell, "Bias Challenges in Investor-State Arbitration: Lessons from International Commercial Arbitration", in C Brown and K Miles (eds), *Evolution in Investment Treaty Law and Arbitration*, Cambridge University Press, Cambridge, 2011, p 445).

An important qualification in Art 57 is the word "manifest". This operates as an evidentiary condition which "imposes a relatively heavy burden of proof on the party making the proposal [to disqualify]" (C Schreuer et al, *The ICSID Convention: A Commentary*, 2nd ed, Cambridge University Press, Cambridge, 2009, p 1202). It has been interpreted to mean "obvious or evident" (*Suez, Sociedad General de Aguas de Barcelona SA and InterAguas Servicios Integrales del Agua SA v Argentine Republic* (ICSID Case No ARB/03/17, Decision on the Proposal for the Disqualification of a Member of the Arbitral Tribunal of 22 October 2007, para 34)), and to "exclude reliance on speculative assumptions or arguments" (*Compania de Aguas del Aconquija SA and Vivendi Universal v Argentina* (ICSID Case No ARB/97/3, Decision on the Challenge to the President of the Committee of 3 October 2001 (*Compania de Aguas v Argentina*), para 25)), but not to bar challenges brought solely on the basis of appearances (ie, "manifest" does not mean "actual": *Compania de Aguas v Argentina* at para 25). It has been observed that the test set forth in Art 57 sets an "extremely high bar for challenging an arbitrator" (L Reed, J Paulsson and N Blackaby, *Guide to ICSID Arbitration*, Kluwer Law International, The Hague, 2004, p 81; see also Luttrell, p 445).

Article 58

The decision on any proposal to disqualify a conciliator or arbitrator shall be taken by the other members of the Commission or Tribunal as the case may be, provided that where those members are equally divided, or in the case of a proposal to disqualify a sole conciliator or arbitrator, or a majority of the conciliators or arbitrators, the Chairman shall take that decision. If it is decided that the proposal is well-founded the conciliator or arbitrator to whom the decision relates shall be replaced in accordance with the provisions of Section 2 of Chapter III or Section 2 of Chapter IV.

COMMENTARY ON SCH 3 ART 58

Procedure for decision on disqualification .... [Sch 3 Art 58-1]
Method of replacement .... [Sch 3 Art 58-2]

[Sch 3 Art 58-1] Procedure for decision on disqualification Article 58 provides that where a proposal for disqualification is made, the decision shall be taken by the other members of the commission or tribunal. In the event that the remaining members of the commission or tribunal are equally divided, and in the event that there is a sole conciliator-arbitrator, the Chairman of the ICSID Administrative Council shall take the decision (C Schreuer et al, *The ICSID Convention: A Commentary*, 2nd ed, Cambridge University Press, Cambridge, 2009, pp 1210–12).

This is a different approach from that adopted in most rules of arbitration. Under the LCIA Arbitration Rules (Art 10(4)), it is the LCIA Court which decides on any challenge; under the ICC Arbitration Rules (Art 11(3)), it is the Secretariat of the ICC Court of Arbitration; and under the ACICA Arbitration Rules (Art 14(4)), it is ACICA.

[Sch 3 Art 58-2] Method of replacement If the two remaining conciliators or arbitrators uphold the challenge, the conciliator or arbitrator in question is to be replaced in accordance with the method used for the original appointment. This is the same procedure that applies under Art 56(1), ie, where a vacancy arises due to the death, incapacity, or resignation of a conciliator or arbitrator.

CHAPTER VI
Cost of Proceedings

Article 59

The charges payable by the parties for the use of the facilities of the Centre shall be determined by the Secretary-General in accordance with the regulations adopted by the Administrative Council.

COMMENTARY ON SCH 3 ART 59
Costs of using ICSID facilities .... [Sch 3 Art 59-1]

[Sch 3 Art 59-1] Costs of using ICSID facilities Article 59 makes provision for the Secretary-General of ICSID to set the charges for the use of ICSID's facilities. The charges payable by the parties for the use of ICSID's facilities are set in accordance with the ICSID Administrative and Financial Regulations. For instance, reg 16 provides that a party wishing to lodge a request for conciliation or arbitration, for example, is required to pay a non-refundable fee as determined by the Secretary-General. The fee for the lodging of a request for conciliation or arbitration is currently set at US$25,000. The fee for a request for a supplementary decision to an award, or for the rectification, interpretation, revision or annulment of an arbitral award rendered pursuant to the Convention, is currently set at US$10,000. This amount is payable by the party requesting the resubmission of a dispute to a new tribunal after the annulment of an award (see ICSID Schedule of Fees, effective 1 January 2008). The ICSID Schedule of Fees also includes information on other fees charged by ICSID in the course of arbitration and conciliation proceedings. Regulation 14 of the ICSID Administrative and Financial Regulations gives further detail on the procedure concerning the payment of funds to cover the costs of the proceedings.

Article 60

(1) Each Commission and each Tribunal shall determine the fees and expenses of its members within limits established from time to time by the Administrative Council and after consultation with the Secretary-General.

(2) Nothing in paragraph (1) of this Article shall preclude the parties from agreeing in advance with the Commission or Tribunal concerned upon the fees and expenses of its members.

COMMENTARY ON SCH 3 ART 60
Fees and expenses of members of Conciliation
   Commissions and Arbitral Tribunals .... [Sch 3 Art 60-1]
Parties to a dispute can agree with Commission or
   Tribunal on fees and expenses .... [Sch 3 Art 60-2]

[Sch 3 Art 60-1] Fees and expenses of members of Conciliation Commissions and Arbitral Tribunals Article 60(1) confers the task of determining the fees and expenses of the conciliators and arbitrators to the commissions and tribunals themselves, although those fees and expenses have to be within limits set forth by the ICSID Secretary-General. The ICSID Schedule of Fees (effective 1 January 2008) sets the limit as being US$3000 "per day of meetings or other work performed in connection with the proceedings, as well as subsistence allowances and reimbursement of travel expenses within limits set forth in Administrative and Financial Regulation 14".

[Sch 3 Art 60-2] Parties to a dispute can agree with Commission or Tribunal on fees and expenses Article 60(2) notes that the parties to a particular dispute have the ability to agree with the commission or tribunal on the fees and expenses of its members. There have been several cases in which the parties and the tribunals have agreed on fees that were higher than those set forth in the Schedule of Fees (C Schreuer et al, *The ICSID Convention: A Commentary*, 2nd ed, Cambridge University Press, Cambridge, 2009, pp 1220–1).

Article 61

(1) In the case of conciliation proceedings the fees and expenses of members of the Commission as well as the charges for the use of the facilities of the Centre, shall be borne equally by the parties. Each party shall bear any other expenses it incurs in connection with the proceedings.

(2) In the case of arbitration proceedings the Tribunal shall, except as the parties otherwise agree, assess the expenses incurred by the parties in connection with the proceedings, and shall decide how and by whom those expenses, the fees and expenses of the members of the Tribunal and the charges for the use of the facilities of the Centre shall be paid. Such decision shall form part of the award.

COMMENTARY ON SCH 3 ART 61

Apportionment of costs in conciliation proceedings	[Sch 3 Art 61-1]
Apportionment of costs in arbitration proceedings .	[Sch 3 Art 61-2]
Inconsistent practice	[Sch 3 Art 61-3]

[Sch 3 Art 61-1] Apportionment of costs in conciliation proceedings Article 61(1) is self-explanatory, providing that in the case of conciliation proceedings, the fees and expenses of the conciliators, as well as the charges for the use of ICSID's facilities, are to be shared equally by the parties. Each party is to bear any additional expenses it incurs, such as its legal fees.

[Sch 3 Art 61-2] Apportionment of costs in arbitration proceedings Article 61(2) deals with arbitration proceedings and provides that unless the parties agree otherwise, it is for the tribunal to assess the expenses incurred by the parties in connection with the proceedings, and to decide how and by whom those expenses shall be paid. The tribunal is also to decide how and by whom the fees and expenses of the tribunal members, and the charges for the use of ICSID's facilities, shall be paid. This decision is to form part of the award.

[Sch 3 Art 61-3] Inconsistent practice The practice of ICSID tribunals in deciding how the costs are to be allocated is inconsistent. Some tribunals have adopted the approach that the losing party is to bear the burden of the proceedings; others have considered the procedural conduct of the parties in deciding how to apportion the costs and expenses of the arbitration; others have apportioned costs relating to parts of the proceeding, but not the entire proceeding; and others have adopted the position that the costs should be borne equally (for an excellent summary, see C Schreuer et al, *The ICSID Convention: A Commentary*, 2nd ed, Cambridge University Press, Cambridge, 2009, pp 1228–36).

CHAPTER VII
Place of Proceedings

Article 62

Conciliation and arbitration proceedings shall be held at the seat of the Centre except as hereinafter provided.

COMMENTARY ON SCH 3 ART 62
Conciliation and arbitration proceedings generally
to take place at ICSID .... [Sch 3 Art 62-1]

[Sch 3 Art 62-1] Conciliation and arbitration proceedings generally to take place at ICSID Article 62 deals with the place of the arbitration or conciliation proceedings. The place of arbitration has no significance in ICSID arbitration, as there is no legal "seat" of the arbitration, due to the self-contained nature of ICSID's system for the review of awards. There is no national law to operate as the *lex arbitri*; the procedure is governed exclusively by the ICSID Convention and the ICSID Arbitration or Conciliation Rules, together with other ICSID Rules and Regulations on certain issues (C Schreuer et al, *The ICSID Convention: A Commentary*, 2nd ed, Cambridge University Press, Cambridge, 2009, pp 1244–5). In accordance with Art 62, most ICSID arbitration and conciliation proceedings are held at the seat of ICSID, at the World Bank, which is located at 1818 H Street, NW, MSN U-3 301, Washington, DC, 20433, United States of America.

Where the proceedings are held under the ICSID Arbitration (Additional Facility) Rules (which apply where only one of the Contracting States party to the dispute, or the State of nationality of the investor party to the dispute, is a Contracting State to the ICSID Convention), the place of arbitration does have legal relevance, as the ICSID Convention, with its self-contained system of review, does not apply. In recognition of this, Art 19 of the ICSID Arbitration (Additional Facility) Rules requires that such arbitration proceedings shall only be held in a State which is a State party to the New York Convention.

Article 63

Conciliation and arbitration proceedings may be held, if the parties so agree,
(a) at the seat of the Permanent Court of Arbitration or of any other appropriate institution, whether private or public, with which the Centre may make arrangements for that purpose; or
(b) at any other place approved by the Commission or Tribunal after consultation with the Secretary-General.

COMMENTARY ON SCH 3 ART 63
Parties can agree to have hearings elsewhere ...... [Sch 3 Art 63-1]

[Sch 3 Art 63-1] Parties can agree to have hearings elsewhere Under Art 63(a), ICSID conciliation or arbitration proceedings may take place at the seat of the Permanent Court of Arbitration (the PCA), in The Hague, or at the seat of any other appropriate institution, with which ICSID may make arrangements.

According to the ICSID website, such arrangements have, in addition to the PCA, also been made with the Regional Arbitration Centres of the Asian-African Legal Consultative Committee at Cairo, Kuala Lumpur and Lagos; the Australian Commercial Disputes Centre; the Australian Centre for International Commercial Arbitration; the Singapore International Arbitration Centre; the Gulf Cooperation Council Commercial Arbitration Centre at Bahrain; the German Institution of Arbitration; and Maxwell Chambers, Singapore.

Article 63(b) further provides that hearings may take place "at any other place" which is approved by the Conciliation Commission or Arbitral Tribunal after consulting with the ICSID Secretary-General. ICSID hearings frequently take place at the Paris office of the World Bank, and at the International Dispute Resolution Centre, which is at 70 Fleet St, London EC4Y 1EU, United Kingdom.

CHAPTER VIII
Disputes between Contracting States

Article 64

Any dispute arising between Contracting States concerning the interpretation or application of this Convention which is not settled by negotiation shall be referred to the International Court of Justice by the application of any party to such dispute, unless the States concerned agree to another method of settlement.

COMMENTARY ON SCH 3 ART 64
Settlement of inter-State disputes concerning interpretation or application of ICSID Convention .... [Sch 3 Art 64-1]

[Sch 3 Art 64-1] Settlement of inter-State disputes concerning interpretation or application of ICSID Convention Article 64 is a compromissory clause in which the States parties to the ICSID Convention agree that any inter-State dispute concerning the interpretation or application of the ICSID Convention which is not settled by negotiation shall be submitted to the International Court of Justice. It is not necessary for both (or all) States parties to the dispute to agree on the submission to the International Court of Justice; the application may be made by "any party to such dispute". If the States agree to another method of settling the dispute, the dispute may not be referred to the International Court of Justice.

This provision (as well as subsequent provisions) does not have the force of law in Australia, as s 32 of the Act only implements Chs II–VII in Australian law.

CHAPTER IX
Amendment

Article 65

Any Contracting State may propose amendment of this Convention. The text of a proposed amendment shall be communicated to the Secretary-General not less than

90 days prior to the meeting of the Administrative Council at which such amendment is to be considered and shall forthwith be transmitted by him to all the members of the Administrative Council.

COMMENTARY ON SCH 3 ART 65
Procedure for amendment of ICSID Convention . [Sch 3 Art 65-1]

[Sch 3 Art 65-1] Procedure for amendment of ICSID Convention Article 65 contains the procedure for amendments to be made to the ICSID Convention. Any State party to the ICSID Convention can propose an amendment by submitting it to the ICSID Secretary-General no fewer than 90 days before a meeting of the Administrative Council. The ICSID Secretary-General then transmits the proposed amendment to all members of the Administrative Council. No amendments have ever been proposed (C Schreuer et al, *The ICSID Convention: A Commentary*, 2nd ed, Cambridge University Press, Cambridge, 2009, p 1263).

Article 66

(1) If the Administrative Council shall so decide by a majority of two-thirds of its members, the proposed amendment shall be circulated to all Contracting States for ratification, acceptance or approval. Each amendment shall enter into force 30 days after dispatch by the depositary of this Convention of a notification to Contracting States that all Contracting States have ratified, accepted or approved the amendment.

(2) No amendment shall affect the rights and obligations under this Convention of any Contracting State or of any of its constituent subdivisions or agencies, or of any national of such State arising out of consent to the jurisdiction of the Centre given before the date of entry into force of the amendment.

COMMENTARY ON SCH 3 ART 66
Further procedure for amendment of ICSID
Convention .... [Sch 3 Art 66-1]

[Sch 3 Art 66-1] Further procedure for amendment of ICSID Convention Under Art 66(1), if the Administrative Council decides by a two-thirds majority to circulate a proposed amendment to the member States, the proposed amendment will be so circulated; however, the amendment will only be made if "all Contracting States have ratified, accepted or approved the amendment". The amendment will enter into force 30 days after the ICSID Convention's depositary notifies the Contracting States that all Contracting States have ratified, accepted or approved the amendment. Under Art 66(2), no amendment can affect the rights and obligations of any Contracting State, or of any national of any Contracting State, arising out of their consent to ICSID's jurisdiction before the date of entry into force of the amendment (see further C Schreuer et al, *The ICSID Convention: A Commentary*, 2nd ed, Cambridge University Press, Cambridge, 2009, pp 1265–6).

CHAPTER X
Final Provisions

Article 67

This Convention shall be open for signature on behalf of States members of the Bank. It shall also be open for signature on behalf of any other State which is a party to the Statute of the International Court of Justice and which the Administrative Council, by a vote of two-thirds of its members, shall have invited to sign the Convention.

COMMENTARY ON SCH 3 ART 67

Signature of ICSID Convention .... [Sch 3 Art 67-1]

[Sch 3 Art 67-1] **Signature of ICSID Convention** Article 67 provides that only States which are members of the World Bank are permitted to sign the ICSID Convention, although a State which is a State party to the Statute of the International Court of Justice (meaning, essentially, a member State of the United Nations) may also sign the ICSID Convention if the Administrative Council, by a two-thirds majority vote, invites that State to do so.

This provision does not contain a time limit within which the ICSID Convention is open for signature. This means that States wishing to become a State party to the ICSID Convention must sign the ICSID Convention, regardless of whether or not the ICSID Convention had already entered into force (Report of the Executive Directors, para 46; C Schreuer et al, *The ICSID Convention: A Commentary*, 2nd ed, Cambridge University Press, Cambridge, 2009, p 1268).

Australia signed the ICSID Convention on 24 March 1975 (ICSID, *List of Contracting States and other Signatories of the Convention* (as of 27 December 2010), Doc ICSID/3, available at www.worldbank.org/icsid).

Article 68

(1) This Convention shall be subject to ratification, acceptance or approval by the signatory States in accordance with their respective constitutional procedures.

(2) This Convention shall enter into force 30 days after the date of deposit of the twentieth instrument of ratification, acceptance or approval. It shall enter into force for each State which subsequently deposits its instrument of ratification, acceptance or approval 30 days after the date of such deposit.

COMMENTARY ON SCH 3 ART 68

Ratification of ICSID Convention .... [Sch 3 Art 68-1]
No provision on reservations .... [Sch 3 Art 68-2]
Entry into force of ICSID Convention .... [Sch 3 Art 68-3]

[Sch 3 Art 68-1] **Ratification of ICSID Convention** Article 68(1) requires that, in addition to States signing the ICSID Convention, they must also ratify, accept or approve the Convention in accordance with their internal constitutional procedures.

[Sch 3 Art 68-2] **No provision on reservations** The ICSID Convention does not contain a provision on reservations, but in practice, no States parties have made a reservation to the ICSID Convention (C Schreuer et al, *The ICSID Convention: A Commentary*, 2nd ed, Cambridge University Press, Cambridge, 2009, pp 1269–70).

[Sch 3 Art 68-3] Entry into force of ICSID Convention In accordance with Art 68(2), the ICSID Convention entered into force on 14 October 1966, being 30 days after the date of deposit of the twentieth instrument of ratification. For each State which subsequently deposits its instrument of ratification, acceptance or approval, the ICSID Convention enters into force 30 days after the date of its deposit. Australia deposited its instrument of ratification on 2 May 1991, meaning the ICSID Convention entered into force on 1 June 1991 (ICSID, *List of Contracting States and other Signatories of the Convention* (as of 27 December 2010), Doc ICSID/3, available at www.worldbank.org/icsid). At the time of writing, 147 States are parties to the ICSID Convention, including Australia.

Article 69

Each Contracting State shall take such legislative or other measures as may be necessary for making the provisions of this Convention effective in its territories.

COMMENTARY ON SCH 3 ART 69
Obligation on Contracting States to implement
ICSID Convention in domestic legislation ..... [Sch 3 Art 69-1]

[Sch 3 Art 69-1] Obligation on Contracting States to implement ICSID Convention in domestic legislation This provision requires States parties to take such legislative or other measures as are necessary to implement the provisions of the ICSID Convention in their territories. In Australia, the ICSID Implementation Act 1990 (Cth) fulfilled this function. In the Explanatory Memorandum to the ICSID Implementation Bill 1990 (Cth), the introduction stated (at p 1) that:

> This Bill, when enacted, will enable Australia to ratify the Convention on the Settlement of Investment Disputes between States and Nationals of other States.
>
> The Convention establishes the International Centre for Settlement for Investment Disputes ("the ICSID") and provides facilities for arbitration or conciliation of investment disputes between States and nationals of other States under the auspices of the Centre. By providing this dispute resolution machinery the ICSID aims to improve the international investment climate and stimulate a larger flow of private international investment.
>
> This Bill will implement Chapters II–VII of the Convention by amendment to the International Arbitration Act 1974 by inserting a new Part IV and a new Schedule (containing the English text of the Convention) into that Act. It will also amend the International Organizations (Privileges and Immunities) Act 1963 to enable effect to be given to the privileges and immunities provisions of the Convention.

Article 70

This Convention shall apply to all territories for whose international relations a Contracting State is responsible, except those which are excluded by such State by written notice to the depositary of this Convention either at the time of ratification, acceptance or approval or subsequently.

COMMENTARY ON SCH 3 ART 70

ICSID Convention to apply to all territories of a State .... [Sch 3 Art 70-1]

[Sch 3 Art 70-1] ICSID Convention to apply to all territories of a State Article 70 "establishes a presumption that the Convention will apply to all territories of a State". A contrary intention would have to be expressed in the form of a written notice to the depositary of the ICSID Convention, at the time of ratification, acceptance or approval or anytime thereafter (C Schreuer et al, *The ICSID Convention: A Commentary*, 2nd ed, Cambridge University Press, Cambridge, 2009, p 1276). The current list of exclusions is ICSID, *Exclusions of Territories by Contracting States* (ICSID Doc 8/B) (available at www.worldbank.org/icsid). Only New Zealand (Cook Islands, Niue and Tokelau) and the United Kingdom (British Indian Ocean Territory, Pitcairn Islands, British Antarctic Territory and the Sovereign Base Areas of Cyprus) have excluded several of their overseas territories (see also Schreuer et al, p 1277). It has been noted above that the International Arbitration Act 1974 (Cth) applies to all of Australia's external Territories (s 2A).

Article 71

Any Contracting State may denounce this Convention by written notice to the depositary of this Convention. The denunciation shall take effect six months after receipt of such notice.

COMMENTARY ON SCH 3 ART 71

Denunciation of ICSID Convention .... [Sch 3 Art 71-1]
Denunciation does not affect pending proceedings . [Sch 3 Art 71-2]

[Sch 3 Art 71-1] Denunciation of ICSID Convention Article 71 provides that States parties to the ICSID Convention may denounce it, ie, withdraw from the ICSID Convention, by giving notice to the depositary of the Convention (being the World Bank, under Art 73 of the ICSID Convention). The denunciation takes effect six months later. On 2 May 2007, Bolivia gave written notice of its denunciation of the ICSID Convention. Its denunciation took effect on 3 November 2007. Further, on 6 July 2009, Ecuador gave written notice of its denunciation of the ICSID Convention. This took effect on 7 January 2010.

[Sch 3 Art 71-2] Denunciation does not affect pending proceedings As Professor Schreuer explains: "A denunciation does not affect pending proceedings. Nor does it affect rights and obligations arising from consent to ICSID's jurisdiction given before receipt of the notice (Art 2). During the six months between receipt of the notice and its taking effect the State in question continues to be bound by such obligations as respect for the Centre's immunities and privileges (Arts 18–24) and recognition and enforcement of awards (Art 54)" (C Schreuer et al, *The ICSID Convention: A Commentary*, 2nd ed, Cambridge University Press, Cambridge, 2009, p 1278).

Article 72

Notice by a Contracting State pursuant to Articles 70 or 71 shall not affect the rights or obligations under this Convention of that State or of any of its constituent subdivisions or agencies or of any national of that State arising out of consent to the jurisdiction of the Centre given by one of them before such notice was received by the depositary.

COMMENTARY ON SCH 3 ART 72

Notices under Arts 70 and 71 do not have
retrospective effect .... [Sch 3 Art 72-1]

[Sch 3 Art 72-1]   Notices under Arts 70 and 71 do not have retrospective effect   Article 72 is an expression of the rule contained in Art 25(1) that "consent, once given, cannot be withdrawn unilaterally" (and see C Schreuer et al, *The ICSID Convention: A Commentary*, 2nd ed, Cambridge University Press, Cambridge, 2009, p 1280). The purpose of this provision is to make it clear that once a State has consented to arbitration proceedings under the auspices of ICSID, the fact that the State later denounces the ICSID Convention does not affect its obligation to go to arbitration if a dispute arises (Schreuer et al, p 1279). If the State has entered into a contractual agreement with an ICSID arbitration clause, that arbitration clause is to "remain valid for the duration of the agreement", notwithstanding the later denunciation of the ICSID Convention by the host State of the investment (Schreuer et al, p 1279). If the State's consent to go to arbitration is in the form of an offer in, for example, a bilateral investment treaty, the investment chapter of a free-trade agreement, or in domestic legislation on foreign investment, then that offer must be taken up by the foreign investor before the notice of denunciation is received by the World Bank (Schreuer et al, pp 1280–1). This has the effect of ensuring that any ICSID proceedings which had commenced prior to the denunciation remain on foot, and the host State is not able to withdraw its consent to the jurisdiction of ICSID.

Article 73

Instruments of ratification, acceptance or approval of this Convention and of amendments thereto shall be deposited with the Bank which shall act as the depositary of this Convention. The depositary shall transmit certified copies of this Convention to States members of the Bank and to any other State invited to sign the Convention.

COMMENTARY ON SCH 3 ART 73

World Bank is depositary for ICSID Convention . [Sch 3 Art 73-1]

[Sch 3 Art 73-1]   World Bank is depositary for ICSID Convention   The purpose of Art 73 is to designate the World Bank as the depositary for the ICSID

Convention. In this capacity, the World Bank "receives instruments of ratification, acceptance or approval in accordance with Art 66(1) and Art 68(1) [and] notices excluding territories in accordance with Art 70 and any notices of denunciation in accordance with Art 71" (C Schreuer et al, *The ICSID Convention: A Commentary*, 2nd ed, Cambridge University Press, Cambridge, 2009, p 1283).

Article 74

The depositary shall register this Convention with the Secretariat of the United Nations in accordance with Article 102 of the Charter of the United Nations and the Regulations thereunder adopted by the General Assembly.

COMMENTARY ON SCH 3 ART 74

ICSID Convention to be registered with United
Nations .... [Sch 3 Art 74-1]

[Sch 3 Art 74-1] ICSID Convention to be registered with United Nations Article 74 provides that the World Bank, as depositary, shall register this Convention with the Secretariat of the United Nations in accordance with Art 102 of the Charter of the United Nations, which provides that:

1. Every treaty and every international agreement entered into by any Member of the United Nations after the present Charter comes into force shall as soon as possible be registered with the Secretariat and published by it.
2. No party to any such treaty or international agreement which has not been registered in accordance with the provisions of paragraph 1 of this Article may invoke that treaty or agreement before any organ of the United Nations.

Article 75

The depositary shall notify all signatory States of the following:
(a) signatures in accordance with Article 67;
(b) deposits of instruments of ratification, acceptance and approval in accordance with Article 73;
(c) the date on which this Convention enters into force in accordance with Article 68;
(d) exclusions from territorial application pursuant to Article 70;
(e) the date on which any amendment of this Convention enters into force in accordance with Article 66; and
(f) denunciations in accordance with Article 71.

COMMENTARY ON SCH 3 ART 75

Functions of depositary .... [Sch 3 Art 75-1]

[Sch 3 Art 75-1] Functions of depositary Article 75 sets out the normal functions of the depositary, which is "to notify the treaty's signatories of legally relevant facts relating to [the Convention]" (C Schreuer et al, *The ICSID*

Convention: A Commentary, 2nd ed, Cambridge University Press, Cambridge, 2009, p 1285). Note that the depositary makes these notifications to the signatory States (ie, all States which have signed the ICSID Convention, of which there are 157), rather than just the States parties (ie, those States which have signed and ratified, or accepted, or approved the ICSID Convention, of which there are 147) (ICSID, *List of Contracting States and other Signatories of the Convention* (as of 5 May 2011), Doc ICSID/3, available at www.worldbank.org/icsid).

DONE at Washington in the English, French and Spanish languages, all three texts being equally authentic, in a single copy which shall remain deposited in the archives of the International Bank for Reconstruction and Development, which has indicated by its signature below its agreement to fulfil the functions with which it is charged under this Convention.

COMMENTARY ON SCH 3 FINAL PROVISION

Three official language versions of ICSID Convention equally authentic ....[Sch.3 Final Provision-1]

[Sch 3 Final Provision-1] Three official language versions of ICSID Convention equally authentic The English, French and Spanish versions of the ICSID Convention are equally authentic. Under Art 33(3) of the *Vienna Convention on the Law of Treaties*, "[t]he terms of the treaty are presumed to have the same meaning in each authentic text" (*Vienna Convention on the Law of Treaties*, opened for signature 23 May 1969, 1155 UNTS 311 (entered into force 27 January 1980)). In the case of a discrepancy in meaning between the authentic texts, Art 33(4) of the *Vienna Convention on the Law of Treaties* further provides that "[e]xcept where a particular text prevails in accordance with paragraph 1, when a comparison of the authentic texts discloses a difference of meaning which the application of articles 31 and 32 does not remove, the meaning which best reconciles the texts, having regard to the object and purpose of the treaty, shall be adopted" (see also C Schreuer et al, *The ICSID Convention: A Commentary*, 2nd ed, Cambridge University Press, Cambridge, 2009, p 1286).

Index

References are to paragraph numbers

Acts Interpretation Act 1901
International Arbitration Act 1974 and . [s 2D-4]
Model Law . . . . [s 17-4]
Agreement in writing
content, recording . . . . [Sch 2 Art 7-6]
definition . . . . [s 3], [s 3-2]
document containing arbitration clause
. . . . [Sch 2 Art 7-8]
exchange of statements of claim and defence, within . . . . [Sch 2 Art 7-7]
introduction of requirement . . . . [s 3-1]
Anti-suit injunctions
issuing . . . . [Sch 2 Art 17-10]
place of arbitration . . . . . . [Sch 2 Art 20-7]
Appeals
decision of court or other authority
. . . . [Sch 2 Art 11-10]
possibility . . . . [Sch 2 Art 11-11]
Arbitral award
see also **Award**
definition . . . . [s 3], [s 3-7]
enforcement, grounds for . . [Sch 2 Art 17I-3]
foreign award . . . . [s 8-27]
interest . . . . [s 25], [s 25-1]
— application of legislative provision . [s 25-6]
— compound interest . . . . [s 25-5]
— implied power . . . . [s 25-2]
— legislative amendments . . . . [s 25-3]
— timing . . . . [s 25], [s 25-4]
Arbitral tribunal
amiable compositeur . . . . . . [Sch 2 Art 28-4]
applicable law . . . . [Sch 2 Art 16-5]
arbitrators *see* **Arbitrator**
choice of "law" . . . . [Sch 2 Art 28-3]
contractual terms, determinations and
. . . . [Sch 2 Art 28-5]
definition . . . . [Sch 2 Art 2-2]
ex aequo et bono . . . . [Sch 2 Art 28-4]
expert, appointment of . . . . [Sch 2 Art 26-1], [Sch 2 Art 26-3]
— participation in hearing . . [Sch 2 Art 26-4]
— scope of power . . . . [Sch 2 Art 26-2]
failure to assist . . . . [s 23A]-[s 23A-2]
ICSID *see* **International Centre for Settlement of Investment Disputes (ICSID)**
interim measures *see* **Interim measures**
international
— interpretation of ICSID awards
. . . . [Sch 3 Art 50-2]
— provisional measures, recommending
. . . . [Sch 3 Art 47-2]
— revision of ICSID award . [Sch 3 Art 51-2]

jurisdiction . . . . [Sch 2 Art 16-1]
— discretion to rule on own . [Sch 2 Art 16-4]
— estoppel and . . . . [Sch 2 Art 16-10]
— hearing by court on . . . . [Sch 2 Art 16-9]
— *kompetenz-kompetenz* principle
. . . . [Sch 2 Art 16-3]
— preliminary issues . . . . . [Sch 2 Art 16-8]
— procedural options following ruling
. . . . [Sch 2 Art 16-6]
jurisdictional challenges
— procedural constraints . . . [Sch 2 Art 16-7]
proceedings *see* **Proceedings**
separability principle . . . . . [Sch 2 Art 16-2]
"usages of trade" . . . . [Sch 2 Art 28-5]
Arbitration
consent to
— agency, by . . . . [Sch 3 Art 25-17]
— conciliation and . . . . . . [Sch 3 Art 26-4]
— constituent subdivision, by . [Sch 3 Art 25-17]
— "exclusive remedy" provision
. . . . [Sch 3 Art 26-1], [Sch 3 Art 26-3]
— withdrawal . . . . [Sch 3 Art 25-16]
— writing, in . . . . [Sch 3 Art 25-15]
definition . . . [Sch 2 Art 1-5], [Sch 2 Art 2-1]
diplomatic protection . . . . . [Sch 3 Art 27-1]-[Sch 3 Art 27-3]
exhaustion of local remedies, requirement
. . . . [Sch 3 Art 26-2]
ICSID *see* **International Centre for Settlement of Investment Disputes (ICSID)**
parties put in position they would have been in
. . . . [Sch 2 Art 11-14]
place . . . . [Sch 2 Art 8-2], [Sch 2 Art 20-1], [Sch 2 Art 20-2]
— agreement as to seat . . . . [Sch 2 Art 20-4]
— anti-suit injunction . . . . . [Sch 2 Art 20-7]
— award to be made at . . . . [Sch 2 Art 20-9]
— common law recognition . [Sch 2 Art 20-8]
— federal State, in . . . . [Sch 2 Art 20-6]
— ICSID proceedings . . . . [Sch 3 Art 62-1], [Sch 3 Art 63-1]
— identification . . . . [Sch 2 Art 20-5]
— laws of the seat . . . . [Sch 2 Art 20-3]
— tribunal determination of . [Sch 2 Art 20-10]
Arbitration agreement
application of Part . . . . [s 30]-[s 30-2]
arising in course of arbitration . . . . . [s 3-5]
court, referral to . . . . [Sch 2 Art 8-1]
death of party . . . . [s 23H]-[s 23H-2]
default by party . . . . [s 23B]-[s 23B-2]

339

Arbitration agreement —*continued*
definition . [s 3], [s 3-3], [s 7-6], [Sch 2 Art 7-1]-[Sch 2 Art 7-3]
— UN recommendation . . . . [Sch 2 Art 7-9]
— UNCITRAL recommendation . . . . [Sch 2 Art 7-9]
dispute *see* **Dispute**
form and content . . . . [Sch 2 Art 7-4], [Sch 2 Art 7-5]
law governing main transaction . . . . . [s 3-6]
Model Law, under . . . . [s 3-4]
rules . . . . [Sch 2 Art 2-4]
scope of agreement . . . . [s 7-11]
— case law . . . . [s 7-11]
substance of dispute . . . . . . [Sch 2 Art 8-6]
validity . . . . [Sch 2 Art 4-3]
writing, in *see* **Agreement in writing**

Arbitrator
appointment
— appointing authority . . . . [s 28-3], [Sch 2 Art 11-6]
— considerations . . . . . . [Sch 2 Art 11-12]
— court, by . . . . [Sch 2 Art 11-9]
— foreign nationals . . . . . [Sch 2 Art 11-1]
— ICSID *see* **International Centre for Settlement of Investment Disputes (ICSID)**
— limitations . . . . [Sch 2 Art 11-3]
— "no grievance is felt" . . . [Sch 2 Art 11-13]
— substitute *see* substitute, appointment *below*
— waiting period . . . . [Sch 2 Art 11-7]
appointment procedure
— agreement on . . . . [Sch 2 Art 11-2]
— court intervention . . . . . . [Sch 2 Art 11-8]
— default . . . . [Sch 2 Art 11-5]
— domestic law, under . . . . [Sch 2 Art 11-8]
— failure to follow . . . . [Sch 2 Art 11-4]
apprehended bias test . . . . [s 18A-2]
— mediation procedure . . . . [s 18A-4]
— *R v Gough* . . . . [s 18A-3]
bias
— impartiality and independence *see below*
— real danger of . . . . [Sch 2 Art 12-7]
challenges to
— agreement of parties . . . . [Sch 2 Art 13-2]
— decisions on . . . . [Sch 2 Art 11-6]
— failure to withdraw following . . . . [Sch 2 Art 13-5]
— grounds . . . . [Sch 2 Art 12-1]
— procedure . . . . [Sch 2 Art 13-1]-[Sch 2 Art 13-4]
— test . . . . [Sch 2 Art 12-6]
conflicts of interest, investigating . . . . [Sch 2 Art 12-5]
contractual release and indemnity . . . [s 28-5]
decision-making . . . . [Sch 2 Art 29-1]-[Sch 2 Art 29-4]
disclosure obligation . . . . . [Sch 2 Art 12-3]
— trigger . . . . [Sch 2 Art 12-4]

dissenting . . . . [Sch 2 Art 29-2]
failure or impossibility to act . [Sch 2 Art 14-1]
— delay and . . . . [Sch 2 Art 14-3]
— meaning . . . . [Sch 2 Art 14-2]
immunity . . . . [s 28]
— appointing authority . . . . [s 28-3]
— common law . . . . [s 28-4]
— history of section . . . . [s 28-1]
— ICSID Convention, under . . . . . . [s 28-6]
— onus of good faith . . . . [s 28-2]
impartiality
— justifiable doubts . . . . . [s 18A], [s 18A-1], [Sch 2 Art 12-4]
— principle, implementation . [Sch 2 Art 12-2]
independence
— justifiable doubts . . . . . [s 18A], [s 18A-1], [Sch 2 Art 12-4]
— principle, implementation . [Sch 2 Art 12-2]
number on arbitration tribunal . [Sch 2 Art 10-1]
— autonomy in determining . [Sch 2 Art 10-2]
— supplementary rule . . . . . [Sch 2 Art 10-3]
signing award . . . . [Sch 2 Art 29-3]
substitute, appointment . . . . [Sch 2 Art 15-1]
— comprehensive approach . [Sch 2 Art 15-2]
— procedure . . . . [Sch 2 Art 15-4]
termination of mandate . . . . [Sch 2 Art 14-4]
— no appeal . . . . [Sch 2 Art 14-5]
withdrawal . [Sch 2 Art 14-6], [Sch 2 Art 15-3]
Australia
definition . . . . [s 3-8]
Australian Centre for International Commercial Arbitration (ACICA)
agreed procedural rules . . . . [Sch 2 Art 6-5]
establishment . . . . [Sch 2 Art 6-3]
Rules . . . . [Sch 2 Art 6-4]
Award
see also **Arbitral award**
agreement to dispense with reasons . . . . [Sch 2 Art 31-5]
annulment
— application, procedural requirements . . . . [Sch 3 Art 52-9]
— effect . . . . [Sch 3 Art 52-15]
— grounds . [Sch 3 Art 52-2]-[Sch 3 Art 52-8]
— power . . . . [Sch 3 Art 52-1]
binding nature of . . . . [s 33]-[s 33-2]
conflict with public policy . . [Sch 2 Art 34-4]
contracting out . . . . [Sch 2 Art 34-5]
correction and interpretation . [Sch 2 Art 33-1]
— claims presented yet omitted . . . . [Sch 2 Art 33-2]
— form and content . . . . . . [Sch 2 Art 33-3]
date and place, statement of . [Sch 2 Art 31-6]
definition . . . . [s 31], [s 31-2]
delivery to parties . . . . [Sch 2 Art 31-7]
dissenting reasons . . . . [Sch 2 Art 31-4]
enforcement . . . . [Sch 2 Art 35-1]-[Sch 2 Art 35-5]
— discretionary power . . . . [Sch 2 Art 36-4]

References are to paragraph numbers

INDEX

— grounds for refusal . . . . [Sch 2 Art 36-1]-[Sch 2 Art 36-6]
— public policy considerations . . . . [Sch 2 Art 36-5]
form and content . . . . [Sch 2 Art 30-2], [Sch 2 Art 31-1]-[Sch 2 Art 31-7]
ICSID . . . . [Sch 3 Art 48-1]
— annulment . . . . [Sch 3 Art 52-1]-[Sch 3 Art 52-15]
— binding force . . . . [Sch 3 Art 50-3], [Sch 3 Art 53-1], [Sch 3 Art 54-3]
— decision as part of . . . . . [Sch 3 Art 49-3]
— definition . . . . [Sch 3 Art 53-5]
— dispatch to parties . . . . . [Sch 3 Art 49-1]
— dissenting opinions . . . . . [Sch 3 Art 48-5]
— enforcement . . . . [Sch 3 Art 53-1]-[Sch 3 Art 53-5], [Sch 3 Art 54-1]-[Sch 3 Art 54-7]
— interpretation . . . . [Sch 3 Art 50-1]-[Sch 3 Art 50-5]
— post-award procedures, time limit . . . . [Sch 3 Art 49-4]
— publication . . . . [Sch 3 Art 48-6]
— questions submitted, dealing with . . . . [Sch 3 Art 48-5]
— recognition . . . . [Sch 3 Art 54-1]-[Sch 3 Art 54-7]
— rectification . . . . [Sch 3 Art 49-2]
— *res judicata effect* . . . . . [Sch 3 Art 53-2]
— revision . [Sch 3 Art 51-1]-[Sch 3 Art 51-6]
— State immunity . . . . [Sch 3 Art 55-1]-[Sch 3 Art 55-3]
— stay of enforcement . . . . [Sch 3 Art 50-5], [Sch 3 Art 51-6], [Sch 3 Art 52-13], [Sch 3 Art 52-14]
— supplementary or additional . . . . [Sch 3 Art 49-2]
— writing, requirement to be in . . . . [Sch 3 Art 48-3]
Investment Convention, under . [s 34]-[s 34-2]
nature and extent of reasons . [Sch 2 Art 31-3]
provisional measure, distinguished . . . . [Sch 3 Art 47-4]
recognition . [s 35]-[s 35-2], [Sch 2 Art 35-1]-[Sch 2 Art 35-5]
— grounds for refusal . . . . [Sch 2 Art 36-1]-[Sch 2 Art 36-6]
recourse
— contracting out . . . . [Sch 2 Art 34-5]
— exclusive . . . . [Sch 2 Art 34-1]
remission to arbitration tribunal . . . . [Sch 2 Art 34-9]
setting aside . . . . [Sch 2 Art 34-1], [Sch 2 Art 34-8]
— application . . . . [Sch 2 Art 34-2]
— discretionary remedy . . . . [Sch 2 Art 34-6]
— grounds . . . . [Sch 2 Art 34-3]
— limitation period . . . . . . [Sch 2 Art 34-7]
statement of reasons . . . . . . [Sch 2 Art 31-2]

Bill of lading
construction and jurisdiction . . . . . . [s 2C-9]
parties . . . . [s 2C-5]
Burden of proof
parties . . . . [Sch 2 Art 19-5]
Carriage of goods
sea, by . . . . [s 2C], [s 2C-12]
— arbitration agreements . . . . [s 2C-3]
— award, making . . . . [s 2C-6]
— bill of lading, parties to . . . . [s 2C-5]
— documentation . . . . . [s 2C-4], [s 2C-10]
— estoppel . . . . [s 2C-7]
— Hague-Visby Rules . . . [s 2C-8], [s 2C-13]
— Hamburg Rules . . . . . [s 2C-8], [s 2C-11], [s 2C-13]
— history of section . . . . [s 2C-1]
— jurisdiction . . . . [s 2C-2], [s 2C-9]
Charterparties
construction and jurisdiction . . . . . [s 2C-10]
Commercial
definition . . . . [Sch 2 Art 1-4]
Conciliation
commencement of proceedings . . . . [Sch 3 Art 28-1]
Conciliation Commission
— constitution of . . . . [Sch 3 Art 29-1]
— failure to constitute . . . . . [Sch 3 Art 30-1]
— function . . . . [Sch 3 Art 34-1]
— jurisdiction . . . . [Sch 3 Art 32-1], [Sch 3 Art 41-2]
— report, requirement to . . . [Sch 3 Art 34-2]
ICSID Convention, procedure in . . . . [Sch 3 Art 33-1]
Panel of Conciliators . . . . . [Sch 3 Art 31-1]
"without prejudice" . . . . [Sch 3 Art 35-1]
Confidential information
confidentiality, interpretation . . . . . [s 23C-2]
definition . . . . [s 15], [s 15-2]
disclosure . . . . [s 23C], [s 23B-1]
— circumstances . . . . [s 23D], [s 23D-1]
— court orders . . . . [s 23G], [s 23G-1]
— New Zealand . . . . [s 23C-3]
— prohibitions . . . . [s 23F], [s 23F-1]
— Tribunal orders . . . . . . [s 23E], [s 23E-1]
Contracting States
disputes . . . . [Sch 3 Art 64-1]
— jurisdiction . . . . [Sch 3 Art 25-13]
Contracts
terms . . . . [Sch 2 Art 28-5]
Contracts of affreightment
construction and jurisdiction . . . . . [s 2C-10]
Convention on the Recognition and Enforcement of Foreign Arbitral Awards
adoption in Australia . . . . [s 3-1]
Convention countries . . . . [s 3], [s 7-7]
enforcement of awards . . . . [s 3]
evidence relating to . . . . [s 10], [s 10-1]
text . . . . [Sch 1]

References are to paragraph numbers

341

Convention on the Settlement of Investment Disputes between States and Nationals of Other States
amendment . . . . [Sch 3 Art 65-1]
— procedure . . . . [Sch 3 Art 65-1], [Sch 3 Art 66-1]
annulment, power of . . . . [s 31-5]
application
— all territories of a State . . [Sch 3 Art 70-1]
— Australia . . . . [s 32]-[s 32-3]
articles . . . . [s 31-11]
awards made under . . . . [s 34]-[s 34-2], [Sch 3 Art 53-3]
— recognition and enforcement regime . . . . [Sch 3 Art 54-2]
denunciation . . . . [Sch 3 Art 71-1]
— effect . . . . [Sch 3 Art 71-2]
domestic legislation, implementation in . . . . [Sch 3 Art 69-1]
entry into force . . . . [Sch 3 Art 68-3]
evidence under . . . . [s 36]-[s 36-3]
exclusion of Chapter 1 . . . . [s 32-3]
ICSID Implementation Act . . . . [s 31-1]
interpretation . . . . [s 31], [s 31-10]
— Judiciary Act, and . . . . [s 38]-[s 38-3]
— power . . . . [s 31-3]
language versions . . [Sch 3 Final Provision-1]
notices . . . . [Sch 3 Art 72-1]
Preamble . . . . [Sch 3 Preamble-1]
ratification . . . . [Sch 3 Art 68-1]
registration with United Nations . . . . [Sch 3 Art 74-1]
reservations . . . . [Sch 3 Art 68-2]
revision, power of . . . . [s 31-4]
settlement of disputes . . . . . [Sch 3 Art 1-4]
signature . . . . [Sch 3 Art 67-1]
text . . . . [Sch 3]
World Bank as depository for . [Sch 3 Art 73-1]
— functions . . . . [Sch 3 Art 75-1]

Costs
agreement of parties . . . . [s 27-2]
discretion to award . . . . [s 27]
— history of section . . . . [s 27-1]
ICSID . . . . [Sch 3 Art 59-1]
— apportionment . . . . [Sch 3 Art 61-1]-[Sch 3 Art 61-3]
— fees and expenses . . . . . [Sch 3 Art 60-1]-[Sch 3 Art 60-2]
limitation of . . . . [s 27-3]

Court
"competent" . . . . [Sch 3 Art 54-6]
definition . . . . [s 3], [s 3-9], [s 7-24], [s 22A], [Sch 2 Art 2-2]
interim measures, ordering . [Sch 2 Art 17J-1]-[Sch 2 Art 17J-4]
international
— interpretation of ICSID awards . . . . [Sch 3 Art 50-2]
— provisional measures, recommending . . . . [Sch 3 Art 47-2]

— revision of ICSID award . [Sch 3 Art 51-2]
intervention . . . . [Sch 2 Art 5-1]
— limitation . . . . [Sch 2 Art 5-3]
— scope of legislative power . [Sch 2 Art 5-2]
matters to consider . . . . [s 39]-[s 39-2]
prescribed . . . . [s 18]
referral to . . . . [Sch 2 Art 8-1]

Data message
definition . . . . [s 3], [s 3-10]

Death
party to arbitration agreement . . . . . [s 23H]-[s 23H-2]

Debt
interest on . . . . [s 26], [s 26-1]
— compound interest . . . . [s 26-3]
— opting out . . . . [s 26-2]

Department of Foreign Affairs and Trade
references to "Department" . . . [s 31], [s 31-7]
Secretary . . . . [s 31], [s 31-8]

Diplomatic protection
Investment Convention provisions . [Sch 3 Art 27-1]-[Sch 3 Art 27-3]

Dispute
Contracting States . . . . [Sch 3 Art 64-1]
— jurisdiction . . . . [Sch 3 Art 25-13]
interim measures . . . . [Sch 2 Art 9-1]
— jurisdiction . . . . [Sch 2 Art 9-3]
— place of arbitration . . . . . . [Sch 2 Art 9-2]
settlement . [Sch 2 Art 30-1]-[Sch 2 Art 30-2]
substance
— rules applicable . . . . [Sch 2 Art 28-1]
— statement of . . . . [Sch 2 Art 8-6]

Electronic communication
definition . . . . [s 3], [s 3-10]

Enforcement
arbitral award . . . . [Sch 2 Art 17I-3], [Sch 2 Art 35-1]-[Sch 2 Art 35-5]
— discretionary power . . . . [Sch 2 Art 36-4]
— grounds for refusal . . . . [Sch 2 Art 36-1]-[Sch 2 Art 36-6]
— public policy considerations . . . . [Sch 2 Art 36-5]
declaratory award . . . . [s 8-6]
definition . . . . [s 3]
foreign agreements . . . . [s 7], [s 7-1]
— application, timing of . . . . [s 7-23]
— arbitrability . . . . [s 7-12]
— "capable of settlement by arbitration", interpretation . . . . [s 7-10]
— conditions, imposition of . . . . . . [s 7-17]
— constitutional validity . . . . [s 7-3]
— court, powers and discretion . . . . [s 7-15], [s 7-17], [s 7-24]
— "determination of matter", interpretation . . . . [s 7-9]
— eligible parties . . . . [s 7-14]
— "incapable of being performed", interpretation . . . . [s 7-22]
— "inoperative", interpretation . . . . . [s 7-21]
— interim or supplementary orders . . [s 7-18]

References are to paragraph numbers

INDEX

— interlocutory orders . . . . [s 7-16]
— legislative amendments . . . . [s 7-2]
— "null and void, inoperative or incapable of being performed", interpretation . . . . [s 7-19]
— "null and void", interpretation . . . [s 7-20]
— procedural law . . . . [s 7-5]
— rights of parties . . . . [s 7-13]
— scope of agreement . . . . [s 7-11]
— stay of proceedings . . . . [s 7-4]
foreign award . . . . [s 8-3], [s 8-5]
— adjournment of proceedings . . . . [s 8-24]
— asset preservation orders . . . . . . [s 8-33]
— common law . . . . [s 8-31]
— composition of authority or procedure . [s 8-16]
— currency . . . . [s 8-28]
— discretion . . . . [s 8-8]
— election . . . . [s 8-11]
— estoppel . . . . [s 8-11]
— failure to give reasonable notice . . . [s 8-14]
— incapacity . . . . [s 8-12]
— interest on award or judgment . . . [s 8-27]
— issue estoppel . . . . [s 8-32]
— limitation statutes . . . . [s 8-29]
— "not capable of settlement by arbitration", interpretation . . . . [s 8-20]
— "not yet binding", interpretation . . [s 8-17]
— onus of proof . . . . [s 8-10]
— partial enforcement . . . . [s 8-18]
— place, laws relating to . . . . [s 8-19]
— public policy . . . . [s 8-21]-[s 8-23]
— reciprocity . . . . [s 8-9]
— refusal to enforce . . . . [s 8-7]
— resumption of proceedings . . . . . [s 8-26]
— scope of submission to arbitration . [s 8-15]
— security, calculation of . . . . [s 8-25]
— security for costs . . . . [s 8-30]
— "set aside", interpretation . . . . . . [s 8-17]
— void for uncertainty . . . . [s 8-13]
— waiver . . . . [s 8-11]
ICSID award . . . . [Sch 3 Art 53-1]-[Sch 3 Art 53-5], [Sch 3 Art 54-1]-[Sch 3 Art 54-7]
interim measures . . . . [Sch 2 Art 17G-1]
— disclosure obligations . . [Sch 2 Art 17G-7]
— history . . . . [Sch 2 Art 17G-4]
— Model Law, under . . . . [Sch 2 Art 17G-2], [Sch 2 Art 17G-3], [Sch 2 Art 17G-6]
— refusal, grounds for . . . [Sch 2 Art 17I-1]-[Sch 2 Art 17I-6]
— security, provision of appropriate . . . . [Sch 2 Art 17G-8]
— "shall be recognised as binding" . . . . . [Sch 2 Art 17G-5]
preliminary orders . . . . . . [Sch 2 Art 17G-1]
— disclosure obligations . . [Sch 2 Art 17G-7]
— history . . . . [Sch 2 Art 17G-4]

— Model Law, under . . . . [Sch 2 Art 17G-2], [Sch 2 Art 17G-3], [Sch 2 Art 17G-6]
— refusal, grounds for . . . [Sch 2 Art 17I-1]-[Sch 2 Art 17I-6]
— security, provision of appropriate . . . . [Sch 2 Art 17G-8]
— "shall be recognised as binding" . . . . . [Sch 2 Art 17G-5]
Estoppel
carriage of goods and arbitration agreements . . . . [s 2C-7]
foreign awards, enforcement of . . . . . [s 8-32]
jurisdiction of arbitral tribunal . [Sch 2 Art 16-10]
Evidence
admissibility . . . . [Sch 2 Art 19-4]
Convention, relating to . . . . . [s 10], [s 10-1]
court assistance . . . . [Sch 2 Art 27-1]
— competence . . . . [Sch 2 Art 27-2]
— foreign courts . . . . [Sch 2 Art 27-6]
— integration with existing procedures . . . . [Sch 2 Art 27-4]
— role of court . . . . [Sch 2 Art 27-5]
— subpoenas . . . . [Sch 2 Art 27-3]
documentary . . . . [Sch 2 Art 22-6], [Sch 2 Art 24-6]
— failure to produce . . . . . [Sch 2 Art 25-6]
foreign agreements *see* **Foreign agreements**
foreign awards *see* **Foreign awards**
ICSID, under
— deemed necessary . . . . . [Sch 3 Art 43-5]
— IBA Rules on the Taking of Evidence in International Arbitration . . . . [Sch 3 Art 43-4]
— national rules, non-application of . . . . [Sch 3 Art 43-6]
— non-mandatory provision . [Sch 3 Art 43-2]
— powers . [Sch 3 Art 43-1], [Sch 3 Art 43-2]
Investment Convention, under . [s 36]-[s 36-3]
materiality . . . . [Sch 2 Art 19-4]
orders . . . . [s 23J]-[s 23J-3]
relevance . . . . [Sch 2 Art 19-4]
weight of . . . . [Sch 2 Art 19-4]
Experts
appointment by tribunal . . . [Sch 2 Art 26-1], [Sch 2 Art 26-3]
— participation in hearing . . [Sch 2 Art 26-4]
— scope of power . . . . [Sch 2 Art 26-2]
reports . . . . [Sch 2 Art 24-6]
Foreign Affairs Department
definition . . . . [s 3], [s 3-11]
delegation by Secretary . . . [s 10A], [s 10A-1]
Foreign agreements
application, timing of . . . . [s 7-23]
arbitrability . . . . [s 7-12]
"capable of settlement by arbitration", interpretation . . . . [s 7-10]
conditions, imposition of . . . . [s 7-17]
constitutional validity . . . . [s 7-3]

References are to paragraph numbers

Foreign agreements —*continued*
  court, powers and discretion . [s 7-15], [s 7-17], [s 7-24]
  "determination of matter", interpretation . [s 7-9]
  eligible parties . . . . [s 7-14]
  enforcement . . . . [s 7], [s 7-1], [s 12]-[s 12-1]
  evidence . . . . [s 9]
  — Convention, relating to . . . [s 10], [s 10-1]
  — history . . . . [s 9-1]
  — Model Law, anomalies . . . . [s 9-3]
  — requirements . . . . [s 9-2]
  "incapable of being performed", interpretation . . . . [s 7-22]
  "inoperative", interpretation . . . . [s 7-21]
  interim or supplementary orders . . . . [s 7-18]
  interlocutory orders . . . . [s 7-16]
  legislative amendments . . . . [s 7-2]
  "null and void, inoperative or incapable of being performed", interpretation . [s 7-19]
  "null and void", interpretation . . . . . [s 7-20]
  procedural law . . . . [s 7-5]
  rights of parties . . . . [s 7-13]
  scope of agreement . . . . [s 7-11]
  stay of proceedings . . . . [s 7-4]
Foreign award
  declaratory award, enforcement . . . . . [s 8-6]
  definition . . . . [s 3]
  enforcement . . . [s 8-3], [s 8-5], [s 12]-[s 12-1]
  — adjournment of proceedings . . . . . [s 8-24]
  — asset preservation orders . . . . [s 8-33]
  — common law . . . . [s 8-31]
  — composition of authority or procedure . [s 8-16]
  — currency . . . . [s 8-28]
  — discretion . . . . [s 8-8]
  — election . . . . [s 8-11]
  — estoppel . . . . [s 8-11]
  — failure to give reasonable notice . . [s 8-14]
  — incapacity . . . . [s 8-12]
  — issue estoppel . . . . [s 8-32]
  — limitation statutes . . . . [s 8-29]
  — onus of proof . . . . [s 8-10]
  — partial enforcement . . . . [s 8-18]
  — place, laws relating to . . . . [s 8-19]
  — public policy . . . . [s 8-21]-[s 8-23]
  — reciprocity . . . . [s 8-9]
  — refusal to enforce . . . . [s 8-7]
  — resumption of proceedings . . . . . . [s 8-26]
  — scope of submission to arbitration . [s 8-15]
  — security, calculation of . . . . [s 8-25]
  — security for costs . . . . [s 8-30]
  — "set aside", interpretation . . . . . . [s 8-17]
  — void for uncertainty . . . . [s 8-13]
  — waiver . . . . [s 8-11]
  evidence . . . . [s 9]
  — Convention, relating to . . . [s 10], [s 10-1]
  — history . . . . [s 9-1]
  — Model Law, anomalies . . . . [s 9-3]
  — requirements . . . . [s 9-2]

form of court order . . . . [s 8-4]
interest on award or judgment . . . . . [s 8-27]
"not capable of settlement by arbitration", interpretation . . . . [s 8-20]
"not yet binding", interpretation . . . . [s 8-17]
recognition . . . . [s 8]
— history . . . . [s 8-1]
— procedure . . . . [s 8-2]
Immunity
  arbitrator . . . . [s 28]
  — appointing authority . . . . [s 28-3]
  — common law . . . . [s 28-4]
  — history of section . . . . [s 28-1]
  — ICSID Convention, under . . . . . . [s 28-6]
  — onus of good faith . . . . [s 28-2]
  State
  — enforcement of ICSID awards . [Sch 3 Art 55-1]-[Sch 3 Art 55-3]
Impartiality
  arbitrator *see* **Arbitrator**
Independence
  arbitrator *see* **Independence of arbitrator**
Interest
  arbitral award . . . . [s 25], [s 25-1]
  — application of legislative provision . [s 25-6]
  — compound interest . . . . [s 25-5]
  — implied power . . . . [s 25-2]
  — legislative amendments . . . . [s 25-3]
  — timing . . . . [s 25], [s 25-4]
  compound
  — arbitral award . . . . [s 25-5]
  — debt . . . . [s 26-3]
  debt under award . . . . [s 26], [s 26-1]
  — compound interest . . . . [s 26-3]
  — opting out . . . . [s 26-2]
  foreign award . . . . [s 8-27]
Interim measures
  anti-suit injunctions . . . . . [Sch 2 Art 17-10]
  applicable provisions . . . . [Sch 2 Art 17D-1]-[Sch 2 Art 17D-4]
  characteristics . . . . [Sch 2 Art 17-8]
  costs and damages . . . . . [Sch 2 Art 17G-1]-[Sch 2 Art 17G-2]
  court-ordered . . . . [Sch 2 Art 17J-1]-[Sch 2 Art 17J-4]
  disclosure obligations . . . . [Sch 2 Art 17F-1]-[Sch 2 Art 17F-3]
  — non-compliance . . . . . . [Sch 2 Art 17F-4]
  enforcement and recognition . . . . [Sch 2 Art 17G-1]
  — disclosure obligations . . [Sch 2 Art 17G-7]
  — history . . . . [Sch 2 Art 17G-4]
  — Model Law, under . . . . [Sch 2 Art 17G-2], [Sch 2 Art 17G-3], [Sch 2 Art 17G-6]
  — refusal, grounds for . . [Sch 2 Art 17I-1]-[Sch 2 Art 17I-6]
  — security, provision of appropriate . . . . [Sch 2 Art 17G-8]

References are to paragraph numbers

INDEX

— "shall be recognised as binding" . . . . . **[Sch 2 Art 17G-5]**
evidence, preservation of . . **[Sch 2 Art 17A-7]**
form . . . . **[Sch 2 Art 17-11]**
grant . . . . **[Sch 2 Art 17-1]**
— conditions . . . . **[Sch 2 Art 17A-1]**-**[Sch 2 Art 17A-6]**
— "harm not adequately repairable". . . . **[Sch 2 Art 17A-3]**
— power, nature of . . . . . **[Sch 2 Art 17-2]**-**[Sch 2 Art 17-5]**
— "reasonable possibility the requesting party will succeed on the merits" . . . . . . **[Sch 2 Art 17A-6]**
— "substantially outweighs". **[Sch 2 Art 17A-4]**
— "urgency" . . . . **[Sch 2 Art 17A-5]**
legislative history . . . . **[Sch 2 Art 17-6]**
Model Law regime, revision of . **[Sch 2 Art 17-7]**, **[Sch 2 Art 17-12]**
modification . . . . **[Sch 2 Art 17D-5]**
request . . . . **[Sch 2 Art 9-1]**
— jurisdiction . . . . **[Sch 2 Art 9-3]**
— place of arbitration . . . . . . **[Sch 2 Art 9-2]**
revocation . . . . **[Sch 2 Art 17D-5]**
scope . . . . **[Sch 2 Art 17-9]**
security, request for . . . . . **[Sch 2 Art 17E-1]**-**[Sch 2 Art 17E-4]**
suspension . . . . **[Sch 2 Art 17D-5]**

International
courts
— interpretation of ICSID awards . . . . **[Sch 3 Art 50-2]**
— provisional measures, recommending . . . . **[Sch 3 Art 47-2]**
— revision of ICSID award . **[Sch 3 Art 51-2]**
definition . . . . **[Sch 2 Art 1-3]**
tribunals
— interpretation of ICSID awards . . . . **[Sch 3 Art 50-2]**
— provisional measures, recommending . . . . **[Sch 3 Art 47-2]**
— revision of ICSID award . **[Sch 3 Art 51-2]**

International Arbitration Act 1974
Acts Interpretation Act 1901 and . . . **[s 2D-4]**
additional provisions, application . . . **[s 22]**-**[s 22-3]**
commencement . . . . **[s 2]**, **[s 2-1]**
construction . . . . **[s 17-2]**
Crown, binding . . . . **[s 2B]**
— common law presumption . . . . . . **[s 2B-2]**
— extended operation of Act . . . . . . **[s 2B-3]**
— history of section . . . . **[s 2B-1]**
interpretation . . . . **[s 2D-5]**
— context . . . . **[s 2D-3]**
objects . . . . **[s 2D6**
— effect . . . . **[s 2D-2]**
— history of section . . . . **[s 2D-1]**
regulations . . . . **[s 40]**-**[s 40-3]**
short title . . . . **[s 1]**, **[s 1-1]**

territories . . . . **[s 2A]**
— extended operation of Act . . . . . . **[s 2A-3]**
— external . . . . **[s 2A-2]**
— history of section . . . . **[s 2A-1]**

International Centre for Settlement of Investment Disputes (ICSID)
Additional Facility
— adoption of . . . . **[Sch 3 Art 6-5]**
— Secretary-General and . . . **[Sch 3 Art 11-5]**
Administrative Council
— Additional Facility, adoption of . . . . **[Sch 3 Art 6-5]**
— adoption of decisions . . . . **[Sch 3 Art 6-2]**
— annual meeting . . . . **[Sch 3 Art 7-2]**
— chairman *see* chairman *below*
— committees, formation . . . **[Sch 3 Art 6-3]**
— composition . . . . **[Sch 3 Art 4-1]**
— meetings . . **[Sch 3 Art 7-1]**-**[Sch 3 Art 7-5]**
— powers and functions . . . . **[Sch 3 Art 6-1]**, **[Sch 3 Art 6-4]**
— quorum . . . . **[Sch 3 Art 7-4]**
— remuneration for members . **[Sch 3 Art 8-1]**
— voting . . . **[Sch 3 Art 7-3]**, **[Sch 3 Art 7-5]**
— World Bank Board of Governors and . . . . **[Sch 3 Art 4-2]**
Annulment Committee . . . . **[Sch 3 Art 52-10]**
— procedure . . . . **[Sch 3 Art 52-11]**
— role . . . . **[Sch 3 Art 52-12]**
arbitration proceedings
— applicable law . . . . . . **[Sch 3 Art 42-1]**-**[Sch 3 Art 42-9]**
— commencement . . . . **[Sch 3 Art 36-1]**
— cost *see* costs *below*
— domestic law, application . **[Sch 3 Art 32-7]**
— *ex aequo et bono* . . . . . . **[Sch 3 Art 42-9]**
— failure to appear or present case . **[Sch 3 Art 45-1]**-**[Sch 3 Art 45-4]**
— international law and . . . **[Sch 3 Art 42-5]**-**[Sch 3 Art 42-7]**
— 90-day time limit . . . . . . **[Sch 3 Art 38-2]**
— no *non liquet* . . . . **[Sch 3 Art 42-8]**
— place . . **[Sch 3 Art 62-1]**, **[Sch 3 Art 63-1]**
— procedural issues, power to decide . . . . **[Sch 3 Art 44-2]**
— request, information included in . . . . **[Sch 3 Art 36-3]**
— rules of procedure . . . . . **[Sch 3 Art 44-1]**
— screening requests . . . . . **[Sch 3 Art 36-4]**
— substantive law . . . . **[Sch 3 Art 42-2]**
— who may commence . . . . **[Sch 3 Art 36-2]**
arbitration tribunal
— admissibility . . . . **[Sch 3 Art 41-7]**
— arbitrators, appointment *see* arbitrators *below*
— constitution procedure . . . **[Sch 3 Art 37-1]**
— corruption . . . . **[Sch 3 Art 52-6]**
— dissenting opinions . . . . . **[Sch 3 Art 48-5]**
— establishment . . . . **[Sch 3 Art 38-1]**
— failure to state reasons for award . . . . **[Sch 3 Art 52-8]**

References are to paragraph numbers

345

International Centre for Settlement of Investment Disputes (ICSID) —*continued*
arbitration tribunal —*continued*
— incidental or additional claims .... [Sch 3 Art 46-1]
— jurisdiction .... [Sch 3 Art 41-1], [Sch 3 Art 41-4]-[Sch 3 Art 41-8]
— "manifestly exceeded its powers" ...... [Sch 3 Art 52-4], [Sch 3 Art 52-5]
— not properly constituted .. [Sch 3 Art 52-3]
— objections to jurisdiction . [Sch 3 Art 41-5], [Sch 3 Art 41-8], [Sch 3 Art 41-9]
— powers and functions ... [Sch 3 Art 41-1]-[Sch 3 Art 41-10], [Sch 3 Art 46-1], [Sch 3 Art 47-1]-[Sch 3 Art 47-6]
— provisional measures, recommending . [Sch 3 Art 47-1]-[Sch 3 Art 47-6]
— questions, taking ...... [Sch 3 Art 48-2]
— "serious departure from fundamental rule of procedure" ..... [Sch 3 Art 52-7]
— summary dismissal procedure .... [Sch 3 Art 41-10]
arbitrators
— appointment .... [Sch 3 Art 37-2], [Sch 3 Art 37-3], [Sch 3 Art 38-4]-[Sch 3 Art 38-5]
— challenges to .... [Sch 3 Art 57-1]-[Sch 3 Art 57-3]
— disqualification .... [Sch 3 Art 58-1]-[Sch 3 Art 58-2]
— nationality . [Sch 3 Art 38-5], [Sch 3 Art 39-1]-[Sch 3 Art 39-4]
— non-Panel .... [Sch 3 Art 40-1]
— qualities .... [Sch 3 Art 40-2]
— replacement .... [Sch 3 Art 56-1]-[Sch 3 Art 56-3]
Archives
— inviolability .... [Sch 3 Art 23-1]-[Sch 3 Art 23-2]
— official communications, protection of .... [Sch 3 Art 23-3]
awards ... [Sch 3 Art 48-1]-[Sch 3 Art 48-6], [Sch 3 Art 49-1]-[Sch 3 Art 49-4]
— annulment . [Sch 3 Art 52-1]-[Sch 3 Art 52-15]
— enforcement .... [Sch 3 Art 53-1]-[Sch 3 Art 53-5], [Sch 3 Art 54-1]-[Sch 3 Art 54-7]
— interpretation .... [Sch 3 Art 50-1]-[Sch 3 Art 50-5]
— recognition .... [Sch 3 Art 54-1]-[Sch 3 Art 54-7]
— revision . [Sch 3 Art 51-1]-[Sch 3 Art 51-6]
— State immunity .... [Sch 3 Art 55-1]-[Sch 3 Art 55-3]
chairman .... [Sch 3 Art 5-1]
— appointment of Annulment Committee .... [Sch 3 Art 52-10]

— appointment of arbitrators . [Sch 3 Art 38-4], [Sch 3 Art 38-5]
— appointment of panellists . [Sch 3 Art 13-5]
— powers .... [Sch 3 Art 5-3]
conciliation .... [Sch 3 Art 28-2]
conciliators
— challenges to .... [Sch 3 Art 57-1]-[Sch 3 Art 57-3]
— disqualification .... [Sch 3 Art 58-1]-[Sch 3 Art 58-2]
— replacement .... [Sch 3 Art 56-1]-[Sch 3 Art 56-3]
costs
— apportionment .... [Sch 3 Art 61-1]-[Sch 3 Art 61-3]
— fees and expenses ..... [Sch 3 Art 60-1]-[Sch 3 Art 60-2]
— using ICSID facilities ... [Sch 3 Art 59-1]
Deputy Secretary-General
— nomination .... [Sch 3 Art 10-1]
— role .... [Sch 3 Art 10-4]
establishment .... [Sch 3 Art 1-1]
evidence gathering
— deemed necessary ..... [Sch 3 Art 43-5]
— IBA Rules on the Taking of Evidence in International Arbitration .... [Sch 3 Art 43-4]
— national rules, non-application of .... [Sch 3 Art 43-6]
— non-mandatory provision . [Sch 3 Art 43-2]
— powers . [Sch 3 Art 43-1], [Sch 3 Art 43-2]
finance
— Contracting States ..... [Sch 3 Art 17-1]
— Memorandum of Administrative Agreement .... [Sch 3 Art 17-1]
jurisdiction . [Sch 3 Art 25-1], [Sch 3 Art 25-2]
— "arise directly" out of "an investment". ... [Sch 3 Art 25-7]-[Sch 3 Art 25-12]
— classes of disputes, notifications .... [Sch 3 Art 25-18], [Sch 3 Art 25-19]
— conditions .... [Sch 3 Art 25-3]
— consent to arbitration *see* **Arbitration**
— dispute, nature of ..... [Sch 3 Art 25-5]
— "legal dispute", determination of .... [Sch 3 Art 25-4], [Sch 3 Art 25-6]
— legal persons, nationality of . [Sch 3 Art 25-14]
— parties both Contracting States .... [Sch 3 Art 25-13]
legal personality .... [Sch 3 Art 18-1]
— "full" international ..... [Sch 3 Art 18-2]
— international recognition .. [Sch 3 Art 18-3]
location .... [Sch 3 Art 2-1]-[Sch 3 Art 2-4]
name .... [Sch 3 Art 1-2]
Panels
— appointment of panellists . [Sch 3 Art 13-5]

References are to paragraph numbers

INDEX

— Australia's panellists . . . . [Sch 3 Art 13-4]
— designation of persons . . [Sch 3 Art 13-1],
    [Sch 3 Art 16-2], [Sch 3 Art 16-3]
— "high moral character", requirement for
    . . . . [Sch 3 Art 14-2]
— maintenance . . . . [Sch 3 Art 12-1]
— membership, cessation of . [Sch 3 Art 56-2]
— membership, overlapping . [Sch 3 Art 13-2],
    [Sch 3 Art 16-1]
— nationality of appointments
    . . . . [Sch 3 Art 13-3]
— purpose . . . . [Sch 3 Art 12-2]
— qualities of members . . . [Sch 3 Art 12-3],
    [Sch 3 Art 14-1]
— "recognised competence" . [Sch 3 Art 14-3]
— succession . . . . [Sch 3 Art 15-3]
— term of appointment . . . . [Sch 3 Art 15-1]
— vacancies . . . . [Sch 3 Art 15-2]
— world representation . . . . [Sch 3 Art 14-4]
privileges and immunities . . [Sch 3 Art 19-1],
    [Sch 3 Art 21-5]
— Australian law, under . . . [Sch 3 Art 19-2],
    [Sch 3 Art 20-3], [Sch 3 Art 21-6]
— certain persons . . . . . . [Sch 3 Art 21-1],
    [Sch 3 Art 21-2]
— legal process, immunity from
    . . . . [Sch 3 Art 20-1]
— limitations . . . . [Sch 3 Art 21-3]
— persons appearing in proceedings
    . [Sch 3 Art 22-1]-[Sch 3 Art 22-2]
— waiver of immunity . . . . [Sch 3 Art 20-2],
    [Sch 3 Art 21-4]
purpose and functions . . . . . [Sch 3 Art 1-3]
Secretariat
— composition . . . . [Sch 3 Art 9-1]
— members . . . . [Sch 3 Art 9-3]
Secretary-General . . . . [Sch 3 Art 9-2]
— Additional Facility and . . [Sch 3 Art 11-5]
— appointing authority . . . . [Sch 3 Art 11-6]
— arbitration decisions . . . . [Sch 3 Art 36-5]
— functions and role . . . . . [Sch 3 Art 11-1]
— independence . . . . [Sch 3 Art 10-2]
— nomination . . . . [Sch 3 Art 10-1]
— publications . . . . [Sch 3 Art 11-4]
— registrar, as . . . . [Sch 3 Art 11-3]
— registration of request for arbitration
    . . . . [Sch 3 Art 36-6]
— representative of ICSID, as . [Sch 3 Art 11-2]
— screening power . . . . . . [Sch 3 Art 36-4]
— World Bank and . . . . . . [Sch 3 Art 10-3]
settlement in accordance with Convention
    . . . . [Sch 3 Art 1-4]
structure . . . . [Sch 3 Art 3-1]
taxation exemptions . . . . . . [Sch 3 Art 24-2]
— Australian law, under . . . [Sch 3 Art 24-3],
    [Sch 3 Art 24-5], [Sch 3 Art 24-7]
— expense allowances . . . . [Sch 3 Art 24-4]
— payments . . . . [Sch 3 Art 24-6]
— persons who are exempt . . [Sch 3 Art 24-1]
— salaries and emoluments . [Sch 3 Art 24-4]
World Bank, relationship with . [Sch 3 Art 2-4],
    [Sch 3 Art 73-1]
Investment
characteristics . . . . [Sch 3 Art 25-12]
— *Salini* criteria . . . . . . [Sch 3 Art 25-12]
definition . [Sch 3 Art 25-9]-[Sch 3 Art 25-10]
— parties, freedom of . . . . [Sch 3 Art 25-11]
Investment Convention *see* **Convention on the Settlement of Investment Disputes between States and Nationals of Other States**
Judiciary Act
enforcement of foreign awards and agreements
    . . . . [s 13]-[s 13-2]
interpretation of Investment Convention . [s 38]-[s 38-3]
Jurisdiction
arbitral tribunal *see* **Arbitral tribunal**
carriage of goods by sea . . [s 2C-2], [s 2C-9],
    [s 2C-12]
— arbitration agreement, effect on . . [s 2C-3]
— award, making . . . . [s 2C-6]
— bill of lading, parties to . . . . . . [s 2C-5]
— documentation . . . . [s 2C-4]
— estoppel . . . . [s 2C-7]
— Hague-Visby Rules . . . [s 2C-8], [s 2C-13]
— Hamburg Rules . . . . . [s 2C-8], [s 2C-11],
    [s 2C-13]
interim measures . . . . [Sch 2 Art 9-3]
Judiciary Act, under . . . . [s 13]-[s 13-2]
Model Law, under . . . . [Sch 2 Art 5-4],
    [Sch 2 Art 8-4]
Mareva relief
foreign awards, enforcement of . . . . . [s 8-33]
Model Law
amendments (2006) . . . . [Sch 2 Art 1-6]
application . . . [s 21]-[s 21-2], [Sch 2 Art 1-1]
— territorial . . . . [Sch 2 Art 1-8]
appointing authority . . . . . . [Sch 2 Art 3-4]
authority, prescribed . . . . [s 18], [s 18-1]
Chapter VIII not to apply . . . . [s 20], [s 20-1]
construction . . . . [s 17-2]
— documents, supporting . . . . [s 17-3]
court . . . . [Sch 2 Art 6-1]
— prescribed . . . . [s 18], [Sch 2 Art 6-2]
definition . . . . [s 15]
force of law . . . . [s 16], [s 16-2]
— history of section . . . . [s 16-1]
international origin . . . . . . [Sch 2 Art 2A-1],
    [Sch 2 Art 2A-2]
interpretation . . . . [s 17]
— Acts Interpretation Act . . . . [s 17-4]
— history of section . . . . [s 17-1]
limitation period . . . . [Sch 2 Art 5-5]
mandatory provisions . . . . . . [Sch 2 Art 4-2]
non arbitral disputes . . . . [Sch 2 Art 1-9]
opting out . . . . [s 21-3]
public policy and . . . . [s 19]-[s 19-2]

References are to paragraph numbers

Model Law —*continued*
  reasonable opportunity to present case . **[s 18C]**
  — development of principle in international arbitration .... **[s 18C-2]**
  — history .... **[s 18C-1]**
  scope .... **[Sch 2 Art 1-2]**
  "subject to", interpretation . . **[Sch 2 Art 1-7]**
  territorial approach ...... **[Sch 2 Art 1-8]**
  text .... **[Sch 2]**
Objections
  delay .... **[Sch 2 Art 4-5]**
  "knows", interpretation ..... **[Sch 2 Art 4-4]**
  silence or inaction .... **[Sch 2 Art 4-7]**
  time limits .... **[Sch 2 Art 4-6]**
  waiver of right .... **[Sch 2 Art 4-1]**
  — deemed .... **[Sch 2 Art 4-8]**
Parties
  burden of proof .... **[Sch 2 Art 19-5]**
  choice of "rules of law" .... **[Sch 2 Art 28-2]**
  default .... **[Sch 2 Art 25-1]**
  — safeguards .... **[Sch 2 Art 25-2]**
  — "without showing sufficient cause" ...... **[Sch 2 Art 25-3]**
  equal treatment .... **[Sch 2 Art 18-1]**
  — history .... **[Sch 2 Art 18-3]**
  — "natural justice" .... **[Sch 2 Art 18-4]**
  — principles .... **[Sch 2 Art 18-2]**
  evidence, failure to produce . **[Sch 2 Art 25-6]**
  failure to appear .... **[Sch 2 Art 25-6]**
  — ICSID arbitration ..... **[Sch 3 Art 45-1]**- **[Sch 3 Art 45-4]**
  failure to communicate
  — statement of claim ..... **[Sch 2 Art 25-4]**
  — statement of defence .... **[Sch 2 Art 25-5]**
  "full opportunity" to present case .... **[Sch 2 Art 18-5]**
  — no reasonable opportunity . **[Sch 2 Art 18-6]**
  hearing, right to .... **[Sch 2 Art 24-2]**
Place of arbitration *see* **Arbitration**
Preliminary orders
  applicable provisions .... **[Sch 2 Art 17D-1]**- **[Sch 2 Art 17D-4]**
  applications .... **[Sch 2 Art 17B-1]**
  — Australian law, under .. **[Sch 2 Art 17B-2]**
  costs and damages ..... **[Sch 2 Art 17G-1]**- **[Sch 2 Art 17G-2]**
  disclosure obligations .... **[Sch 2 Art 17F-1]**- **[Sch 2 Art 17F-3]**
  — non-compliance ...... **[Sch 2 Art 17F-4]**
  enforcement and recognition .... **[Sch 2 Art 17G-1]**
  — disclosure obligations . **[Sch 2 Art 17G-7]**
  — history .... **[Sch 2 Art 17G-4]**
  — Model Law, under .... **[Sch 2 Art 17G-2]**, **[Sch 2 Art 17G-3]**, **[Sch 2 Art 17G-6]**
  — refusal, grounds for ... **[Sch 2 Art 17I-1]**- **[Sch 2 Art 17I-6]**
  — security, provision of appropriate .... **[Sch 2 Art 17G-8]**

  — "shall be recognised as binding" ..... **[Sch 2 Art 17G-5]**
  modification .... **[Sch 2 Art 17D-5]**
  nature of .... **[s 18B]**, **[s 18B-1]**
  regime .... **[Sch 2 Art 17C-1]**
  revocation .... **[Sch 2 Art 17D-5]**
  security, request for ..... **[Sch 2 Art 17E-1]**- **[Sch 2 Art 17E-4]**
  suspension .... **[Sch 2 Art 17D-5]**
Proceedings
  award, making *see* **Award**
  burden of proof .... **[Sch 2 Art 19-5]**
  commencement .... **[Sch 2 Art 21-1]**
  — derogation from provision . **[Sch 2 Art 21-4]**
  — diverse national legal systems .... **[Sch 2 Art 21-2]**
  — rule for determining .... **[Sch 2 Art 21-3]**
  conciliation *see* **Conciliation**
  consolidation ...... **[s 24]**, **[s 24-1]**, **[s 24-5]**
  — difficulties .... **[s 24-2]**
  — institutional rules, under .... **[s 24-3]**
  — optional nature of provision ..... **[s 24-4]**
  counter-claims .... **[Sch 2 Art 23-6]**
  documents, communication of . **[Sch 2 Art 24-5]**
  evidence *see* **Evidence**
  expert reports .... **[Sch 2 Art 24-6]**
  hearings .... **[Sch 2 Art 24-1]**
  — advance notice required .. **[Sch 2 Art 24-4]**
  — control over .... **[Sch 2 Art 24-3]**
  — rights of parties .... **[Sch 2 Art 24-2]**
  language .... **[Sch 2 Art 22-1]**
  — application of chosen ... **[Sch 2 Art 22-5]**
  — autonomy of parties .... **[Sch 2 Art 22-2]**
  — documentary evidence ... **[Sch 2 Art 22-6]**
  — failure to reach agreement on .... **[Sch 2 Art 22-3]**
  — timing for agreement or determination .... **[Sch 2 Art 22-4]**
  "natural justice" .... **[Sch 2 Art 18-4]**
  parties, equal treatment of .. **[Sch 2 Art 18-1]**- **[Sch 2 Art 18-6]**
  persons appearing
  — privileges and immunities . **[Sch 3 Art 22-1]**- **[Sch 3 Art 22-2]**
  reasonable opportunity to present case . **[s 18C]**
  — development of principle in international arbitration .... **[s 18C-2]**
  representation .. **[s 29]**-**[s 29-2]**, **[s 37]**-**[s 37-2]**
  rules of procedure .... **[Sch 2 Art 19-1]**
  — agreement of parties .... **[Sch 2 Art 19-2]**
  — determination by tribunal . **[Sch 2 Art 19-3]**
  set-off .... **[Sch 2 Art 23-6]**
  statements of claim and defence . **[Sch 2 Art 23-1]**- **[Sch 2 Art 23-6]**
  — amending .... **[Sch 2 Art 23-4]**
  — failure to communicate .. **[Sch 2 Art 25-4]**, **[Sch 2 Art 25-5]**
  — supplementing .... **[Sch 2 Art 23-4]**
  termination . **[Sch 2 Art 31-1]**-**[Sch 2 Art 32-2]**

References are to paragraph numbers

tribunal, powers . . . . [Sch 2 Art 8-7]
written . . . . [Sch 2 Art 24-1]
Provisional measures
  award, distinguished . . . . . [Sch 3 Art 47-4]
  binding nature of . . . . [Sch 3 Art 47-6]
  power to grant . . . . [Sch 3 Art 47-1]
  — conditions . . . . [Sch 3 Art 47-5]
  — international courts and tribunals
    . . . . [Sch 3 Art 47-2]
  — purpose . . . . [Sch 3 Art 47-3]
Representation
  international arbitration in Australia . . [s 29-2]
  proceedings, in . [s 29]-[s 29-1], [s 37]-[s 37-2]
Residence
  definition . . . . [s 3], [s 3-12], [s 7-8]
Security for costs
  foreign awards, enforcement . . . . . . [s 8-30]
  orders . . . . [s 23K]-[s 23K-3]
Settlement
  form of award . . . . [Sch 2 Art 30-2]
  Model Law, under . . . . . . [Sch 2 Art 30-1]
Severability
  arbitration agreements . . . . [s 30A]-[s 30A-2]
Stay of proceedings
  application
  — jurisdiction . . . . [Sch 2 Art 8-4]
  — requirements . . . . [Sch 2 Art 8-5]

Subpoenas
  application . . . . [s 23-2]
  court assistance to tribunal . . [Sch 2 Art 27-3]
  obtaining . . . . [s 23]
  — safeguards . . . . [s 23-3]
Third parties
  right to authorise . . . . [Sch 2 Art 2-3]
Tribunal *see* **Arbitral tribunal**
Waiver of rights
  common law under . . . . [Sch 2 Art 9-4]
World Bank
  Board of Governors . . . . [Sch 3 Art 4-2]
  creation and purpose . . . . . . [Sch 3 Art 2-2]
  depository for ICSID Convention
    . . . . [Sch 3 Art 73-1]
  — functions . . . . [Sch 3 Art 75-1]
  hearings . . . . [Sch 3 Art 2-3]
  ICSID, relationship with . . . . [Sch 3 Art 2-4]
  — Secretary-General . . . . . . [Sch 3 Art 10-3]
  President . . . . [Sch 3 Art 5-1]-[Sch 3 Art 5-3]
  — Acting . . . . [Sch 3 Art 5-2]
Writing
  agreement in *see* **Agreement in writing**
  written communications, receipt of
    . . . . [Sch 2 Art 3-1]
  — court proceedings, application to
    . . . . [Sch 2 Art 3-2]
  — subject matter . . . . [Sch 2 Art 3-3]

References are to paragraph numbers